The Official InstallShield® for Windows® Installer Developer's Guide

The Official InstallShield® for Windows® Installer Developer's Guide

Bob Baker

M&T Books

An imprint of Hungry Minds, Inc.

New York, NY • Cleveland, OH • Indianapolis, IN

The Official InstallShield® for Windows® Installer Developer's Guide

Published by
M&T Books
An imprint of Hungry Minds, Inc.
909 Third Avenue
New York, NY 10022
www.hungryminds.com

ISBN: 0-7645-4723-2

Printed in the United States of America

10 9 8 7 6 5 4 3 2

1B/TQ/QU/QR/FC

Distributed in the United States by Hungry Minds, Inc.

Distributed by CDG Books Canada Inc. for Canada; by Transworld Publishers Limited in the United Kingdom; by IDG Norge Books for Norway; by IDG Sweden Books for Sweden; by IDG Books Australia Publishing Corporation Pty. Ltd. for Australia and New Zealand; by TransQuest Publishers Pte Ltd. for Singapore, Malaysia, Thailand, Indonesia, and Hong Kong; by Gotop Information Inc. for Taiwan; by ICG Muse, Inc. for Japan; by Intersoft for South Africa; by Eyrolles for France; by International Thomson Publishing for Germany, Austria and Switzerland; by Distribuidora Cuspide for Argentina; by LR International for Brazil; by Galileo Libros for Chile; by Ediciones ZETA S.C.R. Ltda. for Peru; by WS Computer Publishing Corporation, Inc., for the Philippines; by Contemporanea de Ediciones for Venezuela; by Express Computer Distributors for the Caribbean and West Indies; by Micronesia Media Distributor, Inc. for Micronesia; by Chips Computadoras S.A. de C.V. for Mexico; by Editorial Norma de Panama S.A. for Panama; by American Bookshops for Finland.

For general information on Hungry Minds' products and services please contact our Customer Care Department within the U.S. at 800-762-2974, outside the U.S. at 317-572-3993 or fax 317-572-4002.

For sales inquiries and reseller information, including discounts, premium and bulk quantity sales, and foreign-language translations, please contact our Customer Care Department at 800-434-3422, fax 317-572-4002, or write to Hungry Minds, Inc., Attn: Customer Care Department, 10475 Crosspoint Boulevard, Indianapolis, IN 46256.

For information on licensing foreign or domestic rights, please contact our Sub-Rights Customer Care Department at 212-884-5000.

For information on using Hungry Minds' products and services in the classroom or for ordering examination copies, please contact our Educational Sales Department at 800-434-2086 or fax 317-572-4005.

Please contact our Public Relations Department at 212-884-5163 for press review copies or 212-884-5000 for author interviews and other publicity information or fax 212-884-5400.

For information on using Hungry Minds' products and services in the classroom or for ordering examination copies, please contact our Educational Sales Department at 800-434-2086 or fax 317-572-4005.

For press review copies, author interviews, or other publicity information, please contact our Public Relations department at 317-572-3168 or fax 317-572-4168.

For authorization to photocopy items for corporate, personal, or educational use, please contact Copyright Clearance Center, 222 Rosewood Drive, Danvers, MA 01923, or fax 978-750-4470.

Library of Congress Cataloging-in-Publication Data

Baker, Bob, 1939 Aug. 4-
The official Installshield professional: Window installer edition developer's guide /
Bob Baker.
p. cm.
ISBN 0-7645-4723-2 (alk. paper)
1. Application software--Development.
2. Installshield Professional. 3. Microsoft Windows (Computer file) I. Title.
QA76.76.A65 B34 2000
005.26'9--dc21 00-051571

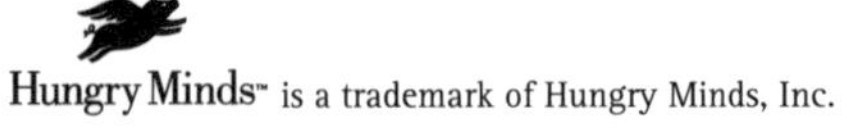

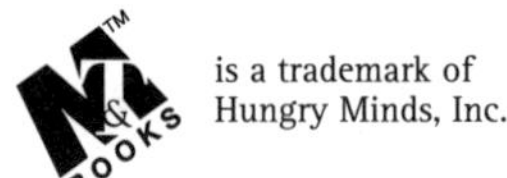

About the Author

Bob Baker is a technical trainer at InstallShield Software Corporation, concentrating on the tools that deal with the Windows Installer service. Bob joined InstallShield at the beginning of 1995 as the program manager for the InstallShield 3 product. Bob has an M.S. degree in computer science, which he received while working as a structural engineer in the power industry prior to joining InstallShield.

Credits

ACQUISITIONS EDITOR
Grace Buechlein

PROJECT EDITOR
Barbra Guerra

TECHNICAL EDITORS
Jim Masson
Rajesh Ramachandran
Alaks Sevugan

COPY EDITORS
S. B. Kleinman
Jerelind Charles

PROJECT COORDINATORS
Louigene A. Santos
Danette Nurse

BOOK DESIGNER
Jim Donohue

PROOFREADING AND INDEXING
York Production Services

COVER IMAGE
® Noma/Images.com

GRAPHICS AND PRODUCTION SPECIALISTS
Robert Bihlmayer
Rolly Delrosario
Jude Levinson
Michael Lewis
Victor Peréz-Varela
Ramses Ramirez

QUALITY CONTROL TECHNICIAN
Dina F Quan

SENIOR PERMISSIONS EDITOR
Carmen Krikorian

MEDIA DEVELOPMENT SPECIALIST
Travis Silvers

MEDIA DEVELOPMENT COORDINATOR
Marisa Pearman

ILLUSTRATORS
Gabriele McCann
Karl Brandt

To Rhonda

With patience and grace, you have borne my continued absences when I've had to conduct training and then on returning home disappeared into the office to work on this book. Without your understanding this book would never have been written.

To my students

I appreciate the many hard questions you have asked. You have spurred me to continue to learn and to never be satisfied with my present level of knowledge.

Foreword

The Windows Installer is one of the cornerstones of Microsoft's desktop management efforts. It is a core component of Windows 2000 – as well as being available for Windows 95, Windows 98, and Windows NT 4.0. The installer is clearly something that Microsoft considers important. It is, indeed, a requirement for building an application that is certified for Windows 2000. The Windows Installer is also something Microsoft's customers consider important – system administrators, in particular. Administrators have been asking for a standard installation technology for a long time, but they can't reap the benefits without the help of software developers. This is where it becomes important for software developers to take advantage of this technology in their applications.

The premise of the installer is simple: Give administrators a consistent way to install the applications that are needed in their environments. By providing a standard installation engine, the installer enables administrators to leverage a single set of tools, and a core set of knowledge and experience, and apply that to the many different applications that they deploy. In addition to standardization, applications that use the installer automatically provide administrators facilities for unattended installations, customization of installs, self-healing applications, and deployment in locked-down environments. The Windows Installer can be used with a variety of software distribution tools – everything from homegrown solutions to large-scale commercial products, such as Microsoft Systems Management Server. The installer is also used in the IntelliMirror feature set of Windows 2000. Using the installer is a key part of making an application easy to deploy in a wide variety of environments, which ultimately reduces the effective cost of the application to customers.

In order to do this, most developers will choose a high level tool like InstallShield for Windows Installer to help them create their installer package. One of the great things about a high-level tool like InstallShield for Windows Installer is that it can hide and abstract away many of the mundane details and complexity that creating an installer package entails. It can put a friendly face on top of the underlying structures of the package, making it possible to very rapidly build installations. This works well for simple packages, but when you want to really exploit the Windows Installer, you not only need to understand the tool you are using, you also need to understand the installation engine itself.

In this book, Bob Baker gives software developers the information that they need to successfully use the Windows Installer in their applications. Bob starts off with a detailed discussion of the Windows Installer engine, giving developers the technological background needed to understand how the installer works, and how the different elements of a Windows Installer package relate to one another. This discussion includes the basics of designing features and components and then goes into more advanced topics such as custom actions. Bob then takes the discussion to the next level, showing how developers can leverage InstallShield for Windows Installer to create these packages. He walks developers through the features of the tool and demonstrates how the concepts presented in the tool map relate to the underlying implementation of the Windows Installer.

The Windows Installer is one part of a larger system of tools and technologies, and in order to fully leverage it, it is important to understand not only the installer engine but also the tools that you use to create packages, and how the tools leverage the engine. Developers who read this book will gain an understanding of both the Windows Installer engine, and the InstallShield for Windows Installer tool, enabling them to fully exploit the capabilities of both.

Jim Masson
Windows Installer Program Manager
Microsoft Corporation

Preface

This book can be viewed as a record of my exploration of the new Windows Installer technology from Microsoft. Software installation on a computer running the Windows operating system has always been a challenging technical effort. I cannot think of a better way to learn about a new technology for installing software than to write a book about it. The writing of this book has been a high-powered learning experience for me, and every day seemed to bring a new epiphany. In the chapters of this book, I have tried to pass on the understanding that I have gained. I have also tried to put emphasis on those subjects with which the students in my classes have had the most trouble.

Please note this book focuses on version 1.52 of the InstallShield for Windows Installer product. Although version 1.52, which was recently released, has many similarities, some of the implementation details and other product features will be different. Please refer to www.installshield.com for information about version 2.01.

Who Is This Book For?

The concept of this book is to lead the reader from today's world of script-based installation programs to the new environment ushered in with Windows 2000. As such, this book is best suited for setup developers who already know what is entailed in the creation of an installation program. This does not mean that you need to be knowledgeable about the creation of installation scripts using InstallScript; a number of chapters are devoted to this language. However, you do need to know about the Windows operating system particularly with respect to Windows NT 4.0 and/or Windows 2000. You also are expected to know about the registry and the basic information that is written to this database. Except for InstallScript, which is covered in detail, you are expected to know at least one programming language such as C++ or VBScript. Examples have been provided in all three of these programming languages, but how to program in either C++ or VBScript is not covered.

The Organization of This Book

This book is divided into five parts and a set of appendixes with the general flow being from the general to the specific. Most chapters discuss the Windows Installer technology followed by a discussion of how to use the InstallShield for Windows Installer authoring tool to manipulate this new technology. The appendixes cover some specific technical subjects that did not fit easily into the main body of the book.

Part I: Introduction to the Windows Installer

In this part I show you where we have been with regard to the installation of software followed by a description of the deployment architecture that has been built into Windows 2000. The prime reason that you will want to use the Windows Installer technology for your installation programs is to be able to make your applications compatible with the new deployment architecture of Windows 2000. In subsequent chapters, I provide an in-depth overview of the Windows Installer technology and show what it takes to create a simple installation without the use of an authoring tool such as InstallShield for Windows Installer.

Part II: Basic Package Creation with Installshield for Windows Installer

The four chapters in this part introduce the InstallShield for Windows Installer authoring tool. Even though these chapters focus on the use of this product, they also cover many important items with regard to the operation of the Windows Installer. These chapters take a detailed walk through the InstallShield for Windows Installer product, pointing out all the features that are available (the actual use of these various features is covered in later chapters of the book); re-create the installation package created in earlier chapters using InstallShield for Windows Installer; get into the details of how you can use InstallShield for Windows Installer to control the operations performed during an installation; and show you how to create the user interface that is displayed during an installation.

Part III: Extending the Windows Installer Functionality

As with any technology, the Windows Installer cannot possibly handle all installation scenarios. Because of this, Microsoft allows you to extend the built-in functionality through the use of what are called custom actions. The beginning chapters in this part discuss the details of custom actions and show how to create custom actions using programming languages such as C++ and VBScript.

Part IV: Advanced Concepts

The early chapters provide a complete tutorial on the InstallScript programming language and how to use it to create custom actions. InstallScript is a powerful scripting language created by InstallShield Software Corporation specifically for the creation of Installation programs. The last two chapters in this part are concerned with some of the core functionality of the Windows Installer. The first of these discusses the creation and use of components. Components are the basic units of any application, and you need to understand components in order to create installations correctly. The final chapter in Part IV discusses transforms, a critical component of the Windows Installer technology. Transforms modify a setup package during an installation, and you can also use them to make permanent changes to a setup package during build time.

Part V: Solving Real-World Problems

This part also contains only two chapters. These chapters tell you how to create localized installations and how to implement the upgrade capabilities that have been designed into the Windows Installer. The first chapter talks about how the Windows Installer handles different languages and how you can use InstallShield for Windows Installer to create various types of localized install packages. The next chapter shows you all the ins and outs of the three types of upgrades that are supported by the Windows Installer.

Appendixes

Four technical appendixes provide you a reference to various subjects that did not fit easily into the main sections of the book. Appendix A gives a detailed description with examples of the command line switches for msiexec.exe, which is the Windows Installer engine. Appendix B provides a handy reference for the properties in the Summary Information Stream found in all windows Installer packages. Appendix C provides you a behind-the-scenes look at the InstallScript run-time architecture, and Appendix D describes the system reboot functionality of the Windows Installer. Appendix E describes the content of the CD-ROM that you can find at the back of the book. On this CD you will find a number of evaluation copies of InstallShield products. You will also find the source code and sample applications that have been described through out the book.

Conventions Used in This Book

From time to time in this book, you'll see icons in the left margin. These are intended to call attention to points that are particularly important.

The Note icons tell you that something is important — perhaps a fundamental concept or something that will build your understanding of subsequent material.

Tip icons indicate a good idea or more efficient way of doing something that may not be obvious.

These icons indicate that an example file is on the companion CD-ROM (see the appendix "What's on the CD-ROM?"). The CD is invaluable, containing code and sample applications that I discuss in the book.

The Caution icons let you know when there's a potential problem if you're not careful.

The Cross-Reference icons refer you to other chapters or other sections in the book where you can find more information on a subject.

More Information

For updates and information related to this book, I am maintaining a special Web site. Check out `www.installshield.com/books/iswidg`.

Acknowledgments

First, I need to thank Viresh Bhatia, CEO of InstallShield Software Corporation. It was Viresh who gave me the opportunity to write this book. Secondly I need to express my gratitude to the Microsoft Windows Installer development team members who willingly provided so much indepth information. These persons are Jim Masson, Ben Chamberlain, Tracy Ferrier, Chetan Parulekar, Carolyn Napier, Chris Gouge, Eugen Daroczy, and John Delo. At InstallShield I had many valuable discussions about how the Windows Installer works with David Thornley and Alaks Sevugan. It was demonstrated time and again that discussing technical concepts with another person promotes understanding much better and faster than when you try to do gain this understanding on your own. I also want to thank Rajesh Ramachandran, the creator of the InstallScript compiler, for the time he spent with me so that I could properly describe the use of the InstallScript language. I need to thank Robert Dickau, the creator of all our training manuals, for the inspiration that I gained for many of the examples that I have used for this book. Finally, I want to thank the IDG staff for their patience with a first time author.

Contents at a Glance

Part V Solving Real-World Problems

Contents

Part I

Introduction to the Windows Installer

Chapter 1

Software Installation, Yesterday, Today, and Tomorrow

IN THIS CHAPTER

- ◆ Defining software installation and deployment
- ◆ Software installation as it was under DOS and 16-bit Windows
- ◆ Installing software under 32-bit operating systems
- ◆ Problems that have arisen with the complexity of operating systems
- ◆ Microsoft's initiative to reduce the total cost of ownership (TCO) of the desktop PC

IN THIS CHAPTER we look at the basics that comprise software installation and show how over time this development activity is getting more complex with each release of the Windows operating system. We will take a little look at the history of the challenges that setup developers have had to face over the years. This is in no way a comprehensive treatment of software installation through the ages but just an attempt to put everyone in the right frame of mind to take the next step. This next step is to understand the Windows Installer service and how to use it properly to enable the installation of software. The Windows Installer service is part of the Windows 2000 operating system. We will discuss the Windows 2000 deployment architecture in Chapter 2 and then get into the real subject of this book, the Windows Installer service, in Chapters 3, 4, and 5.

The Many Faces of Software Installation

Installing an application can be thought of as integrating it with the operating system. The files of an application are copied to the local system, registry entries are made, and the application is exposed to the end-user through the use of shortcuts or other entry points. Software installation can be viewed differently depending on who is involved. The end-user sees software installation through different eyes than does the system administrator. The setup developer has a different viewpoint than either the end-user or the system administrator.

The end-user viewpoint

Most end-users find the installation process long and complex since they tend not to be computer experts. The installation process, in many cases, asks the end-user to answer questions that he or she do not know the answer. These questions concern what features should be installed, whether the features should be installed locally or be run from the source media, where the application is to be installed, and so forth. It is now possible to install software from the Internet and this provides a whole new environment with which the end-user needs to contend. It is not uncommon that an end-user has to contend with a failed installation that leaves the computer in an unknown state where inexplicably applications that used to work no longer work properly if at all.

Modifying or removing an application is part of what is called the maintenance process. During the maintenance process, an original installation of an application has already been made and the end-user wants to modify this installation in some fashion. This mode normally allows the end user to perform the following listed operations:

- Reinstalling all of the components of the application that were installed during the original installation. This might be necessary if necessary files were deleted by mistake or some of the files have been corrupted.
- Installing additional components that were not installed originally.
- Removing components that are no longer needed. This is normally done to free up hard-drive space on the local hard drive.
- Uninstalling the complete application.

Performing a maintenance activity can also be prone to error just as the original installation is. The ideal situation from the end-users standpoint would be for an application to install itself and not require any interaction.

The system administrator's viewpoint

The main challenge facing the system administrator is the mass deployment of software to users in a complex network environment. The problem that is faced is the fact that in many companies the user of the application does not have administrator privileges on their local machine and most installations will fail if they cannot write to certain parts of the registry and/or copy files to certain protected locations on the hard drive. Another challenge that faces the system administrator is the fact that most installations packages are black boxes and cannot be examined or modified except by the original developer. This situation makes it impossible for the system administrator to restrict the features of an application that the end user can access once the installation is complete. Just as with the end-user's situation described in the previous section, the failure of an installation or any maintenance activity leaves the local machine in an unknown state. Because of this the system administrator needs to visit the local machine itself to try and correct the situation. This is not very efficient and contributes greatly to the cost of maintaining the machines in the network.

The setup developer's viewpoint

The main problem that is faced by the setup developer is that the creation of the installation for an application is normally left to the last minute just before the product has to ship. This is because setup is not considered part of the development process. Most complex installations are script-based and the logic that is embedded in the installation script suffers the same fate as the code used to develop the application. This dearth of comment statements means the script tends to get handed from one setup developer to another – thus complicating the process of creating and maintaining the installation through the normal upgrade of the application functionality. Due to the different vendors that provide tools for the setup developer there is no standard set of rules that are followed when creating the installation for an application. Because of this an end-user can see different types of installations depending on the tool that was used to create the install. The ideal situation would be for all installations to look the same thus fostering and expectation in the end-user of what to expect with an installation in the same fashion that the Windows operating system as given users since its inception.

The basic operations when installing software

Regardless of the mode or the system on which you're installing software, a certain set of actions has to take place. These actions are listed below:

- Provide an installation wizard to guide the user in the installation process.
- Determine the user's hardware and software configuration and available disk space.
- Copy files to the specified directories on the system.
- Set up the execution environment for the application by modifying existing files and making entries in the registry.
- Expose the application to the user so that it can be easily launched.
- Provide for changing the install of the application (add/remove features).
- Provide for uninstalling the application when the user no longer needs it so that no artifacts are left behind on the system.

Installing Software in the World of DOS

To look back on the time when everyone was developing software for the DOS operating system is to envision a much simpler world. Since then software has become much more complicated and installing it has become equally so.

In the DOS days all applications were monolithic as was DOS itself. Each application consisted of an executable that was the result of compiling a linking source code. The file system was the operating system and there was no such thing as having multiple processes running at the same time where the sharing of information was performed.

Installing software in this type of environment consisted mainly of copying files and making entries into the AUTOEXEC.BAT and CONFIG.SYS files. Many install programs were just a collection of DOS commands inside a batch file. Users only encountered an installation problem in those rare instances when they needed to install a device driver. For those companies that created something more than a batch file to do their installations the biggest challenge was creating a user interface for the install program. User interfaces for DOS programs sometimes just consisted of a different-colored background and some "windows" made of boxes in which the user was asked to enter certain information. Boxes also displayed the progress of the installation. For larger applications the user interface was more elaborate, with actual pictures drawn on the screen. This is probably where the first use of what we now call *billboards* was implemented.

Then came Microsoft Windows 3.0 . . .

The Environment of 16-Bit Windows

In the PC world, Microsoft Windows 3.0 ushered in a revolution in the area of software application development. We will discuss here only those details of 16-bit Windows that have an impact on the installation of software.

Windows 3.0 introduced the concept of *dynamic linking* to the majority of PC programmers. With dynamic linking, a program gets a large part of its functionality from other files that export this functionality. These other files are called *dynamic linked libraries* (DLLs) because they are only accessed at run time and not at compile time. With the advent of dynamic linking, instead of being a monolith, an application would consist of many different files, thus creating a more complicated installation. In addition, much of the functionality incorporated into an application came from the dynamic linked libraries that comprised the operating system itself.

With dynamic linking came the use of what were termed *initialization files.* These came in two types: those that came with and were used by the operating system and those that were used by the application to store information. The operating system initialization files were SYSTEM.INI and WIN.INI. The initialization files used by an application were termed private .ini files and the information contained in them was of use only to the application itself. The installation program for a software application frequently had to make entries into both the system and the private initialization files.

Windows 3.0 also ushered in the concept of exposing an application to the environment. This meant using icons in the Windows user interface to allow the user to launch an application without the user having to specifically go and find the application's executable. The user could also create an association between a file extension and the application's executable that would know how to interpret a file with that extension. This was made possible by the registration database. The registration database on Windows 3.0 was the forerunner of the registry that is found with 32-bit operating systems. It was used to provide basic OLE functionality and to provide file associations. The installation program for an application would now be able to set up the registration database association between a file extension and what is called the file extension server.

The creation of installations for software now became an important element of the development process, even though it was often done at the end of a development cycle and thus became a critical path item for shipment. This means that it was often the case that the creation of the installation program for an application delayed the actual release of the software due to the problems that were encountered during its development. At the beginning of the 1990s InstallShield Software Corporation shipped its first version of the now-famous development tool for helping developers to create installation programs for their applications. Microsoft also shipped the Setup Toolkit as part of the Windows 3.1 SDK. The purpose of both these products was to provide a standard approach that would make it easier to create installation programs.

The primary challenges that faced the setup developer in the new world of Windows were handling of shared files and creating the user interface for the installation. There is no doubt that Windows provided a much richer graphics capability than was ever possible with DOS. Microsoft launched its Windows Logo Program as part of the introduction of Windows. The Logo Program was an attempt to get developers to create applications that would run successfully under Windows. When first introduced, this program had only the following set of requirements:

- The application had to be written to the Windows API.
- There had to be a Windows-based automated installation program.
- The application had to be tested on Windows, Windows for Workgroups, and Windows NT.
- The application had to pass the Windows Compatibility Survey.

In the year or so before Windows 95 was released, Microsoft added a new wrinkle to the creation of installations for Windows programs: it released a subset of the 32-bit Windows API called Win32s. This was a set of DLLs that exported this API, and applications that used this API could be run under Windows 3.1. Implementing

Win32s was somewhat problematic and it made the creation of an installation program more complex since now it was necessary to find out if these DLLs were already on the system, and if they were not they had to be installed.

The purpose of Win32s was to get developers prepared for a fully functional 32-bit operating system. This 32-bit operating system came in the form of Windows 95. Of course Windows NT was already out there, but it was in its infancy and most users were using Windows 3.1.

The 32-Bit Evolution

The move to a 32-bit operating system started with the release of Windows 95 in the summer of 1995. Windows 95 helped to ease the pain of software development but it also added more complexity to the installation scene. In the late summer of 1996 Windows NT 4.0 was released with the new shell pioneered by Windows 95. Windows NT had always been 32-bit on the backend but until the release of version 4.0 the shell was only 16-bit.

Windows 95 brought with it the Windows 95 registry, which was a unified database for storing system and application data. With the Windows 95 registry it was no longer necessary to store configuration settings in startup configuration and initialization files. In Windows 95 most of the configuration options in SYSTEM.INI were moved to the registry as well as a number of other entries that had always been included in this system initialization file. For WIN.INI all the font and desktop information was moved to the Registry. Both SYSTEM.INI and WIN.INI still existed for the main purpose of compatibility with 16-bit applications, which still ran under Windows 95 but had no access to the Registry since that required the use of the Win32 API.

In Windows 95 the AUTOEXEC.BAT and CONFIG.SYS still existed for compatibility with real-mode system components and to allow users to change certain default system settings, such as the PATH environment variable.

Windows 95 also ushered in the new 32-bit Windows shell, which was COM enabled. It permitted drag-and-drop, the concept of folders, shortcuts, and so forth. Also introduced was the concept of an installable file system that supported file names of up to 260 characters. All these innovations made creating an installation program more difficult.

Prior to the release of Windows 95 Microsoft developed a white paper entitled "Windows 95 Application Setup Guidelines for Independent Software Vendors." The purpose of this paper was to standardize the creation of installation programs. This paper introduced the concept that each installation program should not only provide the capability to install the application but should also provide a method for removing the application from the machine. But providing this capability introduced a new problem: the unintended removal of system files, which could cripple all or part of the operating system.

What Are Installable File Systems?

With MS-DOS, the operating system is the file system and that is all you have. There is no other way to manage files. MS-DOS uses the functions associated with Interrupt 21h to manage files. The MS-DOS file system uses the File Allocation Table (FAT) approach to locating files on the disk. For hard drives it uses what was called the FAT16 implementation and for floppy disks it uses the FAT12 implementation. Since Windows 3.x is tied to MS-DOS, it has the same restrictions as MS-DOS itself.

Windows 95 changes all of this by bringing to the table what is called the Installable File System (IFS) Manager. The IFS Manager uses a form of device driver called a file system driver in order to implement diverse file systems such as FAT, VFAT, CDFS, and so on. FAT is our friend from the MS-DOS days, VFAT is the implementation of a file system that can handle long file names, and CDFS is the CD-ROM file system. Different file system drivers that communicate with the appropriate device drivers for the target I/O hardware implement each of these file systems. VFAT uses a 16-bit addressing scheme to locate files on the hard drive.

By necessity FAT16 is supported by Windows 95/98 and by Windows NT. This is because of backward compatibility issues. However, until Windows 2000 Windows, NT did not support the FAT32 file system; therefore, on multi-boot machines the only way for Windows 95/98 and Windows NT to share drive space is for all drives to be formatted for FAT16. Now that Windows 2000 supports the 32-bit addressing scheme of FAT32 dual-boot machines can share a much more efficient file system.

Writing a file system driver is a complicated process requiring a lot of code. This is probably why it has taken so long for Windows NT/2000 to be able to support the FAT32 addressing scheme.

The potential to remove a system file by accident during an uninstallation was not the only problem that arose. There was also potential to remove files that more than one application needed for it to be able to run. This problem gave rise to the practice of reference counting shareable files in the Registry and not uninstalling them if the shared reference count was greater than zero.

The setup guidelines mentioned above became the forerunner of what became known as the Microsoft Windows 95 Logo requirements. The Logo requirements concerned more than installation and uninstallation, although these were at its core. The basic purpose of the Logo guidelines was to force independent software vendors (ISVs) to create applications that were robust, worked well with the operating system, and was not subject to indiscriminate failure. Such failures greatly increased the cost of managing a corporate network since it forced system personnel to visit the desktop where the problems were occurring.

Microsoft has always had a focus on the desktop computer environment, but during the time when Windows 95 was introduced they were facing a competing concept. This concept came about because of the introduction of the Java programming language. Even though the logo requirements were a step in the right direction, Microsoft recognized that it was not enough for the long term. Microsoft had to keep moving ahead with its technology if it was going to be able to maintain the desktop environment on which its future depended.

The Battle for the Corporate Nervous System

Corporations today continue to fight the age-old battle to increase their return on investment (ROI). With personal computers becoming more prevalent in organizations than ever, a prime sector for reducing costs is the corporate computer network. The term that is used today to identify this cost is *total cost of ownership* (TCO). There are two camps that have formed, both of which promise to lead organizations to this promised land of lower IT costs. Naturally one of these camps is comprised of Microsoft and Intel, which have produced what is called the Wintel model. The other camp is made up of Sun, Oracle, IBM, and others whose approach is based on the use of Java. Both of these camps are sticking to the three-tiered client/server architecture but with different approaches to its future implementation.

The Java-only approach being pushed by Sun and others is the Network Computer (NC). The NC architecture is a three-tiered model of computing wherein data is on database servers, applications are run from application servers, and thin clients run on the NC. The NC is a stateless machine that serves as a terminal in order to run applications and access data on a network. The NC enables the use of any different number of microprocessors since Java is a programming language that is not specific to a particular platform. The stateless nature of this machine means that that no data remain on the client after it is powered down. The data stay on the centralized servers in order to maintain the security of this data and to make the data easier to manage. The idea is that all applications that run on the NC would be developed using the Java API that would come as part of the JavaOS. Both the Java application and the JavaOS would be downloaded to the NC on demand. The main concept here is that the client is very thin and as such the administrative cost of this type of three-tiered client/server system is centered on the server side only with no administrative cost for any deployed client.

The Wintel model proposes some form of the Microsoft Windows operating system running on an Intel CPU. This model comprises a wide range of client models depending on the needs of the customer. The client strategy involves six different devices that go from handheld PCs to high-end workstations. The client model in direct competition with the network computer described above is the network PC. Even though this client will be running the Windows operating system locally it will have a sealed case to prevent the user from modifying the hardware, and the software will be managed remotely from a central IT department. As you can see, the effort to reduce TCO is also focused on the client side of the three-tiered client/server architecture. This effort is comprised of two parts, the development of the network PC specification and the Zero Administration Windows (ZAW) initiative.

The key capabilities that Microsoft's ZAW initiative implements are as follows:

- Automatic system update and application installation.
- Persistent caching of data and configuration information.
- Central administration and system lock.
- Application flexibility to design the best solutions.

These capabilities are part of Windows 2000 Server–run networks, but prior to the release of Windows 2000 Microsoft created the Zero Administration Kit (ZAK), which provides for some of this functionality to be used in networks that are run using Windows NT 4.0 Server.

Defining the New Windows Installer Technology

In support of the ZAW initiative Microsoft has developed a new technology for managing the installation of applications on its 32-bit Windows operating systems. Deploying software has typically been a large source of administrative costs for organizations. Traditional installation programs can cause problems that can normally be solved only by a member of the IT department. Some of these problems include:

Version conflicts — Microsoft Logo requirements dictate that if a setup program contains a more current version of a shared resource (such as a DLL, OCX, and so on) than is presently on the machine, the installation program should always overwrite the existing shared resource with the more current version. This dictate takes for granted that the newer version of the shared resource will work correctly with all other using applications on the system, which may not always be the case. Also, there is the possibility of overwriting the file with an *older* version and potentially disabling other applications on the system.

Failed installations — A failed installation could leave fragments (files, registry entries, and so on) behind, possibly leaving the system in an unstable or unusable state. In traditional setup programs, there were no standardized rollback features for a failed installation.

Broken applications — Users could delete key files (such as DLLs) required by an application and render the application inoperable.

Uninstall problems	Traditional uninstallers might leave fragments of an application behind. Installations were generally application-centric and did not allow for uninstallation of just one portion of the application, such as a thesaurus feature. Moreover, shared files and registry data could be used by multiple applications. This often caused problems when one application uninstalled another application's shared files or data, rendering the remaining application inoperable.
Administration	Often it was difficult to distribute applications to large numbers of client machines. Administrators had to physically visit each machine. There was no standardized method for creating applications to be distributed by administrators over a LAN. Unless the user account running the installer had administrator privileges, there was no guarantee that the installer could correctly update the registry, access network resources, and so on. This often caused installations to leave partially installed applications on the system or fail outright.

Beginning with Windows 2000, the installer service will be a native part of the operating system. Microsoft also provides a system update that allows Windows NT 4, Windows 98, and Windows 95 to use the Windows Installer service capabilities. Microsoft does not intend to make this service available for the Windows 3.x or Windows NT 3.51 operating systems.

Built on top of the Windows installer technology is a deployment architecture that will go a long way toward lowering the TCO for the networked organization. This deployment architecture will greatly facilitate the rollout of new software to the network client machines as well as make it easier to install application or operating system upgrades. This new deployment architecture will be mostly automated, which means it will be a lot less work than the present networked environment. The one drawback is that this deployment capability that comes with the Windows 2000 Server supports only desktop machines running Windows 2000 Professional.

To address the problems listed above Microsoft has created a technology that provides the capability by which installation programs can be created that avoid these problems. All ISVs can use this technology, so you won't need a homegrown installation program that might or might not perform the installation correctly. Using this technology all ISVs can be consistent and at the same time permit the new application deployment capabilities of Windows 2000 Server to implement automated software distribution within the corporate network.

The Future Is Now

Microsoft introduced ZAW with the promise that it would enable companies to significantly reduce the cost of owning PCs while maintaining their existing investments in industry-standard hardware and software. The idea is to help companies automate PC management and deploy the widest choice of applications in an organized manner.

Microsoft's implementation of ZAW includes a new installation architecture called the Windows installer service. Microsoft's Windows Installer service is a key feature of ZAW because it provides developers with system services for creating more intelligent, flexible, and manageable installations. The Windows Installer service will be a native service of Windows 2000 (formerly known as Windows NT 5). It is also available as an add-on service for Windows NT 4.0, Windows 98, and Windows 95. It will not be offered for Windows NT 3.51 or Windows 3.x.

Summary

In this chapter we have seen that the environment in which software is installed is changing, making installation much more complex than it used to be. In the corporation the environment is becoming much more controlled so that individuals do not have free reign over their desktop systems. However, the basic act of installing software is not really changing; it is just being performed differently. The same basic steps are still required.

Chapter 2

The Windows 2000 Deployment Architecture

IN THIS CHAPTER

- Windows 2000 family of operating systems
- Windows 2000 architecture
- Windows 2000 management services
- IntelliMirror
- The key technologies used to implement change and configuration management
- System management server

THIS CHAPTER FOCUSES IN on the deployment aspects of Windows 2000 and those in a Windows 2000 network. We will take a look at Windows 2000 and then investigate the architecture of this newest member of the Windows family. Most of the chapter will be devoted to taking a high-level look at the change and configuration management capabilities of Windows 2000. It is important to understand where the Windows Installer fits into the grand plan that Microsoft has for managing the desktop computer in the corporate enterprise.

Overview of the Windows 2000 Family

The foundation of Windows 2000 is the Windows NT 4.0 architecture. Parts of this architecture are being extended and there are new features being added, but overall the core of Windows 2000 is the same as Windows NT 4.0. This approach to creating Windows 2000 – building off of Windows NT 4.0 – imparts a great deal of stability to this new operating system.

The main focus of the enhancements and added features incorporated into the Windows 2000 family of operating systems is to significantly reduce the total cost of ownership (TCO). The Windows 2000 family consists of four separate versions, which are designed to serve companies of specific sizes, and specific types of applications. These versions are listed below:

- Windows 2000 Professional
- Windows 2000 Server
- Windows 2000 Advanced Server
- Windows 2000 Datacenter Server

Each is discussed in the following subsections.

Windows 2000 Professional

This version of Windows 2000 replaces Windows NT 4.0 Workstation. It is the network client and desktop operating system intended for use by companies of all sizes. This version of Windows 2000 contains the best features of Windows 98 and at the same time has retained and extended the capabilities of Windows NT 4.0 Workstation. Windows 2000 Professional supports up to two microprocessors with up to a total of 4 GB of physical memory.

Microsoft has tried to make this operating system easier to use than any of the past versions. It has created a much simpler installation process for the operating system with a robust plug-and-play capability that essentially does away with the past problems of the operating system not recognizing certain pieces of hardware. The desktop has also become more customizable with such features as personalized menus, an enhanced AutoComplete functionality, better help, and more detailed error messages that actually tell you how to fix the problem instead of just telling you that something is wrong.

Windows 2000 Server

The main use of this version of Windows 2000 is as a file, print, application, or Web server for small to medium-sized companies. Windows 2000 Server supports symmetric multiprocessing (SMP) on computers with up to four microprocessors and 4 GB of physical memory. The new features of this operating system are support for Active Directory, Windows Management Tools, Kerberos and Public Key Infrastructure (PKI) security, Windows Terminal Services, COM+ component services, and enhanced Internet and Web services.

Windows 2000 Advanced Server

Windows 2000 Advanced Server is the equivalent of what used to be called Windows NT 4.0 Server Enterprise Edition. This operating system does everything that Windows 2000 Server can do, with the addition of enhanced network and Internet capabilities. It is designed to be primarily a database server and it provides network and component load balancing. It has a complete clustering infrastructure to enable high availability and scalability.

Windows 2000 Advanced Server supports symmetric multiprocessing for up to eight microprocessors and it can access up to 8 GB of physical memory.

Windows 2000 Datacenter Server

Windows 2000 Datacenter Server is the top end of the line and it is meant for large enterprise operations. It is most appropriate for data warehouse operations or where complex calculations are necessary, such as for econometric analyses and science and engineering simulations. This is the first time that Microsoft is releasing such a powerful operating system. It supports symmetric multiprocessing for up to 32 microprocessors and it can access up to 64 GB of physical memory.

The Windows 2000 Architecture

This section talks about how Windows 2000 works. In particular it will cover the basic layout of the system architecture and will then explain how Windows 2000 manages processes and the memory model that it uses. This will just be a quick overview.

There have been many models used for developing operating systems since the advent of the computer. Four of the more important of these models are the monolithic system, the virtual machine, the layered system, and the client/server model. There is one principle that is common among all these modern operating system models and that is the principle of preventing user programs from accessing the computer hardware in any direct fashion. Based on the design of the central processing unit hardware the programmer can implement two or more privilege levels in an operating system. In the Windows operating systems there are two privilege levels called *user mode* and *kernel mode*. User mode is where application programs run and kernel mode is where operating-system services run. The terminology may vary among operating systems but the meaning is the same. Sometimes kernel mode is called *supervisor mode*.

The Windows 2000 System Components

The architecture of Windows 2000 is a layered system of modules. Figure 2-1 shows a block diagram of this system.

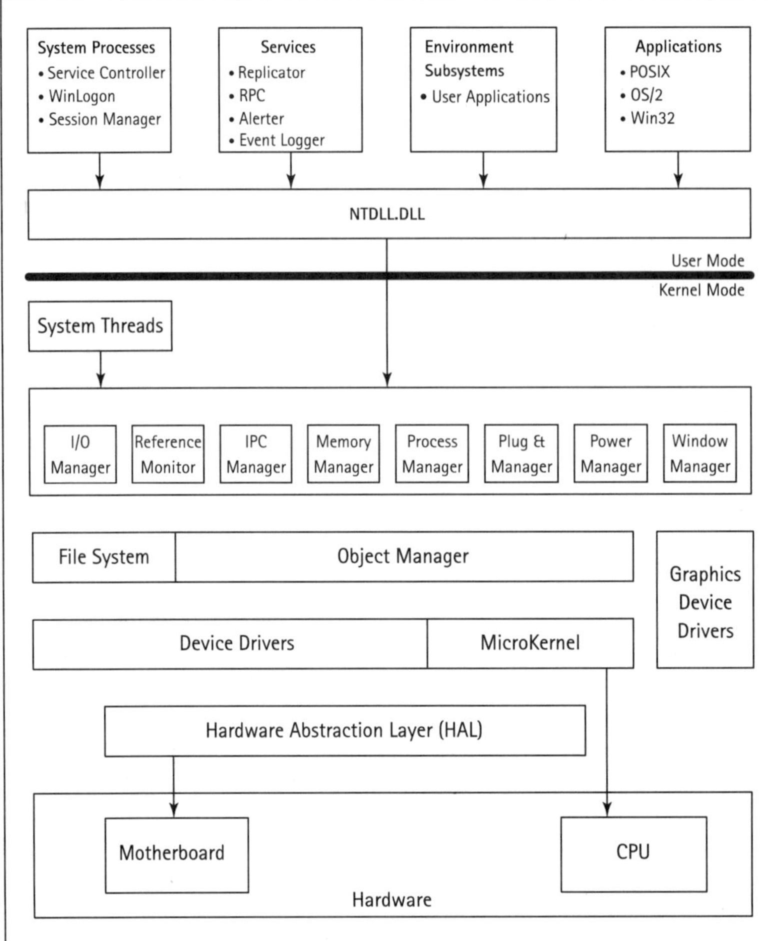

Figure 2-1: Windows 2000 component block diagram

KERNEL MODE COMPONENTS

At the lowest level in the operating system we have the Hardware Abstraction Layer (HAL), which abstracts the motherboard. The HAL is a small layer of software written by the hardware platform manufacturer. It provides the system with a generic function-call hardware interface and does away with the need to write a new operating system for each platform. The abstraction provided by the HAL is binary compatibility of device drivers across different motherboards as long as they have the same CPU architecture. The HAL enables the Windows 2000 operating system to run on either single or multiprocessor computers and allows higher-level device drivers to format data for different kinds of video monitors. In particular the HAL provides an abstraction for off-chip caches, timers, device registers, and interrupt controllers, and is implemented as HAL.DLL.

Similarly, the MicroKernel abstracts the CPU of the computer. This abstraction provides source-code compatibility of drivers across different CPU types. The MicroKernel manages two types of objects, the *dispatcher objects* and the *control objects*. Dispatcher objects control dispatching and synchronization of system operations, which include events, mutants, mutexes, semaphores, threads, and timers. Control objects are used to control the operation of the MicroKernel where dispatching is not involved. Control objects include asynchronous procedure calls, deferred procedure calls, interrupts, processes, and profiles.

In the previous paragraph you will see the terms *mutant* and *mutex*. Mutexes are used only in kernel mode and mutants are used in the Win32 subsystem to implement Win32 API mutexes.

There is a block to the right side of the previous figure called graphics device drivers. This block represents hardware-dependent graphics display drivers, printer drivers, and miniport drivers. Above the MicroKernel and the Device Driver blocks are the Object Manager and the File System blocks. The Object Manager creates, manages, and deletes objects that represent operating-system resources. These resources are such things as processes, threads, and data structures. The Object Manager creates object handles, which consist of access control information and a pointer to the object. The Object Manager also tracks the creation and use of objects and manages the global namespace for Windows 2000.

To the left of the Object Manager block is a special block called File Systems. This represents a special type of device drivers, which are either file system drivers or filter drivers. A file system driver is a driver that takes a file-oriented request and translates it into an I/O request that is bound for a particular input-output hardware device. A filter driver is a driver that intercepts an I/O request and adds value to the request before it is passed on to the I/O device.

The next layer up in our figure is the Executive. The Executive is responsible for implementing operating system functions and for providing a set of common services to all the environment subsystems. The environment subsystems run in user mode. The functionality of the Executive is contained in the file NTOSKRNL.EXE. There are two versions of this file, one for a single-processor machine and one for a multiprocessor machine. The Executive consists of a number of modules, as shown in the previous figure. The following list provides a short description of the function of each of these modules:

I/O Manager — Manages input to and output from different devices. It is made up of the file system, device driver, and cache manager components.

Security Reference Monitor — Enforces security policies on the local computer by validating access to objects and checking user privileges. It also generates audit messages.

IPC Manager	Manages the communication between clients and servers. It consists of the Local Procedure Call (LPC) facility and the Remote Procedure Call (RPC) facility. The LPC facility manages communication between clients and servers on the same computer and the RPC facility manages communications between clients and servers on different computers.
Memory Manager	Implements and controls virtual memory. It is a memory-management system that provides a private address space for each process and protects this address space from incursion by other processes. This module also implements demand paging where disk space is used as a storage area when code and data need to be moved out of physical RAM.
Process Manager	Creates, terminates, and manages processes and threads. These management duties involve suspending and restoring threads as well as retrieving information about processes and threads.
Plug and Play Manager	Coordinates the adding and removal of hardware devices. It maintains control of the central Plug & Play process by communicating with these device drivers for these devices and instructing them to add and start the devices.
Power Manager	Implements power-management policy through the control of the power-management APIs. It coordinates power events and generates power-management requests.
Window Manager	Combines the windowing functionality of the operating system with functions required for drawing on these windows. The Window Manager is implemented by a single device driver implemented in the file WIN32K.SYS. Controlling the windowing capability of Windows 2000 consists of managing screen output and receiving input from devices such as the keyboard and the mouse. Input from these devices is passed as messages to applications.

The last item to be discussed as far as kernel mode implementation is concerned is the block in our figure called System Threads. These are special threads that run only in kernel mode and are housed in the system process. Many of the modules described above use system threads to perform their functions. System threads do not have a user-process address space and therefore must allocate any dynamic memory from the operating-system memory heap. These threads do, however, have all the attributes and contexts of a regular user-mode thread but they only execute code that is loaded into system space.

USER-MODE COMPONENTS

Figure 2-1 shows four basic types of user-mode processes. It also shows a block called NTDLL.DLL. NTDLL.DLL is a special file that provides support for the subsystem DLLs. This file contains functions that are stubs to the Windows 2000 executive system services, and some internal support functions that are used by the subsystem DLLs.

Above the block showing NTDLL.DLL and to the left side there is a block entitled System Processes. The processes shown here are special system processes that run in user mode. These include the WINLOGON.EXE process, which implements the interactive logon functionality, SERVICES.EXE, which is called the Service Control Manager and manages all user mode NT services, and SMSS.EXE, which is the session manager.

The block labeled Services refers to all the NT services that are running on the system. The ones shown in the block are those NT services that come with the operating system, but there could be any number of add-on server applications running as well. Good examples of add-on server applications are Microsoft SQL Server and Microsoft Exchange Server.

The Environment Subsystems block denotes an implementation that exposes some subset of the Windows 2000 executive system services to application programs. This block is combined with the Applications block, which enables applications to run on Windows 2000 even if they were written to run on a different operating system. Windows 2000 supports applications written for Win32, Windows 3.1, MS-DOS, POSIX, or OS/2. Applications can only call those APIs that have been exported by the particular environment subsystem that they are using. For Windows 2000 to run, the Win32 subsystem must always be running. This subsystem is implemented in the file CSRSS.EXE. The OS/2 and the POSIX subsystems are only started if an application needs them in order to run.

Windows 2000 process management

Windows 2000 is a multithreaded, multitasking operating system that is designed to use more than one microprocessor. The Windows 2000 setup detects whether the target system has one or more than one processor. Depending on the situation there are two files that are different even though they will end of with the same name after they get copied to the System32 directory. There will of course be the specific version of HAL.DLL required for the motherboard in the computer and there will be the correct version of NTOSKRNL.EXE. On the Windows 2000 CD-ROM there are two versions of this file, which provides the executive and kernel functionality. There is NTOSKRNL.EXE, which gets copied as is if the machine only has one processor; and there is NTKRNLMP.EXE, which gets copied and renamed NTOSKRNL.EXE if the machine has more than one processor.

When we talk about process management in Windows 2000, we need to talk about both processes and threads. We don't need to talk about programs since a program is just a static set of bits on a disk somewhere. A process is a dynamic entity that can be considered a set of resources that is reserved for the threads that are executing inside the process. A process can be considered to consist of the following items:

- The initial code and data of the program that is being executed.
- A private virtual address space that is only available to the threads in the process unless another process makes part of its address space available through the use of a shred memory section.
- A set of resources that the operating system makes available to the process. These resources can be things such as files, ports, windows resources, and so forth.
- A minimum of one thread of execution running in the process space.
- A unique process ID that defines the process to the operating system.

A process needs to have at least one thread of execution; otherwise the process does not exist. It is a thread that Windows 2000 will schedule for execution. Each thread runs within a process and shares the virtual memory space of the process. Every thread in a process consists of the following components:

- The contents of the registers that represent the state of the processor.
- A stack for the thread to use when executing in user mode.
- A stack for the thread to use when executing in kernel mode.
- A private storage space to be used by subsystems, runtime libraries, and dynamic link libraries.
- A thread ID that uniquely defines the thread to the system and to the process.

Just as a process can contain a group of threads, a job object can contain a group of processes. The basic function of a job object is to permit a group of processes to be manipulated and managed as a single entity. The job object also keeps track of all information for the processes that are or have been associated with the job.

Because Windows 2000 is a multitasking operating system, a process can have more than one thread running at the same time. When there is more than one thread active, the operating system needs to handle which thread gets access to the

CPU and how long the thread can execute before another thread gets access. The same is true when there is more than one process being executed by the operating system. The kernel is responsible for scheduling access to the CPU and it does this through a system of priority levels that are assigned to both processes and threads.

There are 32 different priority levels, numbered 0 to 31, with higher numbers indicating higher priority. Priority levels 0–5 are used for processes and threads running in user mode and levels 15–31 are used for processes and threads running in kernel mode. The Windows 2000 kernel assigns each process a base priority level and a separate base priority level for each thread that is executing within the process. The base priority level of the process stays constant but the level for a thread can range from two levels above to two levels below the base priority level of the process. Depending on the activity that a thread is performing the kernel can raise or lower its priority level.

When there is more than one processor in a computer on which Windows 2000 is running, Windows 2000 uses Symmetric Multiprocessing (SMP). This is considered a more efficient way to implement parallel processing than Asynchronous Multiprocessing (ASMP).

Windows 2000 memory management

Windows 2000 uses a virtual memory management system model, which is based on a flat 32-bit address space. A 32-bit address space permits up to 4 GB of memory addresses. Because almost no PC can have as much as 4 GB of physical memory, Windows 2000 uses a virtual memory management system.

Implementing virtual memory management is the function of the Virtual Memory Manager (VMM) and it involves two primary activities as listed below:

- Mapping a process's virtual address space through the use of a memory-mapping table so as to keep track of what virtual memory address requested by a thread corresponds to what physical memory address. When a thread requests access to memory, it uses a virtual memory address and this gets translated into a physical memory address before data or code is moved.
- Moving code or data to disk when it has to be moved out of physical memory because another thread or process needs that physical location. This activity is normally called *paging*.

Even though there are 4 GB of virtual memory, because of the 32-bit addressing scheme of Windows 2000 only 2 GB of this are available to user-mode processes. The other 2 GB of virtual memory are reserved for use by kernel-mode threads. The lower 2 GB of memory addresses are used by both user-mode and kernel-mode processes and the upper 2 GB of virtual memory addresses are reserved for kernel-mode threads.

Windows 2000 Management Services

Since this book concerns the installation of software we need to focus on those aspects of a Windows 2000 network that deal with this subject. This brings us to a discussion of the management services that are part of Windows 2000. The management services provide the tools that enable the network administrator to maintain servers and networked users from a central location. They can be broken down into the following categories:

- Infrastructure management
- Desktop change and configuration management
- Storage management

Of these three, change and configuration management interests us the most. I will provide a brief overview of the other two categories here and then address change and configuration management in the next section.

Infrastructure management

There are fifteen components that can be considered to comprise the infrastructure management capability of the Windows 2000 server. This capability enables a LAN administrator to manage, from a central location, collections of users, computers, applications, and network resources. These components are discussed briefly in the following subsections.

ADVANCED SYSTEM RECOVERY (ASR)

ASR facilitates disaster recovery. It integrates the various components of backup, restore, repair, and recovery into a unified whole. When using ASR, a user can save the complete state of his or her system so that it can be restored in the event of a disaster.

DISK DUPLICATION

This capability enables you to clone a machine's hard drive onto other machines that have the same hardware and domain configurations. This is much easier and more efficient than setting up a lot of machines individually. This is of value to original equipment manufacturers (OEMs), value-added resellers (VARs), and system administrators.

KERBEROS AUTHENTICATION

This capability fully supports the Kerberos Version 5 authentication protocol, which replaces the Windows NT LAN Manager (NTLM) protocol used in Windows NT 4.0. Kerberos is the primary security protocol for gaining access to all the resources within and across a Windows 2000 Server domain. It provides fast, single login to these resources.

MICROSOFT MANAGEMENT CONSOLE (MMC)

The Microsoft Management Console (MMC) provides a framework that you can extend by creating *snap-ins*. These snap-ins provide the management functionality of the console; MMC does not provide any management functionality of its own. Snap-ins are management components integrated into a common host, the Microsoft Management Console. Each snap-in provides one unit of management behavior and snap-ins can be combined to provide a custom management tool.

MMC is a core part of the Microsoft strategy for managing the corporate network. It simplifies the day-to-day tasks required for system management. The Microsoft Management Console enables the system administrator to create special tools in order to delegate specific administrative tasks to users or groups.

PUBLIC KEY INFRASTRUCTURE (PKI)

The purpose of the Public Key Infrastructure (PKI) in Windows 2000 is to make it easy for e-commerce, intranets, extranets, and Web-enabled applications to use public-key cryptography. Public-key cryptography provides three capabilities that are essential for applications that require distributed security — that is, security in which the participants are not part of the same network and have no common security credentials.

Public-key cryptography provides privacy for data, allows authentication of users and machines, and can prove that a particular user took a particular action. These capabilities can be used to encrypt e-mails, verify visitors to a corporate intranet, and sign legally binding electronic contracts.

PKI is a set of operating-system and application services that makes it easy and convenient to use public-key cryptography. In particular, PKI enables you to do the following:

- Issue new keys
- Review and/or revoke existing keys
- Manage the trust level attached to keys from different issuers
- Locate and retrieve public keys
- Determine whether a specific key is valid or not
- Provide an easy-to-use method for users to use keys

The Windows 2000 PKI is comprised of four main components: Certificate Services; Active Directory; PKI-enabled applications such as Internet Explorer, Internet Information Server, Outlook, and Outlook Express; and the Exchange Key Management Service (KMS).

Certificate Services is a core operating system service that enables businesses to act as their own certificate authority so that they can issue and manage digital certificates. The Active Directory directory service is also a core operating system service that provides a single place to find network resources. With respect to PKI it serves as the publication service. A more complete discussion of Active Directory is provided in a later section of this chapter. The Exchange Key Management Service is a component of Microsoft Exchange that allows for the archiving and retrieval of keys used to encrypt e-mail.

REPAIR COMMAND CONSOLE

This capability is encapsulated in a utility that enables an authorized user to read/write NTFS volumes using the Windows 2000 Server boot floppies. In this mode you can copy files, start and stop services, and repair the system. You can also repair the master boot record, boot sector, and format disk volumes, and repartition volumes using fdisk. This new capability in Windows 2000 obviates the need to perform a parallel or repair installation of the operating system, which saves you considerable time.

SAFE MODE BOOT

Windows 2000 Server supports a safe-mode options screen that you can access from the initial boot loader by pressing F8. It enables a user to prevent the operating system from becoming unbootable after a "badly behaved" driver or an application that uses kernel mode drivers has been installed. If a computer will not start because of this bad driver, the user can start the operating system with minimal services. These minimal services are mouse, monitor, keyboard, mass storage, base video, and default system services. There is no network support provided in this mode. From this mode the user can either change the default settings or remove the installed driver that is causing the problem.

SECURITY CONFIGURATION MANAGER

The Security Configuration Manager is a "define once, apply many times" technology that allows network administrators to define security configurations as a template, which can then be applied to selected computers all in one operation. This can be considered as a one-stop security configuration and analysis tool for Windows 2000 Server. It permits the configuration of various security-sensitive registry settings, access controls on files and registry keys, and security configuration of system services.

SECURITY SERVICES

This capability relates to those security mechanisms that are integrated with the Active Directory. The purpose of this integration is to make security policy easy to configure. It makes controlling the permissions and access rights for large numbers of people fairly simple. Through these services a network administrator can delegate down to the organizational unit (OU) level the rights to manage user and group accounts. The section in this chapter on the Group Policy Editor will talk more about the concept of organizational units.

SERVER CONFIGURATION WIZARD

Windows 2000 Server has a configuration wizard that simplifies the configuration of the various components of the operating system. You can use it to automatically configure Active Directory Server, Networking Server, File Server, Print Server, Web Server, and Clustering Server. These are called scenarios and the configuration wizard will only install the relevant services that are required for the scenario in question.

TASK SCHEDULER

The Task Scheduler automatically invokes a script or application at a specified time. It is a user interface that is fully integrated into the operating system. The Task Scheduler provides a common and fully programmable set of interfaces, which are COM-based. The purpose of the Task Scheduler is to unify a set of disparate tools and enable developers to build their applications automatically. It also enables them to add scheduling services to their applications.

TERMINAL SERVICES

The Terminal Services feature of Windows 2000 Server allows low-end client machines to run Windows applications using terminal emulation. With Terminal Services running on Windows 2000 Server, application execution, data processing, and data storage occur on the server and not on the client desktop. Terminal Services is an implementation of thin-client technology where only an application's user interface is transmitted to the client. Each user who logs on to this service will see only his or her particular session of the application being accessed on the server. Even though this is a thin-client technology, a normal PC (fat client) can also run in this mode for some applications and in the normal mode for other applications. The normal mode for a PC is to have the application execution, data processing, and data storage occurring on the PC itself.

Terminal Services centralizes the management of computing resources for all the clients connected in terminal emulation mode to the server. Using these services enables a faster migration of the desktop to the Windows 2000 environment. It also centralizes the deployment of applications and provides the system administrator with the ability to remotely administer each member of the Windows 2000 family of operating systems. The system administrator can do this from a client machine over a wide area network or via a dial-up connection.

UNATTENDED SETUP

This capability enables original equipment manufacturers (OEMs), value-added resellers (VARs), and system administrators to install Windows 2000 Server without the need for any interaction with the computer. It can also include the unattended setup of scenarios such as Active Directory and Clustering. Using Unattended Setup is faster and easier than having to customize and install each operating system individually.

WINDOWS MANAGEMENT INSTRUMENTATION (WMI)

Windows Management Instrumentation is the Microsoft implementation of the Web-based Enterprise Management (WBEM) standard. WBEM is an industry initiative to develop a standardized and non-proprietary means for accessing and sharing management information in an enterprise network. WBEM specifies standards for a unifying architecture that allows access to data from a variety of underlying technologies and platforms. This data is presented consistently so that management applications can use it to create solutions that reduce the maintenance and life-cycle costs of managing a company's network. WBEM is based on the Common Information Model (CIM) schema, which is an industry standard developed under the auspices of the Desktop Management Task Force (DMTF).

Windows 2000 supports the Windows Management Instrumentation standard. WMI lets management applications from different sources manage all of an organization's devices, drivers, services, and applications consistently.

WINDOWS SCRIPT HOST (WSH)

The Windows Script Host provides a rich capability for creating scripts that can replace the older command or batch file language. WSH enables system administrators to automate tasks such as creating shortcuts or connecting to a network server. The Windows Script Host comes native with scripting engines that support VBScript and JScript. Other scripting languages can be supported if the user provides the necessary scripting engine to support the IActiveScriptParse COM interface. Third-party engines are already available for Perl, TCL, and REXX. We will discuss this in more detail when we discuss creating custom actions using either VBScript or JScript.

Storage management

There are three components that can be considered to comprise the storage management capability of Windows 2000 Server. These components are discussed in the following subsections.

HIERARCHICAL STORAGE MANAGEMENT (HSM)

Hierarchical Storage Management is a new concept that is being introduced as an enhancement to NTFS5. You can use it to keep frequently accessed files readily available and hold down overall storage costs at the same time. HSM does this by keeping the most frequently used files on local storage while moving less frequently used files to slower and less expensive media such as optical drives or tape. HSM works with what are called *reparse points*. A reparse point in this regard is used as a surrogate for a file that is being kept on a remote storage device. The information about the file that is being stored remotely is provided in a stub file that contains the reparse point. This information points to the device where the file is actually located. The NTFS5 file system uses this information to retrieve the file. File retrieval is facilitated through the use of the Remote Storage Service.

REMOVABLE STORAGE MANGER (RSM)

The Removable Storage Manager provides a means for enumerating all removable media in the system except for floppy disks and other low-capacity media. The removable media can be stored off line on a shelf or on line in some type of robotic library. RSM provides a common interface to the removable media through a single set of APIs. It uses *media pools*, which organize the media. Media pools control the selection of media and media type and enable the user to share the media across applications. Media pools also enable the user to track which applications are doing the sharing.

BACKUP UTILITY

The Backup Utility is a set of wizards that enables the system administrator to prepare for disaster recovery. The first task in preparing for disaster recovery is to use the Backup wizard to create a backup for the entire server. The second task is to use the Disaster Recovery Preparation wizard to prepare a set of disaster recovery disks that can be used to fully recover a failed system. Finally the Recovery wizard takes the user through all the steps required to actually recover the system. All these wizards are part of the new Backup Utility.

Desktop Change and Configuration Management

We are now inching closer to the real subject of this book, which is software installation. We are now going to focus on those aspects of the Windows 2000 environment that deal with the deployment of software. What we are talking about here is the management of the desktops that are in the network. The term "change and configuration" represents the reality in today's corporate network. Both hardware and software keep changing and people's needs for these resources also keep changing. Managing this continual change, making sure that the desktops are configured correctly, and doing it all from a central location are the objectives of Change and Configuration Management. Being able to do these things correctly can greatly reduce the total cost of ownership of the network.

Following are the advantages you can get from the proper use of the Change and Configuration Management features in Windows 2000.

- Computing environment settings can be set from a central location. The system administrator can set the computing environment settings to affect groups of computers as well as groups of people. He or she can then be sure that the settings will be enforced as planned.
- When a desktop computer fails and has to be taken out of service, it can be quickly replaced with an identical environment. This means that all data, applications, preferences, and administrative policies are set up on the new desktop.

- Users in a workgroup are able to roam among other computers in the same workgroup, and when they sign onto the network they will be presented with all their data, applications, and preferences.
- Through the process of automatic synchronization between the desktop and the network users can work offline if the network connection is lost. This is because the files that are on the network are cached locally.
- Administrators can manage the installation, upgrade, or removal of software from a central vantage point. This eliminates the need for the end user to intervene with the management of the locally installed software. As we discussed in Chapter 1, improper software installation is one of the major contributors to increasing the total cost of ownership. This is because whenever a desktop computer is left in an unknown state because of a failed installation or uninstallation, system personnel have to visit the machine in order to solve the problem. Windows 2000 circumvents this problem.
- You can upgrade or automatically install the desktop operating system from a remote server. This greatly increases the stability of the operating system. There are now prescribed methods you can use to upgrade the operating system and installations will no longer be able to change system files in the System32 directory.

The Change and Configuration Management capabilities of Windows 2000 are implemented through IntelliMirror, Remote OS Installation, and Microsoft Systems Management Server (SMS). (Microsoft considers SMS to be a value-added solution and not part of the core functionality of Change and Configuration Management.) The important technologies that support these capabilities are Active Directory, Group Policy, and the Windows Installer Service. We discuss these technologies in the following sections. Of course, the remainder of the book is devoted to an in-depth discussion of the Windows Installer Service, so we will not go into any detail about that technology in this chapter.

IntelliMirror

The purpose of IntelliMirror is to enable a user's environment to follow wherever he or she goes. IntelliMirror enables users to roam between machines by mirroring a user's desktop data, applications, and settings on a network server. This keeps the user from having any down time, which in turn enhances the productivity of the entire workgroup. This enhances the productivity of both the user and the administrator; it helps the administrator because this capability can be implemented from a centralized location.

IntelliMirror has three main features: user data management, software installation and maintenance, and user settings management. These features can be used individually or all together, depending on the needs of the organization. We discuss these features in the following subsections.

User data management

User data is, as you might expect, contained in files. When you are implementing this feature of IntelliMirror, user data is stored in specified network locations, but it will appear to the user that this data is stored on the local machine. In this respect it can be said that the user's data will follow the user, which is the objective in what is called a *roaming environment.* You can enable the user's data to roam with the user in three different ways. You can configure the roaming environment manually, set it up on a per-user basis, or use the Group Policy Editor to configure it.

Having a network location look as if it were on the local machine is implemented through what is called *folder redirection.* Folder redirection is discussed later in this chapter.

Software installation and maintenance

This feature of IntelliMirror deals with making software available to the desktops in a controlled way and from a central location. In the controlled environment of a Windows 2000 network the end user cannot install software unless it has been determined that his or her job requires it, or it is otherwise approved for use in the corporation. In addition to being able to centrally manage the installation of applications to be used on the desktop you can also distribute upgrades to these applications using the same centralized management model. The major technologies you can use to implement this feature of IntelliMirror are Group Policy, and the Windows Installer Service. We discuss each of these technologies in its own separate section later in this chapter.

You, the system administrator, have two options as regards deploying software in a Windows 2000 network: you can either *publish* the software or *assign* it. When you assign software, you can make it available to everyone who uses a particular computer or you can make it available to only a specific user. You would typically publish software for those applications that are not necessarily required for a person's job but which might be found useful. An example of an application that would be published is a file compression utility. This allows each person to decide if he or she wants the software and, if so, to install it. If a person required a specific application, then you would assign it instead of publishing it. Table 2-1 provides a complete description of the various software deployment options that you can implement in a Windows 2000 network.

Table 2-1 SOFTWARE DEPLOYMENT OPTIONS IN A WINDOWS 2000 NETWORK

Deployment Option	Description	Implementation
Publish	Installation	The user installs the software by going to the Add/Remove Programs applet and initiating the installation. If the user tries to open a file that requires this software, the software will be installed if it is not already there.
	Uninstallation	The user uninstalls the software by going to the Add/Remove Programs applet and initiating the uninstallation. The software will still be available for reinstallation in the future.
	Supported Format	The installation is described in a Windows Installer Package or in a ZAP file. A ZAP file is a text file that describes how the software is to be installed.
Assign to a user	Installation	The software will be available for installation the next time the user logs onto the network. The user will initiate the installation either from the icon on the Start\Programs menu or from the Add/Remove Programs applet. If the user tries to open a file that requires this software, the software will be installed if it is not already there.
	Uninstallation	The user uninstalls the software by going to the Add/Remove Programs applet and initiating the uninstallation. The software will still be available for reinstallation after the next logon: the reinstallation will be performed like the original installation.
	Supported Format	The installation needs to be described in a Windows Installer Package.
Assign to a computer	Installation	The software will be automatically installed the next time the computer is booted.
	Uninstallation	The only person who can uninstall the software is the person who has local administrator privileges. However, normal users can perform a repair operation on the software.

Deployment Option	Description	Implementation
	Supported Format	The installation needs to be described in a Windows Installer Package.

As shown in the above table, it is possible to publish software even if that software does not have a Windows Installer package. These applications that do not use the Windows Installer will be installed using their own setup routines but before Software Installation and Maintenance feature can use them the installation needs to be described in a ZAW applications package (.zap) file. A .zap file is a text file that contains information on the required command line to be used, the name, version, and language of the application, and the application entry points that need to be entered into the registry. These entry points are file extension, CLSID, and ProgID, and they are the items that would trigger an installation of the application.

When software that does not use the Windows Installer service for its installation is deployed, there are a number of features of deployment that you won't be able to use. You will not be able to use elevated privileges in order to conduct the installation: essentially this means that the end user will have to have administrative privileges on the local system. You will also not be able to assign the software so that it is installed on first use, and you will not be able to have first-use installation of a feature. Finally, you will not be able to instigate a complete rollback of a failed installation or uninstallation. There are other features of the Windows Installer Service that you will also not be able to take advantage of but these are the most significant. The message here is that you should recreate or migrate your installation packages so that they can be compatible with the Windows Installer.

User settings management

A number of items comprise a user's settings. There are four categories of these settings, as shown in Table 2-2.

TABLE 2-2 CATEGORIES OF USER SETTINGS

Category	Description
User-initiated settings	These are settings that the user might change, such as the icons on the desktop, the wallpaper, and the color scheme to be used. These settings will follow roaming users regardless of what machine they are using since the settings are saved on the network server.

Continued

TABLE 2-2 CATEGORIES OF USER SETTINGS *(Continued)*

Category	Description
Administrative settings	Administrators can customize and control a user's computing environment and actually restrict those preferences that a user can personalize. These restricted settings will follow roaming users to any machine.
Temporary information	Temporary information stays with the machine on settings which it was generated and does not roam with the user.
Local computer settings	Local computer information stays with the machine on which it was generated and does not roam with the user.

The concept behind the user settings management feature of IntelliMirror is that users' settings will follow them when they roam from machine to machine. This does not mean that all the settings described above will roam with the user, as that would create unnecessary overhead in the system. Only the vital user and administrative settings roam with the user; the temporary and local settings will not. The temporary and local settings are regenerated as necessary.

This capability is made possible through the use of Active Directory, group policy, offline folders/files, roaming user profiles, and the enhancements that have been made to the Windows shell. We discuss each of these technologies briefly later in this chapter.

Remote OS Installation

Remote OS installation is a feature of Windows 2000 that permits the systems administrator to deploy an operating system throughout an enterprise without having to actually visit each machine. This goes a long way toward Microsoft's goal of minimizing the cost of administering large networks. Combining this capability for remote installation with the features found in IntelliMirror you have the ability to perform machine replacement in the enterprise from a centralized location. By *machine replacement* I mean that a machine can be rebuilt from the bottom up with regard to the OS, the required applications, and a user's data and settings. This not only helps in setting up new machines but can also reduce the cost of disaster recovery operations.

Active Directory, Group Policy, Dynamic Host Configuration Protocol (DHCP), Remote Installation Services, and Domain Name Services (DNS) all combine to enable you to remotely install operating systems. Each of these technologies is briefly described in the following two sections.

The Application Specification for Microsoft Windows 2000 for desktop applications provides an excellent source of information for making your application compatible with the requirements of IntelliMirror. This specification can be downloaded form the Microsoft Web site.

The Key Technologies Used to Implement Change and Configuration Management

There are three major technologies underlying the deployment capabilities in a Windows 2000 network: Active Directory, Group Policy, and of course the Windows Installer Service. There are also ten minor technologies involved. We discuss the three major technologies in this section and the ten minor ones in the next section.

Active Directory

The computing world of today is distributed and I do not think that anyone would argue with that. To use the resources in a distributed environment we have to be able to find them. This is where a *directory service* comes into the picture. A directory service provides a means of storing information about the resources that comprise a network and the various entities that are using these resources. A directory service also provides a mechanism to name, describe, locate, access, manage, and secure the information about these resources and entities. When we refer to the resources in a distributed environment, we are talking about things like applications, files, printers, and so forth. When we refer to entities, we are talking about people, workgroups, organizational units (OU), and so forth.

With all the resources and entities in a modern distributed network there must be something that handles the relationships between them. Once again this is a directory service. A directory enables the system administrator to manage resources and entities. It also works with the security mechanism of the operating system to maintain and strengthen the security of the distributed environment. You need security management for the desktop, remote dial-up users, and external customers that come in to the system via the Internet. Finally, a directory service has to be able to handle synchronization and interoperation with other directory services.

Enter Active Directory, the Windows 2000 Server implementation of a directory service that is used to manage the domains in a Windows 2000 network. Active

Directory provides all users in the distributed environment with access to all the resources in a domain via a single network logon. It also provides a system administrator with a centralized point for administering all the resources and entities on the network. Because we are now in the object-oriented world all resources and entities that make up the distributed environment are called *objects* and that is how we will refer to them from now on.

Microsoft considers Active Directory to be the first enterprise-class directory service that is scalable, built from the ground up using Internet-standard technologies, and fully integrated with the operating system. Active Directory is hierarchical in nature and is object-oriented. It organizes information about the objects in a tree-like structure that has containers and objects and looks a lot like the directories and files in a file system. Figure 2-2 shows how this might look for a particular company.

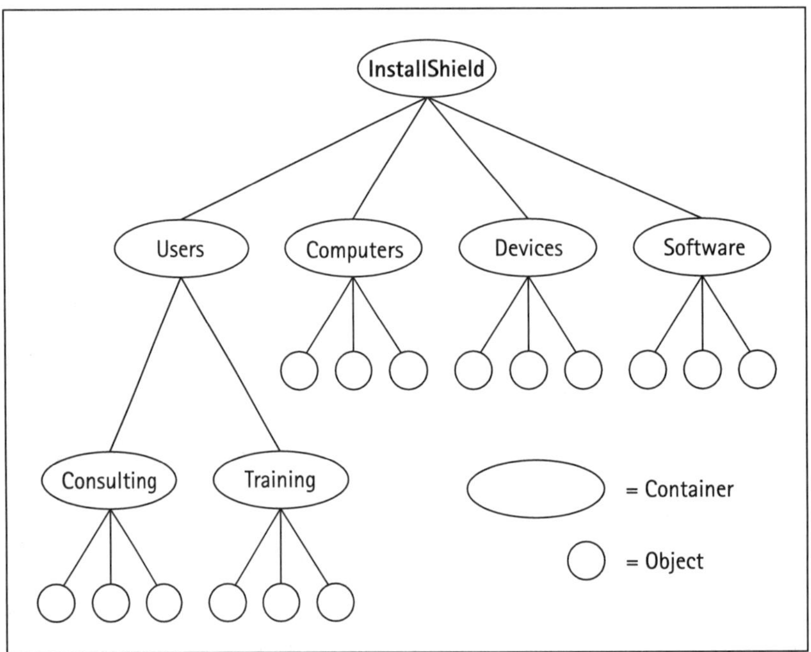

Figure 2-2: Active Directory tree structure defining the containers and objects in a domain

All network objects exist inside a domain and as such the domain is the basic unit of Active Directory. A single domain in Active Directory can span multiple physical locations and to simplify administration Microsoft recommends that system administrators create large domains – if possible, only one domain for the enterprise. When more than one domain is needed, you create what are called *domain trees.* A domain tree consists of two or more domains that share a common schema and configuration and form a contiguous namespace. (I'll define the term *namespace* later in this section.) The domains in a tree are linked together by what are called *trust relationships.* A trust relationship is a relationship established between two domains that allows users in one domain to be recognized by a domain controller in the other domain. Trusts let users access resources in the other domain and also let administrators administer user rights for users in the other domain.

We can also have what is called a *domain forest*, where there are two or more domain trees that do not form a contiguous namespace. However, all trees in the forest share a common schema, configuration, and global catalog.

Through the global catalog for a domain, domain tree, or domain forest users and administrators can find and access any object on the network. Through clients that support the interfaces to Active Directory users can query the global catalog to find the information they need. You can find a user on the network, for example, by initiating a query on first name, last name, e-mail alias, office location, or any other attribute that might be stored for that user's account.

The global catalog is a service and a store that is the repository of all information from all the domains in the enterprise. As described above, the purpose of the global catalog is to serve as the target of any query that is trying to find an object on the network. The global catalog is kept on the domain controllers in the system.

The namespace system used by Active Directory is one that closely adheres to the Domain Naming System (DNS) set of protocols and services used by the Internet and TCP/IP networks. A typical DNS namespace looks like `www.installshield.com`: this standard format allows domain and computers to be given hierarchically friendly names. An example of this is shown in Figure 2-3.

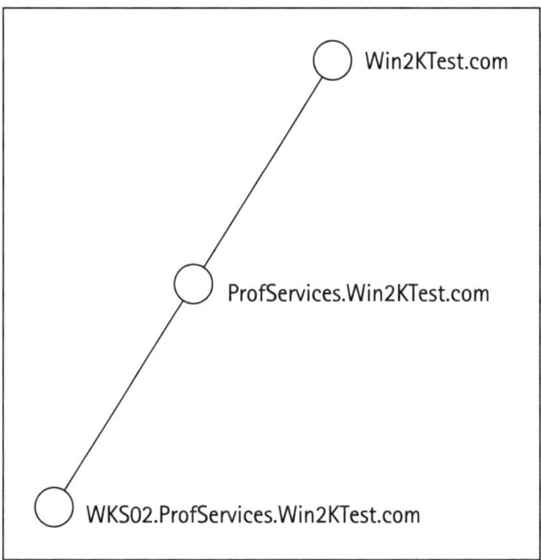

Figure 2-3: A hierarchy of domain and computer names using the DNS naming convention

Since this is supposed to be a brief overview of Active Directory we should not get into any more detail on this subject. However, it is probably important to at least list a few of the other important aspects of this technology.

Security	You control which users can view and access objects in the Active Directory through an Access Control List (ACL). You can grant access on an attribute-by-attribute basis. The security functionality of Active Directory supports both the inheritance and the delegation of authority. With inheritance all the children of an object will have the same security permissions as their parent object. With delegation an administrator can grant administrative rights to other individuals and groups.
Replication	In order to improve fault tolerance, load balancing, and performance, you can replicate the directory to each domain controller in the network that is running Active Directory. If information is changed on one copy of the directory, this information is forwarded to all other domain controllers that are hosting the Active Directory.
Interoperability	Active Directory supports other industry standards so as to allow for interaction between it and other directory services. In particular Active Directory supports the Lightweight Directory Access Protocol (LDAP). It also supports the Name Service Provider Interface (NSPI) and Hypertext Transfer Protocol (HTTP).

Now that we have an idea of what the Active Directory is all about we can proceed to a discussion of Group Policy. Group Policy is heavily dependent on the Active Directory.

Group Policy

When Microsoft Windows NT 4.0 was released, system administrators were introduced to a new tool called the *System Policy Editor.* This tool enabled the administrator to specify Windows NT registry–based policy for both user and computer configurations. You can create system policy in the following ways:

- Create default settings for the computer and user policy for the domain.
- Create custom settings that apply to individual users, groups of users, or individual computers.
- Specify the location from which to download policy and the way in which it will be downloaded for all or some users.

With the System Policy Editor you can set such user policies as access to the control panel, the wallpaper that can be used on the desktop, what can appear on the desktop, and so forth. For instance, a user can have access disabled to such items as the Run and Find commands as well as the registry editors REGEDT32.EXE and REGEDIT.EXE. Computer properties you can set with the System Policy Editor relate to access to system resources such as printers, servers, and so forth.

Windows 2000 brings an extension to the functionality of the System Policy Editor. This enhancement takes the form of the Group Policy Editor that is a snap-in to the Microsoft Management Console (MMC). The Group Policy Editor snap-in enables you to set Group Policy options for registry-based policy, security settings, software installation, scripts, and folder redirection. These items are described at the end of this section. Group Policy settings are contained in what is called a Group Policy Object, which is associated with particular Active Directory directory system containers such as domains and organizational units (OUs). Table 2-3 provides a brief comparison between the System Policy Editor and the Group Policy Editor.

TABLE 2-3 COMPARISON BETWEEN THE SYSTEM POLICY AND THE GROUP POLICY EDITORS

Feature	System Policy Editor	Group Policy Editor
Control	Policies are applied to domains or domain groups only. Policies can be further controlled by user membership in security groups.	Policies can be applied to sites, domains, and organization units. A site is defined as one or more TCP/IP subnets. Policies can be further controlled by user membership in security groups. These policies affect all users and computers in the specified Active Directory container.
Security	Policies are not secure, because they are contained in the registry.	Policies are secure, because they are contained inside Group Policy Objects.
Scope	Policies that can be set are limited to those related to desktop lockdown.	Policies can be used for enhancing desktop lockdown and for enhancing the user's computing environment. Enhancements include software installation, scripts, and folder redirection.
Change Management	Because policies set with this tool are registry-based, only these policies will tend to persist even after a user's group membership is changed. The only way to circumvent this is to manually reverse the specified policy or to have the user edit the registry.	A Group Policy Object contains a description of the policies that have been set and is thus able to automatically clean up the registry when that attributes of the object are changed.

The various policy areas that the Group Policy Editor can set are actually snap-in extensions to the Group Policy Editor snap-in. These extensions are Administrative Templates, Security Settings, Software Installation, Scripts, and Folder Redirection, which are briefly described below:

Administrative Templates	The Administrative Templates are primarily focused on setting registry-based policy. These are the same as described above for the System Policy Editor. In addition, however, these templates also include the capability for setting Disk Quotas and Remote Installation options. These are described in the next section on the supporting technologies.
Security Settings	This extension is used to define the security configuration for all the computers defined within a Group Policy Object. You can define computer, domain, and network security settings with this functionality.
Software Installation	You can use this extension to centrally manage the deployment of software within the organization. This is where the capability to publish and assign applications to groups of users is implemented.
Scripts	Scripts automate the startup and shutdown of computers. You can also automate the network logon and logoff activities. You can write scripts in VBScript or JScript, because the Windows Script Host that comes with Windows 2000 natively supports these script languages.
Folder Redirection	This permits the redirection of special folders on the desktop so that they point to the network. I describe this in more detail in the next section on the supporting technologies.

We now move onto a short discussion of the third key technology that supports the Change and Configuration Management functionality of a Windows 2000 network.

Windows Installer Service

This is the subject of the remainder of this book so this is just an introduction. The Windows Installer Service is a native operating system–resident service that comes with Windows 2000. This service runs on the desktop and provides the capability that IntelliMirror and the Group Policy Editor require to deploy software to the client machines in the network. You can also install Windows Installer on machines running Windows NT 4.0, Windows 95, and Windows 98. The Windows Installer is not supported on any Windows NT platform earlier than version 4.0 and it is not supported on any 16-bit version of Windows.

The Windows Installer concept originated with the Microsoft Office team, which was trying to create an approach to installing Office that was better than the present in-house tools. The team wanted to get away from having to write installation scripts and therefore created a data-driven concept. This approach started to look so promising that the concept was taken out of the Office team's scope and given a life of its own. What has evolved is this installation service, which is part of the operating system that defines a standard format for creating installations and also provides some serious additional functionality to applications through the implementation of a management API function set.

This new installation functionality consists of the description of the product and how it should be installed. This information is contained in a database that the Installer engine knows how to interpret.

Chapter 3 provides a much deeper discussion of this subject even though it does not cover everything that makes up this new technology. When you reach the end of this book, you will know everything about this new approach to installing software.

The Supporting Technologies Used to Implement Change and Configuration Management

In the previous discussion of the three key technologies that are critical to implementing the deployment capabilities of Windows 2000, I mentioned other technologies that are part of this capability. This section provides a brief description of what these supporting technologies are and how they work.

Folder redirection and offline folders

Folder redirection is a feature in Windows 2000 that enables users and administrators to redirect the path of a folder to a new location. This new location can be another folder on the local machine or it can be a directory on a shared network drive.

As an example, let's assume that the My Documents folder has been redirected to a network location. When the user saves a file to this folder, the file is actually being saved in the network location the file is then being stored on the local computer through the process of synchronization. Synchronization occurs in the background and is transparent to the user. If the user is disconnected from the network – either intentionally or unintentionally – he or she can continue to work as if nothing happened. What is actually going on is that the user is working with the synchronized copy of the file that is on the local machine. When the network connection is restored, the network copy is synchronized with the local copy automatically. If both the network copy of the file and the local copy of the file have changed during the time that there was no network connection, the user is prompted as to whether to save both copies or to synchronize one copy with the other.

Synchronization Manager

The Synchronization Manager performs the synchronization operation described above. The Synchronization Manager (SyncMgr) is an operating system infrastructure that provides connectivity functions, system event notification services, and client-side caching. It provides a standard technology for applications to cache and synchronize network resources for local use.

Disk quotas

With Windows 2000 a system administrator can define the amount of data a user can store on an NTFS volume. This new ability comes as part of NTFS version 5.0. At the discretion of the administrator the system can be configured to log an event when a user gets close to the quota that has been set. In addition, the system can be configured to deny further disk space to any user that exceeds the quota. This feature can generate reports and use the event monitor to track quota issues.

Roaming user profiles

The roaming user profile is key to permitting users to roam among machines and to have their customizations available to them regardless of what machine they log on to within the corporate network. In order to be a roaming user, the user must be defined as such by the system administrator. Once this is done and the user logs onto a computer, configures it, and logs off, the profile is copied to a server that has been designated for this purpose. From then on, any time the user logs onto a machine in the network all the profile information will be downloaded to the local computer and the user will see his or her customizations as if he or she were working on the original computer.

Dynamic Host Configuration Protocol (DHCP) and Domain Name Service (DNS)

In Windows 2000 DHCP has been enhanced with a number of new features. However, the only feature that we want to cover in this discussion is the integration of DHCP with DNS.

The Dynamic Host Configuration Protocol (DHCP) is an industry standard that simplifies the administration of TCP/IP networks. In a TCP/IP network each connected computer must have a unique IP address and DHCP keeps the system administrator from having to configure all these computers by hand. The mechanism for implementing this functionality is that the desktop computer (DHCP Client) leases an IP address from the DHCP Server for a period of time. At the end of each IP address lease period the desktop machine can find itself with a new IP address.

DNS maintains the information about the mapping between a computer's Fully Qualified Domain Name (FQDN) and its IP address. A FQDN is a user-friendly name in the format of `server.division.organization.com`. The information needed to perform this mapping is maintained in a distributed database that contains two types of resource records (RR) called A and PTR. The A resource record contains the mapping from the FQDN to the IP address, and the PTR resource record contains the mapping from the IP address to the FQDN.

The problem is that DHCP does not provide any mechanism to update the A and PTR resource records in the DNS-distributed database when a new IP address is assigned to a DHCP Client. This means that the mapping between FQDNs and IP addresses will be incorrect in a very short time. This is where the integration of DHCP and DNS via the implementation of the Dynamic DNS Update protocol comes into play in a Windows 2000 network. The integration of these two technologies means that when a DHCP Client with a particular FQDN acquires an IP address from the DHCP server the A resource record with the FQDN is updated to reflect the new IP address. Likewise, when an IP address is assigned to a DHCP Client with a particular FQDN, the PTR resource record associated with this address is updated to reflect the new FQDN.

Remote Installation Services (RIS)

We have already discussed remotely installing the Windows 2000 operating system. It is the Remote Installation Services that enables you to do this. This service requires three other services that we have already discussed.

- The Active Directory directory service
- The Domain Name Service (DNS) Server
- The Dynamic Host Configuration Protocol (DHCP) Server

Remote installation of the operating system relies on DNS for locating both the directory service and the client machine accounts. RIS also requires a DHCP server to be on the network so that the remote boot-enabled client computers can receive an IP address prior to contacting the remote installation service. RIS depends on the Active Directory directory service for locating existing client machines and for locating any existing RIS servers.

Windows Shell enhancements

The Windows Shell enhancements that have been implemented all relate to the capability to advertise an application on the Start\Programs menu so that it will appear that it is installed when it is not. Launching the application from the icon on this menu will then install the application. In order to be able to advertise an application so that it will get installed on first use, the version of SHELL32.DLL found in the Sytem32 folder needs to be greater than or equal to 4.72.3110.0.

Add/Remove Programs applet

The Add/Remove Programs applet in the Windows 2000 Control Panel has been dramatically enhanced. You can now install, repair, or remove an application from this applet. It now supports publishing software as discussed in the section on IntelliMirror. There is now a comprehensive list of information that can be displayed about any piece of installed or published software.

In the Add/Remove Programs implementation found on Windows NT 4.0 the only information provided was a display name for the application. In Windows 2000 there is a complete list of information such as help for using the application, the name of the manufacturer of the application, and so forth. Also, the applet shows the time the application was last used and the size of the installed image, and it also allows you to sort the list of applications on the machine according to name, size, frequency of use, or date last used.

System Management Server (SMS)

Microsoft sees System Management Server (SMS) as an add-on to the Change and Configuration Management capabilities that come with a Windows 2000 network. When you have a strict Windows 2000 network where all the desktops are running Windows 2000 Professional and all the servers are running Windows 2000 Server, the native management capabilities are all that is required. However, when the enterprise gets more distributed and complex, and the client machines are running other operating systems than Windows 2000, then SMS comes into the picture. With Systems Management Server you can support desktops that are running any of the 16-bit or 32-bit versions of the Windows operating system. SMS also supports environments, whether they are running Windows NT 3.51/4.0 or some version of NetWare.

Systems Management Server provides the following set of capabilities:

Hardware and Software Inventory	Using Windows Management Instrumentation and software scanners, SMS can upload detailed hardware and software inventory information into a SQL Server-based repository. You can also check this inventory to make sure it meets your criteria.

Software Distribution and Installation	Software deployment in SMS is rule-based – that is, integrated with inventory functionality to allow sophisticated targeting. When deploying software, SMS first performs a query of software inventory and collection information and then targets the audience based on rules that have been defined by the system administrator. It then proceeds with the deployment of the software.
Software Metering	SMS enables administrators to track software usage by users, groups, computers, time, or license quota. It can monitor, analyze, and control the use of applications on servers and workstations.
Diagnostics and Troubleshooting	SMS provides a suite of diagnostic tools, which include the capability to monitor and analyze network conditions and performance. It also provides the capability to track critical performance information on a Windows NT server and Microsoft BackOffice.

To put everything into perspective Table 2-4 provides guidelines about when to use IntelliMirror, SMS, or both.

TABLE 2-4 COMPARISON OF INTELLIMIRROR VERSUS SYSTEMS MANAGEMENT SERVER

Usage	SMS	IntelliMirror	Both
Distribution	Yes	No	Yes
Targeting	Collection	Active Directory	Collection of group
Platform	All platforms	Windows 2000	All
Installation	SMS or Windows Installer	Windows Installer	All
Additional management support	Yes	No	Yes

Summary

This chapter has been an overview of the architecture of Windows 2000, with a special emphasis on how it has been designed to facilitate software deployment in the enterprise. What we have seen in this chapter is that with Windows 2000 networks we are entering a whole new world of how software will be managed in the corporate network. The main focus of this new environment is central control of the desktop and the ability to lock down this desktop so that the normal user will not be able to do much damage. This deployment architecture is a major step forward in Microsoft's goal of truly reducing the Total Cost of Ownership of the desktop computer for corporate America.

Chapter 3

Design and Implementation of the Windows Installer Service

IN THIS CHAPTER

- ◆ The design requirements
- ◆ Installation and operation of the Windows Installer Service
- ◆ The enhanced installation environment
- ◆ Products, features, and components
- ◆ Installation package overview
- ◆ Other types of installer packages
- ◆ More about components
- ◆ Getting ready to create an Installer package
- ◆ A word or two about package validation

IN THIS CHAPTER WE delve into the Windows Installer technology and cover the information that you'll need to move on to Chapter 4. This chapter and Chapter 4 provide the background information about this new technology, which you'll need in order to understand the material covered in the remainder of the book.

We begin with a discussion of the design requirements for this new installation technology and then move into an overview of the basic functionality and how it was implemented. We then take a brief look at some of the more advanced features of the Windows Installer before we start to drill down into those subjects that will be essential for moving into Chapter 4. In particular we discuss the important database tables that comprise a Windows Installer package. We also go into some detail about how the installation user interface is implemented in an MSI database. We finish the chapter by talking about the various methods that are available for ensuring that the installation package has been constructed properly.

The Design Requirements

In Chapter 1 you were regaled with a litany of problems with the installation process in use today. It is pretty easy to guess what the design requirements were for the Windows Installer functionality by looking at the functionality that has been developed. In any case let's list the design requirements so we will be able to assess how well the goals set for this new technology have been met.

- First and foremost the new technology was to provide a robust capability to install and uninstall software. It had to be able to keep the machine out of an unknown state if the installation or uninstallation failed because of an error or because the user canceled the operation.
- It was to allow for the control of the desktop, enabling the user to install approved applications but preventing the installation of software that could be potentially harmful. This type of functionality would allow the network administrator to lock down the desktops in the organization. The designers of the Windows Installer felt that this would be a big step toward reducing the total cost of ownership (TCO).
- It was to provide an open architecture so that setup would no longer be a black box to network administrators. With an open architecture the administrator could know in advance what installing a piece of software would do to the system.
- It was to provide the end user with a consistent install experience. It is the Windows tradition to have every Windows application present the same functionality in the same way. For instance, everyone knows that to create a new document or to close an application you go to the File pulldown menu.
- It was to provide a consistent set of installation rules that all setup developers would have to follow. This would help guarantee that all installs created under the new system would operate pretty much in the same way.
- Any new system for installing software had to be able to protect the operating system from having its primary functionality degraded or destroyed. This meant keeping certain operating system components from being replaced with incompatible versions. (This is not a capability that the Windows Installer could implement on its own, but it could be designed to support such functionality once it was added to the operating system.)
- It was to be able to manage all shared resources on the machine. In particular, it needed to be able to identify the clients of all components installed. This capability is critical in preventing one application from disabling another application through an uninstallation action.

- In order for applications to participate in the management of the environment in which they would be operating, there was to be a set of API (Application Programming Interface) functions through which applications could access the necessary functionality of the installation service.
- Last but not least, the Windows Installer was to support all efforts to reduce and eventually eliminate version conflicts between components – sometimes called "DLL Hell." (This is another functionality that had to start with changes in the operating system design.)

This laundry list provides a clear definition of the goals that formed the basis for the development of this new software installation technology. It is now time to take a look at what was actually created out of these requirements.

How the Windows Installer Service Works

The Microsoft Windows Installer comes as an integral part of the Windows 2000 operating system. In addition there is a Unicode version that can be installed on Windows NT 4.0 and an ANSI version that can be installed on Windows 95/98. For the non-Windows 2000 operating systems the Installer engine is distributed via a file with the name InstMsiA.exe or InstMsiW.exe, depending on whether it is the ANSI or the Unicode version. Attempting to install the ANSI version on Windows NT 4.0 or the Unicode version on Windows 95/98 will generate the error message "Wrong OS or OS version for application."

When you're installing the installer service, a number of new and/or updated files are added to the System32 directory. On Windows NT 4.0 a hidden directory named Installer is added to the C:\WINNT directory. It is in this hidden directory that the installation packages for an application are cached after the installation is completed. After uninstallation, these cached packages are marked for removal on the next reboot of the system. Also stored in this location, in special sub-folders, is the file or files that contain the icons used for advertising the product on the Start\Programs menu. We discuss what the term *advertising* means when we discuss what software installation means. On Windows 95/98 this hidden directory is not created until you run the first Windows Installer–based installation.

During the installation of the installer service two file extensions are registered: .msi and .msp. The extension server for both of these file types is msiexec.exe. The .msi extension designates an installation package file and the .msp extension denotes a patch package file. We discuss both types of files in more detail later in this chapter. On Windows NT/2000, msiexec.exe is registered as a service where the image requires the option /V to run as a service. This service is set to have a manual start, which happens the first time that an installation is launched. Thereafter the service continues to run until the machine is shut down. On Windows 95/98 there is, of course, no service functionality, so msiexec.exe runs as a standard process only.

Figure 3-1 provides a simplified picture of how the Windows Installer service operates. You can initiate installation of a product that uses the Windows Installer technology in several ways. First, you can launch it via the command line by running msiexec.exe with the /i option followed by the name of the .msi package file:

```
msiexec /i <package file name.msi>
```

You can also launch it by double-clicking the MSI package in Windows Explorer, or by accessing the .msi file from the Add/Remove Programs applet. The normal method for launching an MSI-based installation for an application is to use a method called bootstrapping. Bootstrapping is the use of a separate application to launch another application.

To provide bootstrapping functionality a setup.exe application must fulfill a number of expectations. First it is called setup.exe because that is what the user is expecting as the way of launching an installation. setup.exe needs to first check to make sure that the Windows Installer service has been installed. If the Windows Installer service has not been installed, setup.exe needs to launch the installation of the correct version of instMsi.exe. It also needs to capture any return codes from the installation of the Windows Installer so that it can handle any reboots necessary because of this installation. If the correct version of the Windows Installer is already present on the system, then setup.exe needs to make sure that there is no other installer-based installation in process. Because there can only be one installation running at a time, setup.exe would need to provide a message and then end the recently initiated installation if there was another one already running. If the correct version of the Windows Installer is present on the system, then setup.exe would launch msiexec.exe with /i option (or call the MsiInstallProduct() API in msi.dll) and then pass the MSI package to it.

Implementing the Windows Installer on Windows NT/2000 as a service allows an installation to run with elevated privileges even if the user performing the installation does not have administrative privileges on the machine. This does not mean that an installation can be performed regardless of a user's privilege level. The Windows Installer service will operate at the privilege level of the user unless a system administrator has advertised the application by using the Group Policy Editor (GPE). What this all adds up to is this: If the user has administrative privileges, then he or she can perform an installation; otherwise the system administrator will have to set the permissions for that particular user and application so that the installation can still take place. This is an implementation of the desktop lockdown functionality.

A Windows Installer package file has an .msi file extension and this file contains all the information required by the Installer to install or uninstall an application or product. We discuss the contents of the installation package file in more depth in a later section.

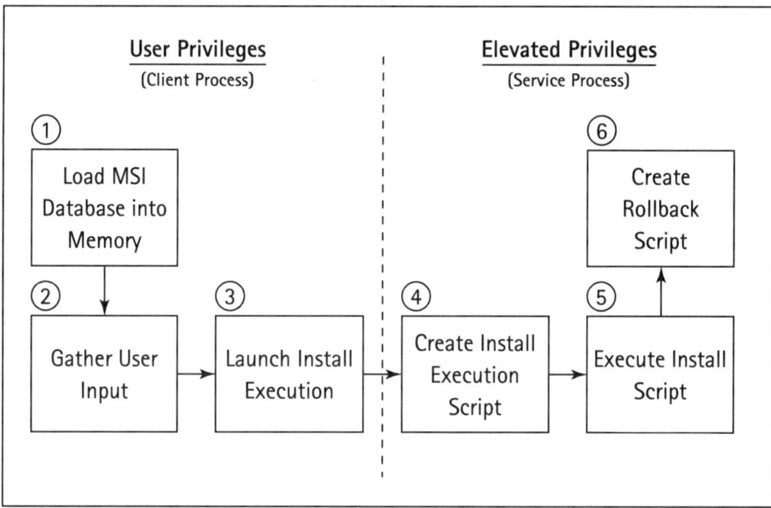

Figure 3-1: Overview of the Windows Installer mechanism

When an installation is launched, the Windows Installer goes into what is called the acquisition phase or the operation that is done at user privileges (as is shown in Figure 3-1). First, a copy of the .msi file is made in the %TEMP% directory on the local system. This copy is made regardless of whether the original .msi package is already on the local machine, on a CD-ROM, or on the network. The copy of the package is given a name unique on the local system. If the original installer package file has the source files compressed inside, the MSI database – along with the source files – is copied to the %TEMP% directory. If the source files are external to the .msi file, then the source files are left in the original location and only the .msi file is copied to the %TEMP% directory.

The acquisition phase, as shown in Figure 3-1, begins with Step 1, where the MSI database is loaded into memory. The process continues with the gathering of input through the end user responding to the queries presented by the installation user interface. This user interface is presented to the user by the msiexec.exe client process displaying the dialogs defined in the MSI database. The user's responses are captured in the database contained in the .msi package file. This corresponds to

Step 2. The final step performed at user privileges, Step 3, is for the client process to launch the installation execution in the process with elevated privileges.

When the service process is launched, it first gathers a little more information from the system. It then creates the script that will be used to process the installation itself. This is Step 4. The script created in the hidden `%WINDIR%\Installer` folder is binary. Step 5 is the actual execution of this script. At the same time the script is being executed, another script is being created. That script is called the *rollback script* and is used to return the system to the state it was in prior to the start of the installation, if the installation does not complete successfully for some reason.

In the *rollback phase* all files, Registry entries, and so forth are restored to the state they were in prior to the start of the installation. You only have this rollback capability during the actual install sequence. After a successful installation, it is not possible to restore the machine to the pre-installation state through rollback. To return to the previous machine state requires the uninstallation of the application that was installed and the re-installation of any applications that might have been changed during the installation in question.

The process that I've just discussed is called the INSTALL top-level action of the Windows Installer. There are two other top-level actions: ADMIN and ADVERTISE. The ADMIN action is the installation of a source image of an application on a network server. Users who have access to this administrative image can then install the product from this source. If users choose to run from source during the installation, most of the application files will be used from the network. The ADVERTISE top-level action refers to the Windows Installer's ability to provide the loading and launching interfaces for an application without physically installing any of the application's files. The actual installation of the files occurs only when a user activates one of the interfaces that has been made available through the ADVERTISE action. Each of these top-level actions is exclusive, meaning that in any one session only one of these actions can be implemented.

We will be talking more about these top-level actions later in this chapter but now we need to take a quick look at some of the functionality that has been added to the Windows Installer.

The Enhanced Installation Environment

We just discussed the basic install and uninstall functionality of the Windows Installer. There is a lot more to this technology than just a basic install and uninstall. This section is a high-level overview of the functionalities that makes this new environment much more robust than the present installation environment. They will all be covered in much more detail throughout the rest of the book.

Resiliency

To be resilient is to be able to recover one's strength quickly. The Windows Installer service is resilient in a number of ways, but they all involve the ability to recover gracefully from errors without presenting the user with error messages. Windows Installer can diagnose problems in its operation and then repair these problems without any action being required from the user. This is called *runtime resource resiliency*. If the Windows Installer service needs to access the source media after the initial installation, it can look for alternative locations where the application source files may be available if the original media is not present. This is called *source resiliency*. The rollback functionality we discussed in the last section is another form of resiliency.

Advertisement

Advertisement is one of the major new capabilities that the Windows Installer service brings to the managed environment envisioned by the Zero Administrative Windows (ZAW) initiative. Advertising is the capability of the Windows Installer to make the interfaces available without actually installing the application. There are two types of advertising: assigning and publishing. Advertisement is made possible through the Installation-On-Demand functionality built into the Installer.

When an application or a feature of an application is advertised, it appears to the user as if that functionality were already installed. For instance, if an application has been advertised, shortcuts and icons have been added to the Start menu, file associations have been made in the Registry, and any Registry entries required by the application have also been added. When a user tries to start an advertised application for the first time, the Windows Installer installs the files for that application. Up until that time the application has only appeared as if it were installed while in actuality it was not consuming any hard drive space. This type of advertisement is called *product level advertisement*. It can be made to a user or to a machine. Typically a network administrator makes the decision to advertise the application based on whether a user needs that application to perform a particular function within the organization.

A second type of advertising is *feature level advertising*. Feature level advertising allows a feature of an application to appear to be available to the user from a toolbar or a menu even though it has not actually been installed. The first time the user tries to make use of that feature, the feature is installed. This type of advertising is implemented by the application itself through access to the Windows Installer API. Because of this it does not require any direct support from the operating system.

How Windows 2000 Uses Advertising to Implement Assigned and Published Applications

In Windows 2000, you can assign and publish applications using IntelliMirror software installation. This technology makes use of the Windows Installer advertising feature.

An *assigned* application is advertised for the user at logon so that it appears to be installed. It is also advertised into Active Directory so that the OS can look it up based on what entry points (that is, file associations) it supports.

A *published* application is only advertised in Active Directory, so users do not see it on their machines. It is still advertised in active directory so the OS can find it when users go to Add/Remove programs or click a document supported by that application.

Before we get into the details of the Windows Installer package file and associated file types it is important to cover some key concepts around which the installer functionality is constructed. These concepts deal with how an application is designed.

Products, Features, Components, and Resources

Microsoft developed the Component Object Model (COM) as the standard approach for product development. This approach centers on the idea that assembling prebuilt components into one package is the most efficient method for creating the desired functionality for the user. The Windows Installer is designed according to a similar philosophy.

Products and features

A *product* is defined as a three-level hierarchy with the top level being the product itself. The product is considered to consist of a number of *features* and each feature is made up of one or more *components*. The component is the atomic unit from which the features are built. The user installing the product sees only the features that have been defined and does not interact directly with the components in any way. It could be said that the feature set of a product is the end user's view and the components that make up these features are the developer's view of the product. Figure 3-2 shows an example of what this hierarchy might look like for a family of graphics programs that share a component.

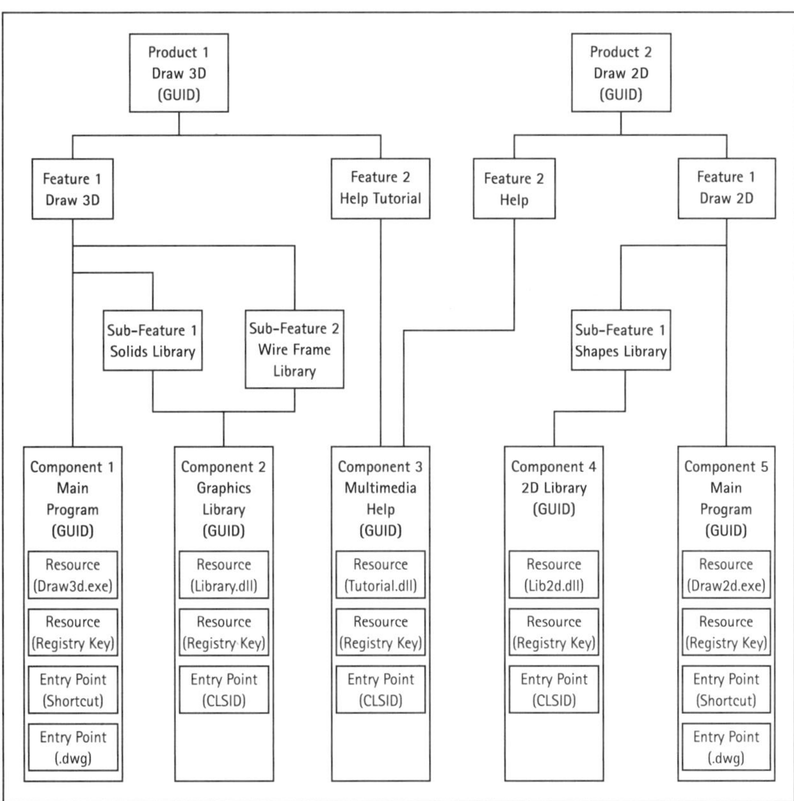

Figure 3-2: Diagram of a typical product, feature, and component hierarchy

Components and resources

A *component* is a collection of installable resources or just resources. A *resource* is a file, Registry entry, shortcut, type library, or the like. When a component is installed, everything that comprises the component is installed. When a component is uninstalled, everything that comprises it is uninstalled. Each component has to be unique and is therefore assigned a component code that is a Globally Unique Identifier (GUID). The Windows Installer looks for a component's *keypath* in order to ascertain whether the component is properly installed. A keypath is normally one of the files that comprise the component but it can also be one of the Registry entries associated with the component. The keypath defines the location of the component on the system. If the keypath for a component is missing, the Windows Installer treats that component as broken and tries to take the necessary action to repair it.

In addition to installable resources, components may also have entry points. An entry point determines how a component is activated. An entry point for a COM server would be the CLSID of the desired interface and the entry point for a main executable would be a shortcut or a registered file extension. The Windows Installer treats entry points specially so that it can support advertising. You can think of advertising as an install that installs only the entry points for your application.

Globally Unique Identifiers

It's fairly easy to generate a unique identifier for a stand-alone machine. All you need to do is create a random number and combine it with a date and time from the system itself. However, when you talk about creating an identifier that will be unique across a network — such as is found with the Internet — then the task becomes much more difficult.

The current method of creating unique identifiers comes from the Open Software Foundation's (OSF) Distributed Computing Environment (DCE) specification. This specification defines the format for creating what is known as a Universally Unique Identifier (UUID), which in the world of COM has come to be known as the Globally Unique Identifier (GUID). A UUID or GUID is 128 bits long and, if it is generated according to the specification mentioned above, it is guaranteed to be different from all other identifiers generated across space and time up until the year 3400 A.D. The UUID/GUID generation algorithm could create 10 million GUIDs per machine per second and still maintain uniqueness. This is possible because the method for getting time from the system uses the FILETIME structure. This is a structure that returns the present time and date as a 64-bit value and it represents the number of 100 nanosecond intervals that have occurred since January 1, 1601. If you do the math you will see that there are 10 million such intervals in each second. This is the reason that the present algorithm will not work past the year 3400 A.D.

A complete discussion of the algorithm for creating the various types of unique identifiers, along with sample C code for generating them, can be found at the following URL:

`http://www.opengroup.org/dce/`

The most significant 80 bits of a UUID/GUID form the time/date stamp part of an identifier. Multiplexed with the time/date stamp portion of the UUID/GUID are information (called the *variant*) that defines how the bits in the identifier are to be interpreted, and version information that defines how the UUID/GUID was created. There are four possible variants with a UUID/GUID:

- Reserved for Network Computing System (NCS) backward compatibility
- Present standard definition
- Reserved for Microsoft Corporation backward compatibility
- Reserved for future definition

There are also four versions of a UUID/GUID:

- Time-based version (the normal version of a UUID/GUID)
- DCE reserved version
- Name-based version
- Randomly generated version

The last 48 bits serve to provide spatial uniqueness. When the computer has a network card, this part of the identifier comes from the IEEE 802 address of the device. If there is no network card, then a randomly generated value is used where the multicast bit is set so as to avoid the possibility of conflict with addresses generated from network cards. The multicast bit is the highest-order bit in the last 48 bits. This bit is never set by an IEEE 802 address, so setting it to 1 will never conflict with a UUID/GUID set on a machine without a network card.

A UUID/GUID has the following human readable form, which is the string representation of this identifier.

```
{7bc70bd5-6635-11d3-8b29-b87f44000000}
```

This is given hexadecimal format with the standard display using lowercase letters for the hexadecimal numbers. For the Windows Installer to use a UUID/GUID for a valid product, package, or component code all the lowercase letters need to be changed to uppercase.

Components are reference counted similarly, as has been done up to now with files that might be shared. Now, however, everything that makes up the component is essentially refcounted together, so no longer will a file be removed during uninstallation and leave the applicable Registry entries still on the system. This refcount is presently kept in the Registry as a list of product codes associated with each component that are also GUIDs. Only when no installed product shows that it is using a component will the component be uninstalled. Figure 3-2 illustrates most of these concepts and shows that a component can be shared across features, across products, and even across companies. This is all possible because of the uniqueness of every component.

There are a number of strict rules you must follow when creating the components. Following these rules ensures that the uninstallation of an application does not cripple some other application that is still on the system. In addition, proper componentization guarantees that all resources that define a component are removed with no orphaned resources left behind. These rules are listed below:

- All files in a component must be installed into the same directory. There can be no subdirectories. You install files in a sub-directory by putting them into a different component.

- Every component must have only one keypath, which can be either a file or Registry key, or the folder in which the component lives (this is the default if you leave the keypath column blank).
- Every .exe, .dll, .ocx, .hlp, and .chm file should be in its own component and these files should be the keypath for the component.
- There can be only one file that is a target for a Start Menu or Desktop shortcut in each component. This means that every file that serves as the target of a shortcut has to be in its own component.
- No file can ever be included in more than one component. This rule applies across applications, products, product versions, and companies. Change the file name if the information must go into a different component.
- No registry entry, shortcut, or other resource can ever be included in more than one component. Change the name if the information must go into a different component.
- Every component that is not backward compatible with previous versions of the component must have a unique component GUID. If the backward compatibility of the component has not been tested, the component GUID should be changed.

It should be noted that there is a close relationship between a component's GUID and the names of a component's resources. If the GUID for a component is changed, then the names of every file, registry key, shortcut, and any other resources in the component must be changed. Conversely, if the name of a resource is changed then the names of all other resources also have to be changed and a new GUID assigned to the component.

Choosing features to install

As I mentioned above, features are the pieces of the product that the end user can choose to install. The end user makes this choice through the Setup Type dialog. With the Windows Installer the end user will be faced with four possible choices when choosing what features to install. A feature can be in one of the following four states:

- Installed to run locally
- Installed to run from source
- To be installed on first use
- Not to be installed

Features can have sub-features and it is up to the developer to determine how granular to make the product. Large applications could easily include many levels of features in order to allow the optimum installation. Features do not have to be globally unique and therefore are not assigned a GUID or feature code.

Installation Package Overview

The installation package is the basic entity that the Windows Installer service uses to obtain the information required to perform an installation or uninstallation. This package contains all the information required to install or uninstall an application, including the source files for the application.

At the center of the installation package is the .msi file that is organized as COM Structured Storage. There are two required parts of this file and there are two optional parts. Every .msi file must have a Summary Information Stream and an installation database. The two optional parts of this file are the source files or pointers to these files that make up all or part of the application, and the transforms that are used to modify the installation database at runtime.

COM Structured Storage

In the early days of computers there was no such thing as a file system. Every computer was created to run a single application and it stored data on a drum, tape, or disk. As computers matured, it became necessary to develop the concept of the file system since now more than one application could to use the computer and there had to be a method for sharing space on a single device for saving data. Thus was born the concept of directories and files, wherein directories could contain directories and files in a hierarchical structure. Applications could view a file as a stream of contiguous bytes without being concerned with where these bytes were physically stored on the disk. In reality these bytes were normally in non-contiguous sectors on the disk.

The file-system concept has served the computer industry well for a long time but recently the world of component software development has forced a further refinement. The solution to today's need for a more robust method for saving (or *persisting*) data is called COM Structured Storage (earlier on it was called OLE Structured Storage). What this approach boils down to is a file system within a file.

With this new approach we get *storages* and *streams*. A storage is the equivalent of a directory in a normal file system and a stream is the equivalent of a file. The following figure depicts the concept of this new type of file.

Continued

COM Structured Storage *(Continued)*

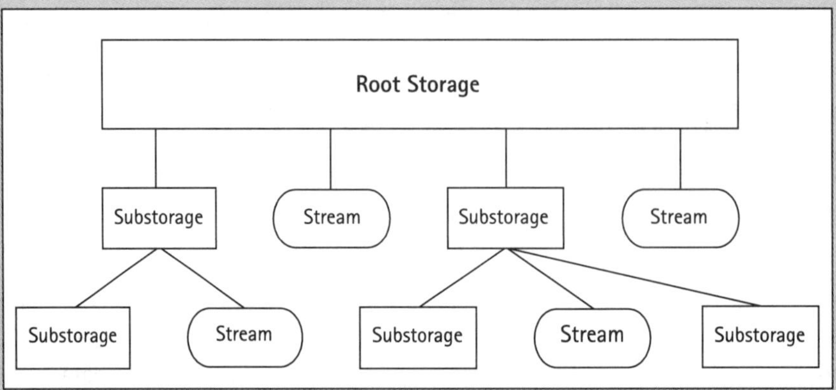

A storage is normally referred to as a storage object and a stream is referred to as a stream object. The root storage in a COM structured storage file maps to a filename in the file system in which the structured storage file exists. One of the major advantages of this type of file is that the hierarchy of storage and stream objects is a standard format. Because of this standard format COM is able to provide standard services that allow any application that is properly constructed to browse the hierarchy of such a file. This does not mean that another application can read the information in this file because the format of the stream objects themselves is still only known to the application that actually created the file in the first place.

There is one exception to this rule, which is that along with the definition of the COM Structured Storage file comes one stream that has a known format. The information contained therein can be read by other applications. This special stream object is called the Summary Information Stream and it is located directly of the root storage. The name of this summary information stream object is \005SummaryInformation. It is made up of a standard common property set and the \005 prefix indicates that it is a property set that is shareable among applications.

You can see the values for the properties that make up this shareable stream object from Windows Explorer when you right-click one of these files and choose Properties from the popup menu. Each property in the standard property set has a name but this name does not necessarily correspond to the type of information that is actually being stored in that property.

The complete collection of the items described above constitutes what is called the *installation package*. When all the application source files are included inside the .msi file the package consists of just this file. We discuss each of the components of the installation package is discussed in the following sections. We also discuss other components of the Windows Installer environment that interface with the installation package.

The Summary Information Stream

There are two purposes for the information stored in the Summary Information Stream. First, it provides information that can be viewed in the Windows Explorer. If you right-click on an .msi file and bring up the Properties dialog, you will see the values that have been authored into the Summary Information Stream.

The second purpose of the Summary Information stream is to provide certain information to the Windows Installer service that it needs to install an .msi package. There are 17 properties that can be set with four of these being required. There are currently four storage formats in use by the Windows Installer: installation packages, merge modules, transforms, and patch packages. Installation packages have the .msi extension, merge modules have the .msm extension, transforms have the .mst extension, and patch packages have the .msp extension. Depending on the storage format, the value of the property in the Summary Information Stream can mean different things.

In the section entitled "Getting Ready to Create an Installer Package" we discuss the Summary Information Stream properties and what they mean when it comes to creating an MSI package.

Now on to a discussion of the mechanism for recording all the information required for performing an installation. This is the installation database.

The installation database

The installation database is a set of relational tables that are linked to each other through the data in the various primary and foreign keys. The data contained in these tables defines the process information, application data, and actions required for the installation of an application or group of applications. There are 79 native tables defined for an MSI database. A few of these tables are temporary, which means they are not persisted with the installation database. An additional four tables can end up in an installation database if components have been added through the mechanism of merge modules. The setup developer can also add custom tables to the database using SQL.

The tables in the installation database can be considered to fall into 10 related groups, as defined in Table 3-1. Some tables fall into more than one group so as to provide a link between groups. You'll note that the work involved in creating an installation database for even a simple application can be overwhelming. That is why there is a need for an authoring tool such as InstallShield Professional–Windows Installer Edition.

TABLE 3-1 INSTALLATION DATABASE TABLE GROUPS

Group Name	Description	Number of Tables
Core Tables	Describe the fundamental features and components of the application for which the installation package is being created.	7
File Tables	Define all the files that comprise the application, actions to be taken relative to these files, and items such as icon files and `.ini` files that need special attention.	18
Registry Tables	Contain all the information for making the various types of Registry entries by COM components, file extensions, MIME types, DCOM/COM+ Application Ids, ProgIDs, and so forth.	16
System Tables	Track the tables, columns, and information in the other tables of the installation database.	6
Locator Tables	Contain the information needed to locate files and applications.	6
Program Information Tables	Contain information that is required during the installation of an application.	5
Installation Procedure Tables	Contain the information that is required to control the tasks performed during the installation.	13

Group Name	Description	Number of Tables
User Interface Tables	Hold that data that is used to create the user interface displayed during an installation, maintenance operation, or uninstallation.	14
ODBC Tables	Define all the information required to install ODBC on a system.	5
NT Services Tables	Define the parameters required for both installing and controlling NT services.	2

Application source files

As I stated previously, the source files for the application to be installed are considered part of the installation package. This is true whether the source files are included inside the .msi file or are external to it. The source files can be included inside the .msi file in either a compressed form (cabinet file) or uncompressed form. They can also be included in compressed or uncompressed form external to the .msi file and there can be a mixture of both compressed and uncompressed files either inside or external to the .msi file. Regardless of the scenario, there are detailed rules to be followed.

Compressed files are inserted into a standard Cabinet file of the type created by the Makecab.exe cabinet file creation tool. The Windows Installer also recognizes cabinet files created in the older Diamond cabinet file structure such as is created by the Cabarc.exe utility.

Other Types of Windows Installer Packages

There are a number of different types of Windows Installer files. All of these files are COM structured storage files but not all of them have the .msi database package format and thus not all of them can be viewed by the normal database editing tools. We briefly discuss other types of Windows Installer in the following subsections. We will cover them in much more detail in later chapters.

Transforms

A *transform* is a template of the differences between two installer databases. A transform can add or replace information in the target database. A transform can be applied at run time to the installation database and essentially change the package only in memory, thus not disturbing the original database. A transform can also be applied at build time and this will permanently change the original database.

A transform might typically be used to create a localized version of an upgraded application. You would do this by first creating a transform of the differences between a base language product and its upgrade, and then applying this transform to the various specific language versions of the product in order to obtain their upgraded versions. For example, say that you presently have a base product in English and it has been localized into German and Japanese. Now assume that a new version of the English product is developed. To use a transform to create the upgrade versions of the German and Japanese products you would create a transform representing the difference between the original and upgraded English versions and apply this transform to the original .msi packages for the German and Japanese products. In this way you have generated the upgrade of the localized products. This is a case of applying a transform at build time.

A good example of applying a transform at install time is the situation where the end user can pick the language in which the installation is to run. In this scenario the transform that is applied is chosen from an initial dialog box and does not permanently change the base installation database since the transform is applied in memory.

Transforms can also be used to modify installations launched from an administrative image on a network drive. In this type of scenario a network administrator might want certain workgroups to get specific configurations of a product. The administrator would distribute the right configurations by creating the appropriate transform so that the product is configured appropriately when an installation is launched. This is another run-time use of transforms. Transforms are also used in patch packages and can be used in merge modules as we discuss a little later in this chapter.

Merge modules

It is possible to merge two installer databases together. An administrator usually does this with a utility that calls the MsiDatabaseMerge database management function exported by msi.dll that is part of the Windows Installer service. Merging two databases in this way only adds information and does not replace any information. The merging will fail if the schemas of the two databases are different. Even if the schemas of the two databases are the same there is the possibility for a *row merge conflict*. A row merge conflict occurs when for the same table in both databases there are two rows, one in each database, that have the same primary key but different data. When the schemas of the two databases are different, no changes are made in the target database and the merge fails. When there is a row conflict, the merge proceeds and the conflicts are reported in another table that is created for that particular purpose.

There is a special application of the capability to merge two databases and that is the use of *merge modules*. A merge module is a simplified form of an installation package and is used to distribute shared code or components to an installation. Merge modules cannot be run separately and are only used to add information to an installation package at design time. After the merge is complete all the information in the merge module is incorporated in the installation package file and the merge module is no longer required for the installation to proceed.

MERGING WITHOUT CONFLICT

Merge modules are used most often in packaging of components that are to be used by many different applications. In fact a merge module cannot define a feature but can only define components. Merge modules can be very useful in allowing development teams to work on their own on different parts of an application and to create merge modules for these parts which can then be combined together to provide the final product. Merge modules also allow for third parties to create redistributable components that other software developers can easily include in their products, knowing that the installation of the component will be performed correctly.

A merge module has the same basic format of an .msi, containing a relational database, a summary information stream, and a cabinet file stored as a stream. The name of this cabinet file is MergeModule.CABinet. Each merge module has a unique identifier that is a GUID. The GUID that uniquely identifies a merge module is also used to create unique names for the primary keys in the tables of the relational database. This circumvents conflicts that can occur when two databases are merged.

MULTIPLE LANGUAGE MERGE MODULES

When a merge module is used to deliver a language dependent component to an installer database, it is sometimes necessary to have language transforms embedded in the merge module. This is sometimes necessary when the default language of the merge module is different from the default language in the target database. The purpose of the language transforms is to provide the capability to change the language of the merge module so that it is compatible with the default language of the target installation database. If the merge module's default language cannot be made compatible, the merge operation will fail.

Multiple language transforms can be embedded in a merge module so that it is compatible with more than one specific installation database. A language transform in a merge module has to follow specific rules as to the naming convention used and the language related database attributes it needs to change.

Patch packages

This is the fourth type of Windows Installer file. This type of file does not contain database tables like an installation package or a merge module. Instead a minimal patch package contains two transforms, a summary information stream, and a cabinet file. Patch packages provide the Windows Installer service with a mechanism for implementing updates and upgrades of installed applications. These applications, of course, must have been installed by the installer service originally.

A patch package is used to provide a small update or minor upgrade to either an administrative image on a network server or a local stand-alone installation. In a small update minor changes are made to one or more application files. A minor upgrade is similar to a small update but here the changes are substantial enough to force a change in the product version. In a major upgrade both the product version and the product code have to be changed.

More about Components

In a previous section we learned that components are the atomic unit of an installation and that there are certain rules you must follow when defining them. In this section we explore components in more detail and look at the various types of special components that you can create. Before we get to that, however, we will take a deeper look at how components can be managed. This is essentially an introduction to some of the important functions available in the Windows Installer API set.

Component management

You can think of the Windows Installer both as a setup service and as a component management system. Component management relates to the use of the API set exported by the Windows Installer service. This API set is provided by msi.dll, which is part of the Windows Installer and can be found in the %SYSTEM% directory. When talking about the management of components we will, of necessity, need to talk about features, since features are nothing but collections of components. As I mentioned in a previous section, the Windows Installer caches a copy of the installation database on the system after the successful completion of the install. This cached package contains the following information:

- The components each feature requires
- The files that comprise each component
- The installation location of each file
- The location of each resource in a component

This readily available information enables a developer to incorporate into an application the capability for self-repair. In other words, if a file contained within a component is either missing or corrupted, the application can automatically initiate actions that will reinstall the file so that the application can function properly. This can all be done without the end user knowing that anything is amiss as long as the application can make use of the source files without the need to ask the user for a CD-ROM or other type of media. In a networked environment it is normal for an application to be installed from an administrative image on a network drive and as long as the network connection is active then this can all happen without any notification to the end user. This cached installation database also provides the application with the necessary information to implement feature level installation-on-demand.

Isolated components

Sharing components among various applications has been one of the major features of Microsoft Windows since introduction. However, the ever-increasing number of applications requiring special versions of these shared components has created a condition known as DLL Hell. This describes a situation where different applications need different versions of the same component. The original concept of shared components was that each component would be completely compatible with previous versions and as such a newer version of a component would never cause an application dependent on an earlier version to fail. In practice this is not often the case: there are many instances of a newer component version breaking an application that was successfully using the earlier version. A typical scenario is a newer version of a component fixing a bug in a previous version, thus causing problems for applications that have come to depend on the side effects that were created by this bug.

Windows 2000 and Windows 98 Second Edition have a new functionality that allows different versions of the same component to reside in memory at the same time. This enables what is called *side-by-side sharing* and is a major step toward eliminating DLL Hell. This new approach to component sharing applies to both COM DLLs and Win32 DLLs. In order to make this new method of sharing work you must author these components correctly. Then they must be installed to the application's installation directory and not to some global location such as the system directory.

The new functionality of Windows 2000 and Windows 98 Second Edition, which permits an application to have a private copy of a COM component, has been implemented in the system loader. The system loader looks for a file with the extension .LOCAL in the Applications folder and if it finds this file it alters its search logic to prefer DLLs that are located in the same folder as the application.

System components

The creators of Windows 2000 have implemented a mechanism whereby system files can no longer be installed when an application is being installed. This mechanism is called Windows File Protection (WFP). It prevents the replacement of critical system files and is considered to be a step toward curing the DLL Hell prevalent on PCs today. If an installation attempts to replace one of the protected system files, the file is replaced and the user is notified that such an attempt was made.

The System File Protection list is comprised of all the .sys, .dll, .exe, .ocx, .ttf, and .fon files that ship on the Windows 2000 CD-ROM. There are approximately 2700 files that fall under this definition. When one of these protected files is overwritten, it is replaced from either the DllCache directory in the System32 folder or the distribution media. On Windows 2000 Professional, the default size of the DllCache directory is 50 MB, but on Windows 2000 Server, Advanced Server, and Data Center Server, all the protected files are cached in DllCache.

There are now only five supported mechanisms for replacing protected system files:

- Windows 2000 service pack installation (UPDATE.EXE)
- Hotfix distributions (HOTFIX.EXE)
- Operating system upgrades (WINNT32.EXE)
- Windows Update
- Windows 2000 device driver installer

This new functionality in Windows 2000 replaces the present concept of Core Components, which plays a large part in the rules for obtaining the "Designed for Windows NT 4 and Windows 98" logo. Core Components are the EXEs, DLLs, and OCXs that populate the System32 folder on pre-Windows 2000 operating systems. The basic rule was that you could install these files but they were never to be uninstalled. The Microsoft MSDN Web site maintains a list of these Core Components, which is now a static list and is being made available for dealing with legacy issues.

Qualified components

Qualified components are a scheme for creating what might be termed a collection of components. In a system that does not implement indirection in any explicit way, qualified components are a method of indirection when it comes to pointing at a particular component by first pointing to the collection of components to which it belongs. The primary function of qualified components is to group together components that share a similar functionality.

As you might expect, each grouping of components is identified by what is called a *category GUID.* Inside a particular collection of components, a qualifier identifies a particular component. A qualifier is a unique text string that can easily be generated when you're searching for a particular component. You only have to maintain the uniqueness of the qualifier within the confines of the component collection.

A typical situation in which you would use qualified components is one in which an application needs to ship a set of resource DLLs. Each of these DLLs is in a different language and only one of these DLLs is needed for any particular localized version of the operating system. These DLLs would be grouped together under one category GUID and the locale identifiers (LCID) would be used as the qualifiers for distinguishing one DLL form the other.

Miscellaneous components

To round off this discussion of components we will discuss several minor component types. These minor components are *transitive components* and *permanent components.*

Transitive components are used to prepare an application to gracefully reinstall during an upgrade from a pre-Windows 2000 operating system to Windows 2000. Assume that an end user upgrades the operating system from Windows 98 to Windows 2000. When the reinstall of the application is implemented, the installer removes the Windows 98 components and installs the Windows 2000 components. This makes it possible to reinstall part of the application instead of all of it.

If you want to install a file, font, or Registry key so that it will not be removed during an uninstallation, then you need to make permanent the component of which these are resources. Setting a certain attribute in the Component table will accomplish this. In addition you need to make a special provision in order to prevent the removal of an empty Registry key. You can do this by writing a dummy value under the key that is not to be removed and entering a plus sign (+) in the name column of the Registry table.

Getting Ready to Create an Installer Package

In the following sections we delve deeper into the makeup of an installation in order to get ready to create a package using a basic database-editing tool. The actual implementation of this MSI package is the subject of Chapter 4. The remainder of this chapter provides you with the basic knowledge to successfully complete the creation of this MSI package.

More about the Summary Information Stream

The Summary Information stream in the .msi file is located off the root storage and contains information about the MSI database that is used for the two purposes discussed earlier in this chapter. Several of the standard properties in the Summary Information property set are not used by the Windows Installer and thus are not authored into the database. These are the *Total Editing Time* and *Thumbnail* properties. There is also one property in an Installer Summary Information Stream that is not in the standard property set and that is the *Codepage* property. This particular property is used to display the other property values in the correct language within Windows Explorer.

The Windows Installer recognizes four different types of databases and the values of the properties that comprise the Summary Information stream can take on different meanings depending on the particular database type that is being created. Table 3-2 describes the meaning of the properties for the Summary Information Stream found in the standard .msi database. It is these properties that you will have to set when you create an installation package for a small application.

For a complete description of the standard properties for all four types of Windows Installer databases see Appendix B.

The properties in Table 3-2 below are listed in ascending order of their Property ID (PID).

TABLE 3-2 MSI DATABASE SUMMARY INFORMATION PROPERTY SET

Property Name	Property Description
Codepage (PID = 1)	Set to the numeric value of the ANSI code page that is to be used for any strings that are stored in the Summary Information Stream. This property identifies the code page to be used when displaying the Summary Information in the property sheet in Windows Explorer. It is also used to translate the strings in the Summary Information Stream into Unicode when calling the Unicode API functions. You must set this property before setting any of the string properties in the Summary Information Stream.
Title (PID = 2)	A short description of the type of Windows Installer package in which this Summary Information Stream resides. For an installation database this string would be something such as "Installation Database." This will inform users about the purpose of the file.
Subject (PID = 3)	The name of the application being installed and is normally set from the Windows Installer ProductName property in the Property table.
Author (PID = 4)	The name of the company that created the product being installed and is normally set from the Windows Installer Manufacturer property in the Property table.
Keywords (PID = 5)	File browsers, such as Windows Explorer, use these values to perform keyword searches for a file. When you enter more than one keyword, separate them by commas. In addition, you can use product-specific keywords here and you can also use this location to perform versioning on the MSI package during development.
Comments (PID = 6)	Conveys the general purpose of the installer database. By convention it is set to "This installer database contains the logic and data required to install <*product name*>."
Template (PID = 7)	Specifies both the platform and the language versions supported by the installer database. For a package that is to be used on an Intel platform and is in English this property would be set as Intel;1033.

Property Name	Property Description
Last Saved By (PID = 8)	The Windows Installer sets this value to the name of the user logged onto the system during an administrative installation. The Windows Installer never uses this property and it should always be NULL in a database that is being shipped. You can use this property while constructing the MSI package to keep track of the last person to modify the database.
Revision Number (PID = 9)	The value of this property is the package code of the Installer package. This code is a GUID.
Total Editing Time (PID = 10)	Not supported by the Windows Installer service but I mention it here since it is part of the standard set of Summary Information Stream properties.
Last Printed (PID = 11)	A date and time that you can set during an administrative installation to record when the administrative image was created. For a normal installation this property is the same as the Create Time/Date property defined next.
Create Time/Date (PID = 12)	Records the time and date when the .msi database was created.
Last Save Time/Date (PID = 13)	Specifies the last time the .msi database was modified (saved). This property is updated every time the database is changed. When the database is created, this value is set to NULL to indicate that no modifications have taken place.
Page Count (PID = 14)	Contains the minimum version of the Windows Installer required for running the installation database. This is stored as the major version times 100 plus the minor version. For Windows Installer 1.1 this value would be 1 times 100 + 10, which equals 110.
Word Count (PID = 15)	A bit field that indicates the type of source file image. This value provides information to the Windows Installer about whether long or short file names are being used, whether the source files are compressed or uncompressed, and whether the source files are from the original media or from an administrative image on a network drive.
Character Count (PID = 16)	Not used for installation packages and must be set to NULL.

Continued

Table 3-2 MSI DATABASE SUMMARY INFORMATION PROPERTY SET *(Continued)*

Property Name	Property Description
Thumbnail (PID = 17)	Not supported by the Windows Installer service but I mention it here because it is part of the standard set of Summary Information Stream properties.
Creating Application (PID = 18)	The name of the application used to author the installation database.
Security (PID = 19)	Identifies how the package should be opened. If the value is 0, there is no restriction; if the value is 2, read-only is recommended; and if the value is 4, read-only is enforced. For installation packages the property value should be set to 2.

The Installer database core

There are in excess of 80 tables in an Installer database but a majority of these have special purposes. There is, however, a core of tables that are used in almost any installation, and these are the ones that we discuss in this section. These are the tables that you will need to populate for the installation package that you will create in Chapter 4. The application for which you are going to create an installation has very few files but one of those files is an ActiveX control and therefore you will need to perform some minimal registration for it to work. This does not make the installation much more complex but it does make it somewhat more realistic than if you were just doing an installation for Notepad. Installing most real-world applications these days involves COM registration.

In order to look at the tables that will be necessary for your installation you need to break them down into several distinct categories. These are different from the table groupings we discussed earlier in this chapter:

Feature-centric tables — Tables that have foreign keys into the Feature table. This group consists of the FeatureComponents, Extension, Class, TypeLib, and Condition tables. Figure 3-3 shows the entity-relationship diagram for this grouping of tables.

Component-centric tables — Tables that have foreign keys into the Component table. This group consists of the FeatureComponents, File, Shortcut, Registry, Extension, Class, TypeLib, and CreateFolder tables. Figure 3-4 shows the entity-relationship diagram for this grouping of tables.

There are many more tables than shown in this diagram that have foreign keys into the Component table but they are not important to the installation that you are going to create.

Directory-centric tables — Tables that have foreign keys into the Directory table. This group consists of the Feature, Component, TypeLib, CreateFolder, and Shortcut tables. The entity-relationship diagram for this grouping of tables is shown in Figure 3-5.

Icon-centric tables — Tables that have foreign keys into the Icon table. This group consists of the ProgId, Class, and Shortcut tables. The entity-relationship diagram for this grouping of tables is shown in Figure 3-6.

Miscellaneous tables group — Tables that do not fit into any of the above categories. These tables are those that have foreign keys into the ProgId, Extension, and Verb tables. There is also the Media table, which is stand-alone for the installation that you will be creating. Figure 3-7 shows the entity-relationship diagram for this grouping of tables.

Entry point tables group — Tables that make up this group are contained in the other table groups described above but it is important to realize that many tables can be part of more than one group. The tables in this particular group define the various types of entry points that an application can have. This group is comprised of the Shortcut, Extension, Class, PublishComponent, and TypeLib tables. Except for the PublishComponent table all the tables in this group are described as part of the other tables groups. The PublishComponent table is a method of creating an array of components and it is discussed in Chapter 17. The entity-relationship diagrams (seen in Figures 3-3 through Figure 3-7) show the tables as the entities with each of the table attribute names listed along with the data type of the attribute. The attributes shown in the top section of each block comprise the primary key for that particular table. Attribute names of which the last character is an underscore (_) are foreign keys into the table of that name.

The following sections provide a brief discussion of each of these table groups. We discuss each of the tables in detail in Chapter 4 when you will need to enter actual values.

THE FEATURE-CENTRIC TABLES GROUP

As I described previously, an application is made up of features, which are in turn made up of components. In Figure 3-3 the Feature table is at the center of the diagram. Since there is a many-to-many relationship between features and components there is a need for an additional table so that this relationship can be broken into two one-to-many relationships. The table that fulfills this need is the FeatureComponents table. You can see in this figure that the *Feature* table refers to itself. That is because features can have sub-features and as such there can be a one-to-many relationship between a feature and its sub-features. In Windows NT 4.0 and Windows 2000 there can be a maximum of 1600 components associated with any one feature. In Windows 95/98 800 components are the maximum allowed per feature.

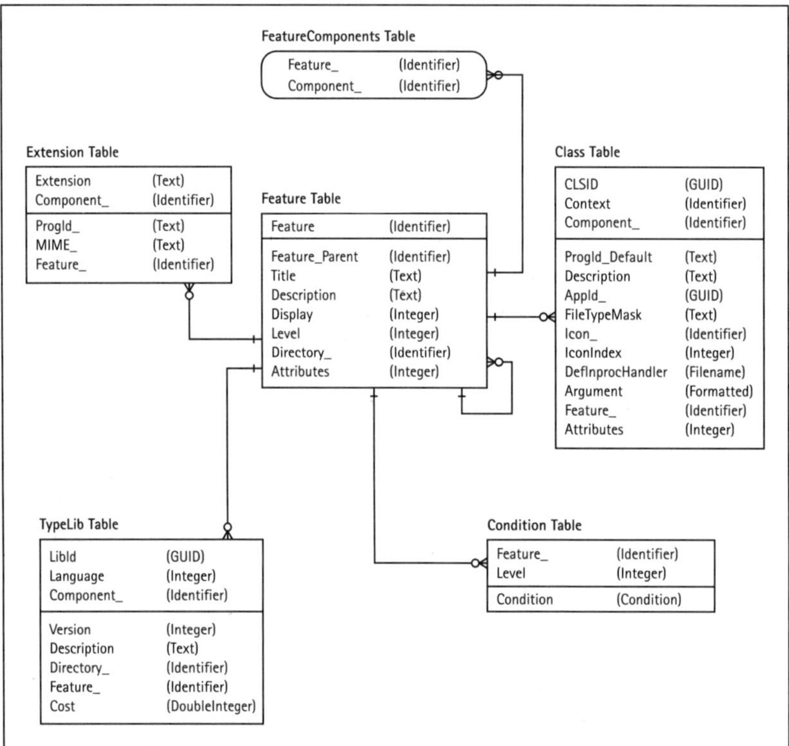

Figure 3-3: The entity-relationship diagram for the Feature Centric table group

The Extension table contains the required information about the file name extension servers. Each row in the Extension table provides the information to the Windows Installer so that a set of registry keys and values can be generated. The reference to the Feature table is necessary since it is a feature providing the service and not just a component by itself. Similarly, the Class and TypeLib tables refer to the Feature table because it is necessary to know the feature that is providing the COM server or type library for the proper registry keys and values to be created.

The Condition table provides a different functionality from that provided by the other tables that relate to the Feature table. This table is used to modify the selection state of a feature based on the evaluation of the condition in the Condition table entry for that feature. Keep in mind that the end user of your application will be deciding on what is installed and what isn't, based on the selections made during the installation. The user typically does this through what is known as the Setup Type dialog, which is one of the dialogs offered as part of the installation's user interface. To understand how this all works under the Windows Installer you need to become familiar with the concept of Install Level.

Every installation has a default Install Level. The value of this Install Level is an integer value that can range from 0 to $2^{15} - 1$ (32,767) and is set in the Property table as the INSTALLLEVEL property. A value of 0 (zero) for an Install Level will hide that feature and not permit it to be installed or even selected. We will be discussing properties in the next section. A feature is installed if its particular Level value is equal to or less than the value of the INSTALLLEVEL property in the Property table. In the Condition table the feature specified in any particular row will have its Level attribute set to the value of Level in the Condition table if the condition for that row evaluates to TRUE. Using the functionality offered by the INSTALLLEVEL property and the Condition table there are a number of ways to manipulate whether a particular feature gets installed or not and under what conditions.

Imagine that an installation offers the end-user the installation options Complete, Typical, and Custom with the default for the Custom installation option being the same as that for the Typical option. Let's assume that we have an application made up of four features and that a Typical install would be for feature 1 and feature 3 to be installed and with feature 2 and feature 4 remaining uninstalled. We could set this up by initially setting the INSTALLLEVEL property in the Property table to a value of 50. This would mean that only those features with a Level attribute of 50 or less would be installed. We would also set the Level attribute for features 1 and 3 to a value of 50 and the Level attribute for features 2 and 4 to a value of 100. Now, if the end user selects a Typical installation, then we don't have to do anything because we have already set everything up for this option to be the default. For a Complete installation, we would set the INSTALLLEVEL property in the Property table to a value of 100, thus ensuring that all features would be installed. For the Custom setup installation option, another dialog box would be presented, allowing the end user to determine which features to install. In a Custom setup dialog the end user, by making selections, manipulates the Level attribute in the Feature table so that it is equal to or less than the INSTALLLEVEL property if the feature is to be installed or greater than this property if the feature is not to be installed.

The Condition table provides further functionality relative to the Install Level of a feature. The Level attribute of a feature can be based on a condition. This condition can be based on the CPU of the target machine, the operating system, the security privileges of the end user, a property in the Property table, and so forth. Let's assume that instead of an application with four features we have an application with eight features where four of the features are available for installation if the operating system is Windows NT 4.0 or Windows 2000 and the other four features are available for installation if the operating system is Windows 95/98. In the Condition table we would define conditions to set to 0 the Level attribute of those particular features that are not to be installed on a particular operating system. Then, based on the installation option chosen by the end user, we would select the features to be installed by setting the appropriate value for the INSTALLLEVEL property in the Property table. Since some of the features would have an Install Level of 0 they could not be installed or even selected in a Custom selection dialog box.

THE COMPONENT-CENTRIC TABLES GROUP

After we define the features that describe the end user's view of our application we need to define the composition of these features in terms that we as developers understand. This means that we have to define the files, registry entries, and other resources that make up the features. These assemblages of resources are called components and they are the atomic units of an application. Figure 3-4 shows an entity-relationship diagram for the tables of interest for the application for which you will create an installation in Chapter 4. There are an additional 15 tables that have foreign keys that reference the Component table, but they are specialized tables that need not concern us at this time.

As already mentioned in the above section on the Feature Centric table group, the FeatureComponents table handles the many-to-many relationship between features and components. The File, Shortcut, Registry, Extension, Class, and TypeLib tables shown in Figure 3-4 represent the resources that you will need to specify in your components when you create your installation in Chapter 4.

The CreateFolder table contains references to a folder that must be created for a particular component. Folders defined here are not folders that will be created as the normal outcome of installing an application; these are folders that must be created during the installation, and generally these are empty folders that would be used by an application. A typical action you will perform in the installation that you are going to create is to create an empty folder for the purpose of saving user data after the application is installed.

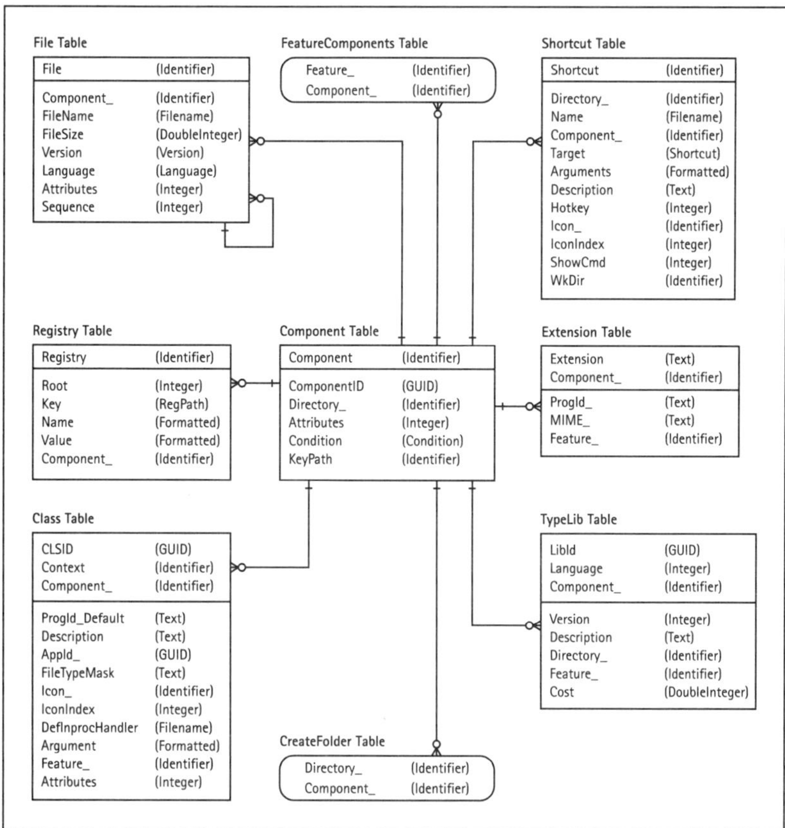

Figure 3-4: The entity-relationship diagram for the Component Centric table group

THE DIRECTORY CENTRIC TABLES GROUP

This group of tables defines both the source of and target for the files to be copied or created during the installation. Figure 3-5 shows the entity-relationship diagram for this group of tables. Several tables that have foreign keys into the Directory table are not shown here because they are specialized tables that do not apply to the installation you are going to create in Chapter 4.

The entry in the Directory table that is referenced from the Feature table is the name of a directory that the end user can configure in a Selection dialog box. Setting a property in the Property table through the selection dialog box typically is how this is accomplished. The entry in the Directory table that is referenced from the Component table is normally the name of the folder where the component is going to be installed under the root target location for the application.

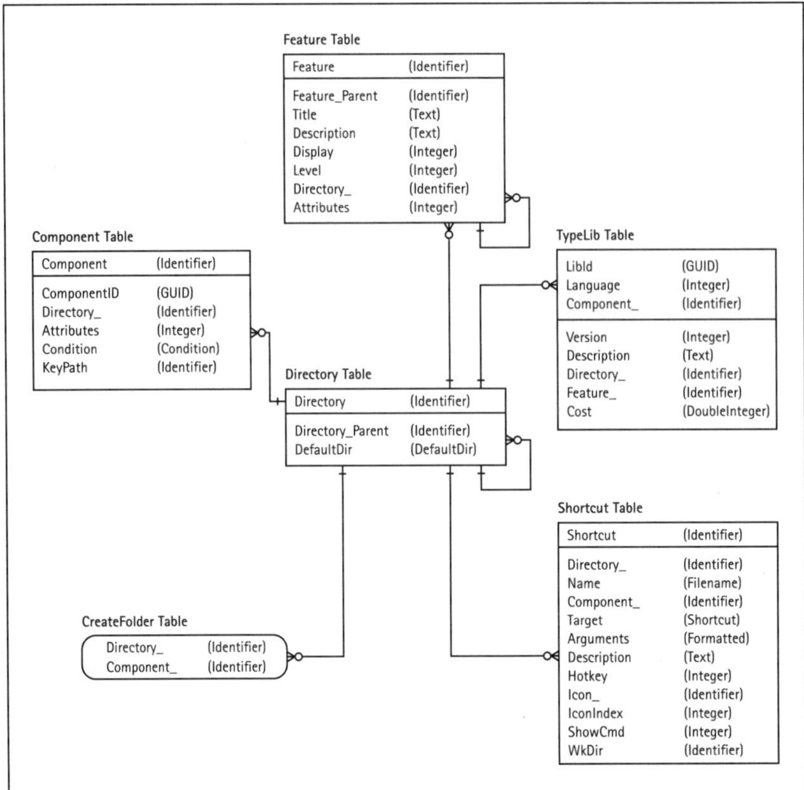

Figure 3-5: The entity-relationship diagram for the Directory Centric table group

For the TypeLib table the Directory table defines the location of the help file for that particular type library. For the Shortcut table the Directory table defines the location where the shortcut file is to be created. For the CreateFolder table the Directory table defines where a particular folder is to be created during the installation. As I mentioned earlier, this is normally an empty folder where, for example, the application data files will be saved by default.

The Directory table itself requires a lot of discussion. We start that discussion here and continue it in the next chapter. The function of the Directory table is to define the complete layout of the installation. This layout definition is relevant to both the location of the source files and the location where these source files are to end up on the target machine. Each row in the Directory table defines both a source location and a target location. When the end user sets the final location for the installation of the application, all the entries in column one of the Directory table become properties in the Property table. The value of each of these properties is a directory path. The Windows Installer also sets a number of properties to system-defined folder paths. This is all done at run time so the persistent version of the database is not changed. The database is only changed in memory. We cover the Directory table in much more detail in Chapter 4.

THE ICON CENTRIC TABLES GROUP

Because of advertisement it is necessary for the icons used on the Start\Programs menu to be contained in separate files. The Icon table contains these icon files. The Shortcut table references the Icon table for the icon to be used when a shortcut is created. The ProgId table references the Icon table for the icon file to be used with a particular ProgId. This is the mechanism that associates a small icon with a particular file extension. For a version-independent ProgId there would be no reference into the Icon table. The Class table references the Icon table for the file to use in conjunction with a particular CLSID. The entity-relationship diagram for this table group is shown below in Figure 3-6.

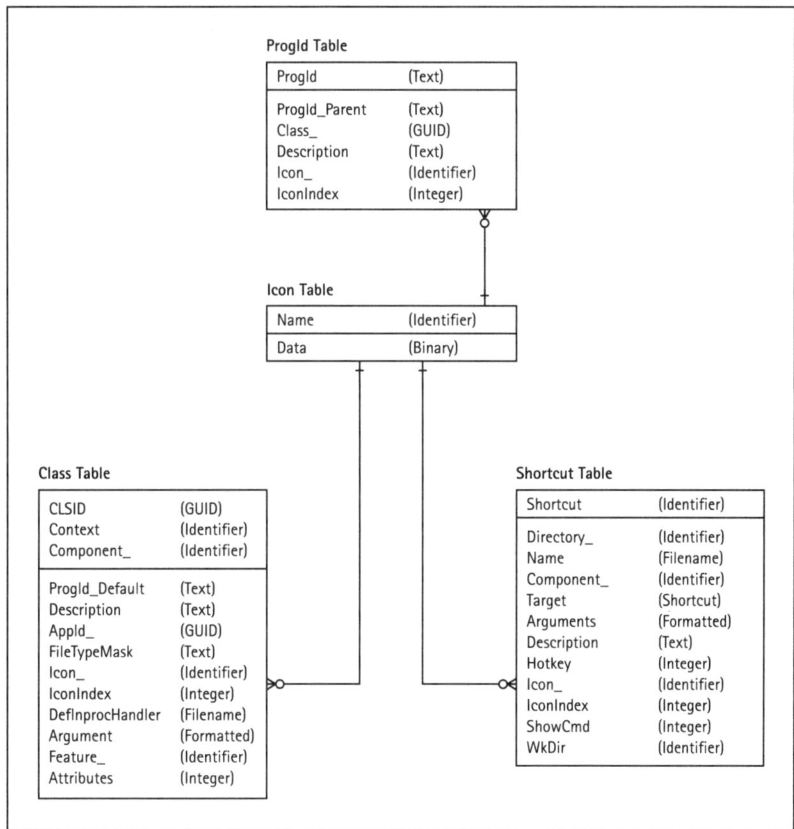

Figure 3-6: The entity-relationship diagram for the Icon Centric table group

The Icon table actually holds the icons in question as binary data. There are specific rules as to how these icon files, and the extensions on these files that are to be used for supplying the icon, are to be created. Icons must be stored in a separate file or files because of the need to be able to advertise a product, file extension, or the like. If the icon came from a resource inside the actual product executable or extension server, there would be no way to show the icon if the main file were not also on the machine. This would invalidate the concept of advertisement, which depends on the idea that only the icon will be displayed without any of the associated product files needing to be on the machine.

Icon files associated strictly with file extensions or CLSIDs can have any extension, such as .ico. Icon files associated with shortcuts must be included as a resource in a file with the Portable Executable (PE) format. This means that the container file for the icon must be either an executable (.exe) or a dynamic link library (.dll) file. In addition, the extension of this icon container file must agree with the extension of the shortcut target. For example, if you have the icon contained as a resource in a dynamic link library but the target of your shortcut is an executable, then all you have to do is change the .dll extension on the icon container file to .exe.

THE MISCELLANEOUS TABLES GROUP

This table grouping describes those table relationships that were too small to rate a separate category of their own. The entity-relationship diagram for this group of tables is shown in Figure 3-7. Except for the Media table all the other tables shown in this diagram have already been discussed as part of the other table groups.

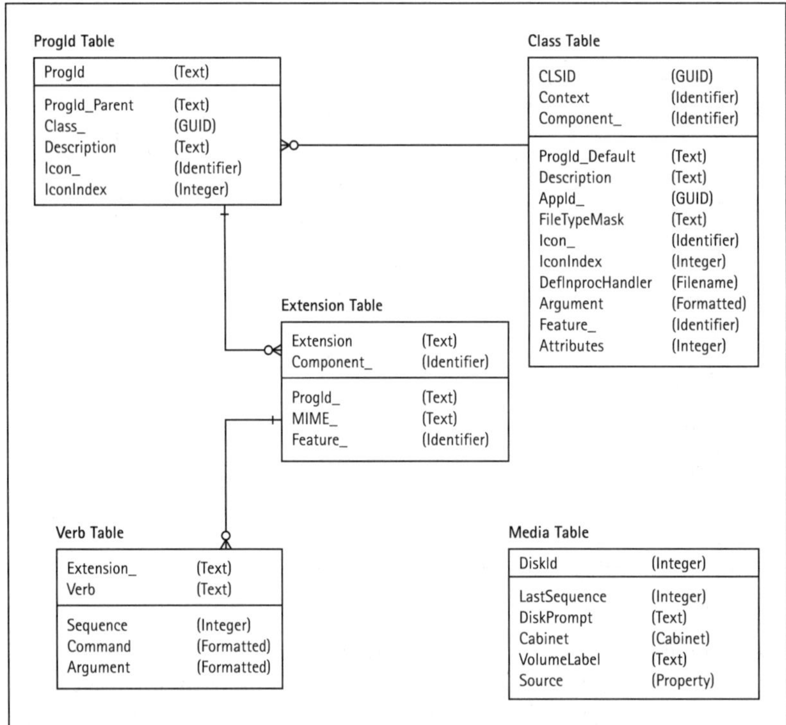

Figure 3-7: The entity-relationship diagram for the Miscellaneous tables group

The function of the Media table is to describe the set of disks that comprise the source media for the installation. Normally a CD-ROM medium is used and as long as the source does not span to a second CD then there will be only one entry in this table. If a floppy-disk distribution is required, there will be as many entries in this table as there are floppy disks in the installation. Each disk will also have to have a volume label that corresponds to the entries in the VolumeLabel attribute of this table.

This table is also used to identify compressed CAB files that contain files needed for an install. These CABs can be embedded in the MSI file, or they can be external.

We have now covered what can be considered the core set of database tables that you need to populate in order to make a simple installation. In the next section we discuss how the information in these core database tables is used to make the installation happen.

Sequences, actions, and properties

We have just discussed the various tables required for defining the information for the installation of a simple application. All these tables did, however, was define what had to be done to the system during the installation. They did nothing toward specifying how the installation itself was to take place. That type of information is defined by actions, which you schedule by placing them in what are called *sequence tables*. An action occurs or does not occur based on the evaluation of a conditional expression. When an action is executed, it uses the information in the database tables (discussed in the previous section) to implement the action. You can think of actions as function calls and the data in the database tables as the arguments to these function calls. A conditional expression is formed from properties, environment variables, and other sources of information. If the conditional expression evaluates to TRUE, the action will take place; otherwise the action does not take place.

Now we need to look at this concept much more closely. In the following sections we take a close look at the sequence tables that you need in an installation database, the types of actions that your simple installation will need to execute, and how properties work. When you finish with this section, you will have a much clearer idea of how this whole technology works. After this you will only have to master some details to be able to implement more sophisticated installations.

SEQUENCING AN INSTALLATION

The sequence of actions that takes place during an installation is specified in sequence tables. In fact there are three pairs of sequence tables, only one of which is active during any installation. The pair of sequence tables that is active is dependent on the top-level action that is initiated. There are three top-level actions or installation modes supported by the Windows Installer service. They are a simple installation, an administrative installation, and an advertisement installation. For each of these installation modes there is a user interface sequence table and an execution sequence table. The actual names of all six of the possible sequence tables are:

- InstallUISequence
- InstallExecuteSequence
- AdminUISequence
- AdminExecuteSequence
- AdvtUISequence (Even though this table forms a part of the database schema, it is not used, as the advertisement of an application would not display a user interface)
- AdvtExecuteSequence

Executing the following command launches a simple installation:

```
msiexec.exe /i  <Fully qualified path to the MSI Package>
```

This command is the command string for the open verb for the .msi file extension. When this command is executed, the Windows Installer issues the INSTALL top-level action and the actions listed in either the InstallUISequence table or the InstallExecuteSequence table are implemented. The specific sequence that is first implemented depends on the user interface level the user has chosen. There are four user-interface levels: full, reduced, basic, and silent. If the user-interface level is either full or reduced, then the actions listed in the InstallUISequence table are implemented first, followed by the actions listed in the InstallExecuteSequence table. If the user-interface level is basic or silent, then only the actions in the InstallExecuteSequence are executed, and the actions in the InstallUISequence table are skipped.

The same process applies to the other two modes of installation. To launch an administrative installation, run the following from the command line:

```
msiexec.exe /a  <Fully qualified path to the MSI Package>
```

A network administrator normally performs this type of installation in order to place an installable image of the application onto a network drive. When the above command is executed, the Windows Installer issues the ADMIN top-level action. Subsequently one or both of the administrative sequence tables are implemented, depending on the user interface level that was chosen.

To advertise an application, use the following command line:

```
msiexec.exe /j [u | m]  <Fully qualified path to the MSI Package>
```

In the above command line the u in conjunction with the /j switch means to advertise the application only for the current user and the m means to advertise the application for all users of the machine.

Advertising is always done with no UI so that only the AdvtExecuteSequence is executed.

To set the user interface to something other than a full interface you need to use the following command-line switches and place them after the path to the MSI package:

`/qr` To run the installation with a reduced user interface level

`/qb` To run the installation with the basic user interface level

`/qn` To run the installation silently

Table 3-3 provides a description of the four user-interface levels mentioned above.

TABLE 3-3 DESCRIPTION OF THE WINDOWS INSTALLER USER INTERFACE LEVELS

User Interface Level	Description
Full UI	All authored dialog boxes are displayed. This means that both modal and modeless dialogs are presented to the user. This user interface runs as a wizard and requests that the user provide input that is captured by the Windows Installer. Even if the all the defaults are selected the user still has to click the Next button on the wizard panels. The user must interact with the wizard for the installation to continue.
Reduced UI	Only the authored modeless dialog boxes are displayed. Since a modeless dialog box requires no action from the user the installation runs without any interaction. Normally this would just be a progress dialog showing the progress of the installation. The UI Sequence is still executed because the modeless dialog(s) that are displayed have been authored into the installation by the setup developer. Also displayed are any of the built-in modal error message dialog boxes. These dialogs come directly from the Windows Installer and not the installation package.
Basic UI	At this user interface level no authored dialog boxes are displayed. Only the built-in modeless dialog boxes that show progress messages are displayed. They will normally be much smaller than authored dialog boxes.
Silent	There is no user interface displayed for this UI level.

All of the sequence tables have the same structure, described in Table 3-4 below.

TABLE 3-4 SEQUENCE TABLE STRUCTURE DESCRIPTION

Column Name	Data Type	Key	Description
Action	Identifier	Yes	This is the name of the action to be conditionally executed based on the results of the condition evaluation. This action can be one of the standard built-in actions, a custom action authored by the setup developer, a single dialog box, or a user interface sequence such as the installation wizard displayed during an installation when using a Full UI user interface level. We discuss standard actions later in this section, and custom actions take up several chapters later in the book.
Condition	Condition		This column contains a conditional statement that must evaluate to either TRUE or FALSE. If it evaluates to FALSE, the action is skipped. If the expression syntax is incorrect, the sequence is terminated. A property by itself is commonly used to define a conditional expression. If the property is not defined in the Property table, the condition evaluates to FALSE. If the condition column is NULL, the action is always executed.
Sequence	Integer		The value in this column defines the position of the action in the sequence. Except for a few special instances these numbers must be positive. The action with the lowest positive sequence number is executed first, depending on the evaluation of the condition statement. The sequence of actions continues in ascending order of the sequence number until the Windows Installer returns a termination flag.

Column Name	Data Type	Key	Description
Sequence *(Continued)*	Integer		The Windows Installer returns four termination codes, which are the only negative numbers permitted in the sequence column. These termination codes are listed below: –1 Successful completion –2 User termination –3 Fatal termination –4 Installation is suspended Any of these termination codes will display a dialog box, which tells the end user what has occurred. Any other negative number, a zero, or a NULL value as a sequence number means that the action is never executed.

You have seen how the various actions that make up an installation are sequenced so that they are executed in the proper order. It is now time to take a closer look at these actions to see what makes them tick.

ACTIONS: THE FUNCTIONS OF THE WINDOWS INSTALLER

As I mentioned before, an action is the equivalent in the Windows Installer world of a function in a normal programming environment. The arguments to these Windows Installer functions are the data in the database tables associated with a certain action. There are two types of actions recognized by the Windows Installer: those that are built-in and those that are authored by the setup developer. The built-in actions are called *standard actions* and those authored by the setup developer are called *custom actions*. We will only be talking about standard actions in this section. Custom actions are a totally different ball game and require several chapters later in this book.

There are approximately 76 standard actions built into the Windows Installer. A small number of these can be placed anywhere in a sequence but the large majority have definite sequencing restrictions. This means that they must occupy a prescribed location in a sequence relative to other actions. In this section you will get your feet wet by looking at the some of the important actions that you will have to deal with when creating your first installation in Chapter 4. Since we talk about various operations relating to the copying of files in the next section we discuss those actions relating to this subject then. Our discussion here involves two different groups of actions: those that define the beginning and end of a sequence of actions that change the system, and those that deal with writing to the Registry.

The InstallInitialize action and the InstallFinalize action mark the beginning and end of a transaction, respectively. The InstallInitialize action then must be sequenced in the sequence table before any actions that change the system. The actions that would normally come before this action are those that are either validating the installation or are completing the task of determining whether there is enough disk space to complete the installation. The actions that would be sequenced to occur after the InstallInitialize action are those that copy files, write to the Registry, and so forth. The InstallFinalize action marks the end of a transaction and when this action is reached in the sequence table there are typically no more actions to execute. Also, it signals that the installation was successful and accordingly the rollback script and the cached files, registry entries, and so forth are removed from the system since there is no more need to be able to roll back the installation.

As shown in Figure 3-1 the actions that make changes to the system are first written into an execution script and then executed when the Windows Installer runs this script. The InstallInitialize and the InstallFinalize actions define the beginning and end of the creation of the execution script. It is only the actions that are placed between InstallInitialize and InstallFinalize that are added to the execution script. It is the InstallFinalize action that causes the Windows Installer to execute this script.

The InstallFinalize action also executes a series of spooled operations in order to clean up the system at the end of the installation. These spooled operations include caching the MSI database in the %Windir%\Installer directory, placing the icon container file in the same location, and deleting the MSI package and source files from their temporary location on the system. If the particular installation scenario that was carried out was a complete removal of the product, the InstallFinalize action automatically removes the Add/Remove Control Panel information, unregisters and unpublishes the product, and marks the cached local .msi database for removal at the time of the next system reboot.

Neither the InstallInitialize action nor the InstallFinalize action uses information from any of the database tables. These actions could be thought of as functions with a NULL argument list.

Table 3-5 defines the group of actions related to writing values to the Registry for the application you will install in Chapter 4. This table describes the functionality of the Registry-related actions as well as the sequencing restrictions that you must follow for the actions.

TABLE 3-5 **REGISTRY-RELATED ACTIONS FOR THE CHAPTER 4 INSTALLATION EXERCISE**

Action Name	Description	Sequence Restrictions
WriteRegistryValues	Writes an application's registry information based on the components that are to be installed either locally or from source. If a component is not to be installed, then the registry information will not be written. This action uses the data in the Registry table to write the registry values.	Must come after both the InstallValidate action and the InstallInitialize action. This sequencing is necessary because there must be knowledge of what components are going to be installed on the system before writing to the Registry. The InstallValidate action confirms that there is room on the target machine for the installation to proceed. The InstallInitialize action must come before any action that changes the system.
RegisterClassInfo	Manages the registration of COM class information with the system. It uses the Class table as the source of data for performing this function. If the system is running Windows 2000, then this action will register all COM classes listed in the Class table if the associated feature is selected to be either installed or advertised. Otherwise this action will only register those COM classes associated with features that have been selected for installation.	Must come after the InstallFiles action and also after the following actions if they occur in the sequence table: UnregisterClassInfo UnregisterExtensionInfo UnregisterProgIdInfo UnregisterMIMEInfo This action must also come before the following actions: RegisterExtensionInfo RegisterProgIdInfo RegisterMIMEInfo

Continued

TABLE 3-5 REGISTRY-RELATED ACTIONS FOR THE CHAPTER 4 INSTALLATION EXERCISE *(Continued)*

Action Name	Description	Sequence Restrictions
Register ExtensionInfo	Manages the registration of extension server information. It uses the Extension table as its source of data. If the system is running an operating system where SHELL32.DLL has a version >= 4.72.3110.0, then this action will register all extension servers listed in the Extension table if the associated feature is selected to be either installed or advertised. Otherwise this action will only register those extension servers associated with features that have been selected for installation.	Must come after the InstallFiles action and also after the following actions if they occur in the sequence table: UnregisterClassInfo UnregisterExtensionInfo UnregisterProgIdInfo UnregisterMIMEInfo RegisterClassInfo This action must also come before the following actions: RegisterProgIdInfo RegisterMIMEInfo
RegisterProgIdInfo	Manages the registration of ProgId information with the system. This action will register all ProgId information for servers specified in the ProgId table as long as the feature for the corresponding class or extension server has been selected for installation.	Must come after the InstallFiles action and also after the following actions if they occur in the sequence table: UnregisterClassInfo UnregisterExtensionInfo UnregisterProgIdInfo UnregisterMIMEInfo RegisterClassInfo RegisterExtensionInfo This action must also come before the following action: RegisterMIMEInfo

Action Name	Description	Sequence Restrictions
RegisterType Libraries	Manages the registration of type libraries with the system. This action uses the TypeLib table for its source of data and it will register every type library associated with a feature that has been selected for installation.	Must come after the InstallFiles action.

The last subject we have to discuss in this section is properties. We then move onto how the Windows Installer actually handles copying files from the source media to the target machine.

PROPERTIES: THE GLOBAL VARIABLES OF THE WINDOWS INSTALLER

If actions are the functions of the Windows Installer and the data in database tables are the arguments for these functions, then properties are the global variables. There are three broad categories of properties: public, private, and restricted public properties. They are all listed in the Property table. These property categories are described below:

- *Public properties*: Public properties are those properties that you can set at the command line, through the user interface, through the application of a transform, by using a standard or custom action, or by authoring it into the database at design time. The names of public properties appear entirely in upper case in the Property table. The INSTALLLEVEL property discussed in a previous section is a public property and would be set at the command line as follows:

  ```
  msiexec.exe /i <path to MSI package> INSTALLLEVEL=100
  ```

  You also need to note that on Windows NT and 2000, only public properties can be passed from the client to the service, so anything that the user set needs to be expressed in public properties by the time you get to InstallExecute in the UI sequence.

- *Private properties*: Private properties are not available to the end user and must be defined either by the setup developer at design time or by the Windows Installer at run time. The name of a private property must contain lowercase letters so that the Windows Installer recognizes the property as being private. The only way a user can interact with a private property is through a control event in the user interface.
- *Restricted public properties*: There are times when you might want to restrict the number of public properties the end user can set. This is the case in a managed environment. (We discuss this type of property in more detail in Chapter 14.)

There are certain restrictions on the creation of property names. A property name is a text string that can contain only letters, numbers, the underscore (_) character, or a period. Every property name can only begin with a letter or a number and cannot begin with an underscore or a period. You can initialize properties at design time by putting them into the Property table with an initial value. Properties built into the Windows Installer do not have to be entered into the Property table with an initial value. This also applies to properties for which a NULL value is acceptable.

The Windows Installer has a defined precedence order for setting properties. The following list gives this order, in descending order of precedence:

1. *Properties specified by the operating environment.* These are properties such as the operating system version, user privileges, and so on.
2. *Properties set from the command line.* These, by definition, are public properties.
3. *Public properties listed by the AdminProperties property and set during an administrative installation.* The AdminProperties property is a semicolon-delimited list of both public and private properties that are set at the time of an administrative installation. Installing from the resulting administrative image uses this set of properties instead of those in the Property table in the `.msi` database.
4. *Public or private properties that are set during the application of a transform.*
5. *Public or private properties that are set by the setup developer when authoring the Property table in the MSI database.*

We meet up with properties again and again throughout the rest of the book. They are very useful in condition statements and are critical for obtaining functionality in the user interface. It is now time to proceed to the discussion about how files are copied under the Windows Installer environment.

File-related operations

When people think of software installation, they normally think of copying files to their local hard drive. Even though this is only one of the actions that must take place during an installation, it is the action that takes the most time and uses the most space on the target machine. In order to copy files in the Windows Installer environment you must first determine whether the target machine has enough space to hold all the files that will be copied. Then you actually copy the files. You can perform other file-related actions in addition to copying files to the target machine, actions such as creating empty directories, moving files, duplicating files, searching for files, and creating shortcut files. We first discuss the actions that go into installing files, and then we touch on how these other actions are handled by the Windows Installer. However, we need to first discuss how files are versioned and the rules used by the Windows Installer for comparing files with the same name.

FILE VERSIONING

The Windows Installer uses the version, date, and language properties in deciding whether a file on the target machine should be overwritten with a file in the installation package. There is a specific format for the version string for a file. This format is as follows:

```
xxxxx.xxxxx.xxxxx.xxxxx
```

Each x represents a digit and the maximum version string allowed is 65535.65535.65535.65535. A version number can be anything less than this and it does not have to have four fields. The number 1 by itself is a valid version number, but none of the fields can exceed five digits and there cannot be more than four fields in the version string.

The Windows Installer uses the following rules for deciding if a file in the installation should replace a file of the same name that is already on the system:

- *Highest version wins*: With all other things being equal the file with the highest version will either be left on the machine or copied to the machine to replace the file that is already there.
- *Versioned file wins*: With all other things being equal a file with a version will always replace a file without a version.

- *Favor product language*: All other things being equal, if the file being installed has a different language from the file on the machine, the file that matches the language of the product being installed will be the file that is either left on the machine or copied to the machine. A language-neutral file is treated just like a file in any other language, so if the product language is also neutral then the file that is language-neutral will win.
- *Mismatched multiple languages*: With all other things being equal in the situation where the file on the system supports a different set of languages from the file being installed, the file that will end up on the machine is the file that best supports the needs of the language of the product being installed.
- *Preserve superset languages*: With all other things being equal the file that gets to be on the machine is the file that supports multiple languages.
- *Non-versioned files and user data*: With all other things being equal, if the modified date of the file on the machine is later than the create date, the file will not be overwritten since it is assumed that user modifications would be destroyed. If the modified and create dates are the same for the file on the machine, the file will be replaced with the file in the installation. If the create date is later than the modified date for the file on the machine, the file will be replaced since it is assumed that the file has not been modified.
- *Non-versioned files using companion files*: With all other things being equal, a non-versioned file that is a companion to a versioned file will follow the rules for a versioned file. The one exception to this rule is that if the versioned file on the machine and the versioned file being installed have the same version and language but the companion file is not on the machine, the companion file being installed is used even though the versioned file on the machine is not replaced.

In the previous list of versioning rules a particular type of file was mentioned. That was a companion file that is a special link, defined in the File table, where the companion file does not depend on its own file version information but on the version of the file to which it is linked. A companion file is defined by using the primary key of the parent file in the version column of the companion file. This links these two files together as companion and parent. (You will not be using this mechanism in the installation that is the subject of Chapter 4.)

The preceding rules are global and apply to all files equally. This does not mean, however, that you cannot override these rules. To override these rules you need to use the REINSTALLMODE property. Even though its name contains the word reinstall you should actually use this property whenever you are installing, reinstalling, or repairing a file. We look at how to use this property to modify the file versioning rules later in the book.

FILE COSTING OR, HOW MUCH SPACE DO I NEED?

Nothing is more annoying when installing software than to get almost through the install and to run out of hard-drive space – or to be told up front that you do not have enough space when you know you do because you are just replacing files and not adding files. Before you copy files you must make sure you have enough space. In the past you could do this with only marginal accuracy. Now the Windows Installer is better able to accurately assess the space needs of the application and to dynamically keep the space needs current based on changes in user selection of features and changes in destination location.

The mechanism used by the Windows Installer for determining the disk space requirements for an installation is called *file costing*. The file costing operation includes in its calculations the disk space required for both installing and removing files, making and deleting registry entries, creating shortcut and other miscellaneous files, and calculating the impact of overwriting files that are already on the system and taking up space. Also included in the file cost calculations are the clustered file sizes as determined by the volume to which the files are to be copied. If the end user changes the location of the installation to another volume, the costs of the installation are recalculated.

The file cost functionality is implemented by the CostInitialize, FileCost, and CostFinalize standard actions, which are entered into both the user interface and execute sequence tables for all installation modes. In addition there is an action that is entered only into the execute sequence table. This is the InstallValidate action. Table 3-6 describes the actions that implement the file costing functionality of the Windows Installer.

TABLE 3-6 THE WINDOWS INSTALLER FILE COSTING IMPLEMENTATION

Action Name	Description	Sequence Restrictions
CostInitialize	Initiates the file costing process by loading the Component and the Feature tables into memory.	Comes before the FileCost and the CostFinalize actions. It also comes before any user interface is presented in the UI sequence tables.
FileCost	Initiates the dynamic costing for the installation. It evaluates the cost for every file listed in the File table on a per-component basis.	Must come after the CostInitialize action and before the CostFinalize action.

Continued

TABLE 3-6 THE WINDOWS INSTALLER FILE COSTING IMPLEMENTATION *(Continued)*

Action Name	Description	Sequence Restrictions
CostFinalize	Ends the internal installation costing process that was started by the CostInitialize action. It queries the Condition table to determine which features are scheduled to be installed and it verifies that all the target directories are writable before allowing the installation to continue.	Must come after the FileCost action and before any user interface sequence that permits the user to modify the feature selections and target directories.
InstallValidate	Verifies that all volumes to which cost has been assigned have sufficient disk space to accommodate the installation. This action will end the installation if any volume is short of disk space. This action also notifies the user if one or more files to be overwritten or removed are in use by an active process.	Must come after the CostFinalize action and any user interface sequence that permits the end user to change the features that will be installed or change the destination for the installation.

FILE INSTALLATION

Once the InstallValidate action has been executed in either the InstallExecute Sequence or the AdminExecuteSequence, we are ready to transfer files. There is only one action that is involved in the transfer of files and that is the InstallFiles action. There are other actions that manipulate files but the InstallFiles action is the only action that copies files from the source media to the target location.

For a file to actually be copied, it is first necessary that the associated component be identified as the one to be installed to the local hard drive. This is determined during the costing process. Which files are transferred depends on the evaluation by the Windows Installer of the file versioning rules.

For files to be transferred, the InstallFiles action must process the File, Component, Directory, and Media tables (shown in the entity-relationship diagrams presented earlier). First the File table is accessed and from this table the associated component in the Component table is identified. Also from the *File* table the sequence number of the file is specified. This tells the InstallFiles action which disk of the media the file is to be found on. The Media table provides media information. (In a later section I discuss the connection between the Files table and the Media table using the sequence number attribute in the Files table.) From the Component table the source and target locations for the file are obtained through the foreign key into the Directory table. The use of the Directory table is rather involved so a later section is devoted to discussing this subject in detail.

DETERMINING THE LOCATION OF FILES ON THE MEDIA The location of a file on the media is determined through the Sequence attribute in the File table and the LastSequence attribute in the Media table. The Sequence attribute in the File table specifies the sequence position of the file on the media. If the files are compressed inside a cabinet file, the sequence numbers in the file table must match the sequence of the files inside the cabinet file. These sequence numbers do not have to be equal to the sequence numbers used inside the cabinet file; they just have to specify the same sequence order as the files in the cabinet.

In the Media table the LastSequence attribute identifies the sequence number of the last file that is available on the particular media defined by this row. Each source media disk contains all the files whose sequence numbers, as specified in the File table, are equal to or less than the value in the LastSequence column of the Media table and greater than the LastSequence value of the previous row in this table. If this is the first entry into the Media table, then the first media disk contains all files that had a sequence number greater than 0 and less than or equal to the value specified in the LastSequence column.

Since your exercise in Chapter 4 will not require you to deal with anything more complex than this, we will not delve into this subject any more deeply. Just be aware that there is more complexity in this business when there is a combination of compressed and uncompressed files that make up the source.

THE FORMAT OF THE DIRECTORY TABLE The Directory table defines the layout of an installation. Each row in the table specifies both a source and a target location, and their being in the same row creates a relationship between the source and the target. When a file must be installed in a target folder, the source folder from the same row of the directory table is used to find it. The Directory table has the columns shown in Table 3-7.

Table 3-7 THE LAYOUT OF THE DIRECTORY TABLE

Column	Data Type	Key	Nullable
Directory	Identifier	Y	N
Directory_Parent	Identifier		Y
DefaultDir	DefaultDir		N

Table 3-8 describes in detail the purpose of each column in this table and how to use it properly. This tends to be a confusing topic so the explanations are fairly extensive and are followed by an example.

Table 3-8 DESCRIPTION OF THE DIRECTORY TABLE ATTRIBUTES

Column Name	Description
Directory	A unique name for a directory or directory path, or it is the name of a property. In the parlance of MSI, an identifier is any text string that may contain letters, digits, underscores, or periods. However, an identifier must start with a letter or an underscore. This column is the primary key for the Directory table and cannot be NULL.
Directory_Parent	Either defines the parent of the directory being defined or it indicates that this row is a root directory. For this attribute to define a root directory the value has to be NULL. This column also has the same data type as the Directory column but it is allowed to be NULL. There can only be one root directory defined in the Directory table and there is a standard format for making this definition. Set the Directory column to the TARGETDIR property, leave this column NULL, and set the DefaultDir column to the SourceDir property.
DefaultDir	Defines the name of the directory under the parent directory defined in the Directory_Parent column. By default this defines both the target and source directories. In this context the term *source* refers to the location of the files on the installation media. To define different target and source locations you would use the following format: *targetname:sourcename*.

Column Name	Description
	If the value of the Directory_Parent column is NULL or has the same value as the Directory column then the value in the DefaultDir column defines the name of the root source directory. If either the target location or the source location is to be the parent directory location without a sub-folder, place a period in this column. In addition, you can format directory names specified in this column as short filename and long filename pairs by using the pipe symbol (|) to separate these filename formats. This column cannot be NULL and it uses the special DefaultDir data type. The DefaultDir data type is a text string that is either a valid filename or a valid identifier. If the Directory_Parent column is NULL, then the DefaultDir data type has to be an identifier; otherwise it has to be a filename or a filename pair. It can also be a period or a period and colon combination (. : .). The DefaultDir data type is only defined for the Directory table.

The above table may have left you more confused about Directory table attributes than you were when you started. So an example is probably appropriate. The example below is taken from the installation for the training application used in the ISWI course. It is only a small extract from the Directory table created during the development of the installation for the ISWI Training App.

Table 3-10 describes how the Windows Installer would resolve the Directory table entries shown in Table 3-9.

TABLE 3-9 EXAMPLE ENTRIES FOR THE DIRECTORY TABLE

Directory	Directory_Parent	DefaultDir
TARGETDIR		SourceDir
ProgramFilesFolder	TARGETDIR	PROGRA~1\Program Files
MyDir	ProgramFilesFolder	MYCOMP~1\My Company
INSTALLDIR	MyDir	MYAPPL~1\My Application

TABLE 3-10 DIRECTORY TABLE TARGET AND SOURCE PATH RESOLUTION

Directory Table Record	Path	Resolution
TARGETDIR	Target	The TARGETDIR property is not defined in the Property table so this value defaults to the value of the ROOTDRIVE property if it is defined. If the ROOTDRIVE property is not defined on the command line or it is not set in the in the Property table, the Windows Installer sets this property. The property will be set, for a non-administrative installation, to the local drive that has the largest free space. This local drive also has to be one to which the system can write.
	Source	The source root path defaults by the Windows Installer to the location of the MSI package.
ProgramFilesFolder	Target	This is a property set by the Windows Installer at initialization. The target directory takes on this full path as defined in the property table. The values in the other two columns have no relevance with regard to the target location path.
	Source	The source location resolves to the following: [MSI Package Location]\Program Files
MyDir	Target	This location resolves to the following: [ProgramFilesFolder]\My Company
	Source	This location resolves to the following: [MSI Package Location]\Program Files\My Company
INSTALLDIR	Target	This location resolves to the following: [ProgramFilesFolder]\My Company\My Application
	Source	This location resolves to the following: [MSI Package Location]\Program Files\My Company\ My Application

You will have to implement the Directory table when doing the example installation in Chapter 4. Now we move on to the final major aspect of creating an installation: developing the user interface.

The user interface

So far we have spent a lot of time discussing how to create an installation database so that we can install files, make registry entries, create shortcuts, and so forth. I have mentioned in passing that there is a user interface and that something called the user interface level helps to determine which sequence table with its actions gets executed when an installation is first started. It is now time to get into the details of how to create a simple user interface in the Windows Installer world. In the past, creating a resource dynamic link library generated a user interface for conducting an installation. The dialog boxes, as well as bitmaps and possibly other items that were shown during the installation, came from this DLL. There was typically a parent window that was also part of the user interface and that displayed a full-screen background. AVI files could be displayed on this background, .wav files could be played, and the background itself tiled with a bitmap.

In the new world of the Windows Installer all this is gone and what we have as a user interface is an Install wizard, which is a set of panels that provides information and/or requests information from the end user. There is no resource DLL required and you no longer have a full screen background on which to display your marketing material or entertain the user with music or videos. The Windows Installer creates the user interface out of the entries made in various database tables. Our installation example in Chapter 4 will not require a complicated user interface so I will only address those specific points it requires.

To discuss how to construct a user interface that is recognized by the Windows Installer I will break the various database tables into three groups. These are the Dialog Centric, Binary Centric, and Miscellaneous UI table groups. For each of these table groups, as with the other table groups above, I will present an entity-relationship diagram to give you an overview of how the various tables interact.

THE DIALOG CENTRIC TABLES GROUP

This group of tables encompasses a large part of the user interface functionality offered by the Windows installer. At the center of this group of tables is of course the Dialog table. Relating to this table are the Control, ControlEvent, ControlCondition, and EventMapping tables. Figure 3-8 shows the entity-relationship diagram for this group of tables.

This group of tables represents the metaphor of a dialog box as a container for controls. These controls can trigger events subject to certain conditions, and can also be triggered by other controls based on what is called *event mapping.* As you can see in Figure 3-8, both dialogs and controls have their dimensions defined in the tables. These dimensions, however, are not dialog units but what are called *installer units.* An installer unit is defined as being equal to one-twelfth of the height of the system font.

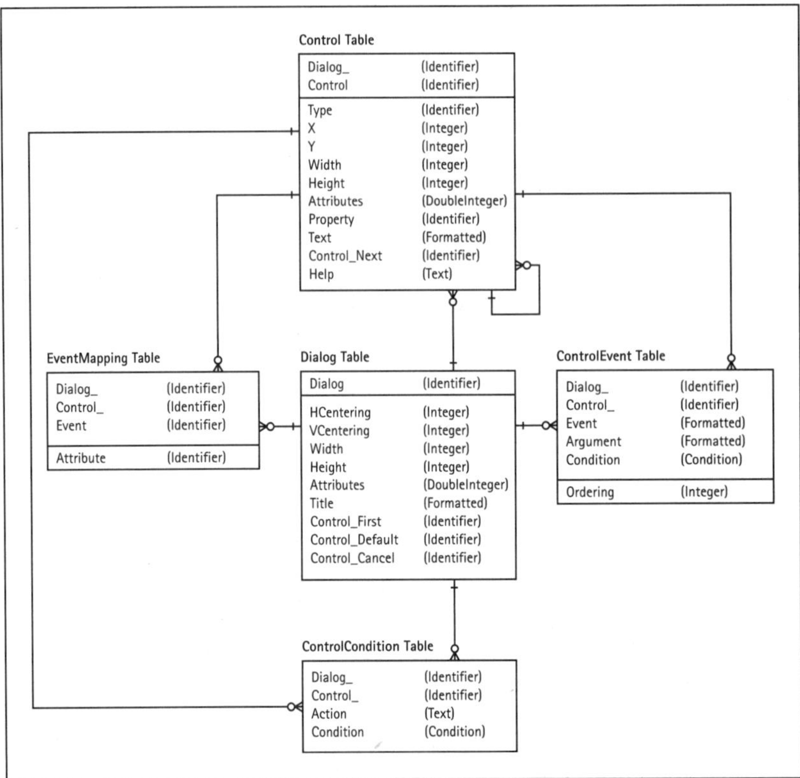

Figure 3-8: The entity-relationship diagram for the Dialog Centric table group

The Windows Installer requires that five dialog boxes be authored into any installation. Two of these required dialog boxes have reserved names and as such do not have to be placed into any of the UI sequence tables. They do, however, have to be entered into the Dialog table. The reserved names and descriptions of these two dialogs are as follows:

FilesInUse Alerts the user that some of the files that are to be copied to the target machine, moved, or deleted as part of the installation are being used by another process. This gives the end user the opportunity to shut down these processes to avoid a reboot at the end of the installation.

FirstRun Collects user name, company name, and product ID information. It does not typically do this during the installation but the first time the application is used. Then it makes a function call to the cached MSI package and the user fills in the information. This highlights the fact that you should build all security into the application itself, because with the Windows Installer there is no licensing enforcement during the installation.

There are no restrictions on the names that you can use in the Dialog table for the three other required dialogs that you need to author into the installation, but you do have to use special sequence numbers in the UI sequence tables. These three dialogs report to the end user the reason for any of the possible termination events that can occur during an installation. Table 3-11 lists the criteria that you must use to create these three dialog boxes.

TABLE 3-11 REQUIRED TERMINATION DIALOG BOXES

Event Type	Sequence #	Description
Fatal error	-3	A modal dialog that will be displayed at the end of an installation if that installation was terminated because of a fatal error. This dialog must describe the situation and have one pushbutton control that allows the user to dismiss the dialog box.
User exit	-2	A modal dialog that will be displayed if the end user cancels the installation. This dialog must describe the situation and have one pushbutton control that allows the user to dismiss the dialog box.
Success	-1	A modal dialog box that will be displayed at the completion of a successful installation. This dialog must describe the situation and have one pushbutton control that allows the user to dismiss the dialog box.

There are other dialogs that typically form the core of an installation's user interface, but these are all optional. These dialogs are as follows:

Disk cost dialog — Appears when an installation is being targeted at a volume that does not have enough space to complete the install. This type of dialog can also be launched as a child dialog from a selection dialog showing the end user the amount of space that will be used by the installation. This is a modal dialog that contains a pushbutton that returns the user to the previous dialog box.

Browse dialog — Allows the user to select and create directories. There are typically a number of combo box and pushbutton controls the user can use to enable the functionality of the Browse dialog box. This is a modal dialog that must have a pushbutton that will dismiss it and return the user to the previous dialog.

Cancel dialog	Confirms that the user actually wants to terminate the installation. This is a modal dialog box that contains a text message and two pushbuttons that permit the user to either confirm the termination or continue with the installation.
License agreement dialog	Displays the license agreement and enables the user to either accept or not accept the terms, typically by pushing one of a pair of radio buttons. If the user accepts, the Next button is enabled so that the user can proceed with the installation. If the user does not accept the agreement, the installation is terminated and the dialog used for ending the installation is presented.
Selection dialog	Allows the user to make selections from a tree control. It implements the custom setup type of functionality. The features that comprise the application are presented in this selection tree. This permits the user to configure the installation of the application. There is normally a button on this dialog that launches the browse type of dialog, which allows the user to change the install location of the application.

There are other dialogs that make up a sophisticated user interface but you don't have to worry about these niceties for your installation example in Chapter 4. You do, however, need to know about the controls you can use to populate a dialog box. There are 22 different types of controls you can use to construct a functioning dialog box. Table 3-12 lists these controls along with a short description of each one. Many controls are associated with a property and the action of the control can change the property. A small group of controls have their own tables because the individual controls act as a group, as is the case with radio buttons. This small group of controls is the subject of the next two sections.

TABLE 3-12 CONTROLS SUPPORTED BY THE WINDOWS INSTALLER

Control Name	Description
BillBoard	Part of a dialog that dynamically changes on progress or through action data messages. This control is not associated with a property. It is a special type of control because it can display other controls as long as they also are not associated with a property. This means that a BillBoard control can display Text, Bitmap, Icon, and other controls of this type.

Control Name	Description
Bitmap	Displays a static picture of a bitmap. The bitmap displayed is stored in the Binary table. This control is not associated with a property.
CheckBox	A two-state control. It is associated with a property and is discussed in more detail later in this chapter.
ComboBox	Displays a dropdown list of predefined values and it also has an edit field where the user can enter values. This control is associated with a property.
DirectoryCombo	Displays a part of the path that is currently displayed in the PathEdit control. It does not show the last segment of the path because it is displayed in the DirectoryList control. This control is associated with the same property associated with the PathEdit and DirectoryList controls.
DirectoryList	Displays a part of the path that is currently displayed in the PathEdit control. It displays those folders below the directory currently displayed by the DirectoryCombo control. It is associated with the same property associated with the DirectoryCombo and PathEdit controls.
Edit	An edit field that is associated with either a string or integer value property.
GroupBox	A static control that consists of a rectangle and an optional caption. It serves to group controls together on the dialog and it is not associated with a property.
Icon	Displays a static picture of an icon that can be stored in the Binary table. It is not associated with a property.
Line	A horizontal line. It is not associated with a property.
ListBox	A regular list box that allows the user to make a single selection from a list of predefined values. It is associated with a property and is discussed in more detail later in this chapter.
ListView	Displays a single column of values, each of which can have an icon associated with it. The user can make a single selection from this list. This control is associated with a property and is discussed in more detail later in this chapter.

Continued

TABLE 3-12 CONTROLS SUPPORTED BY THE WINDOWS INSTALLER *(Continued)*

Control Name	Description
MaskedEdit	An edit field that contains a mask in the text field. You can use it to create a template wherein a user can enter information, such as a product ID. This control is associated with a property.
PathEdit	Displays an edit field that enables a user to select the tail-end section of a path. It is associated with the same property as the DirectoryCombo and DirectoryList controls.
ProgressBar	Displays a bar that changes length as it receives progress messages. This control is not associated with a property.
PushButton	Displays a basic pushbutton. It is not associated with a property.
RadioButtonGroup	A group of radio buttons that work together to make a single selection. It is associated with a property and is discussed in more detail later in this chapter.
ScrollableText	Displays a long string of text such as is found in a license agreement. It is not associated with a property.
SelectionTree	Use in a custom setup-type box that enables the user to change the selection state of a feature. It is associated with a property.
Text	Displays static text that can use a predefined text style. This control is not associated with a property.
VolumeCostList	Presents information about the space required for an installation and the volumes where this space is needed. It is not associated with a property.
VolumeSelectCombo	Enables the user to select a volume from an alphabetical list. It is associated with a property.

The CheckBox, ComboBox, ListBox, ListView, and RadioButton controls each have their own table into which you have to add information in addition to listing them in the Control table. These particular controls require entries into special tables because they are of a type of control that has a multiple selection capability. This group can be broken into two groups: the Binary Centric table group and the Miscellaneous UI table group.

THE BINARY CENTRIC TABLE GROUP

This group consists of the Binary, ListView, and RadioButton tables. The ListView and RadioButton controls are linked to the Binary table because they can display icons. The icons to be displayed in these controls must be stored in the Binary table. Figure 3-9 shows the entity-relationship diagram for this particular table group.

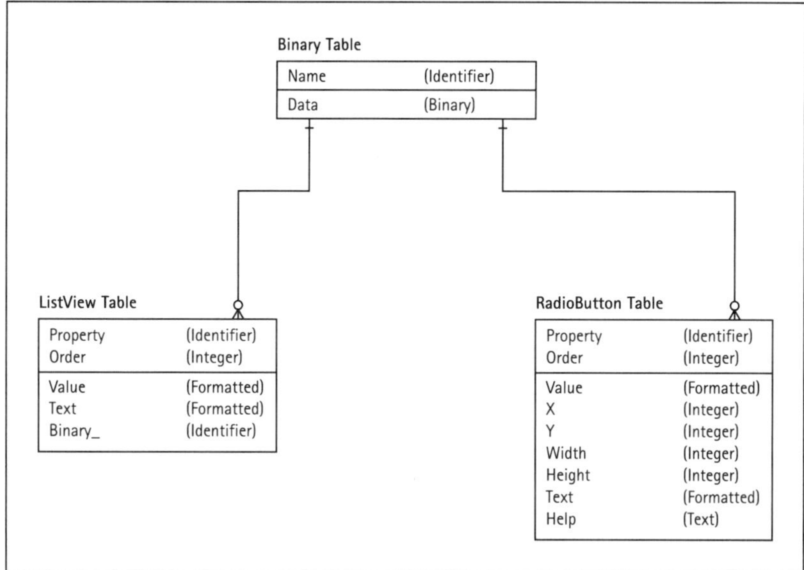

Figure 3-9: The entity-relationship diagram for the Binary Centric table group

Note that one of the attributes that form the primary key in the ListView and RadioButton tables is a property identifier. This is the same property identifier entered for this control in the Control table. In the case of the RadioButton control, every entry in the RadioButton table that has the same property is tied into the RadioButtonGroup, which is identified in the Control table with this same property. For the ListView control every item in the ListView table becomes a member of the same list view if it is assigned to the same property that is identified with this control in the Control table.

THE MISCELLANEOUS UI TABLE GROUP

We now move on to the last of the database tables that is important for the next chapter. This set of miscellaneous tables consists of three tables that deal with group controls in much the same way as the controls discussed in the previous section; additionally, there are two tables that handle text and text styles for the user interface. Figure 3-10 shows the entity-relationship diagram for this group of tables. In this case the term *entity-relationship* is something of a misnomer since these tables have no direct connection to each other.

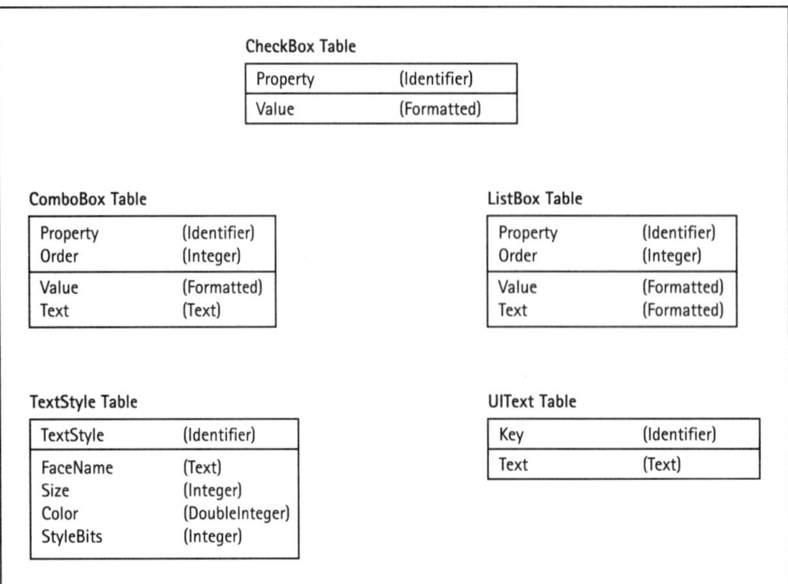

Figure 3-10: The entity-relationship diagram for the Miscellaneous UI table group

The ListBox and ComboBox tables operate in conjunction with the ListBox and ComboBox controls in the same way that the ListView table and the ListView control do. The only difference is that the ListView control can display an icon beside each item in the list and the ListBox control cannot.

The CheckBox table and the CheckBox control are a slightly different proposition. A check box is a two-state control: it is either checked or unchecked. When this control is checked, it sets the value of the property to the formatted string of the Value attribute in the CheckBox table. You have to define the property identifier for this control in the Control table. If there is no value specified in the CheckBox table or if the CheckBox table has not been created, the value of the property is set to the initial value of the property as specified in the Property table. If the property does not have an initial value, the checked state sets the property value to 1. In all the above cases the unchecked state of the control sets the property value to NULL.

A Word or Two About Package Validation

Microsoft strongly recommends that setup developers perform a validation on every new package that they create and on every package they modify. Performing a validation on a package involves three separate activities: internal validation, string-pool validation, and internal consistency evaluation. I only introduce the subject here because you will be performing a validation on the package that we create in Chapter 4.

Chapter 18 provides a complete discussion of package validation.

In Chapter 4 the only validation that you need to worry about is that which checks on the internal consistency among the various tables. This is the only type of validation required by the Windows 2000 Application for desktop applications. This specification gives the rules you need to follow in order to get the Microsoft Windows 2000 logo. Internal consistency evaluators, also called ICEs, are custom actions written in VBScript, JScript, or as a DLL or EXE. When these custom actions are executed, they scan the database for entries in database records that are valid when examined individually but that may cause problems in the context of the whole database. For example, the Component table may list several components that are all valid when tested individually; however, an internal validation would not catch the error when two components use the same GUID as their component code. This type of package validation is called an *internal consistency evaluation.*

Summary

We have slogged our way through a fair amount of detail in this chapter. You now know that the Windows installer uses a complicated database to describe the information needed to run an installation. Windows Installer performs an installation by executing an acquisition phase in order to gather information from the user and to turn the information in the installation database into a script. This script is then executed in an execution phase by the service-side process. The service-side process can have elevated privileges if the network administrator grants them; otherwise the service side will run with user privileges. This is okay if the user has administrative or power-user privileges, but an installation will fail otherwise.

You learned that products are made up of features and components, components being the developer's view of the application and features the end user's view. Features are what the end user is allowed to select or deselect through the custom setup-type dialog box. Components are the atomic unit of an installation and they consist not only of files but of registry entries, shortcuts, and other information required for their proper functioning on the target system.

You also now know the basic concepts involved in constructing an installation package. In particular I have shown you how the important database tables work together to provide the information necessary for performing an installation. Making entries into database tables also creates the user interface for the installation. There is no more use of resource DLLs to create the dialog boxes in an installation wizard.

Chapter 4

Direct Creation of an MSI Package

IN THIS CHAPTER

- Planning the installation
- How to define the product in terms of its features and components
- How to integrate the product with the operating system
- Exposing the product to the end user
- Structuring the order in which the installation is implemented
- Performing the validation of the installation package

NOW THAT YOU'VE GOTTEN an overview of the Windows Installer in Chapter 3, you are going to create an actual installation package for one of the sample applications created for this book. In order to cement what you learned in Chapter 3, you will create this installation package by directly editing an empty database. You will do this using a special tool that comes with the MSI SDK found on the CD-ROM at the back of the book.

Actually, in this chapter you are going to do only half the job: install the sample application. What you create will not have a user interface for the installation. You will add the user interface in Chapter 5.

The combination of Chapters 3, 4, and 5 gives you a foundation that will enable you to learn about the InstallShield for Windows Installer authoring tool and how to use this tool to solve real-world installation problems. You will also see after this chapter and the next why an authoring tool is necessary for any real software-installation development efforts.

The Product to Be Installed

You can find the files that comprise the application to be installed in this example on the accompanying CD-ROM, along with the source code from which these files were generated. This application is called ISWI Artist. It is a basic application that uses COM as one of its components. ISWI Artist draws text or objects on the screen at the location of the cursor when the left mouse button is clicked. The functionality of this application is somewhat trivial but it will demonstrate the complexity of creating an installation without the use of an authoring tool.

Figure 4-1 shows the feature and component layout for this application. This figure shows two top-level features and one sub-feature. The sub-feature is a child of Feature 1. Each of the features is comprised of one component. Feature 1 is the main application and Feature 2 provides the on-line help in the form of an HTML page. Feature 2 is implemented as a standard dynamic-link library that launches Internet Explorer to display the HTML help page. The sub-feature of Feature 1 provides graphics functionality to the product that allows the display of various graphics primitives, shown in different colors. This functionality is implemented as a COM DLL to make it necessary for the user to make the entries in the COM-related tables.

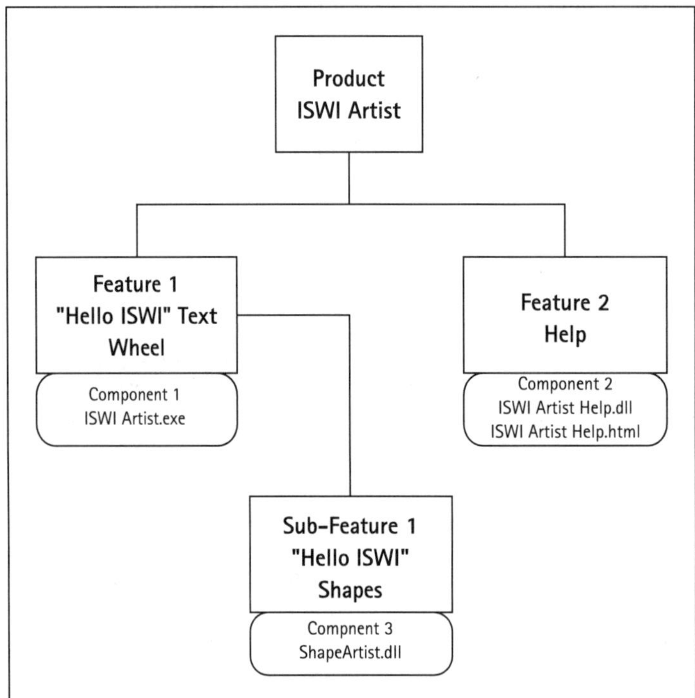

Figure 4-1: Feature and component layout of the example product

Planning the Installation

The installation that you will create will be a Windows Installer package with all the application's files uncompressed and external to the package. This means that the source files will not be streamed into the package. Creating the installation for the ISWI Artist application is broken down into the following activities, which we will discuss briefly here and in more detail in the remaining sections of this chapter:

- Defining the product in Windows Installer terms
- Integrating the product with the operating system
- Exposing the product to the environment
- Structuring the installation
- Creating the installation user interface
- Validating the installation package

A brief description of each of these operations is provided in the following subsections.

Defining the product in Windows Installer terms

Defining a product means describing the features and components that comprise the product. After doing this you must then identify which components go with which features. (Refer to Figure 3-2 in Chapter 3 for an idea of how a product is defined in the world of Windows Installer.) In addition to specifying the features and components that make up the application, you must identify both the product and the components uniquely by giving each a GUID. Features, you will remember, are not unique and thus do not get GUIDs.

Copying application resources to the computer

"Integrating the product with the operating system" means that you copy files to particular locations, create any necessary directories, and make entries in the registry as required by any COM components being installed. None of these actions is explicitly exposed to the end user. For the ISWI Artist application the Windows Installer package you create will perform the following actions:

1. Identify the files that need to be copied.
2. Define the locations to where the files are to be copied.
3. Define the policy to be used when files are to be overwritten.
4. Define the default install action for each component.
5. Create an empty folder where the application's data is to be stored. This empty folder is placed in a different location from where the application.
6. Specify the necessary COM-related registry entries for the COM component.

Exposing the product to the environment

When we expose the application to the environment we are allowing the end user to access the application through various means. The most common method for allowing access to the application is to put an icon on the Start\Programs menu. In addition, however, you will also create an association between the application and a particular file extension and enable the user to launch the application by entering the application's name in the Run dialog found on the Start menu. Finally you need to provide the information which will be exposed in the Add/Remove programs applet on Windows 2000. Unlike on previous versions of the 32-bit operating systems this particular applet now exposes much more information than just the name of the application that performs an uninstallation. It can now provide technical support contact points and enable the end user to perform repair and reinstall operations as well as uninstallation.

Structuring the installation

At this point you have generated all the information required by the product to run correctly on the target machine and enable the end user to access it. What you need to do now is define the sequence of actions necessary to actually get this information onto the computer.

Creating the user interface

The purpose of a user interface for an installation is to solicit input from the end user and provide feedback as to the status of the installation. It is not absolutely necessary to have a user interface if the default values that have been defined are all that is required to get the product onto the target computer successfully. Creating the user interface from scratch using a database-editing tool is a lot of work. To explain the table entries required to author a user interface would take a book by itself. Instead, this book provides a separate .msi file that contains most of the user interface required. In Chapter 5, I will explain how to add those few missing parts; by doing this you should come to understand the low-level details of how a user interface is created in the Windows Installer environment. I encourage you to work through this part of the exercise so that you can appreciate how different creating the user interface for the Windows Installer environment is from what you may be used to in the non-Windows Installer world. For those of you who want a user interface but do not want to go through the effort of creating one from scratch, you can use the basic UI provided in the MSI SDK.

Validating the installation package

The last action that we need to take in this exercise, other than running the installation and the application to see if it works, is to validate the package we have created. You will do this using the tools provided by Microsoft on the MSI SDK, which can be found on the CD-ROM at the back of the book.

Getting Started

The first question you face is how to get started. You certainly do not want to have to create the database tables before you start to enter the necessary data into these tables. You are saved from having to do this by having an empty database created for you by Microsoft. This database, called schema.msi, is provided in the MSI SDK. It provides the latest database schema for creating a valid MSI package. You will want to rename a copy of this file *to* ISWIArtist.msi.

To create this MSI package you will also need a database-editing tool called Orca, also available on the MSI SDK. Orca will need to be installed and its installation is contained in an MSI package. To add the property values to the Summary Information Stream you will need to get the MsiInfo.exe utility. This utility is also available on the MSI SDK.

One additional tool that you will need to create the installation database is one that will allow you to create the necessary GUIDs to uniquely identify the product, components, and other entities contained in the MSI package. The tool you will use to do this is GUIDGEN.EXE, which is available with Visual Studio. GUIDGEN.EXE creates GUIDs in one of four different formats. You will be using the fourth option, the registry format where the GUID is in the following form:

```
{xxxxxxxx-xxxx-xxxx-xxxx-xxxxxxxxxxxx }.
```

When you get to the part of the exercise that deals with creating the user interface you will need to get a special .msi file off the CD-ROM in the back of the book. This file is named ISWIArtistUI.msi and it contains a partially complete installation user interface for the ISWI Artist application. You will need to merge this file with the installation package you are creating. To perform this merge you will need to obtain the MsiMerge.exe utility from the MSI SDK. This utility allows you to merge two databases. You will be completing the user interface using the Orca database-editing tool. We discuss all this in detail in Chapter 5.

Using Orca

Orca is a very easy tool to use. You will be starting with a blank database that has tables without any rows. To add a row to a table you first need to highlight the table in the left-hand panel and then double-click the right-hand panel. A dialog box will appear, enabling you to enter the values required for the row you are adding. You can also add a row from the Tables pulldown menu or by right-clicking the right-hand panel and choosing the Add Row command on the Context menu. To modify an entry in a table row that already exists all you need to do is double-click the appropriate column and perform the edit. You will only see a dialog box when editing an existing entry if the entry is binary data.

I encourage you to experiment with the other functionality in Orca such as adding tables, exporting tables, importing tables, and so on. You will not be using these other capabilities in this example, but you will be using some of them in other places in the book.

Now that you have all the tools you need to create an installation package and have described the product for which the installation is to be performed, you are ready to begin the exercise. You start by defining the product as shown in Figure 4-1.

Defining the Product

As you might expect, features are defined in the Features table and components are defined in the Components table. Features and components are connected through the FeatureComponents table. These two tables are related to many others, but they are the main tables required for this particular activity.

Refer to Figure 3-3 and Figure 3-4 in the preceding chapter for a complete description of the other tables that are related with these three tables.

There is one additional table into which you will enter data for all the parts of this exercise: the Property table. When it comes to defining the product you will be entering information into this table, which identifies the product itself.

Since you are going to build the installation for this product from the top down you start with the creation of the first entries of the Property table. The Property table has two columns and neither is nullable. The following table shows the values that you want to enter into these columns. The values that you enter at this stage of the process define the product-related information. You will set many other properties in this table that deal with other aspects of the installation.

You are required to set five properties for defining a product and there is one property that is highly recommended. Table 4-1 defines the properties and the values that need to be set for the ISWI Artist product. Wherever a GUID is shown as a value you should generate your own instance using GUIDGEN.EXE instead of copying the one shown in the book.

TABLE 4-1 REQUIRED PROPERTY TABLE ENTRIES FOR DEFINING THE PRODUCT

Property Name	Property Value
Manufacturer	ISWI Art Company
ProductCode	{EA6F96C0-9480-11d3-8196-204C4F4F5020}
ProductLanguage	1033
ProductName	ISWI Artist

Property Name	Property Value
ProductVersion	1.0
UpgradeCode	{EA6F96C1-9480-11d3-8196-204C4F4F5020}
INSTALLLEVEL	100

Descriptions of these five required properties is given below:

Manufacturer is the property that specifies the name of the company that is producing the software. This is a required property.

ProductCode is the GUID that uniquely identifies a particular product release. You will need to change the value of this property whenever the product is given a major upgrade (where a product is enhanced with new features and/or components). This is a required property.

Chapter 20 provides a full description of how to upgrade a product.

ProductLanguage indicates the language that the Windows Installer is to use for any strings in the user interface that are not authored into the database. This property is the language identifier for the language and it must be one of the languages listed as one of the values for the Template property that is one of the members of the Summary Information Stream property set. An example of a user-interface string that would not be authored into the database is an error message built into the Windows Installer. This is a required property.

*ProductName*indicates the name of the product being installed. This is a required property.

ProductVersion is the product version provided as a string. The standard format for this string is major version followed by minor version and then (if necessary) build number. The major and minor version numbers must be less than 0xFF (decimal 255) and the build number must be less than 0xFFFF (decimal 65535). This is a required property.

UpgradeCode is another GUID that is used when you create a Windows Installer package that will perform a major upgrade to the product. This property value does not have to be unique among products as long as those products can all be upgraded with the same upgrade package. This is not a required property Microsoft strongly recommends that you assign every product an upgrade code. Otherwise you will not be able to use the upgrade functionality provided by the Windows Installer.

Entering these properties is all you have to do as far as defining the product properties is concerned. You will see the Property table again when you enter values concerning other aspects of the installation.

We now move on to the next task in defining the product. First, you have to identify the features that form the end user's view of the product – the features that the end user can select or deselect through the custom setup type dialog box. Table 4-2 provides the information you need to enter into the Feature table for each of the three features that comprise the ISWI Artist product. Each feature is defined by one row in the Feature table. The Feature table has eight attributes that you need to enter with three of these attributes being non-nullable. As I did with the Property table, I will describe these attributes to show how the Windows Installer uses each during the installation.

TABLE 4-2 FEATURE TABLE ENTRIES REQUIRED TO DEFINE THE ISWIARTIST FEATURE SET

Row #	Column Name	Attribute Value
1	Feature	Main_Feature
	Feature_Parent	
	Title	Text Wheel
	Description	This is the main feature of the application and allows the user to draw a wheel with the string "Hello ISWI."
	Display	5
	Level	100
	Directory_	TARGETDIR
	Attributes	24
2	Feature	ShapeDraw_Feature
	Feature_Parent	Main_Feature
	Title	Shape Drawing
	Description	This feature allows the user to draw the "Hello ISWI" string inside various geometric shapes.
	Display	8
	Level	100
	Directory_	TARGETDIR

Row #	Column Name	Attribute Value
2	Attributes	8
3	Feature	Help_Feature
	Feature_Parent	
	Title	Help Docs
	Description	This feature provides the help for the ISWI Artist application.
	Display	12
	Level	100
	Directory_	TARGETDIR
	Attributes	8

A description of the columns in the Feature table is given below:

The *Feature* column is the primary key for this table and it is an identifier that uniquely names a feature. This identifier is a text string that can contain letters, digits, underscores (_), and periods (.). The scope of the uniqueness of this identifier is only for the product and it is enforced by the fact that a database table cannot contain duplicate primary keys.

The *Feature_Parent* column designates that the feature being defined by this row is a child feature. This identifier is a key into the primary key of this table and points to the row in this table that defines the parent feature to this feature. If a feature is a root feature then this column has to be null. In the operation of the Windows Installer no child feature can be installed if its parent feature is not installed. The value you enter into this column must have the same format as that of the value entered into the Feature column.

Title is a short description that will be displayed in the feature selection tree that the end user will see when performing a custom setup. If this column is null then the Windows Installer will use the identifier for the feature found in the Feature column. Since this is not normally a user-friendly name it is best to enter a better name in this column.

Description is a more complete description of a particular feature that is also displayed when the end user is performing a custom setup. This description is displayed in a text control whenever this feature is highlighted in the feature tree found in the custom setup type dialog.

The entry in the *Display* field is an integer that defines the order in which the features for the product are to be displayed in the feature selection tree found in the custom setup type dialog box. The features with the lowest number will be at the top of the tree or sub-tree. If the number is even then the tree for that feature is initially shown collapsed; if the number is odd then the tree is initially shown expanded. This has no meaning in the case of a feature that is a leaf node in the tree. If the number is 0 or there is no entry in this column then the feature will be hidden and not displayed in the feature tree.

Level is an integer value that defines the install level for this feature. You use it to configure the feature set that will be installed for any predefined setup type options such as Typical, Compact, or Complete. The Windows Installer compares this value with the public INSTALLLEVEL property in the Property table to determine if a feature should be installed or not. If the value entered in this column for the feature is equal to or less than the value of the INSTALLLEVEL property the feature will be installed. Otherwise the feature will not be installed. The user can change this value through the custom setup dialog and either select a feature for installation or change it so that it is not installed. The value you enter into this column can be any number from 1 to 32767. A value of 0 will disable the feature and prevent it from being displayed in a custom setup type feature selection tree.

The *Directory_* column contains the name of a root directory into which this feature will be installed; the end user can change it with a location selection dialog box. Normally a property is used here; it must be a public property so that it can be set from the command line. This value is a foreign key into the Directory table, so any value entered here must also exist in this table.

The *Attributes* column is where you define the default state of the feature. You also design the feature states that the user can set through the custom setup feature tree. There are four feature states: installed to run locally, installed to run from source, advertised, or absent.

A number of pertinent remarks about the entries you are making in the Feature table are provided in the following list. These remarks give some of the background about these entries:

- The values used for the Display attribute in the Feature table provide a feature selection tree where the main feature is at the top of the tree. Since it has a child feature it is initially expanded. This is the effect of using an odd number for this table attribute. The help feature is not expanded since it does not have a child feature, so its display value is an even number.
- The level attribute value of 100 used in this example is the same as the value for the INSTALLLEVEL property that was used earlier in this example.
- The value used for the key into the Directory table is a property that will be set by a custom action that you are going to add later in this example. This is a special property that can be reset from within the custom setup type dialog box.

- The Help_Feature feature and the ShapeDraw_Feature feature are both given an attribute value of 8. This means that it is not possible to set these features to be installed on first use. You need to disallow advertisement for these two features because the ISWIArtist application has not been designed to take advantage of feature-level install on demand. The Main_Feature feature has an attribute value of 24, which means that it cannot be set for installation on first use but also that the user cannot select for this feature not to be installed. The value of 24 comes from the sum of the attribute value of 8 and the attribute value of 16.

The next thing that you have to do is identify the components that form the end developer's view of the product. The end user does not see the components, which are atomic units of the installation. Table 4-3 below provides the information you need to enter into the Component table for each of the three components that make up the ISWI Artist product. Each component is defined by one row in the Component table. The Component table has six attributes that you need to supply, three of these attributes being non-nullable. I will describe the attributes after the presentation of the actual values in order to show how the Windows Installer uses each of these attributes during the installation.

TABLE 4-3 COMPONENT TABLE ENTRIES REQUIRED TO DEFINE THE ATOMIC UNITS THAT COMPRISE ISWIARTIST

Row #	Column Name	Attribute Value
1	Component	Help_Component
	ComponentId	{5774E1F8-939D-11D3-8195-204C4F4F5020}
	Directory_	TARGETDIR
	Attributes	0
	Condition	
	KeyPath	ISWIArtistHelp.dll
2	Component	MainExe_Component
	ComponentId	{5774E1F7-939D-11D3-8195-204C4F4F5020}
	Directory_	TARGETDIR
	Attributes	0
	Condition	
	KeyPath	ISWIArtist.exe

Continued

TABLE 4-3 COMPONENT TABLE ENTRIES REQUIRED TO DEFINE THE ATOMIC UNITS THAT COMPRISE ISWIARTIST *(Continued)*

Row #	Column Name	Attribute Value
3	Component	ShapeDraw_Component
	ComponentId	{5774E1FA-939D-11D3-8195-204C4F4F5020}
	Directory_	TARGETDIR
	Attributes	0
	Condition	
	KeyPath	ShapeArtist.dll

A description of the columns in the Component table is given below:

Component is the primary key for the table and is an identifier that must be unique for the product.

ComponentId is a GUID, which by definition must be unique. This value is used by the Windows Installer to register the component in the registry. If it is null then the component will not be registered and the Windows Installer will not be able to either remove or repair it. Notice that all the letters in the above values are uppercase letters. This is necessary for the component ID to be valid. The GUIDGEN utility generates GUIDs that can have some lowercase letters; you must change these letters to uppercase before using them in this table.

*Directory_* is a foreign key into the Directory table. The value in the Directory table is a property that contains the path to where the component is to be installed.

The value in the *Attributes* column is defines how components are to be handled by the Windows Installer. It can be used to define whether a component can or cannot be run from source or whether this functionality is optional. You can also set other components, such as whether a component is permanent or transitive.

Condition is an expression that evaluates to TRUE or FALSE. If the result of a condition is TRUE, the component will be installed; otherwise it will not be installed. If this column is null, then the result will be the same as if the condition had evaluated to TRUE.

The value in the *KeyPath* column is used by the Windows Installer to detect the existence of the component. Normally this value is what is called the *key file* of the component but it can also be a registry entry. If this column is null, then the value in the Directory_ column is used as the key path.

The following remarks provide background about the entries you are making in the Component table.

- It might seem strange that the ComponentID is not the primary key for this table since it is unique. The scope of this table is only for the product but the scope of the ComponentID has to be across time and space. Since this column can be null it cannot be used as the primary key for the table. When this value is null the Windows Installer will not register the component and it cannot be removed or repaired.
- For the value of the Attribute column in this example we are using zero0, which means that these components can only be run if installed locally.
- In this example we are using the file names as the key paths for the components. In a much larger installation you would want to use some method of making sure that all the file names are unique since in this particular case this column is a foreign key into the File table. InstallShield for Windows Installer will automatically add a unique string to the front of all file names to make sure they are unique identifiers.

Finally, you have to identify which components go with which features. Table 4-4 below provides the information that you need to enter into the Feature Components table for each of the three features and three components that make up the ISWI Artist product. The FeatureComponents table has two attributes that must be supplied, and neither of these attributes is non-nullable. I describe the attributes after the presentation of the actual values in order to show how the Windows Installer uses each of these attributes during the installation.

TABLE 4-4 FEATURECOMPONENTS TABLE ENTRIES REQUIRED TO DEFINE THE RELATIONSHIP BETWEEN FEATURES AND COMPONENTS

Row #	Column Name	Attribute Value
1	Feature_	Help_Feature
	Component_	Help_Component
2	Feature_	Main_Feature
	Component_	MainExe_Component
3	Feature_	ShapeDraw_Feature
	Component_	ShapeDraw_Component

The meaning of the two columns in this table is as follows:
*Feature_* is a foreign key into the Feature table.
*Component_* is a foreign key into the Component table.

Since there is a many-to-many relationship between features and components there must be an additional table in order to create the one-to-many relationship between these two types of entities.

Copying application resources to the computer

It is in this part of the installation creation process that you define the major part of the work that the Windows Installer has to perform in order to get the application onto the target system. You will be defining how to copy files, where to copy them, making the associated registry entries, and making other changes to the system as necessary. To specify all this information for the ISWI Artist application you will need to use six tables. These are the *Class, CreateFolder, Directory, File, Media,* and *ProgId* tables. I cover this material in two separate sections, one on handling files and the file system and the other on working with the registry aspects of COM.

Handling files and manipulating the file system

For this you will need to work with four of the six tables. These will be the File, Directory, CreateFolder, and Media tables. Start with the necessary File table entries. The File table has eight attributes, five of them non-nullable. Table 4-5 shows the entries required for the installation of the ISWI Artist application. There are four files in this application and each file requires a row in the table.

TABLE 4-5 FILE TABLE ENTRIES REQUIRED TO DEFINE THE FILES THAT COMPRISE ISWIARTIST

Row #	Column Name	Attribute Value
1	File	ISWIArtistHelp.htm
	Component_	Help_Component
	FileName	ISWIAr~1.htm|ISWIArtistHelp.htm
	FileSize	2161
	Version	
	Language	
	Attributes	8192 (The particular constant used here is msidbFileAttributesNoncompressed which means that the source file is uncompressed)
	Sequence	1

Row #	Column Name	Attribute Value
2	File	ISWIArtistHelp.dll
	Component_	Help_Component
	FileName	ISWIAr~1.dll|ISWIArtistHelp.dll
	FileSize	28672
	Version	
	Language	
	Attributes	8192
	Sequence	2
3	File	ShapeArtist.dll
	Component_	ShapeDraw_Component
	FileName	ShapeA~1.dll|ShapeArtist.dll
	FileSize	36864
	Version	1.0.0.1
	Language	1033
	Attributes	8192
	Sequence	3
4	File	ISWIArtist.exe
	Component_	MainExe_Component
	FileName	ISWIAr~1.exe|ISWIArtist.exe
	FileSize	36864
	Version	1.0.0.1
	Language	1033
	Attributes	8192
	Sequence	4

The meanings of the eight columns in the File table are described in the following list:

File is a unique identifier for the file being described. It can be the filename or the filename modified with some additional identifier to ensure that it is unique.

This uniqueness needs only to be across the product. This column is the primary key for the File table.

*Component_* is a foreign key into the Component table and is the name of the component that controls the file.

The *FileName* column identifies the actual name of the file that is to be installed.

FileSize indicates the size of the file in bytes.

If the file to be installed has a version, you must enter it in the *Version* column. If the file has no version, leave this column blank.

If the file has a version resource, the *Language* column is a comma-delimited list of the language IDs to be found in this resource. If no language is specified, leave this column blank.

The *Attributes* column provides a number that defines the file's attributes, such as whether the file is read only, whether it is compressed, and so forth.

The *Sequence* column defines the position of the file on the media image. This number specifies the order of installation of the files as well as the source media where the file is to be found.

The following remarks provide background about the entries you are making in the File table:

- In the filename column you are using a special format by which you can specify both the short filename format (8.3) and the long filename format to specify the file. Make sure to use the correct case when giving the file names, not to put spaces between the filenames, and to use the vertical bar to delimit the two filename formats.
- To find out what value to enter into the FileSize, Version, and Language columns right-click on each of these files in Windows Explorer and select Properties from the popup menu. From the General tab on the Properties dialog you get the size in bytes and from the Version tab you get the version number and the name of the language. Knowing the name of the language you can get the Language ID. In our case the Language ID for English (United States) is 1033. If the file has no version resource then the Properties dialog will not have a Version tab and the Version and Language columns will be left blank.
- In the Attribute column you should use the value of 8192 for all files. This means that the source file image is uncompressed. If you do not set the attribute value, you could make the same specification using the Word Count property in the Summary Information Stream.

Before moving on to specifying where the files are to be found and installed you need to define the empty folder that will be created during installation. This empty folder will eventually be used to cache an application preference file for the component that installs the primary executable of the application. To define an empty folder you need to make use of the CreateFolder table. You need to enter one row as shown in Table 4-6. There are only two attributes in this table and neither of them can be null.

TABLE 4-6 CREATEFOLDER TABLE ENTRIES REQUIRED TO DEFINE AN EMPTY FOLDER

Row #	Column Name	Attribute Value
1	Directory_	EmptyFolder
	Component_	MainExe_Component

The following is a description of the two columns in this table.

*Directory_* is a foreign key into the Directory table. In the Directory table you define the location where this folder is to be created.

*Component_* is a foreign key into the Component table. The folder is created when this component is installed. If this folder is empty when the associated component is either moved to run from source or uninstalled, it will be removed.

The following remarks provide background about the entries you are making in the CreateFolder table:

- In this example you are using the component containing the main executable of the ISWIArtist application to house the creation of this empty folder. You could also create a separate component for the sole purpose of creating this empty folder. I mention this to point out the fact that components do not have to contain files.
- You are using this method to create this empty folder because the Windows Installer will delete empty folders not listed in this table. This ensures that this table will only be removed if it is empty at the time the associated component is uninstalled or moved so that it runs from source.
- If a component can be installed to run from source but you still want an empty folder created on the local system, you need to create a special component that is not allowed to run from source to create the empty folder.

You need to make an entry in the RemoveFile table so that the empty folder will be uninstalled if it is empty during an uninstallation of the product. Table 4-7 defines the entries that you need to make in this table in order to implement this functionality.

TABLE 4-7 REMOVEFILE TABLE ENTRIES REQUIRED TO DEFINE THE REMOVAL OF AN EMPTY FOLDER

Row #	Column Name	Attribute Value
1	FileKey	EmptyFolder
	Component_	MainExe_Component
	FileName	
	DirProperty	EmptyFolder
	InstallMode	2

A description of the five columns in this table is given below:

FileKey is the primary key for this table and is a unique identifier for this entry in the table.

*Component_* is a foreign key into the Component table and refers to the component that controls the file or folder to be removed.

FileName provides the name of the file to be removed. If a folder is to be removed, this column is NULL.

DirProperty is the name of a property that will resolve to the full path of the file or folder that is to be removed.

InstallMode defines the whether the removal of the file or folder is to occur when the associated component is being installed, when it is being uninstalled, or both.

The following remarks provide background about the entries you are making in the RemoveFile table:

- The folder that you want to remove if it is empty is associated with the main component, so you have entered the name of this component in the Component_ column and the name of the directory in the Directory table.
- Since you are removing a folder you leave the FileName column empty.
- Since you want this folder to be removed you specify the value of the InstallMode attribute as 2.

You are now ready to define where the Windows Installer will find the files that are to be installed as well as where they should be copied during the installation. You do all this using the Directory table. Using the Directory table can be confusing, so you may want to reread the section on this subject that can be found in Chapter 3.

The Directory table has three attributes, two of which cannot be null. You need to populate four rows of this table, as shown in Table 4-8.

TABLE 4-8 DIRECTORY TABLE ENTRIES REQUIRED TO DEFINE THE SOURCE AND DESTINATION LOCATIONS FOR THE ISWIARTIST APPLICATION

Row #	Column Name	Attribute Value
1	Directory	TARGETDIR
	Directory_Parent	
	DefaultDir	SourceDir
2	Directory	AppDataFolder
	Directory_Parent	TARGETDIR
	DefaultDir	.:APPLIC~1|Application Data
3	Directory	EmptyFolder
	Directory_Parent	AppDataFolder
	DefaultDir	ARTIST~1|ArtistData
4	Directory	ProgramMenuFolder
	Directory_Parent	TARGETDIR
	DefaultDir	.:Programs

Information concerning the columns of the Directory table follows:

The *Directory* column contains an identifier that defines a directory or a directory path. This column can also contain the name of a property, which would need to be set to the full path of a location on the target system. If this value is a property, the Directory_Parent and DefaultDir columns only define the source location. If the value is not a property, then the Directory_Parent and DefaultDir columns define the value of both the target location and the source location.

The entry in the *Directory_Parent* column is the parent directory of the entry in the DefaultDir column. It is also a key into the Directory column. You resolve a directory path by following the values in this column up the tree until you get to a row where the column is either null or equal to the value in the Directory column. When you reach that point then you have arrived at the root of the directory path. You define both the target and the source locations for the application's files this way, with the target location being different if the Directory column contains a property as described in the previous paragraph.

DefaultDir contains the directory name that appears under the directory defined in the Directory_Parent column. If there is only one value in this column, it then defines both the target and the source directory location. To specify different source and target locations delimit these two values with a colon (:), putting the target directory on the left and the source directory on the right. You could replace either of these directories with a period (.), which would indicate that that directory is the same as the directory location defined by the value in the Directory_Parent column. If the value in the Directory_Parent column is null or equal to the value in the Directory column, then the value in this column defines the root source location.

In the following remarks I will go through each of the values entered into the Directory table shown in Table 4-8 and explain what they mean.

- In Row #1 you are defining the root locations for the target of the installation and the source location of the files that comprise the application. You can identify the root by the fact that the directory column is null. In our example the TARGETDIR property will be initialized by a custom action. In this chapter you will just use this custom action without explanation. The entry in the DefaultDir column is a property name that is set by the Windows Installer when the installation is initialized. The value of this property is the location of the cabinet file containing the source files or, if the source files are uncompressed, the root location of the source file tree.
- In Row #2 you are defining the location of the Application Data folder for the current user. AppDataFolder is a property set by the Windows Installer when an installation is initialized. Since this is a property, the target location is set to this value. This has no meaning with regard to the source of the application files since no files are located here but you have made entries into the Directory_Parent and the DefaultDir columns in order to avoid errors when doing the package validation.
- In Row #3 you are defining where we want to create the empty folder where the application's data files will be stored. You do this by defining an identifier named EmptyFolder and then defining this value to mean a folder called ArtistData that is created in the location defined by the AppDataFolder property in Row #2. The Windows Installer will resolve this entry in the Directory table by first taking the entry of ArtistData in the DefaultDir column and seeing that it has a parent directory called AppDataFolder. It will then look for AppDataFolder in the Directory column and find that it is the full path to the Application Data location defined in the Property table. Because it is an entry in the Property table the resolution process stops and the location where the empty folder is created is:

  ```
  [AppDataFolder] ArtistData
  ```
- In Row #4 you are defining the location where the shortcut for ISWIArtist.exe will reside. ProgramsMenuFolder is a property set by the Windows Installer during initialization, but you have made entries into the Directory_Parent and the DefaultDir columns in order to avoid errors during the package validation.

To finish this part of the exercise you need to make an entry into the Media table. You use the Media table to tell the Windows Installer about the disk set that makes up the media for the installation.

The Media table has six attributes, two of which are not allowed to be null. You need to add just one row to this table since you have a small application and do not intend to put this installation onto floppy disks. Table 4-9 shows the input that you need to enter into this table.

TABLE 4-9 MEDIA TABLE ENTRIES REQUIRED TO DEFINE THE INSTALLATION MEDIA

Row #	Column Name	Attribute Value
1	DiskId	1
	LastSequence	4
	DiskPrompt	1
	Cabinet	
	VolumeLabel	Disk1
	Source	

A description of the six columns in the Media table is provided below:

DiskId identifies what disk this is in the set of disks. Normally with a CD-ROM this would be the only entry in this table since most software fits onto one CD-ROM.

LastSequence is the sequence number for the last file that will be found on this particular disk. This sequence number comes from the File table. The sequence numbers of the files on any particular disk will have sequence numbers equal to or less than this value given in this column and greater than the LastSequence value on any preceding disk. It is through the value in this column that the Windows Installer knows which files are on which disk when there is a multi-disk installation.

The *DiskPrompt* entry is combined with the text value of the DiskPrompt property. During the InstallFiles action this value is substituted into the placeholder that is part of the DiskPrompt property. The final message displayed in the message box is the template string associated with Error 1302, which has a placeholder for the DiskPrompt property. The template string is "Please insert the disk: [2]" where [2] is the placeholder for the DiskPrompt property. For a single disk installation such as is found with a CD-ROM this field is normally not used.

The *Cabinet* field contains the name of the cabinet file in which the source files are compressed. If the files are not compressed then leave this field blank.

The *VolumeLabel* field is the volume label of the media on which the associated files reside. Windows Installer uses it to make sure that the proper disk is in the drive before proceeding with the installation. If there is only one disk, this field can be null. If this column has an entry and there is only one disk, this entry will have no meaning to the Windows Installer.

The purpose of the *Source* column is to support patching and it is left blank for all other scenarios.

In the following remarks, I explain the background for the entries that you are making in the Media table.

- Since you have only one disk the value of the DiskId column, which is the primary key for this table, is set to 1.
- You set the LastSequence column to 4 since there are only four files in our example.
- The DiskPrompt column is set to 1 but you do not really need to set it since you will not be presented with a prompt for a disk.
- You gave the VolumeLabel column the value of Disk1 but again this is not really required for our small application.

Now, if you have entered the above information into the ISWIArtist.msi file using Orca, you are ready to address the table entries you need in order to properly register the one COM component in this application.

Initializing the default installation location

One of the things that Windows Installer does not set without some special effort on the part of the setup developer is the default location where the application will be installed. It is this default location that the user can change through the custom setup type dialog box. Microsoft's logo requirements have for a long while identified the ProgramFiles folder as the default location for installing a product. The directory tree under this folder should be the company name followed by the name of the application. This default location for our example application would be something like C:\Program Files\ISWI Art Company\ISWI Artist.

File SETTARGETDIR.DLL (on the CD-ROM at the back of the book under the Chapter04 folder) contains what is called a custom action. You can use this custom action to create the default value for the property TARGETDIR and it is at the location you specify that the application will be installed. To add this custom action to your installation package you need to define it in the CustomAction table and put the file into the Binary table as a binary stream. You will deliver the custom action to the system through the use of the Binary table so that the Windows Installer can execute it. Table 4-10 shows the entries that you need to make into the CustomAction table and Table 4-11 shows the entries that you need to make into the Binary table.

You will want to copy the SetTargetDir.dll file to the folder in which you are creating your installation package. This will make it much easier to enter the data into the Binary table, since you will only have to enter the filename instead of the complete path to the file.

TABLE 4-10 CUSTOMACTION TABLE ENTRIES REQUIRED TO DEFINE THE DEFAULT INSTALLATION LOCATION

Row #	Column Name	Attribute Value
1	Action	DefaultDest
	Type	257
	Source	DefaultDestCA
	Target	SetDefaultTarget

The purpose of each of the four columns in the CustomAction table are described below:

Action is an identifier that uniquely defines the custom action in this table. This is the primary key for this table.

The value entered in the *Type* column identifies to the Windows Installer how it should process this particular custom action.

The *Source* column tells the Windows Installer where to find the custom action.

The *Target* column tells the Windows Installer how to execute the custom action.

In the following remarks I provide some background on the actual entries that you are making in the CustomAction table:

- The 257 in the Type column tells the Windows Installer that this custom action is being implemented in a dynamic link library and that it should execute the action immediately upon encountering it in the sequence table. However, if this custom action is in both the UI sequence table and the execute sequence table then Installer should only implement it the first time Installer encounters it.
- The value entered in the Source column is a foreign key into the Binary table and it is the data identified by this value that the Windows Installer will stream out of this table into a temporary file and execute.

- The value entered into the Target column is the name of the exported function in the dynamic link library that will perform the custom action.

We will take a look at the particular custom action that you are using to initialize the TARGETDIR property at the end of Chapter 10.

TABLE 4-11 BINARY TABLE ENTRIES REQUIRED TO DEFINE THE DEFAULT INSTALLATION LOCATION

Row #	Column Name	Attribute Value
1	Name	DefaultDestCA
	Data	[BinaryData]

The purpose of the columns in the Bianry table are described below:

The *Name* column is the primary key for this table and is a unique identifier for the data that have been streamed into the second field.

The *Data* column holds the streamed-in-binary data that can be any type of file from bitmaps to executable files. These data are unformatted.

The following remarks provide background on the entries that you have made in the above table:

- The value you enter into the Name column is the same value you enter in the Source column of the CustomAction table.
- The value shown in Table 4-11 for the Data column just indicates that there is binary data in this column. Do not enter this into the table; Orca will ask you for the name of the file that is to be streamed in.

Working with COM-related registry input

To provide the necessary COM information for use by the Windows Installer you need only to concern yourself with two tables: the *Class* table and the *ProgId* table. We will come back to the ProgId table again in the next section when you create a file association for the default file extension for the data files created by ISWIArtist.exe.

The Class table has 13 attributes and only four of these cannot be null. For your COM component you need to enter only one row. Table 4-12 shows the values for this one row.

TABLE 4-12 CLASS TABLE ENTRIES REQUIRED TO DEFINE THE COM CLASS INFORMATION

Row #	Column Name	Attribute Value
1	CLSID	{3EECB2C0-90AA-11D3-8191-204C4F4F5020}
	Context	InprocServer32
	Component_	ShapeDraw_Component
	ProgId_Default	ISWIArt.ShapeArtist.1
	Description	Shape Artist Component
	AppId_	
	FileTypeMask	
	Icon_	
	IconIndex	
	DefInprocHandler	
	Argument	
	Feature_	ShapeDraw_Feature
	Attributes	

The columns that comprise the Class table are described below:

CLSID is the class identifier of the COM server.

Context identifies the context in which the COM server will run. This can be LocalServer, LocalServer32, InprocServer, or InprocServer32.

*Component_* is a foreign key into the Component table and it identifies the component in which this COM server is the key file.

ProgId_Default defines the ProgID associated with this COM class.

Description provides the description that the Windows Installer will enter into the registry against this class ID and ProgID.

*AppId_* is a foreign key into the AppId table and is required if the component is a DCOM-enabled component.

The *FileTypeMask* field contains information for the HKCR\CLSID registry key.

*Icon_* is a foreign key into the Icon table that can be associated with this COM class.

IconIndex indicates the icon to be used in conjunction with this COM class.

The *DefInprocHandler* column defines the default in-process handler to be used in the processing of a compound document to provide the required in-process implementation for an out-of-process content object.

Use the *Argument* column when the context of the COM server is LocalServer or LocalServer32. The formatted text string in this column is registered against the OLE server and used by OLE for invoking the server.

*Feature_* is a foreign key into the Feature table and identifies the feature providing the COM server.

The *Attributes* value indicates that the COM server is not to be registered by its absolute path but only its relative path to the client that is going to use it. This is how isolated components are handled.

The following remarks provide you further information about the values that you have entered in to the Class table:

- You must enter exactly the CLSID and other information provided in this table; otherwise this COM DLL will not be registered properly.
- You left the Icon and IconIndex columns null since you are not interested in having an icon associated with this CLSID.
- You left the DefInprocHandler and Argument columns null since there isn't any inter-process communication going on in this application.
- You left the Attributes column null since you are not dealing with isolated (side-by-side) components in this application.

I provide a more detailed discussion of isolated (side-by-side) components in Chapter 17.

In the ProgId table you need to create two rows. The ProgId table has six attributes, only one of which cannot be null. Table 4-13 shows the two rows you need to enter.

The following provides a discussion of the columns that comprise the ProgId table:

The *ProgId* column is the primary key of this table and contains the version-dependent or version-independent Program ID.

Table 4-13 PROGID TABLE ENTRIES REQUIRED TO DEFINE THE COM PROGRAM ID INFORMATION

Row #	Column Name	Attribute Value
1	ProgId	ISWIArt.ShapeArtist.1
	ProgId_Parent	
	Class_	{3EECB2C0-90AA-11d3-8191-204C4F4F5020}
	Description	Shape Artist Component
	Icon_	
	IconIndex	
2	ProgId	ISWIArt.ShapeArtist
	ProgId_Parent	ISWIArt.ShapeArtist.1
	Class_	
	Description	
	Icon_	
	IconIndex	

The *ProgId_Parent* column is only used when a version-independent Program ID has been defined in column 1. This is a key into the first column where you defined the version-dependent Program ID.

The *Class_* column is a foreign key into the Class table for a version-dependent Program ID that identifies a COM class. For a version-independent Program ID this column has to be null.

The *Description* column provides a description of the associated Program ID. This column should be localized so that it conforms to the language of the target operating system if it is a non-English system.

*Icon_* is a foreign key into the Icon table that defines the icon associated with this Program ID. Only use this field if you are making an icon association and it must be null for a version-independent Program ID.

If you give the previous column a value then the *IconIndex* column will specify the index of the icon that is to be used.

The following remarks discuss in more detail the entries that you have made in the ProgId table:

- In Row #1 you are defining the version-dependent Program ID. The CLSID you enter into the third column is the same one that you entered into the Class table.

- In Row #2 you define the version-independent Program ID and in the second column provide a key into the first column of Row #1 in order to associate the version-independent Program ID with the version-dependent Program ID.

You have now completed entries required by the Windows Installer to put the application onto the target system. Now you have to provide the information the Windows Installer requires in order to expose the application to the end user for launching.

Exposing the Product to the Environment

You are going to use three different approaches to making the ISWI Artist application available to the end user. First you will create a shortcut; then you will associate the .isa file extension with the main executable; and finally you will provide a per-application path for this product. The following three sub-sections describe the entries you need to make in the database in order to achieve these goals.

Creating a shortcut for the application

You are going to create a Windows Installer shortcut for the ISWI Artist application, and not a normal shortcut. A Windows Installer shortcut supports installation-on-demand and advertisement whereas a normal shortcut does not. However, you cannot edit the properties of a Windows Installer shortcut as you can edit the properties of a normal shortcut. To create a Windows Installer shortcut you will need to make entries into the Shortcut table and the Icon table. You will start with the Shortcut table.

The Shortcut table contains 12 attributes, five of which cannot be null. Since you are only creating one shortcut you need to enter only one row into this table. Table 4-14 shows the values that you need to enter into this table.

TABLE 4-14 SHORTCUT TABLE ENTRIES REQUIRED TO DEFINE A SHORTCUT FOR ISWIARTIST

Row #	Column Name	Attribute Value
1	Shortcut	Shortcut0
	Directory_	ProgramMenuFolder
	Name	ISWIAR~1|ISWIArtist

Row #	Column Name	Attribute Value
	Component_	MainExe_Component
	Target	Main_Feature
	Arguments	
	Description	This shortcut launches the ISWI Artist application.
	Hotkey	
	Icon_	ISWIArtist.ico
	IconIndex	
	ShowCmd	1
	WkDir	EmptyFolder

The columns of the Shortcut table are described below:

Shortcut is an identifier that serves as the primary key for this table.

*Directory_* is a foreign key into the Directory table that defines the location in which the shortcut file will be created.

Name indicates the name of the shortcut file that will be used to launch the application. This is a name that can be localized and it is the name of the .lnk file.

*Component_* is a foreign key into the Component table that identifies the component with which the target file of the shortcut is associated. The installation state of this component determines whether the shortcut is created or removed and this component must have a key path defined by the shortcut's target file.

Target is a foreign key into the Feature table and this feature is the one that installs the associated component defined in the Component_ column. When this is a key into the Feature table it is what is called an MSI shortcut, which means that it is the type of shortcut that can be advertised. If this is not to be an advertisable shortcut then this is a foreign key into the Property table and this property is expanded into the filename or folder name that is the target of the shortcut. The entry in this column can also use what is called a formatted text string. If you enter [#filekey] where "filekey" is a key into the File table, you will have pointed at the file that you want to be the target of a shortcut. We will be discussing formatted text strings throughout the book.

The *Arguments* column contains a formatted string that defines the arguments you need to use when you activate the shortcut.

Description provides a description of the shortcut that will appear in the property page for this shortcut on a Windows 2000 machine.

The *Hotkey* column defines the hotkey for activating this shortcut.

*Icon_* is a foreign key into the Icon table that defines the icon to be used on the Start\Programs menu with the shortcut.

IconIndex is the index for the icon to be associated with this shortcut.

The *ShowCmd* column defines in what state the application's main window is to appear when it is first launched.

The *WkDir* column defines the working directory for the shortcut. This is the default location for the File\Open and the File\Save As... commands. It can be a foreign key into the Directory table or, if the value entered is enclosed in square brackets, a foreign key into the Property table.

In the following remarks, I discuss in more detail the actual entries that you have made in the Shortcut table:

- In the Shortcut column you just create a string that will uniquely identify this row in the table.
- In the Directory_ column you enter the location for the shortcut. This key into the Directory table identifies an entry, which is the property ProgramMenuFolder, and this defines the location where the shortcut is to be created.
- In the Name column you identify the name of the executable file to be launched with this shortcut. You are using both the short filename and the long filename just in case the SHORTFILENAME property is set from the command line.
- In the Component_ and the Target columns you identify, respectively, the component and feature that contain the file that is the target for the shortcut.
- In the Icon_ column you identify the icon to be used for the shortcut. This icon file is an .ico file and is stored in a binary stream in the Icon table for use during the installation. You have not set an index for this icon because you are using an .ico file and not a file in which the icon is embedded as a resource.
- In the ShowCmd column you place the number 1 so that the application will be launched using a normal window.
- In the WkDir column you have identified a value from the Directory table that defines the location of the empty folder you are creating to hold data files.

The other table necessary to the creation of a Windows Installer shortcut is the Icon table. In order to create a Windows Installer shortcut you need to store the icons for such shortcuts in separate files so that you can implement advertisement. Advertisement of an application is where there is an icon on the Start\Programs menu but none of the files for the application have been installed. For the icon to be shown, however, there does need to be a file containing the icon available on the system.

The Icon table has only two attributes and neither of them can be null. You need to enter one row into this table; Table 4-15 shows the values for this row.

To make things easier you will want to copy the ISWIArtist.ico file to the folder in which you are creating your installation package. Otherwise you will need to enter the full path to this file in Orca.

TABLE 4-15 ICON TABLE ENTRIES REQUIRED TO DEFINE AN ICON FOR A SHORTCUT

Row #	Column Name	Attribute Value
1	Name	ISWIArtist.ico
	Data	ISWIArtist.ico

The following describes the two columns that comprise the Icon table.

Name is the primary key to this table and is normally the name of the file that provides the icon.

Data is a binary stream that contains the file that provides the referenced icon.

In the following remarks I explained in more detail the entries you have made in the Icon table:

- In the Name column you have entered the name of the icon file.
- In the Data column you have entered a filename with an extension .ibd. This extension stands for Installer binary data and it is only shown so that you know that there is a binary stream of data in this column. When you use Orca to enter this data you will be asked to provide the name of the file that is to be streamed in. What you will actually see in Orca in this column is the string "[BinaryData]."

Making these entries into the tables will allow you to advertise this product. You will experiment with this when you finish creating the installation package. Let's now move on to the creation of a file association between the main executable and the .isa file extension.

Creating a file association for the application

When you double-click a file created by your ISWI Artist application you want to launch the application and have that particular file loaded into it. You can do this by making the appropriate entries in the Extension, ProgId, and Verb tables. You will start with the entries required in the ProgId table.

You have already entered several rows into the ProgId table when describing the COM component to the Windows Installer. You now have to add one more row to this table as shown in Table 4-16.

TABLE 4-16 PROGID TABLE ENTRIES REQUIRED TO DEFINE A FILE EXTENSION PROGID

Row #	Column Name	Attribute Value
1	ProgId	isafile
	ProgId_Parent	
	Class_	
	Description	ISWI Artist Document
	Icon_	
	IconIndex	

Since you have already made entries in the ProgId table the following remarks explain in more detail just those new entries that you need to make in order create a file association:

- In this table you enter a value for the ProgId column in what can be considered a standard format for Program IDs associated with file extensions.
- In the Description column you enter a short string that tells someone looking in the registry that this ProgId is associated with an application called ISWIArtist.

The Extension table has five attributes, three of which cannot be null. You need to enter only one row into this table; Table 4-17 shows the values.

The purpose of each of the five columns in the Extension table is discussed in the following:

Extension refers to the extension being registered. You need to enter it without the preceding period.

TABLE 4-17 EXTENSION TABLE ENTRIES REQUIRED TO DEFINE A FILE EXTENSION SERVER

Row #	Column Name	Attribute Value
1	Extension	isa
	Component_	MainExe_Component
	ProgId_	isafile
	MIME_	
	Feature_	Main_Feature

*Component_* is a foreign key into the Component table and designates the component that defines the registry entries used to register the extension. This and the Extension column make up the primary key for this table.

The *ProgId_* column is a foreign key into the ProgId table and defines the Program ID associated with this extension.

*MIME_* is a foreign key into the MIME table and defines the information you must enter in the registry to register a file extension and make it known to a Web browser.

*Feature_* is a foreign key into the Feature table and defines the feature that provides the extension server.

In the following remarks I explain in more detail the entries you have made in the Extension table:

- In the Extension column you enter the .isa extension without the preceding period.
- In the Component_ and the Feature_ columns you enter, respectively, the names of the component and feature that contain the extension server.
- In the ProgId_ column you enter the associated Program ID associated with the .isa extension. You have already entered this into the ProgId table.

The last thing you need to do in order to create this file association is to define the Open verb that will be used to open the .isa file on which you will be double-clicking in Windows Explorer. You create this definition in the Verb table.

The Verb table has five attributes of which two cannot be null. You need to enter only one row into this table; Table 4-18 shows the values for this row.

TABLE 4-18 VERB TABLE ENTRIES REQUIRED TO DEFINE A COMMAND VERB

Row #	Column Name	Attribute Value
1	Extension_	isa
	Verb	open
	Sequence	0
	Command	
	Argument	"%1"

The purpose of each of the five columns in the Verb table is explained below:

The *Extension_* column is a foreign key into the Extension table and identifies the extension for which this verb is associated.

Verb defines the verb associated with the extension defined in the first column. This column and the Extension_ column make up the primary key for this table.

The *Sequence* entry defines the order in which the commands associated with this extension are displayed on the context menu the user obtains by right-clicking a file with this extension in Windows Explorer. The command with the lowest number becomes the default verb. The default verb is shown in bold text at the top of the context menu and is the command executed when the user double-clicks the file in Windows Explorer.

The *Command* column provides the text that will appear on the context menu. If this column is null, then the verb will be displayed on the context menu. This string is localizable.

The *Argument* column specifies the argument to be used on the command line when the command is executed.

In the following remarks I discuss in more detail the entries that you have made in the Verb table:

- In the Verb column you have entered one of the standard verbs associated with Windows Explorer. The standard commands are Open, Print, Find, and Explore.
- The sequence number you set is 0 since you want the Open command to be the default for this extension.
- In the Argument column you have entered "%1" which serves as a placeholder for the file on which you double-click. You need to include the quotes since you need to be able to handle long filenames.

Having made these entries in the ISWIArtist.msi database you have described a file association between your main executable and the file extension .isa. You now have only one more activity to perform in order to complete the three methods of allowing the end user to access this application.

Creating a per-application path

To create a per-application path you need to make an entry in the registry. The concept of a per-application path came with Windows 95 back in 1995; it enables the end user to enter the name of the application's main executable into the Start\Run dialog, and if it is not in the current path the system will be able to find where this application has been installed and launch it. Even more important, if your installation program registers a path, Windows sets the PATH environment to be the registered path when it starts your application. This allows your application executable to find any DLLs that it needs to load without having to have an absolute path to these DLLs. To provide the necessary information to the Windows Installer for creating the proper registry entries you need to use the Registry table.

The Registry table has six attributes, four of which cannot be null. You need to add two rows to this table Table 4-19 shows the values you need to enter.

TABLE 4-19 REGISTRY TABLE ENTRIES REQUIRED TO CREATE A PER-APPLICATION PATH

Row #	Column Name	Attribute Value
1	Registry	Registry0
	Root	2
	Key	Software\Microsoft\Windows\CurrentVersion\App Paths\ISWIArtist.exe
	Name	
	Value	[TARGETDIR]ISWIArtist.exe
	Component_	MainExe_Component
2	Registry	Registry1
	Root	2
	Key	Software\Microsoft\Windows\CurrentVersion\App Paths\ISWIArtist.exe
	Name	Path
	Value	[TARGETDIR]
	Component_	MainExe_Component

A description of each of the six columns that make up the Registry table is given below:

Registry is the primary key for the table and is an identifier that must be unique within the table.

Root is an integer that defines the root key under which the registry entries will be made.

The *Key* column contains the key under which any values will be written by the Windows Installer during installation or uninstallation..

The *Name* column specifies the value name of the location where the value is to be written. If this column is null then the value is written under the default name.

The *Value* column contains the data that is to be written against the value name specified in the previous column.

*Component_* is a foreign key into the Component table. This entry points to the component that contains the information that is to be written to the registry.

Refer to the MSI SDK Help included on the CD-ROM for more information on the format of the information to be included in the Root, Name, and Value columns.

In the following remarks I have elaborated on the entries that you have made in the Registry table:

- For both rows the value in the Key column is the same since you are going to write all your values under this key. This is the App Paths key, which is one of the standard keys to which an installation will write information.
- In Row #2 you are specifying a value name called Path that is the location where an application would look to find its DLLs.
- The entries into the Value column are the path to the ISWIArtist executable and the folder where the ISWIArtist application files are to be installed, respectively.

Now that you've entered these values you have completed the information the Windows Installer needs in order to make the changes to the target system. The next thing you have to do is tell the Windows Installer what actions it needs to perform in order to make these system changes and it should perform them.

Structuring the Installation

You have three separate efforts to perform here. One is to create and populate the execute sequence tables, another is to provide the information in the Summary Information Stream that the Windows Installer needs to work properly, and the third is to populate the user interface sequence tables even though you are not going to display any dialog boxes.

Creating the installation execute sequence tables

You inform the Windows Installer of the actions it needs to execute during an installation by authoring various sequence tables. In these sequence tables you determine when an action will occur by assigning it a sequence number. You can also define a condition so that an action will only be executed under certain circumstances. For this installation of the ISWI Artist application you will be creating all the sequence tables based on the sequences suggested by Microsoft.

There are three sets of sequence tables and which one is executed depends on the top-level action being initiated. Each set of sequence tables has one table associated with the user-interface sequence and one table associated with the execution of the installation. With the INSTALL top-level action, the Windows Installer first processes the actions in the InstallUISequence table and then processes the actions in the InstallExecuteSequence table. With the ADVERTISE top-level action, the Windows Installer always uses a basic or a silent user interface and then processes the actions in the AdvtExecuteSequence table. Even though there is an AdvtUISequence table in the database schema, it is never used. With the ADMIN top-level action, the Windows Installer first processes the actions in the AdminUISequence table and then processes the actions in the AdminExecuteSequence table. I'll address the user-interface sequence tables after you enter the data into the Summary Information Stream.

Refer to Chapter 3, particularly the section "Sequencing an installation," for a more detailed discussion of the functionality of the Windows Installer.

Every sequence table has a standard schema, comprised of the same three attributes:

- The name of a standard action, custom action, or a dialog box or wizard sequence
- An optional condition that determines whether the action gets executed or not

- A sequence number that specifies where in the sequence the action is evaluated for execution

Many standard actions are restricted as to where they can appear in one of the sequence tables, and depending on the type of custom action there may be other restrictions as to where you can place them in the sequence. For now we will not concern ourselves with the ins and outs of proper sequencing. We will follow the recommended Microsoft sequence for the standard actions (there are no custom actions in this example).

The following tables define the values you need to enter into the sequence tables of the ISWIArtist.msi database. You will begin with the execute sequence table associated with the INSTALL top-level action. Each table is followed by a set of remarks that explains some of the more important entries being made in these tables. Each row in the following tables corresponds to a row you need to enter into the appropriate database tables.

TABLE 4-20 ENTRIES FOR THE INSTALLEXECUTESEQUENCE TABLE

Action	Condition	Sequence
LaunchConditions		100
DefaultDest	NOT Installed	150
CostInitialize		200
FileCost		250
CostFinalize		300
InstallValidate		350
InstallInitialize		400
AllocateRegistrySpace	NOT Installed	450
ProcessComponents		500
UnpublishFeatures		550
UnregisterClassInfo		600
UnregisterExtensionInfo		650
UnregisterProgIdInfo		700
RemoveShortcuts		750
RemoveFiles		800
RemoveFolders		850

Action	Condition	Sequence
CreateFolders		900
InstallFiles		950
CreateShortcuts		1000
RegisterClassInfo		1050
RegisterExtensionInfo		1100
RegisterProgIdInfo		1150
WriteRegistryValues		1200
RegisterUser		1250
RegisterProduct		1300
PublishFeatures		1350
PublishProduct		1400
InstallFinalize		1450

In the following remarks I discuss in more detail entries that are shown in the above table:

- Actions in a sequence table will run on install as well as uninstall unless prevented by an appropriate condition. However, even if you provide an uninstall-related action in the sequence table without a condition it will be a no-op because the state of the feature(s) being installed are ABSENT and thus no action will be taken.
- Many actions have sequence restrictions in that some cannot be placed before other actions. The Windows Installer SDK Documentation, found on the CD-ROM at the back of the book, provides the full details of these restrictions.
- The custom action you are using to set the default location for the public property TARGETDIR is the second action in the execute sequence table. You are placing this action before the CostInitialize action because you must define this property in order for file costing to be performed properly. There is condition set on this custom action, so it will not be executed during an uninstallation.

You need to make some entries in the AdminExecuteSequence table in case someone wants to create an administrative image of your sample application on a network drive. You need to launch this type of installation from the command line and it does not actually install the files so that you can run the application. In the creation of an administrative image all source files compressed in a CAB file are uncompressed and laid out in a directory tree structure as defined by the DefaultDir column in the Directory table. Table 4-21 shows the entries in this sequence table.

TABLE 4-21 ENTRIES FOR THE ADMINEXECUTESEQUENCE TABLE

Action	Condition	Sequence
CostInitialize		50
FileCost		100
CostFinalize		150
InstallValidate		200
InstallInitialize		250
InstallAdminPackage		300
InstallFiles		350
InstallFinalize		400

The following remarks provide additional information for the entries in the above table:

- You have not included your custom action in this sequence table because the target location for an administrative installation is a network drive. The proper way to set the install location for an administrative image when there is no user interface is to set the value of TARGETDIR on the command line.
- The important entry here is the InstallAdminPackage action that copies the MSI database to the location specified by the TARGETDIR property and streams any CAB files that might be embedded out of the database. This action also updates the Summary Information Stream by setting the Last Saved By and the Last Printed properties.
- As can be seen the Condition column is empty. This is because for this example there is no need to place a condition on any of the actions.

The last execute sequence table you need to make entries in is the AdvtExecute Sequence table. This table identifies the actions to be executed by the Windows Installer when you're advertising a product.

TABLE 4-22 ENTRIES FOR THE ADVTEXECUTESEQUENCE TABLE

Action	Condition	Sequence
CostInitialize		50
CostFinalize		100
InstallValidate		150
InstallInitialize		200
CreateShortcuts		250
RegisterClassInfo		300
RegisterExtensionInfo		350
RegisterProgIdInfo		400
PublishFeatures		450
PublishProduct		500
InstallFinalize		550

In the following remarks more detail is provided about the entries made in the above table:

- The first thing to notice is that there is no LaunchCondition action in this table. This is because you perform advertisement from a server down to the desktop and it is the responsibility of the person advertising the application not to push it down to a desktop where it cannot be installed. Also, when the end user finally installs the application the LaunchCondition action in the InstallExecuteSequence table will still be executed.
- The second thing to notice about the entries in this table is that the InstallFiles action is missing. This is because files are not installed when an application is advertised.
- The last thing to notice is that the actions CreateShortcuts, RegisterClassInfo, RegisterExtensionInfo, and RegisterProgIdInfo are in this table. This is because these are the items that do get added to the target system when the application is advertised.
- As can be seen the Condition column is empty. This is because for this example there is no need to place a condition on any of the actions.

Adding the summary information

At the time of this writing, Microsoft is still reviewing those properties that it will require you to set in the Summary Information Stream. Therefore we are going to assume that all settable properties are required. The properties you are going to set are the Template, Revision Number, Page Count, Word Count, Title, Subject, Keywords, Author, Comments, Creating Application, Security, Codepage, and Create Time/Date properties. You will use the MsiInfo.exe to add this information to the Summary Information Stream. You will find the MsiInfo.exe tool that comes with the Windows Installer SDK on the CD-ROM at the back of the book. The basic command line for using this tool is as follows:

```
msiinfo  ISWIArtist.msi  {option}  {data}
```

The following table defines the entries that you need to make into the Summary Information Stream for the ISWIArtist.msi installation package, as well as the option you should use with the MsiInfo.exe utility for placing that entry into the Summary Information Stream.

The following remarks provide additional information about some of the entries that your making in the Summary Information stream:

- For the Revision Number property you should enter your own number by having a utility such as GUIDGEN.EXE create it for you. You should not use the one shown here in the book because every package must be unique.
- The value for the Create Time/Date property shown in Table 4-23 is only the format to be used for this property. You should enter your own values based on the system date and time when you created this package.

TABLE 4-23 SUMMARY INFORMATION STREAM ENTRIES

Property Name	Option	Property Value
Template	-P	Intel;1033
Revision Number	-V	{932B9342-A9E7-11d3-81AE-204C4F4F5020}
Page Count	-G	110
Word Count	-W	0
Title	-T	Installation Database
Subject	-J	ISWI Artist

Property Name	Option	Property Value
Keywords	-K	Installer, MSI, Database
Author	-A	ISWI Art Company
Comments	-O	This installer database contains the logic and data required to install ISWI Artist.
Creating Application	-N	Orca
Security	-U	0
Codepage	-C	1252
Create Time/Date	-R	yyyy/mm/dd hh:mm:ss

Chapter 3 provides an introduction to the Summary Information Stream properties and Appendix B gives a complete description of these properties for all four of the different types of MSI-related files that comprise the Summary Information Stream.

Populating the user-interface sequence tables

We do not have to make entries in the any of the user interface tables since when they are empty the Windows Installer will just use a basic user interface level and display a built-in progress dialog box. Chapter 5 discusses in detail the creation of a true user interface for this sample application.

Validating the Installation Package

After completing an MSI package you should always validate it as I mentioned at the end of Chapter 3. The Windows Installer SDK provides you with the Msival2.exe tool for performing just such a validation. Along with Msival2.exe you need the file darice.cub. This .cub file comes along when you run the installation for Msival2.exe, which is contained in the MSI package MsiVal2.msi. The darice.cub file is an internal consistency evaluator (ICE) database, which in actual structure is a standard MSI database that contains only ICEs and their required tables. A .cub file cannot be installed and is only used to store and provide access to ICE custom actions.

To perform a validation of your installation package you must have a special table in the database. This table is the *_Validation* table and it contains the column names and column values for all the tables in the database. You need it to validate your installation package because it ensures that all the columns are accounted for and have the correct values. Luckily, this table comes with the schema.msi file that you used as the starting point for your ISWIArtist.msi package. You can delete this table from the database prior to shipping an application since its only purpose is to perform the internal validation.

To run the validation of the MSI package that you have just created, run msival2.exe using the following command line:

```
msival2 ISWIArtist.msi  darice.cub  -L validation.log
```

When running this command line you will get a log file that contains both informational, warning, and error messages based on the internal consistency evaluators authored by Microsoft into the darice.cub validation library. If you want to eliminate the informational messages, use the following command line:

```
msival2 ISWIArtist.msi  darice.cub  -F -L validation.log
```

The `-F` switch tells the MsiVal2.exe utility not to display any informational messages. You can also use the `-I` switch followed by a list of the ICEs that you want to run and only that list of ICEs will be used to validate the specified MSI package.

When you run the validation of the package you have created, assuming you are not suppressing informational messages, you should get something that looks like the following. This is only a small part of the log file that is created when validating an installation package.

```
ICE01         INFO      ICE01 - Simple ICE that doesn't test anything
ICE01         INFO      Created 04/29/1998. Last Modified 08/17/1998.
ICE01         INFO      Called at 16:24:27.
ICE02         INFO      ICE02 - ICE to test circular references in
File and Component tables
ICE02         INFO      Created 05/18/1998. Last Modified 10/12/1998.
ICE03         INFO      ICE03 - ICE to perform data validation and
foreign key references
ICE03         INFO      Created 05/19/1998. Last Modified 03/30/1999.
ICE04         INFO      ICE04 - ICE to validate File table sequences
according to Media table
ICE04         INFO      Created 05/19/1998. Last Modified 09/24/1998.
ICE04         INFO      Max Sequence in Media Table is 1
ICE05         INFO      ICE05 - ICE to validate that required data
exists in certain tables.
ICE05         INFO      Created 05/20/1998. Last Modified 01/26/1999.
ICE06         INFO      ICE06 - ICE that looks for missing columns in
database tables
ICE06         INFO      Created 05/20/1998. Last Modified 02/18/1999.
ICE07         INFO      ICE07 - ICE that ensures that fonts are
```

```
installed to the fonts folder. Only checked if you have a Font table
ICE07         INFO      Created 05/21/1998. Last Modified 02/18/1999.
ICE08         INFO      ICE08 - Checks for duplicate GUIDs in
Component table
ICE08         INFO      Created 05/21/98. Last Modified 10/08/98.
ICE09         INFO      ICE09 - Checks for components whose Directory
is the System directory but aren't set as system components
ICE09         INFO      Created 05/21/98. Last Modified 1/26/99.
ICE10         INFO      ICE10 - ICE that ensures that advertise
states of feature childs and parents match
ICE10         INFO      Created 05/22/1998. Last Modified 08/17/1998.
ICE11         INFO      ICE11 - ICE that validates the Product Code
of a nested install (advertised MSI) custom action type
ICE11         INFO      Created 05/22/1998. Last Modified 08/17/1998.
ICE12         INFO      ICE12 - ICE that validates the Property type
custom actions
ICE12         INFO      Created 05/29/1998. Last Modified 12/01/1998.
ICE13         INFO      ICE13 - ICE that validates that no dialogs
are listed
```

As you can see by looking through the entire validation.log file, there are no warnings or errors listed against your package. However, if we had actually placed actions into the user interface tables we would have received the nine errors shown below.

```
ICE20         ERROR     Standard Dialog: 'FilesInUse' not found in
Dialog table
ICE20         ERROR     ErrorDialog Property not specified in
Property table. Required property for determining the name of your
ErrorDialog
ICE20         ERROR     FatalError dialog/action not found in
'InstallUISequence' Sequence Table.
ICE20         ERROR     FatalError dialog/action not found in
'AdminUISequence' Sequence Table.
ICE20         ERROR     UserExit dialog/action not found in
'InstallUISequence' Sequence Table.
ICE20         ERROR     UserExit dialog/action not found in
'AdminUISequence' Sequence Table.
ICE20         ERROR     Exit dialog/action not found in
'InstallUISequence' Sequence Table.
ICE20         ERROR     Exit dialog/action not found in
'AdminUISequence' Sequence Table.
ICE31         ERROR     The 'DefaultUIFont' Property must be set to a
valid TextStyle in the Property table.
```

You are now ready to run the installation and see how the product works.

Running the Installation and the Application

In the previous section you made sure that the MSI package contains no validation errors. The final test is to run the install and see if the product works. You probably also want to experiment a little with another installation option to see what happens when you advertise the product. I encourage you to investigate further and refer you to Appendix A, which contains a complete description of the various command-line options that are available with the Windows Installer.

First, however, you should install the package and make sure that the application runs. Before you can do this you need to collect the source files for the application into the same folder where you put your installation package. These files are ISWIArtist.exe, ShapeArtist.dll, ISWIArtistHelp.dll, and ISWIArtistHelp.htm. Since you have no authored user interface in this package you want to run the installation from the command line and log the events so that you can see what happened during the installation. You can run the installation of ISWIArtist using the following command line:

```
msiexec /i ISWIArtist.msi /l*v install.log
```

Below is a small part of the log file created by the Windows installer when using the /l*v switch on the command line shown above.

```
=== Logging started: 12/17/99  16:15:23 ===
MSI (s) (65:51): User policy value 'DisableRollback' is 0
MSI (s) (65:51): Doing action: INSTALL
Action start 16:15:23: INSTALL.
MSI (s) (65:51): Running ExecuteSequence
MSI (s) (65:51): Doing action: LaunchConditions
Action start 16:15:23: LaunchConditions.
MSI (s) (65:51): Note: 1: 2262 2: LaunchCondition 3: -2147287038
Action ended 16:15:23: LaunchConditions. Return value 1.
MSI (s) (65:51): Doing action: CostInitialize
Action start 16:15:23: CostInitialize.
MSI (s) (65:51): Searching for item
Products\3F1E4775D9393D11185902C4F4F40502 in per-user managed key
MSI (s) (65:51): Searching for item
Products\3F1E4775D9393D11185902C4F4F40502 in per-user non-managed
key
MSI (s) (65:51): Searching for item
Products\3F1E4775D9393D11185902C4F4F40502 in per-machine key
MSI (s) (65:51): Did not find item
Products\3F1E4775D9393D11185902C4F4F40502
```

```
Action ended 16:15:23: CostInitialize. Return value 1.
MSI (s) (65:51): Doing action: FileCost
Action start 16:15:23: FileCost.
```

To uninstall this application you would need to run the following command line:

```
msiexec /x ISWIArtist.msi
```

You have to do this by command line because you do not have a user interface authored into the installation package at this time.

When you run the above command lines you should see a small progress dialog and then nothing. This dialog is a built-in dialog provided by the Windows Installer. Also, when you uninstall the application you are presented with a Yes/No message box asking you if you really want to uninstall the application. This message box is also built into the Windows Installer. These dialogs cannot be coming from the database since you have not authored any user interface. Authoring the user interface is the subject of the next chapter.

Summary

In this chapter you experienced first-hand what it takes to directly author an installation database for an application that contains only four files. You have, however, created a robust installation for this application, making sure to include all the items that a real-world installation needs.

We have really only scratched the surface here of what you can accomplish with the Windows Installer. As you might imagine, there is a lot more to learn. In fact, the next thing you need to learn is how to add a user interface to the installation you have just created. We will take a look at this process in the next chapter and see how to create a user interface inside a database.

Chapter 5

Adding the User Interface to Our Installation

IN THIS CHAPTER

- How to create a user interface
- The user interface for a first time installation
- The user interface for a maintenance operation
- Handling installation errors
- When a user cancels the installation
- Package validation
- Running the user interface

THIS CHAPTER BRINGS to a close the investigation of the Windows Installer technology that began with Chapter 3. Here you will add one of the most important components of an installation, the User Interface Wizard that guides the user through the installation process. In this chapter you will see how making entries in database can create a user interface. You will have the opportunity to learn about this new approach to defining dialog boxes through actually adding new dialogs to the UI. You will gain a further appreciation of what an authoring tool can do for you. In the next chapter we will take a look at the InstallShield for Windows Installer authoring tool and you'll start to see how it can relieve the tedium of some aspects of using this new technology.

Creating the User Interface

This section will take you through the generation of several components of a user interface using the Orca database-editing tool. On the CD-ROM at the back of the book is an .msi file named BaseUI.msi, which provides a partial installation user interface for this application. Before you begin to add the missing components of the user interface you will need to merge this database with the ISWIArtist.msi database you have been working on. You can do this using the MsiDb.exe utility with the following command line:

```
msidb -d iswiartist.msi -m baseui.msi
```

After you have completed the user interface using Orca, use the UI preview capability of this tool to see what you have actually created. This enables you to verify that all controls have been placed in the proper location and that everything works properly.

When designing a user interface for installing a product, you have to consider a number of scenarios. The dialogs you need for a new installation are different from those you need for a maintenance type of installation. With a maintenance type of installation, an end user might choose to modify the present installation, repair it, or uninstall the application. In addition, a user interface must be prepared to handle both installation errors and end-user exits. In all there are five categories of user interface design you need to consider when creating an installation package:

- New installations
- Maintenance installations
- Installation errors
- User initiated exits or suspensions
- Administrative installs

The following two subsections cover the first and fourth items. You will be adding a total of four new dialogs to what is already available in the file ISWIArtistUI.msi. Three will be in the new installation category and one in the user initiated exits category. Implementing these four dialogs will also require you to add controls to some of the other dialogs that are in ISWIArtistUI.msi. These additional controls will enable you to navigate to the dialogs you are creating.

Creating the user interface for a new installation

The three dialog boxes you are going to add to the user interface in this section are as follows: a dialog that welcomes the user to the installation, a dialog that asks the end user to provide some input, and a dialog that enables the end user to browse for a location to install the application. These dialogs will provide you with an opportunity to learn to handle Edit and Pushbutton controls, and to understand control events and event mapping. You will also learn how to insert a user interface sequence into a sequence table, as well as how to insert a dialog into a user interface sequence.

The first dialog you are going to create will be named WelcomeDlg. This is the dialog that welcomes the user to the installation of a product. To define this dialog you will need to make entries into three separate tables: the Dialog, Control, and

ControlEvent tables. Table 5-1, Table 5-2, and Table 5-3 show the entries you have to make.

The entries in the Dialog table, as you might expect, define the basic properties of a dialog such as its size, positioning on the screen, and title. Figure 5-1 gives a picture of the welcome dialog you are going to create.

Figure 5-1: The WelcomeDlg dialog box

TABLE 5-1 DIALOG TABLE ATTRIBUTE VALUES FOR THE WELCOMEDLG DIALOG

Row #	Column Name	Attribute Value
1	Dialog	WelcomeDlg
	Hcentering	50
	Vcentering	50
	Width	370
	Height	270
	Attributes	3
	Title	[*ProductName*] [*Setup*]
	Control_First	Next
	Control_Default	Next
	Control_Cancel	Cancel

Dialog: This is the primary key in the Dialog table and it is a unique identifier for the dialog being defined in a row. The required uniqueness is only for the product.

HCentering: This defines where the center of the dialog box is to be located horizontally on the screen. This value can be from 0 to 100.

VCentering: This defines where the center of the dialog box is to be located vertically on the screen. This value can be from 0 to 100.

Width: This specifies the width of the dialog box in pixels.

Height: This specifies the height of the dialog box in pixels.

Attributes: This specifies the style to be used for this dialog box. Typically this attribute defines whether a dialog is modal or modeless. There are a number of other style bits that can be set and for a complete list of these you are referred to the Dialog Style Bits topic in the Windows Installer help file that comes with the SDK found on the CD-ROM at the back of the book.

Title: This is the name to be displayed in the title bar of the dialog box.

Control_First: This is a foreign key into the second column of the Control table and along with the name of the dialog it defines a unique control. This control receives the focus when the dialog is first displayed.

Control_Default: This is a foreign key into the second column of the Control table and along with the name of the dialog it defines a unique control, which responds to the Return key. This column can be blank and if it is then no action will be taken when the user hits the Return key.

Control_Cancel: This is a foreign key into the second column of the Control table and along with the name of the dialog it defines a unique control. Identifying a control in this column enables the System close button in the upper left-hand corner of the dialog box and the close button in the upper right-hand corner. It also makes hitting the Escape key equivalent to clicking on the Cancel button.

The following remarks provide more detail about the entries that are shown in Table 5-1:

- You centered all dialogs on the screen by entering 50 into the HCentering and VCentering columns.
- You entered a value of 3 into the Attributes column. This means that this dialog is to be visible and that it is a modal dialog, which means that the dialog keeps control of the process until the user dismisses it. If dismissing the dialog displays another modal dialog, then the dialog sequence maintains control until the last modal dialog in the sequence is dismissed.
- In the Title column you entered the names of two properties surrounded by square brackets. This will cause the Windows Installer to substitute the value of those properties for the name of the property that is inside the square brackets when the dialog is displayed. When this replacement of the property name for the property value takes place, the square brackets are also removed. In Chapter 4 you defined the value of the ProductName property in the Property table to be the string ISWI Artist. In the BaseUI.msi file you merged with the ISWIArtist.msi installation package you created in Chapter 4 the value of the Setup property was already defined as the string Setup.

- In the Control_First column you defined in the dialog box which control gets the focus first when the dialog is displayed. When this control is described in the Control table, it will point in most instances to another control in the same dialog. You must define all active controls so that the tab order forms a complete cycle. This control defines the first control in that tab order cycle. The remaining controls that comprise the tab order cycle for the WelcomeDlg dialog are defined in Table 5-2.

You must also define seven controls that will populate the WelcomeDlg dialog box. These controls range from pushbutton controls to bitmaps. Table 5-2 shows the entries you need in order to define these seven controls in the Control database table.

TABLE 5-2 CONTROL TABLE ATTRIBUTE VALUES FOR THE WELCOMEDLG DIALOG

Row #	Column Name	Attribute Value
1	Dialog_	WelcomeDlg
	Control	Back
	Type	PushButton
	X	180
	Y	243
	Width	56
	Height	17
	Attributes	1
	Property	
	Text	< &Back
	Control_Next	Next
	Help	
2	Dialog_	WelcomeDlg
	Control	Bitmap
	Type	Bitmap
	X	0
	Y	0
	Width	370
	Height	234
	Attributes	1
	Property	
	Text	[DialogBitmap]
	Control_Next	Back
	Help	

Continued

TABLE 5-2 CONTROL TABLE ATTRIBUTE VALUES FOR THE WELCOMEDLG DIALOG *(Continued)*

Row #	Column Name	Attribute Value
3	Dialog_	WelcomeDlg
	Control	BottomLine
	Type	Line
	X	0
	Y	234
	Width	374
	Height	0
	Attributes	1
	Property	
	Text	
	Control_Next	
	Help	
4	Dialog_	WelcomeDlg
	Control	Cancel
	Type	PushButton
	X	304
	Y	243
	Width	56
	Height	17
	Attributes	3
	Property	
	Text	&Cancel
	Control_Next	Bitmap
	Help	
5	Dialog_	WelcomeDlg
	Control	Description
	Type	Text
	X	135
	Y	70
	Width	220
	Height	30
	Attributes	196611
	Property	
	Text	The [Wizard] will install [ProductName] on your computer. Click Next to continue or Cancel to exit the [Wizard].
	Control_Next	
	Help	

Row #	Column Name	Attribute Value
6	Dialog_	WelcomeDlg
	Control	Next
	Type	PushButton
	X	236
	Y	243
	Width	56
	Height	17
	Attributes	3
	Property	
	Text	&Next >
	Control_Next	Cancel
	Help	
7	Dialog_	WelcomeDlg
	Control	Title
	Type	Text
	X	135
	Y	20
	Width	220
	Height	40
	Attributes	196611
	Property	
	Text	{\VerdanaBold13}Welcome to the [ProductName] [Wizard]
	Control_Next	
	Help	

*Dialog_*: A foreign key into the Dialog table. This entry is the name of the dialog on which the control is being placed. This also forms part of the primary key in this table.

Control: An identifier for the control. It has to be a unique name within the scope of the dialog box and it completes the primary key for this table.

Type: The type of the control. There are presently 22 types of controls supported by the Windows Installer.

X: The horizontal location in pixels of the upper left-hand corner of a rectangular box that bounds this control.

Y: The vertical location in pixels of the upper left-hand corner of a rectangular box that bounds this control.

Width: The width in pixels of the bounding rectangular box for this control.

Height: The height in pixels of the bounding rectangular box for this control.

Attributes: Specifies the bit flags that apply to the control in question. For example, this value can specify that a text field have a transparent background or that an edit field have a sunken (3D) look. Not all attributes apply to all controls.

Property: A property in the Property table that is linked to this control. For example, it is through being linked with a property that all radio buttons can act together as a group.

Text: The text string that will appear on the control. It is localizable.

Control_Next: The control on the dialog that is next in the tab order. The tab order in the dialog has to make a complete cycle.

Help: A text string that provides both ToolTip text and context-sensitive help. The two types of help text must be separated by the pipe (|) symbol.

In the following remarks, I provide more detail about the entries shown in Table 5-2:

- In the Dialog table, you defined the Next button to receive the focus when the dialog is first displayed. With the entries in the Control table as shown in Table 5-2 the tab order would be Next → Cancel → Bitmap → Back → Next.
- In row #1 you have entered a value of 1 in the Attribute column for the Back button. An attribute value of 1 means that this button is visible but disabled, which is appropriate for a dialog that is the starting point for a wizard sequence.
- In rows #2 and #3 you have a bitmap and a line control, respectively, that both have a value of 1 in the Attribute column. This means that these two graphics items are visible.
- For the pushbuttons defined in row #4 and row #6 the value of 3 in the Attribute column means that these controls are both visible and enabled. This means that you must associate a control event with each of these controls. You can do this using the ControlEvent table, which we'll cover in Table 5-3.
- In rows #5 and #7 you have entered a value of 196611 in the Attribute column. This value is made up of the following components:
  - 65536 makes the background of the text control transparent
  - 131072 makes an & appear as is and does not cause the following character to be displayed with an underline
  - 2 enables the text control so that it is not grayed out
  - 1 makes the text control visible
  - Adding the above numbers together gives you 196611 that you have entered as the value in the Attribute column.

- In row #7 in the Text column you entered a string beginning with {\VerdanaBold13}. This modifies the font style of the text that follows. The string VerdanaBold13 is an entry in the TextStyle table and this will display the text in a bolded 13-point Verdana font.

On the WelcomeDlg dialog box there are two active controls. These are the Next and Cancel pushbuttons. When the user clicks these buttons, something must happen. That something is defined by what is called a *control event.*

Control events are analogous to Microsoft Windows messages in Win32-based applications. However, rather than creating a callback function to receive Windows messages and sending Windows messages with the SendMessage function, Windows Installer controls *send* control events specified in the ControlEvent table and *receive* control events specified in the EventMapping table.

To add working controls to dialog boxes, the author of the user interface first selects which control events to use and then associates these with the controls. When a user triggers a control with a control event tied to it, that control event is published to the installer and all controls in the dialog box. If the installer subscribes to the control event, then the publication of the control event results in the installer's executing an action. If any controls in the dialog box subscribe to the control event, then the publication of the control event results in a change in the attributes of these controls, as long as the Windows Installer defines that there is an action to be taken on the subscriber.

The events that you need to define in the ControlEvent table and the required values for the controls in this dialog are given in Table 5-3.

TABLE 5-3 CONTROLEVENT TABLE ATTRIBUTE VALUES FOR THE ACTIVE CONTROLS IN THE WELCOMEDLG DIALOG

Row #	Column Name	Attribute Value
1	Dialog_	WelcomeDlg
	Control_	Cancel
	Event	SpawnDialog
	Argument	CancelDlg
	Condition	1
	Ordering	
2	Dialog_	WelcomeDlg
	Control_	Next
	Event	NewDialog
	Argument	LicenseAgreementDlg
	Condition	1
	Ordering	

Dialog_: This is a foreign key into the Dialog table and in conjunction with the next column defines a unique control in a dialog box.

Control_: This is a foreign key into the Control table and along with the value in the first column defines a unique control in a dialog box.

Event: This is the event that is to be triggered when the user interacts with this control. Events can be such actions as launching a new dialog box, selecting a path, and so forth.

Argument: This is a modifier to the event specified in the previous column. For example, if the event specified is NewDialog then this argument will be the name of the dialog that is to be displayed.

Condition: This is an expression that evaluates to TRUE or FALSE and determines whether the event associated with this control will be executed.

Ordering: This is a value that orders the events if more than one event is associated with the same control.

In the following remarks, I provide more detail about the entries that are shown in Table 5-3:

- In row #1 the event specified in the Event column is SpawnDialog and its argument is CancelDlg. This means that when the Cancel button is clicked the CancelDlg dialog will be launched as a child of the WelcomeDlg dialog. Since the Condition column has a value of 1, this event will always occur.
- In row #2 the event specified in the Event column is NewDialog and its argument is LicenseAgreementDlg. This means that when the Next button is clicked the LicenseAgreementDlg dialog will be launched as the next panel in the Installation Wizard sequence. Since the Condition column has a value of 1, this event will always occur.

The next dialog you'll create is one that that will collect information about the user and ask for a CD Key. Name this dialog UserRegistrationDlg. Figure 5-2 shows what this dialog will look like and Table 5-4 gives the values you need to enter into the Dialog database table to define the basic attributes of this dialog.

In the following remarks, I provide more detail about the entries shown in Table 5-4:

- The Attribute column has a value of 3, which means that this dialog is visible and modal.
- In the Control_First column you are defining a text control to take the focus when the dialog is first displayed. I'll explain the reason for this in the remarks section of Table 5-5.

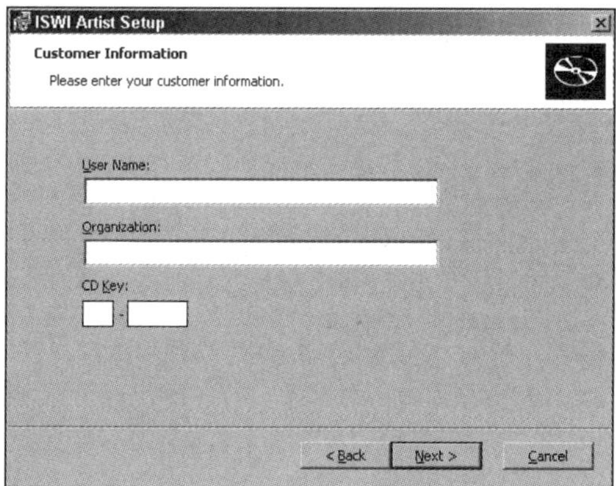

Figure 5-2: The UserRegistrationDlg dialog box

TABLE 5-4 DIALOG TABLE ATTRIBUTE VALUES FOR THE USERREGISTRATIONDLG DIALOG

Row #	Column Name	Attribute Value
1	Dialog	UserRegistrationDlg
	Hcentering	50
	Vcentering	50
	Width	370
	Height	270
	Attributes	3
	Title	[ProductName] [Setup]
	Control_First	NameLabel
	Control_Default	Next
	Control_Cancel	Cancel

You'll define 14 controls to populate the UserRegistrationDlg dialog box. As you can see from Figure 5-2 this is a much more complicated dialog than the WelcomeDlg dialog. Table 5-5 gives the entries you need to make in order to define these 14 controls in the Control database table.

TABLE 5-5 CONTROL TABLE ATTRIBUTE VALUES FOR THE USERREGISTRATIONDLG DIALOG

Row #	Column Name	Attribute Value
1	Dialog_	UserRegistrationDlg
	Control	Back
	Type	PushButton
	X	180
	Y	243
	Width	56
	Height	17
	Attributes	3
	Property	
	Text	< &Back
	Control_Next	Next
	Help	
2	Dialog_	UserRegistrationDlg
	Control	BannerBitmap
	Type	Bitmap
	X	0
	Y	0
	Width	374
	Height	44
	Attributes	1
	Property	
	Text	[BannerBitmap]
	Control_Next	NameLabel
	Help	
3	Dialog_	UserRegistrationDlg
	Control	BannerLine
	Type	Line
	X	0
	Y	44
	Width	374
	Height	0
	Attributes	1
	Property	
	Text	
	Control_Next	
	Help	

Row #	Column Name	Attribute Value
4	Dialog_	UserRegistrationDlg
	Control	BottomLine
	Type	Line
	X	0
	Y	234
	Width	374
	Height	0
	Attributes	1
	Property	
	Text	
	Control_Next	
	Help	
5	Dialog_	UserRegistrationDlg
	Control	Cancel
	Type	PushButton
	X	304
	Y	243
	Width	56
	Height	17
	Attributes	3
	Property	
	Text	&Cancel
	Control_Next	BannerBitmap
	Help	
6	Dialog_	UserRegistrationDlg
	Control	CDKeyEdit
	Type	MaskedEdit
	X	45
	Y	159
	Width	250
	Height	16
	Attributes	3
	Property	PIDKEY
	Text	[PIDTemplate]
	Control_Next	Back
	Help	

Continued

TABLE 5-5 CONTROL TABLE ATTRIBUTE VALUES FOR THE USERREGISTRATIONDLG DIALOG *(Continued)*

Row #	Column Name	Attribute Value
7	Dialog_	UserRegistrationDlg
	Control	CDKeyLabel
	Type	Text
	X	45
	Y	145
	Width	50
	Height	15
	Attributes	3
	Property	
	Text	CD &Key:
	Control_Next	CDKeyEdit
	Help	
8	Dialog_	UserRegistrationDlg
	Control	Description
	Type	Text
	X	25
	Y	23
	Width	280
	Height	15
	Attributes	196611
	Property	
	Text	Please enter your customer information.
	Control_Next	
	Help	
9	Dialog_	UserRegistrationDlg
	Control	NameEdit
	Type	Edit
	X	45
	Y	85
	Width	220
	Height	18
	Attributes	3
	Property	USERNAME
	Text	{80}
	Control_Next	OrganizationLabel
	Help	

Row #	Column Name	Attribute Value
10	Dialog_	UserRegistrationDlg
	Control	NameLabel
	Type	Text
	X	45
	Y	73
	Width	100
	Height	15
	Attributes	3
	Property	
	Text	&User Name:
	Control_Next	NameEdit
	Help	
11	Dialog_	UserRegistrationDlg
	Control	Next
	Type	PushButton
	X	236
	Y	243
	Width	56
	Height	17
	Attributes	3
	Property	
	Text	&Next >
	Control_Next	Cancel
	Help	
12	Dialog_	UserRegistrationDlg
	Control	OrganizationEdit
	Type	Edit
	X	45
	Y	122
	Width	220
	Height	18
	Attributes	3
	Property	COMPANYNAME
	Text	{80}
	Control_Next	CDKeyLabel
	Help	

Continued

TABLE 5-5 CONTROL TABLE ATTRIBUTE VALUES FOR THE USERREGISTRATIONDLG DIALOG *(Continued)*

13	Dialog_	UserRegistrationDlg
	Control	OrganizationLabel
	Type	Text
	X	45
	Y	110
	Width	100
	Height	15
	Attributes	3
	Property	
	Text	&Organization:
	Control_Next	OrganizationEdit
	Help	
14	Dialog_	UserRegistrationDlg
	Control	Title
	Type	Text
	X	15
	Y	6
	Width	200
	Height	15
	Attributes	196611
	Property	
	Text	[DlgTitleFont]Customer Information
	Control_Next	
	Help	

In the following remarks, I provide more detail about the entries shown in Table 5-5:

- In this dialog you can see that there is a different tab order approach because you are including three text controls in this tab order. These text fields are the labels used to identify the three edit fields where the user is able to enter information. You include these particular text controls in the tab order to enable the accessibility functionality required by what are called *screen readers*. (See the sidebar for more about what a screen reader is.) In the Dialog table you set the control that will get the focus when the dialog is first displayed as the NameLabel text control. This is the label that sits just on top of the edit control where users are asked to enter their names. The tab order in this dialog is NameLabel → NameEdit → OrganizationLabel → OrganizationEdit → CDKeyLabel → CDKeyEdit → Back → Next → Cancel → BannerBitmap → NameLabel.

- In rows #9 and #12 you placed the string {80} in the Text column. Since these two rows define the edit fields for a user's name and organization this entry into the Text column defines the length of the string that the edit control will accept.
- In row #14 is an example of the type of redirection that is possible with the Windows Installer. In the Text column you entered the property name [DlgTitleFont] which when replaced with the value of the property becomes {\DlgFontBold8}. This in turn is a foreign key into the TextStyle table that then defines the font to be used for displaying the rest of the text in this column.
- In row #6 you defined a special type of edit control, the MaskedEdit control. This control provides a measure of security during installation. The format of the CDKeyEdit control is defined by the entry made in the Text column. This is a property name that sets the number and length of the fields in the CDKeyEdit control. The name of the property in the Property field is set to the value entered in this control. As I will describe in the Remarks section after Table 5-6, the ValidateProductID control event then sets the ProductID property to a combination of the [PIDTemplate] mask and the PIDKEY property. In a real-world scenario, you will use a custom action to check to see if the ProductID property has the correct value.

On the UserRegistrationDlg dialog box are three active controls: the Back, Next, and Cancel pushbuttons. When the user clicks these buttons, something must happen. That something is defined by what a control event. For this particular dialog you need to make three control event entries for the Next pushbutton. These events are defined in the ControlEvent table and the required values for the controls in this dialog are given in Table 5-6.

TABLE 5-6 CONTROLEVENT TABLE ATTRIBUTE VALUES FOR THE ACTIVE CONTROLS IN THE USERREGISTRATIONDLG DIALOG

Row #	Column Name	Attribute Value
1	Dialog_	UserRegistrationDlg
	Control_	Back
	Event	NewDialog
	Argument	LicenseAgreementDlg
	Condition	1
	Ordering	

Continued

TABLE 5-6 CONTROLEVENT TABLE ATTRIBUTE VALUES FOR THE ACTIVE CONTROLS IN THE USERREGISTRATIONDLG DIALOG *(Continued)*

Row #	Column Name	Attribute Value
2	Dialog_	UserRegistrationDlg
	Control_	Cancel
	Event	SpawnDialog
	Argument	CancelDlg
	Condition	1
	Ordering	
3	Dialog_	UserRegistrationDlg
	Control_	Next
	Event	NewDialog
	Argument	SetupTypeDlg
	Condition	ProductID
	Ordering	3
4	Dialog_	UserRegistrationDlg
	Control_	Next
	Event	SpawnWaitDialog
	Argument	WaitForCostingDlg
	Condition	CostingComplete=1
	Ordering	2
5	Dialog_	UserRegistrationDlg
	Control_	Next
	Event	ValidateProductID
	Argument	0
	Condition	0
	Ordering	1

In the following remarks, I provide more detail about the entries shown in Table 5-6:

◆ In rows #1 and #3 you see an example of how this new dialog box is going to be inserted into the installation user-interface sequence. You're doing this by directing the Back button at the LicenseAgreementDlg dialog and the Next button at the SetupTypeDlg dialog. This, of course, is only part of the operation. You still need to redirect the Next button on the LicenseAgreementDlg dialog at this dialog and likewise with the Back button on the SetupTypeDlg dialog

- In rows #3, #4, and #5 you see that the Next button has three control events tied to it, and that as a result you have to fill in the Ordering column. The values in the Ordering column define the order in which the conditions on the control events are evaluated. If more than one control event has a condition that evaluates to TRUE and they conflict in that they cannot be executed at the same time, then the control event with the highest ordering value will be executed.
- In row #5 you set a value of 0 in the Condition column, so this control event will never be executed. You should do this because you have not set up a format for the CD Key that can be validated.
- In row #4 you launch a child dialog if the costing operation has not been completed before you click the Next button. Since the next dialog is the SetupTypeDlg dialog, which it enables the user to change the destination location for the installation, the Windows Installer must finish the initial costing operation before the user is allowed to do this. With your small application the end user will never get the chance to see this dialog because of the small amount of hard drive space it requires.
- In row #3 is the NewDialog control event, which has as its argument the SetupTypeDlg dialog. This is what you will always see for this small application. In Chapter 9, you will actually implement a validation process for checking a CD Key entered by the user.

What Is a Screen Reader?

A screen reader is an accessibility aid for people who cannot use the visual information displayed on a computer monitor. This information can to some extent be transmitted to the user in other ways. A screen reader takes the displayed information on the screen and redirects it through some alternate medium, such as synthesized speech or a refreshable Braille display. Screen readers are sometimes referred to as *screen review utilities* or *speech access utilities.*

A screen reader only presents textual information. To do this it must determine text labels or descriptions for graphical screen elements. It must also track a user's activities and provide descriptive information about what the user is doing. A screen reader will often monitor system interfaces that support the drawing of the graphical elements on the screen and build an off-screen database of the objects on the screen, presenting some of this information to the user as the screen changes and some only when the user asks for it. Screen readers often include support for configuration files, which are sometimes referred to as *set files* or *profiles.* These are created by the creator of the application for the purpose of providing accessibility to users with visual disabilities.

The next dialog you'll create is a dialog that will enable the user to browse for the location in which to install the product. The name you will give to this dialog is BrowseDlg. Figure 5-3 shows what this dialog will look like and Table 5-7 gives the values you need to enter into the Dialog database table to define the basic attributes of this dialog.

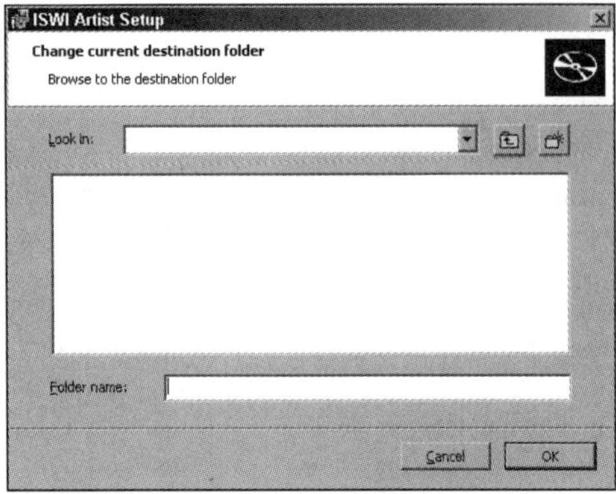

Figure 5-3: The BrowseDlg dialog box

TABLE 5-7 DIALOG TABLE ATTRIBUTE VALUES FOR THE BROWSEDLG DIALOG

Row #	Column Name	Attribute Value
1	Dialog	BrowseDlg
	Hcentering	50
	Vcentering	50
	Width	370
	Height	270
	Attributes	3
	Title	[ProductName] [Setup]
	Control_First	PathLabel
	Control_Default	OK
	Control_Cancel	Cancel

In the following remarks, I provide more detail about the entries shown in Table 5-7:

- The value of 3 in the Attributes column defines that this is a modal dialog box and that it is visible.

- The value in the Control_First column is the label for the PathEdit control. The label for this control is used as the first control to receive the focus; this is because screen readers must be able to tell the user what control has the focus.

You'll want to define 14 controls to populate the BrowseDlg dialog box. As you can see in Figure 5-3, this is also a much more complicated dialog than the WelcomeDlg dialog. Table 5-8 lists the entries required to define these 14 controls in the Control database table.

TABLE 5-8 CONTROL TABLE ATTRIBUTE VALUES FOR THE BROWSEDLG DIALOG

Row #	Column Name	Attribute Value
1	Dialog_	BrowseDlg
	Control	BannerBitmap
	Type	Bitmap
	X	0
	Y	0
	Width	374
	Height	44
	Attributes	1
	Property	
	Text	[BannerBitmap]
	Control_Next	PathLabel
	Help	
2	Dialog_	BrowseDlg
	Control	BannerLine
	Type	Line
	X	0
	Y	44
	Width	374
	Height	0
	Attributes	1
	Property	
	Text	
	Control_Next	
	Help	

Continued

TABLE 5-8 CONTROL TABLE ATTRIBUTE VALUES FOR THE BROWSEDLG DIALOG *(Continued)*

Row #	Column Name	Attribute Value
3	Dialog_	BrowseDlg
	Control	BottomLine
	Type	Line
	X	0
	Y	234
	Width	374
	Height	0
	Attributes	1
	Property	
	Text	
	Control_Next	
	Help	
4	Dialog_	BrowseDlg
	Control	Cancel
	Type	PushButton
	X	240
	Y	243
	Width	56
	Height	17
	Attributes	3
	Property	
	Text	&Cancel
	Control_Next	ComboLabel
	Help	
5	Dialog_	BrowseDlg
	Control	ComboLabel
	Type	Text
	X	25
	Y	58
	Width	44
	Height	15
	Attributes	3
	Property	
	Text	&Look in:
	Control_Next	DirectoryCombo
	Help	

Row #	Column Name	Attribute Value
6	Dialog_	BrowseDlg
	Control	Description
	Type	Text
	X	25
	Y	23
	Width	280
	Height	15
	Attributes	196611
	Property	
	Text	Browse to the destination folder
	Control_Next	
	Help	
7	Dialog_	BrowseDlg
	Control	DirectoryCombo
	Type	DirectoryCombo
	X	70
	Y	55
	Width	220
	Height	80
	Attributes	393227
	Property	BrowseProperty
	Text	
	Control_Next	Up
	Help	
8	Dialog_	BrowseDlg
	Control	DirectoryList
	Type	DirectoryList
	X	25
	Y	83
	Width	320
	Height	110
	Attributes	15
	Property	BrowseProperty
	Text	
	Control_Next	BannerBitmap
	Help	

Continued

TABLE 5-8 CONTROL TABLE ATTRIBUTE VALUES FOR THE BROWSEDLG DIALOG *(Continued)*

Row #	Column Name	Attribute Value
9	Dialog_	BrowseDlg
	Control	NewFolder
	Type	PushButton
	X	325
	Y	55
	Width	19
	Height	19
	Attributes	3670019
	Property	
	Text	New
	Control_Next	DirectoryList
	Help	Create A New Folder|
10	Dialog_	BrowseDlg
	Control	OK
	Type	PushButton
	X	304
	Y	243
	Width	56
	Height	17
	Attributes	3
	Property	
	Text	OK
	Control_Next	Cancel
	Help	
11	Dialog_	BrowseDlg
	Control	PathEdit
	Type	PathEdit
	X	93
	Y	202
	Width	252
	Height	18
	Attributes	11
	Property	BrowseProperty
	Text	
	Control_Next	OK
	Help	

Row #	Column Name	Attribute Value
12	Dialog_	BrowseDlg
	Control	PathLabel
	Type	Text
	X	25
	Y	205
	Width	68
	Height	15
	Attributes	3
	Property	
	Text	&Folder name:
	Control_Next	PathEdit
	Help	
13	Dialog_	BrowseDlg
	Control	Title
	Type	Text
	X	15
	Y	6
	Width	200
	Height	15
	Attributes	196611
	Property	
	Text	[DlgTitleFont]Change current destination folder
	Control_Next	
	Help	
14	Dialog_	BrowseDlg
	Control	Up
	Type	PushButton
	X	298
	Y	55
	Width	19
	Height	19
	Attributes	3670019
	Property	
	Text	Up
	Control_Next	NewFolder
	Help	Up One Level|

The following remarks provide more detail about the entries shown in Table 5-8:

- In rows #6 and #13 the value of 19661 in the Attributes column has the same meaning as described in the Remarks section following Table 5-2.
- The tab order in the BrowseDlg dialog box is PathLabel → PathEdit → OK → Cancel → ComboLabel → DirectoryCombo → Up → NewFolder → DirectoryList → BannerBitmap → PathLabel. You include the labels for the PathEdit and the DirectoryCombo controls in the tab order in order to enable accessibility functionality through a screen reader.
- In rows #9 and #14 you added text to the Help column. This text provides a ToolTip functionality to these two pushbuttons since icons and not text are displayed on these buttons. A screen reader can also use this help text to provide information to visually disabled users. Notice that there is pipe symbol (|) at the end of the text string. This separates the ToolTip text from the context-sensitive help. You did not enter anything to the right of this vertical bar because context-sensitive help has not yet been implemented.
- The value 3670019 in the Attribute column of rows #9 and #14 is comprised of the bit flag components in the following list. These components specify how the buttons defined in these two rows handle the display of icons instead of text.
  - The bit flag 524288 is the Icon control attribute and it specifies that the entry in the Text column is a foreign key into the Binary table and not a text string to be placed on the button.
  - The bit flag 2097152 is the IconSize control attribute and it defines that the icon that is to be loaded is the 16x16 image found in the icon file.
  - The bit flag 1048576 is the FixedSize control attribute and it specifies that the picture is to be centered in the control and that it will be cropped to fit without changing its shape or size.
  - The bit flag 2 is the Enabled control attribute and it specifies that this control will be active.
  - The bit flag 1 is the Visible control attribute and it specifies that this control will be visible.
- In row #7 you entered a value of 393227 for the DirectoryCombo control. This value is comprised of the bit flag components described in the following list:
  - The bit flag 131072 is the FixedVolume control attribute and it specifies that all volumes involved in the current installation and all the fixed internal hard drives will be shown in the combo box.

- The bit flag 262144 is the RemoteVolume control attribute and it specifies that all the volumes involved in the current installation and all the remote volumes will be shown in the combo box.
- The bit flag 8 is the Indirect control attribute and it specifies that the control displays or changes the value of the property that has its identifier listed in the Property column.
- The bit flag 2 is the Enabled control attribute and it specifies that this control will be active.
- The bit flag 1 is the Visible control attribute and it specifies that this control will be visible.

◆ In row #8 you entered a value of 15 for the DirectoryList control. This value has the following effect:

- The Indirect control attribute that specifies that the control displays or changes the value of the property that has its identifier listed in the Property column (8)
- The Sunken control attribute that specifies that the control will appear with a sunken, 3D look (4)
- The Enabled control attribute that specifies that this control is active (2)
- The Visible control attribute that specifies that this control is visible (1)

◆ In row #11 you entered a value of 11 for the PathEdit control. This value has the following effect:

- The Indirect control attribute that specifies that the control displays or changes the value of the property that has its identifier listed in the Property column (8)
- The Enabled control attribute that specifies that this control is active (2)
- The Visible control attribute that specifies that this control is visible (1)

◆ In rows #7, #8, and #11 you entered a value of BrowseProperty in the Property column. This is the name of the property that ties together the DirectoryCombo, DirectoryList, and PathEdit controls. When one of these controls changes this property, the other controls will reflect this change. This property will be used to modify the TARGETDIR property if the user decides to change the default location for the installation.

On the BrowseDlg dialog box are four active controls. These are the Cancel, OK, NewFolder, and Up pushbuttons. For this particular dialog you need to make two Control Event entries for the Cancel pushbutton and the OK pushbutton. I will explain the reason for this will be explained in the remarks section following Table 5-9. These events are defined in the ControlEvent table and the required values for the controls in this dialog are given in Table 5-9.

TABLE 5-9 CONTROLEVENT TABLE ATTRIBUTE VALUES FOR THE ACTIVE CONTROLS IN THE BROWSEDLG DIALOG

Row #	Column Name	Attribute Value
1	Dialog_	BrowseDlg
	Control_	Cancel
	Event	EndDialog
	Argument	Return
	Condition	1
	Ordering	2
2	Dialog_	BrowseDlg
	Control_	Cancel
	Event	Reset
	Argument	0
	Condition	1
	Ordering	1
3	Dialog_	BrowseDlg
	Control_	NewFolder
	Event	DirectoryListNew
	Argument	0
	Condition	1
	Ordering	
4	Dialog_	BrowseDlg
	Control_	OK
	Event	EndDialog
	Argument	Return
	Condition	1
	Ordering	2
5	Dialog_	BrowseDlg
	Control_	OK
	Event	SetTargetPath
	Argument	[BrowseProperty]
	Condition	1
	Ordering	1
6	Dialog_	BrowseDlg
	Control_	Up
	Event	DirectoryListUp
	Argument	0
	Condition	1
	Ordering	

In the following remarks, I provide more detail about the entries shown in Table 5-9:

- In rows #1 and #2 you tied two events to the Cancel button. These are the Reset and the EndDialog control events. The Reset control event forces all controls on the dialog to undo any property changes they might have performed. All properties are returned to the value they had when the dialog was first created. The EndDialog control event with the Return argument acts to destroy the present dialog. It returns control to the dialog that launched it (its parent). Note that the Reset event is executed before the EndDialog event is launched. The condition on both of these control events is set to 1, which ensures that they both will occur.
- In row #3 you defined the DirectoryListNew control event for the NewFolder button. This control event notifies the DirectoryList control that a new folder is to be created, creates a new folder, and then puts the focus on the name field so that the user can name the new folder.
- In row #4 you tied the OK button to the EndDialog control event using the Return argument. This returns control to the parent dialog and, unlike with the Cancel button, retains the property values that you have set or changed.
- In row #5 you also tied the SetTargetPath control event to the OK button. The main reason to use this control event is to notify the Windows Installer to check the validity of the path in the value of the BrowseProperty property. You insert the value of the property by surrounding the property name with square brackets like this: [BrowseProperty]. If the target is valid, the SetTargetPath control event will change the value of the TARGETDIR property.
- In row #6 you tied the Up button to the DirectoryListUp control event. This event notifies the DirectoryList control that the user wants to select the parent of the present directory. The selected directory now becomes the parent unless the present selection is already a volume.

For the BrowseDlg dialog box there is one additional database table you need to use. This is the EventMapping table, which lists those controls that subscribe to an event. I'll explain what this means in the remarks section that follows Table 5-10, which lists the attributes you need to enter into this table.

TABLE 5-10 EVENTMAPPING TABLE ATTRIBUTE VALUES FOR THE BROWSEDLG DIALOG

Row #	Column Name	Attribute Value
1	Dialog_	BrowseDlg
	Control_	DirectoryCombo
	Event	IgnoreChange
	Attribute	IgnoreChange

Dialog_: This is a foreign key into the first column of the Dialog table and forms part of the primary key for this table.

Control_: This is a foreign key into the second column of the Control table and along with the value in the first column identifies a specific control on the dialog.

Event: This is an identifier for the event to which the control is being subscribed. This field, along with the first two columns, forms the primary key for this table.

Attribute: This is the name of the control attribute when the event in the Event column is received by the control.

In the following remarks, I provide more detail about the entries shown in Table 5-10:

- The EventMapping table defines those control events that are published by some other control or by the Windows Installer and that have an impact on the control subscribing to that control event. Here you have the DirectoryCombo control subscribing to the IgnoreChange control event published by the DirectoryList control.
- The effect of subscribing the DirectoryCombo control to the IgnoreChange control event is that the user can highlight a folder in the DirectoryList control and have that highlighted folder reflected in the DirectoryCombo control. This enables the user to change the BrowseProperty property without having to actually open the folder in the DirectoryList control.

In order to integrate the new dialog boxes you just created you need to make some additions and changes to data already in the BaseUI.msi database. You have to add several buttons, change and/or remove some Control Events, and add what is called a control condition to the ControlCondition table. In Table 5-11 you are adding pushbuttons to the CustomizeDlg dialog in order to be able to launch the BrowseDlg dialog. You are also adding a pushbutton to the LicenseAgreementDlg dialog so that you can return to the WelcomeDlg dialog.

Adding new controls to an existing dialog requires a small change to the tab order in order to maintain the circular sequence between controls. The two necessary changes are shown in Table 5-12.

TABLE 5-11 CONTROL TABLE ATTRIBUTE VALUES TO BE ADDED TO EXISTING DIALOGS

Row #	Column Name	Attribute Value
1	Dialog_	CustomizeDlg
	Control	Browse
	Type	PushButton
	X	304
	Y	200
	Width	56
	Height	17
	Attributes	3
	Property	
	Text	&Browse
	Control_Next	Reset
	Help	
2	Dialog_	LicenseAgreementDlg
	Control	Back
	Type	PushButton
	X	180
	Y	243
	Width	56
	Height	17
	Attributes	3
	Property	
	Text	< &Back
	Control_Next	Buttons
	Help	

TABLE 5-12 CONTROL TABLE ATTRIBUTE VALUES TO BE MODIFIED FOR EXISTING DIALOGS

Dialog Name	Control	Old Control_Next	New Control_Next
CustomizeDlg	Tree	Reset	Browse
LicenseAgreementDlg	AgreementText	Buttons	Back

In order to insert the new UserRegistrationDlg dialog into the installation UI sequence you need to make some changes in the ControlEvent table so that the Next button on the LicenseAgreementDlg dialog and the Back button on the SetupTypeDlg dialog will both point at this new dialog. Table 5-13 shows the changes you need to make.

TABLE 5-13 CONTROLEVENT TABLE ATTRIBUTE VALUES TO BE MODIFIED FOR EXISTING DIALOGS

Dialog Name	Control	Old Event Argument	New Event Argument
LicenseAgreementDlg	Next	SetupTypeDlg	UserRegistrationDlg
SetupTypeDlg	Back	LicenseAgreementDlg	UserRegistrationDlg

You need to identify control events for each of the two new controls you just added to the existing CustomizeDlg and LicenseAgreementDlg dialogs. These control events are listed in Table 5-14.

TABLE 5-14 CONTROLEVENT TABLE ATTRIBUTE VALUES FOR THE ADDED CONTROLS

Row #	Column Name	Attribute Value
1	Dialog_	CustomizeDlg
	Control_	Browse
	Event	SelectionBrowse
	Argument	BrowseDlg
	Condition	1
	Ordering	
2	Dialog_	LicenseAgreementDlg
	Control_	Back
	Event	NewDialog
	Argument	WelcomeDlg
	Condition	1
	Ordering	

In the following remarks, I have provided more detail about the entries shown in Table 5-14:

- In the CustomizeDlg dialog the Browse pushbutton is being tied to a special control event associated with the SelectionTree control. Even though the Browse pushbutton is in the CustomizeDlg dialog it is the SelectionTree spawning the BrowseDlg dialog as a child dialog. The SelectionBrowse control event permits the BrowseDlg dialog to modify the path of the item selected in the SelectionTree control.
- The SelectionTree control is used primarily in a dialog that enables the user to select or deselect the features to be installed. The BrowseDlg dialog then enables the user to change the install location of the feature.

Now that you have added the ability to modify the installation location of a feature by adding the BrowseDlg dialog to the user-interface sequence and have added the Browse pushbutton to the CustomizeDlg dialog you need to apply a condition to this Browse pushbutton. The user can launch the CustomizeDlg dialog during the new installation mode or during the maintenance mode, but during the maintenance mode can only select or deselect features to be added to or removed from an application's current installation; the user cannot change the installation location of any of these features. Therefore it is necessary to hide the Browse pushbutton during a maintenance operation. This is what you are going to accomplish by adding a row to the ControlCondition table, as shown in Table 5-15.

TABLE 5-15 CONTROLCONDITION TABLE ATTRIBUTE VALUES FOR THE CUSTOMIZEDLG DIALOG

Row #	Column Name	Attribute Value
1	Dialog_	CustomizeDlg
	Control_	Browse
	Action	Hide
	Condition	Installed

Dialog_: This is a foreign key into the Dialog table and, along with the entry in the Control_ column, identifies a unique control in the dialog box.

Control_: This is a foreign key into the second column of the Control table.

Action: This is the name of the action that will be implemented on the control, depending on the results of the condition defined in the Condition column. Five specific actions are permitted:

Default Sets a control to be the default control in the dialog box.

Disable Disables the control.

Enable Enables the control.

Hide	Hides the control.
Show	Displays the control.

Condition: This is a conditional statement that specifies the circumstances under which the action defined in the Action column will take place.

In Table 5-15 is shown the one and only action you are defining and that is for the Browse pushbutton to be hidden if the installation is in maintenance mode. An installation is in maintenance mode if the installed state of the application evaluates to TRUE. You define the condition simply by placing the term Installed in the Condition column. Installed is a property that gets set by the Windows Installer if it detects that the application has already been installed.

Creating the user interface to handle a user-initiated exit

You are going to create a dialog that is one of the finish dialogs that is given a negative sequence number. The Windows Installer displays this dialog when a user cancels an installation by clicking a Cancel button in one of the modal dialog in the Installation Wizard. This dialog is called UserExitDlg and Figure 5-4 shows what it will look like after you create it. The Windows Installer does not mandate what the name of this dialog is, only that it must have a sequence number of –2 in the sequence tables wherein it is used. Tables 5-16, 5-17, and 5-18 show the values you need to enter to create the UserExitDlg dialog box.

You need to define the eight controls that will populate this dialog box. Table 5-17 shows the values you use to create these eight controls. Only one of these controls, however, is active, because before this dialog is displayed the user has already confirmed that the installation is to be canceled.

TABLE 5-16 DIALOG TABLE ATTRIBUTE VALUES FOR THE USEREXITDLG DIALOG

Row #	Column Name	Attribute Value
1	Dialog	UserExitDlg
	Hcentering	50
	Vcentering	50
	Width	370
	Height	270
	Attributes	3
	Title	[ProductName] [Setup]
	Control_First	Finish
	Control_Default	Finish
	Control_Cancel	Finish

Figure 5-4: The UserExitDlg dialog box

TABLE 5-17 CONTROL TABLE ATTRIBUTE VALUES FOR THE USEREXITDLG DIALOG

Row #	Column Name	Attribute Value
1	Dialog_	UserExitDlg
	Control	Back
	Type	PushButton
	X	180
	Y	243
	Width	56
	Height	17
	Attributes	1
	Property	
	Text	< &Back
	Control_Next	Finish
	Help	
2	Dialog_	UserExitDlg
	Control	Bitmap
	Type	Bitmap
	X	0
	Y	0
	Width	370
	Height	234
	Attributes	1
	Property	
	Text	[DialogBitmap]
	Control_Next	Back
	Help	

Continued

TABLE 5-17 CONTROL TABLE ATTRIBUTE VALUES FOR THE USEREXITDLG DIALOG *(Continued)*

Row #	Column Name	Attribute Value
3	Dialog_	UserExitDlg
	Control	BottomLine
	Type	Line
	X	0
	Y	234
	Width	374
	Height	0
	Attributes	1
	Property	
	Text	
	Control_Next	
	Help	
4	Dialog_	UserExitDlg
	Control	Cancel
	Type	PushButton
	X	304
	Y	243
	Width	56
	Height	17
	Attributes	1
	Property	
	Text	&Cancel
	Control_Next	Bitmap
	Help	
5	Dialog_	UserExitDlg
	Control	Description1
	Type	Text
	X	135
	Y	70
	Width	220
	Height	40
	Attributes	196611
	Property	
	Text	[ProductName] setup was interrupted. Your system has not been modified. To install this program at a later time, please run the installation again.
	Control_Next	
	Help	

Row #	Column Name	Attribute Value
6	Dialog_	UserExitDlg
	Control	Description2
	Type	Text
	X	135
	Y	115
	Width	220
	Height	20
	Attributes	196611
	Property	
	Text	Click the Finish button to exit the [Wizard].
	Control_Next	
	Help	
7	Dialog_	UserExitDlg
	Control	Finish
	Type	PushButton
	X	236
	Y	243
	Width	56
	Height	17
	Attributes	3
	Property	
	Text	&Finish
	Control_Next	Cancel
	Help	
8	Dialog_	UserExitDlg
	Control	Title
	Type	Text
	X	135
	Y	20
	Width	220
	Height	40
	Attributes	196611
	Property	
	Text	{\VerdanaBold13}[ProductName] [Wizard] was interrupted
	Control_Next	
	Help	

In the following remarks, I provide more detail about the entries shown in Table 5-17:

- In rows #1 and #4 you defined two pushbuttons and specified that the value in the Attribute column is 1. This value means that these two pushbuttons are disabled, which means that although they are still visible their text is grayed out.
- I explained the value in the Attribute column for rows #5, #6, and #8 in the Remarks section following Table 5-2.

On the UserExitDlg dialog there is only one pushbutton control for which you have to define control events; all the other pushbuttons are disabled.

TABLE 5-18 CONTROLEVENT TABLE ATTRIBUTE VALUES FOR THE USEREXITDLG DIALOG

Row #	Column Name	Attribute Value
1	Dialog_	UserExitDlg
	Control_	Finish
	Event	EndDialog
	Argument	Exit
	Condition	1
	Ordering	

The entry in Table 5-18 shows you how to tie the Finish pushbutton to the EndDialog control event using the Exit argument. The Exit argument specifies that the installation process is to be terminated by the Windows Installer.

Populating the user interface sequence tables

Now that you have created the additional dialog boxes for the various wizards you need to make them available by placing them into a sequence table. The particular sequence tables of interest here are the InstallUISequence and AdminUISequence tables. You will notice that I make no mention of populating an AdvtUISequence table. That is because Microsoft recommends that no user interface be displayed to the end user when a product is being advertised. Since in Chapter 4 you did not add any actions to the user interface tables you will now add them at the same time, as shown in Table 5-19.

TABLE 5-19 ENTRIES FOR THE INSTALLUISEQUENCE TABLE

Action	Condition	Sequence
FatalErrorDlg		-3
UserExitDlg		-2
ExitDlg		-1
LaunchConditions		100
PrepareDlg		125
DefaultDest	Not Installed	150
CostInitialize		800
FileCost		900
CostFinalize		100
WelcomeDlg	Not Installed	1050
ResumeDlg	Installed And (RESUME Or Preselected)	1100
MaintenanceWelcomeDlg	Installed And Not RESUME And Not Preselected	1150
ProgressDlg		1200
ExecuteAction		1300

In the following remarks, I give more detail about the entries shown in Table 5-19:

- Note the three dialog actions that have the negative sequence numbers. The Windows Installer displays one of them, depending on the reason for the termination of the installation. The name of the action is not important, only the sequence number assigned to the dialog action. The FatalErrorDlg dialog is displayed if there is a Windows Installer run-time error. The UserExitDlg dialog is displayed if the user cancels the installation, and the ExitDlg dialog is displayed if the installation completes successfully.
- Notice that in this table the actions LaunchConditions, DefaultDest, CostInitialize, FileCost, and CostFinalize are the same actions you entered in the top of the InstallExecuteSequence table in Chapter 4. This is because when the installation is being run with a full or reduced user interface option, this table is the first one that is parsed.

Therefore we need to make sure that we check for any launch conditions and that we set the value of TARGETDIR with our custom action.

- The PrepareDlg dialog is a modeless dialog that displays the progress of the initialization of the installation.
- The WelcomeDlg, MaintenanceWelcomeDlg, and ResumeDlg dialogs each start what is known as a *user-interface sequence*. The WelcomeDlg dialog commences a UI sequence for a new installation if the product does not have an installed state of TRUE. The MaintenanceWelcomeDlg dialog begins the UI sequence that enables the user to repair, modify, or remove a product that has already been installed. This A maintenance installation begins whenever the product has an installed state of TRUE and the previous installation was not suspended before it completed. The ResumeDlg begins a UI sequence that completes an installation that was suspended before it completed.
- The ProgressDlg dialog is a modeless dialog that receives the progress information of the installation and displays it to the user.
- The function of the ExecuteAction is to notify the Windows Installer to run the actions in the InstallExecuteSequence table.

The final table you need to populate to complete the user interface for your installation is the AdminUISequence table. Table 5-20 shows the new rows you need to add to this table.

TABLE 5-20 ENTRIES FOR THE ADMINUISEQUENCE TABLE

Action	Condition	Sequence
FatalErrorDlg		-3
UserExitDlg		-2
ExitDlg		-1
PrepareDlg		125
CostInitialize		800
FileCost		900
CostFinalize		1000
AdminWelcomeDlg		1100
ProgressDlg		1200
ExecuteAction		1300

In the following remarks, I provide more detail about the entries shown in Table 5-20:

- The three dialog actions with negative sequence numbers are the same as the dialogs with negative numbers in the InstallUISequence table.
- The file costing actions are required to make sure that the target location for the administrative installation has enough space to hold the files that comprise the application.
- The AdminWelcomeDlg begins the UI sequence that creates an administrative image on a network drive. This sequence consists of this welcome dialog, a dialog that requests the input of a CD Key, and finally a dialog that asks the user to specify the location of the network drive and folder where the administrative image is to be created. In this UI sequence the user cannot define the features to be installed, because this is not a real installation but only an image from which other users can initiate an installation on their local machines.
- The function of the ExecuteAction is to notify the Windows Installer to run the actions in the AdminExecuteSequence table.

Validation of the Package

If you remember from Chapter 4, there were a number of errors in the package when you ran the validation, all of which related to the user interface. Now it is time to make sure that they are gone. Using the same command line you used in Chapter 4 run a validation on your installation package to see if it validates correctly. Use the following command line:

```
msival2 iswiartist.msi darice.cub -F -L validation.log
```

If you did everything shown in this chapter, you should get a log file that has no warnings or errors.

Running the Installation with the User Interface

The final test of your revised installation package is to run the install and test to see if the user interface works in all possible modes of operation. It's particularly important to see if using the BrowseDlg you added in this exercise can change the installation location. I encourage you to investigate further and also to look at Appendix A, which contains a complete description of the various command-line options available to you with the Windows Installer.

Summary

You created dialog boxes and the defined the controls that populate these dialogs. You now have an acquaintance with control events and how controls can subscribe to these control events. In the case of the BrowseDlg dialog you saw how separate controls can be connected through the use of a common property. You will be seeing a lot more about creating and manipulating the user interface when you get to Chapter 9.

Part II

Basic Package Creation with ISWI

Chapter 6

Overview of the ISWI Authoring Tool

IN THIS CHAPTER

- The basic design of ISWI
- The resources in ISWI that will help you understand how to create installation packages
- The menus and toolbar options available for activating the features of ISWI
- The wizards and tools that provide an efficient means for creating installation packages

IN CHAPTERS 4 AND 5 you saw how much work it was to create, by directly editing an MSI database, the installation package for a simple application consisting of only four files. In this chapter I introduce the InstallShield for Windows Installer tool that will make it much easier for you to create installation packages. In particular in this chapter we take a brief look at the various features of ISWI that help in creating installation packages.

What Is InstallShield for Windows Installer?

In Chapters 4 and 5 you worked your way through the creation of an MSI installation package by directly editing a template database. You did this with the Orca tool that comes with the Windows Installer SDK. It turned out to be a lot of work even though the sample application for which you were creating the installation consisted of only four files. In a real-world environment it would take far too long to create installation packages this way. This approach to creating an installation database also creates many opportunities for error. The real-world solution to the problem of creating installation packages, then, is to have a tool that abstracts the information required in the installation database and presents it understandably. This is the role that InstallShield for Windows Installer plays in the creation of Windows Installer installation packages.

InstallShield for Windows Installer (ISWI) is an authoring tool that removes the setup developer from the raw database by several levels. ISWI provides a development environment wherein the setup developer is asked to enter information that that ISWI requests in a user-friendly way. This abstraction of the information you need to enter into a Windows Installer database greatly reduces the time required to develop a working installation package. The installation package that you created in chapters 4 and 5 for the sample application probably took you more than an hour – even when all the database table entries were already identified. You will see in the next chapter that with ISWI this same installation package can be generated in about five minutes.

ISWI is a project-based development tool. This means that it creates an intermediate project file containing all the information required to generate an MSI installation package. The installation package is created only when the setup developer specifically requests that a build be performed. This project approach permits a high level of product management because installation packages for various products can be created from one project file. This is called SKU management – for *Stock Keeping Unit.*

So now let's move on to ISWI and see what it offers you in the way of Windows Installer package creation.

Installing ISWI

This book – in particular this chapter and the next three – is focused on the functionality found in version 1.5 of InstallShield for Windows Installer. An evaluation copy of this version of ISWI can be found on the CD-ROM at the back of the book. An evaluation copy will only let you run installations on the machine on which the installation package was created. All screenshots in this book have been taken using the full retail version of ISWI with the East and West language packs installed. There are a few differences between the release wizard in the evaluation copy and the full retail version. If you have access to it, you should use the full version instead of the evaluation version.

To initiate the installation of the evaluation version of ISWI double-click the file SETUP.EXE. If you are installing the full retail version from a CD-ROM (not the CD-ROM at the back of the book), you will be presented with a browser interface enabling you to click a button to perform the installation. Regardless of whether you are installing the evaluation or the full retail version you need to follow the instructions provided in the installation wizard. By default you will get a complete installation of the product and that is what you want. If for some reason the Windows Installer is not already on the target machine, then the ISWI setup will first install the Windows Installer for you and then prompt you to reboot the system. After the reboot the installation of ISWI will continue automatically. You can take all the default settings offered in the installation wizard.

If there is a previous version of ISWI on your machine, the installation of version 1.5 will appropriately delete and/or update this prior version. Once you have installed ISWI you will want to launch it from the Start→Programs menu.

A First Look at ISWI

A tremendous amount of information must be collected in order to create an MSI package. The user interface for ISWI is modeled after the user interface used by Microsoft for its Outlook product. Figure 6-1 shows the basic design of this user interface. On the far left of the screen is the view panel where you can choose the basic type of information to be manipulated. To the right of the view panel there is a tree control that allows you to select subcategories of the main view, and on the right-hand side of the screen you can see the various default properties and where you can modify them. In some circumstances the right-hand side of the screen is divided horizontally, the top displaying the property sheet and the bottom displaying additional functionality for setting the properties.

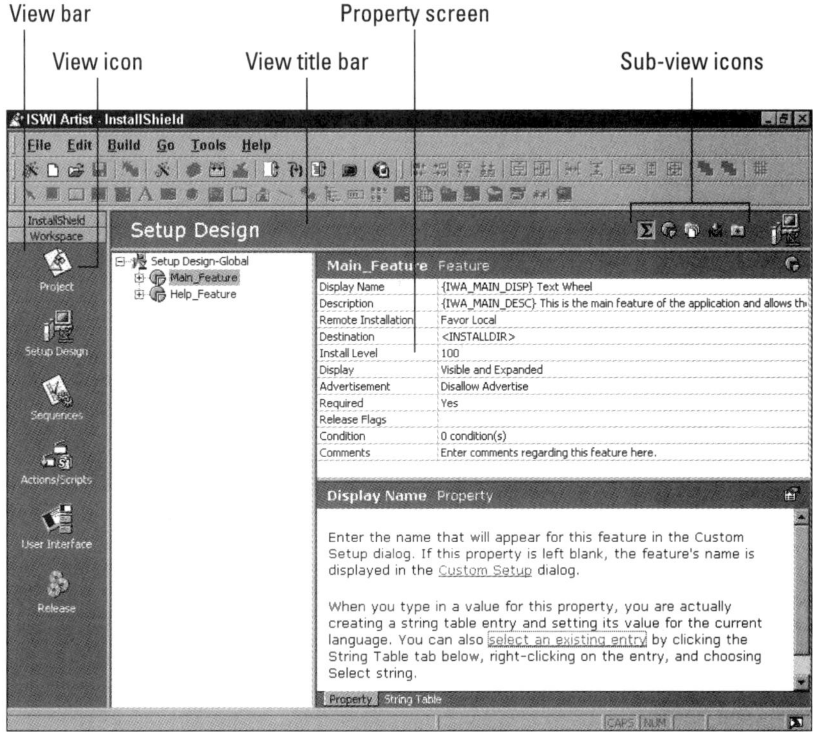

Figure 6-1: The basic user-interface design of ISWI

When you launch ISWI you will be presented with a user interface that enables you to choose various views and screens that provide access to the features of the product. When you launch ISWI without any project association, the left-hand panel icons enable you to choose one of three views: InstallShield Today, Help, and Best Practices. I discuss each of these views in one of the following sections.

The InstallShield Today View

Figure 6-2 shows the default view you see when you first launch ISWI from the Start→Programs menu. This default view is the Welcome screen of the InstallShield Today view. In the screen selection panel are three other screens you can select: Create a new project... and Open a project... and InstallShield on the Web...

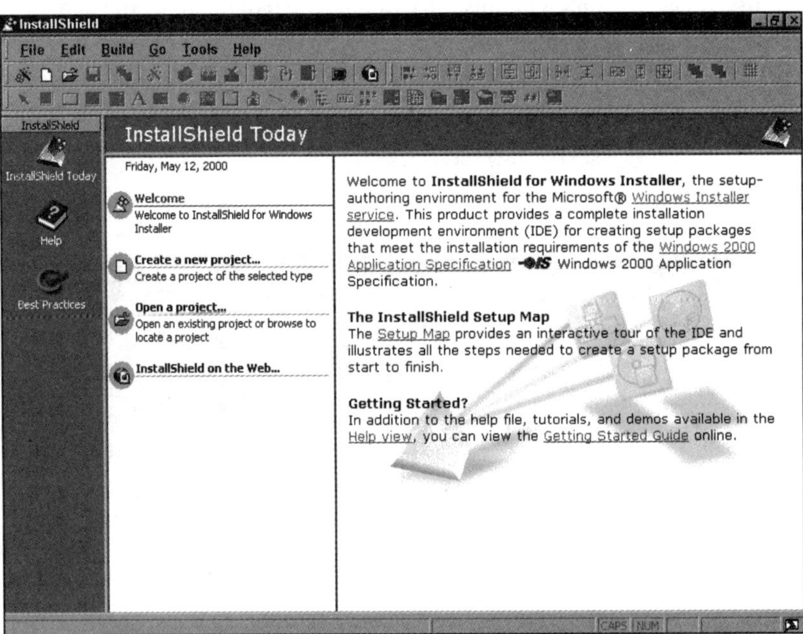

Figure 6-2: The default InstallShield Today screen of ISWI

The Welcome screen provides links to a number of information resources about ISWI, the Windows Installer service, and the requirements for obtaining the "Certified for Windows" logo. These links will take you to other parts of the product or to an associated Web site. In the Welcome screen the Windows Installer service link takes you to the associated topic in the InstallShield for Windows Installer Help Library. The Windows 2000 Application Specification link takes you to the part of the Microsoft Web site where you can download this specification. Of course, to use this link you must have Internet access. This specification lists all the requirements you need to meet in order to obtain the "Certified for Windows" logo. The Setup Map link launches an interactive tour of ISWI. The Help View link takes you to the Help View and the Getting Started Guide link takes you to the Getting Started topic in the InstallShield for Windows Installer Help Library.

Figure 6-3 shows the Create a new project... screen. From this screen you can create either a regular installation project or a merge module project. To create a regular installation project, double-click the Project icon or the Blank Setup Project icon. To create a Merge Module project double-click on the Blank Merge Module Project icon. You can also create these projects by first highlighting the appropriate icon and then clicking the Create pushbutton.

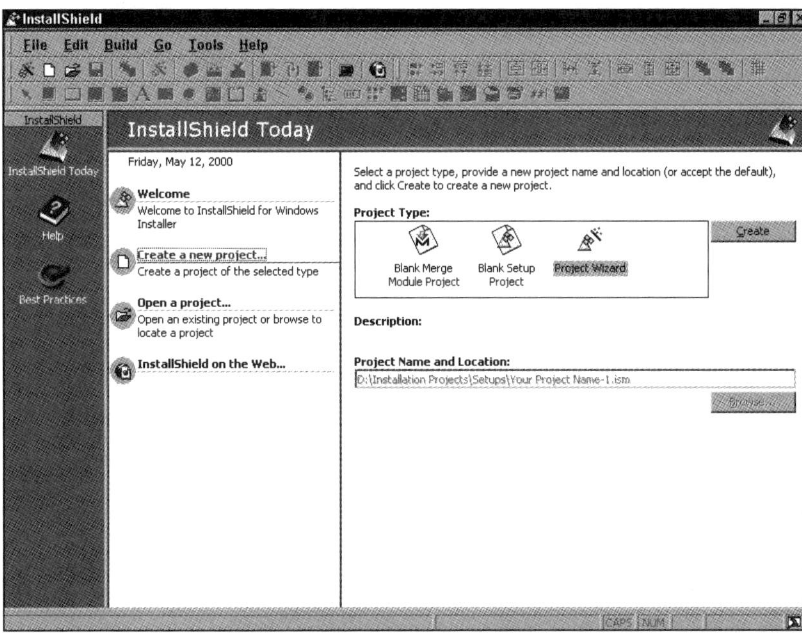

Figure 6-3: The Create a new project... screen of the InstallShield Today view

In this screen there is an edit field you use to set the name and location of the project you are going to create. This edit field is disabled when you have the Project Wizard icon highlighted. This is because the Project Wizard will request that you enter the name of the project you want to create. When creating a new setup project or a merge module project you should first highlight the appropriate icon and then go to the Project Name and Location field and enter the location where you want the project to be created and the name of the project file. Project files always have an .ism file extension so ISWI will add it automatically. After entering this information you can either click the Create pushbutton or double-click the highlighted icon.

Chapter 17 goes into more detail about the creation and use of merge modules.

Clicking the Open a project... link in the screen selection panel will take you to the associated screen, as shown in Figure 6-4. This screen will present you with icons for all the projects you have created and give you ready access to these projects.

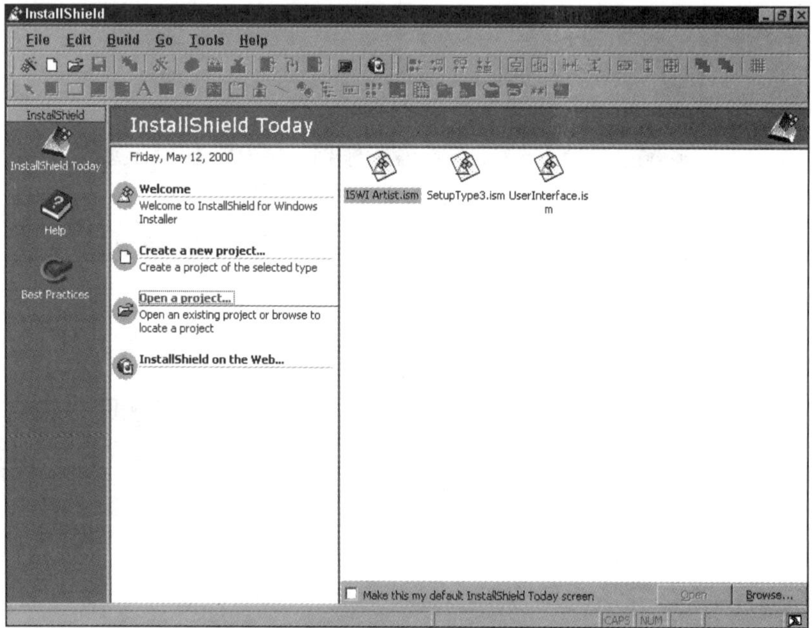

Figure 6-4: The Open a project... screen of the InstallShield Today view

This view shows the projects as large icons, but you can choose a detailed view by clicking the right mouse button and choosing the Details option from the resulting popup menu. In the detailed view you see the name of the project file and the location of this file. Using the same popup menu, you can open the highlighted project or remove it from the screen. You can also browse for another project by choosing the Browse... option on the context menu. If you check the Make this my default InstallShield Today screen option at the bottom of the Open a project... screen, this screen will be the one that appears every time you launch ISWI instead of the Welcome screen. At the bottom of the Open a project... screen there is an Open button and a Browse button. These two buttons provide the same functionality as the same options on the context menu.

The fourth and final screen of the InstallShield Today view is the InstallShield on the Web... screen. This screen provides a number of Web links to various locations on the InstallShield Software Corporation Web site. Of course, you need to have Internet access for these links to work.

The Help View

You can display the Help view by clicking the Help icon in the view selection panel. This icon is directly under the InstallShield Today icon. In this view there is no screen selection panel as with the InstallShield Today view. Here you are presented with a number of help-related icons that link you to various types of help resources, as shown in Figure 6-5.

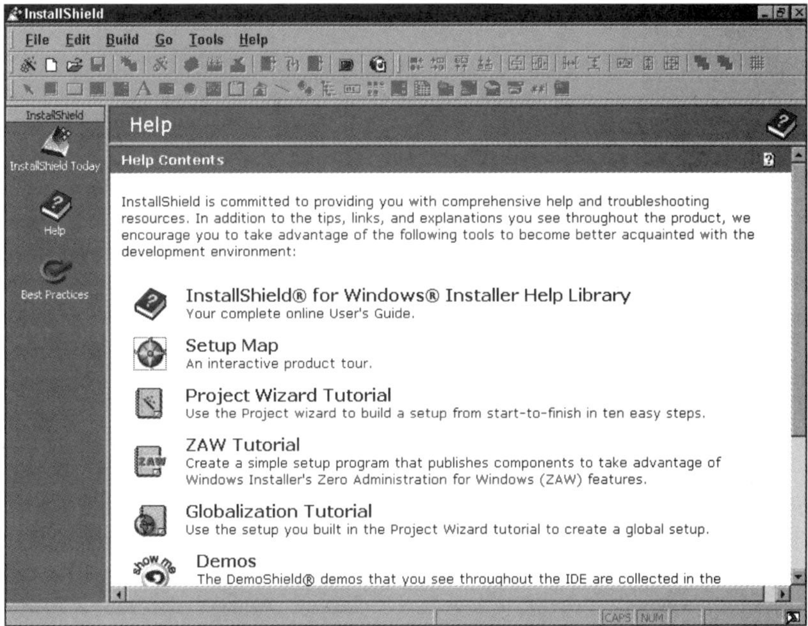

Figure 6-5: The ISWI Help view

In the following subsections I discuss resources you can access from the eight icons provided in this view.

The InstallShield for Windows Installer Help Library

There are three top-level topics in the ISWI Help Library: Getting Started, Getting Results, and the InstallShield IDE Reference. Figure 6-6 shows the opening page of the Help Library.

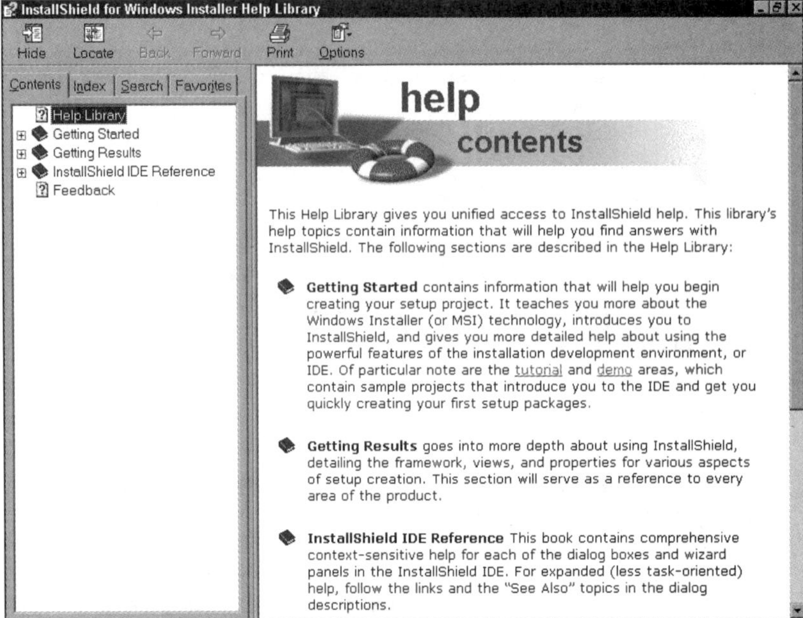

Figure 6-6: The ISWI Help Library welcome page

The Getting Started topic contains information that will help you begin creating a setup project. It teaches you more about the Windows Installer (or MSI) technology, introduces you to InstallShield, and gives you more detailed help about using the powerful features of the installation development environment, or IDE. Of particular note are the tutorial and demo areas, which contain sample projects that introduce you to the IDE and quickly get you creating your first setup packages.

The Getting Results topic goes into more depth about using InstallShield, detailing the framework, views, and properties for various aspects of setup creation. This section will serve as a reference for every area of the product.

The InstallShield IDE Reference topic contains comprehensive context-sensitive help for each of the dialog boxes and wizard panels in the InstallShield IDE. For expanded (less task-oriented) help, follow the links and the See Also topics in the dialog descriptions.

In addition to these three topics the Help Library welcome page provides three important InstallShield Web site links: Feedback, Documentation Update, and Knowledge Base.

The Setup Map

The Setup Map is an interactive tour of the InstallShield for Windows Installer. This interactive tour briefly discusses many of the subjects we examine in this and the next three chapters. Figure 6-7 shows the introductory panel to this interactive tour of ISWI.

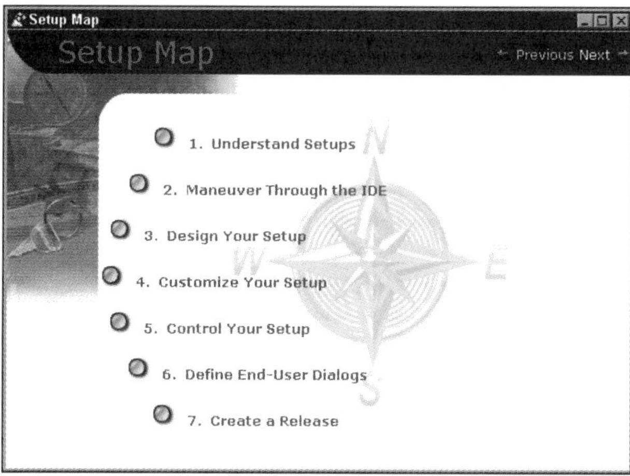

Figure 6-7: The Setup Map overview screen

As you can see in this figure, the Setup Map covers seven topics. The first one, entitled Understand Setups, covers the difference between legacy installations and installations created for the Windows Installer Service. In particular it discusses how features are the end user's view of an application and components are the developer's view of the same application. The Maneuver Through the IDE topic gives an overview of the subject that this chapter is discussing in detail. The Design Your Setup topic discusses how to create features, components, and how to associate the two. The Customize Your Setup topic outlines the steps that follow the creation of features and components. Here you are shown how to add files, define registry entries, create shortcuts, and define advanced settings for the installation. The fifth topic, Control Your Setup, discusses the use of sequence tables for controlling how an installation will function. The Define End-User Dialogs topic discusses the creation of dialog boxes and the various options for configuring the user interface. Finally, the Create a Release topic discusses the use of the Release Wizard to create an MSI package. The Setup Map is an excellent tool for getting acquainted with the high-level features of the ISWI product.

The Project Wizard Tutorial

This Project Tutorial introduces the Project Wizard, which you will make use of in the next chapter to create the initial project for the ISWI Artist application. This tutorial steps you through the creation of a sample application named Othello that comes with ISWI. In addition to the source files for the Othello game application a project file (.ism) is also shipped with ISWI as an example of what a simple project should look like.

The 11 steps in this tutorial match the 11 panels that comprise the Project Wizard. In each step you are provided an explanation of the information that the Project Wizard is requesting. The Summary part of the tutorial explains the actions that you need to take after creating the initial project. (See Figure 6-8.)

Figure 6-8: The Project Wizard Tutorial overview screen

The ZAW Tutorial

The ZAW Tutorial is a step-by-step process that shows you how to create an installation through the IDE without using the Project Wizard. Figure 6-9 shows the Overview screen for this tutorial.

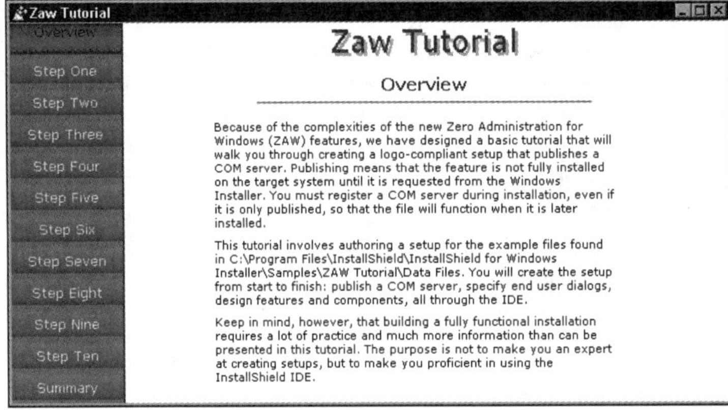

Figure 6-9: The ZAW Tutorial Overview screen

The application installed in this tutorial also comes with ISWI and it consists of a COM client and a COM server. The COM server is a local server and so is an executable, as is the client. This application provides a good example of how to the Component Wizard to create a component for the COM server that demonstrates how to extract COM information so that you can place it in the appropriate tables. It emphasizes the fact that even though the Windows Installer allows the self-registration of COM servers it is better to extract the registration information and place it in tables so that the Windows Installer knows what is taking place. Self-registration is considered a black box since the Windows Installer cannot know what changes have been made to the system if you use self-registration for a COM server and thus does not know how to properly rollback or uninstall what has been done through the use of self-registration.

The Globalization Tutorial

The Globalization Tutorial provides an introduction to the capabilities in ISWI that enable you to create localized installations. Figure 6-10 shows the Overview panel of this tutorial.

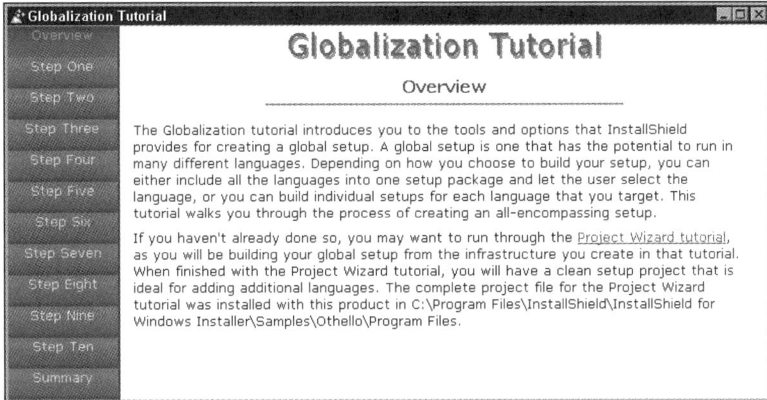

Figure 6-10: The Globalization Tutorial Overview screen

This tutorial addresses four specific issues related to localizing an installation. The first of these issues is the creation of a multilingual installation where the end user can choose the language in which the installation is to be run. The second issue is the creation of different MSI packages based on filtering the components according to language. The filtering process would create different packages for different languages. The third issue is the setting of conditions on the installation of components based on the language of the operating system. A product could be made to install different language versions based on the conditions set on the various components. The final main subject is the use of string tables and how they simplify the creation of multilingual installations.

The demos

There are a number of demos sprinkled throughout the Help Library and the IDE that will walk you through some of the more difficult tasks associated with creating a setup project. If you are looking for information on a certain topic, or you just want to browse the demos, you can launch them from the demos page.

The Windows Installer Programmer's Reference

The Windows Installer Programmer's Reference is shipped with ISWI and you can launch it from the Help view or from the Help pulldown menu. This help file provides the detailed information that an advanced user needs to understand how the Windows Installer works. You can also get the latest Windows Installer Programmer's Reference by downloading the MSI SDK from the Microsoft Web site at `http://msdn.microsoft.com/`.

When you get to this site all you need to do is follow the download links for SDKs to the Platform SDK and from there to the Windows Installer SDK. I recommend that you check this site regularly for the latest information on the Windows Installer.

Help Updates

The Help Updates link in the Help view takes you to the InstallShield Web site where you can download the latest versions of the ISWI help files. I recommend that you update these files regularly.

The Best Practices View

The purpose of the Best Practices view is to define the rules that comprise best practices for a Windows Installer setup. Best practices relate to creating components so that you get the most out of the Windows Installer.

The term *best practices* was used by the draft versions of the Certified for Windows 2000 Application Specification for Desktop Applications, but when this specification was finally released, the term was changed to *componentization rules*. ISWI, however, has continued to use the earlier term.

The Best Practices view describes the rules for creating components, both those checked by the Best Practices Wizard and those not directly checked.

Chapter 17 deals with the subject of components and how they are created, ref counted, and shared. Dealing with components is one of the trickiest things about creating Windows Installer packages.

The Basic Menus and Toolbar

There are six pulldown menus and a basic toolbar in ISWI. Most of the items on these menus and toolbar are disabled unless an active project is open. In the descriptions in the rest of this chapter I assume that there is such a project open. Let's begin with the commands on the File pulldown menu.

The File menu

The File pulldown menu contains 10 command options, described in Table 6-1.

TABLE 6-1 THE FILE MENU OPTIONS

Menu Command	Keyboard Shortcuts	Description
Project Wizard		One of the three methods you can use to launch the Project Wizard.
New Project	Ctrl+N	Takes you to the Create a New Project... screen in the InstallShield Today view.
Open Project	Ctrl+O	Launches a File Open dialog that defaults to the location where your projects are being created. You specify this location in the Options dialog, which we discuss later in this chapter.
Close Project		Closes the currently open project. If the project contains unsaved changes, you will be prompted to save them.
Save Project	Ctrl+S	Saves the currently open project. Only enabled if the project actually has unsaved changes and is disabled otherwise.
Save Project As...		Allows you to save a project under another name. The original project is still available.
Print	Ctrl+P	Prints the text of the script file that is loaded in the Script Editor. Only applicable to the Script Editor and is only enabled when the focus is in this editor. You can use the Script Editor to create Custom Actions using InstallScript.

Continued

Table 6-1 THE FILE MENU OPTIONS *(Continued)*

Menu Command	Keyboard Shortcuts	Description
Print Setup...		Launches the Printer Setup dialog where you can set the print orientation, etc. Enabled only when the focus is in the Script Editor and there is an active printer to which the host machine is connected.
Print Preview		Lets you see what the printed page will look like. Enabled only when the focus is in the Script Editor and there is an active printer to which the host machine is connected.
Exit		Closes the ISWI application prompting you to save changes.

As you can see, the commands in the File menu are somewhat standard for all Windows applications. Now let's move on to the Edit menu.

The Edit menu

On the Edit pulldown menu there are 10 command options and one sub-menu that contains two command options. Table 6-2 describes these commands.

Table 6-2 THE EDIT MENU OPTIONS

Menu Command	Keyboard Shortcuts	Description
Undo	Ctrl+Z	Only applicable to actions that have been performed in the Script Editor. Undoes actions (such as cut, copy, or paste) that have been previously performed.
Redo	Ctrl+Y	Only active when the focus is in the Script Editor; it reverses an Undo action in a script.
Delete	Del	Only active in the Dialog Editor; deletes a selected control or group of controls. (In the Script Editor the Delete key will delete any highlighted portion of a script.)

Menu Command	Keyboard Shortcuts	Description
Cut	Ctrl+X	Active when you have highlighted text in the Script Editor or selected a control or group of controls in the Dialog Editor. Copies text or controls to the clipboard and then deletes the original.
Copy	Ctrl+C	Active when you have highlighted text in the Script Editor or selected a control or group of controls in the Dialog Editor. Copies text or controls to the clipboard.
Paste	Ctrl+V	Active when you have copied text in the Script Editor to the clipboard or when you have copied a control or group of controls to the clipboard in the Dialog Editor. Places text or controls from the clipboard into a script in the Script Editor or onto a dialog box in the Dialog Editor.
Find...	Ctrl+F	Only active when the focus is in the Script Editor. Launches a dialog that enables you to search for a text string in a script.
Replace...	Ctrl+H	Only active when the focus is in the Script Editor. Launches a dialog that enables you to search for a text string in a script and to replace it with another string.
GoTo...	Ctrl+G	Only active when the focus is in the Script Editor. Launches a dialog that enables you to immediately jump to a designated line number.
Repeat...		Only active when the focus is in the Script Editor. Launches a dialog that enables you to define how many times to repeat the next action.
Insert		Only active when the focus is in the Script Editor. It has two options on a sub-menu. The first sub-menu option launches the InstallScript Function Wizard, which enables you to insert one of the supported InstallScript functions into the script.

Continued

TABLE 6-2 THE EDIT MENU OPTIONS *(Continued)*

Menu Command	Keyboard Shortcuts	Description
		The other sub-menu function enables you to insert a string ID into a script so that the script can use directly the text associated with that string ID.

The next pulldown menu we need to discuss is the Build menu.

The Build menu

The Build menu contains those commands used to turn an ISWI project file (.ism) into an MSI package. It also contains commands related to the use of InstallScript to create custom actions. Table 6-3 describes these commands.

TABLE 6-3 THE BUILD MENU OPTIONS

Menu Command	Keyboard Shortcuts	Description
Release Wizard		Launches the Release Wizard used to build new releases.
Compile	Ctrl+F7	Compiles an InstallScript that is being used to implement a custom action.
Build	F7	Rebuilds the present build that was originally created with the Release Wizard. If there is no active release then this will create a new release using default values.
Batch Build...		Launches a dialog that enables you to choose a set of Release labels to be built in sequence.
Stop Build	Ctrl+Break	Stops a build in progress.
Test	Ctrl+T	Tests the user interface of the current build and release.
Debug	F5	Debugs the InstallScript custom actions of the current build and release.

Menu Command	Keyboard Shortcuts	Description
Run	Ctrl+F5	Runs the installation for the current build and release.
Compiler Settings...		Launches a dialog that enables you to define certain settings for the InstallScript compiler.

The next section addresses the Go menu.

The Go menu

The Go menu provides a set of navigational commands that enable you to move around the IDE efficiently. Table 6-4 describes these navigational commands.

TABLE 6-4 THE GO MENU OPTIONS

Menu Command	Description
InstallShield Today	Takes you to the InstallShield Today view, described earlier in the section of the same name.
Help/Support	Takes you to the Help view, described earlier in the section of the same name.
Best Practices	Takes you to the Best Practices view, described earlier in the section of the same name.
Project	Only available when there is an open project. Takes you to the Project view where the basic properties that relate to the whole project and product are set.
Setup Design-Global	Takes you to the Global sub-view of the Setup Design view. In this view you can see all features, components and merge modules that comprise the design of the product.
Setup Design-Features	Takes you to the Features sub-view of the Setup Design view. In this view you can see only the features that are part of the product design.

Continued

TABLE 6-4 THE GO MENU OPTIONS *(Continued)*

Setup Design-Components	Takes you to the Components sub-view of the Setup Design view. In this view you can see only the components that are part of the product design.
Setup Design-Merge Modules	Takes you to the Merge Modules sub-view of the Setup Design view. In this view you can see only the merge modules that are part of the product design.
Setup Design-Destination	Displays all the parts of the product design according to the defined target destination.
Sequences	Takes you to the Sequences view where you can control the operation of the installation.
Actions/Scripts	Takes you to the Actions/Scripts view where you can create both standard and InstallScript-based custom actions.
User Interface	Takes you to the User Interface view where you can design and modify the user interface to be used in the installation.
Release	Takes you to the Releases view where you can create new builds or releases, or rerun builds and releases that have already been created.

You can also access the Go menu commands through the View bar at the far left of the IDE. You can access the sub-views of the Setup Design view from the icons in the top title bar of the view. These icons are on the far right of this title bar when you are in the Setup Design view.

The Tools menu

The Tools menu contains nine command options; seven of these options launch wizards that help to create various parts of an installation project. Table 6-5 briefly describes these commands. Later sections describe the wizards in more detail.

The majority of the tables in an MSI database are abstracted in one form or another in the IDE. This means that by entering the properties through the IDE you are defining the entries that are to be made in the various database tables when a build is run. However, there are certain tables not exposed through the IDE; to make entries in these tables you need another mechanism. This mechanism is the Power Editor. It appears to make entries directly into the database, but actually it makes additional entries into the project file, which are turned into database entries at build time.

TABLE 6-5 THE TOOLS MENU OPTIONS

Menu Command	Description
Power Editor	Launches an editor that enables you to make entries into various tables that have not been exposed through other parts of the IDE.
Import Visual Basic Project...	Launches a wizard that enables you to import a Visual Basic project and create an ISWI project.
Validate Project...	Performs a validation against the project file much as an MSI package is validated by Microsoft's Msival2 utility.
Convert Source Paths...	Launches a wizard that helps you convert absolute paths in your project to path variables.
Create/Apply Transforms...	Launches a wizard that enables you to generate and/or apply a transform.
Add New Language...	Enabled only when there is no project open. Creates a new language and adds it to the languages that will be available in future projects.
Create Patch...	Launches a wizard that enables you to create a patch package you can use to update one or more installations.
DemoShield Designer...	Launches the DemoShield designer that you can use to create a browser for your product's installation.
Options...	Launches a dialog in which you can set various global options for the projects you create.

The Options dialog launched with the Options... command on the Tools menu enables you to define certain global functionality for all projects you create. The Options dialog has four tabs: General, File Locations, Path Variables, and Dialog Editor.

The General tab enables you to have the Best Practices Wizard on whenever you create a project. It also enables you to always have the help file on top and the SETUP.EXE launcher always created. On the File Locations panel you can define the default locations for both installation projects and where Merge Modules will be copied after they are created. On the Path Variables panel you can define whether you want to be prompted for a path variable or not while working with paths for source files. On the Dialog Editor panel you can choose to be prompted to save unsaved changes in the Dialog Editor upon exiting.

The Help menu

The Help pulldown menu supplies you with a set of commands that provide support in using ISWI as well as keeping it up to date. Table 6-6 describes the commands in this menu.

TABLE 6-6 THE HELP MENU OPTIONS

Menu Command	Description
Help View	Takes you to the Help view where you have direct access to all the tutorials.
Help Library	Launches the ISWI Help library.
MSI Help Library	Launches the MSI Help library.
Setup Map	Takes you to the Setup Map that provides a guide through the ISWI IDE.
Readme	Launches the release notes for the present version of ISWI.
InstallShield on the Web	Takes you to the InstallShield Web site. (You need an Internet connection for this command to work.)
Update...	Gives you access to a sub-menu where you can take advantage of the capabilities of Web Update. The two commands on the sub-menu enable you to configure the product to be updated over the Web and to perform this update.
About InstallShield	Launches the About box for the current version of ISWI.

The Toolbar

Many of the commands on the pulldown menus are mimicked on the Toolbar. The Toolbar provides you with faster and more efficient access to these commands, described in Table 6-7.

TABLE 6-7 BASIC TOOLBAR FUNCTIONALITY

Tool Icon	Tool Name	Description
	Project Wizard	Launches the Project Wizard.

Tool Icon	Tool Name	Description
	New Blank Setup Project	Creates a blank setup project.
	Open Project	Opens an existing project.
	Save Project	Saves a project after changes have been made.
	Insert InstallScript Function	Launches the InstallScript Function Wizard.
	Release Wizard	Launches the Release Wizard.
	Compile	Compiles an InstallScript that has been created to implement custom actions.
	Build	Initiates a re-build on an existing project.
	Stop Build	Stops a build in process.
	Test	Runs a test of the user interface of the present install package.
	Debug	Launches the debugger for an installation that includes a custom action created with InstallScript.
	Run	Runs the current installation.
	DemoShield Designer	Launches the DemoShield Designer. (DemoShield must be installed on the computer for this command to work.)
	InstallShield Home Page	Takes you to the InstallShield Web site if you have an Internet connection.

Now that we have examined all the menu and toolbar items we need to investigate the various parts of a project workspace.

The Project Workspace

You can create two types of projects in ISWI: main installation projects and Merge Module projects. These two types of projects are similar in many ways, but because of the nature of an MSI package and a Merge Module there are significant differences as well. In the following sections we briefly discuss the workspaces for both a main installation project and a Merge Module project.

Installation project workspace

The installation project workspace has six views that give you access to the property screens by means of which you can create a main installation project. These are the Project, Setup Design, Sequences, Actions/Scripts, User Interface, and Release views. You can access them by clicking the icons in the left viewbar. Figure 6-11 shows the Project view of the Installation Project Workspace.

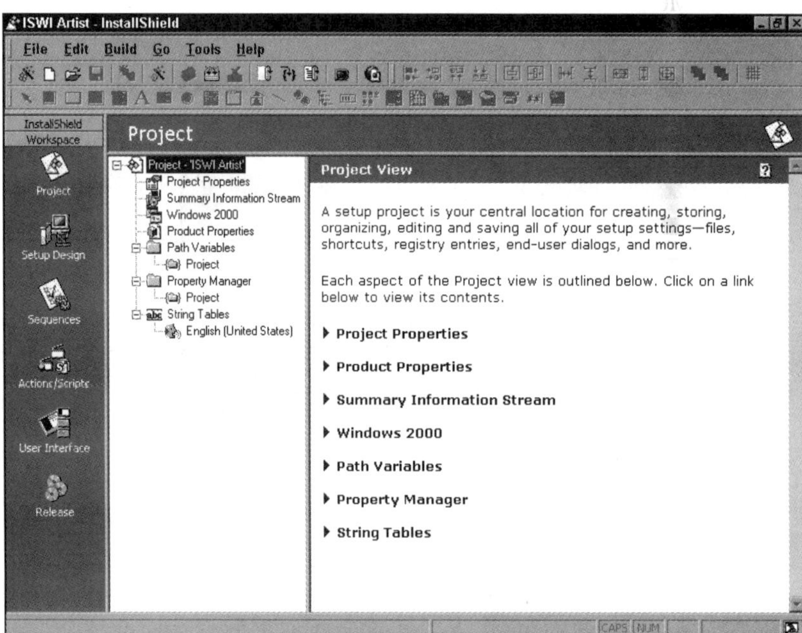

Figure 6-11: The Install Project Workspace

You can use the Project view to define properties that impact the global operation of the installation as well as the build environment. The Setup Design view is where you put together the product design, which you define by creating features and components. The Sequences and Actions/Scripts views are where you can exert control over the installation process. The User Interface view enables you to define the user interface to be used during the installation and the Release view enables you to control the build process used to create the installation package.

Chapters 7, 8, and 9 address the Project Workspace in detail.

Merge Module workspace

The other type of workspace in ISWI is the one in which you create and build a Merge Module project. In this workspace there are five views, which you can access from the icons in the viewbar on the left of the screen. Figure 6-12 shows the Project view of the Merge Module workspace.

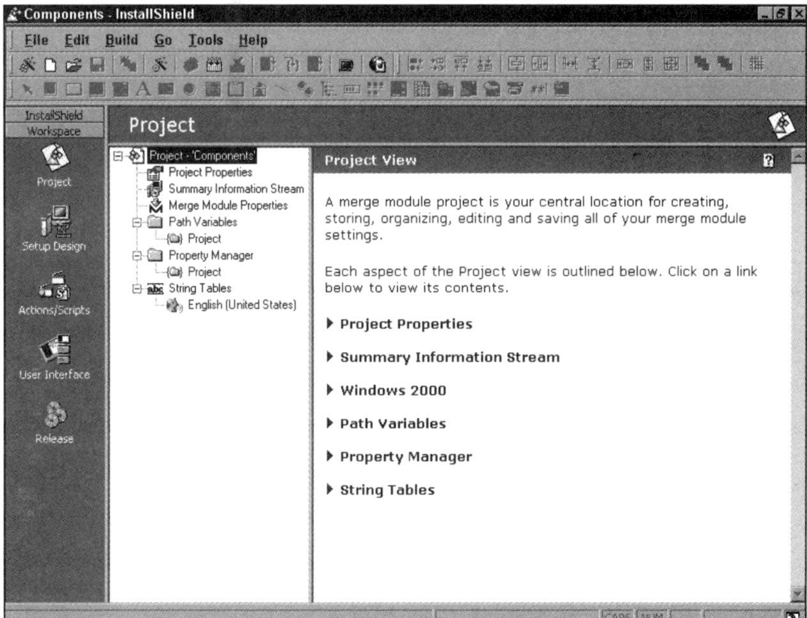

Figure 6-12: The Merge Module Workspace

The available views in the Merge Module workspace perform like the analogous views in the Installation Project workspace, with the single exception that there is no Sequences view in the Merge Module workspace.

Chapter 17, where we discuss the concept of shared components, covers Merge Module creation in detail.

Project Creation Wizards and Tools

ISWI contains many wizards and tools to help you create installation projects. This section provides an overview of each of these wizards and tools, most of which you'll use throughout the book to create actual projects.

The wizards

A wizard is series of dialog boxes linked together to provide you with step-by-step instructions that lead us through performing a given activity. Some wizards consist of only one or two dialogs; others consist of many dialogs. The length of the wizards depends on the complexity of the task. However, even though a wizard will give you step-by-step instructions, it does not do away with the need to know the underlying technology. Wizards ask many questions and the only way you can answer these questions is by knowing what the wizard is trying to accomplish. Now let's take a look at each of the available wizards and see the purpose of each.

THE PROJECT WIZARD

The Project wizard creates an InstallShield setup project by prompting you for information about the application and providing us with *smart defaults*, such as suggested features and components, and standard dialogs. You can also open an existing project in the Project wizard in order to edit it.

You can launch the Project wizard by doing any of the following:

- Clicking the Project Wizard button on the toolbar
- Selecting the Project Wizard option from the File pulldown menu
- Clicking the InstallShield Today shortcut on the viewbar to open the InstallShield Today view and then clicking the Use the Project Wizard option
- Selecting the New Project option from the File menu and then double-clicking the Project Wizard icon

The Welcome dialog of the Project Wizard is shown in Figure 6-13. In this first dialog of the Project Wizard are listed all the dialogs that comprise this wizard. By placing the mouse cursor over the name of any of the dialogs in you will get a description of the purpose of the dialog. Once you have run through the wizard, you can save the project or build the first release. The project will then open in the IDE so you can add the additional project properties that you couldn't enter in the Project Wizard.

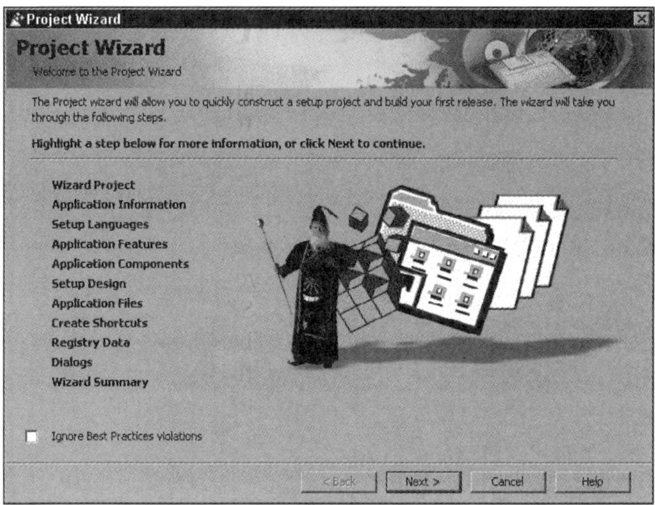

Figure 6-13: The Project Wizard Welcome Dialog

THE RELEASE WIZARD

The Release wizard provides an easy way for you to build a release for a product and specify the settings particular to that release.

You can launch the Release Wizard by doing any of the following:

- ◆ Clicking the Release Wizard button on the toolbar
- ◆ Selecting the Release Wizard option from the Build pulldown menu
- ◆ Right-clicking the Release icon in the Release view and selecting the Release Wizard option from the Context menu
- ◆ Highlighting a build label in the Release view and then clicking on the Release Wizard action item in the right-hand panel
- ◆ Right-clicking a release label in the Release view and selecting the Release Wizard option from the context menu

The Welcome dialog of the Release Wizard is shown in Figure 6-14. There is also a build option that builds the release highlighted in the Release view. This option will also build a product's first release using default settings. Any of the following will access the rebuild functionality:

- ◆ Clicking the Build button on the toolbar
- ◆ Selecting the Build option from the Build pulldown menu

- Right-clicking on a release label in the Release view and selecting the Build option from the context menu

All builds performed in the IDE will provide output in an output window at the bottom of the screen. The output window will show any errors or warnings generated during the build. An alternative to using the Release Wizard or the rebuild function is to perform builds from the command line. Using the command-line options to build a release can help automate the build process.

Figure 6-14: The Release Wizard Welcome Dialog

THE BEST PRACTICES WIZARD

This wizard is invoked whenever you violate Setup Best Practices while adding files to a component – that is, whenever you have broken one of the rules associated with creating components. The wizard tells you which Best Practices you are not adhering to and prompts you for a correction. The wizard is only enabled if you have activated it through either the Best Practices check box in the Options dialog or the Welcome panel of the Project Wizard.

The Best Practices Wizard monitors three componentization rules:

- Every .exe, .dll, .ocx, .hlp, and .chm file has to reside in its own component.
- No component should ship a file with the same name as the name of a file in another component.
- No component should contain a file that is also available in a Merge Module.

The Welcome dialog of the Best Practices Wizard is shown in Figure 6-15. Using the Welcome dialog of the Best Practices Wizard, you can turn off the Best Practices Wizard for all future file-add operations.

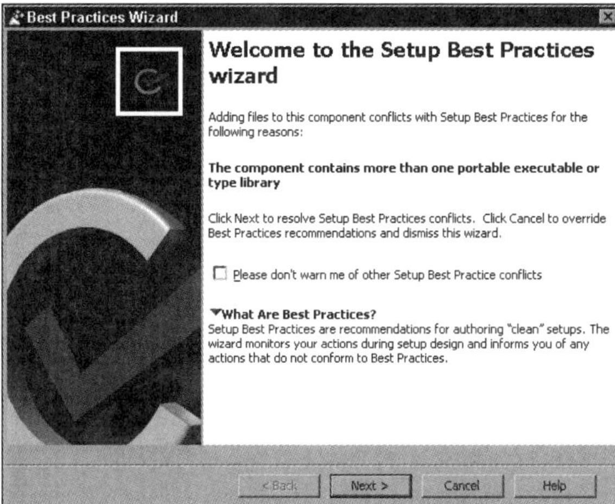

Figure 6-15: The Best Practices Wizard Welcome Dialog

THE OPEN PROJECT WIZARD

The Open Project Wizard enables you to import an InstallShield Professional project (version 5.5 or later) into InstallShield for Windows Installer. Most of the information in the Professional project can be migrated over, but some of the information is either not supported by the Windows Installer service or supported differently.

When this wizard has completed, you will have a new InstallShield for Windows Installer project that contains all of the settings and files and much of the logic in the InstallShield Professional project.

You can launch the Open Project Wizard by following these steps:

1. Click the Open File button on the toolbar or select Open Project from the File menu.
2. In the dialog that appears, select InstallShield Professional Projects (*.ipr) from the Files of Type option.
3. Navigate to the Professional project that you want to open and click Open.

The Welcome dialog of the Open Project Wizard is shown in Figure 6-16.

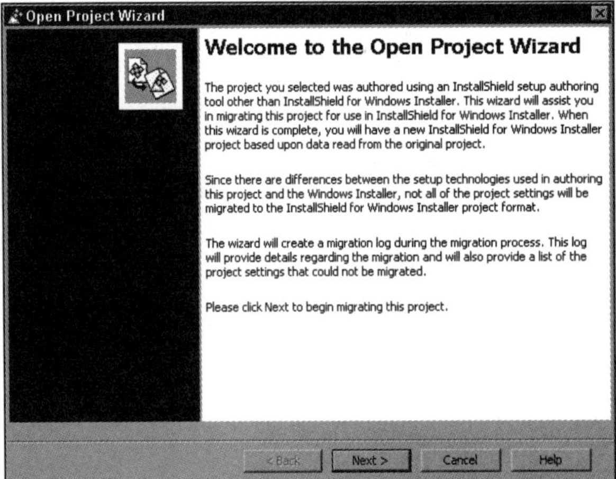

Figure 6-16: The Open Project Wizard Welcome Dialog

THE OPEN MSI/MSM WIZARD

The Open MSI/MSM Wizard enables you to import setup packages and merge modules into ISWI. The wizard walks you through importing an .msi or an .msm file.

You can launch the Open MSI/MSM Wizard by following these steps:

1. Select the Open Project button on the toolbar and browse to the location of the .msi or .msm file.
2. Select either Windows Installer Packages (*.msi) or Windows Installer Modules (*.msm) from the Files of Type list provided in the browse dialog.
3. Select the MSI package or Merge Module you want to open and click the Open button.

The Welcome dialog of the Open MSI/MSM Wizard is shown in Figure 6-17. Once the desired Windows Installer database is selected the Open MSI/MSM wizard gathers the options for converting the file and then tells you if it has been successful in creating the setup or merge module project.

THE COMPONENT WIZARD

The Component Wizard provides two options for creating components. You can create components using Best Practices or you can select a component type and define the component properties yourself.

Figure 6-17: The Open MSI/MSM Wizard Welcome Dialog

When you create components using Best Practices you give the wizard all of your application's files and have it create all the necessary components according to the Setup Best Practices. With the second option you select a specific component type and then define the special treatment required for the component during installation and uninstallation. The special types of components you can create with this option are:

- COM server
- Install NT services
- Control NT service
- Fonts
- ODBC resources

The Welcome dialog of the Component Wizard is shown in Figure 6-18. The Component Wizard is not intended for modifying existing components. Once you create a component using the Component Wizard you need to do any further editing of the properties, files, advanced settings, and the like in the Setup Design view.

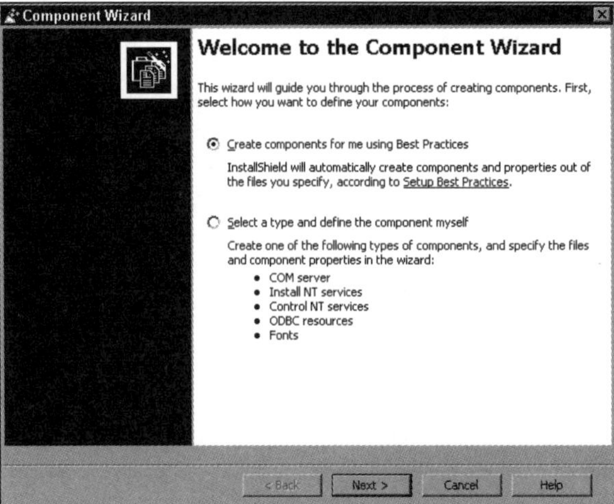

Figure 6-18: The Component Wizard Welcome Dialog

THE IMPORT REG FILE WIZARD

InstallShield enables you to import an existing REG file that you obtained from other setup projects or created outside the IDE. To import a REG file into a component you need to launch the Import REG File Wizard by following these steps:

1. In the Setup Design view, click a component's Registry Data icon to display its visual registry editor.
2. Right-click Registry Data icon in the registry editor and select the Import REG File option from the context menu.

The Welcome dialog of the Import REG File Wizard is shown in Figure 6-19. When you import a REG file into a component, that registry data will be added to the component's registry data and written to the end user's system when the component is installed.

THE EXPORT REG FILE WIZARD

InstallShield also enables you to export to a REG file the existing registry data that has been defined for a component. To export a REG file from a component you need to launch the Export REG File Wizard by following these steps:

1. In the Setup Design view, click a component's Registry Data icon to display its visual registry editor.
2. Right-click the Registry Data icon in the registry editor and select the Export REG File option from the Context menu.

The Welcome dialog of the Export REG File Wizard is shown in Figure 6-20.

Figure 6-19: The Import REG File Wizard Welcome Dialog

Figure 6-20: The Export REG File Wizard Welcome Dialog

THE MERGE MODULE WIZARD

The Merge Module Wizard associates merge modules with one or more of the features defined in an application. When running this wizard you are presented with a gallery of all the merge modules that have been saved to the Merge Module locations defined on the File Locations tab of the Options dialog. To launch the Merge Module Wizard, follow these steps:

1. Go to the Global sub-view of the Setup Design view.
2. Right-click an existing feature or subfeature and select the Merge Module Wizard option on the context menu.

The Welcome dialog of the Merge Module Wizard is shown in Figure 6-21.

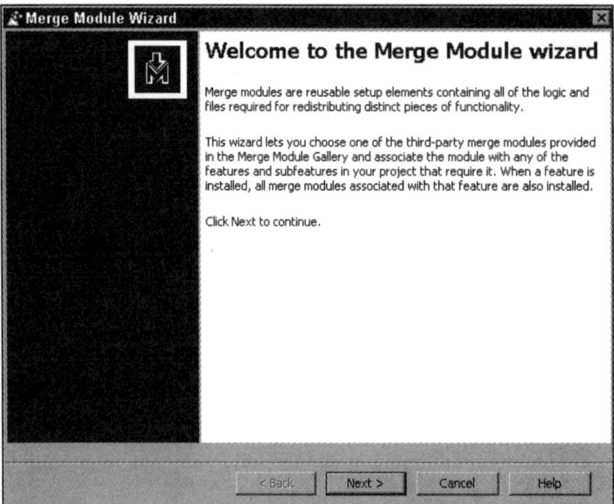

Figure 6-21: The Merge Module Wizard Welcome Dialog

THE CUSTOM ACTION WIZARD

The Custom Action Wizard enables you to define custom actions to be used during the running of the installation package. Custom actions are the means by which you can extend the built-in capabilities of the Windows Installer. To launch the Custom Action Wizard, follow these steps:

1. Open the Actions/Scripts view.
2. Right-click the Custom Action icon in the Actions/Scripts view and select the Custom Action Wizard option from the Context menu.

The Welcome dialog of the Custom Action Wizard is shown in Figure 6-22. When you complete the definition of a custom action you need to go to the Sequences view and put this custom action where it will be executed by the Windows Installer.

THE VISUAL BASIC WIZARD

The Visual Basic Wizard enables you to import Visual Basic projects into an InstallShield setup. The wizard scans the Visual Basic project and determines all file dependencies. It then displays the results of the scan, showing the files that it will add to the ISWI project. You can also create a new setup project by scanning a Visual Basic project when there is no setup project open in ISWI. The Visual Basic Wizard requires that Visual Basic be installed on the build system. Selecting the Import Visual Basic Project option from the Tools menu launches the Visual Basic wizard. The Welcome dialog of the Visual Basic Wizard is shown in Figure 6-23.

Figure 6-22: The Custom Action Wizard Welcome Dialog

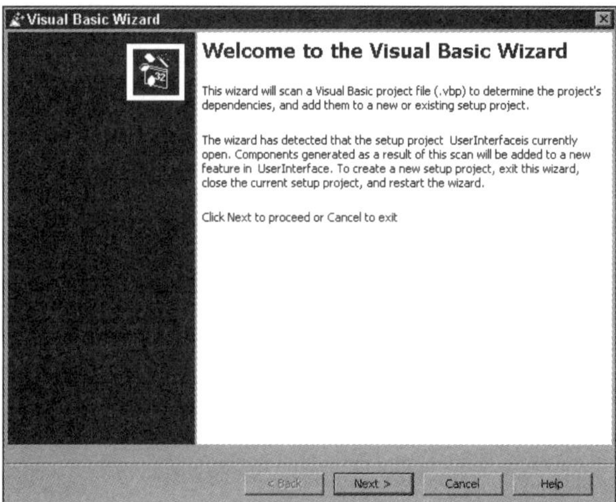

Figure 6-23: The Visual Basic Wizard Welcome Dialog

THE VALIDATE PROJECT WIZARD

The Validate Project Wizard performs an internal consistency evaluation on an InstallShield project (.ism) file. This wizard scans the ISWI project file for compliance with a set of rules modeled after the internal consistency evaluators developed by Microsoft for validating an actual MSI database. Selecting the Validate Project option from the Tools menu launches the Validate Project wizard. After the wizard has completed the validation process, it generates a report alerting you to any instances of noncompliance with the rules. The Welcome dialog for the Validate Project Wizard is shown in Figure 6-24.

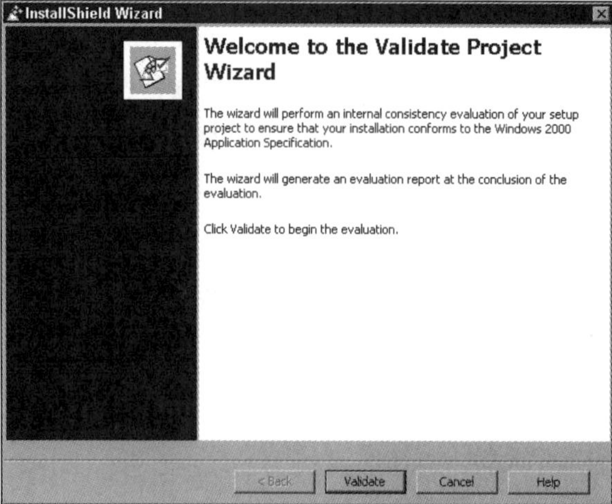

Figure 6-24: The Validate Project Wizard Welcome Dialog

THE CONVERT SOURCE PATHS WIZARD

The Convert Source Paths Wizard enables you to convert existing hard-coded paths into path variables. By creating path variables for locating the source files of an application you can enhance the portability of a setup project. Selecting the Convert Source Paths option from the Tools menu launches the Convert Source Paths wizard. The Welcome dialog of the Convert Source Paths Wizard is shown in Figure 6-25.

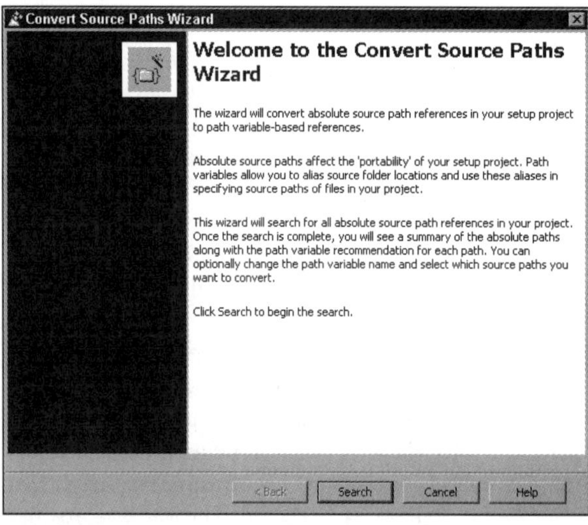

Figure 6-25: The Convert Source Paths Wizard Welcome Dialog

THE ADD NEW LANGUAGE WIZARD

If you need your setup to run in languages that aren't supported by InstallShield's international versions, or would like to create your own translations for some of the supported languages, you can add support for those languages with the New Language Wizard. This wizard enables you to select the languages you would like to support and the projects to which you would like to add these languages. It then adds the languages you have chosen to the list of available languages for the setup. Selecting the Add New Language option from the Tools menu launches the New Language Wizard, which is only enabled when there are no open projects in the IDE. The Welcome dialog of the Add New Language Wizard is shown in Figure 6-26.

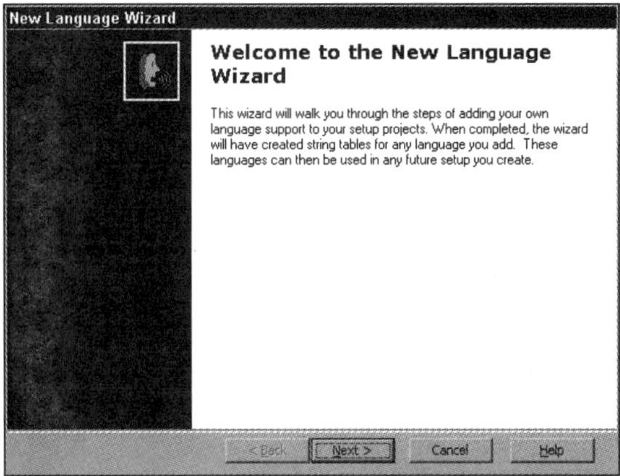

Figure 6-26: The Add New Language Wizard Welcome Dialog

THE TRANSFORM WIZARD

The Transform Wizard walks you through the steps involved in creating and applying transforms. Transforms represent the difference between two MSI databases. When you apply a transform to an MSI database you are permanently changing the target MSI database.

Selecting the Create/Apply Transform option on the Tools menu launches the Transform Wizard. After launching the Transform Wizard, you can choose whether to create a transform or to apply a transform in the Welcome dialog. The Welcome dialog of the Transform Wizard is shown in Figure 6-27.

THE PATCH WIZARD

The Patch Creation Wizard builds a patch package (.msp) file capable of updating earlier versions of an installed product. Specifically, you can use a patch package to update or upgrade an installed image for an earlier version of a product. Selecting Create Patch from the Tools menu launches the Patch Wizard. The Welcome dialog of the Patch Wizard is shown in Figure 6-28.

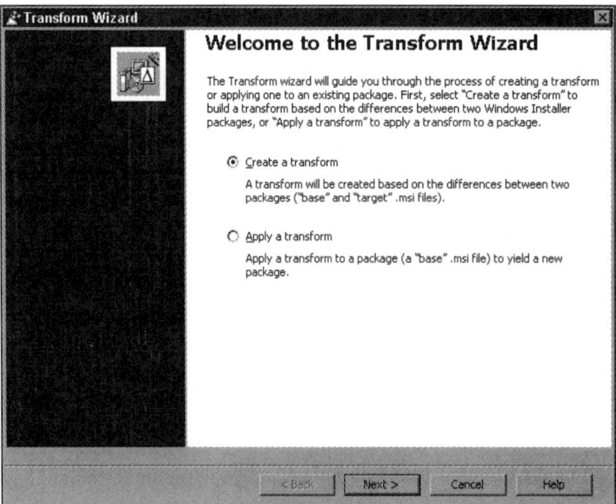

Figure 6-27: The Transform Wizard Welcome Dialog

The wizard is independent of any setup or merge module projects that may be open in the IDE. It does not affect the current project, and you can create a patch for a completely different release from the current one. All settings for creating the patch package are stored in a patch creation project (.pcp) file, which is completely separate from any ISWI project (.ism) file.

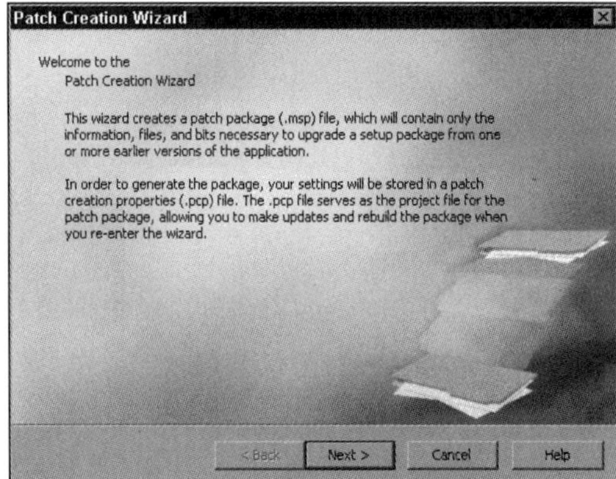

Figure 6-28: The Patch Wizard Welcome Dialog

The tools

In addition to the wizards that help you create installation projects, ISWI also provides you with various tools for the same purpose. These tools do not run as wizards and as such fall into another category. This section provides a brief overview of each of these tools.

THE DIALOG EDITOR

The Dialog Editor is a visual resource editor similar to the one in Visual C++ or Visual Basic. Using the ISWI Dialog Editor you can create a new dialog box or modify an existing dialog by editing its properties and controls. You get to the Dialog Editor through the User Interface view in the IDE.

The User Interface explorer manages versions of the dialog for each of a project's supported languages. To edit an existing dialog you need to select a language-specific version of the dialog. The different language versions of a dialog remain identical except for any changes to a control's size.

There are two toolbars associated with the Dialog Editor: the alignment and sizing toolbar, and the controls toolbar. Enable them by entering the Dialog Editor.

In Chapter 9 we take a detailed look at the Dialog Editor and how you can use it to modify existing dialogs as well as create new ones.

THE SCRIPT EDITOR

The ISWI installation development environment (IDE) includes a full-featured text editor that is activated automatically whenever you open a script file for the purpose of implementing a custom action. The InstallShield script editor operates much like other standard Windows editors. The script editor includes the following functionality:

Over 120 separate edit commands — More than 120 separate edit commands can be assigned to keystrokes that you can invoke when developing scripts.

Keystroke macros — You can record a series of keystrokes as a macro and run the macro to play back the keystrokes whenever desired. You can record up to 10 macros.

Drag-and-drop text manipulation — You can drag and drop highlighted text among any windows supporting OLE text drag-and-drop. You may copy or move text.

Multiple split views — You can create up to four separate views of the same edit buffer and scroll each view independently.

Unlimited undo/redo — All edit actions are fully undoable and redoable, though you can set a limit on the number of edit actions that may be undone.

Auto indentation	As you enter code, the editor automatically indents lines to follow the rules you have chosen.
Column selection and manipulation	You can select columns of text with the mouse and then manipulate them. You can select empty columns (columns with a width of zero characters), causing subsequent typing and deletion to occur over multiple lines at the same time.
Microsoft IntelliMouse support	With the Microsoft IntelliMouse you can easily scroll as well as select lines or words.

DEMOSHIELD DESIGNER

This tool is actually a separate product that you can launch from the ISWI IDE, provided you have ISWI installed. You can use the DemoShield Designer to create a browser front end for an installation package. Discussing how to create browsers using DemoShield is unfortunately beyond the scope of this book.

SPY

NetInstall Spy is an application that will track a target system and produce a list of changes. You can then open InstallShield for Windows Installer to create a setup project based on those changes.

Although you can run Spy and ISWI on the same machine, it is not recommended. Spy will provide a much more accurate snapshot of the changes to the system if it is run on a clean machine.

More specifically, Spy will evaluate all the files, registry entries, shortcuts, services, and system settings, and just about anything else that is part of an installation. Once it has completed this initial system evaluation, you can run any installation that you would like to capture. If you want to bundle multiple installations, just run them one after the other. Finally, you need to run Spy again, this time to check for changes in the system since the last time you ran Spy. When Spy has completed, it will create an .inc file, which contains references to all the changes that took place. You can then open this .inc file with InstallShield for Windows Installer to create a new setup project based on the changes.

WEB UPDATE

Web Update enables you to distribute the latest versions of all of your applications to any customers who have bought your software before. When an end user installs any of your Web Update–enabled applications, the Web Update Client is also installed, and enabling the user to see if a newer version of the application is currently available for download. When an end user checks for updated versions of your applications, the Web Update client compares the latest version of the application available on your Web server to the version installed on the customer's computer. If the version on the Web server is newer, the end user can install it.

Summary

In this chapter we have looked into every corner of the InstallShield for Windows Installer product, albeit briefly. In the next three chapters you'll get much closer to ISWI as you create an actual installation and learn how to work with all the capabilities of ISWI.

Chapter 7

Basic Installation Package Creation with ISWI

IN THIS CHAPTER

- Using the Project Wizard
- Modifying the String Table Editor to create new string IDs
- Adding additional feature and component properties using the IDE
- Modifying the shortcut properties in the IDE
- Creating a file extension association for the application
- Using the Release Wizard to create an installation package

THIS CHAPTER INTRODUCES YOU to creating a basic installation package using Install Shield for Windows Installer. Essentially you will be repeating the work that you did in chapters 4 and 5.

The Product to be Installed

You can find the files that comprise the application you'll install in this example on the accompanying CD-ROM, along with the source code from which these files were generated. The name of this application is ISWI Artist. It is a basic application that uses a COM DLL for one of its components. The functionality of this application is somewhat trivial but it will demonstrate the complexity of creating an installation without an authoring tool. This application draws certain text or objects on the screen at the location of the cursor when the left mouse button is clicked. Figure 7-1 shows the feature and component layout for this application.

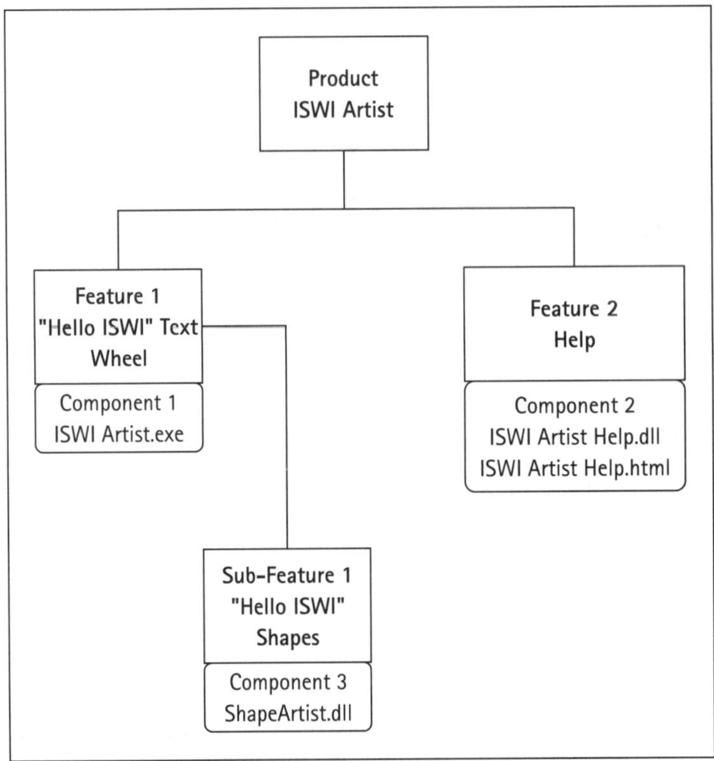

Figure 7-1: Feature and component layout of the example product

Figure 7-1 shows two top-level features and one sub-feature. The sub-feature is a child of Feature 1. All the features are comprised of one component each. Feature 1 is the main application and Feature 2 provides the on-line help in the form of an HTML page. Feature 2 is implemented as a standard dynamic-link library that launches Internet Explorer to display the HTML help page. The sub-feature of Feature 1 provides more graphics functionality to the product that enables you to display various graphics primitives. These graphics primitives are shown in different colors when this sample application is run. This functionality is implemented as a COM DLL to necessitate making the entries in the COM-related tables.

Creating the Initial Project with the Project Wizard

You are going to create the initial cut of the project using the Project Wizard, and then finish off the project using some of the wizards available by making entries directly in some of the property screens in the IDE. By the time you finish creating and building this project you will have used many of the various features in ISWI.

Get started by launching the Project Wizard. You can do this by double-clicking the Project Wizard icon in the Create a new project... screen of the InstallShield Today view. You can also access the Project Wizard from the File pulldown menu or by clicking the Project Wizard icon in the toolbar. When you launch the Project Wizard, you will see the Welcome panel of the wizard as shown in Figure 7-2.

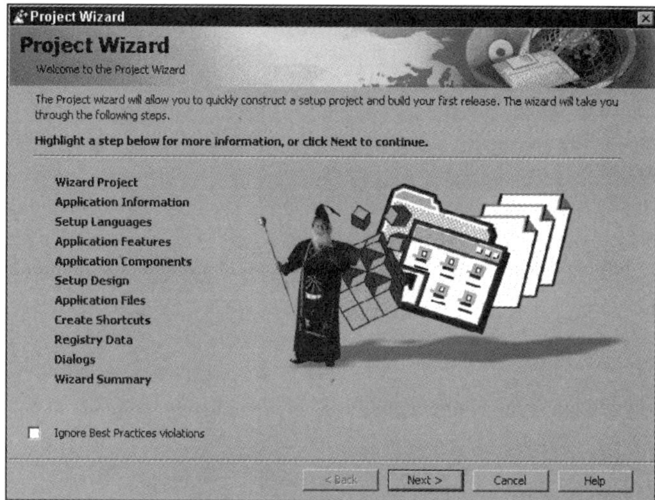

Figure 7-2: The Project Wizard Welcome dialog

This first panel of the Project Wizard provides a list of all the panels in the wizard. As you can see, there are a total of 11 panels in this wizard. If you place your cursor over the name of any of these panels, you will see a description of the purpose of the panel. At the bottom of this first panel you can see a check box with the caption Ignore Best Practices violations. This enables you to have ISWI warn you of any violations of what are called Best Practices.

Best Practices are explained in the Best Practices view. They relate to the rules you need to follow when creating components to be installed by the Windows Installer. In essence, when creating components you need a separate component for every file that has an .exe, .dll, .ocx, .hlp, or .chm extension. Each of these files must also be the key path for its component. In addition, no component can be the target for more than one shortcut and all files in any component must have the same destination.

The term Best Practices refers to what the draft versions of the "Certified for Windows 2000" requirements called the rules for creating components. When these requirements were finally released, the requirements used this term for something else, but in ISWI it stuck around and still relates to the rules for creating components.

The Options... command is at the bottom of the Tools pulldown menu. On the General tab of the resulting dialog box there is an option for setting the default approach used to handle Best Practices violations. If you uncheck this box in the Options dialog, every time you launch the Project Wizard the check box at the bottom of panel 1 will be checked. For this exercise you should have ISWI warn you of any violations of the Best Practices rules so you will want to have the Enforce Setup Best Practices checkbox checked in the Options dialog.

Let's click the Next button and go to the second wizard panel. This is where you will enter the name of the project to be created. Enter the project name ISWI Artist as shown in Figure 7-3.

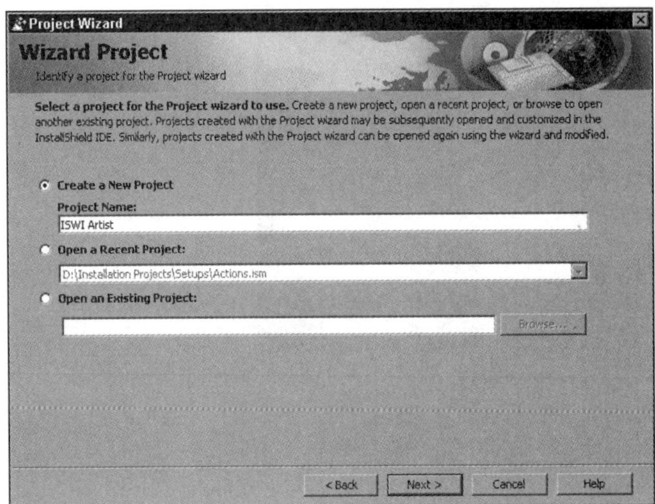

Figure 7-3: Entering the project name in the second dialog of the Project Wizard

From this panel you can create a new project or open a recently created project. You also can browse for a project in another location by choosing the third option on this panel.

Clicking the Next button takes you to the third panel in the Project Wizard. On this panel you make entries that set certain properties that will be entered into the Property table at build time. This wizard panel is shown in Figure 7-4.

You need to make the entries shown in this figure. The Project Wizard will not let you leave any of these properties empty. The top three entries in this panel are part of the set of five required properties that every MSI package must contain. The Default Destination Folder edit field is where you set the initial value of the INSTALLDIR Directory table entry. In Chapter 4 you used a custom action to set the default value for the TARGETDIR Now INSTALLDIR is being used to serve the same function as TARGETDIR did in Chapter 4. The difference is that you do not have to use a custom action to set the default value of INSTALLDIR.

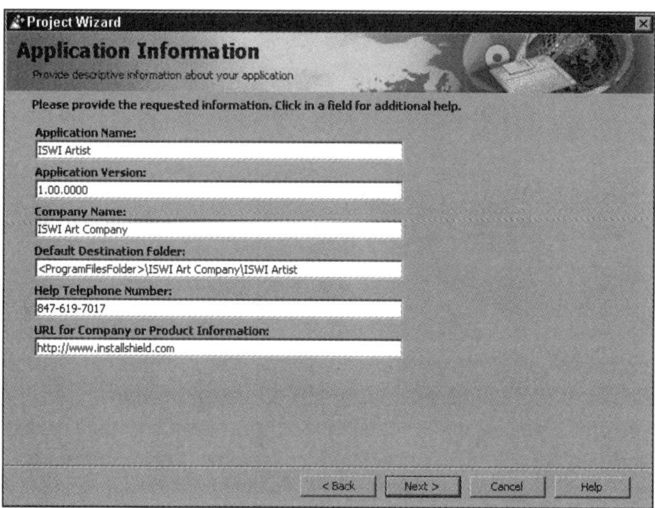

Figure 7-4: Providing basic property values in the Application Information dialog

The setting of the default destination of a product comes from the format required by the "Certified for Windows" application specification. The general format for the installation location for an application is the program files folder followed by a folder with the name of the company that creates the application and finally a folder with the name of the application being installed. Since the location of the Program Files folder depends on where the operating system is installed this location is treated as a project path variable. As you will notice, the Default Destination Folder is filled in automatically when you enter the values in the Application Name and Company Name edit fields.

In the Help Telephone edit field you need to enter the telephone number that the user can call for technical support for the product being installed. The entry made here sets the value of the ARPHELPTELEPHONE public property. The value of this property is displayed in the Add/Remove Programs Applet in Windows 2000. The final edit field on this wizard panel is the URL of the company or the product. This entry sets the value of the ARPURLINFOABOUT public property, which is also displayed in the Add/Remove Programs Applet in Windows 2000.

Chapter 8 discusses properties and the types of properties you can find in an MSI database.

Now let's move on to the next panel. Click on the Next button to get the panel shown in Figure 7-5.

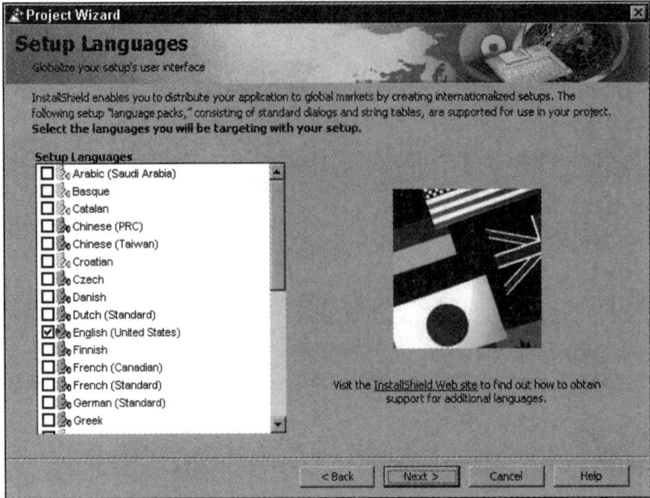

Figure 7-5: Selecting the languages in the Setup Languages dialog

In this panel you can choose additional languages in which to run your setup. The appropriate language packs must be installed for this functionality to work. If you do not have the appropriate language pack and you try to select a language, you will be given an error message box containing a link to the InstallShield Web site where the language packs are sold. For this example application you will create an installation in English, which is the default language.

Chapter 19 discusses how to localize an installation.

Now let's move on to the next panel in the Project Wizard. This panel, the Application Features panel, is where you start to actually design the structure of the application. This panel is shown in Figure 7-6.

When this panel is first displayed, you are presented with three default feature names. For your example application you will change these default features to the ones shown in Figure 7-6. You need to make sure to make the ShapeDraw_Feature feature a child of the Main_Feature feature. You can use the Add, Delete, and Rename buttons to add, delete, and rename the features shown in the Features panel. You can also right-click a feature and get a context menu that enables you to do the same thing. On this context menu you also get options that enable you to restructure the feature tree. You can move a feature up or down and this changes things in the Features panel. It will also change the order of how these features appear in the custom setup type dialog in the user interface. You can also change the relationship between features by choosing the Move Left or Move Right options on the context menu. Use the Move Up or Move Down options to position a feature relative to another in order to then change the relationship by using the Move Left or the Move Right options.

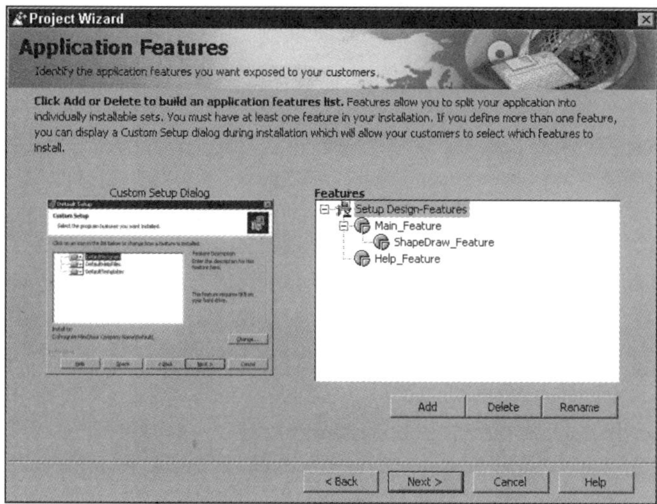

Figure 7-6: Defining the application features in the Application Features dialog

When you create a feature name, you cannot use spaces or any other characters you can't include in the name of a feature in the Feature table. The names that you create are used as the names of the features in the Feature table. A feature name can be any string that contains letters, digits, periods (.), or the underscore (_), as long as it begins with an underscore or a letter.

After you generate the feature structure for your application you need to define the components that make up the application. You can do this in the next panel of the Project Wizard, shown in Figure 7-7.

When this panel is first displayed, it contains four default components. Delete these and create new components with the names shown in Figure 7-7. Instead of deleting all four default components you could delete just one of them and give the remaining components to the names that we want. When naming components in this panel, you need to follow the same rules you followed when naming the features in the previous panel.

You can click the right mouse button on a selected component and get a context menu that enables you to either delete or rename the component. If you right-click the topmost item in the Components panel, you are given the option to create a new component; you can also either have the components sorted in this view or have them displayed in the order in which they are created. Except for toggling the sorting of the components in the Components panel, you can perform all the same actions using the buttons at the bottom of the Components panel.

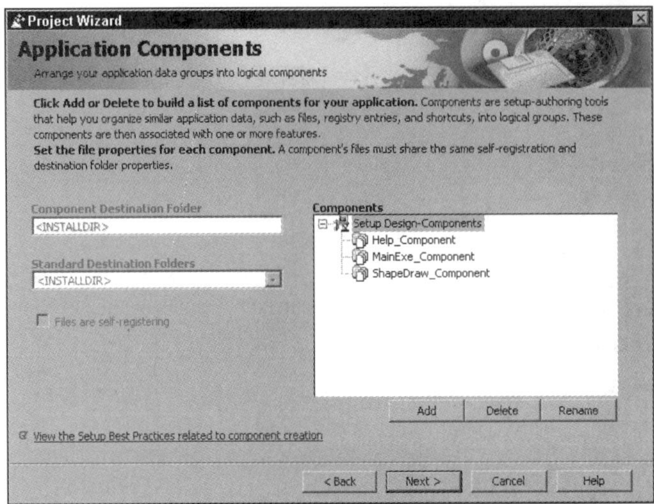

Figure 7-7: Defining the application components in the Application Components dialog

When you highlight a component in the Components panel of the Application Components dialog, the Component Destination Folder edit field, the Standard Destination Folders combo box, and the Files are self-registering check box are all enabled. By default, the destination of any component is set to be the same as prescribed by the INSTALLDIR variable. You can change this destination by adding a sub-folder to the default using the following format: <INSTALLDIR>\Docs. Doing this forces the creation of a folder named Docs under the root installation location of the application. You can also choose a Windows Installer–defined location by choosing a different install location from the Standard Destination Folders drop-down combo box. Doing this forces the component to a specific location defined by the operating system. The component goes to this location regardless of the final install location for the feature that contains the component.

In the Application Components dialog you can define a component as being self-registering. Do this by checking the check box located below the Standard Destination Folders combo box. When you have identified a component as self-registering, the Windows Installer will call the exported function DllRegisterServer, which will perform all the registration of the COM server DLL. Similarly, on uninstallation the Windows Installer will call the function DllUnregisterServer to remove the registry information for the COM component.

I strongly recommend that installation package authors not use self-registration. Instead they should register modules by authoring one or more of the other tables provided by the installer for this purpose. Using the component wizard in ISWI makes it easy to extract the COM information from a COM server. Many of the benefits of having a central installer service are lost with self-registration because self-registration routines tend to hide critical configuration information. The following list shows the reasons why you do not to use the self-registration for COM servers:

- You cannot safely roll back installation done with self-registered modules using DllUnregisterServer because there is no way to tell if the self-registered keys are being used by another feature or application.
- Your ability to use advertisement is reduced if class or extension server registration is performed within self-registration routines.
- The installer automatically handles HKCR keys in the registry tables for both per-user and per-machine installations. DllRegisterServer routines currently do not support the notion of a per-user HKCR key.
- If multiple users are attempting to use a self-registered application on a computer, each one will have to install the application on first run because the installer cannot easily determine that the proper HKCU registry keys exist for that user.
- The DLLRegisterServer can be denied access to network resources such as type libraries if a component is both specified as run-from-source and listed in the SelfReg table. This can cause an administrative installation to fail.
- Self-registering DLLs are more susceptible to coding errors because the new code required for DllRegisterServer is often different for each DLL. Instead, use the registry-related tables in the database to take advantage of existing code provided by the installer.
- Self-registering DLLs can sometimes link to auxiliary DLLs that are not present or are the wrong version. In contrast, the installer doesn't need to depend on the current state of the system to register the DLLs using the registry-related tables.

In this example application you have one COM server DLL but do not want it to be identified as self-registering. Therefore you do not check the check box.

Now that you have finished creating the components that comprise your application you need to associate these components with the proper features. You do this in the next dialog box in the Project Wizard, shown in Figure 7-8.

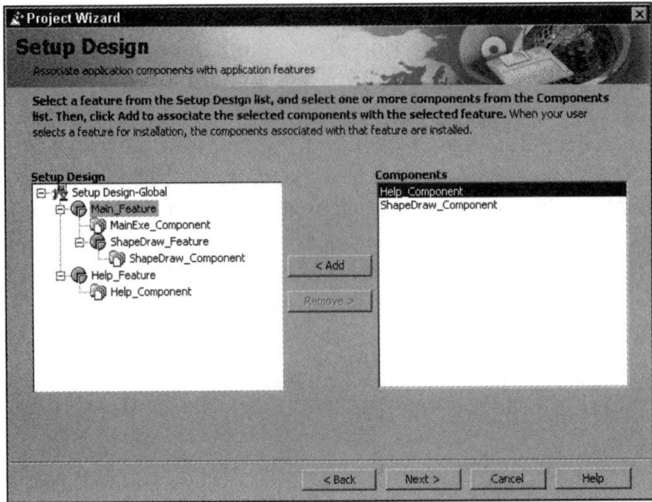

Figure 7-8: Finalizing the setup design by associating components with features in the Setup Design dialog

When you highlight a feature in the Setup Design panel of this dialog, you get a list of all the components in the Components panel that have not already been associated with the highlighted feature. You need to remember that components can be shared among features within an application or between the features of two separate products. This is why you will always get a list of all components not used by the feature in question. You need to make the feature/component association shown in Figure 7-8.

Next you have to add files to each of the components you have created. When you click the Next button on the Setup Design dialog, you are taken to the dialog shown in Figure 7-9. In this dialog you are given a dropdown combo box that contains a list of all the components that have been created in the project. For each of the components in the list you can add files by using the Add Files... button on the right of the dialog, by right-clicking in the Files panel and choosing the Add... option, or by dragging files from a Windows Explorer view and dropping them into the Files panel of this dialog.

When you add files to a component from a location not defined by one of the preset path locations, you are presented with a dialog that asks you to define a path variable for this location or to use the absolute path of the file to include it in the build process. It's a good idea to define path variables for all an application's files because you can then change the location this path variable points to. This makes it easy to change the location on the build system where the application files are located. The dialog that is presented is shown in Figure 7-10.

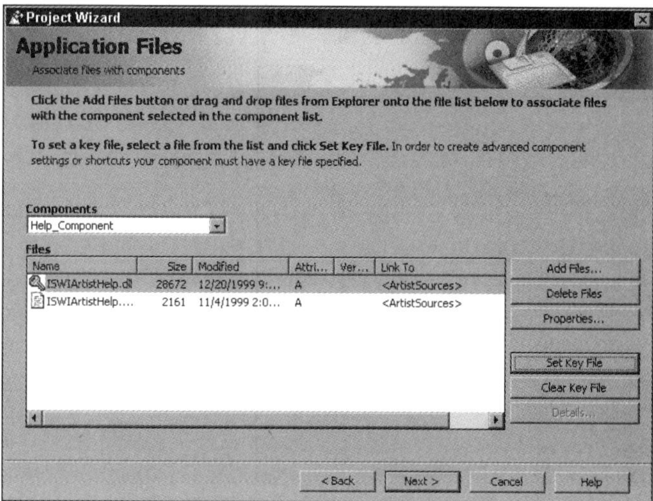

Figure 7-9: Adding files to the components using the Application Files dialog

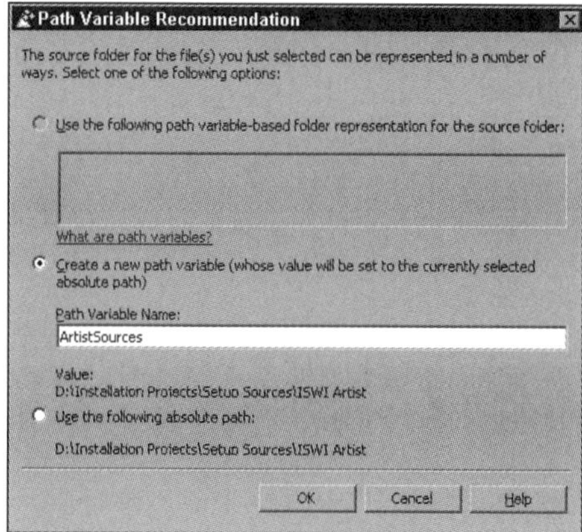

Figure 7-10: The Path Variable Recommendation dialog

You can delete files from the component in the Application Files dialog by using the push button to the right of the Files panel, or you can right-click the file you want to delete and choose the Delete option on the context menu. When you add files to a component, you need to remember to set one of the files as the key file for the component. You can do this by highlighting the file to be set as the key file and then clicking the Set Key File button to the right of the Files panel. You can also clear a file as the key file by using the Clear Key File button. If you try to set a file as a key file when there is already a key file, you get a message box asking whether you want to change the present key file. Table 7-1 shows the files you must add for each of the components you have created.

TABLE 7-1 COMPONENT AND FILE ASSOCIATION FOR THE ISWI ARTIST APPLICATION

Component	Associated Files
Help_Component	ISWIArtistHelp.dll
	ISWIArtistHelp.htm
MainExe_Component	ISWIArtist.exe
ShapeDraw_Component	shapeartist.dll

If you highlight a file in the Files panel and click the Properties... button, you get the dialog shown in Figure 7-11. This dialog enables you to set the attributes of the highlighted file that will be in effect when the file is installed.

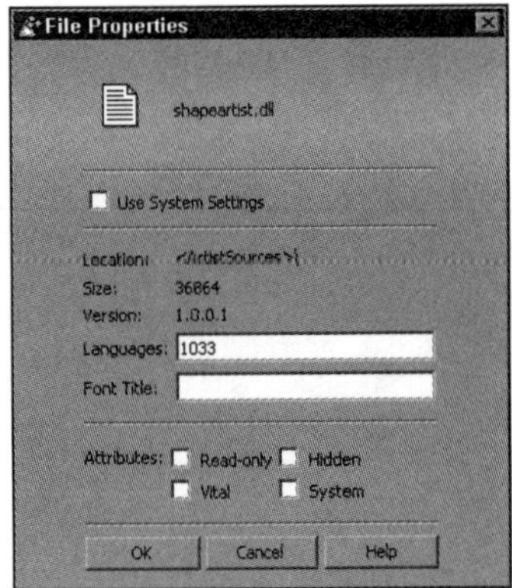

Figure 7-11: The File Properties dialog

By default a file included in an installation will be installed with the same attributes it has on the build system. Unchecking the Use System Settings check box will enable you to change the default attribute settings. At the bottom of the File Properties dialog is a set of four check boxes that enable you to set the individual attributes of the highlighted file. Read-only, Hidden, and System are the standard file attributes with which everyone is familiar. The other attribute, Vital, is a special attribute used by the Windows Installer to determine whether a file missing from a component can safely be ignored or whether the installation must be terminated because the file is not available.

If the Vital attribute is set and the component to which the file belongs is selected for installation, the installer must be able to install this file for the installation to be completed successfully. If the installer is unable to install the file for some reason (for example, if the source file cannot be located within the source image), an error dialog box will appear with the options Retry and Cancel. For a file for which this attribute is not set, the options in case of an install error will be Abort, Retry, and Ignore (that is, the user can complete the install successfully without installing that file).

In the File Properties dialog are two edit fields – Languages and Font Title. The Languages edit field enables you to enter a comma-delimited list of language identifiers that indicate the languages supported by the highlighted file. The Font Title edit file enables you to identify a font title for font files that do not have an embedded font title. TrueType Fonts (.ttf) and TrueType Collections (.ttc) have embedded font titles; you should not specify a font title for these types of files in this edit field. For a standard font file (.fon) you will need to specify the font title in the Font Title edit field.

Before we move on to the next dialog in the Project Wizard there is one last button we should discuss. This is the Details... button, which under most circumstances is disabled. If you violate the rules for creating components, the offending file will be indicated with a warning icon in the Files panel and when you select this file the Details... button will become enabled. Clicking this button will display a message box that describes the error generated when you added the file to the component. For example, if you add a file to a particular component that is already part of another component the error message will tell you that the file is already part of another component.

Now that you have added files to your components and set any properties that you want the files to have when they are installed, we move on to the next dialog in the Project Wizard. The next dialog is where you create a shortcut for your application. This dialog is shown in Figure 7-12.

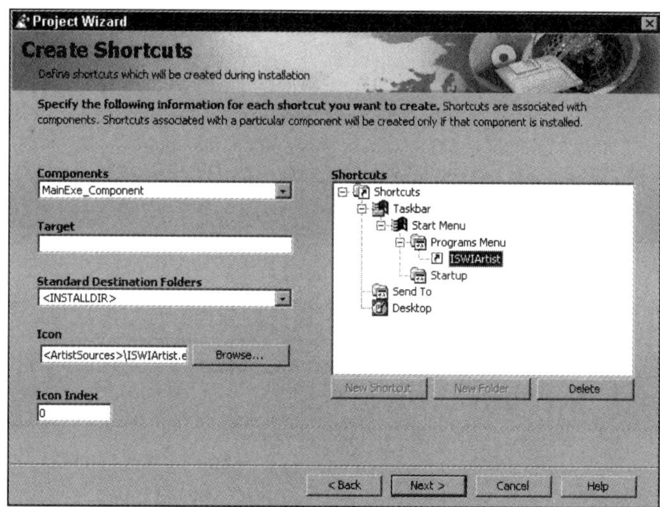

Figure 7-12: Creating a shortcut in the Create Shortcuts dialog

When creating a shortcut, you need to decide whether you want a shortcut that can be advertised or a standard shortcut only. A shortcut that can be advertised is often referred to as an MSI shortcut. To create an MSI shortcut for the ISWI Artist application, first select the component with which the shortcut is to be associated. You can do this using the Components combo box where all the components that have been created are listed. To associate the shortcut with the main executable select the MainExe_Component and then create the name of the shortcut under the Programs Menu icon in the Shortcuts panel of the Create Shortcuts dialog. Because this component is to be installed wherever the <INSTALLDIR> variable points you do not have to make any changes in the Standard Destination Folders combo box. However, you do have to identify the source of the icon that is to be used to on the Start→Programs menu. You can do this by browsing to the ISWIArtist.exe file using the Browse button next to the Icon edit field. Since you want the first icon in ISWIArtist.exe, leave the icon index at the default value of 0.

Do not identify a target for the shortcut because the key file for the MainExe_Component will automatically be used as the target for the MSI shortcut. If you wanted to create a standard shortcut, you would now identify a specific target for the shortcut; then only a standard shortcut would be created. An MSI shortcut is one that can be advertised because it contains extra information to implement this functionality. Once installed an MSI shortcut cannot be edited and will be approximately three times the size of a standard shortcut. If you right-click an MSI shortcut and select the Properties option, you will see that on the Shortcut tab of the Properties dialog all the edit fields are disabled so that you cannot change any of the shortcut attributes.

After completing the input required to create the shortcut for the ISWI Artist application, go to the next dialog in the Project Wizard. This dialog enables you to import a .reg file for each of the components you have created. This dialog is shown in Figure 7-13.

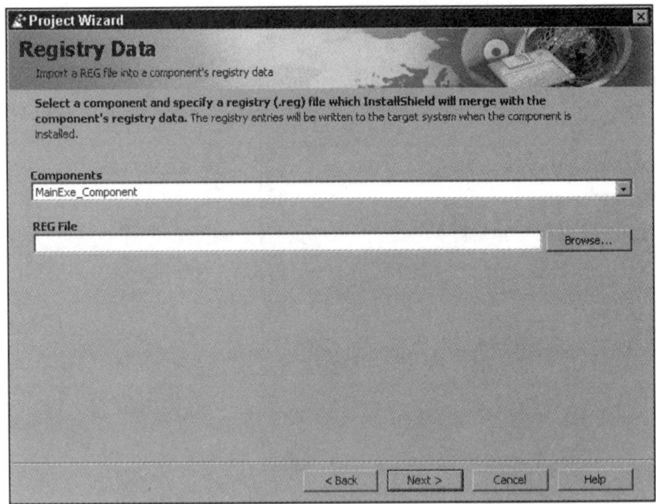

Figure 7-13: Importing registry data using the Registry Data dialog

In the Components combo box you get a list of all the components that have been created for the application. For each of these components you can browse to a .reg file and import the information it contains. The information in the .reg file becomes a permanent part of the project file when it is imported. For the ISWI Artist application you do not have any need to import registry information, so you can just move on to the next dialog in the Project Wizard. This dialog enables you to determine the dialogs to be displayed when the application is installed. This is the Dialogs dialog and it is shown in Figure 7-14.

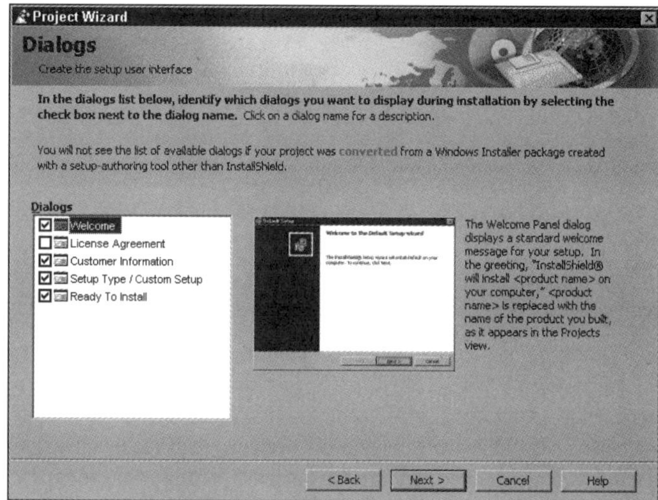

Figure 7-14: Modifying the Installation Wizard using the Dialogs dialog

In the Dialogs panel is a list of five dialogs that you can decide to include or exclude from the installation wizard sequence. You can highlight each of the dialogs in the list and see the design of that particular dialog along with a description of its purpose. For the installation of the ISWI Artist application you will deselect the License Agreement dialog. This dialog requires an .rtf file and displays the End User License Agreement (EULA) for the application. Because you do not have a EULA for the application, you do not need to include this dialog in the installation you are creating.

The last dialog in the Project Wizard is the Wizard Summary dialog where all the input you made in the other wizard dialogs is summarized. In this final dialog you can save the project and make an initial build of the installation package, or you can just save the project. Choose to just save the project because you need to input more information before completing the project. The Wizard Summary dialog is shown in Figure 7-15.

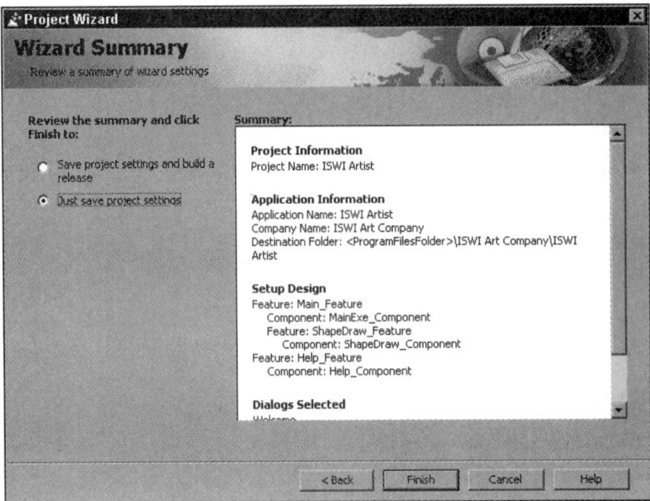

Figure 7-15: The Wizard Summary dialog of the Project Wizard

Completing the Installation Project in the IDE

You have generated the initial installation project using the Project Wizard. To finish this project off you need to go into the IDE and finalize a number of settings. You will work down through all the views in the IDE making entries in each of the property pages.

The Project view

In the Project view you need to set a number of properties that configure the overall project and the installation package. Let's start with the Project Properties page.

PROJECT PROPERTIES

For the Author Name property enter the name of the setup developer creating the setup package; in the Comments property enter a general string that identifies the general purpose of the setup project. You do not have to do anything with the Setup Languages property because you have already identified in the Project Wizard that the setup language is to be English. Table 7-2 provides a description of the three properties that can be set for the project. The picture following Table 7-2 shows these three properties in the ISWI IDE.

TABLE 7-2 PROJECT PROPERTIES IN THE PROJECT VIEW

Property	Value	Discussion
Setup Author Name	Bob Baker	Saved in the project file only; does not make its way into the MSI package.
Setup Languages	English (United States)	In the international editions of ISWI you will be able to select additional languages. For each language selected a string table is generated under the String Table Editor.
Authoring Comments	This project demonstrates the creation of an MSI installation package using both the Project Wizard and the IDE.	Saved in the project file only; does not make its way into the MSI package.

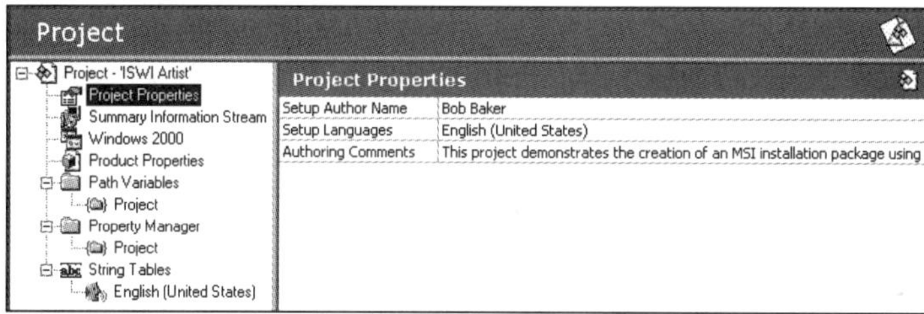

SUMMARY INFORMATION STREAM PROPERTIES

Moving on to the Summary Information Stream properties, you need to enter values for some of the properties that were not covered by the Project Wizard input. You need to modify the entries as shown in Table 7-3. The properties that you enter here are used to create the Summary Information Stream in the Windows Installer package when you build your project. The figure following Table 7-3 shows the Summary Information Stream properties as they appear in the ISWI IDE.

TABLE 7-3 SUMMARY INFORMATION STREAM PROPERTIES IN THE PROJECT VIEW

Property	Value	Discussion
Title	Installation Database for ISWI Artist	Describes the type of package being created. Other types of packages would be merge modules, transforms, and patches.
Subject	ISWI Artist	Provides to Windows Explorer the name of the product that will be installed with the MSI package. This is not the same as the ProductName property in the Property table.
Author	ISWI Art Company	Provides to a file browser the name of the company that created the MSI package. This is not the same as the Manufacturer property in the Property table.
Keywords	Installer;MSI; Database	Windows Explorer can be used to perform a search for files containing the keywords that are specified here.
Package Code	{051F5172-1586-11D4-823A-204C4F4F5020}	The unique identifier for the package; it must be different for every package created. Stored in the Revision Number property of the Summary Information Stream.
Template Summary		Defines both the CPU and the language supported by the MSI package. Since you have not entered any value here ISWI will provide a default string of Intel;1033, which means that the package is for an Intel processor and the supported language is English.
Comment	Contains the logic and data required to install ISWI Artist.	This string, displayable in a file browser, should convey the general purpose of the MSI package. By convention it reads "This installer database contains the logic and data required to install *<product name>*."

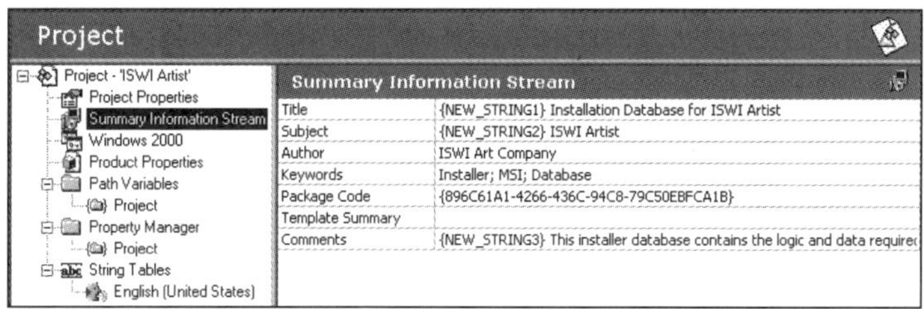

When you enter strings in the Summary Information Stream properties, you will see that ISWI adds a default string ID in the form of {NEW_STRING1}. This will happen every time you enter a string that the end user can see during the installation of the product. These strings are localized when you develop installations in other languages. String IDs enable you to create localized installations. One of the things you will do before completing this project is change these default string IDs into something more readable.

WINDOWS 2000 PROPERTIES

In Windows 2000 there is a much more robust Add/Remove Programs applet than you have seen in Windows NT 4.0 and Windows 9*x*. The properties that you enter here are displayed in this new Windows 2000 feature. When you used the Project Wizard, you already entered two of these properties, but you have to make other entries directly in the IDE. All the properties you need to set in the Windows 2000 property page are described in Table 7-4. The figure following this table shows the properties as they appear in the ISWI IDE.

TABLE 7-4 WINDOWS 2000 PROPERTIES IN THE PROJECT VIEW

Property	Value	Discussion
Display Icon	*<ArtistSources>*\ISWIArtist.ico	The location of the icon that will be shown beside the product name in the Add/Remove Programs applet in Windows 2000. This must be an icon and not a file from which an icon is to be extracted. This sets the ARPPRODUCTICON property in the Property table, which is a foreign key into the Icon table into which this icon is streamed.

Continued

TABLE 7-4 WINDOWS 2000 PROPERTIES IN THE PROJECT VIEW *(Continued)*

Property	Value	Discussion
Disable Change Button	No	Disables the Change button in the Add/Remove Programs applet in Windows 2000 if set to Yes. When set to Yes, it sets the ARPNOMODIFY property in the Property table to a value of 1.
Disable Remove Button	No	Disables the Remove button in the Add/Remove Programs applet in Windows 2000 if set to Yes. When set to Yes, it sets the ARPNOREMOVE property in the Property table to a value of 1.
Disable Repair Button	No	Hides the Repair button in the Add/Remove Programs applet in Windows 2000 if set to Yes. You can find this button in the Support Info dialog. When set to Yes, it sets the ARPNOREPAIR property in the Property table to a value of 1.
Publisher	ISWI Art Company	Sets the value of the Manufacturer property in the Property table.
Publisher/Product URL	`http://www.installshield.com`	Sets the value of the ARPURLINFOABOUT property in the Property table.
Product Version	1.00.0000	Sets the value of the ProductVersion property in the Property table.
Support Contact	Bob Baker	Sets the value of the ARPCONTACT property in the Property table.
Support URL	`http://www.installshield.com`	Sets the value of the ARPHELPLINK property in the Property table.
Support Phone Number	847-619-7017	Sets the value of the ARPHELPTELEPHONE property in the Property table.

Property	Value	Discussion
Read Me		Sets the value of the ARPREADME property in the Property table. This information is displayed in the Support Info dialog. If the readme file is being installed with the product and you want to show the location of this file, you need to use a custom action to set this property. ISWI provides a custom action for this purpose that we will discuss in Chapter 11. No value is entered here for the ISWI Artist application since the help file is triggered from within the product.
Product Update URL	`http://www.installshield.com`	Sets the value of the ARPURLUPDATEINFO property in the Property table. Here users can find update information about the product.
Comments	All problems with the ISWI Artist application should be e-mailed to Bob Baker at `robertb@installshield.com`.	Sets the value of the ARPCOMMENTS property in the Property table. These comments are shown in the Support Info dialog of the Add/Remove Programs applet.

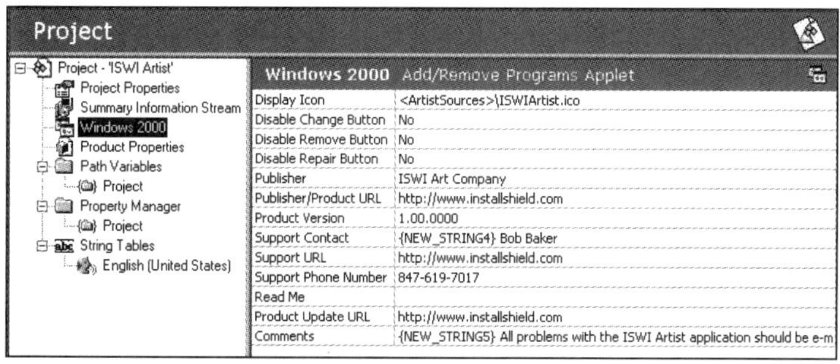

Except for the Change and Remove buttons all information in the Windows 2000 Add/Remove Programs applet is shown in the Support Info dialog box.

PRODUCT PROPERTIES

The Project Wizard has created all the necessary entries on the Product Properties page, but you do not want to use the Product Code and the Upgrade Code properties that have been created for you. If you have already created an installation for ISWI Artist using the steps outlined in chapters 4 and 5, you need to use the Product Code and Upgrade Code you used in that installation package. Table 7-5 shows the correct Product Code and Upgrade Code values and also describes the other product properties.

TABLE 7-5 PRODUCT PROPERTIES IN THE PROJECT VIEW

Property	Value	Discussion
Product Name	ISWI Artist	Sets the value of the ProductName property in the Property table.
Product Version	1.00.0000	Sets the value of the ProductVersion is property in the Property table. This the same value that was set in the Windows 2000 property sheet described in Table 7-4.
Product Type	Internet Application	Not used at this time. Leave it at the value provided by default by ISWI.
Product Code	{EA6F96C0-11D3-8196-204C4F4F5020}	Sets the value of the ProductCode property in the Property table. You to use the same value you used in want Chapter 4, so do not use the value that ISWI generated for you when you created the project using the Project Wizard.
Upgrade Code	{EA6F96C1-11D3-8196-204C4F4F5020}	Sets the value of the UpgradeCode property in the Property table. You want to use the same value you used in Chapter 4, so do not use the value that ISWI generated for you when you created the project using the Project Wizard.

Property	Value	Discussion
Install Condition	0 conditions(s)	If you want to specify any conditions for the LaunchCondition table, enter them here. Chapter 8 discusses launch conditions.
Destination Folder	*<ProgramFilesFolder>* \ISWI Art Company\ ISWI Artist	Sets the value for the INSTALLDIR variable.This is where the application will be installed if the end user does not specifically change the location in the Custom Setup dialog box in the Installation wizard.

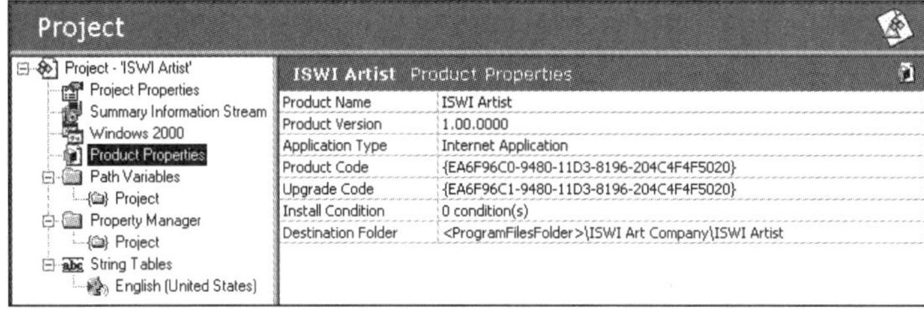

PATH VARIABLES

Path variables enable you to find the source files for creating your build without having to use hard-coded paths. You can then change the location of the source files on your build system and just modify the value of your path variable and the build will still be able to locate the files it needs to make the build. This is much more convenient than having to go and reset the build location of each file in your setup project. Path variables are also useful if we want to move the project to a different machine and build the project just by changing the value of the path variable instead of changing the source location of each file in the project.

Every project you create has six predefined path variables that are set based on the configuration of the build machine on which ISWI is installed. The values of these predefined path variables cannot be altered. You can create and modify additional path variables as necessary. When creating the initial project using the Project Wizard, you were asked to define a path variable when we first added a file to a component. Thereafter, all files added from the same location used this same path variable. The path variable you created when running the Project Wizard appears in the Path Variable property page and you can edit it as required. Table 7-6 describes the predefined path variables that come with each project you create.

TABLE 7-6 PREDEFINED PATH VARIABLE PROPERTIES IN THE PROJECT VIEW

Predefined Path Variable	Description
ProgramFilesFolder	The location of the Program Files folder on the build machine
WindowsFolder	The location of the Windows folder on the build machine
SystemFolder	The location of the System32 folder on the build machine
CommonFilesFolder	The location of the Common Files folder on the build machine
ISProjectFolder	The location of the folder on the build machine where the current project can be found
ISProductFolder	The location of the folder on the build machine where ISWI is installed

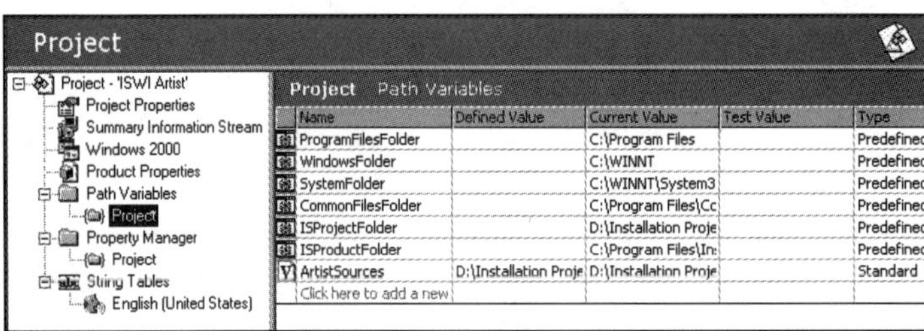

You can create path variables of three different types: Standard, Environment, and Registry. Selecting one of the three types in the Type column of the Path Variables property page sets the type of the path variable. This column is the one farthest to the right in the property page. When you were adding files to the ISWI Artist components, you were presented with the Path Variable Recommendation dialog shown in Figure 7-10. The ArtistSources path variable you created in this dialog shows up as a Standard path variable in the Path Variables property sheet.

STANDARD PATH VARIABLES You can use the Predefined path variables to construct Standard path variables. To do this, enclose the Predefined path variable in angle brackets (<>) and use it as the first part of the value definition for the path variable. For example, if you wanted to move the source files for the ISWI Artist application into the directory where the project file is found you would create the following definition for the ArtistSources path variable:

```
<ISProjectFolder>\Setup Sources\ISWI Artist
```

In the Current Value column you would see the value of the absolute path to where the source files are on the build machine.

ENVIRONMENT VARIABLE-BASED PATH VARIABLES To create a path variable of the Environment type you first need to create the environment variable using the System applet in the Control Panel. In Windows 2000 the Environment Variables dialog is launched from the Advanced tab of this applet. After you have created the environment variable, enter the name of the path variable in the Name column and the name of the environment variable in the Defined Value column. In the Type column, set the type to Environment. When entering the name of the environment variable in the Defined Value column, do not enclose this name in angle brackets. Path variables of the Environment type can be useful when you're performing builds on different machines on different nights and the source files are in a different location depending on the machine. You can use a batch file to set the value of the environment variable to depend on the machine that is being used.

REGISTRY-BASED PATH VARIABLES You can also define a registry key where the location of the source files for an application is specified. The first step in creating the Registry type of path variable is to create a key in the registry. The best place to do this is under the HKEY_LOCAL_MACHINE \SOFTWARE key, even though you can use the HKEY_CURRENT_USER\SOFTWARE key as well. After creating the key, either specify the location for the source files as the data for the default Value Name of the key or create a specific Value Name and specify the location of the source files as the Value Data for this Value Name. How you construct the registry key and associated data determines how you will enter the information in the Defined Value column in the Path Variables property sheet.

For example, assume there are the following entries in the registry:

```
[HKEY_LOCAL_MACHINE\SOFTWARE\Sources]
@="D:\\Installation Projects\\Setup Sources\\ISWI Artist"
"Sources"="C:\\Installation Projects\\Setup Sources\\ISWI Artist"
```

If you set the type of your ArtistSources path variable to be Registry and enter HKEY_LOCAL_MACHINE\SOFTWARE\Sources in the Defined Value column of the Path Variable property sheet, the Current Value of the ArtistSources path variable will be set as follows:

```
D:\Installation Projects\Setup Sources\ISWI Artist.
```

This becomes the definition of the ArtistSources path variable, because the last item of the entry you made in the Defined Value column is the name of a key; therefore the Current Value for the path variable is set to the default value for that key.

If instead you enter HKEY_LOCAL_MACHINE\SOFTWARE\Sources\Sources in the Defined Value column of the Path Variable property sheet, the ArtistSources path variable is set to

```
HKEY_LOCAL_MACHINE\SOFTWARE\Sources\Sources.
```

This is because the last item you made in the Defined Value column is a Value Name; therefore the Current Value shown in the path variable property sheet for the ArtistSources path variable becomes the Value Data of that Value Name.

When entering path locations in the registry, do not use quotes even if you are specifying a long path name.

TEST VALUES For any particular build you can override the location specified by the environment variable or the registry entry by setting a test value in the Test Value column. The value you enter in this column needs to be a hard-coded path to a location that contains a copy of the source files you used to make the build. You can set the test value of a path variable prior to setting either the environment or registry values for a path variable.

Even though you can enter a location in the Test Value column for a Standard path variable, test values will only work for path variables of the Environment and Registry types.

CONVERTING SOURCE PATHS TO PATH VARIABLES If you decide to use absolute paths for some or all of the files in our project, you can later convert them all to path variables with the Convert Source Paths Wizard, which is launched from the Tools pulldown menu. This wizard will scan the project file and find all locations where an absolute path is being used to access a source file. When it finds such a location, it recommends the name of a path variable you can use, but also enables you to change this name if you wish. Once you have either accepted the recommendations or made your own path variable names the Convert Source Paths Wizard re-links all source files using these path variables.

PROPERTY MANAGER

The Property Manager is the feature that enables you to modify or add new properties that will be built into the Property table in the MSI database. The Property Manager and the properties included by default with a new project are shown in Figure 7-16.

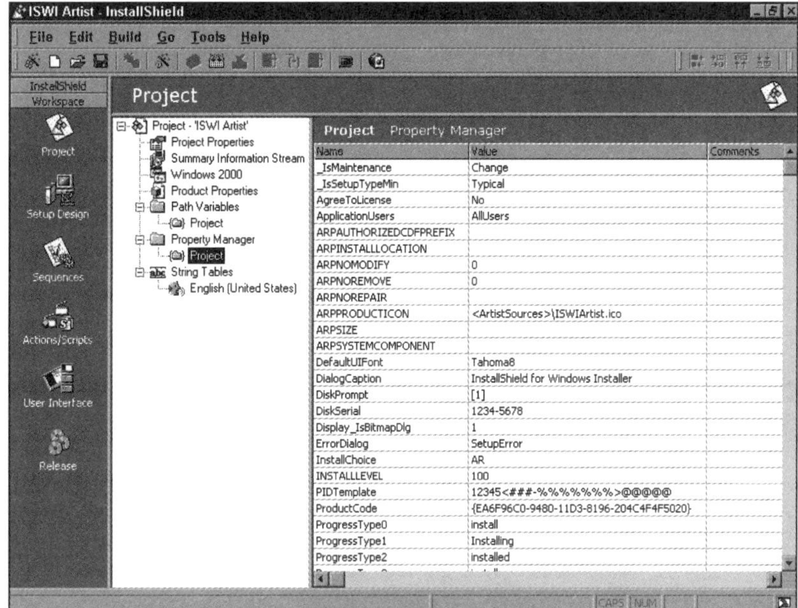

Figure 7-16: The Property Manager in the Project view

You need to do one thing in the Property Manager: delete the ARPNOREPAIR property value. This will prevent this property from being built into the Property table. You should do this to make sure that the Repair button is enabled in the Windows 2000 Add/Remove Programs Applet. Just setting this property to 0 will not enable this particular button. Table 7-7 shows all the default properties in the Property Manager. We will eventually discuss each of these properties; for now you need to look at only a few of these properties as they relate to creating the installation for the ISWI Artist application. Table 7-7 includes this discussion.

Table 7-7 THE DEFAULT INSTALLER PROPERTIES IN A NEW PROJECT

Property	Value
_IsMaintenance	Change
_IsSetupTypeMin	Typical
AgreeToLicense	No
ApplicationUsers	AllUsers
ARPAUTHORIZEDCDFPREFIX	

Continued

Property	Value
ARPINSTALLLOCATION	
ARPNOMODIFY	0
ARPNOREMOVE	0
ARPNOREPAIR	
ARPPRODUCTICON	*<ArtistSources>*\ISWIArtist.ico
ARPSIZE	
ARPSYSTEMCOMPONENT	
DefaultUIFont	Tahoma8
DialogCaption	InstallShield for Windows Installer
DiskPrompt	[1]
DiskSerial	1234-5678
Display_IsBitmapDlg	1
ErrorDialog	SetupError
InstallChoice	AR
INSTALLLEVEL	100
PIDTemplate	12345<###-%%%%%%%>@@@@@
ProductCode	{EA6F96C0-9480-11D3-8196-204C4F4F5020}
ProgressType0	install
ProgressType1	Installing
ProgressType2	installed
ProgressType3	installs
RebootYesNo	Yes
Registration	No
ReinstallFileVersion	o
ReinstallModeText	omus
ReinstallRepair	r
SetupType	Typical
UpgradeCode	{EA6F96C1-9480-11D3-8196-204C4F4F5020}

The following remarks describe in more detail the entries shown in Table 7-7:

- When you build the MSI database, any property without a defined value (like ARPINSTALLLOCATION) will not be built into the database.
- As I mentioned earlier, you need to delete the ARPNOREPAIR property value so that it will not be built into the Property table.
- The INSTALLLEVEL property defines the global installation level of the MSI package; it is the determining factor by which any particular feature will get installed. Each feature in an application is assigned its own install level and if this value is equal to or less than the value of the INSTALLLEVEL property then that feature will be installed. If the feature install level value is greater than the value of the INSTALLLEVEL property, then that feature will not be installed unless the end user goes to the Custom Setup dialog and selects that feature.
- Note that the changes you made to the Product Code and the Upgrade Code in the Product Properties property page have been reflected in the Property Manager.

Most of the properties shown in the Property Manager relate to the function of the user-interface dialogs; these properties will be covered in Chapter 9. A full description of all these properties is provided in Chapter 8.

STRING TABLES

The last thing you need to deal with in the Project view is the String Tables editor. In the other property pages you have entered a number of strings that are considered localizable into other languages. This means that when you created these strings ISWI assigned them a default string identifier or *string ID*. The function of a string table is to provide a single identifier that can reference different language strings, which is a functionality you need when you want to translate a string into a number of languages. Through one string ID you can reference any of the various translations of a particular string.

When ISWI creates a default string ID, it is in the form of *NEW_STRINGX* where *X* is a sequential number. This default string ID is not very informative; you need to change it so it will give you an idea of where it is being used. You can modify these string IDs in the String Tables editor. Figure 7-17 shows the state of the string table after you have made all the entries in all the other Project view property sheets.

Before you start creating new string IDs you should first develop a standard format. I suggest that you begin every string name with the prefix IWA_ followed by the name of the property page and the name of the property. For example, NEW_STRING1 refers to the Subject property in the Summary Information Stream property page. Using my suggested format the string ID for this particular string would be IWA_SIS_SUBJECT. The renamed default string IDs are shown in Figure 7-18.

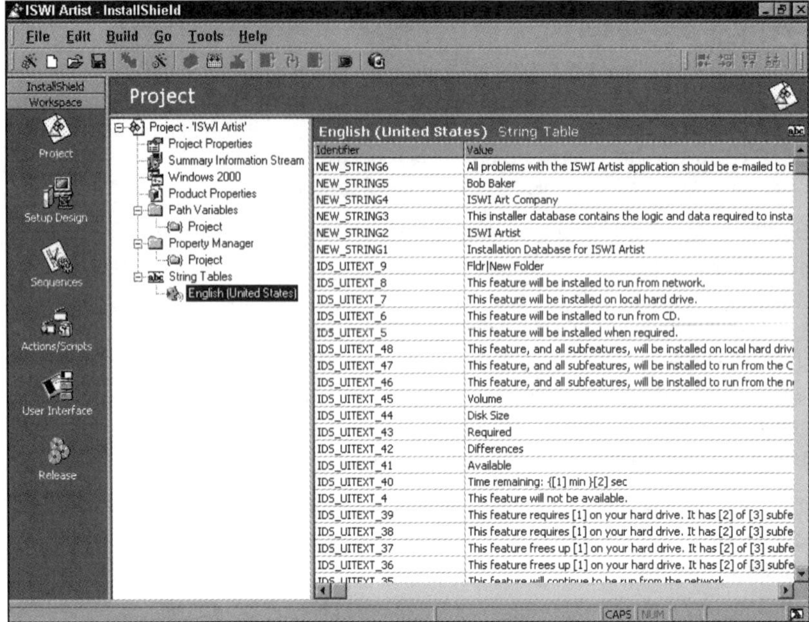

Figure 7-17: The String Tables editor

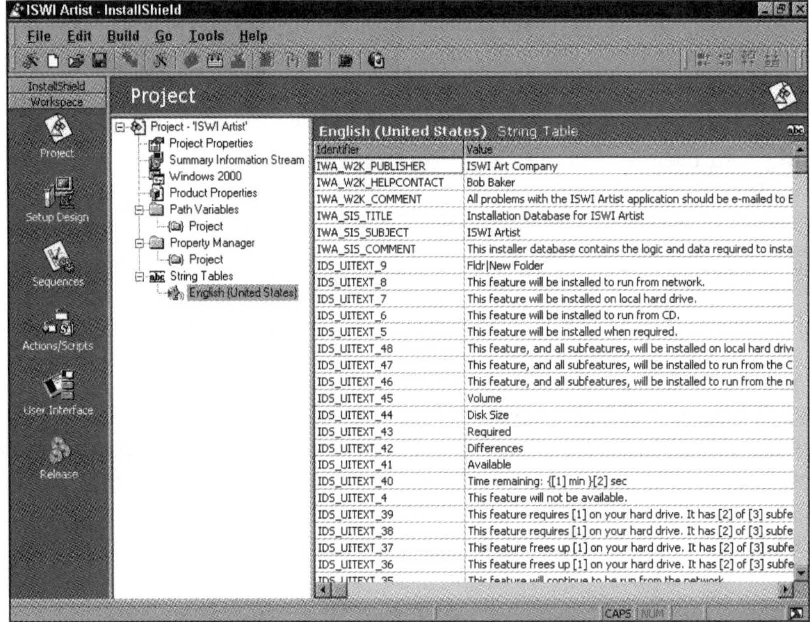

Figure 7-18: The modified default string IDs of the localizable strings in the Project view

It is interesting to note that every time you create or modify a string ID the String Tables editor records the date and time of the action. This information is stored in the Modified column, which is the column farthest to the right in the String Tables editor.

With the String Tables editor you can also create new string IDs and use them later in other views in the IDE. Before we move on to the Setup Design view you should create the strings that you will use for the feature, shortcut, and file type display names and descriptions. You will use these string IDs when finalizing the input for the three features in the ISWI Artist application and the one shortcut that launches the application. Table 7-8 shows the string IDs for the feature, shortcut, and file type display names and descriptions.

TABLE 7-8 STRING IDS FOR FEATURE, SHORTCUT, AND FILE TYPE DISPLAY NAMES AND DESCRIPTIONS

String ID	String
IWA_MAIN_DESC	The main feature of the application; enables the user to draw a wheel with the string "Hello ISWI"
IWA_MAIN_DISP	Text Wheel
IWA_HELP_DESC	Provides the help for the ISWI Artist application
IWA_HELP_DISP	Help Docs
IWA_SHAPEDRAW_DESC	Enables the user of the application to draw the "Hello ISWI" string inside various geometric shapes
IWA_SHAPEDRAW_DISP	Shape Drawing
IWA_SHORTCUT_DISP	ISWI Artist
IWA_SHORTCUT_DESC	Launches the ISWI Artist application.
IWA_FILETYPE_PROGID_DESC	ISWI Artist File
IWA_FILETYPE_OPENCOMMAND_DISP	Open with ISWI Artist

You can create these strings in the string table by clicking the right mouse button and selecting the Create & Set... option on the resulting context menu. This option will give you a dialog box where you can enter both the string ID and the string itself. If you want you can also provide a comment for the string ID that lets you identify more clearly where the string will be used. A string table has a Modified column that is updated with the date and time that a string has been entered and/or modified. The default strings that come with each project do not get an entry in this column. You can sort on this column so that you get all the strings that have been modified or created in one location. After you have finished creating these entries into the string table you can move on to the Setup Design view where you will complete the input for the features and the components that you created in the Project Wizard.

The Setup Design view

In the Setup Design view you will be making the necessary changes and additions to finalize the features and components. As I mentioned in Chapter 6 the Setup Design view is the only major view that has sub-views. For our purposes you need to work only in the global view, where you can see both features and components at the same time.

FINALIZING THE FEATURE PROPERTIES

There are a number of feature properties that you need to either modify or add. These properties relate to the display of a feature in the Custom Setup dialog. The first thing you should do is select the strings you created in the String Tables editor for the display name and description of each of the features. Figure 7-19 shows how to select strings for the Main_Feature feature.

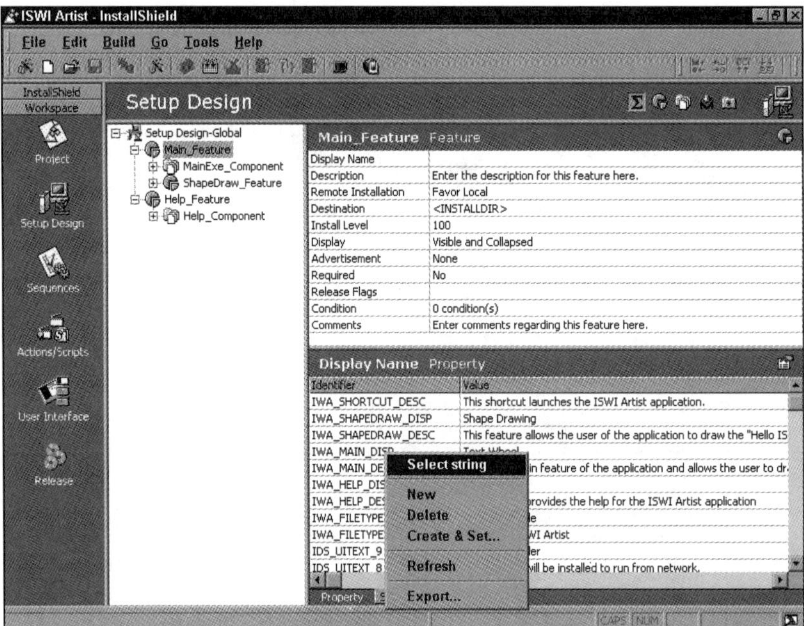

Figure 7-19: Selecting strings with identifiers into a feature property

The first thing to do when selecting a string into a localizable property is to make sure that the string table is visible by clicking on the String Table tab at the bottom of the property page. Once the String Table is visible, first left-click on the property into which you want to select the string and then right-click on the string ID you want to select. You get a context menu of which the top option is Select string. Choosing this option selects the string as the value of the property you first clicked with the left mouse button. Perform this operation for each feature so that both the display name and description are tied to a string with a string ID.

For the Main_Feature feature you need to modify three of the default property values that were set for you by the Project Wizard. You should change the Display property to Visible and Expanded, the Advertisement property to Disallow Advertise, and the Required property to Yes. For the ShapeDraw_Feature and the Help_Feature you need only change the Advertisement property to Disallow Advertise. You should do this because the ISWI Artist application is not designed to perform a feature-level installation on demand. Table 7-9 describes the properties for a feature.

TABLE 7-9 PROPERTY VALUES FOR THE FEATURES

Property	Value	Description
Display Name	Main_Feature: The text associated with the IWA_MAIN_DISP string ID ShapeDraw_Feature: The text associated with the IWA_SHAPEDRAW_DISP string ID Help_Feature: The text associated with the IWA_HELP_DISP string ID	Defines the text string that will be inserted into the Title field of the Feature table. This is the text displayed in the feature selection tree in the Custom Setup dialog.
Description	Main_Feature: The text associated with the IWA_MAIN_DESC string ID ShapeDraw_Feature: The text associated with the IWA_SHAPEDRAW_DESC string ID Help_Feature: The text associated with the IWA_HELP_DESC string ID	Defines the text string that will be inserted into the Description field of the Feature table. This is the string displayed in the Custom Setup dialog when a user highlights the feature in the selection tree.

Continued

TABLE 7-9 PROPERTY VALUES FOR THE FEATURES *(Continued)*

Property	Value	Description
Remote Installation	All Features: Favor Local	Sets one of the bit flags in the Attributes field of the Feature table. This specifically defines the default state of the feature to be installed on the local machine.
Destination	All Features: *<INSTALLDIR>*	The configurable destination property that the end user can change in the Custom Setup dialog. This property sets the value of the Directory_ field in the Feature table.
Install Level	All Features: 100	The feature installation level compared with the INSTALLLEVEL property to determine if the feature is to be installed by default. If this value is greater than the value of the INSTALLLEVEL property, the feature will not be installed unless the end user goes to the Custom Setup dialog and selects to have the feature installed. This property sets the value of the Level field in the Feature table.
Display	Main_Feature: Visible and Expanded This setting has no meaning for the other features, because they do not have sub-features.	Sets the value of the Display field of the Feature table. If the numeric value in this field is odd, the feature tree is initially expanded in the Custom Setup dialog. If the value is even, the feature tree is initially collapsed if it has sub-features.
Advertisement	All Features: Disallow Advertise	Sets another bit-flag in the Attributes field of the Feature table. This prevents the end user from selecting to install the feature on first use.

Property	Value	Description
Required	Main_Feature: Yes ShapeDraw_Feature: No Help_Feature: No	Sets another bit-flag in the Attributes field of the Feature table. If you choose Yes for this property, the end user will not be able to deselect the feature in the Custom Setup dialog.
Release Flags	All Features: Leave null	Not related to the MSI database. This enables you to make builds that only include features with certain release flags. The Release Wizard provides a dialog you can use to insert the release flags that identify the features you want in the build. Of course any feature not identified with a release flag will be included in all builds.
Condition	All Features: Leave as default, which is 0 condition(s)	Enables you to make entries into the Condition table where you can change the value of the Level property in the Feature table to another value based on whether the associated condition evaluates to true or false. When you click in this property, you are provided with a Condition property editor that enables you to define the conditions that will be built into the Condition table.
Comments	All Features: None required	An internal comment that is only inserted into the project file and never built into the MSI database.

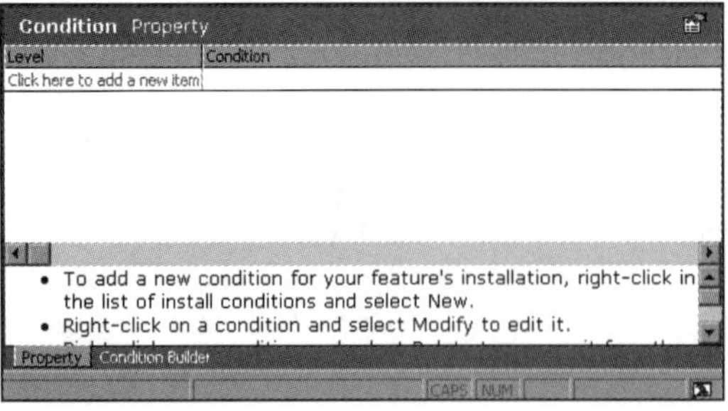

Once you have made these changes you are ready to finalize the component properties.

FINALIZING THE COMPONENT PROPERTIES

You have only one property to change for the ShapeDraw_Component: the Registration property. The ShapeDraaw_Component is a COM DLL and you need to extract the COM information so the build process will populate the proper tables in the Windows Installer package. There are three choices for the Registration property: Use Advanced Settings, Extract at Build, and Self-Register. When you created the ShapeDraw_Component with the Project Wizard, it did not enable you to extract the COM registration information; therefore you have to extract this information at build time. Select the Extract at Build option for the Registration property. You could delete the component and recreate it using the Component Wizard. This wizard would put the COM information in the Advanced Settings; you would then need to select the Use Advanced Settings option for the Registration property.

For a look at the tables that will be created when you extract the COM information at build time you need to look back at Chapter 4 and the section entitled "Working with COM-Related Registry Input." You need only two tables for your COM component: the Class and ProgId tables.

None of the other components is a COM component so you do not have any registration issues with them. Since this is a new application you do not have any legacy installation issues and so we can leave the Shared property with its default value of No. For all the components you want to use the Component Codes you used in the Chapter 4 exercise. This is because the components you are creating here are the same as the components you created in Chapter 4, and they need to have the same Component Codes.

We discuss the creation of components and when Component Codes should change in Chapter 17.

The properties for a component are described in Table 7-10.

TABLE 7-10 PROPERTY VALUES FOR THE COMPONENTS

Property	Value	Description
Destination	All Components: *<INSTALLDIR>* Here you make all the files in each component go to the root install location of the product.	Sets the value of the Directory_ field in the Component table. You can add hard-coded folders to be beneath this location, which the end user can configure through the Custom Setup dialog.
Registration	MainExe_Component: Use Advanced Settings ShapeDraw_Component: Extract at Build Help_Component: Use Advanced Settings	Relates to COM servers and how the server is to be registered at the time of installation. For components that are not COM servers this setting is meaningless. In your installation project you have chosen to have the COM information extracted when you create the Windows Installer package.
Component Code	MainExe_Component: {5774E1F7-939D-11D3-8195-204C4F4F5020} ShapeDraw_Component: {5774E1FA-939D-11D3-8195-204C4F4F5020} Help_Component: {5774E1F8-939D-11D3-8195-204C4F4F5020}	The GUID that makes each component unique. The GUIDs shown here are the ones that you used to create these same components in Chapter 4. These GUIDs are not the same GUIDS you used to define COM class IDs. This property sets the value of the ComponentId field of the Component table.

Continued

TABLE 7-10 PROPERTY VALUES FOR THE COMPONENTS *(Continued)*

Property	Value	Description
Shared	All Components: No	Sets a bit flag in the Attributes field of the Component Table. The purpose of this bit flag is to maintain compatibility with legacy applications that may be installing the same files that make up this component. This compatibility is maintained in the SharedDLL key in the registry that keeps count of all the applications that use the same shared file.
Permanent	All Components: No	Sets another bit flag in the Attributes field of the Component table that determines whether this component will be uninstalled or left on the machine.
Condition	All Components: Leave null	Controls whether a component is installed or not. This property sets the value of the Condition field in the Component table.
Remote Installation	All Components: Favor Local	Sets another bit flag in the Attributes field of the Component table that determines whether this component can be run from source, run locally, or both.
Languages	All Components: Language Independent	Relates to the build environment of ISWI wherein it is possible to filter components based on the language set here. A build can be made to bring in only components identified with a set of languages. Components designated as Language Independent will be included in all builds.

Property	Value	Description
Reevaluate Condition	All Components: No	Sets another bit flag in the Attributes field of the Component table that determines whether the condition in the Condition field of the Component table is reevaluated on a reinstallation of the application. Primarily used when the OS has been upgraded and the component originally installed must be switched out with another component. Setting this property to Yes identifies the component as transitive. If this bit flag is not set, the condition statement will not be reevaluated during the reinstallation.
Never Overwrite	All Components: No	Sets another bit flag in the Attributes field of the Component table that determines whether this component will be overwritten during an installation or a reinstallation.
Source Location	All Components: Leave null	An ISWI-specific property that enables you to configure the media layout to be different from the layout of folders of the installed product. By default the media layout of files will be the same as what you'll see after installing the product.
Comments	All Components: Leave null	An internal comment only inserted into the project file and never built into the MSI database.

Under each component name in the Setup Design view is a tree of icons where you can create additional input related to that particular component. You need to set the properties for several of these property types that relate to the MainExe_Component component.

For the MainExe_Component you need to go to the Shortcut property page and add a display name and description. Since you have already created string IDs for the two strings that you want you can use the same process for selecting the shortcut display name and description that you used for the feature display names and descriptions. Click the Shortcuts icon under the MainExe_Component and expand the tree under the Programs Menu icon. Click the shortcut name you created in the Project Wizard to display the Shortcut property page. Click the Display Name property in this property page to show a String Table tab at the bottom of the screen, and click on this tab to display the string table. Using the same process you used before, left-click the property value into which you want to select the string and then go to the string table, right-click the appropriate string, and choose the Select String option. Also, for the shortcut you need to add *<EmptyFolder>* as the value for the Working Directory property of the shortcut. (You need to include the angle brackets as part of the string that you enter.) You will be creating this particular property in the next section using the Power Editor. The property settings for a shortcut are shown in Table 7-11.

TABLE 7-11 PROPERTY VALUES FOR THE SHORTCUT ASSOCIATED WITH THE MAINEXE_COMPONENT COMPONENT

Property	Value	Discussion
Display Name	The string identified by the IWA_SHORTCUT_DISP string ID	Shown on the Start→Programs menu. This property sets the value of the Name field in the Shortcut table.
Description	The string identified by the IWA_SHORTCUT_DESC string ID	Shown as the comment in the Properties dialog when you right-click the shortcut in Windows Explorer. This property sets the value of the Description field in the Shortcut table.
Arguments	Leave null	Identifies any command line argument that the target of the shortcut is to use when it is launched. This property sets the value of Arguments field of the Shortcut table

Property	Value	Discussion
Target	Leave null	Identifies the target of the shortcut if the shortcut is not to be a standard shortcut (that is, not able to be advertised). In this case you are creating what is called a MSI shortcut so the implementation automatically uses the key file of the component as the target of the shortcut.
Icon File	*<ArtistSources>*\ISWIArtist.exe	Identifies the file from which the icon for the shortcut is to be extracted. The icon is extracted and streamed into the Icon table. This sets the value of the Icon_ field of the Shortcut table. You need a separate icon if a shortcut is to be advertised.
Icon Index	0	Identifies the index of the icon used for the shortcut and sets the value of the IconIndex field in the Shortcut table.
Run	Normal Window	Can be either Normal Window, Maximized Window, or Minimized Window. These define the size of the window when the application is launched. They also set the value of the ShowCmd field in the Shortcut table.
Working Directory	*<EmptyFolder>*	Sets the value of the current directory. This is the location the Open and Save As... dialogs will default to when first launched.

Continued

TABLE 7-11 **PROPERTY VALUES FOR THE SHORTCUT ASSOCIATED WITH THE MAINEXE_COMPONENT COMPONENT** *(Continued)*

Property	Value	Discussion
Hot Key	0	Where the hotkey is defined if one is needed for launching the shortcut. Generally used only to implement accessibility functionality. This property sets the value of the Hotkey field in the Shortcut table.
Comments	Null	For internal use only; only saved in the project file and never built into the MSI database.

The property sheet for the shortcut is shown in Figure 7-20.

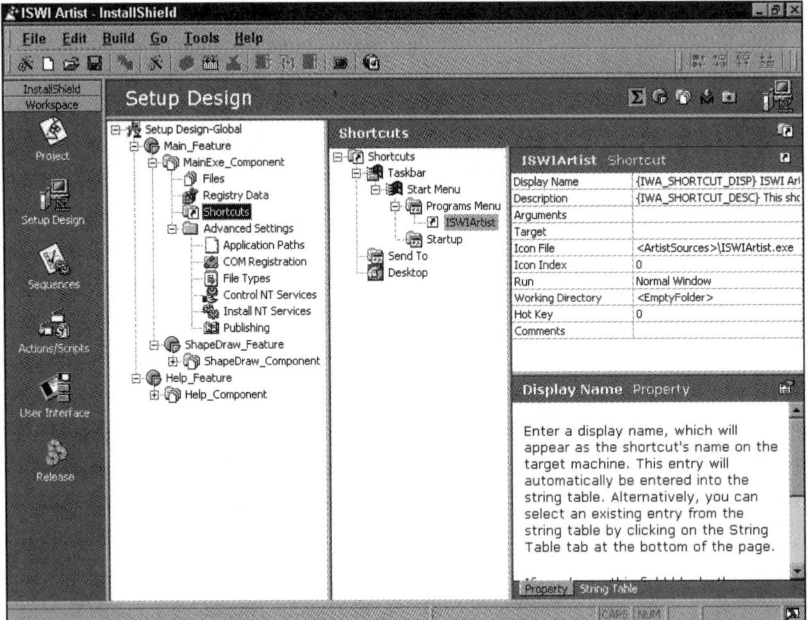

Figure 7-20: The shortcut property sheet for ISWI Artist

For the MainExe_Component you will also want to create a per-application path and a file type for the files created by the ISWI Artist application. You can create both of these by clicking on the Application Paths icon under Advanced Settings for the MainExe_Component. In the property page you need to identify the file for which the application path is to be created. Under the File column in the property page you get a dropdown list of all the files in the component; select the one you want. Of course in your case there is only one file, so select ISWIArtist.exe. In the Application Path column you can enter search paths and use them to find any DLLs that the application needs; you can also select from the dropdown menu any of the standard locations known to the operating system or you can select the destination directory of the application as defined by the INSTALLDIR property. The Application Paths property sheet is shown in Figure 7-21.

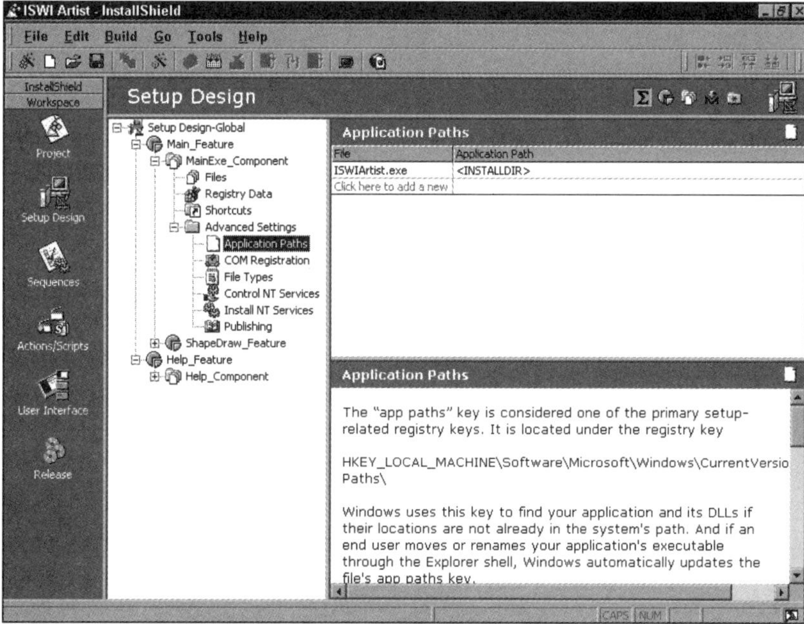

Figure 7-21: The Application Paths property sheet

To create a file association click on the File Types icon under Advanced Settings. The file association will also be created for the component installing ISWIArtist.exe. You want to register the .isa file extension so that it shows up in Windows Explorer with an appropriate icon a description telling you what application created it. Also, when you right-click this type of file you'll want to be able to open the file without first identifying an application to open it. You should also be able to double-click the file and have the application automatically open it.

To make all this happen you need to first create a ProgID and enter all its properties. Then you need to create a file extension and fill in all its properties. When you clicked the File Types icon under Advanced Settings, you saw two icons on the right, one labeled ProgIDs and the other labeled Extensions. To create a new ProgID right-click the icon labeled ProgIDs and select the New ProgID option. Enter the ProgID isafile as the name of this new ProgID. When you click this ProgID you can see that you need to enter five properties in the property sheet. The values of the properties are shown in Table 7-12.

TABLE 7-12 FILE TYPE PROGID PROPERTY VALUES

Property	Value	Description
COM Class	Leave null	Not associated with a COM class.
Description	ISWI Artist File	Describes files with the associated extension that will be displayed in Windows Explorer. You created this string earlier using the String Table editor, so all you have to do is select that string as you did the display names of the features.
Icon File	Path to ISWIArtist.exe in the build environment	The file from which the icon will be extracted. This icon will be displayed in Windows Explorer beside files with the .isa extension.
Icon Index	0	Identifies that the first icon in the Icon File is to be used.
Icon Extraction	Yes	Extracting the icon from the Icon File makes the icon available so that a product that is advertised and not actually installed will still be able to show the proper icon in Windows Explorer beside files with the .isa file extension.

When you've entered these properties for the ProgID, you've completed the first part of creating the registration information for defining a file type. Now let's move on to the Extensions icon: right-click this icon and select the New Extension option. When you create an extension, you do not include the period, so you need to enter isa as the extension and not .isa. When you create an extension the canonical open verb is automatically generated for you under the extension you created. You need to associate the extension itself in the property sheet with the ProgID you have created. Click in the Value field beside the ProgID property name and from the dropdown list of all the ProgIDs you have created in the project select the appropriate ProgID to link the extension and ProgID together. Now you need to select the open verb and enter the three properties associated with this verb. The properties are shown in Table 7-13.

TABLE 7-13 FILE EXTENSION OPEN VERB PROPERTY VALUES

Property	Value	Description
Command Sequence	0	The default value. Defines where on the right-click context menu the command will be displayed. A value of 0 makes the open verb the default command; it will be shown in bold text at the top of the context menu.
Display Name	Open with ISWI Artist	Displayed on the context menu. You created this string earlier using the String Tables editor, so all you have to do is select that string as you did the display names of the features.
Argument	"%1"	The placeholder for the file that will be launched by ISWI Artist when you choose the Open command on the context menu or double-click the file in Windows Explorer.

The three property sheets you have just dealt with are shown in Figure 7-22.

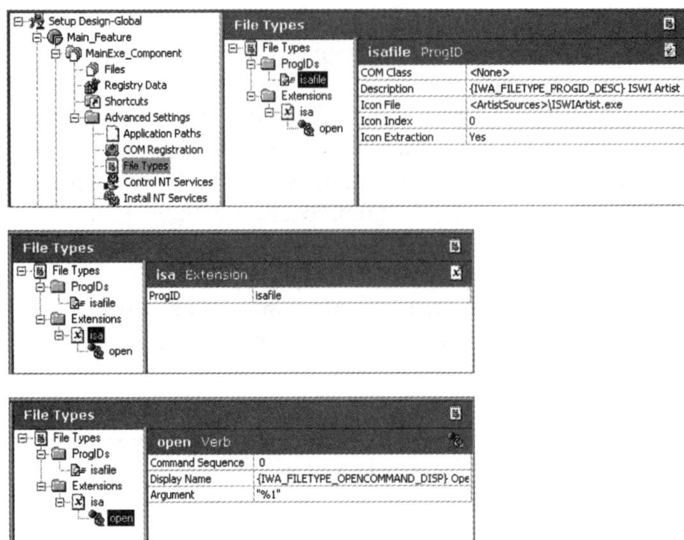

Figure 7-22: The File Types property sheets

Using the Power Editor

One of the things you'll want to do is to create a folder in which to save the data files created with the ISWI Artist application. After you create this empty folder you will make it the working directory of the shortcut. This will cause the Open and Save As... options on the File pulldown menu to default to this location. To create this folder you need to make one entry in each of the Directory, CreateFolder, and RemoveFile tables using the Power Editor. These entries are shown in Table 7-14.

TABLE 7-14 REQUIRED POWER EDITOR ENTRIES

Table	Column Name	Attribute Value
CreateFolder	Directory_	EmptyFolder
	Component_	MainExe_Component
Directory	Directory	EmptyFolder
	Directory_Parent	AppDataFolder
	DefaultDir	Artist~1 | ArtistData
RemoveFile	FileKey	EmptyFolder
	Component_	MainExe_Component
	FileName	
	DirProperty	EmptyFolder
	InstallMode	2

The following remarks describe in more detail the entries that you have made using the Power Editor:

- In the CreateFolder table you enter the foreign key into the Directory table that defines the location and name of the folder to be created. You also identify the component that will create the folder when the component is installed. This is a foreign key into the Component table.
- In the Directory table you identify the folder to be created by entering an appropriate identifier in the Directory column. You then define the location of this folder by specifying the parent and child directories in the second and third columns respectively. These entries will resolve correctly because the Windows Installer sets the location of AppDataFolder at install time. This is a standard location associated with the install location of the operating system. The entry in the DefaultDir column is the name of the folder that will be created; and you have defined it using both a short and a long filename format.
- In the first column of the RemoveFile table you enter a unique identifier. In this example we are using the same identifier we used in the Directory table, but you don't have to use this identifier. The second column is again a foreign key into the Component table indicating the component that, when it is uninstalled, will also remove the data folder if it is empty. Leave the third column null to indicate that it is a folder and not a file to be removed. The fourth column identifies the name of the property to be created that contains the value of the full path to the folder to be removed. This is a property because all entries in the Directory table become properties when the Directory table is resolved at the end of the file costing-related actions. The fifth column just tells the Windows Installer that the folder is to be removed only when the associated component is being removed. You can remove a folder during the installation of a component during both installation and uninstallation.

The entries described above now make the *<EmptyFolder>* name, which you used as the working directory for the shortcut, a valid project property. The location of the *EmptyFolder* entry in the Directory table will be resolved at run time to the location of the AppDataFolder Windows Installer with the sub-directory named ArtistData.

You have now completed all the input required to create a valid installation package for the ISWI Artist application. Next you'll perform the build using the Release Wizard.

Building the MSI Package

To build the project you have just created you need to use the Release Wizard. This is because you did not make a build after you completed the pass through the Project Wizard, but instead just saved the project file. You can access the Release Wizard from the toolbar or from the Build pulldown menu. The first dialog you see is the Welcome dialog, and the next dialog is the Build Label dialog shown in Figure 7-23.

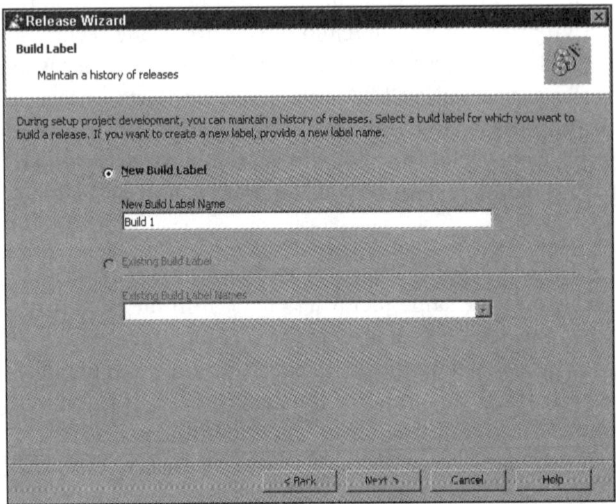

Figure 7-23: The Build Label panel of the Release Wizard

In this panel you define the top level in a two-tier release hierarchy by providing what is called a *build label*. If you had already created previous builds, you would have the option to make a new release of a previous build. Call your first build Build 1 as in Figure 7-23.

The next dialog in the Release Wizard is where you specify a release name that will become the next level in the release hierarchy. As with build labels you can also select a previously created release if any has been generated. The Release Label dialog is shown in Figure 7-24. Call this first release Release-1.

The next dialog in the Release Wizard is where you can filter the particular release you are making and only include features that have been assigned a certain set of release flags. This is one of the feature properties that you can set in the feature property sheet. If you assign release flags to your features, you can provide a comma-delimited list of the flags and the release will only include those features whose flags match what you enter in this dialog. It will also include all the features without a release flag. This dialog is shown in Figure 7-25.

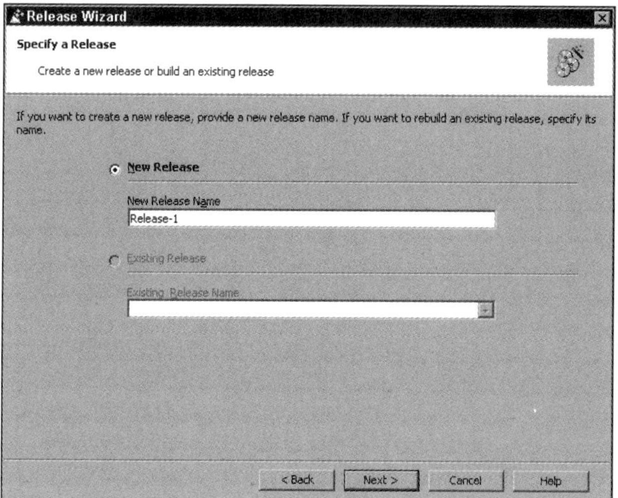

Figure 7-24: The Release Label panel of the Release Wizard

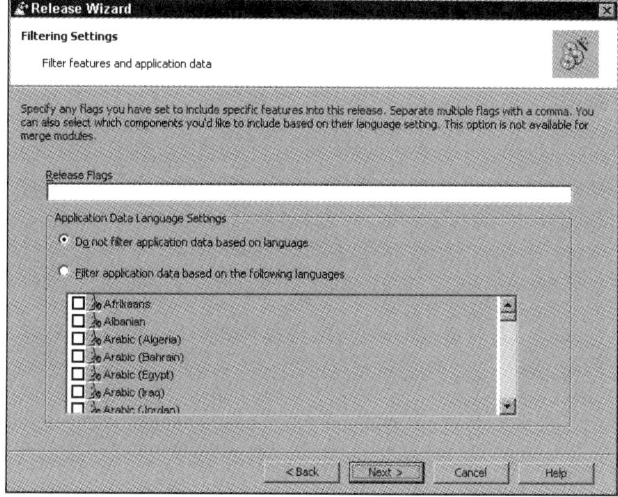

Figure 7-25: The Filtering Settings panel of the Release Wizard

You can also filter components based on language. To designate language-based filtering of components select the second radio button and then check off the languages you want to include in the release. The release will include all components whose language property matches any of the selected languages, and all components designated as language independent.

The next dialog is the Media Type & Patch Optimization dialog where you specify the size of the media image you are going to create. This dialog is shown in Figure 7-26.

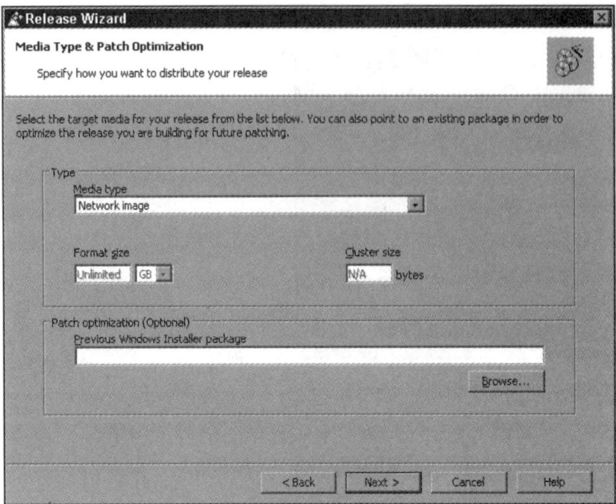

Figure 7-26: The Media Type & Patch Optimization panel of the Release Wizard

In the Media Type dropdown combo box you are given a selection of different sizes of media that you can create. Except for the Network image option the release will be broken into the number of disks required to hold the complete installation image. The Network image option is an unlimited size and therefore would never occupy more than one disk. For the release you are creating, take the default media type of Network image.

We will discuss the use of the Patch Optimization edit field in Chapter 20 where we will also discuss upgrading a product that is already installed.

The next dialog is where you can choose whether you want the source files to be compressed, uncompressed, or some combination of both. When source files are compressed, they are compressed into a Microsoft cabinet (CAB) file structure that the Windows Installer knows how to unpack at installation time. If the media type chosen is a Network image, the compressed files will be stored inside the MSI package. Otherwise the compressed CAB files will be kept separate from the MSI package. This dialog is shown in Figure 7-27.

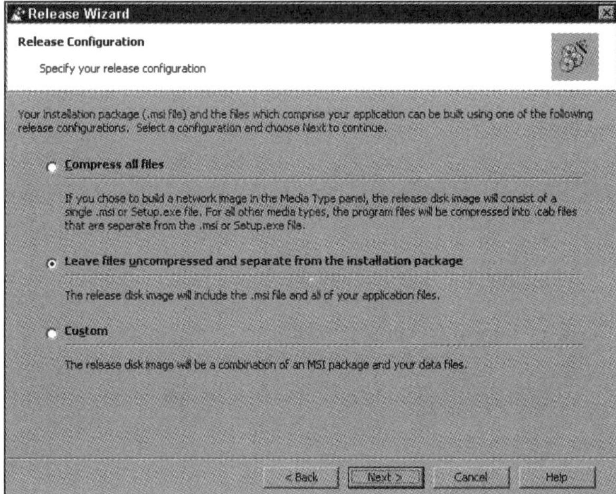

Figure 7-27: The Release Configuration panel of the Release Wizard

For the release you are creating, leave the files uncompressed and separate from the MSI package. This is the default option for this dialog.

The next dialog is the Setup Languages panel. This dialog is used when you want to create a multilingual installation wherein you can give the end user the option to select the language in which the installation user interface is to be displayed. This dialog is shown in Figure 7-28.

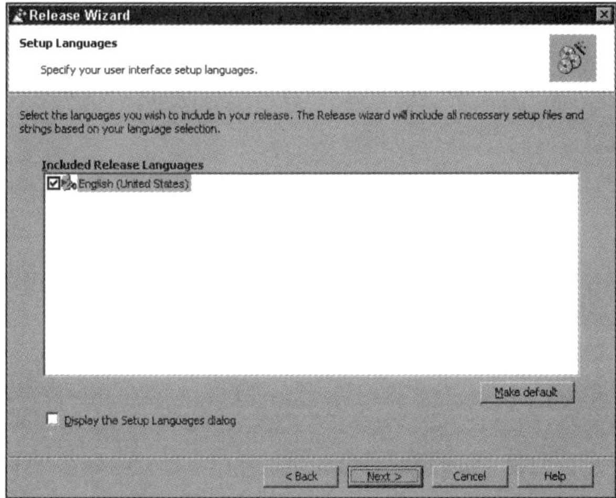

Figure 7-28: The Setup Languages panel of the Release Wizard

Since you are only creating an installation in English you have nothing to select in this dialog.

We will take a close look at how to use this dialog when we discuss creating international installations in Chapter 19.

The next dialog is the Advanced Settings panel and here you have a lot of choices. The first thing you can do is change the release location for this particular build. This does not change the default location but only the location where the present release will be saved. This dialog is shown in Figure 7-29.

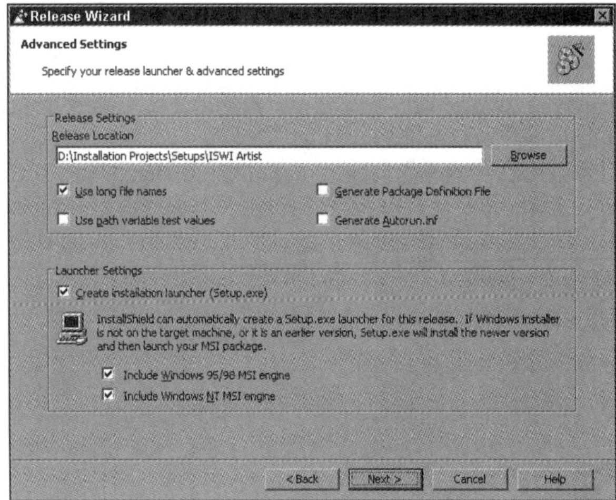

Figure 7-29: The Advanced Settings panel of the Release Wizard

Along with setting the release location for this particular build we have the option of specifying four other items as listed below:

Use long filenames	You can choose to have the media built using long or short filenames. Most of the time you will probably use the default option of long filenames but there may be instances where you want to create an installation that will be installed on a system that does not support long file naming; then you would need to use the short filenames in creating the media image.

Use path variable test values	If you select this option, the Release Wizard will look for the source files in the location specified by the Test Value specified against an Environment or Registry type path variable in the Path Variable property sheet. The location of to where the Test Value points can be found in the Project View and was discussed earlier in this chapter when I talked about the creation of path variables.
Generate Package Definition File (PDF)	If you select this option, the build will include a PDF file you can use when deploying the package using Microsoft's System Management Server (SMS).
Generate Autorun.inf	If you select this option, the build will include a file named Autorun.inf. This file automatically launches the installation of the application from a CD-ROM when the CD-ROM is inserted.

At the bottom of the Advanced Settings dialog you can specify certain launcher settings. Here you can add a Setup.exe file to the build. Setup.exe performs a bootstrapping function in that when it is launched it will in turn launch the MSI installation. If you also choose to have the MSI engines included in the build, Setup.exe will also install the Windows Installer service on any system on which it is not already installed. There are two versions of the Windows Installer engine, one for Windows 95/98 systems and one for Windows NT 4.0 systems. The Windows Installer comes as part of the Windows 2000 operating system.

Take the default settings as presented in Figure 7-29. The final dialog in the Release Wizard is the Summary panel. Here you can review all the selections you made while running the wizard, and if necessary go back and make changes before clicking on the Build pushbutton. This dialog is shown in Figure 7-30.

When you build the project, there is an output window at the bottom of the screen that provides feedback on the progress of the build. After the build completes successfully, install the application to see if everything works. During the installation, if we go to the Custom Setup dialog by choosing the Custom option in the Setup Type dialog you will see something like what is shown in Figure 7-31.

When you look at the selection tree in this dialog, you can see that the tree is expanded, as you wanted it to be. Also, if you click on the Text Wheel feature you can see that this feature cannot be deselected like the other features. You'll also notice that these features can only be installed to the local hard drive. This is because for each component you selected the Favor Local value for the Remote Installation property. When you highlight a feature in the selection tree, the description of that feature appears in the static text field on the right side of the Custom Setup dialog. At the bottom of the Custom Setup dialog you'll see that you can change the installation location of the application. When you make changes here, you are modifying the value of the INSTALLDIR property.

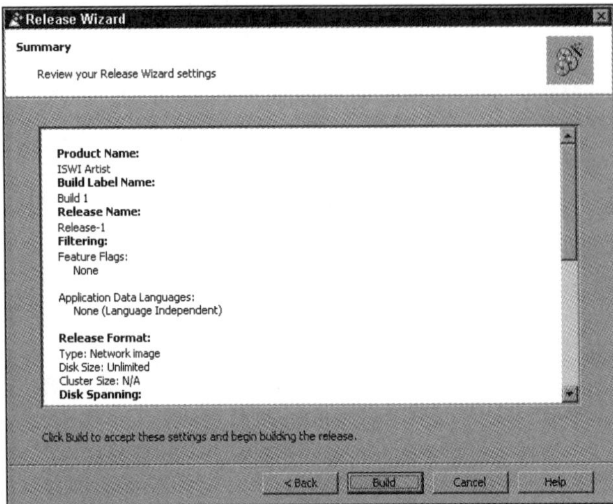

Figure 7-30: The Summary panel of the Release Wizard

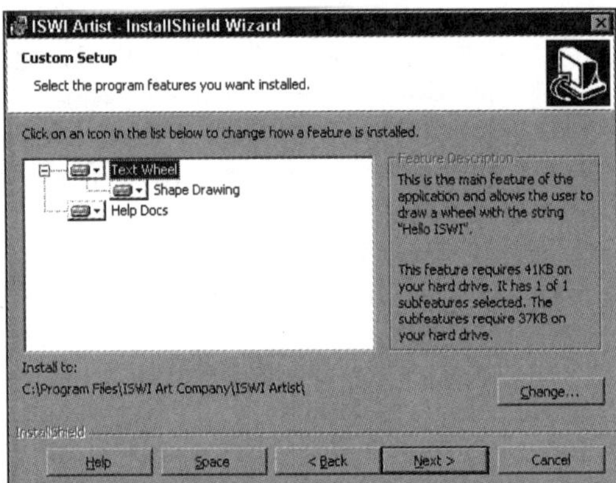

Figure 7-31: The Custom Setup dialog in the Installation Wizard for the ISWI Artist application

Once you complete the installation you should run the application to make sure that it works. Essentially this is the same installation you created in chapters 4 and 5 using the Orca database-editing tool. Finally, check your installation package to see if it validates correctly.

Validating the Installation Package

To validate the MSI package you have just created, run msival2.exe using the following command line:

```
msival2 ISWIArtist.msi  darice.cub  -L validation.log
```

When running this command line, you will get a log file that contains both informational, warning, and error messages based on the internal consistency evaluators authored by Microsoft into the darice.cub validation library. If you wanted to eliminate the informational messages, you would use the following command line:

```
msival2 ISWIArtist.msi  darice.cub  -F -L validation.log
```

The –F switch tells the MsiVal2.exe utility not to display any informational messages. You can also use the –I switch followed by a list of the ICEs that you want run, and only that list of ICEs will be used to validate the specified MSI package.

When you run the validation of the package using the –F switch you have created, you should get a package that shows you have no errors.

Summary

In this chapter you took a fairly extensive look at much of the IDE. In addition, you learned how to kick off a project using the Project Wizard. You also saw that there are many other areas of the ISWI IDE that you still need to investigate. The main thing you learned is the importance of an MSI package-authoring tool that relieves you from having to work directly with the database using a tool such as Orca. You are now ready to move on to manipulating the user interface using the Dialog Editor. This is the subject of the next chapter.

Chapter 8

Controlling the Installation

IN THIS CHAPTER

- The relationship between the old and the new installation technologies
- The built-in actions provided by the Windows Installer
- Sequencing actions
- The properties provided and set by the Windows Installer
- Creating conditions
- Creating custom actions

THE PURPOSE OF this chapter is to show the mechanism by which you can make a Windows Installer–based installation do what you want it to do. In particular we take a look at *properties, actions,* and *sequence tables.*

Basic Concepts

Before the Windows Installer came along, installations were essentially programming implementations wherein the lines of a script were executed in sequential order to perform the activities required of the installation. As in all programming environments calls were made to various functions and the values of global variables were set and read. These functions of course were passed arguments, which carried out the function.

The Windows Installer, as you have seen, is a database technology: on the surface, it would appear to have done away with the need to write scripts. Even though no explicit scripts are now required, except those needed to implement custom actions, the operation of the Windows Installer closely parallels the execution of a script. Table 8-1 shows the relationship between the items that comprise a Windows Installer database and those involved in the legacy approach of implementing an installation via writing a script.

TABLE 8-1 THE RELATIONSHIP BETWEEN A SCRIPT-DRIVEN INSTALLATION AND A WINDOWS INSTALLER DATABASE

Script-Driven Installation	Windows Installer Database
Global variables	A Windows Installer database has *properties*, which are stored in the Property table. Properties are so important that there are two special functions in Windows Installer API that set and get properties from the Property table. These two functions are MsiSetProperty and MsiGetProperty. You will use these two functions a lot when you create custom actions.
Built-in functions	Windows Installer has Standard Actions. Now instead of using built-in functions or calling ComponentMoveData you can use the Standard Action called InstallFiles.
User-defined functions	With any script-based tool you can create your own functions. This enables you to extend the basic functionality of the tool. In the Windows Installer environment you can create Custom Actions, which enable you to extend the functionality of the Windows Installer. Chapters 10 through 16 focus on the many ways to create Custom Actions.
Function arguments	In Windows Installer the arguments to your Standard or Custom Actions come from the data you author into the various database tables that comprise the MSI package.
Procedural execution of lines of script	In a scripting environment you order the progress of an installation by writing your script so that certain tasks are performed before others. With Windows Installer–based installations you order the way an installation executes by placing your Standard and Custom actions in special database tables called *sequence tables*. You also display end-user dialogs by placing them into the appropriate sequence tables. Actions are executed and dialogs displayed according to the sequence number they have been assigned.

As you can see, the old approach and the new approach to creating an installation package have a lot in common. The packages look different on the outside but underneath the operation is almost the same.

In this chapter we are going to concern ourselves with the Sequences view and the Actions/Scripts view in the InstallShield for Windows Installer IDE. In the Actions/Scripts view you can manipulate or create the actions available for use in generating an installation package. Of course, even though you cannot add new standard actions to those already shown in this view you can add comments to these actions. These comments are stored only in the project file and can be considered equivalent to the comment statements in a script that describe the purpose of a function. Standard actions are those that are built in to the Windows Installer and cannot be modified except by the developers of the Windows Installer. Figure 8-1 shows the Actions/ Scripts view.

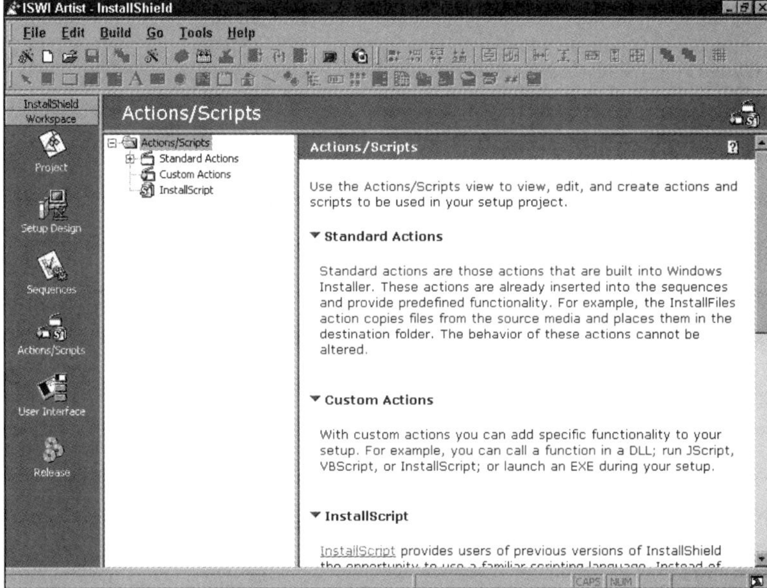

Figure 8-1: The Actions/Scripts view in the ISWI IDE

In this view you can see a tree of three folders, the top folder being Standard Actions. If you expand this folder, you get a list of all the standard actions built into version 1.1 of the Windows Installer. The only thing that you can do with the standard actions in this view is to provide comments. Also in this view there are two folders that pertain to the creation of custom actions.

We take a quick look at custom actions later in this chapter and then dig into them in much more detail in Chapters 10 through 16.

The other view we are concerned with in this chapter is the Sequences view. It is in this view that you can schedule when actions are executed during the installation process. Figure 8-2 shows this view.

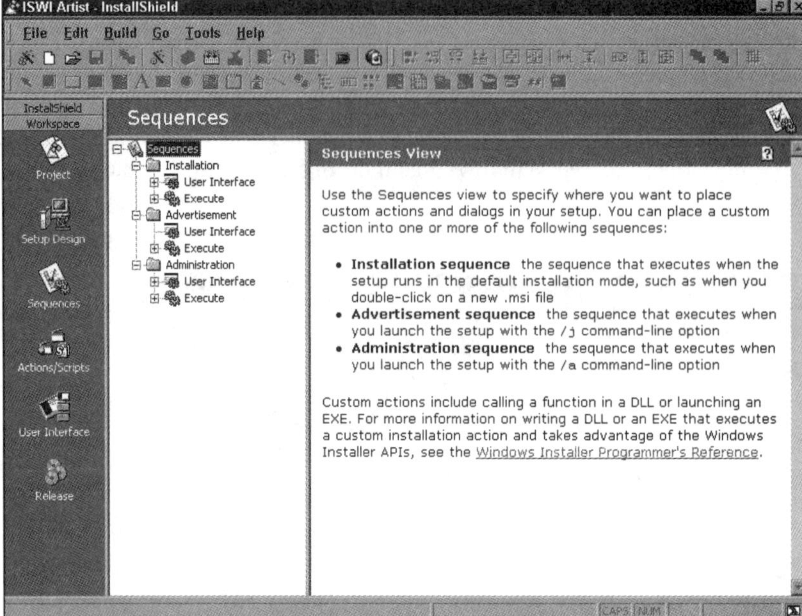

Figure 8-2: The Sequences view in the ISWI IDE

In this view there is a tree of three top-level folders, each of which has two subfolders. The three top-level folders correspond to the three top-level actions that are part of the Windows Installer: the INSTALL, ADVERTISE, and ADMIN top-level actions. You may remember from the discussion in Chapter 3 that each of the three top-level actions has two associated sequence tables. One of these sequence tables is where the user interface of the installation is run and the other sequence table is where the actions that actually change the target system are executed.

If you expand one of these subfolders under the Installation folder, such as the one labeled User Interface, and click one of the actions in this sequence, you get something like what is shown in Figure 8-3.

In the panel to the right of the sequence tree you can see a property sheet that carries the title of the action you have clicked. In this panel you can see that the action has a sequence number; you can place a condition on this standard action as well as create an internal comment statement for it. The sequence number tells the Windows Installer when a particular action is to be executed relative to all the other actions in any particular sequence table.

If you look closely at Figure 8-3, you will see that the User Interface sequence shows more than one style of icon. Some of these icons look like miniature dialog boxes and that is what they actually represent. In fact, in the User Interface sequence you can insert standard actions, custom actions, and dialog boxes. In the Execute sequence you can only insert standard actions and custom actions.

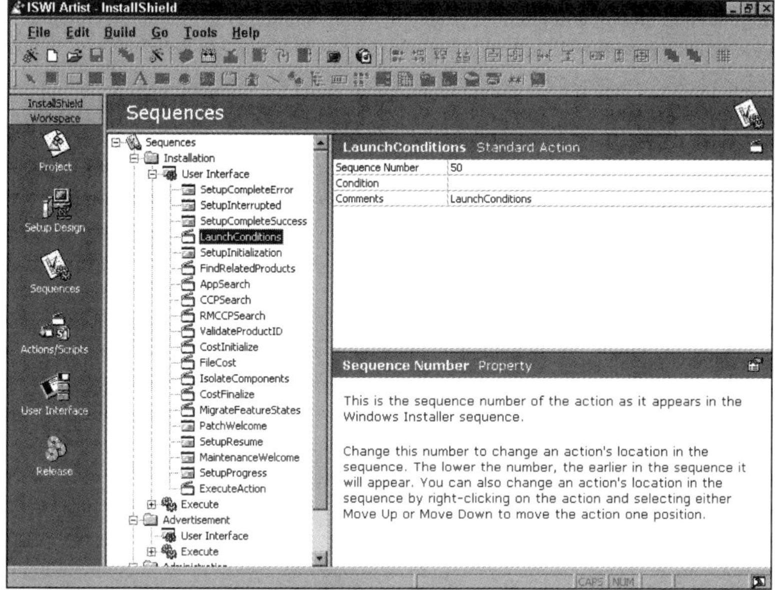

Figure 8-3: The User Interface sequence under the Installation top-level action

Keep in mind that you are dealing with a relational database when you are dealing with the Windows Installer. Because of this you can't enter more than one row with the same primary key. In the case of the sequence tables the name of the action that has been entered into the sequence table is the primary key for these tables. Therefore no action or dialog can ever appear more than once in the same sequence table.

The Built-in Actions

There are numerous standard actions built in to the Windows Installer. These standard actions give you many options when you perform the most common types of installation-related functions. It is possible to group most of the built-in actions into one of six categories. These categories are listed below:

Windows Installer data store — The actions in this category write into the registry information about the Product, Features, and Components. When these actions are executed, components are identified with features and products, and feature states are recorded.

File searching	File searching consists of looking for a particular file on a system. You search for a file primarily to determine whether an installation should proceed or be terminated.
File costing	The purpose of the file costing actions is to determine the total disk space required for an installation. File costing in Windows Installer is a fairly sophisticated operation in that it considers the space required not only for new files being added to the system but also shortcuts, registry entries, and files that are to be overwritten or removed.
File installation	The actions in this category relate to the duplication, movement, and installation of files, the creation of folders not related to installing files, and the removal of files and folders.
Registry and configuration settings	These actions create all registry entries required for the components and files that are installed. They can remove registry entries that an installation no longer needs. They also work with initialization files and environment variables.
Installation configuration	This category of actions covers all actions that do not fit into the previous categories. These actions control reboots of the system, handle qualified components, identify the start and end of the actions to be included into the execution script, and so on.

There are restrictions on where most of these built-in actions can be placed. The restrictions are on where they can be placed relative to other actions. We look more closely at most of these built-in actions in the following sections. (There are a few miscellaneous actions that we do not cover.)

The help file for the Windows Installer that comes with the Windows Installer SDK provides detailed descriptions for all the standard actions that are supported. The Windows Installer SDK can be found on the CD-ROM that comes with this book.

Windows Installer data store

When a product is installed using the Windows Installer service, there are a number of entries that are made in the Registry by the Windows Installer during installation so that the Windows Installer can manage the application. The Windows Installer API functions use many of these entries to perform programmatic actions. We can divide the associated Standard Actions in to three sub-categories according to the various types of information that is placed into the Registry: general product and user data, component information, and product and feature state information. Each of these is discussed in the following subsections.

GENERAL PRODUCT AND USER DATA

There are two standard actions that are of concern here: the RegisterProduct and RegisterUser actions. The main location in the Registry to which these two actions write is in the following key:

```
HKLM\Software\Microsoft\Windows\CurrentVersion\Uninstall\
```

The RegisterProduct action creates a key under this location that uses the ProductCode as the name of the key. Under this key this action writes all the values and data displayed in the Add/Remove Programs applet on Windows 2000. The RegisterProduct action also identifies where the cached MSI package is installed and gives the name the Windows Installer has created for this package. This information is written to the following Registry key:

```
HKLM\Software\Microsoft\Windows\CurrentVersion\Installer\
LocalPackages\
```

Under this key the Windows Installer generates a key using a packed version of the ProductCode. A packed GUID is one from which the surrounding curly braces and the dash separators have been dropped. Then the resulting value is rearranged by the Windows Installer in order to make searching more efficient. The value name is the machine ID or the User SID depending on whether it was a per-machine or a per-user installation, and value data is the path to the cached MSI package.

The RegisterUser action adds the data for the ProductID, RegOwner, and RegCompany value names under the Uninstall key I referred to previously. Both the value names and data are created by this action.

There are no sequence restrictions for either of these actions. However, they should be in the InstallExecuteSequence table and placed near to the end of that sequence, as is the case with any project created in ISWI. These two actions use data from the Property table in order to write the data into the registry.

COMPONENT INFORMATION

In this sub-category we are dealing with three Standard Actions: the ProcessComponents, PublishComponents, and UnpublishComponents actions. The ProcessComponents action provides a reference count for all components that have been installed to either run from source or run locally. This action also identifies the name and location of the key path for each installed component. This information is stored under the following key in the Registry:

```
HKLM\Software\Microsoft\Windows\CurrentVersion\Installer\Components\
```

Under this registry key is a key generated from the packed component codes of every component installed on the machine. The value names created for this registry key are the packed product codes of every product using that component. The data for each of these value names is the definition of the key path for the component. If a value name is comprised of all zeros, then that particular component has been made permanent: the reference count for the component will still be decremented on an uninstallation but the component itself will never be uninstalled.

The PublishComponents and UnpublishComponents actions deal with the Registry entries needed to implement *qualified components.* A qualified component is a method of grouping components with the same functionality into categories. It can be thought of as a method of single-level indirection somewhat similar to a pointer. The information with regard to qualified components is entered under one of two Registry keys, depending on whether the installation is being performed for the current user or for the machine. The registry key for an installation for the current user is as follows:

```
HKCU\Software\Microsoft\Installer\Components\
```

The registry key for an installation being performed for the machine is as follows:

```
HKLM\Software\Classes\Installer\Components\
```

The PublishComponent table provides the information for generating the sub-keys, value names, and data. The sub-keys are the ComponentIds from this table in packed form, as I explained earlier. The value names are the qualifiers associated with this particular ComponentId and the data is something called a *Darwin Descriptor* followed by the information from the AppData column of the PublishComponent table. A Darwin Descriptor is a compressed string comprised of the product code, feature name, and component code. The UnpublishComponents action just removes the described registry entries for all features selected for uninstallation.

There are no sequence restrictions imposed on these actions, but they should be in the InstallExecuteSequence table and located between the InstallInitialize and InstallFinalize actions so that they are included in the execution script created by the Windows Installer. The ProcessComponents action queries the Component table to get the information it needs to write the values to the registry. The PublishComponents and the UnpublishComponents actions query the PublishComponent table to get the information needed to write values to the registry.

PRODUCT AND FEATURE STATE INFORMATION

The actions that we need to investigate relative to the generation of feature and product information are the PublishFeatures, PublishProduct, and UnpublishFeatures actions. The purpose of these actions is to identify the state of the feature or product. Also, for features a mapping of parent feature to sub-feature is provided.

The PublishFeatures action writes the selection state of each feature into the registry in one of two locations, depending on whether the installation is being performed for the current user or for the machine as a whole. If the installation is being performed for the current user, the registry location that is being written is as follows:

```
HKCU\Software\Microsoft\Installer\Features\
```

If the installation is being performed for the machine as a whole, the registry key is as follows:

```
HKLM\Software\Classes\Installer\Features\
```

The sub-keys created under this location are packed Product Codes for all products that have been installed per-user. The value names are the names of all features with a selection state of absent, advertised, local, or run-from-source. The data for each value name is the parent feature of the feature given in the value name. If the feature has no parent, the value data is a null string.

The PublishFeatures action also provides a mapping between the features and components of all features that have been installed. The location of this registry key is as follows:

```
HKLM\software\Microsoft\Windows\CurrentVersion\Installer\Features\
```

The sub-keys under this location are packed Product Codes with features that have been installed either locally or to run from source. The value names are the names of the features, and the data is a concatenated list of compressed Component Codes that are contained in the feature. A compressed Component Code is one in which the GUID is compressed into an unreadable form for the sake of saving space in the registry. At the end of the list of compressed Component Codes are a delimiter and the name of the parent feature of the feature named in the value name. If the feature has no parent, the delimiter and the parent name are omitted.

The PublishProduct action writes the state of a product into the registry in one of two locations. If the product is being installed for the current user, the registry key is as follows:

```
HKCU\Software\Microsoft\Installer\Products\
```

If the product is being installed for the machine as a whole, the registry key where the information is written is as follows:

```
HKLM\Software\Classes\Installer\Products\
```

For each product that has been installed or advertised there will be a sub-key consisting of the packed Product Code. Under this key will be a sub-key called SourceList, and if the product has one or more patches associated with it there will be a Patches sub-key as well.

The values, names, and data associated with each product sub-key identify basic information about the product and its install state. The SourceList sub-key identifies the various locations where the Windows Installer can find the MSI package that installs the product.

Unlike with the other actions we discuss in this section, with these actions you have to follow some sequence restrictions. The PublishFeatures action has to come before the PublishProduct action. The UnpublishFeatures action can be placed anywhere in the sequence. However, since all these actions make changes to the target system they must be in the execute sequence and positioned between the InstallInitialize and the InstallFinalize actions so that they are written into the execution script created by the Windows Installer when the installation is run. As shown in the ISWI Sequences view, the UnpublishFeatures action is placed early in the sequence and the PublishFeatures and PublishProduct actions are placed late in the sequence.

The PublishFeatures action queries the Feature, Component, and FeatureComponents tables to obtain the information for writing values to the registry. The UnpublishFeatures action queries the FeatureComponents table to remove the values written to the registry. The reminder of the information required to perform the removal is found in the registry itself. The PublishProduct action gets all the information it needs from the information written by PublishFeatures action in the registry.

File searching

There are three Standard Actions that pertain to searching for applications that are already installed on the target system. The basic approach for searching for an application is for you to provide a number of signatures that identify the application. If the Windows Installer finds the application, the value of a public property is set with the path to the defined signature. You can use this property in a condition to prevent some action from happening if the property is not set.

You can use the AppSearch action to search for existing versions of products that might be on the system. This action uses the information entered into the AppSearch and Signature tables. In addition, you can use the CompLocator, IniLocator, RegLocator, and DrLocator tables to provide additional information for the search process. There are no restrictions identified in the Windows Installer help on where in the sequence you can place the AppSearch action. However, if you place the AppSearch action after the CostInitialize action then your Windows

Installer package will fail validation. This means that you will want to place this action early in the sequence table.

The other two actions that deal with searching for a file are the CCPSearch and the RMCCPSearch actions. These actions search for qualifying products that will enable you to install the product. You can use these actions when you're shipping a competitive upgrade version of a product and you want to see if the end user possesses the competing product. CCP stands for *compliance checking program* and RMCCP stands for *removable media compliance checking program.*

The CCPSearch action uses the information in the CCPSearch, Signature, CompLocator, RegLocator, IniLocator, and DrLocator tables to conduct its search. You must place this action before the RMCCPSearch action in the sequence table. The RMCCPSearch action uses the information in the CCPSearch, Signature, and DrLocator tables to conduct its search. If these actions are successful, they set a predefined property to 1; you can use this property in condition statements to prevent the installation if the qualifying product is not found.

The CCPSearch action, as with the AppSearch action, needs to be placed prior to the CostInitialize action in order to avoid a failed package validation.

File costing

File costing is the determination of how much space an application will require on the local hard drive. The five Standard Actions described in Table 8-2 implement the file costing activity that takes place during an installation. These actions are shown in the order in which they should be sequenced. (ISWI sequences these actions in this order.)

TABLE 8-2 FILE COSTING ACTIONS

Action	Description	Tables Used
CostInitialize	Initiates the costing activity.	Interfaces with the Feature and Component tables.
FileCost	Conducts an analysis of each file to be installed locally and determines its space requirements. Takes into account files that already exist on the target system.	Queries the File, Component, ReserveCost, DuplicateFile, and MoveFile tables.

Continued

TABLE 8-2 FILE COSTING ACTIONS *(Continued)*

Action	Description	Tables Used
IsolateComponents	Identifies all files to be copied to a private location in addition to a shared location.	Queries the IsolatedComponent table.
CostFinalize	Ends the costing process initiated by the CostInitialize action.	Queries theCondition and Component tables.
InstallValidate	Verifies that all volumes to which a cost has been attributed have enough space for the installation. Also identifies any files to be over-written that are also in use at the time of the installation.	Does not query any table in the database.

File costing is carried out in both the UI sequence and the execute sequence. Costing is performed in the UI sequence based on the default feature selection states built into the installation package. The costing in the execute sequence finalizes the costing based on any changes the end user may have made using the custom setup dialog.

File installation

There are 17 Standard Actions that can be considered related to the actual installation of files on the target system. To discuss these adequately we need to define four different categories of actions based on their specific purpose. The first category consists of those actions that perform the standard actions of copying files, deleting files, creating folders, and so forth. The second category consists of those actions related specifically to the installation and uninstallation of ODBC. The third category consists of those actions that install and control NT Services. The final category is a special action that populates the Import Address Table for imported DLLs. Each of these categories is the subject of one of the following subsections.

STANDARD FILE MANIPULATION

There are ten Standard Actions included in this category, each of which is restricted with regards to where it can be placed in the sequence. These actions can only be in the InstallExecuteSequence table and they have to be between the InstallInitialize and the InstallFinalize actions so that they are written into the execution script created by the Windows Installer. These actions are shown in the Table 8-3 in the relative order in which they must be placed in the sequence table.

TABLE 8-3 STANDARD FILE MANIPULATION ACTIONS

Action	Description	Tables Used
RemoveShortcuts	Handles the removal of an advertised shortcut for a feature that will be uninstalled. Also manages the removal of a non-advertised shortcut where the associated component will be uninstalled.	Queries the Shortcut table.
RemoveDuplicateFiles	Deletes files created using the DuplicateFiles action.	Queries the DuplicateFile table.
RemoveFiles	Removes files installed with the InstallFiles action. Can also be used to remove folders.	Queries the File table and the Component table.
RemoveFolders	Removes empty folders.	Queries the CreateFolder table and the Component table.
CreateFolders	Creates empty folders for components to be installed on the local hard drive.	Queries the CreateFolder table and the Component table.
MoveFiles	Locates files on the target machine and moves or copies those files to a new location. (Files moved or copied with this action are not deleted during an uninstallation.)	Queries the MoveFile table.
InstallFiles	Performs the basic file copy during an installation. Files are only copied if the associated component is to be run locally and not from source.	Queries the File table and the Component table.
PatchFiles	Applies all appropriate patches and also performs the byte-wise patching of files.	Queries the Patch table.
DuplicateFiles	Duplicates files installed with the InstallFiles action.	Queries the DuplicateFile table.
CreateShortcuts	Manages the creation of both standard shortcuts and MSI shortcuts.	Queries the Shortcut table.

The default sequence that you get with a new project in ISWI has the DuplicateFiles action before the PatchFiles action. You need to move the PatchFiles action so that it comes before the DuplicateFiles action. This prevents the duplication of unpatched files.

HANDLING ODBC

There are only two basic actions in the Windows Installer for handling the installation of ODBC. The Windows Installer does nothing with ODBC except turn over the responsibility of the installation and uninstallation to the ODBC Driver Manager. Table 8-4 shows the two actions that work with ODBC.

TABLE 8-4 ODBC-RELATED ACTIONS

Action	Description	Tables Used
RemoveODBC	Removes the data sources, translators, and drivers listed for removal during an installation.	Queries the ODBCDataSource, ODBCTranslator, and ODBCDriver tables.
InstallODBC	Installs the data sources, translators, and drivers listed for removal during an installation.	Queries the ODBCDataSource, ODBCTranslator, and ODBCDriver tables.

There is no sequence restriction on the placement of the RemoveODBC action, but typically it is placed early in the execute sequence after the InstallInitialize action. The InstallODBC action must be placed after the InstallFiles action, because this action does not copy files but only passes on the necessary information to the ODBC Driver Manager.

INSTALLING AND CONTROLLING NT SERVICES

Windows Installer provides four actions for working with NT services. Three of these actions are related to the control of a service and one action actually installs the service. These actions are shown in Table 8-5 in the relative position in which they must be placed in the sequence table. These actions must be in the InstallExecuteSequence table between the InstallInitialize and InstallFinalize actions.

TABLE 8-5 ACTIONS FOR INSTALLING AND CONTROLLING NT SERVICES

Action	Description	Tables Used
StopServices	Stops a service running on the target system.	Queries the ServiceControl table.
DeleteServices	Deletes a service on the target system.	Queries the ServiceControl table.
InstallServices	Registers a service on the system. (It does not actually copy any files to the system.)table.	Queries the ServiceInstall
StartServices	Starts a service installed on the target system.	Queries the ServiceControl table.

Since none of these actions actually transfers files to the target system, you must include one of the file manipulation actions between the DeleteServices and InstallServices actions in the sequence table. It is recommended that you also sequence the StartServices action just before the RegisterUser action.

All of these actions require that the end user be an administrator, that the installation have elevated privileges with permission to control services, or that the installation be a managed application on a Windows 2000 network.

IMAGE BINDING

The action that implements image binding is the BindImage action. This action speeds up the loading of an executable image when it depends on a number of other DLLs. Binding an image consists of computing the virtual address of each imported function, which is then saved in the importing image's Import Address Table (IAT). As a result, the image is loaded much faster than it would otherwise be, particularly if it uses many DLLs, because the system loader does not have to compute the address of each of the imported functions.

For more information on this subject you are referred to descriptions of the BindImage, BindImageEx, and StatusRoutine APIs that are described in the MSDN Library.

The BindImage action must come after the InstallFiles action. This action queries the BindImage table.

Registry and configuration settings

The Standard Actions that fall into this category create and remove registry entries, create and remove entries in initialization files, and set and delete environment variables. There are 22 actions in this category. In order to explain these actions, I create a number of subcategories that relate specifically to implementation: creating basic COM information, creating COM+ information, registering type libraries, implementing self-registration of COM modules, registering fonts, creating standard registry entries, creating entries in .ini files, and creating or modifying environment variables. Each of these subcategories is the subject of one of the following subsections.

COM REGISTRATION

Eight Standard Actions work to generate or remove COM information in the registry. You must use these actions in a specific relative sequence, shown in Table 8-6. You must place all of these actions in the InstallExecuteSequence table between the InstallInitialize and InstallFinalize actions.

TABLE 8-6 BASIC COM REGISTRATION ACTIONS

Action	Description	Tables Used
UnregisterClassInfo	Removes COM class information from the registry.	Queries the Class table.
UnregisterExtensionInfo	Removes extension-related information from the registry.	Queries the Extension table.
UnregisterProgIdInfo	Removes ProgId information from the registry.	Queries the ProgId, Extension, and Class tables.
UnregisterMIMEInfo	Removes MIME-related information from the registry.	Queries the MIME table.
RegisterClassInfo	Removes COM class information from the registry.	Queries the Class table.
RegisterExtensionInfo	Removes extension-related information from the registry.	Queries the Extension table.

Action	Description	Tables Used
RegisterProgIdInfo	Registers COM class information in the registry.	Queries the ProgId table.
RegisterMIMEInfo	Registers COM class information in the registry.	Queries the MIME table.

In addition to the relative positioning of these actions, there are a few other sequence restrictions that you should keep in mind. The RemoveRegistryValues action must be placed before any of the actions that unregister information from the registry. As you might expect, all the actions that add information to the registry must come after the InstallFiles action.

COM+ REGISTRATION

There are two Standard Actions for managing the registration of COM+ applications. As with all the remaining actions that we discuss in this chapter this is a pair of actions, one for removing registration information from and one for adding registration information to the registry. Table 8-7 shows these actions in the order in which they are to appear in the InstallExecuteSequence table. As with all the other actions that make changes to the system, you must place these actions between the InstallInitialize and InstallFinalize actions.

TABLE 8-7 COM+ REGISTRATION ACTIONS

Action	Description	Tables Used
UnregisterComPlus	Removes all COM+ .information from the registry	Queries the Complus table.
RegisterComPlus	Adds COM+ information to the registry.	Queries the Complus table.

The RegisterComPlus action must come after the InstallFiles action.

TYPE LIBRARY REGISTRATION

These two actions remove and register type libraries. Table 8-8 shows them in the order in which they are to appear in the InstallExecuteSequence table. As with all the other actions that make changes to the system, you must place these actions between the InstallInitialize and InstallFinalize actions.

TABLE 8-8 TYPE LIBRARY REGISTRATION ACTIONS

Action	Description	Tables Used
UnregisterTypeLibraries	Removes the registration for type libraries from the registry.	Queries the TypeLib table.
RegisterTypeLibraries	Adds the registration for type libraries to the registry.	Queries the TypeLib table.

The UnregisterTypeLibraries action must be placed before the RemoveFiles action and the RegisterTypeLibraries action must be placed after the InstallFiles action.

SELF-REGISTRATION OF COM SERVERS

These two actions unregister and register self-registering COM servers. Table 8-9 shows them in the order in which they are to appear in the InstallExecuteSequence table. As with all the other actions that make changes to the system you must place these actions between the InstallInitialize and InstallFinalize actions.

TABLE 8-9 SELF-REGISTRATION ACTIONS

Action	Description	Tables Used
SelfUnregModules	Unregisters all self-registering modules that are scheduled for uninstallation.	Queries the SelfReg table.
SelfRegModules	Registers all self-registering modules that have been installed.	Queries the SelfReg table.

The SelfUnregModules action must be placed before the RemoveFiles action and the SelfRegModules action must be placed after the InstallFiles action. Because the self-registration of COM servers is a black box to the Windows Installer it is not recommended that these tables be used. The COM registration information needs to be placed in the tables as described earlier. Using self-registration breaks the roll-back functionality of the Windows Installer and tends to reduce other Windows Installer capabilities such as advertisement.

FONT REGISTRATION

These two actions unregister and register font files. Table 8-10 shows them in the order in which they are to appear in the InstallExecuteSequence table. As with all the other actions that make changes to the system, you must place these actions between the InstallInitialize and InstallFinalize actions.

TABLE 8-10 FONT REGISTRATION ACTIONS

Action	Description	Tables Used
UnregisterFonts	Removes registration information about installed fonts from the registry.	Queries the Font table.
RegisterFonts	Adds registration information about installed fonts to the registry.	Queries the Font table.

The UnregisterFonts action must be placed before the RemoveFiles action and the RegisterFonts action must be placed after the InstallFiles action.

BASIC REGISTRY MANIPULATION

These two actions unregister and register normal registry entries. Table 8-11 shows them in the order in which they are to appear in the InstallExecuteSequence table. As with all the other actions that make changes to the system, you must place these actions between the InstallInitialize and InstallFinalize actions.

TABLE 8-11 BASIC REGISTRY MANIPULATION ACTIONS

Action	Description	Tables Used
RemoveRegistryValues	Removes an application's specific information from the registry	Queries the Registry table.
WriteRegistryValues	Adds an application's specific information to the registry	Queries the Registry table.

The RemoveRegistryValues action must be placed before the UnregisterProgIdInfo and UnregisterMIMEInfo actions.

WORKING WITH INITIALIZATION FILES

These two actions remove information from and add information to initialization files. Table 8-12 shows them in the order in which they are to appear in the Install ExecuteSequence table. As with all the other actions that make changes to the system, you must place these actions between the InstallInitialize and InstallFinalize actions.

TABLE 8-12 INITIALIZATION FILE ACTIONS

Action	Description	Tables Used
RemoveIniValues	Removes information in an initialization file during either an installation or an uninstallation of the associated component.	Queries the RemoveIniFile table.
WriteIniValues	Writes information to an initialization file during an installation when the associated component is set to be installed locally or from source.	Queries the IniFile table.

There are no other sequence restrictions on these actions.

WORKING WITH ENVIRONMENT VARIABLES

These two actions, shown in Table 8-13, modify environment variables. Unlike with the other actions in this chapter, there are no restrictions as to where you can place these actions relative to each other in the sequence table. However, as with all the other actions that make changes to the system, you must place them between the InstallInitialize and InstallFinalize actions.

TABLE 8-13 ENVIRONMENT VARIABLE ACTIONS

Action	Description	Tables Used
RemoveEnvironmentStrings	Modifies the value of an environment variable during an uninstallation.	Queries the Environment table.

Action	Description	Tables Used
WriteEnvironmentStrings	Modifies the value of an environment variable during an installation.	Queries the Environment table.

The only sequence restriction on these actions is that they must come after the InstallValidate action.

Installation configuration

There are 14 Standard Actions that you can use to configure the overall installation. For discussion purposes we can break these 14 actions down into four subcategories: the actions used to configure a basic installation process, the actions that provide verification that the installation should continue, the actions that control the initiation of system reboots, and the actions used to control an upgrade installation. Each of these subcategories is the subject of one of the following subsections.

BASIC INSTALLATION CONFIGURATION

Six Standard Actions fall under this category. One difference between these actions and most of the other Standard Actions is that they do not query any of the database tables. There are a few sequence restrictions for a few of these actions; they are given in Table 8-14. The order of appearance in Table 8-14 represents the normal or default relative sequence of these actions.

TABLE 8-14 INSTALLATION CONFIGURATION ACTIONS

Action	Description	Sequence Restrictions
ExecuteAction	Initiates the implementation of the execute sequence. Passes the value of all public properties from the user interface sequence to the execute sequence.	Is normally placed at the end of the user-interface sequence after all user input has been collected.
InstallInitialize	Marks where the Windows Installer will start to generate the execution script.	Comes before any action that will make changes to the target system.

Continued

Table 8-14 INSTALLATION CONFIGURATION ACTIONS *(Continued)*

Action	Description	Sequence Restrictions
InstallExecute	Runs all actions that placed into the execution script up to the point where this action is encountered. Does not terminate the installation process that continues after the Windows Installer returns from executing the script. A new script is started at this point.	Must be placed between the InstallInitialize and InstallFinalize actions.
InstallExecuteAgain	Has the same function as the InstallExecute action, which allows for two of these types of operations to occur in the same sequence table.	Must be placed between the InstallInitialize and InstallFinalize actions.
SEQUENCE	Executes a custom sequence table named with the SEQUENCE property. The custom sequence table must have the same schema as the built-in sequence tables.	None.
InstallFinalize	Forces the execution of the execution script and marks the end of the transaction that began with the InstallInitialize action.	Must come after the InstallInitialize action.

You should keep in mind that you are dealing with a relational database and that you cannot have duplicate primary keys in any of these tables. This is why there are two actions that do the same thing but have different names – InstallExecute and InstallExecuteAgain. The name of the action in a sequence table is the primary key for that table and thus you cannot repeat the name of any action in a sequence table.

VERIFICATION

Two actions determine whether an installation should proceed or not. One of these actions validates that the environment on the target system is correct and the other validates that the user has the rights to install the product. These actions are shown in Table 8-15.

TABLE 8-15 INSTALLATION VALIDATION ACTIONS

Action	Description	Tables Used
LaunchCondition	Evaluates all the conditions in the LaunchCondition table and terminates the installation with an error message if any of these conditions evaluates to false.	Queries the LaunchCondition table.
ValidateProductID	Sets the value of the ProductID property if the user enters the correct product identifier.	Works with the Property table.

You should place both of these actions in both the user interface and execute sequence tables, normally near or at the top of each sequence. To add conditions to the LaunchCondition table in ISWI, go to the Product Properties icon in the Project View and click the Install Condition property. When you do this, ISWI enables you to enter both the condition and the associated message, as shown in Figure 8-4.

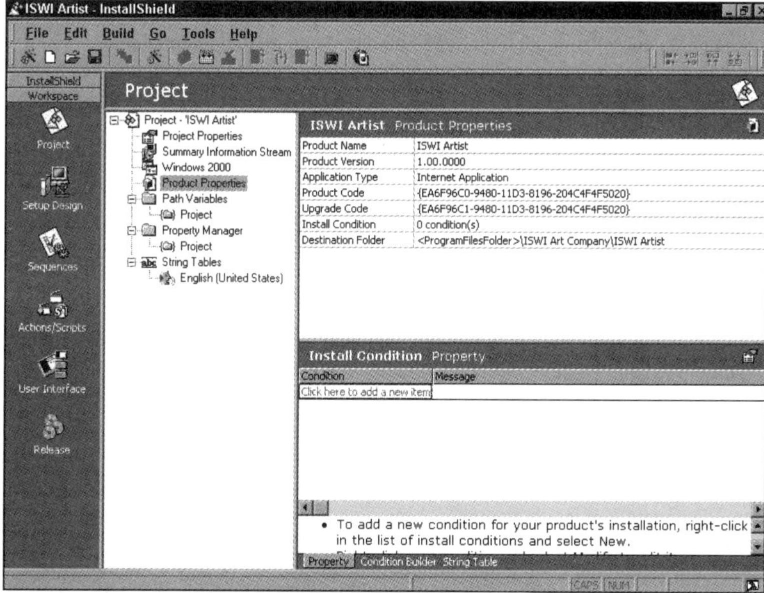

Figure 8-4: Setting conditions in the LaunchCondition table

You must provide a message for each condition you define. If you do not, you will get a build error. There are only two columns in the LaunchCondition table and neither of these columns can be null. If you click the Condition Builder tab at the bottom of the screen, you get a view that helps you create conditions from some of the important properties set by the Windows Installer. You also get a list of all the allowed operators from which you can create more elaborate conditions.

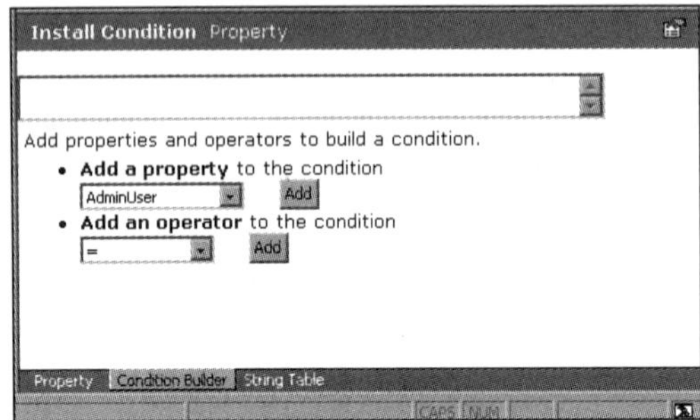

When using the Condition Builder, make sure that you add a space between the property name and the operator; otherwise the Windows Installer will not be able to parse the condition properly.

SYSTEM REBOOTS

There are two actions that control whether a system reboot should occur at the end of an installation or in the middle. These actions are shown in Table 8-16.

TABLE 8-16 SYSTEM REBOOT ACTIONS

Action	Description	Tables Used
ScheduleReboot	Initiates a prompt for a system reboot at the end of the installation.	Does not query any of the database tables.
ForceReboot	Forces a reboot in the middle of an installation.	Does not query any of the database tables.

The ScheduleReboot action is typically placed at the end of the execute sequence, but you can place it anywhere because it is not subject to any sequencing restrictions. The ForceReboot action must be placed between the InstallInitialize and InstallFinalize actions. It is highly recommended that you place it after the RegisterProduct action; otherwise the Windows Installer will require the source of the installation package to continue with the installation.

CONFIGURING AN UPGRADE INSTALLATION

There are four actions that relate to performing an upgrade installation. These actions are shown in Table 8-17.

TABLE 8-17 UPGRADE INSTALLATION ACTIONS

Action	Description	Tables Used
FindRelatedProducts	Based on the entries in the Upgrade table, finds all products installed on the system that match the criteria in this table.	Queries the Upgrade table.
PreventInstall	Prevents an upgrade installation based on the existence of certain conditions.	Works with the Property table.
MigrateFeatureStates	Retains feature states when an upgrade installation is performed.	Queries the Upgrade table.
RemoveExistingProducts	Removes all products found by the FindRelatedProducts action.	Queries the Upgrade table.

You need to place the FindRelatedProducts action in both the user interface sequence and the execute sequence. You must place this action before the MigrateFeatureStates and RemoveExistingProducts actions. You need to place the MigrateFeatureStates action in both the user interface sequence and the execute sequence tables. You can place the RemoveExistingProducts action only in the execute sequence table, normally after the InstallFinalize action.

Sequencing the Actions

Now that you know what built-in actions are and that there are restrictions on where most of them can be placed in a sequence table, let's look at how to manipulate the placement of these actions in a sequence. As you saw in Figure 8-3, many of the built-in actions have already been placed in the various sequences. The default sequences that you get when you create a new project are based on the recommended sequences documented in the Windows Installer SDK help. However, these recommended sequences do not always do what you want; you need to be able to modify them, either by removing actions you don't need, inserting new actions, or modifying the present placement of actions.

To manipulate the default sequences go to the Sequences view, as shown in Figure 8-3, and highlight an action. Then click the right mouse button to get a context menu with four options. These options enable you to insert a new action after the highlighted action, remove the highlighted action, or move the highlighted action up or down in the sequence. The Insert... option on the context menu launches the Insert Action dialog box, shown in Figure 8-5.

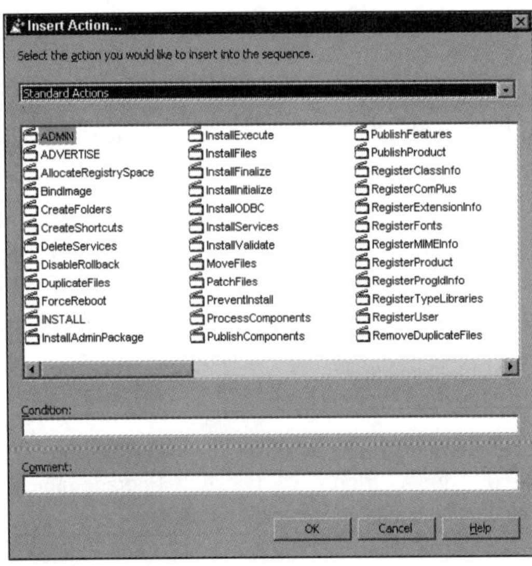

Figure 8-5: The Insert Action dialog box

At the top of this dialog is a combo box from which you can select the type of action you want to insert into the sequence. When you are in the user-interface, you can select any of the following actions:

Standard actions	Built-in actions (discussed in the preceding section).
Custom actions	User-defined actions created in the base installation project to extend the functionality of the Windows Installer. These custom actions are listed in the CustomAction table of the base installation package.
Merge module custom actions	User-defined actions created by the Merge Module author and merged into the base installation package.

Dialogs	Dialogs available within the base installation project.
Merge module dialogs	Dialogs created by the Merge Module author and merged into the base installation project.

In the execute sequence you can insert the actions but not the dialogs. This is only reasonable, because the user is not supposed to interact with the Windows Installer in the execute sequence.

In the list box below the combo box is a list of all the actions or dialogs not already inserted into the sequence. Remember that there can only be one instance of an action or a dialog in any particular sequence because the name of the action or dialog is the primary key for the sequence tables.

Below the list box are two edit fields. The upper edit field enables you to place a condition on the action or dialog you are inserting into the sequence. (A condition is an expression that evaluates to the value of true or false.) You do not have to enter a condition; if you leave this field empty the action or dialog will always be executed. We talk about conditions in more detail later in this chapter. The lower edit field is where you can enter a comment that will be inserted into the project file but does not find its way into the final MSI package. This comment is only for the setup developer's use.

For the purpose of this discussion we have really been looking at the actions that make up the Installation top-level action. There are two other top-level actions you can manipulate. As with the Installation default sequence, the default sequences for the Advertisement and the Administration top-level actions are also those that are recommended in the Windows Installer SDK documentation. It is interesting to note that there are no actions or dialogs in the user-interface sequence of the Advertisement top-level action.

The Insert Action dialog allows you to insert an action or dialog anywhere in a sequence, which means that it will not stop you from making the insertion in the wrong place.

Working with Properties

Before we discuss the creation of conditions, which are so important in controlling the actions that implement an installation, we need to discuss properties, which act as the global variables for an installation. Properties fall into two major categories: properties authored into the installation database and properties set at run time. The properties set at run time are not persisted in the database and as such are only set in memory. All authored properties are set in the Property table and all run-time properties are set in the run-time version of the Property table. Properties are pivotal in the creation of conditions.

Public and private properties

Windows Installer has defined many properties. You can also create properties of your own. Properties come in two styles, private and public. You can tell a public property because its name will be in all uppercase letters. The names of private properties are rendered in a mixture of uppercase and lowercase letters. A property name can consist of letters, numbers, periods, and underscores; the first character in the property name must be either a letter or an underscore.

Only a public property can be set from the command line. Also, only public properties can be sent across the process boundaries when the Windows Installer switches from the user-interface sequence to the execute sequence. This, of course, is meaningful only in Windows NT 4.0 and Windows 2000, where there is both a client process and a service process. On Windows 95/98 only one process is running and this transfer of public properties has no meaning. The following is an example of how to set a public property at the command line:

```
msiexec /i C:\Temp\MyApp.msi INSTALLLEVEL=50
```

This command line sets the installation install level to 50.

In the case of a managed installation you may need – or simply want – to restrict the number of public properties that can be passed to the service process via the ExecuteAction action. You would do this in order to maintain a secure environment when an application is being installed in a managed environment. If the following conditions are all met, the list of public properties that the user can change at the command line defaults to a list of restricted public properties.

- The system is Windows NT 4.0 or Windows 2000
- The user is not a system administrator
- The application being installed is using elevated privileges

The number of public properties that are on the default list of restricted public properties is a small subset of all public properties that are defined by the Windows Installer.

Properties defined by the Windows Installer

The built-in properties, both public and private, can be divided into 11 categories. These categories are as follows:

Component location properties	Defines the root location of the source files on the media and the location of the installation package location after the execution of an administrative install. There are only two properties in this category.

Configuration properties	Relates to those items that enable you to configure the installation. These properties include the ability to configure the user-interface level to be used during the installation, the ability control any system reboots that may be necessary, and so forth. There are 39 properties in this category.
Date, time properties	Set by the Windows Installer at run time to be the system date and time.
Feature installation options properties	Thirteen properties that define the features and components and how they will be installed – locally, advertised, run-from-source, and so forth.
Hardware properties	Eleven properties set by the Windows Installer at run time with the physical values relating to such items as screen height and width, processor type, text dimensions, and so forth.
Installation status properties	Eighteen properties that define the status of the installation by determining whether the product is already installed, whether there is sufficient disk space to accommodate the installation, the user interface level being used, and so forth.
Operating system properties	Seventeen properties that define such things as the type and version of the operating system, the computer name of the target system, the service pack that has been installed, and so forth.
Product information properties	Eleven properties that provide information such as the product name, product version, technical support contact information, and so forth.
Summary information update properties	Three properties that relate to the updating of the summary information stream of an administrative image.
System folder properties	When an operating system is installed, it defines the location of a set of standard folders on the computer. This set of properties contains the location of these folders and the Windows Installer sets these properties at run time. There are 21 of these predefined locations.

User information properties	Six properties that contain information such as the name of the user, the name of the company where the user works, the default language of the user, and so forth.

The complete definition of these built-in properties is provided in the MSI Help file that can be found on the CD-ROM at the back of the book.

REQUIRED PROPERTIES

All MSI packages must have the five properties described in Table 8-18.

TABLE 8-18 REQUIRED PROPERTIES

Property Name	Description
ProductCode	A unique identifier in the form of a GUID that makes this product distinguishable from all other products installed by the Windows Installer.
ProductLanguage	A numeric language identifier that identifies to the Windows Installer the language it should use for all strings that have not been authored into the database.
Manufacturer	The name of the company that developed the application being installed.
ProductVersion	The version of the product provided as a string. The format of this string is AA.BB.CCCC where the first field is the major version, the second field is the minor version, and the third field is the build number.
ProductName	The name of the product being installed.

The ProductCode, ProductVersion, and ProductLanguage properties are vital to the implementation of upgrades using the Upgrade table. The ProductName property identifies the product in the Add/Remove Programs applet.

PROPERTY PRECEDENCE

The installer sets properties using the following order of precedence. A property value in this list can override a value that comes after it and be overridden by a value coming before it in the list.

- Properties specified by the operating environment
- Public properties set on the command line
- Public properties listed by the AdminProperties property set during an administrative installation
- Public or private properties set during the application of a transform
- Public or private property that you set by authoring the Property table of the MSI package

Creating your own properties

When you want to author a property into the Property table using ISWI, you need to use the Property Manager in the Project view. Go to the Project view and click the Project icon under the Property Manager folder. You will see the default set of properties that you get with every new project, as shown in Figure 8-6. These are not the only properties that are built into the MSI database. There are other sources for some of the properties, such as the entries made under the Product Properties screen in the Project view.

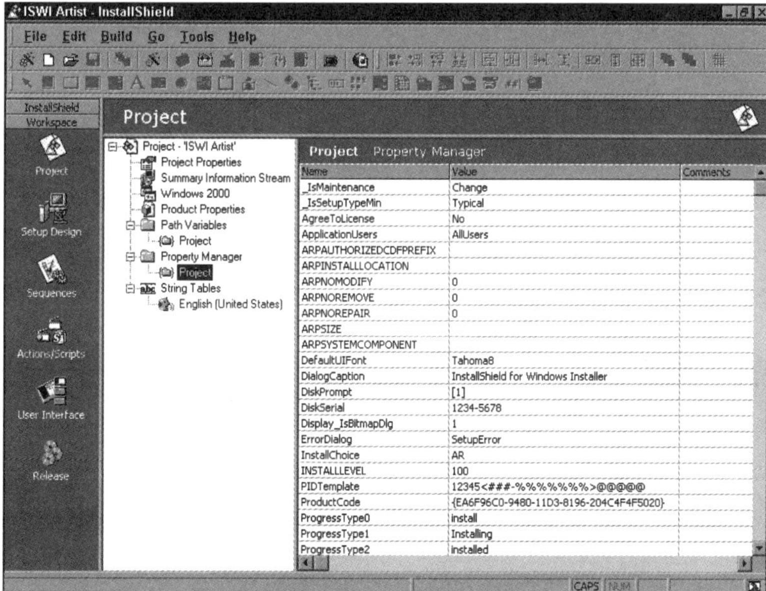

Figure 8-6: The ISWI Property Manager

To add a new property you need to double-click the line at the bottom of the Property Manager screen and then type in your property name and the initial value you want to associate with this property. A property without a value will not be built into the MSI database. The Windows Installer treats both the property name and the property value as strings. The property name should be 72 characters or less but there is no limit to the length of the property value.

The default properties

When you create an installation and do not author any additional properties, you get a set of default properties in the MSI database, as described in Table 8-19.

TABLE 8-19 DEFAULT PROPERTIES CREATED BY ISWI

Property Name	Property Value	Description
_IsMaintenance	Change	Tied to the radio-button group in the Maintenance Type dialog. It makes the radio button labeled Modify the default in this group.
_IsSetupTypeMin	Typical	Tied to the radio button group in the Setup Type dialog. It makes the radio button labeled Complete the default in this group.
AgreeToLicense	No	Tied to the radio button group in the License Agreement dialog. It makes the radio button labeled "No, I do not agree" the default for this group.
ApplicationUsers	AllUsers	Tied to the radio button group in the Customer Information dialog. It makes the radio button labeled "Install this application for all users" the default for this group.
ARPAUTHORIZEDCDFPREFIX		Windows Installer public property that you can set to the URL of the update channel for the application being installed.

Property Name	Property Value	Description
ARPINSTALLLOCATION		Windows Installer public property that you can set to the full path to the primary folder of the application being installed.
ARPNOMODIFY	0	Windows Installer public property that if set disables the Modify button for the product in the Add/Remove Programs applet on Windows 2000.
ARPNOREMOVE	0	Windows Installer public property that if set disables the Remove button for the product in the Add/Remove Programs applet on Windows 2000.
ARPNOREPAIR	0	Windows Installer public property that if set to 1 disables the Repair button for the product in the Add/Remove Programs applet on Windows 2000.
ARPPRODUCTICON		Windows Installer public property that specifies the foreign key to the Icon table that will be used as the primary icon for the install package.
ARPSIZE		Windows Installer public property that represents the estimated size of the application in kilobytes.
ARPSYSTEMCOMPONENT		Windows Installer public property that if set to 1 prevents the product from being displayed in the Add/Remove Programs applet.
DefaultUIFont	Tahoma8	Windows Installer private property that sets the default font style for controls in dialog boxes.
DialogCaption	InstallShield for Windows Installer	This is a custom property in ISWI and is not presently used.

Continued

TABLE 8-19 DEFAULT PROPERTIES CREATED BY ISWI *(Continued)*

Property Name	Property Value	Description
DiskPrompt	[1]	Windows Installer private property that holds a string displayed in a dialog that prompts the user to insert a disk.
Display_IsBitmapDlg	1	Used as a condition on the back button on the InstallWelcome and PatchWelcome dialogs that enables the user to go back to the splash bitmap. By default the back button on these two dialogs is disabled.
ErrorDialog	SetupError	Windows Installer property that defines the dialog that is to be used to display error messages.
INSTALLLEVEL	100	Windows Installer public property that is set to a default value of 100 and represents the installation level for the installation package.
PIDTemplate	12345<###-%%%%%%%>@@@@@	Windows Installer private property that sets the format of the MaskedEdit control when you use one to enter a serial number or other product-security code. It is against this value that a user's input is validated.
ProductCode	GUID	A GUID generated when a new project is created. This is one of the properties that every Windows Installer package must have.
ProgressType0	install	Displays a certain static control during an installation-related action.
ProgressType1	Installing	Displays a certain static control during an installation-related action.

Property Name	Property Value	Description
ProgressType2	installed	Displays a certain static control during an installation-related action.
ProgressType3	installs	Displays a certain static control during an installation-related action.
RebootYesNo	Yes	A custom property that is not presently used by ISWI.
Registration	No	A custom property that is not presently used by ISWI.
ReinstallModeText	omus	Sets the REINSTALLMODE property when the end user selects the Repair option in the Maintenance Type dialog.
SetupType	Typical	A custom property that is not presently used by ISWI.
UpgradeCode	GUID	Generated when a new project is created. This is not one of the required properties but you'll need it if you want to implement upgrades.

If a property in the Property Manager is not given a value, it will not appear in the Property table of the resulting MSI package when the database is built. We discuss the one exception to this rule in Chapter 9 when you add the serial-number functionality to the installation for the ISWI Artist application.

Using Conditions to Add Control

There are ten tables in an MSI database that have columns where you can enter a condition in order to add another level of control to the functionality of an installation. Of these ten tables, six are the sequence tables. Table 8-20 describes the tables where you can enter conditions.

Table 8-20 TABLES WITH COLUMNS FOR SETTING A CONDITION

Table Name	Description
Condition	Uses a condition to modify the selection state of a feature by modifying its install-level value. A feature with an install-level value greater than the value of the INSTALLLEVEL property will have a state of Absent. An install level of 0 disables and hides the feature.
ControlCondition	Determines whether a control in a dialog box can be hidden, shown, disabled, or enabled.
ControlEvent	Determines whether a particular control event tied to a control in a dialog box will be triggered or not.
LaunchCondition	Read by the LaunchConditions action; if any of the conditions returns a value of false the installation is terminated.
InstallUISequence	If the condition entered into this table evaluates to false, the Windows Installer will not execute it.
InstallExecuteSequence	If the condition entered into this table evaluates to false, the Windows Installer will not execute it.
AdminUISequence	If the condition entered into this table evaluates to false, the Windows Installer will not execute it.
AdminExecuteSequence	If the condition entered into this table evaluates to false, the Windows Installer will not execute it.
AdvtUISequence	If the condition entered into this table evaluates to false, the Windows Installer will not execute it.
AdvtExecuteSequence	If the condition entered into this table evaluates to false, the Windows Installer will not execute it.

You can see that a condition is an expression that evaluates to either true or false. You can create condition statements from properties, environment variables, component action states, component install states, feature action states, and feature install states. The following list summarizes the syntax requirements of a condition statement:

- Case-sensitive symbol names and values
- Case-insensitive environment variable names

- Literal text enclosed between quotation marks ("*text*")
- Non-existent property values treated as empty strings
- No floating-point numeric values
- Operators and precedence the same as in the BASIC and SQL languages
- Arithmetic operators are not supported
- Parentheses to override operator precedence
- Case-insensitive operators
- For string comparisons, a tilde ~ prefixed to the operator performs a case-insensitive comparison
- Comparison of an integer with a string or property value that cannot be converted to an integer always false, except for the comparison operator <>, which returns true.

For a complete description of the conditional statement I refer you to the topic "Condition Statement Syntax" that can be found in the MSI Help on the CD-ROM at the back of the book.

Introduction to Custom Actions

A custom action enables you to extend the built-in functionality of the Windows Installer. Even though many of the chapters in this book are devoted solely to custom actions it is a good idea to take a quick look at them now. Figure 8-1 showed the Actions/Scripts view. In this view, under the Actions/Scripts folder, there is an icon with a Custom Actions label. If you highlight this icon and click the right mouse button, you get a context menu with two options, New and Custom Action Wizard... If you choose the latter, you are launched into a wizard that leads you through the creation of a custom action. If you click the Welcome panel of this wizard, you get the panel shown in Figure 8-7.

In the Basic Information panel of the Custom Action Wizard you enter the name of the custom action and provide internal comments to describe it. In the remaining panels you will be asked to define the type of custom action, the location where the Windows Installer can find the implementation of the custom action, and other information about how the custom action is to be executed.

Once you have created a custom action you have to insert it into one of the sequences so that it will be executed. You can also put a condition on the custom action so that it will be executed only under certain circumstances.

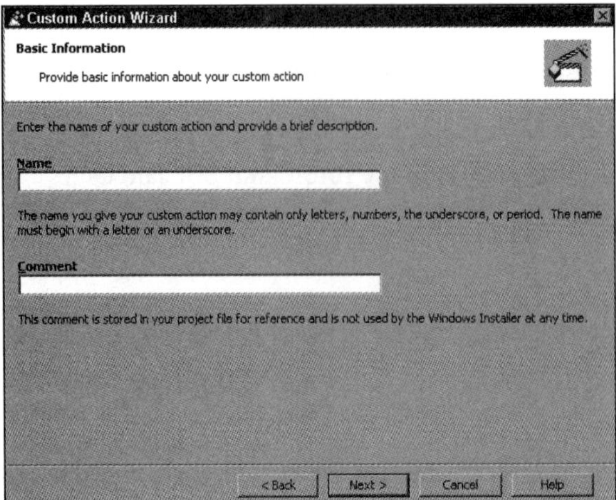

Figure 8-7: The Basic Information panel of the Custom Action Wizard

Part III of this book is devoted solely to the description and creation of all the types of custom actions you can use.

Summary

In this chapter you have seen that under the covers there are many similarities between the current script-based installations and the new Windows Installer approach. Actions serve the same purpose as functions and read the various database tables to get the information they need. You can create a procedure for performing an installation by placing actions in sequence tables. You can also put a higher level of control on these actions by creating specific conditions under which they will be executed. Finally you learned to extend the built-in functionality provided by the Windows Installer by creating custom actions.

Chapter 9

Creating the Installation User Interface

IN THIS CHAPTER

- Understanding the user interface in the Windows Installer Service
- Investigating the dialog boxes that come with ISWI
- Using the Dialog Editor in InstallShield for Windows Installer
- Modifying an existing dialog using the Dialog Editor
- Creating a new dialog with the Dialog Editor and inserting it into a wizard sequence

WE ARE GOING TO EXTEND our knowledge of package creation using ISWI in this chapter by taking a close look at how to manipulate the user interface.

The Windows Installer User Interface

In Chapter 3 we discussed the user interface in Windows Installer in a fair amount of detail. The important thing to keep in mind is that just like all other aspects of an MSI package the user interface is authored into the database tables. Unlike with legacy applications you no longer have full-screen backgrounds with your billboards, AVI files, or WAV files playing to keep you entertained while the installation proceeds. All you have is a wizard sequence and a final setup progress dialog that lets you know how the installation is proceeding.

Take a look at Chapter 3 for a complete discussion on the subject of user-interface levels. User-interface levels are important relative to what the user will see during an installation.

There are three components that make up the user interface in a Windows Installer database. These are dialog boxes, controls, and control events. The definition of each of these entities is contained in the Dialog, Control, and ControlEvent database tables respectively. There are seven database tables that supplement the information in the Control table. These are the BBControl, Billboard, CheckBox, ListBox, ListView, ComboBox and RadioButton tables. The main purpose of most of these supplemental tables is to populate the respective controls with values or other information. For instance, the ListBox table has a separate row in it for each row that is to be displayed in the list box control. Except for the BBControl and the Billboard tables all these tables tie the control to a particular property in the Property table. An action on the control will set the specified property to a particular value.

There are two other tables that are important with respect to the user interface: these are the EventMapping and ControlCondition tables. The EventMapping table defines those actions to which a certain control is subscribed and the Control Condition table defines the conditions under which a particular control is to be enabled, disabled, made visible, hidden or made the default control of a dialog. Through the Dialog Editor you will be seeing the impact of each of these tables by creating certain types of dialogs and controls. It is important, however, to discuss in more detail this business of control events and subscription.

Control Events and Subscription

Control events are analogous to Microsoft Windows messages in Win32-based applications. However, rather than creating a callback function to receive Windows messages and sending Windows messages with the SendMessage function, Windows Installer controls send control events specified in the ControlEvent table and receive control events specified in the EventMapping table.

To add working controls to dialog boxes, the author of the user interface first selects which control events to use and then associates these with the controls. When a user triggers a control with a control event tied to it, that control event is published to the installer and all controls in the dialog box. If the installer subscribes to the control event, the publication of the control event results in the installer's executing an action. If any controls in the dialog box subscribe to the control event, then the publication of the control event results in a change in the attributes of these controls as long as the Windows Installer defines that there is an action to be taken on the subscriber.

For example, consider a dialog that contains a progress bar and a text control that needs to display a description of the actions that are taking place during an installation. To implement this you would need to subscribe the text control to the ActionText. You would also need to make string entries in the ActionText table so that when a certain action is being executed the text string from the ActionText table describing that action is displayed in the text control. Each control event is published either by the installer or one of the controls in a dialog box. You author this type of functionality into the dialog box by listing the control together with the name of the control event in the ControlEvent table.

Although only the installer or a single control publishes a control event, the installer and controls can subscribe to multiple control events. This is accomplished by listing the control together with the control event in the EventMapping table. The value in the Attribute column of this table is the control attribute that is set when the subscribing control receives the control event. However, for the majority of control events no action is taken on controls that subscribe to these events. The main use of subscription is either during the selection of features in the custom setup type dialog or in the dialog that shows the progress of an installation.

If a control subscribes to a control event that is not published by the installer or a control in the same dialog box, an error may result. For a more information about particular control events, see the list of standard control events in MSI Help file.

Looking at the ISWI Built-In Dialogs in Detail

When you look at the built-in dialogs that come with ISWI you need to look at both the basic dialogs themselves and the wizard sequences into which they have been organized. The basic dialogs themselves are displayed in the User Interface view and you can see how they are used in the Sequences view.

The User Interface view

If you go to the User Interface view in the ISWI IDE you will see a complete list of the dialogs that come with your installation of ISWI. These dialogs are listed in alphabetical order and this does not tell you anything about the sequence of the dialogs in any particular wizard. The User Interface view is shown in Figure 9-1.

In this view under the All Dialogs icon you can see an alphabetical list of dialogs that have either come with ISWI or been imported in one way or another. If you highlight the All Dialogs icon or the User Interface icon above it and right-click, you get a context menu with four options. These options are New Dialog..., Import Dialog..., Import Dialogs from Resource DLL..., and Export Dialogs to Resource Script... Each of these options is the subject of one of the following subsections.

THE NEW DIALOG OPTION

Selecting this option launches a dialog that displays a gallery, which presents a selection of available dialogs including a blank dialog. You can use the blank dialog to build new dialogs from scratch. You can also use any of the other dialogs in the dialog gallery as a starting point for constructing a new dialog. Other than the blank dialog form all the other dialogs that appear in the dialog gallery come from dialogs exported from a project. If you click a dialog other than the blank dialog form and a dialog with the same name is already in the project, the dialog name will be changed before it is imported. The new name will be the same as the name of the existing dialog except that a number will be appended to it.

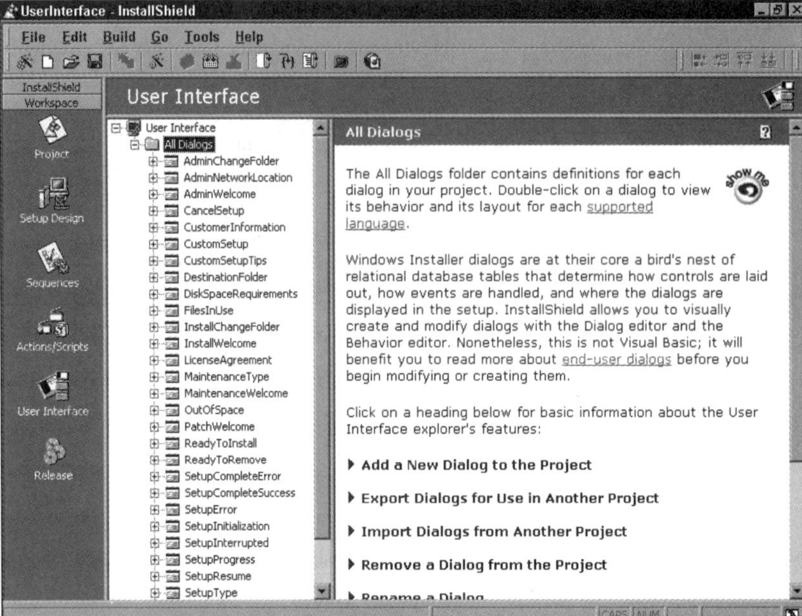

Figure 9-1: The User Interface view in the ISWI IDE

THE IMPORT DIALOG OPTION

When you select this option you are presented with a file open dialog that gives you a list of .isd files. An .isd file contains the description of a dialog stored in a proprietary binary format that can only be read by ISWI. Unlike with the dialog gallery you get with the New Dialog option, with this dialog you can browse for a .isd file anywhere on the system. Also, using this option will prevent you from importing a dialog if there is already a dialog with the same name in the project. This dialog enables you to add dialogs and not templates that can be used for creating new dialogs.

For each string displayed in a dialog created by ISWI a string ID is used to uniquely identify the string for the purposes of easy localization. When you import a dialog that contains a string ID that is being used by another dialog, the dialog importing mechanism warns you of this and lets you decide how to handle the clash of string Ids.

IMPORTING DIALOGS FROM A DYNAMIC LINK LIBRARY

You can also import dialogs defined as resources in a DLL. For best results you need to make sure that the dialogs in the resource DLL consist only of those controls that are supported by the Windows Installer.

EXPORTING DIALOGS TO A RESOURCE SCRIPT

All dialogs that have been defined in a project can be exported to a resource script. This is a file that has an .rc extension and can be added to a Visual C++ project and compiled into a DLL. To see how all this works, export all the dialogs in a standard project to an .rc file. Then create a simple DLL project in Visual C++, add this .rc file to the project, and compile the DLL. If you open this DLL as a resource in Visual C++, you will see all the dialogs that were in the ISWI project. Next, delete all the dialogs in your project and then import them again from the DLL that you just created.

WORKING WITH INDIVIDUAL DIALOGS

When you highlight an individual dialog in the User Interface view and right-click you have three options that affect only the highlighted dialog. One, you can export the dialog as an .isd file. This file will be saved in a Dialogs folder that is created in the root directory where all the project files are being saved. Two, you can delete the dialog, or three, you can rename it. You can also delete a dialog by pressing the Delete key. When you delete a dialog entered in one of the sequence tables this dialog is deleted from the sequence as well.

The Sequences view

If you look at the Sequences view and expand the Installation User Interface tree, you will see only a few of the dialogs that you see in the User Interface. If you expand the Administration User Interface view, you will see the same thing, except that there will be much fewer dialogs in this sequence. The question is, How do all the other dialogs get displayed if you don't put them into the any of the sequence tables?

In general, inserting the first dialog in the wizard sequence into the sequence table starts a wizard sequence. Then the remaining dialogs in any sequence are displayed via the control events assigned to the pushbuttons in each dialog. In a simple wizard sequence the Next pushbutton will trigger a NewDialog control event that displays the next dialog in the sequence. The Back pushbutton will trigger a NewDialog control event that displays the previous dialog. You can think of a wizard sequence as being similar to a doubly linked list.

Before taking a closer look at each of the wizard sequences you need to look at each of the dialogs in the sequence tables and understand why they are there. You also need to look at the conditions that have been set to control whether these dialogs even get displayed. Table 9-1 explains the dialogs in the Installation/User Interface tree in greater detail.

TABLE 9-1 DIALOG BOXES IN THE INSTALLATION USER INTERFACE

Dialog Name	Condition	Description
SetupCompleteError		The dialog that the Windows Installer launches when it detects an error during the installation and has to terminate the process. The Windows Installer knows to launch this particular dialog because it has a -3 sequence number. This is a modal dialog.
SetupInterrupted		The dialog that the Windows Installer launches when the user decides to cancel the installation. The Windows Installer knows to launch this particular dialog because it has a -2 sequence number. This is a modal dialog.
SetupCompleteSuccess		The dialog that the Windows Installer launches when the installation completes successfully. The Windows Installer knows to launch this particular dialog because it has a -1 sequence number. This is a modal dialog.
SetupInitialization		The first dialog that is displayed, and it stays active while the Windows Installer is performing its up-front actions (file costing, searching for files, and so on). In other words, all actions that precede the display of the starting dialog for one of the wizard sequences are performed while this dialog is on the screen. This is a modeless dialog so that other actions can occur while it is on the screen.

Dialog Name	Condition	Description
PatchWelcome	PATCH	The welcome panel to the start of an operation designed to update or upgrade a product through the use of a patch package. This wizard sequence will be launched if the PATCH public property is set. This is a modal dialog.
InstallWelcome	Not Installed And Not PATCH	The welcome panel for the start of an installation wizard sequence. This wizard sequence will be launched if the PATCH public property is not set and the Windows Installer has not found the product already registered on the machine. This is a modal dialog and all the other dialogs in the sequence will be displayed based on the control events associated with the Next and Back buttons.
SetupResume	Installed And (RESUME Or Preselected) And Not PATCH	The welcome panel for the start of an installation being resumed after suspension.
MaintenanceWelcome	Installed And Not RESUME And Not Preselected And Not PATCH	The welcome panel for the start of a maintenance installation wizard sequence. This wizard sequence will be launched if the PATCH public property is not set and the Windows Installer has found the product already registered on the machine, provided that this is not the resumption of a suspended installation. This is a modal dialog and all the other dialogs in the sequence will be displayed based on the control events associated with the Next and Back buttons.

Continued

TABLE 9-1 DIALOG BOXES IN THE INSTALLATION USER INTERFACE *(Continued)*

Dialog Name	Condition	Description
SetupProgress		A modeless dialog that contains a progress bar control. This progress bar control receives the information that allows it to display the progress of the installation.

There are four wizard sequences in the Installation/User Interface tree in the Sequences view. These are the sequences that start with either the InstallWelcome, the MaintenanceWelcome, the PatchWelcome or the SetupResume dialogs. All the other dialogs in this sequence table are individual dialogs only and do not start a wizard sequence.

In the Administration/User Interface tree in the Sequences view, you will find the dialogs you can use when performing an administrative installation. Table 9-2 describes the dialogs in this sequence.

TABLE 9-2 DIALOG BOXES IN THE ADMINISTRATION USER INTERFACE

Dialog Name	Condition	Discussion
SetupCompleteError		See Table 9-1.
SetupInterrupted		See Table 9-1.
SetupCompleteSuccess		See Table 9-1.
SetupInitialization		See Table 9-1.
AdminWelcome		The welcome panel for the start of an administrative installation wizard sequence. This wizard sequence will be launched if the top-level action has been set to ADMIN. This is a modal dialog and all the other dialogs in the sequence will be displayed based on the control events associated with the Next and Back buttons.
SetupProgress		See Table 9-1.

In the Administration/User Interface tree of the User Interface view there is only one wizard sequence, the one starting with the AdminWelcome dialog.

As described in Chapter 3 there is a tabled named AdvtUISequence in the database schema, but this table is not used since there is no need to have a user interface for performing the advertisement of an application. When an application is advertised there is no information that is needed from the end user. Since no files are being installed there is no need to select features and there is no destination location that needs to be configured. The only thing that happens during advertisement is that registry entries are made and shortcuts are created on the Start/Programs menu

In the next five sections you will look at the four wizard sequences that arer possible in the InstallUISequence table and the one wizard sequence that is possible in the AdminUISequence table. The description of each of these wizard sequences is accompanied by a figure that shows the dialog at which the Next and Back buttons are pointed. Also shown is the condition on the NewDialog control event that determines which new dialog will be displayed. The name of the dialog that will be displayed is given in the rectangle. You need to remember that only the first dialog of a wizard sequence is inserted into the sequence table and all other dialogs in the wizard sequence are displayed through the use of the NewDialog control event, which takes as its argument the name of the new dialog to be displayed. Now let's take a look at the individual wizard sequences and how they are constructed, starting with the InstallWelcome sequence.

The InstallWelcome dialog sequence

Figure 9-2 is a flow chart that shows the dialogs in the main wizard sequence that begins with the InstallWelcome dialog. I'll explain the design of each of the dialogs in the sequence. Some of the dialogs in this sequence can spawn other dialogs that are not part of the main sequence, and I'll explain each of these internal sequences as part of the discussion of the dialog that initiates it.

This is the most complicated of the wizard sequences. It is also the one most frequently used. Because of this I will explain each of the dialogs in this sequence in detail since many of the actions you perform in this sequence you will repeat in the other sequences. We'll begin with the InstallWelcome dialog box.

THE INSTALLWELCOME DIALOG

This is a simple dialog with no functionality other than that implemented by the Next and Cancel buttons. Figure 9-2 shows that you can get to the SplashBitmap panel by clicking the Back button. The Back button is disabled by default so this will not work unless you go into the Dialog Editor and enable this button.

The condition on the Back button's NewDialog control event is the existence of the Display_IsBitmapDlg property. This property is set by default in the Property Manager of the Project view. The SplashBitmap dialog has only a basic bitmap on it and if you want to display this dialog you should exchange this bitmap for something relevant to the product you are installing.

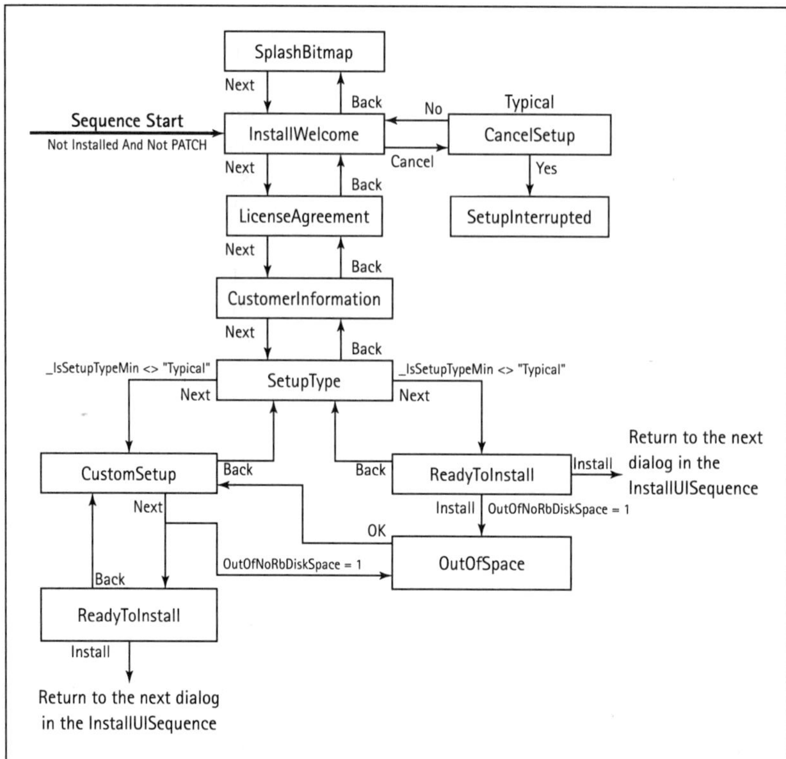

Figure 9-2: The main Installation Wizard sequence

The Cancel button on the InstallWelcome dialog spawns a child dialog that asks for confirmation before terminating the installation. This is the CancelSetup dialog. This dialog will either terminate the installation or return the user to the parent dialog. The Cancel buttons on all dialogs function in the same way.

THE LICENSEAGREEMENT DIALOG

This dialog prevents a user from continuing with the installation unless he or she specifically agrees to the End User License Agreement (EULA) that is displayed. The EULA is displayed in a Scrollable Text control, which requires a text string in Rich Text Format (RTF). In the ISWI Dialog Editor this text string must be provided as an RTF file.The user accepts the EULA through a RadioButtonGroup control associated with the AgreeToLicense property. The default value of this property in the Property Manager is No. The condition on the NewDialog control event tied to the Next button is AgreeToLicense = "Yes." Unless the end user selects the I agree radio button the Next button will not launch the next dialog in the wizard sequence.

THE CUSTOMERINFORMATION DIALOG

This dialog contains two edit fields and a radio button group. The edit fields are tied to the USERNAME and COMPANYNAME public properties. If these two properties are not authored into the Property table or set from the command line, the Windows Installer will set these properties using information from the registry. Entering information into these edit fields will change the values of these two properties.

The RadioButtonGroup control enables the end user to choose whether to install the product for everyone who uses the machine or just for the current user. Under certain circumstances, however, the RadioButtonGroup control is hidden and the user is not given the choice. The control is hidden under any of the following circumstances:

- When the ProductState property has a value greater than 0. This will be the case if the product has been advertised but not installed, installed for a different user, or installed for the current user previously. The last situation would launch the maintenance dialog sequence so the user would never see the CustomerInformation dialog.
- When the user does not have administrative privileges on the target machine. Under these circumstances the HKEY_LOCAL_MACHINE registry hive cannot be written and therefore only an installation for the current user is possible.
- When the target operating system is Windows 95/98. On these two systems there are no such concepts as a per-user or a per-machine installation.

The RadioButtonGroup control is associated with the ApplicationUsers property, which is set to an initial value of AllUsers in the Property Manger. This forces the default selection to be an installation for all users of the machine. If the Application Users property is set to AllUsers and the user has administrative privileges, then the Next button will set the ALLUSERS public property to a value of 1. This will cause the Windows Installer to perform a per-machine installation. If the ALLUSERS public property is not set because of a certain set of conditions then the Windows Installer will perform an installation for the current user.

THE SETUPTYPE DIALOG

The setup type dialog that comes with ISWI enables the user to select either a complete install or a custom setup. This functionality is implemented with a RadioButton Group control that is associated with the _IsSetupTypeMin property defined in the Property Manager. The default value of this property is Typical, which makes the default setup type a complete installation. The Next button has two control events defined that will launch either the ReadyToInstall dialog or the CustomSetup dialog depending on the radio button selected by the user.

THE CUSTOMSETUP DIALOG

This dialog enables the end user to change the default selection of the features to be installed. The visible features to be installed are displayed in the SelectionTree control. The remote installation and advertisement properties set for a feature and the remote installation property set for the components that are associated with a feature define the possible action states for a feature. The end user would then be able to select one of these action states in the CustomSetup dialog or could decide to accept the default action state.

The user can also change the installation location for each of the features in the SelectionTree control. This functionality is implemented by the Change button, which uses the SelectionBrowse control event to launch the InstallChangeFolder dialog. Using this dialog the user can browse to a new location and create new folders. The location defined with the InstallChangeFolder dialog becomes the new install location for the feature highlighted in the SelectionTree control.

In addition to the standard Back, Next, and Cancel buttons, there are several others that provide information to the user. The Help button spawns a dialog that displays the various types and meanings of the icons that are used for features in the SelectionTree control. There is also the button with the label Space launches the DiskSpaceRequirements dialog that contains a VolumeCostList control. This control displays all the volumes involved in the current installation and will highlight any volumes that do not have enough space to accommodate the selected features.

The Next button on the CustomSetup dialog is tied to two NewDialog control events, which you condition using the OutOfNoRbDiskSpace private property. If the value of this property is False, the Next button will launch the ReadyToInstall dialog, where the user initiates the installation. If the value of this property is True, the Next button will launch the OutOfSpace dialog, which is described in a later section. The Windows Installer sets the OutOfNoRbDiskSpace property to True if any of the target volumes do not have enough disk space for the selected features.

When setting the value of the OutOfNoRbDiskSpace property the Windows Installer does not take into account the space that is required for caching files and other information required for implementing rollback. It is the OutOfDiskSpace property that takes into account the impact of caching files for rollback purposes. The OutOfNoRbDiskSpace property is dynamically updated any time the total install cost is reevaluated.

THE READYTOINSTALL DIALOG

This dialog launches the installation with the Install button and is the last dialog in the InstallWelcome wizard sequence. The Install button is tied to the EndDialog control event with the Return argument. This control event returns control to the Windows Installer and the next action or dialog in the InstallUISequence table is executed. Under normal circumstances the modeless SetupProgress dialog will be launched and then the ExecuteAction action will be executed. The ExecuteAction action initiates the executionof the actions listed in the InstallExecuteSequence table. In addition to launching the installation clicking the Install button sets a series of three properties that are used later to define conditions that will either hide or display text in the SetupProgress dialog and in the SetupCompleteSuccess dialog. These properties are ProgressType1, ProgressType2, and ProgressType3, and they are defined with default values in the Property Manager.

THE OUTOFSPACE DIALOG

This dialog is exactly like the DiskSpaceRequirements dialog except for the positioning of the text control. It is displayed when the OutOfNoRbDiskSpace property is set to True. This dialog provides feedback through the VolumeCostList control about what volumes do not have enough space to accommodate the current selection of features and their target locations. When users click the OK button, they are returned to the CustomSetup dialog where they can reconfigure the installation to complete successfully.

The MaintenanceWelcome dialog sequence

In Figure 9-3 is a flow chart that shows the dialogs in the main wizard sequence that begins with the MaintenanceWelcome dialog. I'll discuss the design of each of the dialogs in this sequence separately – I've already discussed some of them in their roles as part of the InstallWelcome wizard sequence. It is interesting to note that a number of the dialogs you see in the User Interface view are used in more than one sequence. Displaying a dialog in more than one wizard sequence is accomplished by placing different conditions on the pushbutton control events. Depending on how these dialogs are launched, they can have slightly different functionalities.

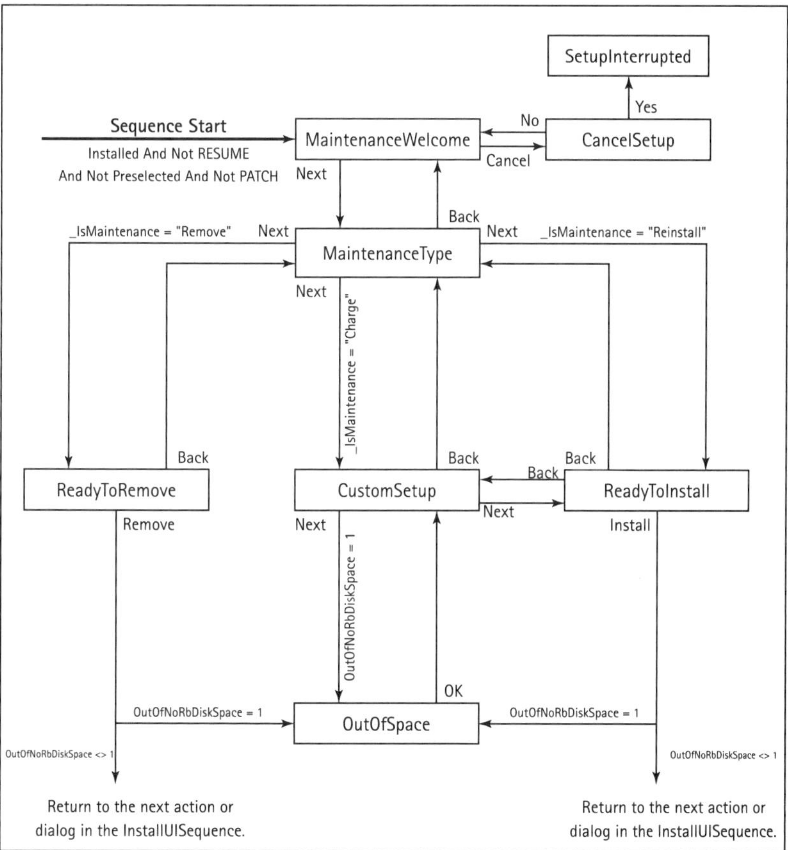

Figure 9-3: The Maintenance Wizard sequence

THE MAINTENANCEWELCOME DIALOG

This dialog is almost the same as the InstallWelcome dialog except that it displays different text and it does not have the Back button pointing at the SplashBitmap dialog. The Next button launches the MaintenanceType dialog using the NewDialog control event.

THE MAINTENANCETYPE DIALOG

In this dialog the user is presented with three options for performing a maintenance type of operation. These three options are presented in a RadioButtonGroup control associated with the _IsMaintenance property. The default value for this property as set in the Property Manager is Change, which makes the radio button with the Modify label the default when the dialog is first displayed. The three options that the user has in this dialog are Modify, Repair, and Remove. When the Modify option is selected the _IsMaintenance property is set to Change; when the Repair option is selected the property is set to Reinstall; and when the Remove option is selected the property is set to Remove. The _IsMaintenance property is used in a condition statement on the NewDialog control event associated with the Next button. Based on the value of the _IsMaintenance property one of three dialogs is displayed: ReadyTo Remove, CustomSetup, or ReadyToInstall.

When the user selects the Repair option the ReinstallMode control event is also executed, with the argument being the value of the ReinstallModeText property as defined in the Property Manager. This control event specifies the modes to be used during the reinstall operation based on the text string used as an argument to this control event. The value of the ReinstallModeText property is omus. Each of the letters in this string specifies a certain operation to be carried out with regard to files, registry entries, and shortcuts. A complete list of all the possible values is provided in the MSI Help for the REINSTALLMODE public property.

THE READYTOREMOVE DIALOG

This dialog is the last dialog in the MaintenanceWelcome wizard sequence. The user initiates the uninstallation of the product by clicking on the Remove button. A number of control events are associated with the Remove button on this dialog, the most important being the Remove control event that has an argument that consists of the string ALL. This defines that all installed features are to be uninstalled. There is also an EndDialog control event with the Return argument. This control event returns control to the Windows Installer. The Windows Installer then displays the modeless SetupProgress dialog and then executes the ExecuteAction action. The ExecuteAction action initiates the execution of the actions in the InstallExecuteSequence table and these actions actually perform the uninstallation operation.

THE CUSTOMSETUP DIALOG

We have already looked at this dialog in the section on the InstallWelcome wizard sequence. The possible sequence of events is the same as described in that section, the only difference being that the Back button will take the user to the MaintenanceType dialog instead of to the SetupType dialog. The condition that controls this functionality is the value of the Installed property. The Windows Installer sets this property when an operation is first launched and the product has already been installed.

THE READYTOINSTALL DIALOG

This is another dialog that has the same type of functionality as described in the section on the InstallWelcome wizard sequence. The main difference here is that if this dialog is launched from either the MaintenanceType dialog or the CustomSetup dialog, pressing the Back button returns the user to the dialog from which the ReadyToInstall dialog was launched.

The SetupResume dialog sequence

This sequence is one that you will very rarely see. This sequence normally appears only if an installation is interrupted by some event not initiated by the user. You might see it, for instance, if you are doing an installation from a network server and the connection gets lost during the installation. Figure 9-4 shows the wizard sequence for a resumed installation.

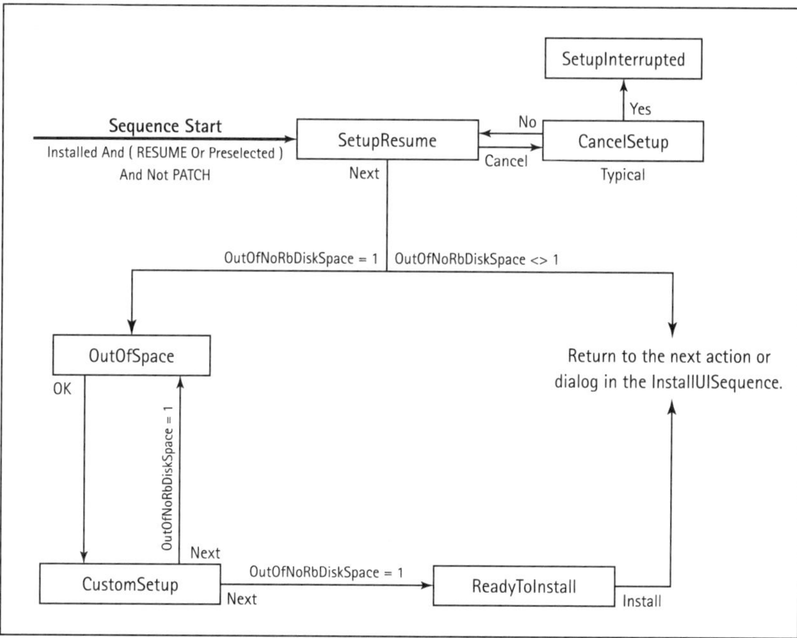

Figure 9-4: The Installation Resume Wizard sequence

THE SETUPRESUME DIALOG

This dialog is the only one in the default sequence for the resumption of a suspended installation. The only time there will be more dialogs displayed in this sequence is when the OutOfNoRbDiskSpace property has been set by the Windows

Installer. When this occurs then the OutOfSpace and CustomSetup dialogs come into play just as described in the section on the InstallWelcome wizard sequence.

The PatchWelcome dialog sequence

The PatchWelcome Dialog is the only dialog in this sequence. As in the Install Welcome dialog, the Back button is pointed at the SplashBitmap dialog and this button is also disabled (See Figure 9-5).

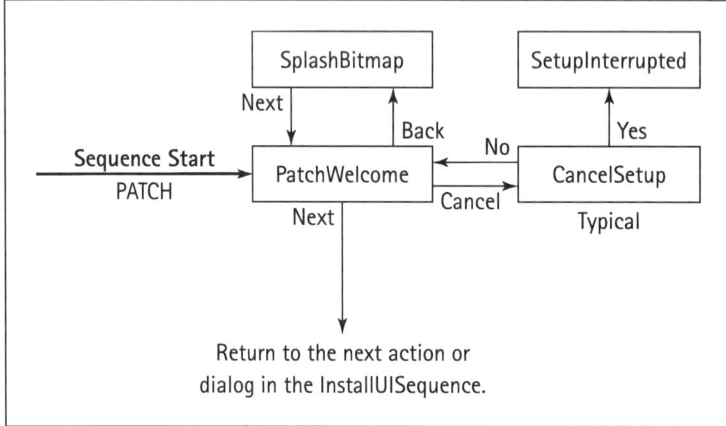

Figure 9-5: The Installation Resume Wizard sequence

The AdminWelcome dialog sequence

The final wizard sequence we'll look at is the one you use when performing an administrative installation to a network drive. In this type of installation no files are actually installed. All that happens is that any source files compressed into CAB files are uncompressed into a source directory structure as dictated by the Directory table. Figure 9-6 shows this sequence.

THE ADMINWELCOME DIALOG

This dialog is the same as all the other welcome dialogs that kick off wizard sequences. The text displayed is different according to the objective of the sequence and the Next button points to different dialogs, but they're all basically the same. In this case the Next button points at the AdminNetworkLocation dialog.

THE ADMINNETWORKLOCATION DIALOG

This dialog provides browse functionality for the purpose of finding a location where a network image is to be located. The browse functionality is implemented by the AdminChangeFolder dialog, which is the same as the InstallChangeFolder dialog. I discussed the InstallChangeFolder dialog in the section on the InstallWelcome wizard sequence.

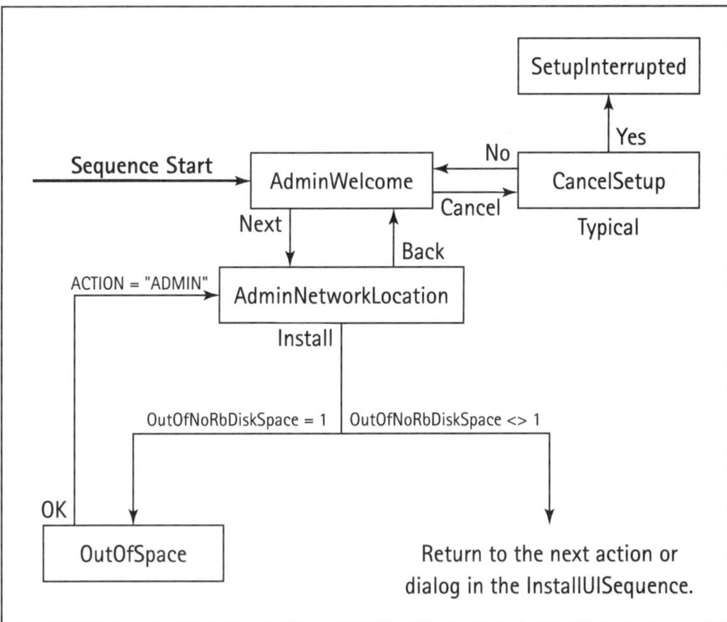

Figure 9-6: The Administrative Installation Wizard sequence

When the Install button is clicked two control events that are implemented if the space requirements for the image can be accommodated by the network drive. The first control event is the SetTargetPath event that sets the value of the TARGETDIR public property. This property contains the location of the installation package for the network image. The other control event just returns control to the Windows Installer so that the installation can be implemented. If the OutOfNoRbDiskSpace property is set to True then clicking the Install button will take the user to the OutOfSpace dialog. This is the same dialog displayed whenever the target volume lacks sufficient space for the installation to take place. Clicking the OK button on the OutOfSpace dialog returns the user to the AdminNetworkLocation dialog, where he or she can find a new location for the installation.

The Dialog Editor

A visual resource editor is part of the User Interface view shown in Figure 9-1. This editor is used to create and modify the dialog boxes used in an installation. Figure 9-7 shows the dialog editor with a blank form for creating a new dialog. You can generate this view by first creating a new dialog as described in the first section of this chapter, dragging the splitter bar to the left as far as you can, and finally dragging the alignment toolbar to the left and the control toolbox toolbar down and to the left.

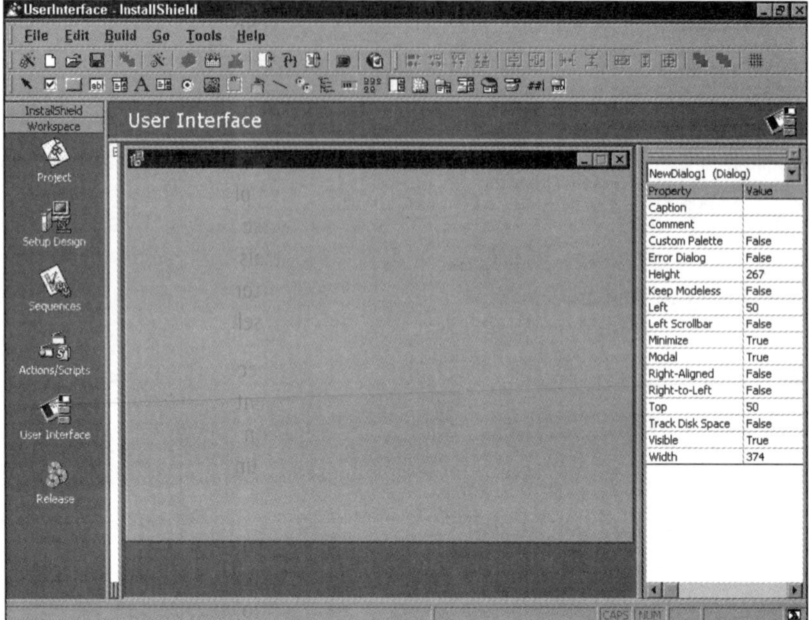

Figure 9-7: The Dialog Editor with a blank form

The controls toolbar

On the controls toolbar are 24 icons representing the functionality that you can add to a dialog box. There are actually 23 controls and one selection tool. All of these controls have properties and most of these properties are given default values when you first place them on a dialog. You will have to change many of these default properties in order to obtain the desired functionality. You will be working with a number of these controls when you modify or create dialogs at the end of this chapter. A complete description of all the properties pertaining to a particular control can be found in the MSI Help, available from the ISWI Help pulldown menu. Table 9-2 describes the tools, listed as they appear from left to right on the toolbar.

This table shows those controls that are supported by the Windows Installer. The Windows Installer does not support all the standard controls found in Windows. Also, you cannot create custom controls since the Windows Installer will not recognize them.

Table 9-2 WINDOWS INSTALLER CONTROLS AND THE CONTROL TOOLBAR

Control Icon	Control Name	Description
	Select Tool	Used to select, move, and size controls that have been placed on the dialog. You can also use this tool to select multiple controls by holding down the left mouse button and fencing in the controls to be selected.
	CheckBox	A two-state check box that you can use to implement an on-and-off functionality. An operation on this control sets or unsets the value of a property.
	PushButton	A typical command button. One of the few controls that can be used to execute a control event.
abl	Edit	Enables the end user to input text. Associated with a property that is set to the value entered into the control. This control can be either single or multi-line. There is no change notification issued by this control so there's no way to know if something has been entered or not.
	ComboBox	Displays a dropdown list of predefined values and an edit field into which the user can enter a value. Associated with a property that is set to the value in the control selected by the user. The Windows Installer does not support scroll bars for this control.
A	Text	Displays static text. Can be subscribed to various control events and display action data and action text messages.

Continued

TABLE 9-2 WINDOWS INSTALLER CONTROLS AND THE CONTROL TOOLBAR *(Continued)*

Control Icon	Control Name	Description
	ListBox	A regular list box that enables the user to make a single selection from a list of predetermined values. Displays the values that have been entered into the Listbox table. Each ListBox control is associated with a specific public property and it is this property that defines which values in the ListBox table are displayed in any particular ListBox control.
	RadioButton	Not actually a separate control but considered to be part of a RadioButton Group. To define a RadioButton control you must define it in the RadioButton table and associate it with a group through the defined property for the group.
	Bitmap	Similar to the Text control except that it displays a static bitmap image instead of static text.
	GroupBox	Displays a rectangle around a group of controls and can optionally have a text description.
	Billboard	Used to display other controls that can be added and removed from the dialog box by control events. Only controls that do not have associated properties can be placed on a billboard control. Controls that would typically be placed on a Billboard control are Text, Bitmap, and Icon controls.
	Line	You can't make this anything but a horizontal line.

Control Icon	Control Name	Description
	RadioButtonGroup	Consists of a group of radio buttons from which a user will set the value of the property associated with the radio button group. A RadioButtonGroup control can only set a property value; it cannot be used to send a control event.
	SelectionTree	Enables a user to change the selection state of features. Normally used in a custom setup dialog. Associated with a property that the user can set through a browse dialog.
	ProgressBar	Displays a bar graph that changes length as it receives progress messages. Subscribes to the SetProgress control event so that it receives the information related to the progress of the installation via the change in the Progress attribute.
	ListView	A standard ListView control that displays a single column of values with an icon next to each item. Displays the values in the ListView table that are associated with specific properties.
	ScrollableText	Displays a long string of text in Rich Text Format (RTF). Often used to display an End User License Agreement (EULA).
	Icon	Displays a static picture of an icon where the background of the image is transparent.
	DirectoryList	Displays a part of the path currently displayed in the PathEdit control, and the folders below the directory currently displayed by the DirectoryCombo control. The PathEdit, DirectoryCombo, and DirectoryList controls are tied together through the use of a string-valued property. This property defines the path selected by the user.

Continued

TABLE 9-2 **WINDOWS INSTALLER CONTROLS AND THE CONTROL TOOLBAR** *(Continued)*

Control Icon	Control Name	Description
	DirectoryCombo	Displays all the available volumes in alphabetical order and the all the levels of the current path. This control, along with the PathEdit and DirectoryList controls, is designed to be used in a browse dialog where the user can change the install location for the product.
	VolumeCostList	Presents information about the cost associated with the selection of features for installation. Shows all the volumes involved in the current installation, and can also be used to show all other volumes. If the required disk space exceeds the amount available, the volume is highlighted.
	VolumeSelectCombo	Enables the user to select a volume from an alphabetical list of volumes. You can control the types of volumes displayed by changing the properties that define this control.
	MaskedEdit	An edit field that you can configure by using a mask. Associated with a property, the value of which is set to the text entered in this control.
	PathEdit	Used to display an edit field that enables a user to select the tail-end section of a path or enter a path using either a logical drive letter or (if a drive has no drive letter) a Universal Naming Convention (UNC) path.

Editing the dialog design

After you place controls on the dialog you can manipulate these controls in a number of different ways. You can copy and paste controls, align controls with each other, center them in the dialog, and so forth. The editing functionality in the Dialog Editor is contained in the Alignment and Sizing toolbar and the Edit pulldown menu. There is also a context menu you get when you right-click in the dialog.

THE ALIGNMENT AND SIZING TOOLBAR

On the Alignment and Sizing toolbar are 14 options for manipulating the controls that you place on a dialog. Table 9-3 describes these options, listed as they appear from left to right on the toolbar.

TABLE 9-3 OPTIONS AVAILABLE ON THE ALIGNMENT AND SIZING TOOLBAR

Tool Icon	Tool Name	Description
	Align Left	Enabled when more than one control has been selected. All the selected controls will be lined up on their left edge with the left edge of the last control selected.
	Align Right	Enabled when more than one control has been selected. All the selected controls will be lined up on their right edge with the left edge of the last control selected.
	Align Top	Enabled when more than one control has been selected. All the selected controls will be lined up on their top edge with the left edge of the last control selected.
	Align Bottom	Enabled when more than one control has been selected. All the selected controls will be lined up on their bottom edge with the left edge of the last control selected.
	Center Vertical	Centers a control vertically in the dialog box.
	Center Horizontal	Centers a control horizontally in the dialog box.
	Space Across	Enabled when more than one control has been selected. All the selected controls will be evenly spaced between the control farthest to the left and the one farthest to the right.

Continued

TABLE 9-3 OPTIONS AVAILABLE ON THE ALIGNMENT AND SIZING TOOLBAR *(Continued)*

Tool Icon	Tool Name	Description
	Space Down	Enabled when more than one control has been selected. All the selected controls will be evenly spaced between the control that is closest to the top and the one closest to the bottom.
	Make Same Width	Enabled when more than one control has been selected. All the selected controls will be made the same width as the last control selected.
	Make Same Height	Enabled when more than one control has been selected. All the selected controls will be made the same height as the last control selected.
	Make Same Size	Enabled when more than one control has been selected. All the selected controls will be made the same height and width as the last control selected.
	Bring To Front	An authoring help when you're working on overlapping controls. Brings a control that is behind another control to the top. Has no effect on the order in which controls are painted at run time.
	Send To Back	An authoring help when you're working on overlapping controls. Sends a control in front of another control to the back. Has no effect on the order in which controls are painted at run time.
	Toggle Grid	Turns a grid on the base form of the dialog on or off. When the grid is turned on it provides a snap-to functionality, making all controls drawn on the grid align with it along all edges. Controls drawn before the grid is turned on do not snap to the grid unless they are moved. Then they will change size so that all edges align with the grid.

These alignment tools constitute the standard set of tools found in all visual resource editors. Knowing how to use these tools will enable you to efficiently create professional-looking dialogs.

USING THE EDIT AND CONTEXT MENUS

On the Edit pulldown menu you have access to the typical Delete, Cut, Copy, and Paste options. The keyboard shortcuts for these options are also the standard ones for any Windows-based application. You can copy and paste controls on the same dialog box and you can also copy controls from one dialog to another. At this time you cannot undo or redo any of these actions but the next version will provide the ability to undo changes made in the Dialog Editor.

On the context menu you will see the Copy, Cut, and Paste options and also Bring to Front and Send to Back options, which are the same as the options on the Alignment and Sizing toolbar. The only new option in this context menu is one that enables you to select all controls on the dialog.

When you use the copy option to duplicate a particular control such as a pushbutton, the paste operations will put the copy of the control directly on top of the control that was copied. All you need to do is to drag the control that was pasted off the original control.

Modifying an Existing Dialog

Before you get into the business of creating a new dialog using the Dialog Editor, you should get some experience by modifying one of the standard dialogs. As an example, add a check box to the SetupCompleteSuccess dialog. When this check box is checked and the Finish button is clicked, the Windows Installer will launch another dialog. You will find that doing this is not as easy as it may sound.

In this example you will use the state of the check box to decide whether the Windows Installer will spawn the CancelSetup dialog or not when the user clicks the Finish button in the SetupCompleteSuccess dialog. In Chapter 11, which covers custom actions you will be able to see that this type of functionality could be used to launch a Web site or a readme file. The modified dialog box will look like what is shown in Figure 9-8.

Most of the effort will be related to setting properties and defining control events and conditions. Before we proceed you need to know how to place controls on top of a bitmap, which you will have to do in this example. If you do not do things exactly so, the check box will cover this control and it will not be visible when the dialog is launched.

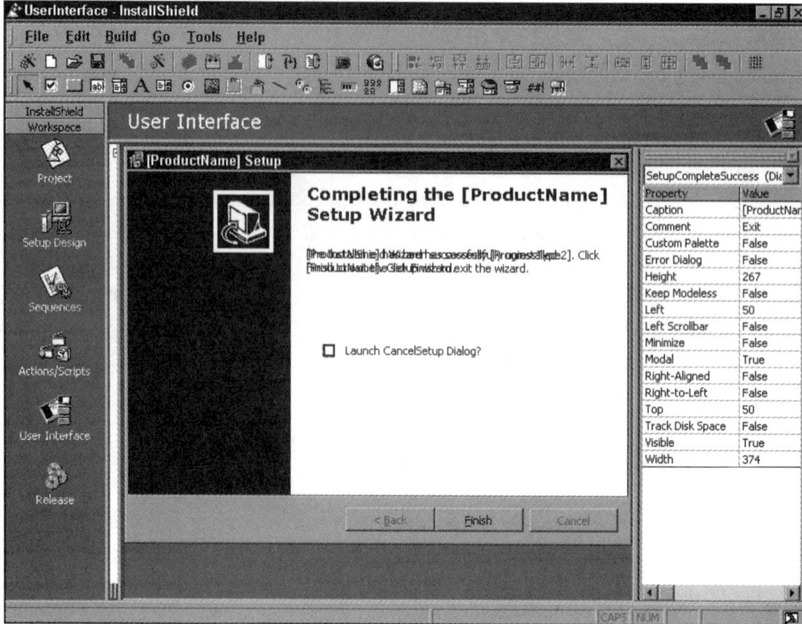

Figure 9-8: The Modified SetupCompleteSuccess dialog

The Windows Installer paints controls in a certain order, starting with the control that is designated in the Dialog table as the Control_First attribute. This will be the first control painted, after which each control in the tab order will be painted in sequence. The key to making a control appear on top of a bitmap is to make sure that the controls on top of the bitmap have a higher tab order than the bitmap. There are two basic rules:

- The bitmap must be earlier in the tab order than any of the controls to be placed on the bitmap. You can arrange this using the Tab Index property. In the case of the SetupCompleteSuccess dialog the easiest solution is to give the bitmap control a Tab Index of 0.
- All controls plus the bitmap must have their Tab Stop properties set to True.

Following these two rules you need to make modifications to the Image (Bitmap) control that forms the background to this dialog. The Tab Index property must be set to 0 and the Tab Stop property must be set to True. After you have done this, add the check box control on top of the bitmap. In addition to the check box control you must also add a static text control beside it in order to display the usage of the check box. Do not use the text property of the check box itself: it does not have a Transparent property and would appear as the same color as the dialog form itself. The text control does have a Transparent property, which you can set so that the bitmap color will show through. Table 9-4 shows the non-default values for the properties for the check box and text controls.

TABLE 9-4 NON-DEFAULT PROPERTIES FOR THE CHECK BOX AND TEXT CONTROLS

Control Name & Type	Property	Value
LaunchCheckBox (CheckBox)	Height	10
	Left	146
	Property	LaunchDialog
	Sunken	False
	Tab Index	1
	Top	125
LaunchCheckBox (CheckBox)	Value	Yes
	Width	10
CheckBoxText (Text)	Height	11
	Left	164
	Tab Index	2
	Text	Launch CancelSetup Dialog?
	Top	125
	Transparent	True
	Width	135

The following remarks provide more detail on the entries described in Table 9-4:

- You have associated the LaunchDialog property with the check box control. We have not defined any default value in the Property Manager for this property, so when the check box is not checked the value of the property will be null. This way the property name itself can be used as a condition.
- For the check box control you have turned off the Sunken property in order to hide the fact that this control has a gray background. Since there is no transparent property to be set this is the only way to get rid of this background when placing the control on top of a bitmap. You have also made the control square so that the text portion of the control is hidden.
- In order to provide a caption beside the check box you have used a static text field, the Transparent property of which you can set to True so that the color of the bitmap can show through.

Now you have to click on the Behavior icon for this dialog in order to add some functionality to your check box. All the Windows Installer is going to do is launch the CancelSetup dialog if the check box is checked and the user clicks on the Finish button. You can do this by adding another control event to the Finish button, as shown in Figure 9-9.

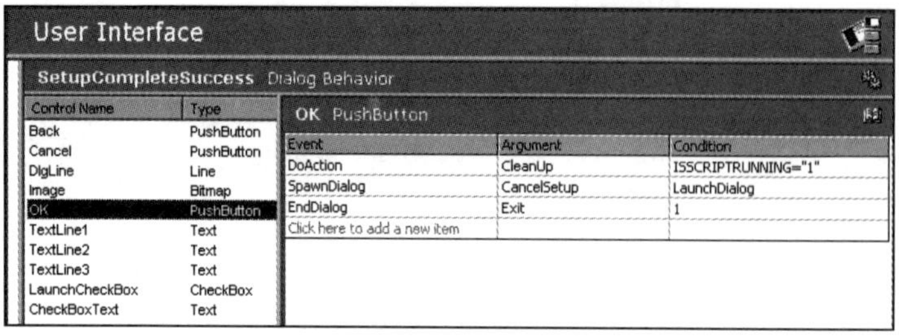

Figure 9-9: Adding a control event to the Finish button

As you can see, you condition the SpawnDialog control event based on whether the LaunchDialog property has been set or not. This is the property you have associated with the check box control. When the check box is not checked then the value of the LaunchDialog property will be null; when the check box is checked the value of LaunchDialog will be Yes.

You should do one more thing in order to modify the standard behavior of your modified dialog: hide the two new controls when an uninstallation is being performed. To do this you need to click on the Conditions tab at the bottom of the Behavior screen. In this screen you can assign an action and a condition on that action that will be applied to the highlighted control. The actions available to you are Enable, Disable, Hide, or Show. The action you are interested in is the Hide action, which you want to be executed when the Installed property is set. Set this condition on the LaunchCheckBox and CheckBoxText controls. This will cause these controls to be hidden when the SetupCompleteSuccess dialog is displayed at the end of an uninstallation.

Creating a New Dialog

A useful exercise in creating a new dialog box is to create a setup type dialog that has three options instead of just the two provided with the built-in SetupType dialog. In this example you will enable the user to choose a Typical, Complete, or Custom setup. Since the main point of this example is for you to learn how to create a new dialog, you should first create an installation that has a number of features that can be configured for a Typical and a Complete install. This installation package only has to copy files, so that you can see that the functionality you create actually works as designed.

You should create a setup that has at least four features, each of which should have at least one component with at least one file to be installed. Set the Typical installation scenario to be that features one and three are installed. You can do this by setting the install level property for features two and four to be 101. Since the INSTALLLEVEL property is set by default to 100, features two and four will not be installed unless the INSTALLLEVEL property is reset to 101 or the end user goes to the custom setup dialog and specifically chooses to install those two features. Once you have created the basic install package, you are ready to create the new setup type dialog box and then to insert it into the installation wizard sequence.

To create your new dialog box you need to go to the User Interface view, select the All Dialogs icon, and right-click the mouse. From the resulting context menu select the New Dialog... option. This launches the Dialog Gallery from which you should choose the Blank Dialog icon. Double-clicking this icon will give you an entry in the User Interface view with the title NewDialog1, which you should rename SetupType3. Now that you have created a blank dialog form you can start to populate it with controls. Figure 9-10 shows the final dialog that you will create.

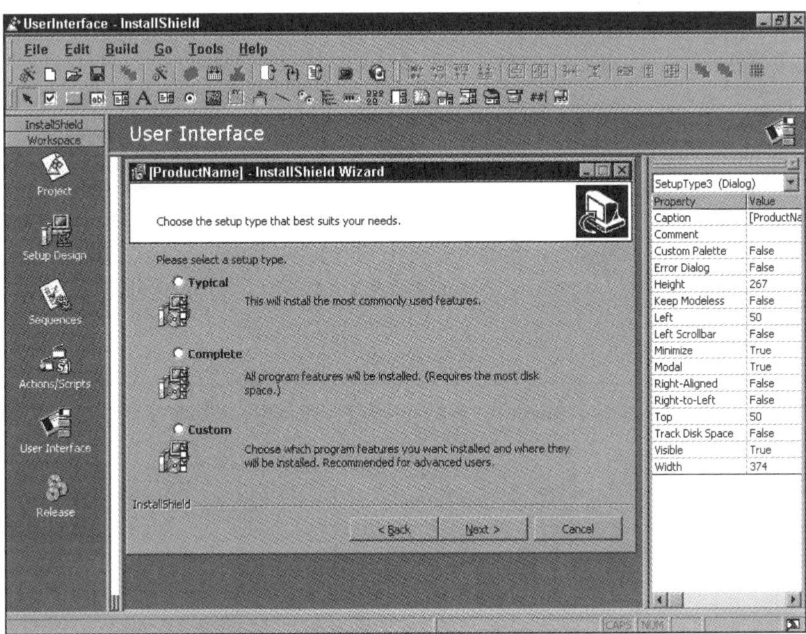

Figure 9-10: The three-way setup type dialog box

You are going to place a total of 21 controls on this blank form to create the SetupType3 dialog box. You can break these controls into three categories: creating the basic design, constructing the radio button functionality, and creating the navigational controls. Each of these categories will be described in more detail later in the chapter, but the first thing you need to do is add a caption to the dialog itself. You define the caption for the dialog by entering a value for the Caption dialog property. To enter the string for the dialog caption, click in the value field for the Caption property and then click on the small button with the ellipsis on the right side of this field. This button takes you to a String Table Editor, where you can add a new string ID with which to associate the caption text. Since you will be associating all the text you enter into this dialog with string IDs you should create a standard format for creating a set of uniform IDs. A format that works is one that has the following format:

```
IUI_<CONTROL NAME OR PROPERTY NAME>_SETUPTYPE3
```

For the caption property use the string ID `IUI_CAPTION_SETUPTYPE3`. Associated with this string ID would be the text string [ProductName] – InstallShield Wizard. The part of the string enclosed in square brackets indicates that the value of the ProductName property will be inserted at that location at the time of installation. For the dialog this is the only property that you need to enter; for all the other properties we can accept the default values.

Now you need to get in and start adding the controls to this dialog. The entries you need to make are described in the following subsections. Only those properties that you need to alter are described.

The basic dialog design

The controls associated with the basic design of the dialog box are those that provide general text relating to the overall purpose of the dialog, placement of bitmaps that make the dialog more pleasant to view, and the branding of the dialog that ensures that everyone knows that InstallShield was used to create the installation package. Table 9-5 shows the property values for the controls to be added to create the basic dialog design.

TABLE 9-5 BASIC DESIGN CONTROLS AND NON-DEFAULT PROPERTY VALUES

Control Name & Type	Property	Value
Banner (Bitmap)	Enabled	False
	File Name	<GraphicSources>\Banner.bmp
	Height	44
	Left	0
	Tab Stop	False
	Top	0
	Width	374
DlgLine (Line)	Enabled	False
	Height	0
	Left	0

Control Name & Type	Property	Value
DlgLine (Line)	Top	44
	Width	374
DlgTitle (Text)	Base Text Style	MSSansBold8
	Height	15
	Left	13
	Tab Stop	False
	Text	Setup Type
	Top	6
	Transparent	True
	Width	292
DlgDesc (Text)	Base Text Style	Tahoma8
	Height	14
	Left	21
	Tab Stop	False
	Text	Choose the setup type that best suits your needs.
	Top	23
	Transparent	True
	Width	292
DlgText (Text)	Base Text Style	Tahoma8
	Height	10
	Left	21
	Tab Stop	False
	Text	Please select a setup type.
DlgText (Text)	Top	51
	Width	326
Branding1 (Text)	Base Text Style	MSSWhiteSerif8
	Height	13
	Left	4
	Tab Stop	False
	Text	InstallShield
	Top	229
	Width	50

Continued

TABLE 9-5 BASIC DESIGN CONTROLS AND NON-DEFAULT PROPERTY VALUES *(Continued)*

Control Name & Type	Property	Value
Branding2 (Text)	Base Text Style	Tahoma8
	Height	13
	Left	3
	Tab Stop	False
	Text	InstallShield
	Top	228
	Transparent	True
	Width	50
BrandingLine (Line)	Enabled	False
	Height	0
	Left	48
	Top	234
	Width	326

In the following remarks more detail is provided with regard to the entries shown in Table 9-5:

The file Banner.bmp can be found on the CD-ROM at the back of the book.

- Banner.bmp can also be found as an .ibd file in C:\Program Files\InstallShield\InstallShield for Windows Installer\Redist\Language Independent\OS Independent\IsDialogBanner.ibd. An .ibd file is the type of file you get when you use Orca to export the Binary table. You can open this file using Visual C++ and resave it as a .bmp file.
- In creating the InstallShield branding you should note that the Branding1 text control where the text style was MSSWhiteSerif8 kept the Transparent property as False. The Branding2 text control changed the Transparent property to True and moved the left coordinate one unit to the left. This is how the sunken look was created.

Constructing the radio button functionality

The main functionality of this dialog resides in the radio button group that you will create. As is the case with all active controls, a radio button group is associated with a property in the Property table. The value of this property is set depending on the specific radio button in the group that is selected. There are 10 specific controls you need to add to the dialog box in order to complete the radio button functionality. Table 9-6 describes the values of the properties for which you are not going to use the defaults provided.

TABLE 9-6 RADIO BUTTON-RELATED CONTROLS AND NON-DEFAULT PROPERTY VALUES

Control Name & Type	Property	Value
SetupType3RBG (RadioButtonGroup)	Has Border	False
	Height	160
	Left	22
	Property	SetupType3RBG
SetupType3RBG (RadioButtonGroup)	Top	65
	Width	286
SetupType3RBG1	Base Text Style	MSSansBold8
(RadioButton)	Height	15
	Left	31
	Order	1
	Text	Typical
	Top	65
	Value	Typical
	Width	276
SetupType3RBG2 (RadioButton)	Base Text Style	MSSansBold8
	Height	15
	Left	31
	Order	2
	Text	Complete
	Top	117
	Value	Complete
	Width	276

Continued

TABLE 9-6 RADIO BUTTON–RELATED CONTROLS AND NON-DEFAULT PROPERTY VALUES *(Continued)*

Control Name & Type	Property	Value
SetupType3RBG3 (RadioButton)	Base Text Style	MSSansBold8
	Height	15
	Left	31
	Order	1
	Text	Custom
	Top	172
	Value	Custom
	Width	276
Typical (Icon)	Enabled	False
	File Name	<GraphicSources>\Typical.ico
	Height	26
	Left	21
	Tab Stop	False
	Top	80
	Width	26
Complete (Icon)	Enabled	False
	File Name	<GraphicSources>\Complete.ico
	Height	26
	Left	21
	Tab Stop	False
	Top	133
	Width	26
Custom (Icon)	Enabled	False
	File Name	<GraphicSources>\Custom.ico
	Height	26
	Left	21
	Tab Stop	False
	Top	186
	Width	26
TypicalText (Text)	Base Text Style	Tahoma8
	Height	31
	Left	86
	Tab Stop	False
	Text	This will install the most commonly used features.

Control Name & Type	Property	Value
TypicalText (Text)	Top	81
	Width	245
CompleteText (Text)	Base Text Style	Tahoma8
	Height	31
	Left	86
	Tab Stop	False
	Text	All program features will be installed. (Requires the most disk space.)
	Top	136
	Width	245
CustomText (Text)	Base Text Style	Tahoma8
	Height	31
	Left	86
	Tab Stop	False
	Text	Choose which program features you want installed and where they will be installed. Recommended for advanced users.
	Top	188
	Width	245

The following remarks provide additional information about the entries shown in Table 9-6:

The icon files Typical.ico, Complete.ico, and Custom.ico can be found on the CD-ROM at the back of the book.

- In the Windows Installer there is only a RadioButtonGroup control with no separate RadioButton control. You create radio buttons by making entries in the RadioButton table and associating the entries in the table to a group through the use of a common property name. The fact that there is a separate radio button on the control toolbar in the Dialog Editor is just a visual mechanism for creating the entries in the RadioButton table.
- The order of the three radio buttons corresponds to the order of their creation. Since you created them from top to bottom the order is from top to bottom.

- The entry for the Value property is what the SetupType3RBG property is set to when the user selects that particular radio button. In order to have a default selection when the end user launches the SetupType3 dialog box you author the SetupType3RBG into the Property table with an initial value of Typical. You can do this using the Property Manager. Actually, when you created the RadioButtonGroup control you specified a property of which the name was entered into the Property Manager; all we have to do is give it an initial value.

Creating the navigational controls

There are three navigational controls you need to place on the dialog box: Next, Back, and Cancel. Unlike with the other controls you have placed on this dialog you not only have to place them in the dialog, but you also have to assign them a certain behavior. To make a control perform a particular action, click on the Behavior icon under the dialog name in the User Interface view. Here you are provided with a list of all the controls in the dialog, and you can select a control and assign a control event to it. First you need to add the pushbuttons to the dialog: Table 9-7 shows the values of the properties for these buttons.

TABLE 9-7 NAVIGATION-RELATED CONTROLS AND NON-DEFAULT PROPERTY VALUES

Control Name & Type	Property	Value
Cancel (PushButton)	Base Text Style	Tahoma8
	Cancel	True
	Height	17
	Left	301
	Text	Cancel
Cancel (PushButton)	Top	243
	Width	66
Next (PushButton)	Base Text Style	Tahoma8
	Default	True
	Height	17
	Left	230
	Text	&Next >
	Top	243
	Width	66

Control Name & Type	Property	Value
Back (PushButton)	Base Text Style	Tahoma8
	Height	17
	Left	164
	Text	< &Back
	Top	243
	Width	66

The following remarks provide additional information for creating the Next and Cancel buttons on the dialog.

- For the Cancel button you need to set the Cancel button to True. This enables the Close title-bar button on the dialog so that clicking on this button or hitting the Escape key performs the same function as clicking the Cancel button itself.
- For the Next button, set the Default property to True. Setting this property makes the Next button the default; as a result, hitting the Enter key has the same effect as clicking the Next button.

You now have to assign the proper control events to these push buttons that you have added to the dialog. Also, in order to insert this new dialog into the installation wizard sequence in place of the standard SetupType dialog you need to make changes to the control events on the upstream and downstream dialogs in the wizard sequence. First you should set the control events for the new dialog.

For the Cancel button you have only one control event to define: for the Cancel button to launch a child dialog that asks the user if he or she really wants to terminate the installation. Figure 9-11 shows this control event.

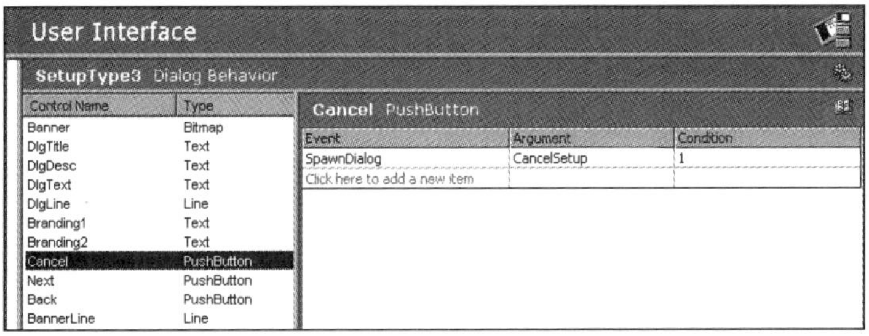

Figure 9-11: The control event for the Cancel button

The control event is the SpawnDialog event and the argument is the name of the child dialog to be launched. The name of the standard child dialog is CancelSetup and the condition you place on this control event is 1, which means that this event will always happen when the user clicks the Cancel button.

You need to define a number of control events for the Next button because the action of this button will depend on which radio button the end user selects. Figure 9-12 shows the three control events you need to define.

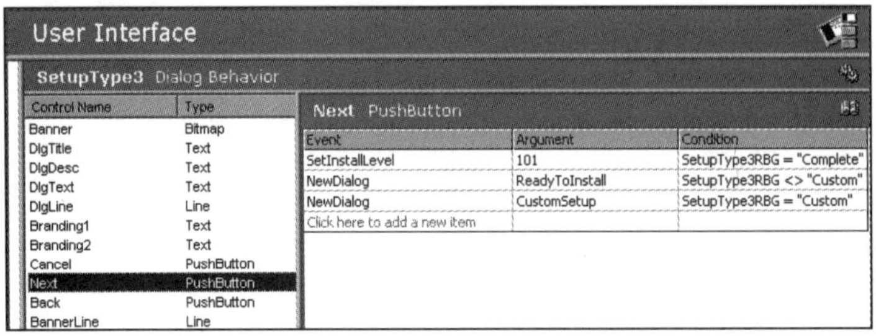

Event	Argument	Condition
SetInstallLevel	101	SetupType3RBG = "Complete"
NewDialog	ReadyToInstall	SetupType3RBG <> "Custom"
NewDialog	CustomSetup	SetupType3RBG = "Custom"

Figure 9-12: The three control events for the Next button

For all of these control events you define conditions based on the value of the SetupType3RBG property. The value of this property is set according to the radio button selected by the end user. If the user opts to do a complete installation then the value of the SetupType3RBG property is set to Complete. In this case you use the SetInstallLevel control event to change the value of the INSTALLLEVEL property to 101, thus ensuring that all features will be installed. Remember that you set the install level property for features two and four to 101 to prevent their installation during a Typical installation.

When clicking the Next button you go to the ReadyToInstall dialog if the user has not chosen to perform a Custom installation and to the CustomSetup dialog if a custom install is selected. The condition placed on the launching of a new dialog determines which dialog is displayed, as shown in Figure 9-12.

You need to define only one control event for the Back button. This is simply to return to the CustomerInformation dialog if the user clicks this button. Figure 9-13 show this control condition.

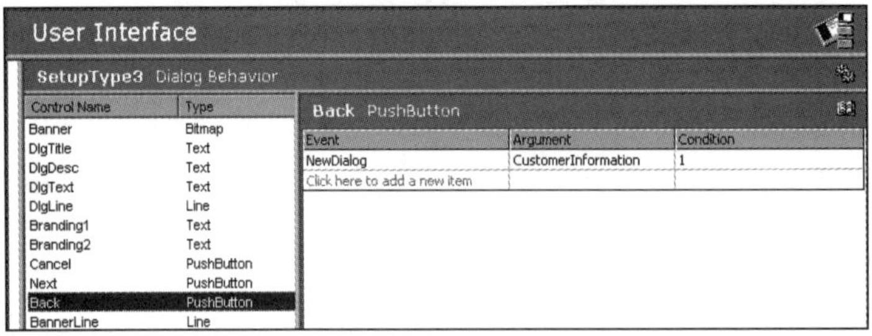

Event	Argument	Condition
NewDialog	CustomerInformation	1

Figure 9-13: The control event for the Back button

The condition placed on this control event ensures that it will always take place when the Back button is clicked.

In order to put this new dialog into the installation wizard sequence you need to adjust the control events on three other dialogs: CustomerInformation, ReadyTo Install, and CustomSetup. For the CustomerInformation dialog you need to set the argument of the NewDialog control event associated with the Next button to be SetupType3. You need to perform a similar operation for the Back buttons on the other two dialogs. These Back buttons must also point at the SetupType3 dialog through the NewDialog control event. Then there is one final action you need to take, to modify a control event associated with the Next button in the CustomSetup dialog. You need to change the [_IsSetupTypeMin] control event to [SetupType3RBG]. The argument must be changed to Custom. The condition for this control event will remain the same as before. The purpose of this control event is to ensure that the if the CustomSetup dialog is entered from a dialog that is not the SetupType3 dialog, the value of the property will be set to Custom.

Once you have completed these actions we have successfully inserted the new dialog box into the installation wizard sequence and all you have to do is test this sequence to make sure everything is working.

Summary

In this chapter you have taken a close look at the user interface implemented by the Windows Installer. You have investigated the user interface functionality from the viewpoint of ISWI. In particular you have seen the Dialog Editor implemented in ISWI, and have used it to modify one of the standard dialogs that come with ISWI. You have also used the Dialog Editor to create a new dialog and have inserted this new dialog into the InstallWelcome wizard sequence. You have gained some knowledge about how the user interface is implemented in the Windows Installer. This information will come in handy in later chapters when you implement real-world solutions that involve the user interface.

Part III

Extending the Windows Installer Functionality

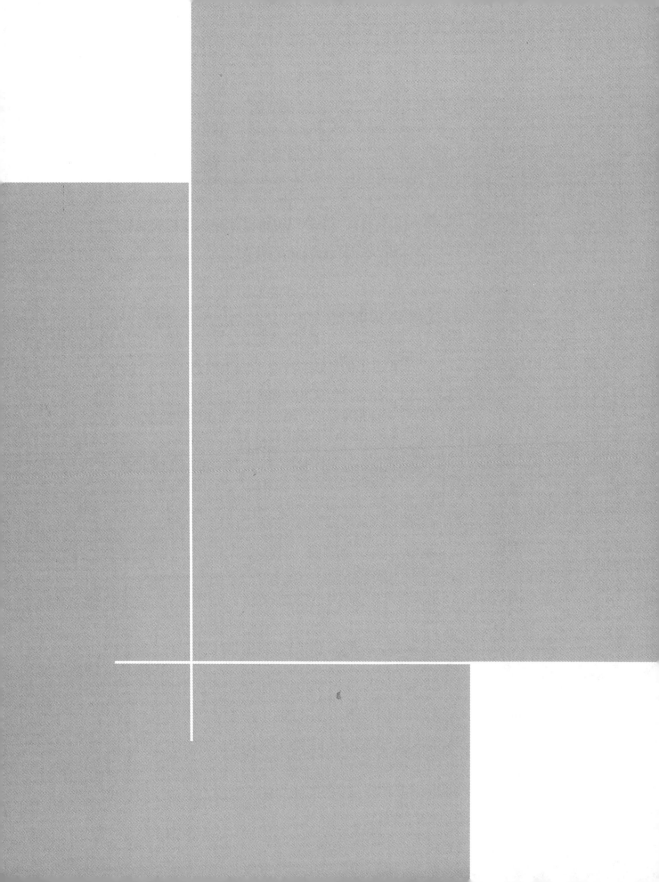

Chapter 10

Extensibility Through Custom Actions

IN THIS CHAPTER

- Custom action basics
- The Windows Installer mechanism
- The categories of custom actions
- The types of custom actions
- How custom actions are processed
- Advanced issues with the use of custom actions

THIS CHAPTER PROVIDES an introduction to extending the built-in functionality of the Windows Installer. You can do this by using what are called *custom actions*. This chapter prepares you to move forward to Chapters 11 and 16 where you will learn how to create custom actions that solve real-world problems. In this chapter you will learn about the various types of custom actions you can create and how to specify the options that define how the Windows Installer is to invoke them.

Custom Action Basics

When you as a setup developer find that a certain functionality is not offered by the Windows Installer as a standard action, you have the option of creating a custom action. Custom actions are the means that Microsoft has created to enable you to extend the capabilities built into the installer. Here are some ways to use custom actions:

- To determine if a reboot is necessary based on whether a particular file was replaced or a particular component was installed
- To perform license verification
- To clean up temporary files created during an installation
- To remove an old product that used a legacy install

- To enable or disable a component after the CostFinalize action has completed
- To validate a serial number entered during an installation
- To initiate a custom sequence that contains actions that change the system
- To set the value of a property to be equal to the value of another property
- To sequence the order of self-registration of COM servers
- To set the ARPINSTALLLOCATION property to the full path of the application's primary folder
- To set the CCP_DRIVE property to the full path to the removable volume
- To create internal consistency evaluators for database validation
- To display an error message and then terminate an installation
- To run a nested installation

Custom actions are identified in the CustomAction table and it is through this table that you integrate the custom code and data into the installation. Custom action code can be in the form of an executable, a dynamic link library, a script, or a formatted text string.

Every custom action is a separate thread from the main installation thread being run by the Windows Installer, and some types are run in a separate process. A custom action thread can be run synchronously or asynchronously. When a custom action is run synchronously the main installation process thread waits for the custom action to complete before it continues. When it is run asynchronously, the main installation process thread continues simultaneously with the custom action execution. There is no way to synchronize an asynchronous custom action and the main installation thread. You can see that you should not run a custom action asynchronously if its function is to perform actions on the results of which other custom or standard actions would depend.

With one exception custom actions only run with user privileges and as such they will have only limited access to the system if the user is not an administrator. The one exception is when a custom action is allowed to run in the system context and thus does not impersonate the user. When the user does not have administrator privileges then the only way for you to create a custom action that will make changes that require elevated privileges is to tap into the Windows Installer through manipulation of the database tables. You would do this by inserting temporary rows into the appropriate database tables to be used as input to standard actions specified in the sequence tables.

Custom actions are sequenced like standard actions. That is, the name of the custom action is placed in a sequence table and given a sequence number that tells the Windows Installer when the action is to be executed relative to other actions. There are six sequence tables in the Windows Installer database schema but only four of these sequence tables can legitimately have custom actions. These four sequence tables define the INSTALL and ADMIN top-level actions. Also, just as with standard actions, you can place a condition on a custom action and it will be executed only if that condition evaluates to TRUE.

You can use four methods to invoke a custom action. As I mentioned just now, the most common invocation method is to insert the name of the custom action into a sequence table. There are two functions that can be called from a custom action that will invoke another standard or custom action and then there is a control event that will call a custom action from a control in a dialog box. We'll discuss these in more detail later in this chapter and give some actual examples in Chapters 11and 16.

Before we go any further in this discussion of custom actions, we need to revisit the discussion in Chapter 3 about the mechanism used by the Windows Installer to perform installations. In the next section, I will go into this subject in more detail because you'll need this background in order to truly understand how custom actions operate.

The Windows Installer Mechanism

In Chapter 3 we discussed in detail the mechanism that the Windows Installer uses to perform a standard installation. To completely understand the operation of various custom actions you need to have a deeper understanding of the details of this mechanism. Figure 10-1 shows a more detailed picture of the Windows Installer run-time architecture.

Instead of dividing user privileges from elevated privileges as in Figure 3-1, here the line divides the picture between the client process and the server process. There are five important concepts that you should understand about the run-time environment of the Windows Installer on Windows NT and Windows 2000. These can have a major impact on how you use custom actions:

- The client process initiates the total mechanism of the Windows Installer.
- The user-interface level you specify when initiating a top-level action has a major impact on how the Windows Installer proceeds with executing that action.
- The Windows Installer database is open in both processes.
- Only public properties are carried across from the client-side database to the service-side database.
- At the end of the execution of any top-level action control is always passed back to the client side. This happens regardless of success or failure of the operation.

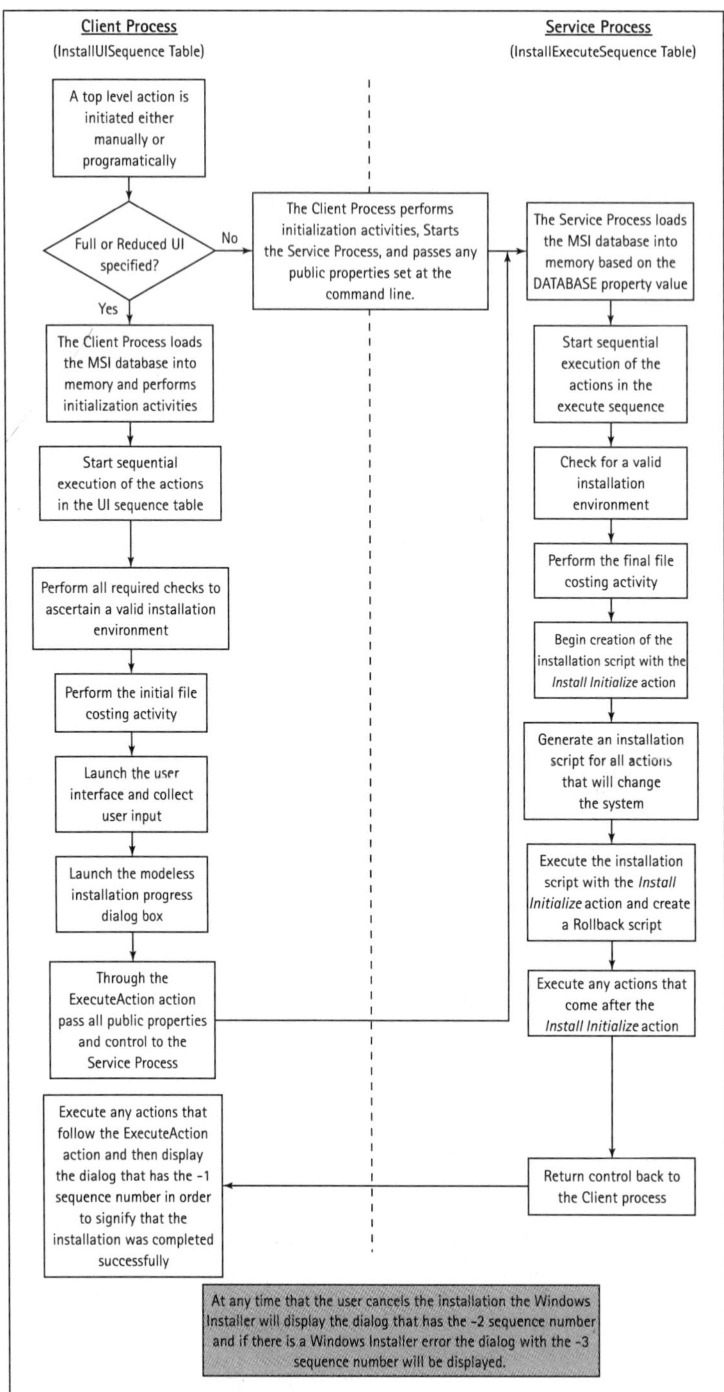

Figure 10-1: Details of the Windows Installer run-time architecture

The focus of this book is Windows 2000 and you need to understand that the Windows Installer operates in a different mode on a Win 9x machine. On Win 9x both the user interface sequence and execute sequence are run in the same (client) process. This means that both private and public properties are available in both sequence tables since there is only one copy of the database that is being used.

User Impersonation and the Windows Installer Service

As we discuss in Chapter 3 and again in this chapter the Windows Installer is a client/server operation with the main functionality of an installation being carried out on the server side as an NT service. When the Windows Installer is installed on Windows NT 4.0 or it comes natively with Windows 2000, its access token is the token of the local system. This means that the service process can do anything that a local administrator can do.

Now this can be a problem because when a user without administrator privileges initiates an installation it is possible for the service side to do a lot more on the systems than the user could do. This is definitely not what you want to happen, because it would completely destroy the objective of being able to lock down the desktop except for authorized applications. What you really want is for the service process to operate as if it had the same access to the system resources as the user has — unless some higher authority overrides this default security mechanism of custom actions. In this case the higher authority is the system administrator using the system Policy Editor or the Group Policy Editor, depending on whether we are talking about a Windows NT 4.0 or Windows 2000 network. The question is how is such functionality implemented?

The service process uses the access token of the client process to try to access the resources necessary to perform the installation. The security mechanism in Windows NT/2000 operates so as to compare the access token of the client with the security descriptor of the resources being accessed. This authentication and authorization process is part of the basic security infrastructure of Windows NT/2000. This act of the service process pretending to be the client is called *user impersonation.*

It is important to understand that when an application is installed for the machine, then the install is elevated for all users of the machine. So if you have a system administrator install an application for a particular machine, all users of the machine — even those who do not have administrative privileges — can perform maintenance mode operations for the application. This means that non-admin users of the machine can perform repair, change, and/or remove operations.

Custom Action Categories

Custom actions can be categorized according to when and in which process of the installation they are executed. You can run custom actions during the UI sequence and/or the execute sequence. They can be executed as the install script is being created, they can be executed when the install script is being executed, they can be executed during a rollback operation, and they can be executed after the successful completion of the installation. There are two major categories of custom actions: *immediate* and *deferred*. The deferred category is made up of four subcategories: *install*, *rollback*, *commit*, and *system context*. Each of these categories and subcategories is the subject of one of the following subsections.

Immediate execution custom actions

An immediate custom action is executed as soon as the Windows Installer encounters it when processing the sequence tables. Immediate is the default category for custom actions. Custom actions in this category can be placed in any sequence, except for advertise execute. There are a few sequencing restrictions on where certain types of immediate custom actions can be used. These restrictions are discussed in the section "Custom Action Types" later in this chapter. In general, you can use immediate category custom actions to set properties, feature states, component states, and target directories by manipulating the rows in various database tables. You can also use them to schedule system operations by inserting rows into the sequence tables or run and schedule other actions directly by using the MsiDoAction() API. You should *not* use them to make changes directly to the system or to call any system services directly. You should schedule these types of actions to occur when the install script is actually executed; we discuss deferred execution custom actions in the next subsection.

To summarize, you should only use immediate custom actions to modify the MSI database, and other aspects of the install session like setting properties, and not to perform any direct action on the system. The Windows Installer will then use the database entries created by immediate custom actions to make the required changes to the system. Remember that immediate custom actions only execute with user privileges and can have only limited access to the system. The Windows Installer can have elevated privileges in cases where the user does not have administrative privileges. The installer can therefore make changes to the system if those changes have been identified in the database.

Deferred execution custom actions

A deferred custom action is one whose execution is delayed until the install script is itself executed. This type of action differs from the immediate custom action in the previous section; that type of custom action is executed as soon as the Windows Installer encounters it in the sequence table. A deferred custom action is created so as to make direct changes to the system. Because a deferred custom action is written into the execution script, the database has already been processed and the install script generated before it is executed. A deferred custom action allows the setup developer to specify system operations to be carried out at a particular point during the installation.

INSTALL CUSTOM ACTIONS

Because you have to write this category of custom action into the install script, you can only sequence it in the execute sequence table. There you must place it in that portion of the execute sequence that is the target of script generation. This section is bounded by the InstallInitialize and InstallFinalize actions: therefore deferred custom actions must come after the InstallInitialize action and before the InstallFinalize action. Placing them in any other location will generate a Windows Installer error during the installation process.

Deferred custom actions can be particularly challenging depending on the type of deferred custom action. This is because of the possibility that an installation script, under certain circumstances, can be executed outside the installation session in which it was written. This creates a problem for the type of deferred custom action that requires a handle to the session object. I'll address this particular problem with deferred custom actions in the section on advanced issues later in this chapter.

ROLLBACK CUSTOM ACTIONS

As I already described, the Windows Installer creates a rollback script as it is processing the installation script. At the same time, it is caching all the files it deletes from the system as part of the installation. This makes it possible to return the system back to its original state if the installation fails or is canceled by the user. Once the installation is completed successfully the rollback script and the cached files are deleted from the system. In the previous section you learned that deferred custom actions are those that change the system directly and do not work through the Windows Installer by changing the database. System changes made by this category of custom action cannot be automatically rolled back by the Windows Installer because the Installer does not know what those system changes were. Because of this, there must be a way to reverse these changes during the rollback action.

You use the rollback category of custom action to reverse the system changes made by a normal custom action during the installation process. A rollback custom action is a type of deferred custom action in that it is not executed when the Windows Installer encounters it in the execute sequence table. The Windows Installer copies this type of custom action into the rollback script, and the action is only executed if a rollback becomes necessary.

COMMIT CUSTOM ACTIONS

Commit custom actions are the complement of rollback custom actions. They are executed upon successful completion of the installation script. This means that they are run after the completion of the InstallFinalize action. Since they are executed only after a successful installation these are only temporary changes made by other custom actions – for example rollback related data that is now no longer needed.

Commit custom actions are the complement of rollback custom actions. When rollback is disabled, neither commit nor rollback custom actions are executed. By default, rollback is enabled but there is a public property that can be set at the command line to disable this functionality. When rollback is disabled, the Windows Installer sets the RollbackDisabled property. If an installation cannot be completed successfully with rollback disabled, then the RollbackDisabled property must be used in a condition to prevent the installation from proceeding. The proper place for this condition is in the LaunchCondition table. You need to create the condition in the LaunchCondition table and to set a condition on the LaunchConditions action so that this action is executed when rollback has been disabled.

Now that I have described the four categories of custom actions we need to get into the details of the various types of custom actions and how they are actually invoked. This is the subject of the next two sections. The types of custom actions are explained in the next section and then the processing of custom actions is discussed in the section after that. Later on we will get into actually creating custom actions of all types.

SYSTEM CONTEXT CUSTOM ACTIONS

By default the Windows Installer runs a custom action at the privilege level of the user who is doing the installation. This will be the case even if the user who does not have administrative privileges is granted elevated privileges by the system administrator. This default functionality can be changed if a custom action is defined to run in the system context. Running in the system context is considered to be running the custom action without any user impersonation. The most common cases where elevated privileges are granted are as follows:

- A per-machine installation of an application that is performed by an administrator is then elevated for all users of the machine so that they can perform maintenance operations on the application.
- A per-user installation of an application is performed using the assignment and publishing capabilities of IntelliMirror. IntelliMirror was discussed extensively in Chapter 2.
- A per-user installation of an application is performed after an administrator has set the per-user and per-machine AlwaysInstallElevated system policy.

Running a custom action in the system context is the way to get around the default security model for custom actions. If a user has administrative privileges on his or her local machine, a system context custom action has no meaning, because all custom actions will run in the system context. However, if the user only has user privileges then a system context custom action will only run at elevated privileges if the user has been granted elevated privileges by the system administrator. Of course, this only has meaning on Windows NT/2000 since Windows 95/98 do not have privilege levels.

On Windows NT 4.0 for a system context custom action to run in the system context the system policy AlwaysInstallElevated (Per-User) and the AlwaysInstallElevated (Per-Machine) must both be set to 1. You can set them using the System Policy Editor found in a Windows NT 4.0 Server-run network. The registry key under which the per-user value is defined is as follows:

```
HKEY_CURRENT_USER\Software\Policies\Microsoft\Windows\Installer
```

The registry key under which the per-machine value is defined is as follows:

```
HKEY_LOCAL_MACHINE\Software\Policies\Microsoft\Windows\Installer
```

On Windows 2000 the execution of system context custom actions is pretty much the same functionality as just described for Windows NT 4.0. If an application is managed in a Windows 2000 network and a user not included in the authorized group of people who have been designated to have this application installs this application, a system context custom action will still only run with user privileges and not in the system context. However, this is a difference that has no real meaning because even if an application itself would only need to write to the HKEY_CURRENT_USER registry key the Windows Installer still needs to write to the HKEY_LOCAL_MACHINE registry key in order to enter the data that it stores with regard to what products are using which components, and so forth.

Basically, if you have a system context custom action and you only have user privileges then you will not be able to run the installation unless the system administrator has granted you permission. In this scenario the system context custom action will run with elevated privileges and all other types of custom actions will run with user privileges. If you have administrative privileges, then all custom actions will run in the system context regardless of their type. This will be true on either Windows NT 4.0 or Windows 2000.

The Custom Action Database Tables

There are ten database tables involved with custom actions. They are the CustomAction, Binary, Directory, Error, File, InstallUISequence, InstallExecute Sequence, AdminUISequence, AdminExecuteSequence, and Property tables. The CustomAction table is the central point in all this functionality and it provides the means by which custom actions and data are integrated into an installation. It is this table that uses the other tables listed for identifying the location of the source of the code that implements the custom action. Figure 10-2 provides the schema for six of these database tables used in defining custom actions. The sequence tables are not shown in the schema since they serve only to define when a custom action is to be executed.

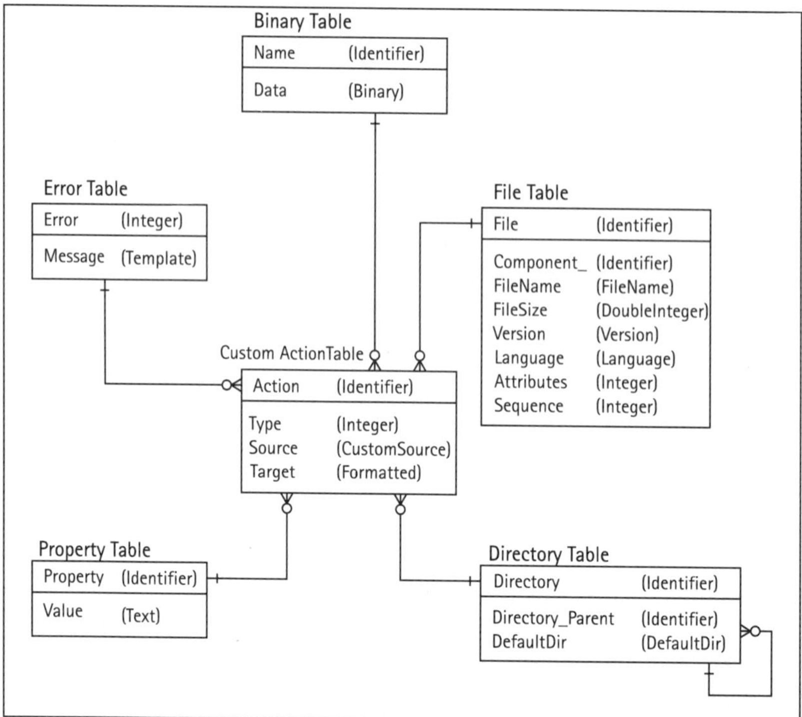

Figure 10-2: Schema of the custom action related database tables

Since the CustomAction table is the controlling entity for the custom action functionality, we are going to look at this table in detail. Table 10-1 defines the various columns in this table.

TABLE 10-1 ATTRIBUTE DESCRIPTION FOR THE CUSTOMACTION TABLE

Column Name	Data Type	Description
Action	Identifier	Specifies the name of the action, which is entered into the first column of the applicable sequence table. If this custom action was only called by another custom action, the name of the custom action will still be entered in this table but will not be entered into the sequence table.

Column Name	Data Type	Description
		When the Windows Installer encounters a name in the sequence table, it first looks for a standard action of that name and then looks for a custom action specified in this table. If the name provided in this table is the same as the name of a standard action, then the custom action will never be called.
Type	Integer	Defines the type of custom action as well as the options to be used in processing this custom action. The options specified with this value are how the Windows Installer is to treat the return value from a custom action; how the custom action is to be scheduled to run and in which process; and the category of the custom action as defined earlier in this chapter.
Source	CustomSource	Specifies the location of the custom action code. In most cases this field is a foreign key into the Binary, Directory, Property, or File table where the location of the source code is defined. For some types of custom actions the code for the custom action is given in the Target field of the CustomAction table and in these cases this field is NULL. The full details of the parameters used in this column are given in the following subsections.
Target	Formatted	Normally the definition of the calling parameters for the custom action code. For example, if the custom action is a DLL this field would specify the DLL entry point. The full details of the parameters used in this column are given in the following subsections.

Streaming the files that implement custom actions into the Binary table is the most convenient method of delivering a custom action to the system so that it can be executed. It is the method used by Microsoft for handling the custom actions that comprise the validation .cub files. Table 10-2 describes the two columns that comprise this table.

TABLE 10-2 DESCRIPTION OF THE BINARY TABLE ATTRIBUTES AS THEY RELATE TO CUSTOM ACTIONS

Column Name	Data Type	Description
Name	Identifier	The primary key for the table and a unique identifier for accessing the binary data being stored in the table. When the file implementing the custom action is being stored in the Binary table, this value is used in the Source column of the CustomAction table to identify the file.
Data	Binary	Contains a binary stream that comprises the bits that make up the file that is to implement the custom action. Using the MsiRecordSetStream and the MsiViewModify database functions creates the binary data stream.

If the file containing the implementation of the custom action is to be installed with the application, you must make an entry in the File table. Table 10-3 describes the columns of this table and how they relate to custom actions.

TABLE 10-3 DESCRIPTION OF THE FILE TABLE ATTRIBUTES AS THEY RELATE TO CUSTOM ACTIONS

Column Name	Data Type	Description
File	Identifier	The primary key for this table and a unique identifier. When the file implementing the custom action is being installed with the installation, this value is used in the Source column of the CustomAction table to identify the file.
Component_	Identifier	A foreign key into the Component table that identifies the component controlling the file that will implement the custom action.
FileName	Filename	The actual name of the file being used to implement the custom action.

Column Name	Data Type	Description
FileSize	DoubleInteger	The size of the file in bytes. This is the same value you see when looking at the properties of the file using the right-click context menu in Windows Explorer.
Version	Version	The version number of the file. This is the same value you see when looking at the properties of the file using the right-click context menu in Windows Explorer.
Language	Language	The language of the file. This is the same value you see when looking at the properties of the file using the right-click context menu in Windows Explorer.
Attributes	Integer	Identifies the properties of the file. These properties include Read Only, Hidden, System, and so on.
Sequence	Integer	Identifies the position of the file on the media image.

The Directory table comes into play in two different ways when it comes to custom actions. You can use it to identify where the Windows Installer can find the file that is implementing the custom action, and it can be the target of the custom action. When the Directory table is the target of a custom action, then the custom action is acting on this table to make an entry in it.

When using a Directory table–based custom action, you need to make sure that it is not inserted into the sequence prior to the table's initialization. If you insert it before this, you will get a 2732 run-time error saying that the Directory Manager is not initialized. This will happen if the costing actions have not been completed.

Table 10-4 provides a description of the Directory table columns and how to use them when implementing custom actions.

Table 10-4 DESCRIPTION OF THE DIRECTORY TABLE ATTRIBUTES AS THEY RELATE TO CUSTOM ACTIONS

Column Name	Data Type	Description
Directory	Identifier	Either a unique name for a directory or directory path or the name of a property. This column is the primary key for this table. This identifier is used in the Source column of the CustomAction table for two different types of custom actions: To identify a directory that provides the working location of an executable that is to implement the custom action To identify a directory whose location will be set using a formatted text string entered into the Target column of the CustomAction table.
Directory_Parent	Identifier	Defines the parent of the directory being defined or indicates that this row is a root directory. A NULL value in this column indicates a root directory.
DefaultDir	DefaultDir	Defines the name of the directory under the parent directory defined in the Directory_Parent column. By default this column defines both the target and source directories.

The Property table comes into play with three types of custom actions. You can use it to provide a location where the Windows Installer can find the file that is implementing the custom action; you can use it to contain the actual script implementing the custom action; or you can make it the target of a special type of custom action to set a property using a formatted text string. You need to understand that there are two versions of the Property table, the one that is persisted in the Windows Installer database and the one that gets created in-memory when at the start of an installation. The one that is created in-memory at run-time goes by a different name that is not documented. When you enter properties into the Property table during the creation of an installation package, you are entering them into the persisted version of the Property table. When you create properties during the running of an installation, you are making these entries only in the in-memory version of the Property table. Table 10-5 provides a description of the columns of the Property table and how they are used to implement custom actions.

TABLE 10-5 DESCRIPTION OF THE PROPERTY TABLE ATTRIBUTES AS THEY RELATE TO CUSTOM ACTIONS

Column Name	Data Type	Description
Property	Identifier	The primary key for this table; a unique identifier. Used in the Source column of the CustomAction table for three different types of custom actions: To identify a property whose value gives the complete path to an executable that is to implement the custom action To identify a property whose value contains the complete script text for either a VBScript- or a JScript-implemented custom action To identify a property whose value will be set using a formatted text string entered into the Target column of the CustomAction table
Value	Text	The value of the property, which can either be the path to an executable implementing a custom action or contain the script text that implements a custom action. You can set this value using a formatted string in the Target column of the CustomAction table.

Table 10-6 describes the columns in the Error table and how they are used to implement custom actions. The Error table is used to implement a special type of custom action. This is a custom action that displays an error message and then terminates the installation.

The Binary table contains the source for the custom actions contained in files. The advantage of using the Binary table is that the file containing the custom action functionality is always available. This is not the case when you use the File table to identify the location of the custom action, because in this case you have to install the file first before the custom action can be executed. The Directory and Property tables define the location of the custom action that is to be run. In two cases these tables have a value set by a particular type of custom action. The Error table is used for a special type of custom action that just displays an error message.

We are now ready to delve into the details of each type of custom action. In this discussion we'll look at particular groupings of the custom action types. Most of these groupings will be based on the format by which the custom action is implemented.

TABLE 10-6 DESCRIPTION OF THE ERROR TABLE ATTRIBUTES AS THEY RELATE TO CUSTOM ACTIONS

Column Name	Data Type	Description
Error	Integer	Contains the error number and is the primary key for this table. A special type of custom action will display an error message based on an entry in the Target column of the CustomAction table. If the formatted string in the Target column evaluates to an integer, then the error message associated with that integer in the Error table will be displayed. Error numbers from 25000 to 30000 are reserved for this type of custom action.
Message	Template	The error message template that will be displayed if a custom action references the error number in the Error column.

Custom Action Types

There are six distinct types of custom actions documented in the Windows Installer help. An additional type of custom action is provided by InstallShield for Windows Installer. This type of custom action is the subject of Chapters 12 and 13. For now we will only discuss what might be termed the native custom action types. The types are defined by the mechanism used to implement their functionality. These custom action types are listed in the following sections.

Custom actions implemented in an executable file

The actions to be performed are implemented in an .exe file. Four subtypes comprise this custom action type. The subtypes are defined by the source used to locate the applicable executable file. The executable file custom action is the only type of custom action for which the code can already reside on the machine that is the target of the installation. In all other types of custom actions the implementation code must either be installed as part of the installation or be incorporated into one of the database tables shown in Figure 10-2.

If the category of custom action is immediate, the executable that implements the custom action is created with the CreateProcessAsUser() API. This function is passed the security token of the user so that the custom action will only run with user privileges. This is also how the install, rollback, and commit subcategories of deferred custom actions are launched. However, if the custom action is the system context subcategory of deferred custom action then it will be launched with the

CreateProcess() API function if the user has been granted elevated privileges. If the user tries to install a managed application without authorization, the custom action will be launched with the CreateProcessAsUser() API. If the user has administrative privileges, the performance of the custom action and the resources to which it has access will be the same regardless of which API function is used.

A custom action implemented as an executable is the only type of custom action that can continue beyond the point of termination of the Windows Installer. In order for this to happen the executable custom action must be defined to run asynchronously.

Custom actions implemented in a dynamic link library

The actions to be performed by this type of custom action are implemented in a .dll file. Two subtypes comprise this type. As with the executable file type of custom action the subtypes are defined by the source used for locating the dynamic link library being used for the implementation. The one thing about this type of custom action is that it must be installed with the application. Because of this you cannot call directly to a Windows API. You have to create the custom action .dll file and then call a Windows API if that is what you want to do.

Using the information provided in the CustomAction table the Windows Installer knows the path of the dynamic link library and proceeds to call first the LoadLibrary() API function to get the handle to the module and then the GetProcAddress() API function to get the address of the exported function that implements the custom action. Using this function address the Windows Installer then calls this function to execute the custom action. In order to call the function the Windows Installer has defined the prototype of this function.

```
UINT __stdcall MyActionName(MSIHANDLE hInstall)
```

Since this type of information is not provided in the CustomAction table you can pass only a predefined parameter to this function. The only parameter that the Windows Installer knows to pass is the handle to the current install session and this is the only parameter that is allowed when defining this exported function. Also, when defining the exported function that will implement the custom action you will need to specify that it use the __stdcall calling convention. You need to make sure you know what the exported name of the function will be so you can enter it into the CustomAction table correctly. See the sidebar on this subject later in this chapter.

Custom actions implemented in script

You can implement custom actions using either VBScript or JScript. You can implement custom actions in VBScript either in a .vbs file or by entering the script text in one of the appropriate tables. You can implement custom actions in JScript either in a .js file or by entering the script text in one of the appropriate tables. Four subtypes comprise either the VBScript or the JScript custom actions. These subtypes are defined by the source used for locating the source of the code to implement the custom action.

In order for a custom action defined in script to run it must have VBSCRIPT.DLL on the system if the script being used is VBScript, or JSCRIPT.DLL if the script being used is JScript. You need the file SCRRUN.DLL regardless of what script language you're using. All of these files should be on all supported operating systems, but it is possible that a custom action will need an updated version of these files if a syntax is being used that is not supported by earlier versions. This could be the case on a Windows 95 system. In some cases you may need to install these files along with the application files so that custom actions implemented in script will function properly.

Custom actions implemented as formatted text

This type of custom action can change the values of properties and change directory paths. The changes that are made by these custom actions are all made in the in-memory version of the Property table. All the information required to implement this type of custom action is contained in the CustomAction table. There are two subtypes of this custom action type defined by the possible targets of the action. In the Source column of the CustomAction table is specified either a key into the Directory table or into the Property table. In the Target column of the CustomAction table you would place the formatted text string that would set these values.

A formatted text string is a string that has embedded in it certain parameters that are replaced by values from the MSI database or from the system. All parameters replaced during the resolution of the formatted text string are surrounded by square brackets (`[]`). The formats to use for these parameters are as follows:

[property name]	Resolved when it is replaced by the value of the property in the Property table.
[%environment variable]	Resolved when it is replaced by the value of the environment variable as defined by the system.
[#file key]	Resolved when it is replaced by the value of the full path to the file defined by this primary key in the File table.

[$component key]	Resolved when it is replaced by the value of the full path to the installation location of the component defined by this primary key in the Component table. This installation can have one of three different values depending on the install state of the component. If the component is to be run locally, this is the path to the installation folder on the local system. If the component is to run from source, this will be the value of the source location for the component. Finally, if the component is not selected to be installed then a null string will replace this sub-string.
[\c]	Replaced by the character that immediately follows the backslash. If more than one character follows the backslash, only the first character will be inserted into the string and all other characters are ignored. You would be most likely to use this sub-string if you wanted to insert a literal `[` into the string.

We will take a look later in the chapter at how this type of custom action could be used in place of the dynamic link library we used in Chapter 4 to initialize the default location for the TARGETDIR property.

Custom actions that display error messages

This is a special type of custom action whose sole purpose is to display an error message and then terminate the installation. It can display the message from the CustomAction table or the Error table. For this type of custom action the Source column of the CustomAction table is left blank and the Target column contains a formatted text string that will resolve either to a text string or to a pure numeric value. If the formatted text string resolves to a string that has non-numeric characters, the string itself is displayed as the error message. However, if the formatted string resolves to a pure numeric value, then it is used as an entry into the Error table and the message associated with that error number is displayed as the error message. The formatting of the text string to be placed in the Target column of the CustomAction table follows the same rules as described in the previous section on custom actions implemented using formatted text.

Custom actions that perform nested installations

This custom action type does just what the name implies: It is able to nest a child installation inside a parent installation. Three subtypes comprise this custom action type. These subtypes are defined by the location of the installation package that implements the nested installation.

The Windows Installer package that contains the nested installation can be inserted as a sub-storage into the main installation package. It can also be located at the root of the source tree, or it can be an MSI package that has already been either advertised or installed on the target machine. There are severe sequencing restrictions on where a nested installation custom action can be placed in the sequence of the main installation. The user interface of the nested installation will not be displayed and all progress messages for the nested installation will be shown by the progress dialog of the main installation. A nested installation custom action can only be run as an immediate category of custom action and it can only be run synchronously with the main installation.

We will get into detail about how nested installation custom actions are to be implemented in Chapter 11.

In the following subsections each of these types of custom actions will be described in detail. The next subsection kicks off this detailed discussion by looking at the database tables involved in the definition and execution of custom actions.

Basic Custom Action Implementation

There are 20 basic types of custom actions and these are the focus in this section. You can modify the performance of most of these basic custom action types with certain additional options that define special scheduling, invocation, and return value processing. These additional options are discussed in the next section. This section addresses where custom actions can be stored, which is the key element in defining these 20 basic custom action types.

Storing custom actions in the binary table

You can store four types of custom actions in the Binary table. These are described in Table 10-7. In order to be in the Binary table these types of custom actions must be defined in a file and they must have an .exe, .dll, .vbs, or .js file extension. The files that implement the custom action are streamed out into a temporary file created in the TEMP directory. This file's name will begin with msi followed by a unique number and the extension .tmp. The Windows Installer knows how to invoke this file based on the custom action type. For all of these custom actions the Source column of the CustomAction table contains a foreign key into the Binary table.

TABLE 10-7 BASIC CUSTOM ACTION TYPES STORED IN THE BINARY TABLE

Custom Action	Description
Type 1	A dynamic link library and the Target column of the CustomAction table containing the name of the exported function that will implement this custom action.
Type 2	An executable file and the Target column of the CustomAction table containing any command line string that this executable needs to run correctly. This column can be blank if no command line is required.
Type 5	A custom action written in JScript and the Target column containing the name of an optional function that will be called after the Windows Installer parses the script text. This column can be blank.
Type 6	A custom action written in VBScript and the Target column containing the name of an optional function that will be called after the Windows Installer parses the script text. This column can be blank.

Copying custom actions to the system during installation

Four types of custom actions can be copied to the system during the installation. These are described in Table 10-8. Just like the custom action types that can be stored in the Binary table these types of custom actions also must be defined in a file and they must have a recognized file extension. Since these types of custom actions depend on the file that implements the functionality to be copied to the system they must be deferred category custom actions. Being deferred custom actions they must be placed after the InstallInitialize action and, because the file must be copied to the system before it can be executed, it can only be placed after the InstallFiles action in the execute sequence. Since these files will be removed during an uninstallation it is important to place a condition on these custom actions so that they only run during installation.

TABLE 10-8 BASIC CUSTOM ACTION TYPES COPIED TO THE SYSTEM DURING INSTALLATION

Custom Action	Description
Type 17	A dynamic link library and the Target column of the CustomAction table containing the name of the exported function that will implement this custom action.
Type 18	An executable file and the Target column of the CustomAction table containing any command line string that this executable needs to run correctly. This column can be blank if no command line is required.
Type 21	A custom action written in JScript and the Target column containing the name of an optional function that will be called after the Windows Installer parses the script text. This column can be blank.
Type 22	A custom action written in VBScript and the Target column containing the name of an optional function that will be called after the Windows Installer parses the script text. This column can be blank.

Calling Conventions, Exporting Symbols, and Name Decoration in Dynamic Link Libraries Created with Microsoft Visual C++

In order to understand how an executable or dynamic link library links to functions defined in a dynamic link library and compiled with Microsoft Visual C++, you need to know the four calling conventions supported by the Visual C/C++ compiler; the three methods for exporting functions from a dynamic link library; and how the Visual C/C++ compiler decorates the function names for internal use.

The four calling conventions are __cdecl, __stdcall, __fastcall, and thiscall. The __cdecl calling convention is the default calling convention for C and C++ programs compiled with Microsoft Visual C++. The argument passing order is from right to left. With this calling convention the caller of the function cleans up the stack. This means that the function doing the calling will pop the arguments from the stack. Because of this, functions that use the __cdecl calling convention can have a variable number of arguments.

The __stdcall calling convention is used to call Win32 API functions. The argument passing order is from right to left, just as for the __cdecl calling convention. Here the called function is responsible for cleaning up the stack. Since this calling convention does not allow a variable argument list, a function that uses this modifier but has a variable set of arguments is automatically compiled as __cdecl. Functions that use this calling convention require a function prototype.

The __fastcall calling convention specifies that arguments are to be passed in registers whenever possible. The implementation of this calling convention is for the first two DWORD or smaller arguments to be passed in the ECX and EDX registers with all other arguments being passed from right to left. With this calling convention the clean up of the stack is done by the called function. The compiler defines the use of these registers, and new versions of the compiler could possibly change the registers used for passing arguments.

The thiscall calling convention is the default calling convention for functions that are members of a C++ class. In this case the arguments are placed on the stack from right to left with the this pointer being placed on the stack last. The this pointer is not an explicit member of the argument list and it points to the object itself. Functions declared with the static keyword do not have the implicit this pointer argument.

C and C++ symbols define variable and function names. When Microsoft Visual C++ compiles a C or C++ program, the symbols are encoded so as to include type information. This encoding is required in C++ since this language permits the overloading of function names. When a function is overloaded, there can be more than one function with that name as long as the argument lists between the two functions are different. This encoding allows the linker to distinguish between different versions of the overloaded function. This name encoding spills over to programs written in the C language.

This encoding of symbols performed by the Microsoft Visual C++ compiler is called *name decoration* or *name mangling*. The algorithm used for creating these decorated names is contingent on the calling convention being used for the function. It's important to know what the decorated name of the function is when you're creating dynamic link libraries for functions being exported and the client of the exported function is linking explicitly to the DLL.

A function name can be exported using the __declspec(dllexport) keyword in the source code; an EXPORTS statement in a module definition file (.def); or an /EXPORT specification in a command to LINK.EXE.

Continued

Calling Conventions, Exporting Symbols, and Name Decoration in Dynamic Link Libraries Created with Microsoft Visual C++ *(Continued)*

The purpose of the __declspec(dllexport) keyword is to simplify the handling of decorated names, particularly in C++. Every compiler has a proprietary algorithm for creating decorated names for exported functions in a dynamic link library. In fact, this algorithm can change among different versions of a compiler. This is true for Microsoft Visual C++. To account for name changes that occur when you upgrade your compiler, all you have to do is recompile the DLL and the EXE to account for the name changes.

When you use C++ the decorated names generated by Microsoft Visual C++ are somewhat long and, as I mentioned before, they are proprietary and subject to change at a moment's notice. However, when you're programming in C the decorated names are predictable, although they differ depending on the calling convention being used. In fact, you can make C++ functions predictable by using the extern "C" modifier when defining your function. The only place you cannot use this modifier is on a function that is a class method. It is, of course, not recognized as a valid keyword in a C language file since its only purpose is to force the C naming convention to be used from a C++ program.

For the __cdecl calling convention the compiler decorates the name by just prefixing the underscore (_) character to the function name. However, if you use the __declspec(dllexport) keyword then the underscore is stripped from the exported name and all that is left is the original name used in the DLL.

When you use the __stdcall calling convention, you create the decorated name by prefixing the underscore character to the function name, appending the at symbol (@) to the end of the function name, and then adding the decimal number that represents the number of bytes in the argument list. Using the __declspec(dllexport) keyword does nothing in this case to change the exported function name. For example, a function that is declared as `int __stdcall function( char c, int a, double b)` would have a decorated name of _function@13.

When you use the __fastcall calling convention, you create the decorated name by prefixing and appending at symbols (@) to the function name and then following the last at symbol with the decimal number of bytes in the argument list. Using the __declspec(dllexport) keyword does nothing in this case to change the exported function name. For example, a function that is declared as `int __fastcall function( char c, int a, double b)` would have a decorated name of @function@13. The thiscall calling convention cannot export the function names using the C calling convention since it is used only for C++ member functions and thus you cannot use the extern "C" modifier.

So what do you do if you cannot accept a decorated name because of the implementation you're using? This is where the module definition file or the /EXPORT specification for LINK.EXE come in. Unlike the __declspec(dllexport) keyword a .DEF file or the /EXPORT specification permit the definition of the name to be used for the exported function to be the same as the name used in the source code. This can be very useful when the client has to explicitly link to the DLL. In such a case the client will be using the LoadLibrary to load the DLL into the address space of the client and then using GetProcAddress to get the address of the exported function. GetProcAddress uses the handle to the DLL obtained by calling LoadLibrary and the exported name of the function to be called. This can only be done if the exported name of the function is known at run time. It is important to be able to provide to the client the exported name of the function to be called and this is much easier when you can control the name during the build.

Identifying the custom action via the directory table

There is only one type of custom action that has its location specified in the Directory table. This type of custom action depends on an executable file being on the system before the installation commences. As such this custom action can be either immediate or deferred. The Windows Installer locates this file through a key to the Directory table. This custom action is described in Table 10-9.

Table 10-9 CUSTOM ACTION TYPES LOCATED BY A KEY INTO THE DIRECTORY TABLE

Custom Action	Description
Type 34	An executable such as NOTEPAD.EXE that is guaranteed to be on the system prior to installation. The Source column of the CustomAction table contains a foreign key into the Directory table that defines where the Windows Installer can find this file. The Target column of the CustomAction table contains the name of the executable file followed by any command line string that the executable file will need.

Identifying the custom action via the property table

Three types of custom actions have their locations stored in the Property table. Defining the location of a custom action as a property concerns executable files and custom actions that are implemented in either JScript or VBScript. In the case of an executable file the Property table defines where on the system this file can be found. In other words, this is an instance where the file that is to implement the custom action is already on the target system. However, in the case of the custom actions implemented in VBScript or JScript, it is the script itself that is contained in the Property table. In all three cases the Source column of the CustomAction table contains a foreign key into the Property table. The types of custom actions that use the Property table for defining their source are described in Table 10-10.

TABLE 10-10 BASIC CUSTOM ACTION TYPES LOCATED VIA THE PROPERTY TABLE

Custom Action	Description
Type 50	Identifies an executable that already exists on the target system as the file that will implement the custom action. In the Property table the value of the property provided in the Source column is the full path to the executable. The Target column of the CustomAction table contains any command line required by the executable in order for it to implement the custom action.
Type 53	Implemented in JScript; the script text is the value of the property name specified in the Source column of the CustomAction table. The Target column of the CustomAction table contains the name of an optional script function that is called after the Windows Installer parses the script text.
Type 54	Implemented in VBScript; the script text is the value of the property name specified in the Source column of the CustomAction table. The Target column of the CustomAction table contains the name of an optional script function that is called after the Windows Installer parses the script text.

Storing custom actions as strings in the database

Five types of custom actions are stored as strings in the CustomAction table. With all five types, a string entered in the Target column of the CustomAction table provides the implementation of the custom action functionality. In three of these custom actions the Source column of the CustomAction table is null and in the other two the Source column specifies the target of the custom action. The target of the custom action can be either the Directory table or the Property table. The types of custom actions where the implementation is stored directly in the CustomAction table are described in Table 10-11.

TABLE 10-11 BASIC CUSTOM ACTION TYPES STORED IN THE CUSTOMACTION TABLE

Custom Action	Description
Type 19	Displays an error message and then terminates the installation. The Source column of the CustomAction table is null and the Target column contains a formatted text string. If this string evaluates to a pure numeric value, then it will be used as an entry into the Error table and the associated error message will be displayed. If the string evaluates to something that contains non-numeric characters, then the string itself will be the error message.
Type 35	Sets a value for a directory in the Directory table. The Source column of the CustomAction table defines the key in the Directory table to be set. The Target column of the CustomAction table contains a formatted text string that resolves to the value for the directory location.
Type 37	Implements its functionality through the use of JScript code. The Source column of the CustomAction table is null and the Target column contains the JScript text.
Type 38	Implements its functionality through the use of VBScript code. The Source column of the CustomAction table is null and the Target column contains the VBScript text.
Type 51	Sets a property in the Property table with formatted text. The Source column of the CustomAction table defines the name of the property to be set. The Target column is a formatted text string that resolves to the value for the designated property.

Performing nested installations

Three types of custom actions perform other installations as child installs of the main installation. These nested installations are themselves defined by MSI packages. There are severe restrictions on how and where these types of custom actions can be used.

The full details of these types of custom actions will be covered in Chapter 11. These custom actions are briefly described here in Table 10-12.

TABLE 10-12 BASIC CUSTOM ACTION TYPES THAT PERFORM NESTED INSTALLATIONS

Custom Action	Description
Type 7	The MSI package containing the child installation is streamed into the main installation package as a sub-storage. The Source column of the CustomAction table designates the name of this sub-storage. The Target column contains a list of property settings to be passed to the child install.
Type 23	The MSI package containing the child installation is located at the root of the source tree for the main installation. The Source column of the CustomAction table designates the name of this child MSI package. The Target column contains a list of property settings to be passed to the child install.
Type 39	The child installation is already installed or advertised. The Source column of the CustomAction table designates the product code for this child installation. The Target column contains a list of property settings to be passed to the child install.

The Processing of Custom Actions

There are three basic steps to specifying the process that the Windows Installer is to use in executing a custom action. They are: scheduling when the custom action is to be executed, invoking the custom action, and processing the return values from a custom action. You identify these processing options to the Windows Installer by modifying the Type field in the CustomAction table. The modifications you can make are subject of the following subsections.

Scheduling custom actions

In this section we will discuss the various options that a setup developer has for specifying when a custom action is to be executed. This is where a clear understanding of the Windows Installer mechanism becomes important. You may want to look back at the section in this chapter entitled "Windows Installer Mechanism" that goes into this subject in detail.

Specifying when a custom action is to be run in the context discussed here has nothing to do with putting conditions on the custom action in the sequence table. What we are talking about here is telling the Windows Installer in which process the custom action is to be run. This scheduling option is only applicable to the Immediate category of custom action, because any of the categories of deferred custom actions can only run in the execute sequence.

You have to keep in mind here that on Windows NT/2000 two processes are running and on Windows 95/98 only one process is running. On Windows NT/2000 the UI sequence table is run in the client process and the execute sequence table is run in the service process. On Windows 95/98 the actions in both sequence tables are run in the client process because no service process is possible on these particular operating systems. The same custom action cannot appear in any sequence table more than once since the name of the custom action is the primary key for that particular row of the sequence table. The Windows Installer will not permit duplicate entries in the database.

You can specify four mutually exclusive options for defining the execution scheduling of an immediate category of custom action. Two of these relate strictly to the sequence table in which the custom action has been defined. The other two relate to the process in which the custom action will be executed. Table 10-13 describes each of the various scheduling options and gives the value that you need to add to the Type field in the CustomAction table.

Table 10-13 EXECUTION SCHEDULING OPTIONS

Option Name	Option Value	Description
Default	0	The default functionality is for the custom action to run whenever it is encountered in a sequence table. If it is in both the UI and the execute sequence tables and both of these tables are executed, it will run twice during an installation or an uninstallation. This will not happen only if a condition that does not evaluate to TRUE has been entered against the custom action.

Continued

TABLE 10-13 EXECUTION SCHEDULING OPTIONS *(Continued)*

Option Name	Option Value	Description
First sequence	256	Under this option the custom action will only be executed when it is encountered in the UI sequence table, and not when it is encountered in the execute sequence table. If the UI sequence table is not run because of the user-interface level, the custom action will run in the execute sequence if encountered. It will never run in both sequences. If a condition prevents the custom action from running in the UI sequence, it will still not run in the execute sequence. The only thing that matters for this option is the sequence table into which the custom action has been entered and not the process in which the sequence table is being run.
Once per process	512	Prevents a custom action from running more than once in the same process. If a custom action is in both the UI sequence and the execute sequence tables and the installation is being run on Windows 98, the custom action will only run when encountered in the UI sequence table (as long as the user interface level is high enough).
Repeat in same process	768	Permits a custom action to run more than once in the same process. If a custom action is in both the UI sequence and the execute sequence tables and the installation is being run on Windows 98, the custom action will run when encountered in the UI sequence table and then again when it is encountered in the execute sequence (as long as the user interface level is high enough).

Using these descriptions for the custom action scheduling options, Table 10-14 describes the functionality for the possible scenarios that can occur.

TABLE 10-14 OPERATION OF THE CUSTOM ACTION SCHEDULING OPTIONS

Option	Windows NT/2000	Windows 95/98
Default	*In UI sequence only:* The custom action will run when encountered in the UI sequence unless prevented by a condition or if the sequence is not run because the user-interface level was set at either basic or none.	*In UI sequence only:* The custom action will run when encountered in the UI sequence unless prevented by a condition or if the sequence is not run because the user-interface level was set at either basic or none.
	In execute sequence only: The custom action will run when encountered in the execute sequence unless prevented by a condition.	*In execute sequence only:* The custom action will run when encountered in the execute sequence unless prevented by a condition.
	In both sequences: The custom action will run when encountered in both sequences. It will not run in the UI sequence if prevented by a condition or if the UI sequence is not run because the user-interface level was set at either basic or none. It will not run in the execute sequence if prevented by a condition.	*In both sequences:* The custom action will run when encountered in both sequences. It will not run in the UI sequence if prevented by a condition or the UI sequence is not run because the user-interface level was set at either basic or none. It will not run in the execute sequence if prevented by a condition.
First sequence	*In UI sequence only:* The custom action will run when encountered in the UI sequence unless prevented by a condition or if the sequence is not run because the user-interface level was set at either basic or none.	*In UI sequence only:* The custom action will run when encountered in the UI sequence unless prevented by a condition or if the sequence is not run because the user-interface level was set at either basic or none.
	In execute sequence only: The custom action will run when encountered in the execute sequence unless prevented by a condition.	*In execute sequence only:* The custom action will run when encountered in the execute sequence unless prevented by a condition.

Continued

Table 10-14 OPERATION OF THE CUSTOM ACTION SCHEDULING OPTIONS *(Continued)*

Option	Windows NT/2000	Windows 95/98
First sequence	*In both sequences:* The custom action will run only in the UI sequence. However, it will not run in the UI sequence if prevented by a condition or if the UI sequence is not run because the user-interface level was set at either basic or none. It will then run in the execute sequence unless prevented by a condition.	*In both sequences:* The custom action will run only in the UI sequence. However, it will not run in the UI sequence if prevented by a condition or if the UI sequence is not run because the user-interface level was set at either basic or none. It will then run in the execute sequence unless prevented by a condition.
Once per process	*In UI sequence only:* The custom action will run when encountered in the UI sequence unless prevented by a condition or if the sequence is not run because the user-interface level was set at either basic or none.	*In UI sequence only:* The custom action will run when encountered in the UI sequence unless prevented by a condition or if the sequence is not run because the user-interface level was set at either basic or none.
	In execute sequence only: The custom action will run when encountered in the execute sequence unless prevented by a condition.	*In execute sequence only:* The custom action will run when encountered in the execute sequence unless prevented by a condition.
	In both sequences: The custom action will run when encountered in both sequences. It will not run in the UI sequence if prevented by a condition or the UI sequence is not run because the user-interface level was set at either basic or none. It will not run in the execute sequence if prevented by a condition.	*In both sequences:* The custom action will run only in the UI sequence. However, it will not run in the UI sequence if prevented by a condition or if the UI sequence is not run because the user-interface level was set at either basic or none. It will then run in the execute sequence unless prevented by a condition.

Option	Windows NT/2000	Windows 95/98
Repeat in same process	*In UI sequence only:* This is not applicable on Windows NT/2000.	*In UI sequence only:* The custom action will not run in the UI sequence.
	In execute sequence only: This is not applicable on Windows NT/2000.	*In execute sequence only:* The custom action will run when encountered in the execute sequence unless prevented by a condition.
	In both sequences: This is not applicable on Windows NT/2000.	*In both sequences:* The custom action will run when encountered in the execute sequence unless prevented by a condition.

Invoking custom actions

This section deals with the different ways of invoking a custom action. In this same context we need to discuss how to define when a custom action is to be executed. We have already discussed the fact that there are two primary categories of custom actions, immediate and deferred. An immediate custom action is executed as soon as the Windows Installer encounters it in the Sequence table. This is the default and you can place this category of custom action at any location, with a few exceptions, within either the UI sequence table or the execute sequence table. The exceptions have already been noted in the previous discussions of the various basic types of custom actions.

With deferred custom actions, the custom action is executed only upon being encountered in either the execution script or the rollback script. The following script segment shows how a deferred custom action would appear in the execution script for an installation.

```
InstallProtectedFiles(AllowUI=1)
ActionStart(Name=DeferredExe_Binary,,)
CustomActionSchedule(Action=DeferredExe_Binary,ActionType=1026,Sourc
e=BinaryedEx,,)
ActionStart(Name=RegisterUser,Description=Registering
user,Template=[1])
```

I named this custom action DeferredExe_Binary. It launches Notepad.exe directly after the completion of the InstallFiles standard action. Lines 2 and 3 of the script show how the Windows Installer enters this information into the execution script. You will notice the entry `ActionType=1026`, which tells the Windows Installer how to treat this custom action. Table 10-15 lists the various options you can define to tell the Windows Installer when to execute a custom action. In the terminology of the Windows Installer these are called the *in-script execution options.*

TABLE 10-15 IN-SCRIPT EXECUTION OPTIONS

Option Name	Option Value	Description
Immediate	0	Specifies that the Windows Installer will execute the custom action immediately when it is encountered in the sequence table.
Execution	1024	Specifies that the custom action will be written into the execution script and will be executed when the execution script is run. Unless a condition is placed on this custom action it will run both during installation and uninstallation.
Rollback	1280	Specifies that the custom action will only be run if the installation or the uninstallation has to be rolled back, which can happen if there is a run-time error or if the user cancels the action.
Commit	1536	Specifies that the custom action is to run only if the installation completes successfully.
System context	3072	Specifies that the custom action is to run with elevated privileges as long as the user has been granted elevated privileges by the system administrator.

Up to now we have been talking about invoking custom actions that have been entered into the various sequence tables. Entering a custom action into a sequence table is the most common method of invoking a custom action. Custom actions can, however, invoke other custom actions – or standard actions, for that matter – through either the Installer API or through the Installer automation interface.

The name of the Installer API you can use to invoke a custom action is MsiDo Action. The prototype for this function is as follows:

```
UINT MsiDoAction(MSIHANDLE hInstall, LPCTSTR szAction)
```

Where

```
hInstall is the handle to the installation
szAction is the name of the action to execute
```

MsiDoAction is a database function that is part of the Windows Installer API set. It can execute a standard action, a custom action listed in the CustomAction table, or a user-interface wizard action. A common way to use this function is to call it from within a custom action that is sequenced in the InstallExecuteSequence table between the InstallInitialize and the InstallFinalize actions. In this way you can use the function to invoke another custom action.

You can access a method through the automation interface that provides the same functionality as MsiDoAction. The syntax of this method is as follows:

```
object.DoAction(action)
```

where `object` is the session object and `action` is the string name of the action to execute.

This is one of the methods of the Session object that is part of the Windows Installer automation interface. Just like the MsiDoAction method, this method can execute a standard action, a custom action that is listed in the CustomAction table, or a user-interface wizard action. A common way to use this method is to call it from within a custom action that is sequenced in the InstallExecuteSequence table between the InstallInitialize and the InstallFinalize actions. In this way you can use the method to invoke a standard action that makes changes to the system.

The final way to invoke a custom action is to use the DoAction control event. A control event is tied to a control found in a dialog box. The argument to this particular control event is the name of a custom action listed in the CustomAction table. Typically this control event is tied to a pushbutton control; clicking on the pushbutton invokes the specified custom action.

Processing the return values from custom actions

The last step in defining a custom action's behavior to the Windows Installer is to define how the custom action thread is to run and how return values are to be handled. A custom action can be run synchronously or asynchronously and the Windows Installer can be told how to handle any exit codes that may be returned from the custom action. When a custom action is run synchronously, the Windows Installer will suspend any further actions until the custom action has finished and its thread has been terminated. Asynchronous execution means that the custom action thread and the main installation thread run in parallel; what happens at the end of the execution of the sequence depends on how you have specified the custom action exit code is to be handled by the Windows Installer. Table 10-16 shows the possible options for specifying how the Windows Installer is to run a custom action.

TABLE 10-16 RETURN PROCESSING OPTIONS

Option Name	Option Value	Description
Synchronous wait	0	Specifies that the installation process will wait on the custom action to complete and that the return value must be 0 for the main installation to proceed. If the custom action does not return 0, the installation will be terminated.
Synchronous continue	64	Specifies that the installation process will wait on the custom action to complete and that any return value from the custom action will be ignored. The Windows Installer will continue with the installation after the custom action has completed.
Asynchronous wait	128	Specifies that the custom action will proceed in parallel with the main installation but that the Windows Installer will wait at the end of the sequence for the custom action to return an exit code. If the exit code is not 0, the installation will be terminated.
Asynchronous continue	192	Specifies that the custom action will proceed in parallel with the main installation and that the Windows Installer will not wait at the end of the sequence for the custom action to return an exit code.

Now we can discuss how to put all this information together so that the Windows Installer knows how to process the custom action.

Telling the Windows Installer how to process a custom action

You tell the Windows Installer how to process a custom action through the Type attribute in the CustomAction table. You can do this by taking the basic custom action type number and adding it to the execution scheduling option to be used, and finally by adding this sum to the in-script execution option and then to the return processing option. This will only work properly if the in-script execution option is 0, specifying that the custom action is to be executed in immediate mode and not written into the execution script. If the custom action is specified as deferred, you would not want to add in the execution scheduling option; otherwise you would define an invalid type. For each type of custom action there are rules for what can be combined to make a valid type. As an example you can create the following pseudo-code that defines how the type specification should operate for the dynamic link custom action you used in the example installation in Chapter 4.

```
If(category != deferred AND basic type != nested installation custom
action) then
Type = Basic Type + Execution Scheduling Option + Return Processing
Option
Else
Type = Basic Type + In-Script Execution Option + Return Processing
Option
Endif
```

For the example installation in Chapter 4 you have a custom action that you are storing in the Binary table and even though you are placing it in both sequence tables you want it to run only once and you want the Windows Installer to wait for a successful exit code before it continues with the processing of the sequence tables. Since you are placing this custom action into both sequence tables it is not a deferred custom action. You would enter the following Type value in the Custom Action table:

```
Type = 1 + 0 + 256 + 0 = 257
```

Example Custom Action

In this section we take a close look at the custom action you used in Chapter 4 to set the default installation location. We also take a look at a different method for implementing this same type of functionality. This other approach, which we did not use in Chapter 4, sets the TARGETDIR property using a formatted text string.

If you remember, you implemented the custom action you used in Chapter 4 as a dynamic-link library. The code for this DLL is as follows:

```
/*-----------------------------------------------------------------+
|                                                                  |
|     File Name: SetDefault.cpp                                    |
|     Description:     Set the default value of TARGETDIR          |
|     Author:    Bob Baker                                         |
|                                                                  |
+-----------------------------------------------------------------*/
```

```
#include <windows.h>
#include <msi.h>
#include <msiquery.h>

UINT __stdcall SetDefaultTarget(MSIHANDLE hInstall)
{
     LPCTSTR    TargetDirProp = TEXT("TARGETDIR");
     LPCTSTR    ProgFileFolderProp = TEXT("ProgramFilesFolder");
     LPCTSTR    ManufProp = TEXT("Manufacturer");
     LPCTSTR    ProdNameProp = TEXT("ProductName");
     TCHAR      szValueBuf[MAX_PATH+1] = { 0 };
     TCHAR      szTargetPath[MAX_PATH+1] = { 0 };     DWORD
ncharCount = MAX_PATH+1;


// Get the location of the program files folder
// This value will already have a directory separator
// since it is a directory-related property
MsiGetProperty(hInstall, ProgFileFolderProp, szValueBuf,
                                                 &ncharCount);
     lstrcpy(szTargetPath, szValueBuf);
     ncharCount = MAX_PATH + 1;

// Get the name of the company publishing the software
MsiGetProperty(hInstall, ManufProp, szValueBuf, &ncharCount);
     lstrcat(szTargetPath, szValueBuf);
     lstrcat(szTargetPath, "\\");
     ncharCount = MAX_PATH + 1;

// Get the name of the product
MsiGetProperty(hInstall, ProdNameProp, szValueBuf,
                                             &ncharCount);
     lstrcat(szTargetPath, szValueBuf);
     ncharCount = MAX_PATH + 1;

// Set the concatenated values of the above properties as the
// default value of the TARGETDIR property
MsiSetProperty(hInstall, TargetDirProp, szTargetPath);
return ERROR_SUCCESS;
}
```

If you wanted to define TARGETDIR using formatted text, you could make the entries into the CustomAction table as shown in Table 10-17.

TABLE 10-17 CUSTOMACTION TABLE ENTRIES REQUIRED TO DEFINE THE DEFAULT INSTALLATION LOCATION USING FORMATTED TEXT

Row #	Column Name	Attribute Value
1	Action	DefaultDest
	Type	307
	Source	TARGETDIR
	Target	[ProgramFilesFolder][Manufacturer]\[ProductName]

The following remarks explain in more detail the entries that you have made in the CustomAction table shown in Table 10-17.

- In the Action column you use a text string to uniquely identify the custom action in the table. Here you show that you are using the same name that you used to define the custom action as a dynamic link library.
- In the Type column you want to define this custom action to run only in the first sequence table in which it is found, but you want to make sure that if the UI sequence table is skipped the custom action will run in the execute sequence. The basic type of this custom action is 51 and to it you need to add the 256 scheduling option. Since you want this custom action to run synchronously with the main installation and you want it to run in immediate mode you create the type as follows:

  ```
  Type = 51 + 256 + 0 + 0 = 307
  ```
- In the Source column you specify that the property you want to set is TARGETDIR.
- In the Target column you provide the formatted text string that will create the directory path that would for the example install in Chapter 4 be as follows:

  ```
  C:\Program Files\ISWI Art Company\ISWI Artist
  ```

  You will notice that there is no directory divider (backslash) between the ProgramFilesFolder property and the Manufacturer property. This is because the ProgramFilesFolder property, being a directory-related property, comes with a trailing directory divider (\). There must be a backslash, however, between the Manufacturer and ProductName properties.

Advanced Issues

Because of the complex mechanism of custom actions a number of advanced issues have not been covered in this chapter. We will cover these in detail in Chapter 11. Here I just give a brief overview of what they are.

Context information for deferred custom actions

It is possible that a deferred custom action be executed outside the session that defined it. Because of this a deferred custom action only has access to the information written into the execution script. This can cause a problem if the custom action is expecting the session object, which is the case with custom actions both implemented as dynamic link libraries and using script. You can use a limited number of methods in deferred custom actions where the context information is required.

Nested installation custom actions

An installation can be run as a child install of a main installation through the use of a custom action. You need to understand many things before you can run nested installation custom actions – such things as how and where nested installations can be scheduled, how to use custom actions within a nested installation, how to pass properties to a child installation, how to provide a user interface for the child installation, and so forth.

Disabling rollback and its impact on custom actions

It is possible to disable rollback if there is not enough space on the target machine to temporarily cache files being overwritten during the installation. However, this can have a major impact on certain types of custom actions.

Debugging custom actions

There will be times when you have to debug a custom action created as a dynamic link library or as an executable file.

Adding temporary data to the database

Using a custom action it will be possible to add non-persistent data to some of the tables of the database in memory. This can be important if you want to dynamically create items that will be displayed in the user interface. In Chapter 11 we'll discuss how you can add this temporary data using the special SQL syntax understood by the Windows Installer API. Function set.

Summary

In this chapter you learned about the various types of custom actions you can create, and (I hope) you learned that creating and using custom actions is not a trivial matter. In particular you saw that one category of custom action is executed immediately and that another category of custom action is deferred so that it is executed only when the actual installation is run. You now know that to understand the use of custom actions you need to clearly understand how the Windows Installer works, what happens in the client process, and what happens in the service process.

In the following chapters you will have the opportunity to create and run custom actions of various types. This will continue to cement your understanding of the Windows Installer functionality. You will also learn how to capitalize on your knowledge of InstallScript and how to use InstallScript to create custom actions.

Chapter 11

Creating and Using Custom Actions

IN THIS CHAPTER

- Syntax and use of the Windows Installer SQL
- The ISWI Custom Action Wizard
- Creation and use of the custom tables
- How to use custom actions with the user interface
- Special problems in working with deferred custom actions
- How to run installations from within an installation
- Creation and use of various miscellaneous custom actions
- How to debug custom actions

IN THIS CHAPTER YOU'LL extend the knowledge you gained in Chapter 10 about the categories and types of custom actions. In this chapter you create a number of different types of custom actions and become familiar with a number of techniques that you can use to create these custom actions.

Preliminaries

Creating and using custom actions can be complicated. Before you get into actually creating example custom actions you need to take a look at a number of technical details. First we will look at the valid return values that are recognized by the Windows Installer, and then we will take a tour through the version of SQL supported by the Windows Installer. Then before we move on we will look at several issues related to working with the Windows Installer package at run time.

Custom action return values

There are two sets of return values depending on whether the custom action has been created with C++ in a dynamic link library or with either VBScript or JScript.

If a custom action is identified as being of the type for which the Windows Installer is expecting to handle a return value, then one of the valid return values must be returned. Table 11-1 shows the return values that are valid for a DLL and for script custom actions.

TABLE 11-1 VALID RETURN VALUES FOR DLL AND SCRIPT CUSTOM ACTIONS

Constant	Description
Visual C++ return constant ERROR_FUNCTION_NOT_CALLED VBScript or Jscript return value 0	Identifies to the caller that an action was not executed. This is not a failure condition. This is most useful if a custom action is calling another DLL; this return value tells the caller that a certain action was not taken. When returned to the Windows Installer, this return value is treated just like ERROR_SUCCESS.
Visual C++ return constant ERROR_SUCCESS VBScript of JScript return value IDOK = 1	Indicates that the action completed successfully. The Windows Installer will continue to process all the other actions in the sequence table.
Visual C++ return constant ERROR_INSTALL_USEREXIT VBScript or Jscript return value IDCANCEL = 2	Indicates that the user canceled the installation. When the Windows Installer receives this return value, it will immediately terminate the installation and run the action that has a –2 sequence number. If the custom action is in the execute sequence, the Windows Installer will then return control to the client process where the action that has the –2 sequence number is executed. Default setups created by ISWI will display the SetupInterrupted dialog box that tells the user that the setup was interrupted before the installation was completed. All actions up to this point will be rolled back unless the rollback functionality has been disabled.

Constant	Description
Visual C++ return constant ERROR_INSTALL_FAILURE VBScript and JScript return value IDABORT = 3	Indicates that a fatal error occurred. When the Windows Installer receives this return value, it will immediately terminate the installation and run the action that has the -3 sequence number. If the custom action is in the execute sequence, the Windows Installer will then return control to the client process, where the action that has the -3 sequence number is executed. Default setups created by ISWI will display the SetupComplete Error dialog box that tells the user that the setup was interrupted before the installation was completed. All actions up to this point will be rolled back unless the rollback functionality has been disabled.
Visual C++ return constant ERROR_INSTALL_SUSPEND VBScript and JScript return value IDRETRY = 4	Indicates that the user canceled the installation. When the Windows Installer receives this return value, it will immediately terminate the installation and run the action that has the -4 sequence number. If the custom action is in the execute sequence, the Windows Installer will then return control to the client processwhere the action that has the -4 sequence number is run. Default setups created by ISWI do not have any actions associated with this sequence number. When the Windows Installer receives this return value, the installation will be terminated but no rollback or cleanup will be performed. The user will have to restart the installation manually. The InProgress key in the registry provides the settings needed to resume the suspended installation. This is an obsolete return value and is not used.
Visual C++ return constant ERROR_NO_MORE_ITEMS VBScript and JScript return value IDIGNORE = 5	Tells the Windows Installer to stop processing any more actions in the sequence table. If this custom action is in the user interface sequence, control will be passed immediately to the execute sequence. If the custom action is in the execute sequence, control will be passed back to the client process and the SetupCompleteSuccess dialog will be displayed indicating that the installation completed successfully.

Script-based custom actions are different from those written in C++ because the script text can be contained directly in either the CustomAction table or the Property table. Being able to include a script-based custom action in a database table is in addition to implementing a script custom in a file that can either be installed with the product or stored in the Binary table. A script custom action does not have to be implemented as a script function; it can be a scriptlet similar to what might be contained in a Web page. When the custom action is just a scriptlet, the return values described in Table 11-1 cannot be used and you should tell the Windows Installer to ignore the return value from the custom action. Checking the appropriate check box in the Additional Options dialog of the Custom Action Wizard does this

The next subject that you need to investigate is the version of SQL implemented in the Windows Installer. Many of the custom actions that you will need to create will have to use SQL in order to interface with the MSI database.

Windows Installer SQL

SQL stands for Structured Query Language and was developed at IBM in the 1970s. It is by far the most popular relational database query language and it is what you have to use to access the tables in an MSI database. The only exception to this is accessing the Property table, which has several special functions for setting and retrieving individual records. Even with the Property table you have to use SQL if you want to work with more than one record at a time.

Standard SQL is divided into three parts: a Data Definition Language (DDL), a Data Manipulation Language (DML), and a Data Control Language (DCL). The version of SQL used with MSI databases only contains a Data Definition Language and a Data Manipulation Language. Using the Data Definition Language you can change the schema of a database by adding or dropping tables. You can also alter a table by adding columns. With the Data Manipulation Language you can work with the records in the database tables. You can select, add, delete, and update records.

The SQL language is made up of various types of statements and associated clauses. Now you should take a closer look at the statements and clauses that comprise the Data Definition Language and the Data Manipulation Language as implemented by the Windows Installer.

THE DATA DEFINITION LANGUAGE

In the Data Definition Language there are three statements. Using these statements you can create a new table, delete a table, or add a column to a table. These three commands are described in Table 11-2.

TABLE 11-2 DATA DEFINITION LANGUAGE STATEMENTS SUPPORTED BY WINDOWS INSTALLER

Statement	Description
CREATE TABLE *<table-name>* (*<column-specifications>*)	Used to create a new table in the MSI database. This statement is followed by the name of the table to be created and a definition of the columns that make up the new table.
DROP TABLE *<table-name>*	Used to delete a table from the MSI database. The only parameter used with this statement is the name of the table.
ALTER TABLE *<table-name>* ADD *<column-specification>*	Used to add a column to a table in the MSI database. Like the CREATE TABLE statement, this statement takes a number of parameters that describe the new column to be added.

In all three of these commands, the name of a table cannot exceed 31 characters and the table name is case-sensitive.

When you use the CREATE TABLE or ALTER TABLE statements, you need to provide a column definition, which includes the specification of the type of data to be contained in the column. In an MSI database there are only three types of data you can use: strings, integers, and binary streams. The data type keywords you can use with the CREATE TABLE and the ALTER TABLE statements are described in Table 11-3. You must specify the data type of a column. If you don't, you'll get a Windows Installer SQL query (1615) error indicating that the query contains an invalid type specifier.

TABLE 11-3 COLUMN DATA TYPE SPECIFICATION KEYWORDS

Keyword	Description
CHAR [(*column-size*)]	Defines the column to be a string data type. You can specify any size from 1 character to a 255 characters. If no size is specified, this data type will default to be a string of unlimited length.

Continued

TABLE 11-3 COLUMN DATA TYPE SPECIFICATION KEYWORDS *(Continued)*

Keyword	Description
CHARACTER [(*column-size*)]	Operates like the CHAR keyword.
LONGCHAR	Defines a string data type that can have unlimited length.
SHORT	Defines a column data type that is a two-byte integer.
INT	Defines a column data type that is a two-byte integer.
INTEGER	Defines a column data type that is a two-byte integer.
LONG	Defines a column data type that is a four-byte integer.
OBJECT	Defines a binary data type. Only one column in a table can have this data type.

In Table 11-3 you saw the basic keywords you can use to define the data type of a column. Only one of these data types can be specified for any particular column. There are other attributes, however, that you can also use to modify a column. These attributes determine whether a column is to be treated as temporary or permanent, whether it can have a null value or not, and so on. The three modifiers available with Windows Installer are described in Table 11-4. All of the keywords shown in Table 11-4 are optional.

TABLE 11-4 COLUMN MODIFIER KEYWORDS

Modifying Keyword	Description
NOT NULL	Identifies a column that cannot be null.
TEMPORARY	Identifies a column that will only exist in memory and will not be persisted in the database when it is closed. When using this keyword, it is important to also use the HOLD keyword so that this column will get a refcount. Without a refcount this column will not be accessible.
LOCALIZABLE	Identifies a column as one that holds a string that must be localized. The purpose of this keyword is to allow a localization utility to query for the attribute and only allow the columns that have the LOCALIZABLE attribute to be localized. No column designated as a primary key can be marked as being localizable.

When you are creating a new table using the CREATE TABLE statement, you need to identify the column or columns that comprise the primary key for the table. There are a few rules you need to follow when defining the primary key for a table. First, to designate those columns that form the primary key, you need to use the PRIMARY KEY clause, which is a comma-delimited list of the column names. Also, when you create the table you need to define the columns that will form the primary key first before you define any of the other columns. When creating both persistent and temporary columns in a table, you need to define all the persistent columns before you define any temporary columns. One final rule for creating a table is that there can only be one column in a table that has the object data type.

Before we start looking at a few examples of SQL statements that create tables and add columns we need to discuss the subject of refcounting temporary tables and columns. Using the HOLD and FREE keywords you can control the lifetime of temporary columns and tables. When you use the HOLD keyword, the hold count on a table is incremented, and when you use the FREE keyword, the hold count is decremented. When the last hold count on a table is released, then all temporary columns become inaccessible. If all the columns in a table are temporary, the table itself becomes inaccessible.

When you use the CREATE TABLE statement, you can only use the HOLD keyword. It would not make any sense to use the FREE keyword when first creating a table or adding a column. You can use the ALTER TABLE statement to increment or decrement the hold count on a particular table outside of the action to add a column. The format for this use of the statement is as follows:

```
ALTER TABLE <table-name> HOLD
ALTER TABLE <table-name> FREE
```

Now let's take a look at a few example SQL statements for creating new tables and adding columns to an existing table.

CREATING A NEW TABLE For the first example you will create a simple table that can be used to implement the creation of user accounts on a system. The SQL statement to do this is as follows:

```
CREATE TABLE `CustomUserAccounts` (`UserName` CHAR(72) NOT NULL,
    `TempPassWord` CHAR(25) NOT NULL, `Attributes` LONG PRIMARY KEY
        `UserName`)
```

The most important thing to notice about this SQL statement is that the name of the table and the names of the columns are enclosed in grave accent marks. This circumvents any possibility of a clash with an SQL keyword. This use of the grave accent marks is recommended in all cases, even if there is no possibility of a clash, since it will enhance performance. If you have to qualify a column name with the table name in order to make it clear what table the column belongs to, you must use the grave accent marks around both the table name and the column name. This would look like the following if you needed to make sure you were using the UserName column from the CustomUserAccounts table and not some other table:

```
`CustomUserAccounts`.`UserName`
```

You will be using these SQL statements in your C++ code so they have to be converted to strings. Typically the above SQL statement will be used in our C++ code as follows:

```
const TCHAR *const sqlCreateTable = TEXT("CREATE TABLE
     CustomUserAccounts` (`UserName` CHAR(72) NOT NULL,
        `TempPassWord` CHAR(25) NOT NULL,
            `Attributes` LONG PRIMARY KEY `UserName`)");
```

For a second example, suppose that you need to create a temporary table to be used at install time to hold special attributes of the target system. This table will have two columns where the first column is the name of the attribute and the second column is the value of the attribute. Both columns hold string values with the first column being restricted to a string length of 36 and second column being able to hold a string of any length. The name of this table will be SystemAttributes. The SQL statement to create this table is as follows:

```
CREATE TABLE `SystemAttributes` (`AttributeName` CHAR(36) NOT NULL
    TEMPORARY, `AttributeValue` LONGCHAR NOT NULL TEMPORARY
        PRIMARY KEY `AttributeName`, `AttributeValue`) HOLD
```

The first thing that you should note from this SQL statement is that to create a temporary table you need to identify each and every column as being temporary. Also, you need to use the HOLD keyword in order to increment the hold count for this table. If you do not do this, this table will not be accessible because it will have a 0 hold count. To use this SQL statement in C++ code you would format it as follows:

```
const TCHAR *const sqlTempTable = TEXT("CREATE TABLE
     `SystemAttributes` (`AttributeName` CHAR(36) NOT NULL
        TEMPORARY, `AttributeValue` LONGCHAR NOT NULL TEMPORARY
           PRIMARY KEY `AttributeName`, `AttributeValue`) HOLD)");
```

ADDING A COLUMN TO AN EXISTING TABLE For this example assume that you want to add a temporary column to the CustomUserAccounts table that will hold the results of calculations necessary during the installation. For you to do this temporary column must have an integer data type. The SQL statement to create this temporary column is as follows:

```
ALTER TABLE `CustomUserAccounts` ADD `Result` LONG TEMPORARY HOLD
```

This SQL statement will add a temporary column named Result to the CustomUserAccounts table.

THE DATA MANIPULATION LANGUAGE

Four statements comprise the Data Manipulation Language implemented in the Windows Installer. The purpose of these four statements is to work with rows in an existing database. You can add, delete, and modify the data in rows and you can query a database table in order to select a group of rows. Table 11-5 shows the four Data Manipulation Language commands.

TABLE 11-5 DATA MANIPULATION LANGUAGE STATEMENTS SUPPORTED BY WINDOWS INSTALLER

Statement	Description
SELECT *<column-name-list>* FROM *<table-name-list>*	Obtains a group of records from one or more tables. If you want to obtain a result set that includes all the columns in a table or table list, you can use an asterisk (*) instead of providing a list of the all the column names.
DELETE FROM *<table-name>*	Deletes rows from a table. A WHERE clause is necessary if only some of the rows are to be deleted.
UPDATE *<table-name-list>* SET *<update-specification>*	Modifies existing rows in one or more tables.
INSERT INTO *<table-name>* *<column-name-list>* VALUES *<value-list>*	Adds new records to a table.

There are two keywords and two clauses that you can use with these SQL statements in order to modify the results obtained from the basic statements. The two keywords, both optional, are described in Table 11-6.

TABLE 11-6 DATA MANIPULATION LANGUAGE KEYWORDS

Modifying Keyword	Description
DISTINCT	Prevents duplicate records from appearing in a result set generated by an SQL query.

Continued

TABLE 11-6 DATA MANIPULATION LANGUAGE KEYWORDS *(Continued)*

Modifying Keyword	Description
TEMPORARY	Identifies a column that will only exist in memory and will not be persisted in the database when it is closed. When using this keyword, you must also use the HOLD keyword so that this column will get a refcount. Without a refcount this column will not be accessible.

The two clauses that we need to discuss in detail are the WHERE clause and the ORDER BY clause. These are discussed in the following two subsections.

THE WHERE CLAUSE Several of the Data Manipulation Language statements use a WHERE clause to filter the rows that are the subject of the operation. This optional clause can be used with the SELECT, DELETE FROM, and UPDATE statements. The basic format of the WHERE clause is as follows:

```
WHERE <operation-list>
```

The structure of the operation list that follows the WHERE keyword is the essence of the WHERE clause. The valid operation types that can make up an operation list are shown in Table 11-7.

TABLE 11-7 VALID OPERATION TYPES

Operation	Description
<column-name> = *<column-name>*	Compares the values in two different columns; if they are equal then the row is added to the result set. If the columns being compared are in two different tables, the result set is called an inner join.
<column-name> operator *<constant>*	Compares the value in a column with a constant value. Following this table is a description of the operators that can be used and with which data types they are valid.
<column-name> operator *<marker>*	Compares the value in a column with a variable (marker). A record passed to the MsiViewExecute function provides a value for the variable. Following this table is a description of the operators that can be used and with which data types they are valid. You will also see how to use markers when you are executing a view.

Operation	Description
<column-name> IS NULL	Checks to see if a particular column is null. All rows that have a null value in the specified column are added to the result set.
<column-name> IS NOT NULL	Checks to see if a particular column contains a value. All rows that have a value in the specified column are added to the result set.

The valid relational operators that can be used are the equal to (=), not equal to (<>), greater than (>), greater than or equal to (>=), less than (<), or less than or equal to (<=). All of these operators can be used when comparing numerical values, but only the equal (=) and the not equal (<>) operators can be used when comparing string values. None of the operators can be used to compare columns that contain the object data type. For object data types it is only possible to determine if the column is null or not null. You can group operations by using the AND and OR logical operators. You can change the order of evaluation of operations by using parentheses.

A marker is a means by which you can create queries that contain parameters that will be filled in later. The token used to represent a parameter for which a value will be provided at a later time is the question mark (?). When a SELECT statement is created using markers, there is no restriction on where these markers can be placed relative to the non-parameterized values that are part of the statement. However, when markers are used with either the INSERT INTO or the UPDATE statements, the use of markers must come before the first use of any hard-coded values. A record passed to either the MsiViewExecute function or the Execute method of the View object supplies the values that replace the markers that are part of a parameterized statement. When we discuss the WHERE clause, we need to talk about what to do when this clause is referencing more than one table, which can happen when you're using the WHERE clause in either a SELECT or an UPDATE statement. When you are comparing the columns in different tables, you are creating what is called a join. In the Windows Installer only inner joins are supported. It is not possible to perform circular joins or outer joins. In a circular join, three or more tables are linked together and the final linking returns to the first table in the operation list. In an outer join records are included even if they do not have related records in the joined table. An example of this from the MSI help is as follows:

```
WHERE Table1.Field1=Table2.Field1 AND Table2.Field2=Table3.Field1
                                   AND Table3.Field2=Table1.Field2
```

Since this WHERE clause refers back to table 1 in a circular fashion this is called a circular join. An outer join is not possible because the Windows Installer does not support the special syntax required. A valid inner join would be the above WHERE clause with just the first two operations, as follows:

```
WHERE Table1.Field1=Table2.Field1 AND Table2.Field2=Table3.Field1
```

THE ORDER BY CLAUSE You can use this clause to order the results obtained from a SELECT statement. The basic format for this clause is as follows:

```
GROUP BY <column-list>
```

The column list is a comma-delimited list of column names. This clause is the means by which you can sort the result set obtained by a SELECT statement. Using this clause will cause a slight delay because of the sorting that is necessary.

Accessing the current Installer session

In Chapter 10 you saw that there are two major categories of custom actions, immediate and deferred. Only DLL and script-based immediate custom actions have access to the current installer session. If you want to make temporary changes to the MSI database during the installation, you need to use a DLL, VBScript, or JScript immediate custom action. It is not possible to use an executable based custom action to access the current Windows Installer session, because this type of custom action runs in its own process and there isn't a way to pass an install session handle to it.

A DLL custom action is passed a handle to the current installer session. This handle is then used in a number of the Windows Installer functions to work with the MSI database during the installation. The format for a DLL custom action function is as follows:

```
UINT __stdcall <exported-function-name>(MSIHANDLE <variable-name>)
```

The name of the function that will be called when the custom action is executed can be whatever you want it to be, as can be the variable name that receives the session handle. The remainder of the format for this exported function has to be as shown in the previous code example. For example, to declare a function MyAction where the install session handle is called hInstall, you would use

```
UINT __stdcall MyAction(MSIHANDLE hInstall)
{
//my code here...
}
```

When you're using an immediate custom action written in VBScript or Jscript, you access the current Installer session using the Session object. When you're using a deferred custom action, you still get a session handle — it's just a much more limited session and you only have access to what has been written into the execution script.

The Windows Installer attaches this object to the script with the name of Session. This object has a number of methods and properties that enable the manipulation of the active database during an installation. Figure 11-1 shows the Windows Installer object model. Note that the two Installer object methods that can be used to create a Session object cannot be used in a custom action. This is because there can only be one Session object in any particular process and during an installation the Windows Installer automatically creates a Session object, so any attempt to create another one will cause an error.

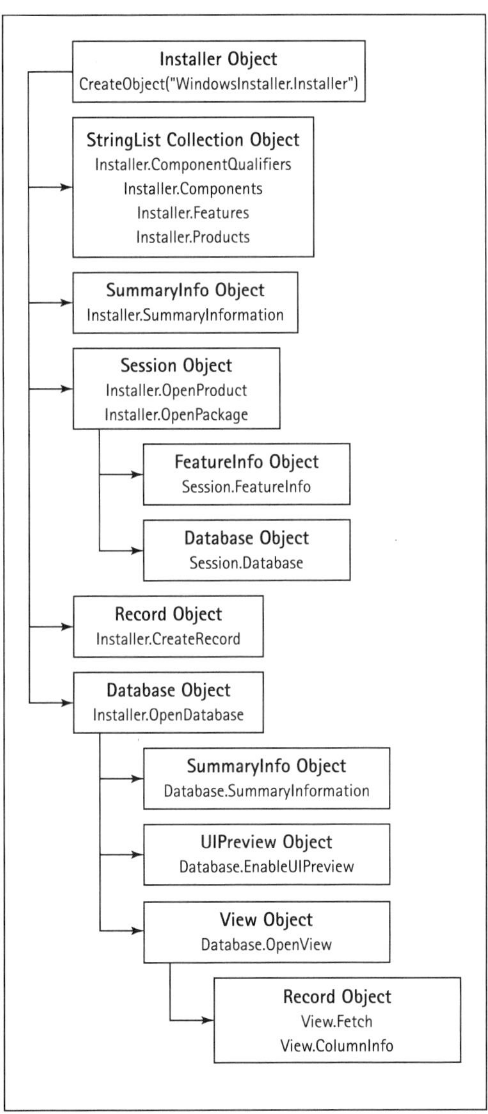

Figure 11-1: The Windows Installer object model

When you need to use a deferred custom action, you cannot access the current installer session. This is because a deferred custom action is written into the execution script created by the Windows Installer; during the execution of this script the installation may be temporarily suspended. When the installation is resumed, the Windows Installer session that was created when the installation was initially invoked will no longer be available. This temporary suspension might happen, for example, when the system needs to be rebooted during the installation.

Because of this, a deferred custom action only has access to information written into the execution script. This is a complex subject and it is covered in the Deferred Custom Actions section later in this chapter. If a deferred custom action does not need to obtain information from the database and only implements changes to the target system, there is no additional effort required.

It is not possible to access an installer session from a custom action that is not the current installer session. Custom actions can only work with the active database of the current session and cannot access another MSI database. Because of this there are a number of Windows Installer database functions that you cannot use within a custom action since they require a handle to a database that is not the database of the current session. The Windows Installer help provides a list of these particular functions.

Working with the MSI database at install time

Unless you're working with the Property table, working with the active database during an installation session requires the creation of a view. The Property table has a set of special access functions you can use for access that do not require the creation of a view. When accessing the active database, you need to follow these steps:

1. Obtain a handle to the active database using the MsiGetActiveDatabase function. This function requires the handle to the current installer session. It returns the handle to the active database.
2. Create a view object using the MsiDatabaseOpenView function. It takes the handle to the active database, an SQL query that defines the result set required, and a pointer to the view handle that is to be returned.
3. Once a handle to a view object is available, execute the view object using the MsiViewExecute function in order to obtain the result set. If markers were used in the SQL query, this where they are given actual values through the passing of a record containing the replacement values for the markers used. An example of this is shown later in this section.

4. Having executed the view you can fetch each record in turn and manipulate it however you want. To fetch a record you use the MsiViewFetch function, which takes the handle to the view, and a pointer to a record in which the fetched information will be returned.

5. Access the fetched records with the functions provided for the purpose of working with each field in a record. These functions are of the form MsiRecordGet* and MsiRecordSet* where the asterisk can be, with one exception, String, Integer, or Stream. The one exception is that the function that would be called MsiRecordGetStream is instead called MsiRecordReadStream.

6. If any particular record is to be added to the table, call the function MsiViewModify, passing it the new record that is to be added. You must use the modify mode MSIMODIFY_INSERT_TEMPORARY because the MSI database during an installation session is read-only and you can add only temporary records to tables. You cannot modify records that have been authored into the database when the MSI package was created.

7. If you are going to execute another view and you have not fetched all the records in the current view, you must close the current view using the MsiViewClose function. To follow good programming practices, always close your views – regardless of whether you need to execute another view.

If the only thing you want to do is add records to an empty table, then you can skip steps 3 and 4. All you need to do in that case is get the handle to the active database, open a view, create the record that is to be added, and then use the MsiViewModify function to add the new record to the table. This record will be temporary, meaning that it will not be persisted in the database when it is closed.

Before you leave this section you need to take a look at an example of how to use markers in your SQL queries. The following skeleton code that might be found in a DLL custom action provides a good description of the use of markers in an SQL query. This example code shows how to extract from the RadioButton table the entries associated with an array of property names. For a complete description of the columns in this table, see the MSI help.

```
int i;
MSIHANDLE hDatabase, hView, hRecord, hRec=0;
TCHAR* szPropertyNames[] = {TEXT("RBProp1"), TEXT("RBProp2"),
                                              TEXT("RBProp3")};

// Use a marker (?) in place of the property name in the
// following SQL statment
const TCHAR* sqlRadioButton = TEXT("SELECT `Order`, `X`, `Y`,
`Width`, `Height`, `Text` FROM `RadioButton` WHERE `Property`=?");

// With this function call you get a handle to the database
```

```
// being used by the current installation
hDatabase = MsiGetActiveDatabase(hInstall);

// Once you get a handle to the running database you
// create a view object based on the SQL query
MsiDatabaseOpenView(hDatabase, sqlRadioButton, &hView);

// You need to create a record that will be used to
// replace the marker in the SQL query with an actual value.
// This record only needs one column since you are using only
// one marker in our SQL query
hRecord = MsiCreateRecord(1);

// You now need to loop through the array of property names
// that will be used to replace the marker in the SQL query
for(i=0; i<3; i++)
{
    // Now set the value of the record to each
    // property name in order
    MsiRecordSetString(hRecord, 1, szPropertyNames[i]);

    // You need to execute the view in order to supply
    // the missing property names before you can get
    // a valid result set from the SQL query
    MsiViewExecute(hView, hRecord);

    // For the view that has been executed you need to loop
    // through each record in the result set and do
    // something with it
    while(ERROR_NO_MORE_ITEMS != MsiViewFetch(hView, &hRec)
    {
        // Do something with the fetched records
    } // end while loop
} // end for loop
```

The previous code shows that you need to execute a new view for every change in the value of the marker. Note that the marker is changed for each of the property names that you want to use in getting a different result set from the RadioButton table. Since radio buttons are joined together into a radio button group by a common property name, there will be more than one row in the RadioButton table that uses the same property name. To loop through any particular result set you can use the MsiViewFetch function until it returns a value that says that it can find no more items in the result set. Because you have fetched all the records in the view you do not have to close the view to generate another one. However, if you want to follow good programming practices then you should always explicitly close any views that you create.

An alternate way to look at actions in the sequence tables

In Chapter 8 you saw how with the use of the sequence tables you can exert control on the installation procedure. We discussed the fact that the Windows Installer executes the actions listed in the sequence tables in the order of their sequence numbers, starting with the action that has the lowest positive sequence number and ending with the action that has the highest sequence number. It is instructive to look at this process a little more closely and see what is really going on behind the scenes.

The Windows Installer uses many of the API functions that you use to create our custom actions. This is definitely the case when the Windows Installer executes the actions placed in the sequence tables. The following pseudo-code shows how the Windows Installer actually runs an installation.

```
// First, a SQL query is created that
// will select all the rows in the sequence table. Ignore
// for this example the fact that there are possibly negative
// sequence numbers that identify actions that are only
// executed under certain circumstances.
sqlQuery = SELECT `Action`, `Condition` FROM
                   `InstallExecuteSequence` ORDER BY `Sequence`

// Using the above query a view object is created.
MsiDatabaseOpenView(hDatabase, sqlQuery, &hView)

// The view is executed passing a null record since no markers
// are used in the SQL query.
MsiViewExecute(hView, 0)

// In a while loop all the records in the view are fetched one
// at a time and the condition on the action is evaluated.
while(ERROR_NO_MORE_ITEMS != MsiViewFetch(hView, &hRecord)
{
    // Retrieve the condition string from the record. It is
    // the second field.
    MsiRecordGetString(hRecord, 2, szCond, 255)

    // Evaluate the condition to see if is TRUE or if no condition
    // was entered in the sequence table for the action.
    // If the condition is NULL or if it evaluates to TRUE
    // execute the action.
    // an optimization here to only call EvaluateCondition once
result = MsiEvaluateCondition(hInstall, szCond);
if(MSICONDITION_TRUE == result ||
       MSICONDITION_NONE == result)
```

```
        {
            // Retrieve the name of the action from the fetched record.
            // The name of the action is the first field in the record.
            MsiRecordGetString(hRecord, 1, szAction, 72)

            // Execute the action.
            MsiDoAction(hInstall, szAction)
        }

        // If the condition has a bad syntax or the session handle
        // is not valid terminate the installation.
        else if(MSICONDITION_ERROR == result)
        {
            return ERROR_INSTALL_FAILURE
        }
}
```

The preceding example code demonstrates that using the sequence tables is actually an indirect way of calling the MsiDoAction function. The name of the action passed to this function can be the name of a standard action, a custom action, or the name of a dialog. If the name of the action is a deferred custom action, the MsiDoAction function writes the custom action into the execution script. I'll go into more detail about this functionality in the section "Deferred Custom Actions" later in this chapter.

Introduction to the ISWI Custom Action Wizard

When you create custom actions, you will probably use the Custom Action Wizard. You can access this wizard from the Actions/Scripts view by right-clicking the Custom Actions icon and selecting the Custom Actions Wizard option from the context menu. For some types of custom actions you can use the New option from this context menu, but this requires you to know exactly how the CustomAction table needs to be authored. The first dialog that comes up when you launch the Custom Action Wizard is the Welcome dialog shown in Figure 11-2.

When you click the Next button, you get the Basic Information dialog where you provide a name for the custom action and an optional comment that will help you remember its purpose. The name you enter here will be used to identify the custom action in the Action field of the CustomAction table when the MSI package is built. The Basic Information dialog is shown in Figure 11-3.

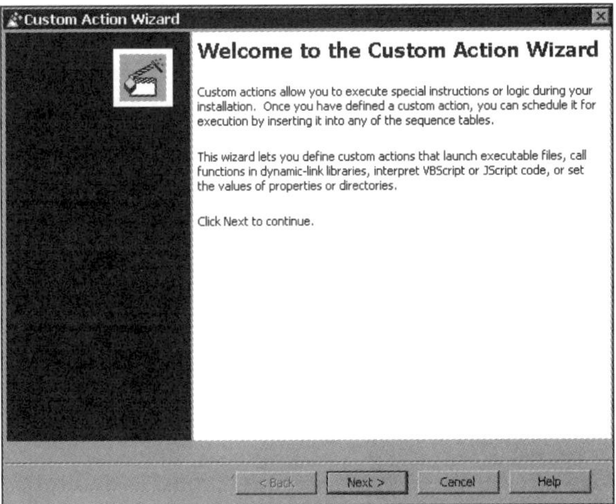

Figure 11-2: The Welcome dialog of the Custom Action Wizard

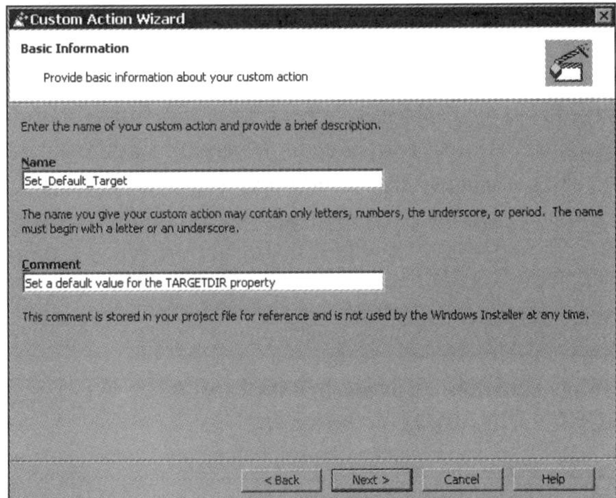

Figure 11-3: The Basic Information dialog of the Custom Action Wizard

The next dialog in the wizard is the Action Type dialog. In this dialog you select the basic type of custom action you are going to create. This dialog is shown in Figure 11-4.

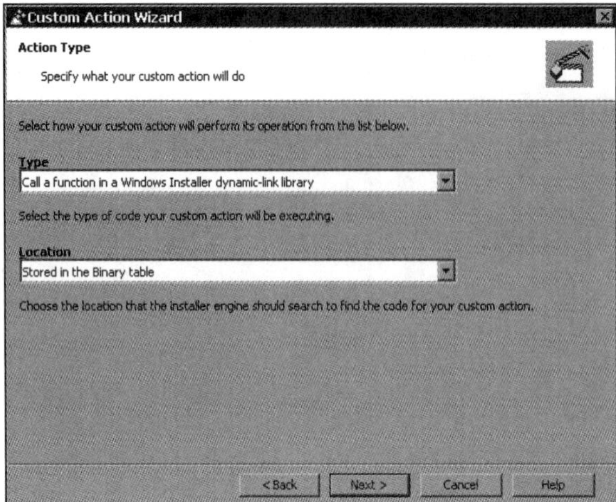

Figure 11-4: The Action Type dialog of the Custom Action Wizard

For example, if you define a type of custom action as being a Windows Installer DLL to be stored in the Binary table then it is a basic type 1 custom action. If you define a DLL custom action to be installed with the product, then it is a basic type 17 custom action. Selections made in later dialogs of the wizard can modify the basic type identified in this dialog. Depending on the type of custom action you choose in the Type combo box a different set of selections is available in the Location combo box. For certain types of custom actions there are no choices in the Location combo box. Table 11-8 describes the possible custom action types along with the available location choices.

TABLE 11-8 SUMMARY OF THE BASIC CUSTOM ACTION TYPES AVAILABLE WITH THE ISWI CUSTOM ACTION WIZARD

Type	Location	Description
Launch an executable	Stored in the Binary table Installed with the product Stored in the Property table Stored in the Directory table	The only type of custom action that can exist on the system prior to the start of the installation. When the executable, such as Notepad.exe is already on the system, the location of this file is then specified in either the Property table or the Directory table.

Type	Location	Description
Call a function in a standard dynamic link library	Stored in the Binary table Installed with the product Destination machine search path	A special type of custom action implemented by ISWI to allow the calling of a DLL function in any DLL. Behind the scenes is a Windows Installer DLL stored in the Binary table that reads from an initialization file all the information required to actually call the standard DLL function. This type of custom action is covered in the section "Calling functions in a standard link library" later in this chapter.
Call a function in a Windows Installer dynamic-link library	Stored in the Binary table Installed with the product	Calls a function in a DLL that is either stored in the Binary table or installed with the product. The format of the function has to conform to the description given in the section "Accessing the current Installer session" earlier in this chapter.
Run VBScript code	Stored in the Binary table Installed with the product Stored in the Property table Stored directly in the custom action	Implemented in a .vbs file when stored in the Binary table or installed with the product. When the script code is stored in the Property table or in the CustomAction table, the script code is written into either the Value column of the Property table or the Source field of the CustomAction table.
Run JScript code	Stored in the Binary table Installed with the product Stored in the Property table Stored directly in the custom action	Implemented as a .js file when stored in the Binary table or installed with the product. When stored in the Property table or in the CustomAction table, the script code is written into either the Value column of the Property table or the Source field of the CustomAction table.

Continued

Table 11-8 SUMMARY OF THE BASIC CUSTOM ACTION TYPES AVAILABLE WITH THE ISWI CUSTOM ACTION WIZARD *(Continued)*

Type	Location	Description
Run InstallScript code	No options available	No location option since an InstallScript custom action is implemented behind the scenes as a DLL stored in the Binary table. This functionality is described in Appendix A. Using InstallScript to create custom actions is the subject of Chapters 12–16.
Set a property	No options available	No location options to be set since this type of custom action is totally contained within the fields of the CustomAction table.
Set a directory	No options available	No location options to be set since this type of custom action is totally contained within the fields of the CustomAction table.
Launch another .msi package	Included within your main setup Stored on the source media An application that is advertised or already installed	A nested installation custom action is provided by the Windows Installer that you can have child installations to the main installation. A nested installation that is included in the main setup is incorporated as a sub-storage in the MSI package. When it is stored on the source media the nested installation package is external to the main MSI package but is in a location that is relative to the main package. When the nested install custom action is for a product that is either advertised or installed, all you have is the ProductCode for that product.

Once you have selected the basic type of custom action we want to create you move on to the next dialog in the wizard. With a few exceptions the next dialog asks you to provide the entries to be used in the Source and Target fields of the CustomAction table. Figure 11-5 shows the next wizard dialog, the Action Parameters dialog.

For each type of basic Windows Installer custom action the Custom Action Wizard can create the entries required in the Source and Target fields of the CustomAction table are different. Table 11-9 describes the entries required based on the type of custom action being created.

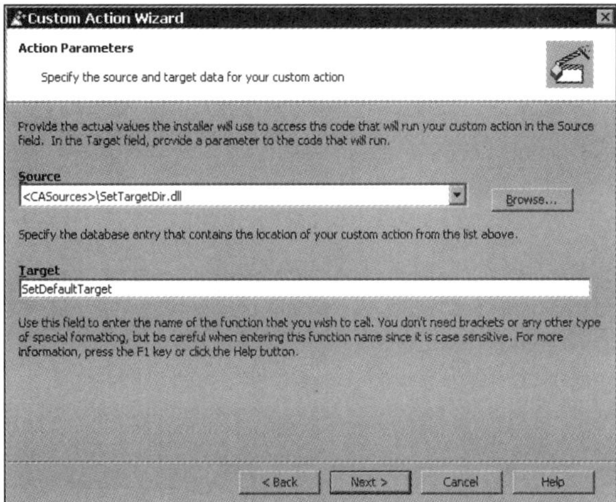

Figure 11-5: The Action Parameters dialog of the Custom Action Wizard

TABLE 11-9 SUMMARY OF THE ACTION PARAMETERS REQUIRED FOR EACH CUSTOM ACTION TYPE

Type	Source	Target
Launch an executable stored in the Binary table	Contains a key to the Binary table that identifies the row from which the executable will be streamed out into a temporary file.	If the executable is to be run with a particular command line option, this command line is entered in this field. For example, you could use it to identify a text file that is to be displayed by the executable.

Continued

TABLE 11-9 SUMMARY OF THE ACTION PARAMETERS REQUIRED FOR EACH CUSTOM ACTION TYPE *(Continued)*

Type	Source	Target
Launch an executable installed with the product	Contains a key to the File table that identifies the component with which the file is associated. The install location for the component provides the location of the executable file on the system. This type of custom action would most likely be run as a deferred category custom action since the InstallFiles action must run before this type of custom action can be executed.	If the executable is to be run with a particular command line option, this command line is entered in this field. For example, you could use it to identify a text file to be displayed by the executable.
Launch an executable with a fully qualified path identified by a property	Contains the name of a property. The value of this property includes the complete path, including the name of the executable. By definition this type of custom action is for an executable already on the target system.	If the executable is to be run with a particular command line option, this command line is entered in this field. For example, you could use it to identify a text file to be displayed by the executable.
Launch an executable located by an entry in the Directory table	Contains a key to the Directory table. The entry in the Directory table provides the location to the executable but does not provide its name. By definition this type of custom action is for an executable already on the target system.	Contains the name of the executable to be launched; it can also include a command-line string with which the executable will be run. For example, you could use it to identify a text file to be displayed by the executable.
Call a function in a Windows Installer dynamic-link library stored in the Binary table	Contains a key to the Binary table that identifies the row from which the DLL will be streamed out into a temporary file.	Contains the name of the exported function that will be called by the Windows Installer to implement the custom action.

Type	Source	Target
Call a function in a Windows Installer dynamic-link library installed with the product	Contains a key to the File table that identifies the component with which the DLL is associated. The install location for the component provides the location of the DLL file on the system. This type of custom action would most likely be run as a deferred category custom action since the InstallFiles action must be run before this type of custom action can be executed.	Contains the name of the exported function that will be called by the Windows Installer to implement the custom action.
Run VBScript code in a .vbs file stored in the Binary table	Contains a key to the Binary table that identifies the row from which the .vbs file will be streamed out into a temporary file.	Contains the name of a script function that can be called. this function is also implemented inside the .vbs file but it need not be called from within this file. If the .vbs file contains only a function, this column must contain the name of the function.
Run VBScript code in a .vbs file installed with the product	Contains a key to the File table that identifies the component with which the .vbs file is associated. The install location for the component provides the location of the .vbs file on the system. This type of custom action would most likely be run as a deferred category custom action since the InstallFiles action must be run before this type of custom action can be executed.	Contains the name of a script function that can be called. This function is also implemented inside the .vbs file but it need not be called from within this file. If the .vbs file contains only a function, this column must contain the name of the function.

Continued

TABLE 11-9 SUMMARY OF THE ACTION PARAMETERS REQUIRED FOR EACH CUSTOM ACTION TYPE *(Continued)*

Type	Source	Target
Run VBScript code in a .vbs file already on the system and located by an entry in the Property table	Contains the name of a property in the Property table. The value of this property includes the complete path, including the name of the executable. By definition this type of custom action is for a .vbs file that is already on the target system, an unlikely scenario.	Contains the name of a script function that can be called. This function is also implemented inside the .vbs file but need not be called from within this file. If the .vbs file contains only a function, this column must contain the name of the function.
Run VBScript code stored in the CustomAction table	There is no entry in this field for this type of custom action.	The VBScript text that comprises this custom action is contained in this field of the CustomAction table.
Run JScript code in a .js file stored in the Binary table	Contains a key to the Binary table that identifies the row from which the .js file will be streamed out into a temporary file.	Contains the name of a script function that can be called. This function is also implemented inside the .js file but need not be called from within this file. If the .js file contains only a function, this column must contain the name of the function.
Run JScript code in a .js file installed with the product	Contains a key to the File table that identifies the component with which the .js file is associated. The install location for the component provides the location of the .js file on the system. This type of custom action would most likely be run as a deferred category custom action since the InstallFiles action must be run before this type of custom action can be executed.	Contains the name of a script function that can be called. This function is also implemented inside the .js file but need not be called from within this file. If the .js file contains only a function, this column must contain the name of the function.

Type	Source	Target
Run JScript code in a .js file already on the system and located by an entry in the Property table	Contains the name of a property in the Property table. The value of this property includes the complete path, including the name of the executable. By definition this type of custom action is for a .js file already on the target system, an unlikely scenario.	Contains the name of a script function that can be called. This function is also implemented inside the .js file but need not be called from within this file. If the .js file contains only a function, this column must contain the name of the function.
Run JScript code stored in the CustomAction table	There is no entry in this field for this type of custom action.	The VBScript text that comprises this custom action is contained in this field of the CustomAction table.
Set a property	A property the value of which will be set be set by the formatted text string provided in the Target field.	Contains a formatted text string that will be used to set the value of the property named in the Source field. The formatting of this string must follow the rules used by the MsiFormatRecord API function.
Set a directory	A key into the Directory table that will be set by the formatted text string provided in the Target field.	Contains a formatted text string that will be used to set the value of the property named in the Source field. The formatting of this string must follow the rules used by the MsiFormatRecord API function.
Launch another .msi package contained as a sub-storage in the main installation package	Contains the name of the sub-storage inside the MSI package that contains the MSI package, which implements the nested installation custom action.	Contains a string that identifies the public properties and their values that are to be used on the command line when the nested installation is executed.

Continued

TABLE 11-9 SUMMARY OF THE ACTION PARAMETERS REQUIRED FOR EACH CUSTOM ACTION TYPE *(Continued)*

Type	Source	Target
Launch another .msi package that has the install package located on the source media	Contains the path on the source media where the MSI package, which implements the nested installation custom action, can be found. This path must be relative to the location of the MSI package that contains the main installation.	Contains a string that identifies the public properties and their values that are to be used on the command line when the nested installation is executed.
Launch another .msi package for an application that is advertised or already installed	Contains the ProductCode property value for the product that is the target of the nested installation custom action.	Contains a string that identifies the public properties and their values that are to be used on the command line when the nested installation is executed.

Table 11-9 did not mention the special type of custom action implemented by ISWI where a function in any DLL can be called. This is because this particular type of custom action is covered separately in the section "Calling functions in a standard dynamic link library" later in this chapter. As Table 11-8 showed, this type of custom action is a special implementation of a Windows Installer DLL custom action that is stored in the Binary table. I also did not cover the InstallScript type of custom action since this type is the subject of Chapters 12 through 16.

After entering the necessary action parameters for the custom action you are creating you move on to the Additional Options dialog by clicking the Next button. This dialog is shown in Figure 11-6.

This is the final dialog of the wizard where you can enter information to define your custom action. It is in this dialog that the basic type is modified according to the return processing, in-script processing, and execution scheduling options that you choose. The return processing options enable you to define whether the custom action will run synchronously or asynchronously. It also enables you to tell the Windows Installer to ignore the return code from the custom action. The In-Script Execution and Execution Scheduling options are described in detail in Chapter 10.

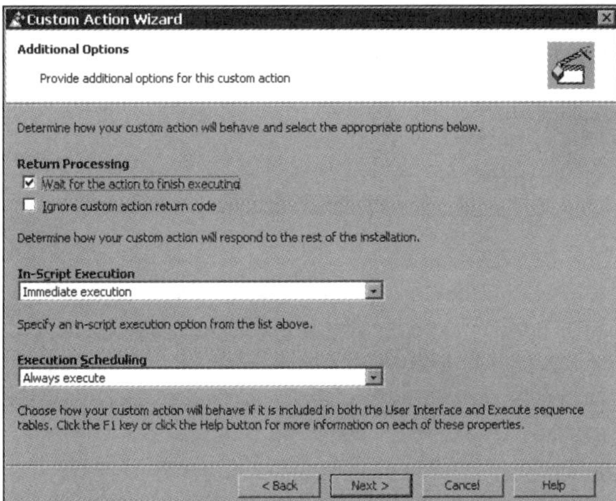

Figure 11-6: The Additional Options dialog of the Custom Action Wizard

After you make your selections in the Additional Options dialog and click the Next button you get the Summary dialog, shown in Figure 11-7.

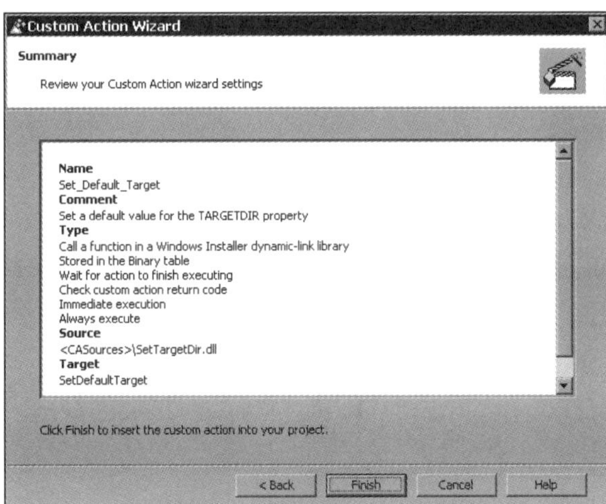

Figure 11-7: The Summary dialog of the Custom Action Wizard

When you click the Finish button on this dialog, the custom action is created in the ISWI project file and the entries that are going to be made in the CustomAction table are shown in the Actions/Scripts view when you click on the name of the custom action. Figure 11-8 shows the CustomAction table entries.

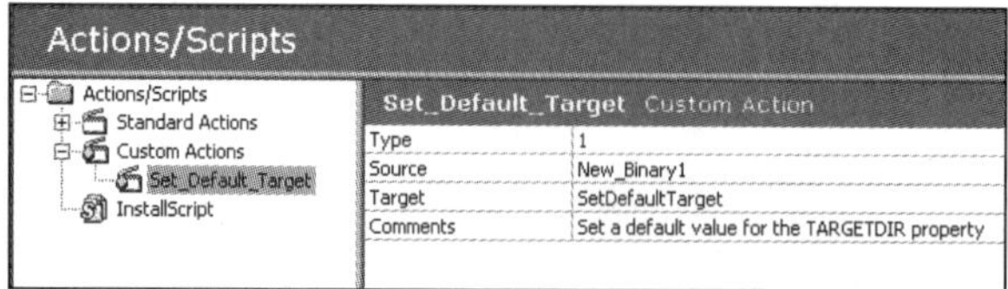

Figure 11-8: The CustomAction table entries for the Set_Default_Target custom action

The custom action you created in the preceding example was a Type 1. This is a DLL custom action where the DLL is stored in the Binary table. The Source property row shows the foreign key into the Binary table, New_Binary1. This key is created by ISWI and it will identify the entry in the Binary table from which this DLL will be temporarily streamed out. The Target property row shows the name of the exported function from this DLL that will be called by the Windows Installer to implement the custom action. The Comments property row in Figure 11-8 shows the comments you entered when you first started to create the custom action. The entry in this row is only stored in the project file and is not used in the MSI database.

The only type of custom action that cannot be created by the ISWI Custom Action Wizard is the Error custom action (Type 19). You must create this type of custom action directly in the IDE by selecting the New option from the context menu where you launched the Custom Action Wizard. We will look at an example of this type of custom action in the "Miscellaneous Custom Actions" section later in this chapter.

Working with Properties

Windows Installer provides two special functions to work with properties in an install session. In the next section we take a close look at these two functions. You need to keep in mind that the function of properties in the Windows Installer environment is to act as global variables to the installation.

The MsiGetProperty and MsiSetProperty APIs

Two primary database functions are provided by the Windows Installer for working with the Property table. These functions are MsiGetProperty() and MsiSet Property().These two functions are prototyped in the header file msiquery.h, which is in the Include subfolder of the Windows Installer SDK installation location.

The MsiGetProperty() function retrieves the value of an installer property. It has the following format:

```
UINT MsiGetProperty(
MSIHANDLE hInstall,      // handle to installer session
LPCTSTR szName,          // case-sensitive property name
LPTSTR szValueBuf,       // buffer for returned property value
DWORD pchValueBuf        // in/out buffer character count
);
```

When you use this API to obtain the value of a property, you need to tell the function the number of characters in the property value, including the null terminator. The best way to set the size of the buffer passed to this function is to first pass an empty string in order to get back the actual size of the number of characters that make up the property value. Then call the function again with the buffer sized to just accommodate the property value, making sure to increment this size in order to accommodate the null terminator. If a property is not defined, you will get an empty string returned as the value of the buffer and a buffer size of 0. The following is typical C++ code that would retrieve the value of a property:

```
LPCTSTR szPropName = TEXT("ADDLOCAL");
LPTSTR szPropValue = 0;
DWORD  dwBufSize = 0;

::MsiGetProperty(hInstall, szPropName, TEXT(""), &dwBufSize);
szPropValue = new TCHAR[++dwBufSize];

if(ERROR_SUCCESS != ::MsiGetProperty(hInstall, szPropName,
                                     szPropValue, &dwBufSize))
{
    if(szPropValue)
        delete [] szPropValue;
    return ERROR_INSTALL_FAILURE;
}
```

The MsiSetProperty() function sets the value of an installer property. It has the following format:

```
UINT MsiSetProperty(
MSIHANDLE hInstall,      // handle to installer session
LPCTSTR szName,          // case-sensitive property name
LPCTSTR szValue          // property value to set
);
```

You can use this function to remove a property as well as to set the value of a property. To remove a property all you need to do is set the value of the existing property to an empty string. This will remove the property from the Property table.

Two additional functions retrieve information from the Property table. These are the MsiGetMode and MsiGetLanguage APIs. The MsiGetMode function determines whether the installer is running in a specified mode. This function returns a Boolean value of TRUE or FALSE depending on whether the specified mode passed into the function is currently set or not. The Windows Installer help defines those properties that can be passed to this function. The MsiGetLanguage function returns the value of the ProductLanguage property.

An example custom action using the Property table

A good example of using a DLL custom action to manipulate properties in the Property table is one that shows how you can change the selection of features programmatically. For this example you need a simple setup project with four features, each feature containing several components. You can find this project and the source code for this custom action on the CD-ROM at the back of the book.

The project you are going to work with here is called Features. It has four features, each with three components. The fourth feature is hidden and its install level property has been set to 101 so that it will not be installed. In this scenario you want the fourth feature to be installed only if the end user deselects the third feature, and you can arrange this with a simple DLL custom action that manipulates the ADDLOCAL property. You are going to search the value of the ADDLOCAL property to see if contains the string Feature3. If it does, then you do not have to do anything, but if it does not then you need to concatenate the string ,Feature4 to the value of the ADDLOCAL property. This way you will force the installation of the fourth feature if the user has deselected the third feature.

The source code for this custom action is as follows:

```
/*----------------------------------------------------------------+
|
|   File Name:  Features.cpp
|
|   Description: Custom action to control the feature set of an
|                installation
|   Author: Bob Baker
|
+----------------------------------------------------------------*/

#include "stdafx.h"

BOOL APIENTRY DllMain( HANDLE hModule, DWORD  ul_reason_for_call,
                                               LPVOID lpReserved)
{
    return TRUE;
}
```

```
//
// This custom action will force the installation of Feature4
// if Feature3 is deselected
//
UINT __stdcall SetFeatureFour(MSIHANDLE hInstall)
{
    LPCTSTR      LocalFeatureProp = "ADDLOCAL";
    TCHAR*       szFeatureThree = TEXT("Feature3");
    TCHAR*       szFeatureFour = TEXT(",Feature4");
    TCHAR*       szFeatureBuf;
    DWORD        ncharCount = 0;
    UINT         uiReturn;

    // Get the list of features to be installed
    // First send an empty string in order to get the
    // correct size of the buffer needed to hold the property value
    uiReturn = MsiGetProperty(hInstall, LocalFeatureProp, TEXT(""),
                                                         &ncharCount);

    switch(uiReturn)
    {
    case ERROR_INVALID_HANDLE:
    case ERROR_INVALID_PARAMETER:
        // don't call message boxes from within your CA, use
MsiProcessMessage() instead. Message boxes break no UI installs,
don't encourage folks to do it. ProcessMessage also works with the
logging system, and external UI, so it is a way better way to go.

MessageBox(NULL,
              "An error occurred when getting the buffer size",
                                                 "Error", MB_OK);
        return ERROR_INSTALL_FAILURE;
    }

    // Increment the character count to account
    //for the null terminator
    ++ncharCount;

    // Allocate memory for the property value return buffer
    szFeatureBuf = (LPTSTR) malloc(ncharCount);
    uiReturn = MsiGetProperty(hInstall, LocalFeatureProp,
                                      szFeatureBuf, &ncharCount);

    switch(uiReturn)
```

```
    {
    case ERROR_INVALID_HANDLE:
    case ERROR_INVALID_PARAMETER:
        MessageBox(NULL,
             "An error occurred when getting the buffer size",
                                                   "Error", MB_OK);
        return ERROR_INSTALL_FAILURE;
    }

    // If Feature3 is not being installed install Feature4
    // by adding the , Feature4
    // string to the ADDLOCAL property
    if(!strstr(szFeatureBuf, szFeatureThree))
    {
        strcat(szFeatureBuf, szFeatureFour);

        uiReturn = MsiSetProperty(hInstall, "ADDLOCAL",
                                                   szFeatureBuf);

        switch(uiReturn)
        {
        case ERROR_INVALID_HANDLE:
        case ERROR_INVALID_PARAMETER:
        case ERROR_FUNCTION_FAILED:
            MessageBox(NULL,
                 "An error occurred when getting the buffer size",
                                                   "Error", MB_OK);
            return ERROR_INSTALL_FAILURE;
        }

    }

    return ERROR_SUCCESS;
}
```

You need to add this custom action to the InstallExecuteSequence table as an immediate category type of custom action. You can place it right after the LaunchConditons action in this sequence and create a condition in the Condition column so that it will only run on installation and not on uninstallation. The condition you place on this custom action is Not Installed. You cannot place this custom action in the user-interface sequence because the ADDLOCAL property is not created until the ExecuteAction action runs. The entries you need to make in the Custom Action Wizard to create this custom action are shown in Table 11-10.

TABLE 11-10 CREATING THE SET_FEATURE_SELECTION CUSTOM ACTION

Wizard Dialog	Selections
Basic Information	Name: Set_Feature_Selection
	Comments: Add Feature4 if Feature3 not selected
Action Type	Type: Call a function in a Windows Installer dynamic-link library
	Location: Stored in the Binary table
Action Parameters	Source: <*Sources*>\Features.dll
	Target: SetFeatureFour
Additional Options	Return Processing: The "Wait for the action to finish executing" option is checked and the "Ignore custom action return code" option is unchecked
	In-Script Execution: Immediate execution
	Execution Scheduling: Always execute

To insert this custom action into the execution sequence go to the Sequences view and expand the sequence of actions under the Execute icon. Highlight the LaunchConditions action, right click and then select the Insert... option on the context menu. This will give you a dialog box where you can choose to insert custom actions from the combo box at the top of the dialog. There should only be one custom action to select but before you close this dialog you should enter the condition in the edit field below the list of custom actions. When you close the dialog by clicking the OK button, the custom action is inserted into the sequence and this custom action is given a sequence number halfway between the sequence number for the LaunchConditons action and the FindRelatedProducts action.

To build the Features project on the CD-ROM you will probably need to modify the path variable used to locate the files and the custom action during the build. In a real-world scenario you would have to concern yourself with the all the public properties that control what gets installed where. These public properties are ADDLOCAL, REMOVE, ADDSOURCE, ADDDEFAULT, REINSTALL, ADVERTISE, COMPADDLOCAL, COMPADDSOURCE, FILEADDLOCAL, FILEADDSOURCE, and FILEADDDEFAULT. The MSI help provides a detailed description of these properties and explains the order in which they are evaluated.

The preceding method for controlling the feature set to be installed requires that the features not be disabled. In other words, if you had set the install level of Feature4 to 0 then it would still not have been installed even after you added it to the ADDLOCAL property value.

Creating and Using Custom Tables

There will be many times when you want to create custom tables to be used by custom actions that you develop. Even though these custom actions could be created in memory at install time you will probably want to create these tables and enter data into them at build time. The custom actions you call at run time will use the data in these custom tables to perform their intended function.

ISWI version 1.5 cannot create custom tables and therefore to create a custom table that will be persisted in the database you need to perform post processing on the MSI package after it is built using ISWI. You can add a custom table to a Windows Installer database in two ways. You can create a text archive file and then import this text archive file using the Orca utility that comes with the Windows Installer SDK. This is more work than the second option, which is to use a VBScript file created to perform this particular function. The name of this script file is WiRunSQL.vbs and you can find it in the Samples\Scripts folder under the location where the Windows Installer is installed. This operation requires that the Windows Scripting Host (WSH) be installed and it must use the console executable that comes with the WSH. The format of the command line for using this script file is as follows:

```
cscript wirunsql.vbs "<path-to-msi-database >" "<sql-statement>"
```

Once you have added the table to a copy of the original MSI database you can use Orca to enter the data into this table. Since you do not want to have to repeat this whole operation every time you build a new package using ISWI, you need to use the ISWI Transform Wizard to create a transform between the original package and the package that has the new table or tables. Now every time you build a new package you can then use the Transform Wizard to apply the transform to the new package. This will add the new table or tables and associated data to the newly created database. If some of the data must be modified, we can open up the transformed database with Orca and make the changes.

Chapter 18 includes a complete discussion of transforms and how to create and apply them.

For example, you might want to create a custom table in order to mimic the standard actions that search for files and directories. The Windows Installer provides a standard action called AppSearch the purpose of which is to search for the existence of files, folders, registry entries, and initialization file entries. The only problem with this standard action is that it can only be placed in a sequence table prior to the CostInitialize standard action. This sequence restriction is imposed by ICE27, which is one of the Internal Consistency Evaluators used in validating a package for the "Certified for Windows" logo. If you want to search for a file or folder based on the value of the INSTALLDIR property, you need to run your search after the CostFinalize standard action. In this case you would need to create your own search functionality.

Custom Actions and the User Interface

There will be many times when you will want to create custom actions that work with the user interface. You will want to have custom actions that are launched when the user clicks a button. If you want to populate a control at run time, you will need to create a custom action to do this. In the following two sections you will create one custom action that will launch a Web site when a button is clicked and another custom action that will dynamically populate a combo box control. Since in the previous custom actions you used C++ you will now use VBScript for these custom actions.

Using the DoAction control event

One of the things you might want to do is launch a custom action with a button is click. To do this you use the DoAction control event. This control event takes as an argument the name of the custom action to be launched. For this to work, this custom action has to be of the immediate category; it cannot be a deferred custom action. For this custom action you will store the VBScript code directly in the CustomAction table. Table 11-11 show the selections you need to make in the Custom Action Wizard for this custom action.

Table 11-11 CREATING THE OPEN_WEB_PAGE CUSTOM ACTION

Wizard Dialog	Selections
Basic Information	Name: Open_Web_Page
	Comments: Launches the InstallShield Web site
Action Type	Type: Run VBScript code
	Location: Stored directly in the custom action
Additional Options	Return Processing: The "Wait for the action to finish executing" option is unchecked and the "Ignore custom action return code" option is checked; tell the Windows Installer to ignore the return code because you are creating a VBScript custom action that cannot return a code because no function is being invoked
	In-Script Execution: Immediate execution
	Execution Scheduling: Always execute

For this particular type of custom action the Custom Action Wizard does not provide you with a dialog in which to enter the Source and Target fields of the CustomAction table; instead you get a dialog where you can enter the VBScript that will go into the Target field of the CustomAction table. From Table 11-9 you can see that for this type of custom action the Source field is empty. Figure 11-9 shows the VBScript editor dialog and the VBScript text you need to enter for this custom action.

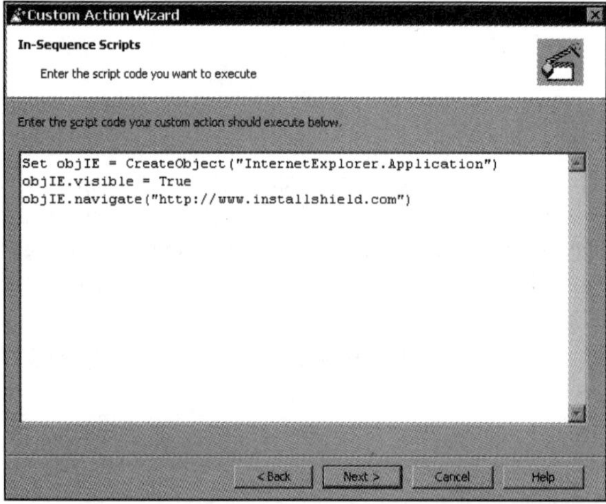

Figure 11-9: The In-Sequence Scripts dialog of the Custom Action Wizard

The dialog shown in Figure 11-9 is only displayed when you are creating either a VBScript or JScript custom action where the script code is to be stored in the Target field of the CustomAction table. The code that has been entered for this custom action is very simple, creating an Internet Explorer object and then using the navigate method of this object to launch the Web site. Setting the visible property of this object to True just ensures that when the Web site is launched you will be able to see it.

Now you need to attach this custom action to a button on a dialog. The best way to do this is with the Finish button on the SetupCompleteSuccess dialog displayed after a successful installation. Since you already have a project named Features that you used earlier for running other custom actions you might as well continue to use it for this example. To add this custom action to the project go to the User Interface view and expand the tree under the SetupCompleteSuccess dialog. Click on the Behavior icon: this displays all the controls so that you can assign control events to them. You need to make sure that the Events tab is active at the bottom of the screen.

Since you want to add this control event to the Finish button click on the control named OK. When you click in an empty row in the Event column, you get a dropdown list of control events to choose from. The one you want is the DoAction control event. In the Argument column for this control event you get a dropdown list of all the custom actions you have created in the project. The one you want to select is the Open_Web_Page custom action. Since you only want this custom action to run during an installation, place the condition Not Installed on this control event. This will prevent the custom action from launching the InstallShield Web site at the end of an uninstallation. Figure 11-10 shows the User Interface view for the control event you just selected. You'll notice that this new control event has been moved to the top. You can do this by right-clicking on the control event and selecting the Move Up option.

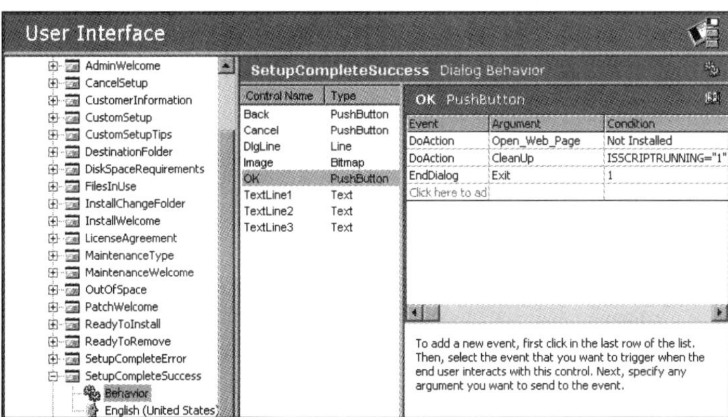

Figure 11-10: Creating the control event for launching the InstallShield Web site

Now that you have created a small custom action using VBScript you need to see how to use this programming language to populate a control dynamically at run time.

Dynamically populating a combo box during an install

In this example you are going to enumerate the mapped network drives on the target machine and then display this enumeration in a combo box control. To enumerate the network drives that are mapped to a particular machine you will use the Network object of the Windows Scripting Host. The object model for the Windows Scripting Host is shown in Figure 11-11.

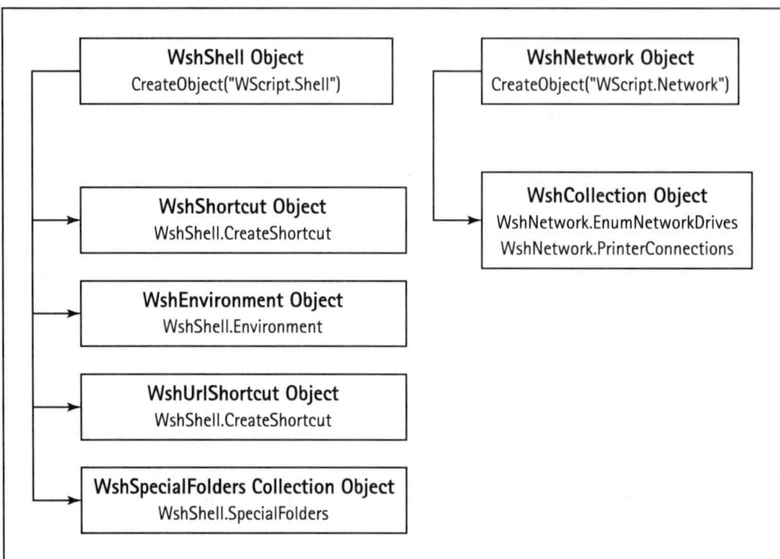

Figure 11-11: The Windows Scripting Host object model

This example, of necessity, is comprised of the creation of a VBScript file and the creation of a dialog box that contains a combo box control and a pushbutton. You will place both the custom actions you create using the .vbs file and the dialog that you create in the user interface sequence so that you can verify that what you have done actually works. You do not need to insert this dialog into a wizard sequence but can place it directly in the sequence table itself.

The first thing we need to do is to create the VBScript file that will implement the functionality you want. The following VBScript code is what you want to create in order to populate the ComboBox table at run time with the list of mapped network drives.

The code described in the next section can be found on the CD-ROM in a file named ENUMNETDRIVES.VBS. The custom action that uses this file has been created in the Features project that is on the CD-ROM as well.

CREATING THE VBSCRIPT FILE

The process followed by this script file is much the same as what I described in the section "Working with the MSI database at install time" earlier in this chapter. Here you are using the methods and properties made available through the Windows Installer Automation interface. When you use the automation interface, the Session object is provided to you by the Windows Installer. You do not have to create this object. It comes to you with the name Session. You use the Session object and the Database and the Installer properties to create a Database object and an Installer object. Once you have these two objects you do not need to use the Session object anymore.

```
' This VBScript is used to populate the ComboBox table with
' a list of the mapped network drives on the target machine
Function GetNetworkDrives()

    ' You need to create an installer object
    ' so that you can create a record object.
    ' The Session object is given to you by
    ' the Windows Installer so it does not have to be created.
    Set objInstaller = Session.Installer

    ' Create an object for the currently running
    ' database using the Database property of the Session object.
    Set objDB = Session.Database

    ' Create a view object for all the columns
    ' in the ComboBox table.
    Set objView = objDB.OpenView("SELECT * FROM `ComboBox` WHERE
                                `Property` = 'NETWORKDRIVES'")

    ' You need to execute the view so that you can
    ' iterate through it to find how many rows may
    ' have been authored into the database.
    objView.Execute

    j = GetStartingIndex(objView)

    ' Create a record object that you will use to
    ' enter data into the ComboBox table.
```

```
Set objRec = objInstaller.CreateRecord(4)

' Create a Windows Scripting Host network object
' that you will use to enumerate all the network drives.
Set WshNetwork = CreateObject("WScript.Network")

' Create a collection of network drives
' that you will iterate in order to populate the
' ComboBox table.
Set objDrives = WshNetwork.EnumNetworkDrives

' Initialize an index that will be used to order
' the appearance of items in the combo box control.
' Now iterate through the collection of network drives
' and use this information to add records to the ComboBox table.
' The network drives collection comes in two parts. First is the
' mapped drive letter followed by the UNC path to the network
' server.
' This is why you need to step through the collection with
' a step value of 2.
For i = 0 to objDrives.Count - 1 Step 2
    ' Create a string that includes both the drive letter
    ' and the server path.
    ' This will be the text that is displayed in the
    ' combo box control.
    strMapDrive = "Drive " & objDrives.Item(i) & " = "
                                          & objDrives.Item(i+1)

    ' The first column of the ComboBox table is the name of the
    ' property that will identify all the records
    ' to be displayed.
    objRec.StringData(1) = "NETWORKDRIVES"

    ' The second column of the ComboBox table is an index
    ' that orders how the records in the table
    'are to be displayed.
    objRec.IntegerData(2) = j

    ' The third column of the ComboBox table is the
    ' value to which the property NETWORKDRIVES
    ' will be set when a selection is made
    ' from the list in the combo box control.
    ' For this example this is just the string
    ' equivalent of the order index.
    objRec.StringData(3) = CStr(j)
```

```
        ' The fourth column is the string that will be
        ' displayed in the combo box control.
        objRec.StringData(4) = strMapDrive

        ' Using the Modify method of the view object
        ' you add a temporary record to the ComboBox table.
        ' This record will not be persisted in the table
        ' when the databse is closed.
        objView.Modify 7, objRec

        ' Clear the data from the record so that you can
        ' use it again for the next row to be inserted.
        objRec.ClearData

        ' Increment the index.
        j = j + 1
    Next

    ' Return success to the Windows Installer.
    GetNetworkDrives = 1

End Function

' This function returns the value to be used
' for the starting index in the ComboBox table.
' It is necessary to have a function like this
' in case there are already records in this table
' associated with the NETWORKDRIVES property.
Function GetStartingIndex(view)

    ' The index will never be less than 1
    j = 1

    ' You need to loop through the view to make sure
    ' that there are no existing records
    ' for your particular property.
    ' There is no way to get the number of records
    ' in a view except to loop through the view
    ' and increment a counter.
    Do
        Set rec = view.Fetch
        j = j + 1
    Loop Until rec Is Nothing
```

```
    GetStartingIndex = j

End Function
```

Using the Database object you can create a view object using the following SQL statement:

```
SELECT * FROM `ComboBox` WHERE `Property` = 'NETWORKDRIVES'
```

Using this statement the OpenView method of the Database object creates a View object that will include all the columns of the ComboBox table and those rows where the Property column has the value of NETWORKDRIVES. Create this view using the WHERE clause to make sure that any new rows that you add start with the correct index in the Order column. You do not want to have two rows with the same index number.

Use the CreateRecord method of the Installer object to create a Record object with four columns. This is the record you will use to add the temporary rows to the ComboBox table. Then create a Windows Scripting Host Network object using the VBScript CreateObject function. Using the EnumNetworkDrives method of the Network object, create a collection object that enumerates the mapped network drives on the target machine. Once you have the drives collection you can loop through it and create the records you want to place into the ComboBox table. Do this by setting the either the StringData or the IntegerData property of the Record object to the appropriate value. These properties take as an argument the field number being set. The field numbers of a record are 1-based since field 0 is reserved for Windows Installer–specific information.

Once the fields of the Record object have been populated, add the record to the ComboBox table using the Modify method of the View object. Because you are dealing with the run-time database you can only add temporary rows to a table and these will not be persisted when the database is closed. Accordingly you need to use the temporary action available with the Modify method, which has a value of 7. Once you have added a row to the table, clear the data in the record and loop back to pick up the information for the next record you want to add. It is interesting to note that the drives collection has two parts, the drive letter and the UNC path to the server. Each has a separate index number, which is why the For loop in the code has a Step value of 2.

CREATING THE CUSTOM ACTION

Now that you have created the code that will implement the custom action you need to create the custom action itself. You can do this using the Custom Action Wizard, making the entries shown in Table 11-12.

Table 11-12 CREATING THE ENUM_NETWORK_DRIVES CUSTOM ACTION

Wizard Dialog	Selections
Basic Information	Name: Enum_Network_Drives
	Comments: Populates the ComboBox table with a list of the network drives
Action Type	Type: Run VBScript code
	Location: Stored in the Binary table
Action Parameters	Source: <Sources>\enumnetdrives.vbs
	Target: GetNetworkDrives
Additional Options	Return Processing: The "Wait for the action to finish executing" option is unchecked and the "Ignore custom action return code" option is also unchecked
	In-Script Execution: Immediate execution
	Execution Scheduling: Always execute

After creating this custom action you need to insert it into a sequence so that you can test its functionality. To make things simple and quick you can insert it into the user interface sequence immediately after the FindRelatedProducts action. After creating the custom dialog box you can insert it immediately after the custom action. Now you need to create this dialog box.

CREATING THE CUSTOM DIALOG

In order to see whether our custom action actually populates the ComboBox table with a list of mapped network drives you need to create a dialog that has at a minimum a combo box control and a pushbutton. Such a dialog box is shown in Figure 11-12.

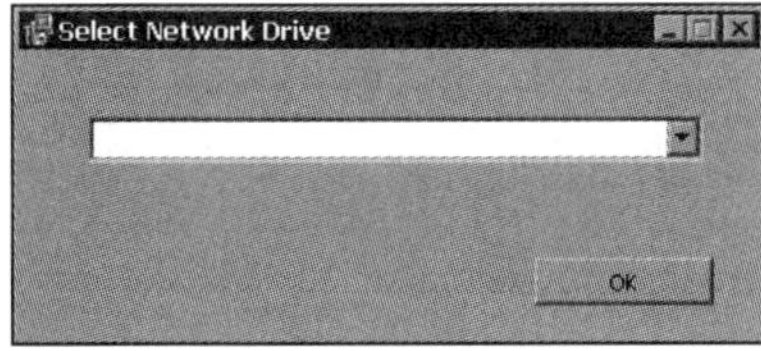

Figure 11-12: The Select Network Drive dialog box

When you add the combo box control to this dialog, you will be asked to identify the name of the property with which the control is to be associated. You need to make sure to enter the name of the property you used in the VBScript code, NETWORKDRIVES. When you enter this property name, it will appear in the Property Manager in the Project view. If you want to have this combo box control show a default value when the dialog is launched, you need to give this property a value. The simplest thing to do is to give it a value of 1. This means that the first item in the list of mapped network drives will be shown as the default value. The last thing you need to do to this combo box control is to make sure to set the height of the control to a size that will contain at least three or four items. A good height is 100. If you do not set the height, the combo box will not show any values when you drop it down.

You need to add a pushbutton so that you can dismiss the dialog after selecting the network drive. You can use the EndDialog event with the Return argument to do this. You should also make sure to set the condition to 1 so that it will always be true. Now you can insert this dialog directly into the user interface sequence after the Enum_Network_Drives custom action. Then you can build the project and test it to make sure that it works.

This custom action and dialog have been included with the Features project that is on the CD-ROM at the back of the book.

Deferred Custom Actions

Up until now you have creating custom actions of the immediate category. These custom actions run as soon as the Windows Installer encounters them in the sequence table. As I mentioned earlier, deferred custom actions are first written into the Windows Installer execution script and then executed. A custom action written into the Windows Installer execution script no longer has access to the MSI database and has to rely on the information that has been written to the CustomActionData property. In the following example you will learn how to create this special property value.

Both DLL and script-based custom actions require a handle to the installation session. In the case of a DLL the handle is in the form of a value of type MSIHANDLE; in the case of script-based custom actions it is an object with the name Session. When one of these types of custom actions is defined as being deferred, it will still be passed a valid handle or object but will have greatly reduced access to any context information. Table 11-13 describes available information for deferred custom actions.

TABLE 11-13 CONTEXT INFORMATION AVAILABLE TO DEFERRED CUSTOM ACTIONS

Function/Method Name	Description of Available Context Information
MsiGetProperty or Session.Property	The only properties that can be accessed by these functions are the ProductCode property and a special property named CustomActionData.
MsiGetMode or Session.Mode	MsiGetMode can identify whether the custom action is running as part of an installation, rollback, or commit operation. Session.Mode can only identify whether the custom action is running as part of an installation. It does not have access to either rollback or commit operations.
MsiGetLangauge or Session.Language	These functions return the value of the ProductLanguage property as a numeric language ID.
MsiProcessMessage or Session.ProcessMessage	This function is used by the custom action to send messages to the Windows Installer, which in turn can display them on the progress bar to indicate the status of the custom action.

Now you should take a look at a simple example of a deferred custom action and its use of the CustomActionData property.

In this example you will create the CustomActionData property that will have as its value a string that you want to display using a deferred DLL custom action. You'll need two custom actions for this example: one immediate category custom action that will define the CustomActionData property and one deferred DLL custom action that will display the value of this property in a message box. To create the string value for the CustomActionData property you will use a Type 51 custom action. This type of custom action sets the value of a property based on a formatted text string. You will not actually use the name CustomActionData when setting the property value; you'll use the name of the custom action that will be accessing this value. The custom action that is going to display the value of the property will do an MsiGetProperty call on the property name CustomActionData. Once again you will use the Features project to create this example. First, create the Type 51 custom action. Table 11-14 show the entries you need to make in the Custom Action Wizard for this custom action.

TABLE 11-14 CREATING THE TYPE 51 CUSTOM ACTION

Wizard Dialog	Selections
Basic Information	Name: Set_CAD_Prop
	Comments: Set the value of the CustomActionData property
Action Type	Type: Set a property
	Location: Null
Action Parameters	Source: Display_CAD_Prop
	Target: This string is the value of the CustomActionData property
Additional Options	Return Processing: The "Wait for the action to finish executing" option is checked and the "Ignore custom action return code" option is unchecked (these selections cannot be changed)
	In-Script Execution: Immediate execution (cannot be changed)
	Execution Scheduling: Always execute

As you can see, the custom action being used to set the value of the CustomActionData property is of the immediate category. In the source field of the Action Parameters dialog of the wizard you have entered the name of the deferred custom action you are going to create next. The value of the property is the string "This string is the value of the CustomActionData property." And this is what will be displayed in the message box launched from the deferred custom action.

The deferred custom action that will read the value of the CustomActionData property is implemented in a DLL. The code for the exported function in the DLL is shown below:

```
UINT __stdcall DisplayProperty(MSIHANDLE hInstall)
{
    LPCTSTR     PropertyName = "CustomActionData";
    TCHAR*      szPropertyBuf;
    DWORD       ncharCount = 0;
    UINT        uiReturn;


    // First, send an empty string in order to get the
```

```
    // correct size of the buffer needed to hold the property value
    // Note that the name of the property being accessed
    // is CustomActionData
    uiReturn = MsiGetProperty(hInstall, PropertyName, TEXT(""),
                                                        &ncharCount);

    switch(uiReturn)
    {
    case ERROR_INVALID_HANDLE:
    case ERROR_INVALID_PARAMETER:
// never do this in a deferred CA. It totally breaks unattended
installs. MsiProcessMessage()
MessageBox(NULL, "An error occurred when getting the buffer
                                            size", "Error", MB_OK);
        return ERROR_INSTALL_FAILURE;
    }

    // Allocate memory for the property value return buffer
    szPropertyBuf = (LPTSTR) malloc(++ncharCount);
    uiReturn = MsiGetProperty(hInstall, PropertyName, szPropertyBuf,
                                                        &ncharCount);

    switch(uiReturn)
    {
    case ERROR_INVALID_HANDLE:
    case ERROR_INVALID_PARAMETER:
        MessageBox(NULL, "An error occurred when getting the
                              property value", "Error", MB_OK);
        return ERROR_INSTALL_FAILURE;
    }

    MessageBox(NULL, szPropertyBuf, "Property Display", MB_OK);

    return ERROR_SUCCESS;
}
```

The DLL that implements this functionality is on the CD-ROM as well as the source code for the DLL. Table 11-15 shows the entries you need to make in the Custom Action Wizard to create this deferred custom action.

TABLE 11-15 CREATING THE DISPLAY_CAD_PROP CUSTOM ACTION

Wizard Dialog	Selections
Basic Information	Name: Display_CAD_Prop
	Comments: Disp lay the value of the CustomActionData property
Action Type	Type: Call a function in a Windows Installer dynamic-link library
	Location: Stored in the Binary table
Action Parameters	Source: <*Sources*>\PropertyDisplay.dll
	Target: DisplayProperty
Additional Options	Return Processing: The "Wait for the action to finish executing" option is checked and the "Ignore custom action return code" option is unchecked
	In-Script Execution: Deferred execution
	Execution Scheduling: Always execute (cannot be changed)

Note that the name of the custom action you have just created is the same as the name of the property that you set with the formatted text (Type 51) custom action.

Finally, you need to insert these two custom actions into the execute sequence table. Since you are working with a deferred custom action you need to insert them between the InstallInitialize and the InstallFinalize actions in this sequence. Insert the custom action that is setting the value of the property first and then insert the deferred custom action right after it. In the Features project the two custom actions are inserted immediately after the MoveFiles action and just before the InstallFiles action. Place the formatted text custom action so the property is set before the deferred custom action is run.

Running Secondary Installations within a Main Installation

You often need to run another installation as part of a main installation. You might be installing a third-party application as part of your application. If this secondary installation is also a Windows Installer package and you want the progress of this secondary installation to be reflected in the progress of the main installation, you can only do this installation by using a nested installation custom action. It is possible to execute a secondary installation in the user interface sequence, but this is not a good idea because the secondary installation will not run if the user decides to implement an install using either a basic or silent user-interface level.

The Windows Installer prevents additional MSI-based installations from running at the same time under two different scenarios. The Windows Installer will not allow the processing of more than one execute sequence table at the same time. Preventing the processing of more than one sequence table at the same time is accomplished by setting the _MSIExecute mutex when it starts to process any of the execute sequence tables. Setting this mutex prevents the Windows Installer from executing a second installation in the execute sequence. More than one installation can be run in the user interface sequence at the same time as long as all the installations are in separate processes. However, if you try to launch another installation package to run as a thread in the same user-interface process, you will generate a Windows Installer error. For instance, if you try to run another installation from a DLL custom action placed in the user interface sequence table by calling the MsiInstallProduct function you will get an error that informs us that another installation is already running.

Because nested installation custom actions are the primary means provided in Windows Installer for running secondary installations you need to take a close look at how to use them. There are three types of nested install custom actions. All of these three types are categorized according to where the main installation can find the MSI package that implements the nested install custom action. Table 11-16 lists these three types.

TABLE 11-16 THE TYPES OF NESTED INSTALLATION CUSTOM ACTIONS

Custom Action Type	Description
Type 7	The MSI package that implements the nested install custom action is incorporated in the main installation package as a sub-storage. The name of this sub-storage is entered into the Source field of the CustomAction table. The Target field of the CustomAction table provides a list of the public properties to be set when the nested install custom action runs. See the list after this table for the public properties that can be set on the command line.

Continued

Table 11-16 THE TYPES OF NESTED INSTALLATION CUSTOM ACTIONS *(Continued)*

Custom Action Type	Description
Type 23	The MSI package that implements the nested install custom action is separate from the main package but is located relative to the root location of the main package. The relative location of this nested install custom action is entered into the Source field of the CustomAction table. The Target field of the CustomAction table provides a list of the public properties to be set when the nested install custom action runs. See the list after this table for the public properties that can be set on the command line.
Type 39	The application has already been either advertised or installed. The Source field of the CustomAction table contains the value for the ProductCode property of this application. The Target field of the CustomAction table provides a list of the public properties to be set when the nested install custom action runs. See the list after this table for the public properties that can be set on the command line. This type of nested installation custom action is restricted in that it can only perform a reinstall or removal of a product that was originally installed with a nested installation custom action. You cannot just specify any product code and remove it with the Type 39 custom action.

There are many rules and restrictions you need to follow when using nested installation custom actions:

- A nested installation shares the same user interface and logging settings as the main installation.
- A nested installation can only be run as an immediate custom action. The Windows Installer will automatically combine the rollback information for the main installation and the secondary installation.
- Nested installation custom actions have the same return values as described earlier in this chapter for other non-script-based custom actions. This means that if a nested installation custom action fails then the main installation will be terminated unless the Windows Installer has been told to ignore the return values.

- A nested installation custom action can only be executed as a synchronous custom action. However, it is possible to tell the Windows Installer to ignore any return codes from the nested install custom action.
- Since a nested installation is performed within the same context as the main installation and in a sense owns the process it can have a nested installation itself. In other words, there is nothing to prevent a nested install from launching another nested install.
- The main installation cannot call itself as a nested installation custom action.
- It is possible to initiate system reboots from within a nested install custom action just as they can be performed from within the main installation.
- Windows Installer cannot query a nested installation for its cost. Because of this it is necessary to add rows in the ReserveCost table to account for the worst-case cost associated with the components that comprise the nested install custom action.
- To control the feature state of a nested installation custom action you need to set the ADDLOCAL, ADDSOURCE, REINSTALL, and REMOVE properties on the command line for the nested MSI package. Enter this command line in the Target column of the CustomAction table. Only those public properties that reference features can be set in this way for a nested installation custom action.
- If a per-machine installation attempts to run a per-user nested installation, the Windows Installer registers the parent installation as per-user by default. This can cause the installer to incorrectly remove the application, because it attempts to uninstall the application per-machine when it is actually registered as per-user. To force the state of a nested installation to track the state of its parent installation, enter ALLUSERS=[ALLUSERS] in the Target column of the CustomAction table. In this case, the nested installation is per-machine if the parent is per-machine, and the nested installation is per-user if the parent is per-user.
- You cannot place a nested installation custom action in either the AdminUISequence table or the AdminExecuteSequence table.
- Patching and upgrading will not work with nested installations.
- A main installation and the associated nested installation cannot install the same component.
- There will only be one progress bar with the total installation but it will not integrate the actions from the main install and the nested install. The progress of the nested install will be shown as a separate action.
- A nested install custom action cannot install any of its resources in an advertise mode.

Now that know the rules you need to follow when using nested installation custom actions, you need to look at a few examples of running secondary installations from within a main installation. The first example does not use a nested installation custom action, but the second example does.

I mentioned at the beginning of this section that you could run a secondary install from the user interface sequence without using a nested installation custom action: You can do this by creating an executable custom action that runs MSIEXEC.EXE. Table 11-17 shows the entries you can make to create this type of secondary installation. You can only run a secondary installation using MSIEXEC.EXE in the user interface sequence since this type of secondary installation would be locked out in the execute sequence.

TABLE 11-17 CREATING A SECONDARY INSTALLATION CUSTOM ACTION USING MSIEXEC

Wizard Dialog	Selections
Basic Information	Name: *<custom-action-name>*
	Comments: *<comment>*
Action Type	Type: Launch an executable
	Location: Stored in the Directory table
Action Parameters	Source: SystemFolder
	Target: Msiexec.exe /i *<path-to-MSI-package>* /qn (You can install the secondary MSI package to be installed with the product or stream it into the Binary table; if you stream it into the Binary table you will have to stream it out to a known location in order to provide a path)
Additional Options	Return Processing: The "Wait for the action to finish executing" option is checked and the "Ignore custom action return code" option is unchecked
	In-Script Execution: Immediate execution
	Execution Scheduling: Always execute

Now let's move on and cover the other custom actions available to you with the Windows Installer.

Miscellaneous Custom Actions

Up to now we have looked at some of the major types of custom actions that you will use most of the time. A few other types of custom actions deserve a little attention. In this section we will look more closely at the formatted text type of custom action and the Type 19 or error custom action. Finally we will look at a utility provided by ISWI to allow you to call a function in any DLL, not just those DLLs that have been formatted to meet the requirements of the Windows Installer.

Using formatted text custom actions

You have already used a formatted text custom action in the example related to deferred custom actions. This was a very simple example since it did not really use any formatting at all, but just provided a string that would be displayed. Before we discuss this type of custom action further you should look at the conventions used to create a formatted text string.

FORMATTING A TEXT STRING

Formatting a text string involves replacing tokens in the string with values from one or more of the database tables. The tokens to be replaced are enclosed in square brackets ([*token*]). The square brackets can be iterated because the substitutions are resolved from the inside out. This enables you to set the value of one property to the value of another property.

Curly braces ({ }) in addition to the square brackets have a special meaning when it comes to the creation of a formatted text string. If a part of the string being formatted is enclosed in curly braces and contains no square brackets, it is left unchanged, including the curly braces. If a part of the string is enclosed in curly braces and contains one or more property names, and if all the properties are found, the text (with the resolved substitutions) is displayed without the curly braces. If any of the properties is not found, all the text in the braces and the braces themselves are removed.

There are four ways to format a taken using the square brackets to get different values from the database or from the system. You can insert the value of a property, file path, a component path, or an environment variable into a string using the square brackets. You need to use a special character if the substitution is not to come from the Property table. The formatting of the various types of tokens are as follows:

- The inclusion of a property name between the square brackets without any initial character means that the value of the property will be substituted into the text string. The format for this token is [*property-name*].
- The inclusion of an environmental variable name between the square brackets with an initial % character means that the value of the environmental variable will be substituted into the text string. The format for this token is [%*environment-variable-name*].

- The inclusion of a key into the File table between the square brackets with an initial # character means that the full destination path of the file will be substituted into the text string. The first column of the File table is the primary key into this table. Finding the associated component and then getting the value of the key into the Directory table will resolve the actual path for the file. Because the value substituted here depends on the Directory table being resolved, you cannot use this type of substitution in a custom action that is placed in the sequence table before the CostFinalize action. The format for this token is [*#file-table-key*].
- The inclusion of a key into the Component table between the square brackets with an initial $ character means that the full installation path of the component will be substituted into the text string. The first column of the Component table is the primary key into this table. Finding the associated value of the key into the Directory table will resolve the actual path for the component. Because the value substituted here depends on the Directory table being resolved, you cannot use this type of substitution in a custom action that is placed in the sequence table before the CostFinalize action.

  When the substitution of the component installation path is made, the action state of the component is taken into account when making the substitution. If the action state of the component is to be installed locally, the target directory replaces the token in the text string. If the action state of the component is to be installed to run from source, the source directory replaces the token in the text string. If the component is not selected or if the component is missing, the token is replaced by a null string. The format for this token is [$*component-table-key*].
- The Windows Installer will replace, by the character without any further processing, a token in the text string of the form [\c]. Only the first character after the backslash is kept; everything else is removed.

Now that you have seen how a formatted text string is created you need to look at two of the three types of custom actions that use a formatted text string. The third type of custom action that can use a formatted text string is the error message custom action. A separate section is devoted to this type of custom action.

SETTING A DIRECTORY USING A FORMATTED TEXT STRING (TYPE 35)

The CostFinalize action resolves the Directory table and all entries are entered into the in-memory version of the Property table as properties that have an ending backslash. Normally this resolution of the Directory table happens only once in each process. Using a Type 35 formatted text custom action forces a re-resolution of the Directory table and a subsequent update of the Property table. None of these operations affect the persistent version of the database; they only happen in memory. In fact, only with this type of custom action or the direct use of the

MsiSetTargetPath API function is it possible to force this re-resolution of the Directory table and update of the Property table.

This type of custom action identifies the key into the Directory table in the Source field of the CustomAction table. The formatted text string that will be used to update the entry in the Directory table is placed in the Target field of the CustomAction table when you build your project. This type of custom action can only be of the immediate category. Also, since it depends on the Directory table already being resolved, this type of custom action must come after the CostFinalize action in the sequence table.

A good example of the use of this type of custom action is the modification of the default installation location for an application. The "Certified for Windows" logo requirements state that the default location for the installation of a product must be *<ProgramFilesFolder>\<Company Name>\<Application Name>* unless the application has already been installed, in which case the default location for installation can be the actual location of the installed product. You would probably want to change the default location of an installation when doing a major upgrade of a product. It would create a more efficient upgrade if you installed into the same location as the product version being upgraded.

In order to change the default location of the installation, you would first use the AppSearch action to find the installation location of the old product. This would set a property to the location of the old installation if the product were found on the system. Let's assume for this example that the name of this property is APPSEARCHPROP and that all the tables associated with the AppSearch action have been properly authored. As I mentioned earlier, you can only run the AppSearch action prior to the CostInitialize action in the sequence and you can only run a Type 35 custom action after the CostFinalize action. What you want to do is create a Type 35 custom action so that it redefines the location of the INSTALLDIR location based on the value of the APPSEARCHPROP property. Table 11-18 describes the entries you need to make in the Custom Action Wizard to create this custom action.

TABLE 11-18 CREATING A TYPE 35 CUSTOM ACTION TO MODIFY INSTALLDIR

Wizard Dialog	Selections
Basic Information	Name: Set_INSTALLDIR
	Comments: Modify the installation location of a product to be the same as that of the one already installed
Action Type	Type: Set a directory
	Location: Null (no entry possible here)

Continued

TABLE 11-18 CREATING A TYPE 35 CUSTOM ACTION TO MODIFY INSTALLDIR *(Continued)*

Wizard Dialog	Selections
Action Parameters	Source: INSTALLDIR
	Target: [APPSEARCHPROP]
Additional Options	Return Processing: The "Wait for the action to finish executing" option is checked and the "Ignore custom action return code" option is unchecked (no changes possible here) In-Script Execution: Immediate execution (no change possible here)
	Execution Scheduling: Always execute

This custom action redefines the value of INSTALLDIR to be the value of the APPSEARCHPROP property. You can simulate the results of the AppSearch action by authoring the Property table to have a value using the Property Manager in the Project view of ISWI. This has been done in the Features project on the CD-ROM. In this project the default installation location is <ProgramFilesFolder>\InstallShield\Features, which you can see in the Product Properties dialog of the Project view. The location C:\Features\ has been authored into the project to be the value of the APPSEARCH-PROP property.

You'll want to insert the Set_INSTALLDIR custom action in the user interface sequence immediately after the MigrateFeatureStates action. You need to place a condition on this custom action of APPSEARCHPROP in order to prevent it from executing if a previous install location for the product was not found by the AppSearch action. You can verify that this works by running the installation and going to the CustomSetup dialog and looking at the install location defined there. If you have defined the above value for the APPSEARCHPROP property, you will see that the install location for Features application will be C:\Features\ unless you change it.

SETTING A PROPERTY USING A FORMATTED TEXT STRING (TYPE 51)

You have already used a simple version of a Type 51 custom action so now you need to look at another example where you implement some indirection using this type of custom action. The Property table does not allow any indirection in that the value of one property will not resolve to the value of another property even if you use the square brackets around the property name. For example, if you had a property called PROP1 and it had a value of [PROP2], and you had a property called PROP2 with a string value of "This is the value of PROP2," the value of the property PROP1 would just be [PROP2] and not the string “This is the value of PROP2.” This prevents circular references in the Property table.

Using a Type 51 custom action you can implement indirection and set the value of a property to be equal to the value of another property. The following example is somewhat contrived but it does illustrate the capability of this type of custom action. What you want to do in this example is implement double indirection, which will set the value of a property to the value of another property and that property to the value of a third property. Here you want to author into the Property table, using the Property Manager in ISWI, a property called PROP1 with a value of PROP2. You also want to author a property called PROP2 and give it a value of “This is the value of PROP2.” Now you want to create a Type 51 custom action that sets the value of PROP3 but starts with the PROP1 property. Table 11-19 shows the entries you need to make in the Custom Action Wizard.

TABLE 11-19 CREATING A TYPE 51 CUSTOM ACTION TO INDIRECT PROPERTY VALUES

Wizard Dialog	Selections
Basic Information	Name: Indirect_Properties
	Comments: Set the value of one property to be equal to the value of another property
Action Type	Type: Set a property
	Location: Null (no entry possible here)
Action Parameters	Source: PROP3
	Target: [[PROP1]] (note the use of double square brackets)
Additional Options	Return Processing: The "Wait for the action to finish executing" option is checked and the "Ignore custom action return code" option is unchecked (no changes possible here)
	In-Script Execution: Immediate execution (no change possible here)
	Execution Scheduling: Always execute

In order to check that the value of PROP3 has been set to the value of PROP2 you can place the following text in a text control on the InstallWelcome dialog: **PROP3: [PROP3]**. You can insert this custom action prior to the InstallWelcome dialog and then when this dialog is displayed the value of PROP3 will be substituted in the location where you have placed [PROP3] in the text control. The point of this example is that you can nest property names and the resolution of the formatted text string will occur from the innermost set of square brackets to the outermost set of square brackets. This custom action has also been implemented in the Features product on the CD-ROM.

Now let's move on to a discussion of one additional formatted text custom action, the error message custom action. This is discussed separately since it has a unique functionality.

The error message custom action (Type 19)

The Type 19 custom action is special in that it has only one purpose: to display an error message and then terminate the installation. It is also the only type of custom action that you cannot create with the Custom Action Wizard. This is because it is so simple that it does not merit a wizard for its creation. The type will always be 19 and you can't modify it by any other options since none of the other options applies to this type of custom action. It can only be of the immediate category and there is no return type except the ERROR_INSTALL_FAILURE return type; the Windows Installer cannot be told to ignore this.

To create a Type 19 custom action in ISWI you need to select the New option from the context menu when you right click on the Custom Actions icon in the Actions\Scripts view. Then, enter the values directly in the dialog that represents the fields in the CustomAction table. In the Type field enter the number 19. In the Source field do not enter anything since this field is to be left null. Finally, in the Target field enter the formatted text string that will resolve to the error message to be displayed in the message box when the custom action is executed. The rules for formatting this text string are the same as those described earlier for the "Set a property" and "Set a directory" custom actions. This formatted text string can either resolve to the message to be displayed or to an integer. If it is a text string, this string is what will be displayed in the error message box. If it resolves to a number, this number needs to be a key into the Error table and the message associated with the error number will be displayed in the error message box.

This type of custom action must always be conditioned since once it is executed there is no way to avoid the termination of the installation.

A good example of the use of this type of custom action is provided in Chapter 20 in the section "Preventing the Downgrading of a Higher Version with a Lower Version." There it is used to terminate an installation if there is a situation where installing the product will downgrade the product to one of a lower version.

Calling functions in a standard dynamic-link library

There is an additional capability in ISWI that enables you to directly create custom actions that can call many functions in normal DLLs. This can assist setup developers who already have many functions implemented in DLLs in their legacy installations in using these DLLs so they do not have to reformat these functions to conform to the calling requirements of the Windows Installer. A special wrapper DLL that does conform to the Windows Installer calling requirements has implemented this functionality. This wrapper DLL gets the information it needs about the standard function calls to the normal DLLs from an .ini file created by the Custom Action Wizard. In any one project it is possible to have up to 1001 calls to various DLL functions.

It is possible to directly call many Windows APIs as well as those functions in DLLs that have been created for legacy installations. It is not possible to call any function, however, that requires the passing of a structure or pointer to a structure. Since return values and in/out arguments to any function called are treated as properties in the Property table it is only possible to work with values that can be handled as numbers or strings.

To implement this type of functionality you need to choose the "Call a function in a standard dynamic-link library" type in the Action Type dialog of the wizard. For this type there are three possible selections for the location. "Stored in the Binary table" and "Installed with the product" are the ones that apply to the DLLs created by the setup developer. The "Destination machine search path" is the location selection that you need to use when calling a Windows API. The machine search path is the one Windows typically uses when it searches for a DLL. This search path is as follows:

- The directory where the executable module for the current process is located
- The current directory
- The Windows system directory
- The Windows directory
- The directories listed in the PATH environment variable

When calling a Windows API, you must be aware that when any function takes a string the appropriate Windows DLL exports both an ANSI and a Unicode version of the function. These are exported with either an A or a W appended to the base name of the function. For example, the DeleteFile() function exported by Kernel32.dll takes as an argument a string that is the fully qualified path to the file to be deleted. To use this function you would need to identify the name of this function as DeleteFileA.

To get a better handle on this ISWI functionality and the additional dialog in the Custom Action Wizard where the definition of the function being called is made, you need to work through an example. In this example you will call a function in a DLL that reverses the characters in a string. This is not a Windows DLL so you will include it with the MSI package by streaming it into the Binary table. Table 11-20 shows the selections you need to make in the Custom Action Wizard.

TABLE 11-20 CREATING A CUSTOM ACTION TO CALL A STANDARD DLL FUNCTION

Wizard Dialog	Selections
Basic Information	Name: Reverse_String
	Comments: Reverse the characters in a string
Action Type	Type: Call a function in a standard dynamic-link library
	Location: Stored in the Binary table
Function Definition	(See Figure 11-13 for the entries to be made in this dialog)
	Action Parameters Source: *<Sources>*\revstr.dll
	Target: (This field is disabled and shows the calling specification for the DLL function)
Additional Options	Return Processing: The "Wait for the action to finish executing" option is checked and the "Ignore custom action return code" option is unchecked
	In-Script Execution: Immediate execution
	Execution Scheduling: Always execute

The Function Definition dialog of the Custom Action Wizard is a dialog that you have not seen before. It is in this dialog that you define the arguments and return values for the function that will be called as a custom action. The information you enter goes into the .ini file that the wrapper DLL reads to set up the call to the actual function. The declaration of the function you are calling is as follows:

```
STDAPI ReverseString(LPCSTR szStr, LPSTR svStr)
```

The first argument is the constant string you are passing to the function and the second argument is the first argument returned with all the characters reversed. Figure 11-13 shows the entries you need to make in the Function Definition dialog of the wizard.

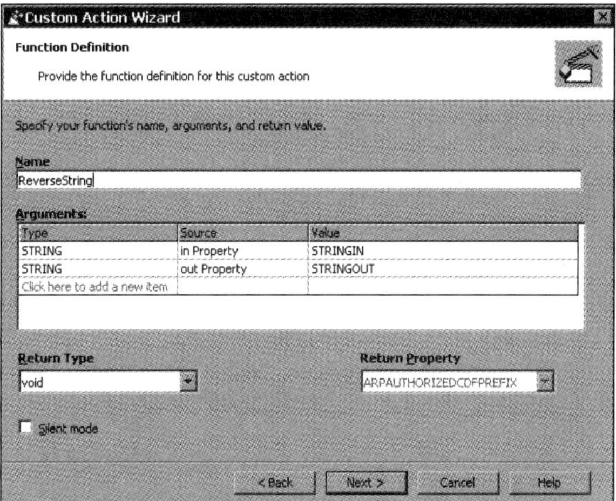

Figure 11-13: The Function Definition dialog entries for the ReverseString function call

In the Function Definition dialog you enter the name of the function being called in the Name edit field. In the arguments dialog you define both arguments as being of type STRING. The Source for the first argument is an in Property and the Source for the second argument is an out Property. You identify the property names to be used to hold these arguments in the Value column. You use STRINGIN for the first argument and STRINGOUT for the second argument. When you enter these property names, they are created in the Property Manager where you can give them values if required. You need to give the STRINGIN property a value so that something will be passed to the ReverseSring function. The STRINGOUT property will be populated when the custom action is run.

To complete this example you need to give a value to the STRINGIN property using the Property Manager in the Project view. You also need to insert the custom action in a sequence and then provide some means for displaying the results. This has been done in the Features project on the CD-ROM. The value given to the STRINGIN property is "This is the input string." The custom action is inserted immediately before the PatchWelcome dialog in the user interface sequence. You can display the value returned in the STRINGOUT property by placing the string **Reversed String: [STRINGOUT]** in a static text control in the InstallWelcome dialog. When the installation is run, the input string will be displayed in this dialog with all the characters reversed.

Debugging Custom Actions

To enable the debugging of a custom action, set the environment variable MsiBreak to the name of the designated action, which is case-sensitive, just as it appears in the CustomAction and sequence tables. For DLL custom actions, a user breakpoint is called just prior to the entry point call. If the current session is not running under a debugger, the standard exception dialog box is invoked with an option to debug. This brings up the debugger registered for JIT debugging (to enable MSDEV for this, select Just-in-time debugging from the Options menu). Single-step a few times and you will be inside the custom action code.

If you want to enable source-level debugging, the PDB file must be available, either at the original build location for the DLL or in the directory where the DLL is executing. Custom actions stored in the Binary table are saved to a new temporary file and executed from the system TEMP directory. The temporary file name begins with MSI. This separate file is created to prevent conflict with other temp files. If you want source-level debugging and you are not running on the same machine where the DLL was built, you need to copy the PDB file to the TEMP directory under the same name as the new custom action file. A separate thread is created to call the custom action to support asynchronous execution, to provide cleanup after the action is called, and to provide recovery in the case of an exception during execution. The mechanism is similar with EXE custom actions, except that the debug break occurs just prior to the CreateProcess call. You cannot step into the EXE code, and you cannot attach the debugger to the process until it is running. If you want to debug custom actions executing in the service, you must attach the debugger to the service process (MsiExec.exe) ahead of time.

Summary

In this chapter you got your hands dirty and created a number of different types of custom actions. You started off by looking at the valid return codes that certain types of custom actions can use to communicate with the Windows Installer. Then you reviewed the SQL syntax you need to use in a custom action when you interface with the tables of the database. We discussed how to interface with the Windows Installer during the installation and how to access the installation session from either a DLL custom action or a custom action implemented in VBScript or JScript.

After going through these preliminary subjects you worked through the Custom Action Wizard in ISWI to see the various dialogs that comprise it. Once you finished with that you looked at the special means provided for accessing the values in the Property table. You saw that there are two special functions for getting and setting values in the Property table without having to use SQL statements. We briefly discussed the creation of custom tables.

You spent some time creating several custom actions that worked with the user interface. One of these custom actions would launch a Web site when a button was pushed. The other custom action would show how to dynamically populate a combo box control at run time. This custom action enumerated the list of mapped network drives on the target system and supplied this list in the combo box. You created a special dialog to show this list of mapped network drives. You then looked at the special considerations required for running deferred custom actions and how this category of custom action can obtain the values it needs. Because a deferred custom action can run after the original installation session has ended, it only has access to the information written into the execution script. You looked at how to add the information required by your custom actions to this execution script.

At the end of the chapter you looked at a special type of custom action that can perform a secondary installation during the install of the main product. These types of custom actions are called *nested install* custom actions. You saw that there are many restrictions on the implementation of these types of child installations. Finally, you looked at several miscellaneous types of custom actions and created several examples of them.

Chapter 12

The ISWI Scripting Environment

IN THIS CHAPTER

- What is InstallScript
- The script editor
- Compiler settings
- Compiling at the command line
- Compiler directives
- The script debugger

THIS IS THE FIRST of four chapters to delve into the InstallScript language and its use. In particular, we discuss the scripting environment provided in InstallShield for Windows Installer: the script editor, the script compiler, and the script debugger. These are all things you need to know about before you start investigating the language itself and how to use it in creating custom actions.

What Is InstallScript?

InstallScript is a powerful scripting language designed to enable the functionality required for creating a software installation package. InstallScript in many ways appears to be similar to the C language but it is definitely not "C." Also, unlike VBScript or JScript, InstallScript has to be compiled before it can run. However, it is not compiled into native code but into something similar to Java's bytecode format. The InstallScript bytecode looks a lot like machine code but is only understood by the scripting engine. The scripting engine is added to the system on which the installation is being run: it interprets the InstallScript bytecode and then passes the correct machine code to the processor in order to implement the actions in the script.

> Appendix C provides a complete description of how the InstallScript engine is added to the target machine and how it provides functionality for creating custom actions.

InstallScript provides many of the basic data types found in other programming languages. It also provides a robust API function set. These functions provide an installation-focused capability that enables you to easily implement the various actions you'll need when creating an installation package.

Creating and Compiling Scripts

To work through this section you need to create a sample project in ISWI. Name this project ScriptTest. After creating this project, go to the Actions/Scripts workspace view and left-click the InstallScript icon in the tree view. Then go to the InstallScript panel to the right of the tree view and right-click to bring up the context menu. From this context menu select the New Script File command and you will get something that looks like what is shown in Figure 12-1.

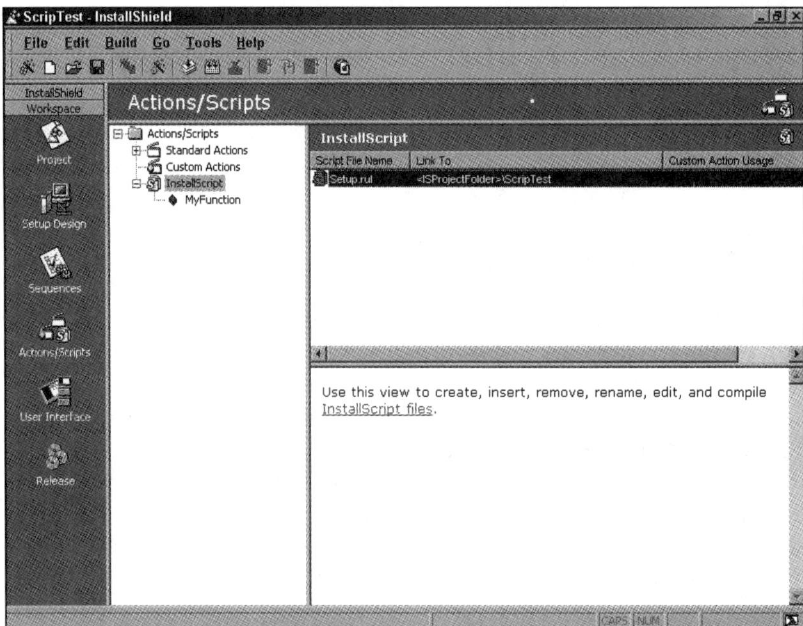

Figure 12-1: Creation of a new Setup.rul script file

A skeleton file named Setup.rul will be created for you in the folder ScriptTest that was created when you created the project. This location is defined by the ISProduct Folder path variable. Now double-click the script file name and you will be launched into the script editor. You can also right-click the script file name and you will get a context menu that provides the following commands:

Edit Script Opens the script editor just as when you double-click the file name.

Compile Compiles the script code into a file with an .obs extension. This object file will be located in the same folder as the .rul file and will have the same name as the .rul file. The keyboard shortcut for this command is Ctrl+F7. You can also compile a script using the Compile command from the Build pulldown menu or by clicking the Compile icon on the toolbar.

Remove Removes the file from the project but does not delete it; if you were to remove Setup.rul and then create a new script file you would get a file named Script1.rul, and then Script2.rul, and so on.

Rename Allows you to rename the script file that is created for you when you select the New Script File command. The keyboard shortcut for this command is F2.

You must not remove or rename the script file Setup.rul. This is the required filename for creating the final compiled script. Other script files may have any name you choose; you can incorporate them into Setup.rul using the #include statement.

New Script File Allows you to create a new empty script file that can be edited by the script editor.

Insert Script Files... Allows you to browse for script files that already exist and that you want to include in your project.

Let's take a brief look at the skeleton Setup.rul file and make a few changes so that you will be able to use it to explore the script editor, the Compiler, the Debugger, and the InstallScript language. The initial Setup.rul file is shown in the following code.

```
//////////////////////////////////////////////////////////////////////
//
//  IIIIIII SSSSSS
//    II    SS                          InstallShield (R)
//    II    SSSSSS (c) 1996-2000, InstallShield Software Corporation
//    II        SS                     All rights reserved.
//  IIIIIII SSSSSS
//
//
//  This template script provides the code necessary
//  to build an entry-point function to be called in an
//  InstallScript custom action.
//
//    File Name:  Setup.rul
//
//  Description:  InstallShield script
//
//////////////////////////////////////////////////////////////////////

// Include Isrt.h for built-in InstallScript function prototypes.
#include "isrt.h"

// Include Iswi.h for Windows Installer API function prototypes and
// constants, and to declare code for the OnBegin and OnEnd events.
#include "iswi.h"

    // The keyword export identifies MyFunction() as an
    // entry-point function. The argument it accepts must be a
    // handle to the Installer database.
    export prototype MyFunction(HWND);

    // To Do:  Declare global variables, define constants,
    // and prototype user-defined and DLL functions here.


// To Do:  Create a custom action for this entry-point function:
// 1.  Right-click on Custom Actions in the Actions/Scripts view.
// 2.  Select Custom Action Wizard from the context menu.
// 3.  Proceed through the wizard and give the custom action
//     a unique name.
// 4.  Select Run InstallScript code for the custom action type,
//     and in the next panel select MyFunction (or the new name of
//     the entry-point function) for the source.
// 5.  Click Next, accepting the default selections until the wizard
//     creates the custom action.
```

```
//
// Once you have made a custom action, you must execute it in your
// setup by inserting it into a sequence or making it the result of
// a dialog's control event.

///////////////////////////////////////////////////////////////////
//
// Function:  MyFunction
//
//  Purpose:  This function will be called by the script engine when
//            Windows(R) Installer executes your custom action
// (see the "To Do," above).
//
///////////////////////////////////////////////////////////////////
function MyFunction(hMSI)
    // To Do:  Declare local variables.
begin

    // To Do:
    // Write script that will be executed when MyFunction is called.

end;


// To Do:
// Handle initialization code when each sequence (User Interface and
// Execute) starts.
// function OnBegin()
// begin
// end;

// To Do:
// Write clean-up code when each sequence (User Interface
// and Execute) ends.
// function OnEnd()
// begin
// end;
```

You want to change the name of the entry-point function from MyFunction to ScriptTest. You will do this in two places: once where the function is being prototyped and once where the function is being defined. You should change the prototype so that it looks like this:

```
export prototype ScriptTest(HWND);
```

Now change the entry point-function implementation line to look like this:

```
function ScriptTest(hMSI)
```

The quickest way to do these changes is to use the Replace... command in the Edit pulldown menu. Now you're ready to get into the script editor and see how this tool works.

The script editor

The script editor in ISWI is automatically invoked when you open a script file for editing. This editor encompasses most of the features that you'd expect in a text editor for code creation. When you double-click the Setup.rul filename, you enter the script editor and get something that looks like what is shown in Figure 12-2. The only difference that you might see is that the left margin in Figure 12-2 is a different color from the color in the script window. The normal functionality at the time of this writing is that the left margin is same color as the script window. In Figure 12-2 you can see that the tree view shows the new name of your ScriptTest entry-point function. When you click this icon in the tree view, the script editor will take you directly to the first line of the function's implementation.

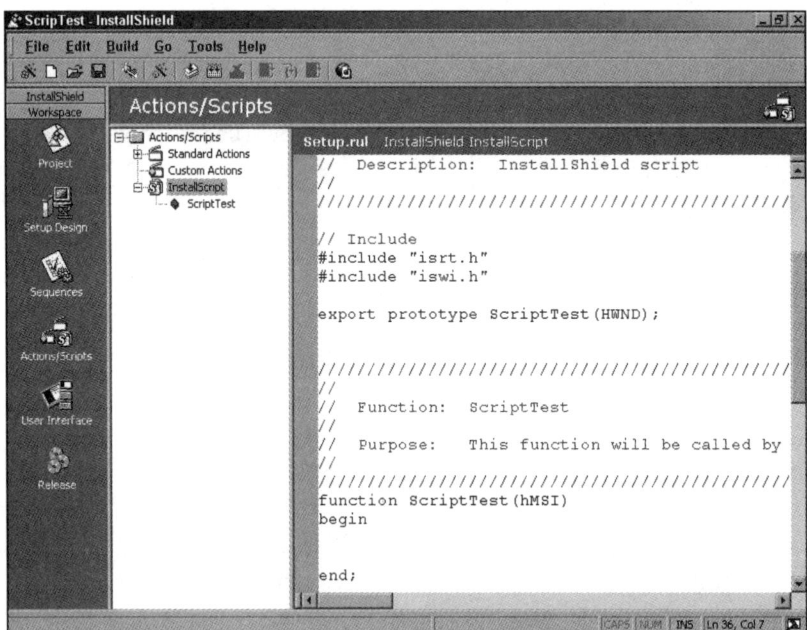

Figure 12-2: Script editor showing skeleton script after function name change

SCRIPT EDITOR PROPERTIES

You are going to start your tour of the script editor by bringing up the Properties sheet. Do this by right-clicking in the script editor and selecting the Properties command at the bottom of the context menu. This will bring up a tabbed properties dialog, which will look like what is shown in Figure 12-3.

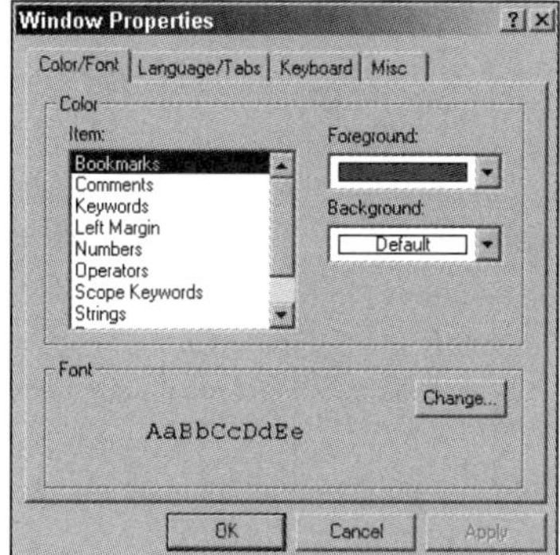

Figure 12-3: Tabbed dialog for setting color and font properties in the script editor

There are two sections in the dialog shown in Figure 12-3. At the top is the section where you can change the default syntax coloring, and at the bottom is the section where you can change the font used in the script editor. First we will discuss the items for which you can define the display colors to be used in the script editor. Table 12-1 provides a description of the items for which colors can be assigned.

TABLE 12-1 ITEM DESCRIPTIONS AND DEFAULT COLOR SCHEMES IN THE SCRIPT EDITOR

Item	Description	Default Color
Bookmarks	A marker displayed in the left margin, which allows you to traverse your script with a minimum of keystrokes.	Teal
Comments	All text in your script that explains what's happening in the script to those using it. Comments are identified by either a set of enclosing characters /* ...*/ or by a set of double slashes (//).	Green

Continued

TABLE 12-1 ITEM DESCRIPTIONS AND DEFAULT COLOR SCHEMES IN THE SCRIPT EDITOR *(Continued)*

Item	Description	Default Color
Keywords	Reserved words that you are not allowed to use in your script for variable names because the compiler expects these words to have a special meaning.	Blue
Left Margin	The space to the left of the script window in which your bookmarks can be displayed. It is also where your cursor will turn to an arrow and allow you to select a complete line of the script.	Default color of the script window
Numbers	A numeric value not contained in quotes or in a comment statement.	Teal
Operators	One of the symbols you can use to execute actions in your script, such as the plus sign (+).	Red
Scope Keywords	Reserved words that define the beginning and end of a block of script. In the script editor, these particular keywords are not separated out and thus are treated as normal keywords.	Blue
Strings	A set of displayable characters contained within a pair of double or single quotes.	Dark Red
Text	A set of displayable characters not contained within double or single quotes. Such text strings will be variable names, function names, and the like.	Black
Window	The background color of the script window. You can change this as you wish but you will have to make sure that the other syntax coloring will be compatible or some text may not be visible.	Windows default color

At the bottom of the dialog shown in Figure 12-3 you can change the font used in the script editor and see a sample of the current font style. When you click the Change... button, you get the dialog shown in Figure 12-4, which looks a lot like the typical font-selection dialog available in most Windows applications. One thing you will notice is that the selection of fonts is limited those with fixed spacing. Also at the bottom of this dialog is a dropdown combo box labeled Script. In this combo box you have the choice of Western, Hebrew, Arabic, Greek, Turkish, Baltic, Central European, Cyrillic, or Vietnamese script languages.

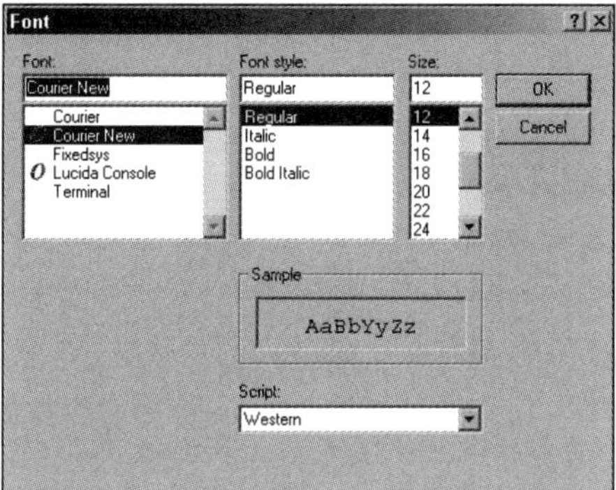

Figure 12-4: The Font dialog in the script editor

The next tab on the Properties dialog is the Language/Tabs tab. On this panel (shown in Figure 12-5) are three sets of properties that you can configure. These property sets are Auto Indentation, Tabs, and Language. You can also define three styles of Auto Indentation, but the default style is to use the same indentation as was used for the previous line.

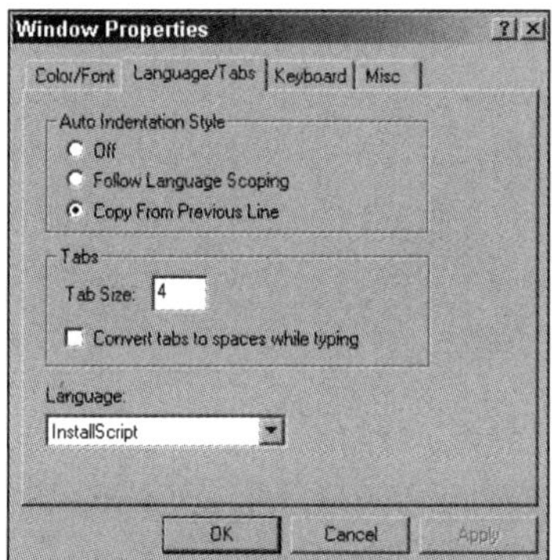

Figure 12-5: The Language/Tabs property page in the script editor

The second Property set defines the number of spaces that comprise a tab. You can also have all tabs turned into spaces as you enter them. This means, of course, that when you use the backspace or arrow keys to traverse a line you will move a space at a time and not in tab-sized increments. The final property set you can define is the language in which the file is being created. The default is InstallScript but the dropdown combo box allows you to choose among a number of other languages with built-in rules as far as what keywords are to have syntax coloring. These other languages are C/C++, Basic, Java, Pascal, SQL, and <none>. Choosing <none> means that the file to be created is straight ANSI text and there are no keywords defined.

The third tab on the Properties dialog is where you can define keyboard shortcuts for a number of built-in commands. There are 125 commands for which you can define keyboard shortcuts. Of these 125 commands, 67 have default settings. In some cases more than one keyboard shortcut is assigned to the same command.

Figure 12-6 shows the third panel in the Properties dialog.

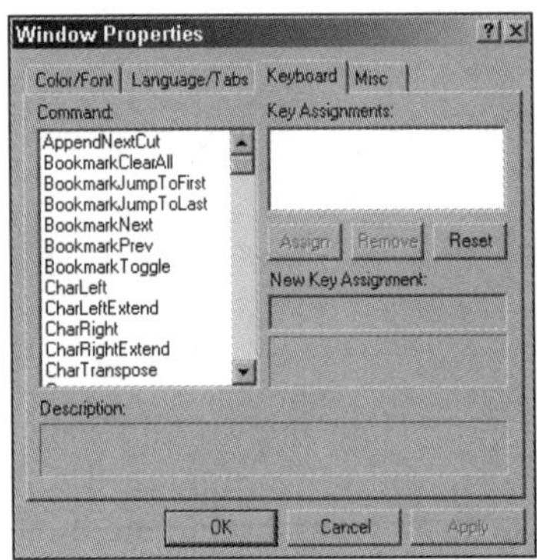

Figure 12-6: The Keyboard property page in the script editor

Let's take a look at how to set the keyboard shortcut for a command that does not have a default value. For this example, look at the BookmarkClearAll command, which clears all bookmarks in the edit window, as shown in the following steps.

1. Highlight the command in the Command list box.
2. Place the cursor in the New Key Assignment edit box and press the keys that you want to use as the keyboard shortcut. For this example, use the combination Ctrl+Alt+F12; press and hold down each of these keys in succession. When the F12 key is pressed, you will see this key combination in the New Key Assignment edit box.
3. Click the Assign button, which has now been enabled, and this keyboard shortcut is entered into the Key Assignments edit box.

4. Click the Apply button to finalize this action. If you had chosen a keyboard shortcut that was already in use, you would have been notified in the sunken text field directly below the New Key Assignment edit box. If you highlight the key assignment in the Key Assignments edit box, the Remove button is enabled, which enables you to undo this keyboard shortcut.

In the fourth and final panel of the Properties dialog you can enable or disable certain types of functionality in the script editor. This panel is shown in Figure 12-7.

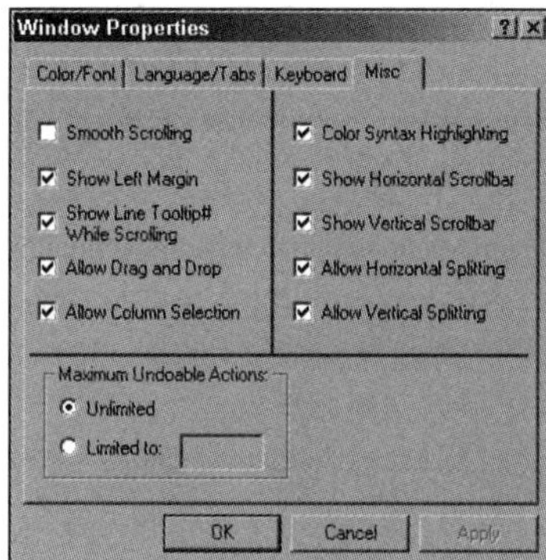

Figure 12-7: The Misc property page in the script editor

At the bottom of this property page you can limit the number of undoable actions you can have. You might want to do this to conserve limited memory resources. You can also undo an Undo by using the Redo capability that is also available in the script editor.

You can set ten additional options with this page in the Property dialog. Table 12-2 describes these options.

TABLE 12-2 MISCELLANEOUS SCRIPT EDITOR OPTIONS

Option	Description
Smooth Scrolling	Slows down some scrolling operations for the smooth vertical scrolling of a large script file.
Show Left Margin	Turns off the left margin so the script text goes all the way to the left side of the script window.

Continued

Table 12-2 **MISCELLANEOUS SCRIPT EDITOR OPTIONS** *(Continued)*

Option	Description
Show Line Tooltip# While Scrolling	Turns off the Tooltip display that shows the line number of the top line in the script window when you're scrolling with the vertical scroll bar.
Allow Drag and Drop	Enables the capability to drag and drop within your script any highlighted sections of text.
Allow Column Selection	Enables the capability to select columns of text by using the Alt key in conjunction with the mouse.
Color Syntax Highlighting	Turns off the color syntax of the various types of words in the script so everything is displayed in the default Windows foreground color, normally black.
Show Horizontal Scrollbar	Displays the horizontal scrollbar. When the horizontal scrollbar is not shown, the only way to move horizontally is to use the keyboard.
Show Vertical Scrollbar	Displays the vertical scrollbar. When the vertical scrollbar is not shown, the only way to move vertically is to use the keyboard.
Allow Horizontal Splitting	Enables the capability to split the script window horizontally.
Allow Vertical Splitting	Enables the capability to split the script window vertically.

We have now finished the discussion of the various properties you can set for the script editor. In the next section we will get into the various things you can do with the script editor to make your life easier when creating scripts.

USING THE SCRIPT EDITOR

In this section I am only going to briefly address some of the important features of the script editor. I'm assuming that everyone is familiar with the normal navigation capabilities of a text editor or word processor. I want to concentrate on those features that might be considered a little out of the ordinary.

THE CONTEXT MENU We'll start with some of the commands available in the context menu you bring up by right-clicking in the script editor. To enable the items on this context menu enter some text in the script editor and then highlight the line of text. With the cursor in this highlighted line right-click and you will see that most of the options on this menu are enabled. The most interesting commands are the ones in the middle section of this context menu, and they are described in Table 12-3.

TABLE 12-3 CONTEXT MENU COMMANDS

Command	Description
Show Whitespace	Displays all spaces with a dot, which appears midway in the height of the uppercase characters. This menu command is a toggle.
Make Uppercase	Only active when text has been highlighted. If a word or string has been highlighted, this command will enable you to change all characters to upper case.
Make Lowercase	Only active when text has been highlighted. If a word or string has been highlighted, this command will allow you to change all characters to lower case.
Tabify	Converts spaces to tabs of the currently set tab size. The groups of spaces to be converted to tabs must be highlighted; otherwise no conversion will take place. If the group of spaces is smaller than the current tab size, no action is taken. If the number of spaces is greater than the tab size, groups of spaces equal to the tab size will be converted to tabs. After this operation, any group of spaces smaller than the tab size will be left as spaces.
Untabify	Converts all tabs in highlighted text to spaces.

THE EDIT MENU In addition to those commands on the context menu, two interesting commands are found on the Edit pulldown menu. These are the Repeat... and Insert commands. Selecting the Repeat... command brings up a small dialog where you are asked to define the number of times you want the next action to be repeated. To see how this works, select this command and choose the default value of 10 in the edit field. Now type a letter and you will see that this letter appears 10 times on the same line. Now highlight this line, making sure that there is a carriage return at the end of the line, and copy it to the clipboard. Now place the cursor on the line following the line that you just copied to the clipboard, go to the Repeat... option again, and choose the default value of 10 again. Now hit Ctrl+V to copy this line from the clipboard and you will see that the line has been copied 10 times.

When you select the Edit→Insert menu option, you will see a sub-menu containing the options InstallScript Function... and String Table Entry.... Choosing the InstallScript Function... option launches the Function Wizard. The Function Wizard enables the easy insertion of a call to one of the InstallScript APIs mentioned at the beginning of this chapter. Figure 12-8 shows the first panel of this wizard, which lists the available function categories and the function names that comprise these categories.

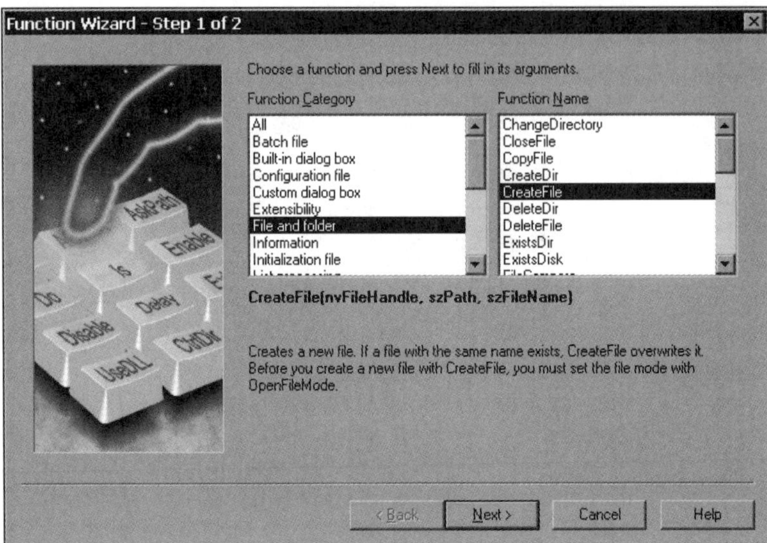

Figure 12-8: Panel one of the InstallScript Function Wizard

The prototype of the selected function and a short description of the function's purpose are provided below the two list boxes in this dialog. Clicking the Next button brings up the second and final panel in this wizard. In this panel you can edit the names of the parameters to be passed to the function; this panel also provides, where appropriate, a list of the valid constants that you can pass. Placing the cursor in each of the edit fields on this panel gives you a short description of the purpose of the parameter. Figure 12-9 shows the second panel of the Function Wizard.

In the above two figures the function name that selected is the CreateFile API. When I click on the Finish button, the following string will be entered into the script at the point where I have my cursor:

```
CreateFile ( nvFileHandle , szPath , szFileName );
```

Of course it is still your responsibility to make sure that all parameters passed to a function have been properly initialized. You will use the Function Wizard in this chapter and the next as you explore the InstallScript language and see how to create custom actions with it.

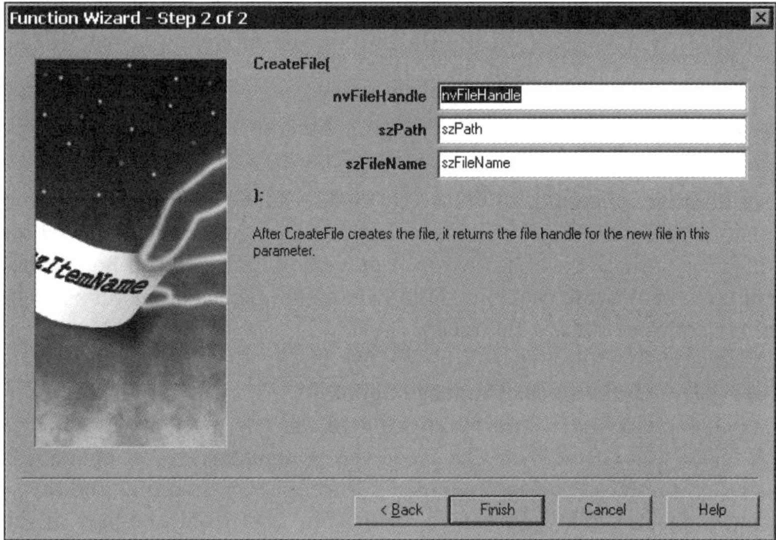

Figure 12-9: Panel two of the InstallScript Function Wizard

The other option on the Edit → Insert submenu is the String Table entry... command. When you select this option, a dialog box is launched that enables you to select a string from the string table and to have it inserted into your script with the proper format. This format is for the string ID, preceded by the @ symbol, to be inserted into the present location of the cursor. This location must be a place where this format will be recognized. For example, this format can be used to pass a string to a function that requires a string constant. Figure 12-10 shows this dialog box.

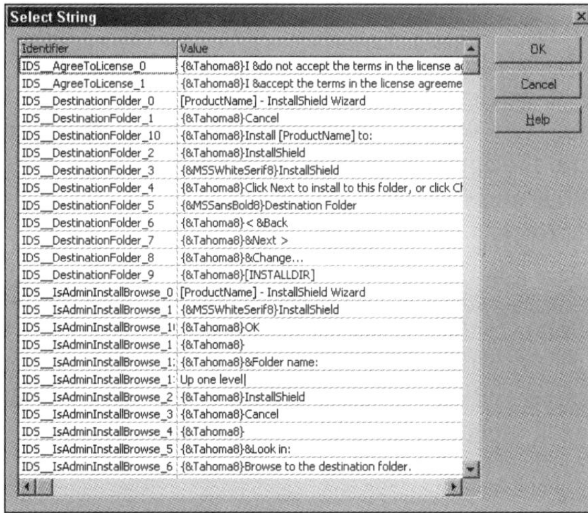

Figure 12-10: The Select String dialog box

In this figure you can see that the selected string identifier is IDS__ DestinationFolder_5. When I click on the OK button, the following string will be inserted in my script at the location of the cursor.

```
@IDS__DestinationFolder_5
```

We have not discussed the Find..., Replace..., Goto..., Cut, Copy, Paste, Undo, and Redo options since these are standard commands and operate in the script editor just as they do in any other text editor or word processor. You will also notice that there is a Print command on the File pulldown menu. This command is only enabled when the script editor has the focus.

USING THE MOUSE All the normal mouse operations are available in the script editor. These include selecting a line by clicking in the left margin, dragging to select multiple lines, and so on. You can, however, implement several operations with the mouse that might not be so obvious. First we'll cover dragging and dropping text. Using drag-and-drop you can move or copy text from one part of the script to another and you can also move or copy text to and from applications that are OLE Drag and Drop enabled, such as Visual C++. To move text you need to first highlight it, click the left mouse button over the highlighted text, and drag the text to the new location. If you want to copy the text instead of move it, hold down the Control key as you drag the text. This will copy the text to the new location while leaving it in the original location.

Another handy functionality you can implement with the mouse is to select columns of text. To do this, first hold down the Alt key, left-click in the column and line where you want to start selecting columns, and with the left button still down drag the cursor to the line and column where you want to end the selection. You can now cut, copy, paste, and/or delete this selection.

With the mouse you can also create a split window. The script window can be split vertically, horizontally, or in both directions to create four windows. You can scroll each of these windows individually, meaning that you can work on as many as four different areas of the script. You can also use the drag-and-drop functionality to move or copy text among these windows. To create the split window you need to move your mouse cursor to the upper end of the vertical scroll bar or to the left end of the horizontal scroll bar and find the location where the cursor turns into a double-headed arrow. Then you can either double-click the left mouse button to split the window exactly in half or drag the splitter bar to any location you desire. To remove the split window you can double-click the left mouse button on the splitter bar or drag it to the top or to the left until it disappears.

Finally, you can use the mouse to vertically scroll the text in the editor. When you hold down the left mouse button and then drag the vertical scroll bar, you will see what is called a Tooltip#, which identifies the number of the line presently at the top of the script editor window.

USING THE KEYBOARD Appendix D goes into detail about all the keyboard shortcuts implemented by default. In this section we'll take a close look at only two of these areas of functionality, because they can be very useful when creating a script. These two areas are bookmarks and macros. Bookmarks are handy devices for navigating quickly to important parts of a large script. There are six bookmark-related commands, three of which are assigned a default keyboard shortcut. The first thing to do is assign keyboard shortcuts to the three commands that do not have them. Table 12-4 shows all six commands related to bookmarks, the first three with their default keyboard shortcuts and the second three with the shortcuts I suggest you assign them.

TABLE 12-4 KEYBOARD SHORTCUTS FOR IMPLEMENTING BOOKMARKS

Command	Keyboard Shortcut	Description
BookmarkToggle	Ctrl+F2 (default)	Toggles a bookmark for the current line on and off.
BookmarkNext	F2 (default)	Moves to the line containing the next bookmark.
BookmarkPrev	Shift+F2 (default)	Moves to the line containing the previous bookmark.
BookmarkClearAll	Ctrl+Shift+F2	Clears all bookmarks in the script window.
BookmarkJumpToFirst	Alt+F2	Moves to the first line containing a bookmark.
BookmarkJumpToLast	Ctrl+Alt+F2	Moves to the last line containing a bookmark.

To set the keyboard shortcuts for the last three commands, go to the Properties dialog and click on the Keyboard tab. Then put the focus in the New Key Assignment edit field and press the keys that will make up the shortcut. Click the Assign button and then the Apply button and the assignment is complete.

To turn a bookmark on, place the cursor in the line you want the bookmark associated with and press Ctrl+F2. An arrowhead will appear in the left margin pointing at the line. Enter a number of bookmarks and then see how the other keyboard shortcuts will help you navigate in the script.

Using the Find functionality enables you to define a string that can be used to identify any line for which you want to set a bookmark. All you do is enter the string and then click on the Mark All button. For instance, you could bookmark all functions by entering the string "function" and then clicking the Mark All button. All lines with the word "function" in them would then be set with a bookmark.

The other keyboard-implemented functionality we'll discuss here is the creation of macros. A macro is a recording of keystrokes, which you can play back by executing the assigned keyboard shortcut. You'll create three macros that will save you time when you create custom actions using InstallScript. These macros will contain the standard formatting and information for creating new files and functions.

To create a macro you need to go into record mode, enter the keystrokes that will be recorded, and assign a keyboard shortcut to the macro. The script editor will allow you to create a maximum of ten macros. To initiate the record mode you need to press the Ctrl+Shift+R keys. When you do this, a small modeless dialog will be displayed, containing one button. You use this button to end the recording session. When you end the recording session, you will be presented with a dialog box that asks you to assign the keyboard shortcut to the macro you just created. This dialog box is shown in Figure 12-11.

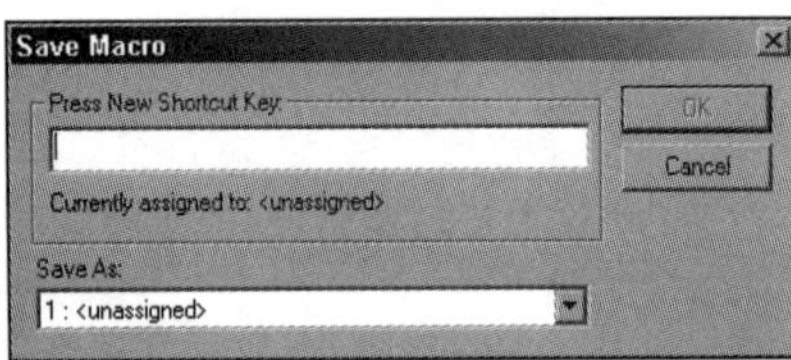

Figure 12-11: Dialog box for assigning a keyboard shortcut to a macro

The macro you're about to create is a standard header for a private function that you'll use whenever you create a helper function for your entry-point functions. The code for this standard template for a private function is as follows.

```
///////////////////////////////////////////////////////////////////////
//
//     Function Name:
//
//     Parameters:
//
//     Purpose:
//
//     Implementation:
```

```
//
///////////////////////////////////////////////////////////////////////

function <name>(<parameter_list>)

begin


end;
```

You can assign any keyboard shortcut you want for this macro if it is not already in use for some other purpose. I have used Ctrl+F12 in the environment that I have set up on my machine.

The compiler

When you build your project, your script is automatically compiled. You can also compile your script without having to build your project, by using the Compile button on the toolbar just to the left of the Build button. You can also initiate a compile using the Ctrl+F7 keyboard shortcut or by going to the Compile option on the Build pulldown menu. When your script is compiled, it is turned into an object file with an .obs extension. This file will be located in the root folder of your ISWI project. When you perform a straight compile, you will get an output window at the bottom of the screen where all warnings and errors will be displayed. When you perform a build of the project, the same output window provides you with the output of the build process. The output window will first provide the results of the script compilation and then these results will scroll off the screen to be replaced with the results of the build. The script results are not displayed at the bottom of the output window along with the build results. You will need to scroll to the top of the output window to see the results of the script compilation and linking.

Always compile your scripts separately first before building your project. This way you won't be surprised with a bad script when you go to test your installation.

COMPILER SETTINGS

On the Build pulldown menu is the option for Compiler settings..., which launches a dialog box enabling you to define how you want the compiler to behave. You make settings in this dialog for every project. The Compiler Settings dialog is shown in Figure 12-12.

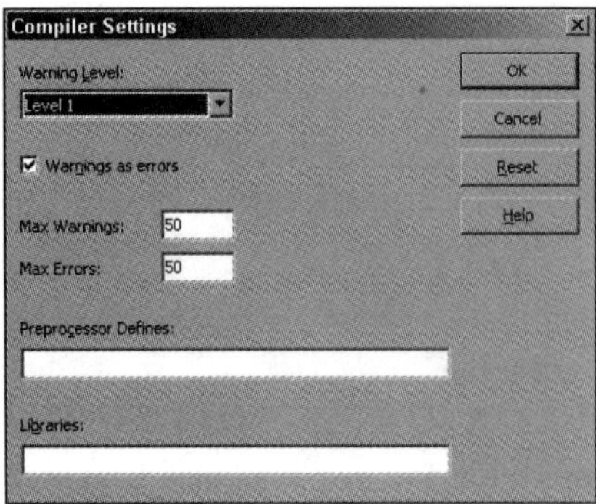

Figure 12-12: The Compiler Settings dialog

In the Warning Level combo box are four levels to choose from and they are described in Table 12-5. The default warning level is Level 1.

Table 12-5 COMPILER WARNING LEVELS

Warning Level Option	Description
None	No warning messages displayed
Level 1 (Default)	Displays all system warning messages that cannot be handled by the InstallScript compiler
Level 2	Displays all system warning messages that cannot be handled by the InstallScript compiler and any warnings that relate to string lengths that exceed the limit
Level 3	Displays all warning messages

Check the "Warnings as errors" check box if you want the compiler to treat a warning as an error and not create the .obs file. Warnings will still be displayed as warnings in the output window but they will prevent the correct compilation of the script. Below this check box are two edit fields where you can specify the maximum number of warnings and errors to be displayed in the output window.

In the edit field labeled Preprocessor Defines you can set a constant identifier to a numeric value. Entries look like the following:

```
CONSTANT1=1234,CONSTANT2=5678
```

There cannot be any spaces between the constant name and the equals (=) sign, but there can be spaces to the right of the equals sign. There can also be spaces after the value and before the comma separator, but not to the right of the comma separator. The following input into this edit field would also be valid:

```
CONSTANT1,CONSTANT2
```

The following statement in your script would be valid if you were to make these entries in the Preprocessor Defines edit box of the Compiler Settings dialog. However, in this case you need to avoid spaces on either side of the comma separator.

```
#ifdef CONSTANT1
      statements to perform some actions
#endif
```

With these entries in your script and CONSTANT1 defined in Compiler Settings dialog box then the statements between #ifdef and #endif will be compiled; if CONSTANT1 is not defined then these statements will not be compiled.

We discuss preprocessor directives in detail later in this section.

At the bottom of the Compiler Settings is another edit field labeled Libraries. Here you can enter the fully qualified path(s) to script libraries that you have created for commonly used code. Script libraries are linked into the final compiled script. In order to keep the size of the final compiled script as small as possible only those functions from the library are used are brought into the compiled script and not all the code in the library. A script library will have an .obl extension and the compiled script will have an .inx extension. You can use libraries created using InstallShield Professional 6.0 or higher or you can create these libraries with ISWI. There is no way to create libraries using the ISWI IDE so you will need to do this at the command line. You'll learn how in the next section.

THE COMPILE OUTPUT WINDOW

When you compile your script, an output window will open up across the bottom of the ISWI IDE, providing the following information:

- The version of the script compiler being used
- The name of the file being compiled (in most cases Setup.rul)
- A list of the errors and warnings generated by the compiler. Each error or warning will be accompanied by the name of the file in which the error or warning occurred, the line number in the script that may be generating the error or warning, the error or warning number being generated, and a short description of the error or warning.
- The name of the object file being created followed by the location of the file being compiled

If you click the right mouse button in this window, you will get a context menu that gives you three choices. You can copy the contents of the window to the clipboard by selecting the Copy All option or you can clear the window by selecting the Clear All option. You can paste the information copied to the clipboard into a text file for permanent reference. You can also close this window by selecting the Hide option, or by grabbing the top edge with the left mouse button and dragging it down to the bottom. You can open this window by running the compiler or by grabbing the top edge of the window in the closed position and dragging it upward with the mouse using the left button.

As I mentioned earlier, the settings made in the Compiler Settings dialog are on a per-project basis. If you have a standard set of script libraries that you want to use across all of your projects, you must enter this same information in the Compiler Settings dialog for every project. There, however, is a way around this: you can make entries into the Compile Folders.ini file. You can find this initialization file in the Support folder of the installation location for ISWI. The default entries in this file are as follows:

```
[Folders]
Folder0=<ISProductFolder>\Script\Include
Folder1=<ISProductFolder>\Script\ISRT\Include
Folder3=<ISProductFolder>\Script\ISWi\Include

[Libraries]
Libraries1=<ISProductFolder>\Script\ISWi\Lib\iswi.obl
Libraries2=<ISProductFolder>\Script\ISRT\Lib\isrt.obl
```

The `[Folder]` section provides the search path for all the include files. You can add to this section the location of your own include files, particularly those that prototype the functions in your own script libraries. To add the location for your own script libraries you just need to make entries under the `[Libraries]` section using the format shown above. The order in which functions are linked is the order in which the libraries are identified. If you have two functions with the same name in two different libraries, the one that will actually get linked will be the one in the library listed last.

COMPILING AT THE COMMAND LINE

You can do a lot from the command line that you can't do from the IDE. Most importantly, you can create script libraries. The compiler is named COMPILE.EXE and you'll find it in the following location:

```
C:\Program Files\Common Files\InstallShield\IScript
```

The command line syntax is as follows:

```
compile [options] [filename(s)] [@commandfile]
```

The arguments on the command line are not order-dependent and you can place them at any location on the command line. Table 12-6 describes the command-line options you can use. There can be no space between an option and its parameter.

TABLE 12-6 COMMAND LINE COMPILE OPTIONS

Option	Description
/Q or /q	Suppresses the copyright message and the information about the file being created during the compilation.
/O<filename> or /o<filename>	Changes the name of the output file being created. Keep in mind that the main script must be compiled to have the name Setup.inx. You can only control the naming of the .inx file from the IDE by starting off with the script file being named Setup.rul.
/G or /g	Creates the debug information files that have .dbg and .map file extensions.
/I<directory path> or /i<directory path>	Defines a directory where a script will search for an include file. You need to use this option for each location that you want to include in the search path.
/D<name>=<num> or /d<name>=<num>	Defines a numeric constant or constants. To define more than one constant you need to use this option for each.
/E<num> or /e<num>	Sets the number of errors that will be displayed. The default value is 50.
/W<num> or /w<num>	Sets the number of warnings that will be displayed. The default value is 50.
/V<num> or /v<num>	Sets the warning level to be used. This determines the type of warnings to be displayed. The default value is Level 1.
/C or /c	Specifies that the .rul file is only to be compiled and that it is not to be linked. The file created will be an object file with an .obs extension.
/L or /l	Specifies that the specified files be compiled into a script library. The file created will have an .obl extension.

The one thing that you cannot do on the command line that you can do in the IDE is have the compiler treat warnings as errors and prevent compilation of the script. The /C and /L options cannot be used together. When you use neither the /C nor the /L option, the default behavior of the compiler is to compile and link, thus creating an .inx file.

The `[filename(s)]` parameter on the command line specifies the file or files that are the target of the action being taken with the compiler. You can specify one .rul file along with .obs and .obl files. These files do not need to be in the same position on the command line. They can be separated by one or more of the options described in Table 12-6. If you specify more than one .rul file, the compiler will only work with the first one it finds and will skip any subsequent .rul files.

The `[@commandfile]` parameter is a special file in which you can provide the compiler with all the other command-line parameters required to perform the compilation activity. This prevents the command line from becoming too long and unwieldy. The command line using this facility would look like the following:

```
compile @parameters.txt
```

A typical parameters.txt file would look like the following:

```
"D:\Installation Projects\Setups\ScriptTest\Setup.rul"
"/iC:\Program Files\InstallShield\InstallShield for Windows
Installer\Script\Include"
"/iC:\Program Files\InstallShield\InstallShield for Windows
Installer\Script\isrt\Include"
"/iC:\Program Files\InstallShield\InstallShield for Windows
Installer\Script\iswi\Include"
"C:\Program Files\InstallShield\InstallShield for Windows
Installer\Script\iswi\lib\iswi.obl"
"C:\Program Files\InstallShield\InstallShield for Windows
Installer\Script\isrt\lib\isrt.obl"
```

Note that the option switches are inside the double quotes and that each quoted string should be on a separate line in the command file.

COMPILER DIRECTIVES

The InstallScript preprocessor is a text processor that manipulates the text of a script file as the first phase of the compilation process. A number of directives are recognized by the preprocessor. Some of these directives are called *preprocessor directives* and others are called *conditional-compilation directives*. Some predefined macros are also defined during the compilation process. These three types of directives are the subjects of this section.

The preprocessor directives are #include, #define, #undef, #warning, and #error. The conditional-compilation directives are #if, #ifdef, #ifndef, #else, #elif, and #endif. The predefined macros are __LINE__, __FILE__, and _ISCRIPT_VER.

No directive can span more than one line in the script and this line is limited to a total of 250 characters, including the directive itself. The line on which a directive is being defined has no terminator. In other words, do not use a semi-colon (;) at the end of the line defining a directive.

THE #INCLUDE DIRECTIVE The #include directive is a preprocessor directive that instructs the preprocessor to add the contents of a specified file to the file in which this directive is contained and at the point at which it appears. This means that the contents of the specified file replace the directive. The syntax for this directive is as follows:

```
#include "path-spec"
#include <path-spec>
```

The path-spec identifier can be a simple filename or it can include a fully qualified path or a relative path to the file. The syntax of this directive determines the search algorithm used to find the file when `path-spec` does not contain a complete path to its location.

When you use the quoted form, the preprocessor searches for the specified file in the directory where the file being compiled is located. Then it looks for the file in the folders specified in the Compile Folders.ini file (if the compiler is being invoked from the IDE) or in the folders specified by the /I option (if the compiler is being run from the command line). The angle-bracket form has the same search algorithm that you use with double quotes. This is different from the implementation in the C language.

Include files can be nested. This means that a #include directive can appear in a file that is itself named by a #include directive in another file. When a #include directive is nested, you need to watch out for a situation where there is a multiple declaration of a constant, variable, function prototype, or the like. When we discuss the conditional-compilation directives, you will learn how to avoid this situation.

In InstallScript you will commonly use the #include directive to incorporate declarations as well as script code. Declarations are contained in files with the .h extension (header files) and script code is contained in files with the .rul extension. Header files are normally included at the top of the script file and script files are included at the bottom of the script file. However, if you are including script files where you are not using all the code, you may want to consider creating a script library instead. Including the script library as part of your compiler settings will only statically link that code that is actually used and not all the code in the library. This gives you a smaller .inx file.

You should only #include header files created with InstallScript since some of the C/C++ constructs in header files are not supported by the InstallScript compiler.

THE #DEFINE DIRECTIVE The #define directive gives a meaningful name to a constant that you are going to use in your program. There is only one construct for the #define directive, as follows:

```
#define identifier token-string
```

The identifier is the name of a constant and wherever in the script code this name appears the preprocessor replaces it with "token-string." The only exceptions occur where the identifier forms part of a comment statement, is part of string, or forms part of a longer identifier. By convention identifiers are in upper case using the underscore character (_) to separate words, but they can be any combination of lowercase and uppercase letters. You can also use numbers and the underscore character to create an identifier, as long as the first character of your identifier is not a number. You need to limit your identifier to a maximum of 63 characters.

You don't need a token-string when defining an identifier. If you define an identifier without providing a token-string, you remove any occurrences of the identifier from the source file where the definition has been made. The identifier is still defined and you can still test for its existence. When you specify a token-string, there must be at least one space between it and the identifier. The token-string can be either a numeric value or a string value. A numeric value can be a decimal number or a hexadecimal value. To identify a numeric value as hexadecimal you need to precede the value with 0x so the compiler will know how to treat it. The following are valid uses of the #define directive:

```
#define DEBUG
#define CONSTANT 0xFFFF
#define PATH_LENGTH 260
#define PROGRAM_FILES_FOLDER "C:\\Program Files"
```

If you redefine a constant within your code, you will get compiler warning C7502 to tell you that you have a macro redefinition.

THE #UNDEF DIRECTIVE The #undef directive removes the definition of an identifier previously defined with the #define directive. The syntax for this directive is as follows:

```
#undef identifier
```

This directive removes the current definition of *identifier* and the preprocessor ignores further instances of this identifier. If there are any more instances, you will get compiler error C8025 to tell you that you have an undefined identifier. When you use the #undef directive, you only provide the identifier and do not add the token-string.

THE #ERROR DIRECTIVE The #error directive produces a compile-time error message. When an #error directive is encountered, compilation of the script is terminated.

The syntax of this directive is as follows:

```
#error token-string
```

The argument to the #error directive is an optional string that provides a message that describes the reason for the error. There must be at least one space between the #error directive and the token-string argument. This directive is useful for detecting constraint violations during the preprocessing of the script. The following is an example of the use of this directive:

```
#if    _ISCRIPT_VER < 0X600
#error "Script compiler version 6.10.100.1265 is required."
#endif
```

You cannot use macro expansion in the string-token argument to #error.

THE #WARNING DIRECTIVE The #warning directive is similar to the #error directive, but it gives a warning and does not terminate compilation unless you have specified that warnings are to be treated as errors. The syntax for this directive is as follows:

```
#warning token-string
```

As with the #error directive, this directive is useful in detecting pre-defined constraints during the preprocessing of the script.

THE #IF, #ELIF, #ELSE, AND #ENDIF DIRECTIVES This set of directives controls the compilation of portions of the script. The syntaxes for the #if and #elif directives are as follows:

```
#if constant-expression
#elif constant-expression
```

or

```
#if constant-expression)
#elif (constant-expression)
```

The constant-expression argument to these two directives can be either an expression that evaluates to a numeric value or a predefined constant that is a numeric value. If the expression or constant has a nonzero value, then the lines following the directive are included in the compilation of the script. Otherwise these lines are not included in the compilation. Each #if directive must be matched with a closing #endif directive prior to the end of the file; otherwise you will get an error message.

You can use the defined processor operator with the #if and #elif directives. The syntax for this operator is as follows:

```
defined(identifier)
```

In this expression *identifier* must be a macro. This expression evaluates to TRUE if *identifier* is currently defined and to FALSE if it is not defined. The defined operator can be modified with the unary NOT (!) operator.

The syntaxes for the #else and the #endif directives are as follows:

```
#else
```

and

```
#endif
```

These two directives do not take any arguments.

One way you can use these directives is to make sure that you do not get macro redefinition when you have nested include files. The iswi.h header file, with a slight modification, provides a good example:

```
#if !defined(_ISWI_H_)
#define _ISWI_H_

#include "ISMsiQuery.h"

external prototype void OnBegin();
external prototype void OnEnd();

NUMBER __hMsiInstall;

#endif // _ISWI_H_
```

In the preceding code sample the header file `ISMsiQuery.h` will only be included once and after that the identifier `_ISWI_H_` will show as being defined and the preprocessor will not include the lines between the #if and the #endif directives.

THE #IFDEF AND #IFNDEF DIRECTIVES These two directives perform the same function as the #if directive when it is used with the defined (*identifier*) operator. The syntaxes for these directives are as follows:

```
#ifdef identifier
```

and

```
#ifndef identifier
```

These are equivalent to

```
#if defined(identifier)
```

and

```
#if !defined(identifier)
```

The example in the previous section would look like this if you were to use these two directives:

```
#ifndef _ISWI_H_
#define _ISWI_H_

#include "ISMsiQuery.h"

external prototype void OnBegin();
external prototype void OnEnd();

NUMBER __hMsiInstall;

#endif // _ISWI_H_
```

THE PREDEFINED MACROS Three predefined macros are generated by the preprocessor. These are __LINE__, __FILE__, and _ISCRIPT_VER. You can use them wherever a numeric constant is valid. The __LINE__ expands to be equal to the line number wherever this macro is located. The following code snippet demonstrates what this means. (The numbers in the left-hand column represent the line numbers in the script.)

```
50    nArg = __LINE__;
51    SprintfBox(INFORMATION, "Title", "nArg = %d", nArg);
52    SprintfBox(INFORMATION, "Title", "Line = %d", __LINE__);
```

The first call to SprintfBox will display nArg = 50 and the second call will display Line = 52. Using the __LINE__ macro can be quite beneficial when you're using message box displays to help debug a script. If you are using multiple script files, it would be handy not only to have the line number printed out but also to know the name of the file that contains the line number. This is where the __FILE__ macro comes in. The value of the __FILE__ macro is set by the preprocessor to the name of the file that is being compiled. The name of the file includes the full path to the file. You can use the __FILE__ macro wherever a string constant can be used.

The final predefined macro is _ISCRIPT_VER, which identifies the version of the compiler being used. At the time of this writing, the value to which this macro was expanded was 0x600 hex or 1536 decimal.

The debugger

The InstallShield Visual Debugger is a source-level debugger; it displays debugging controls and your setup script in different panes of the same window. In the script pane of the window, the statement to be executed next is indicated with a visual marker, called the *execution point.*

From the Visual Debugger you can execute your script, statement by statement, and trace the flow of control by watching the execution point as it moves in the script pane of the Visual Debugger window. You can also monitor the value of any variable in your script at any point during script execution. With these methods, you can more easily identify sources of script error and inefficiency.

LAUNCHING THE DEBUGGER

The debugger is only useful in debugging script run-time errors. You cannot use the debugger to find the source of any compilation errors. A script that will not compile will not be added to an installation project at build time. You can launch it from the Build pulldown menu, by pressing the F5 key, or by clicking the Debug icon in the toolbar. Debugging is made possible during the build by the creation of the .dbg file. The .dbg file is created when you compile and build from the IDE a script that is associated with a custom action that you have defined. You must also have inserted this custom action into a sequence table before you can debug. If no InstallScript custom action has been defined, this file is not created and no debugging can occur. If an InstallScript custom action has been defined but not inserted into a sequence table, there is nothing to execute and the debugger will not be launched. During the build process the linker creates a file with a .map extension. This file enables you to perform a manual inspection to find out which module's version of a function was linked into the final image. Since the .map file is a text file you can view it using any text editor. This file can be valuable if you are using a number of different modules and a function with the same name defined is in more than one module.

When compiling from the command line, you need to remember to include the /G switch; otherwise the debug information will not be created. When you're compiling from the IDE, the .dbg and .map files are created in the Interm folder under the Build Label folder in your project location. When you compile from the command line using the /G option, the .dbg and .map files will be created in the same location as your Setup.rul file. This file is located in the root of your project location.

You can also run the debugger from the command line when you launch an installation package using msiexec.exe, as shown in the following code:

```
msiexec /i <msi package> ISSCRIPTDEBUG=1
ISSCRIPTDEBUGPATH="path to folder where the .dbg file is located"
```

This functionality allows for remote debugging as long as the debugger has been registered on the remote machine. To debug a script on a remote machine you need to copy Isdbg.exe to that machine and run this file with the /REGSERVER command-line parameter. This will register this executable on the remote machine. You will find Isdbg.exe in the Program Files\Common Files\InstallShield\IScript folder. You will also have to make sure that your MSI package and associated source files are on the remote machine.

If you embedded the MSI package into Setup.exe, you use the following command line to launch the installation in debug mode:

```
setup /v"ISSCRIPTDEBUG=1 ISSCRIPTDEBUGPATH=\"path to folder where
the .dbg file is located\""
```

Note that the complete command line is enclosed in double quotes and that the quotes around the path to the .dbg file are preceded with the backslash.

If you are debugging from the command line and the .dbg file is in the default location as determined by the build, then you do not need to use the ISSCRIPTDEBUGPATH public variable.

When you launch the installation in debug mode, either from the ISWI IDE or from the command line, you will get the Debugger interface, as shown in Figure 12-13.

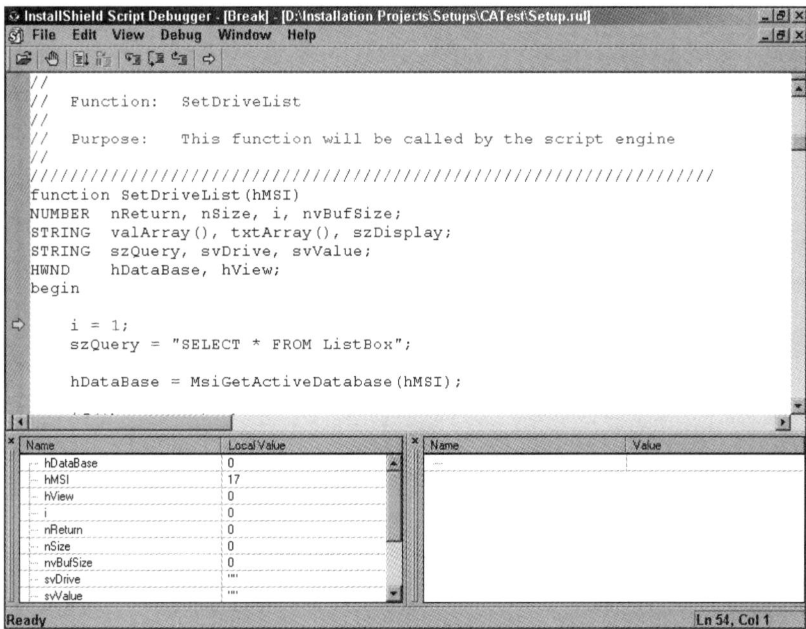

Figure 12-13: The InstallScript Debugger window

THE DEBUGGER USER INTERFACE

The user interface of the Debugger provides three main windows, which provide feedback during the debugging process. There are also a menu and toolbar that provide the command selection that enables you to control the various actions you take while debugging a script.

THE MENU, TOOLBAR, AND CONTEXT MENU COMMANDS The Debugger interface provides you with six menus: File, Edit, View, Debug, Windows, and Help. Table 12-7 describes the commands on each of these menus.

TABLE 12-7 DEBUGGER MENU COMMANDS

Menu	Option	Description
File	Open...	Opens a text file in read-only mode. You cannot make changes to a text file when it is displayed in the script window. The keyboard shortcut for this command is Ctrl+O.
	Close	Closes the topmost script window.
	Exit	Exits the Debugger and shuts down the debugging process.
Edit	Copy	Copies a highlighted section of text in the script window to the clipboard. Within the Debugger you can paste what you have copied to the clipboard in the Local Value field of the Variable Window or the Name field of the watch window. The Paste command is available from this context menu. The keyboard shortcut for this command is Ctrl+C.
	Find...	Brings up a basic dialog for entering the string on which you want to perform the search. There is no Find Next functionality so you need to use this command for repeated searching on the same string. The keyboard shortcut for this command is Ctrl+F.
View	Toolbar	Toggles the toolbar so that it is either enabled or disabled and not visible.
	Status Bar	Toggles the status bar so that it is either enabled or disabled and not visible.
	Watch	Toggles the watch window so that it is either enabled or disabled and not visible.
	Variable	Toggles the Variable Window so that it is either enabled or disabled and not visible.

Menu	Option	Description
View (continued)	Options...	Displays a property dialog where you can set the various properties that determine how the script window is to display various items. The functionality of this property dialog is exactly the same as that of the property dialog available for the script editor.
Debug	Go	Instructs the Debugger to run the script until it encoun-encounters a breakpoint. The keyboard shortcut for this command is F5. (You can use this same keyboard short-cut to initiate a debugging session from the ISWI IDE.)
	Break	Inserts a break when the Debugger is running. This command is only enabled when the Debugger is running and when this is the case you will see the word [Run] in the title bar of the Debugger. When you select the Break command, you might then also see the phrase [Waiting for a Break] flashing in the title bar. This indicates that the Debugger has not reached the point where it is going to break — possibly because a modal dialog has been displayed and the breakpoint is to be the next executable statement after the dialog. The keyboard shortcut for this command is the Break key.
	Step Into	Steps into a user-defined function and traces through the code that comprises this function. You cannot step into a built-in function or a Windows API function that you are calling. The keyboard shortcut for this command is F11.
	Step Over	Steps over a user-defined function so that you will not trace through the code that comprises this function. The keyboard shortcut for this command is F10.
	Step Out	Steps out of a user-defined function when you are finished tracing through the code that comprises this function. The keyboard shortcut for this command is Shift+F10.
	Run to Cursor	Runs the Debugger from the current location to the location in the script where the cursor has been placed. When you select this command, a blue circle is placed in the left margin and the Debugger moves to this location.

Continued

TABLE 12-7 DEBUGGER MENU COMMANDS *(Continued)*

Menu	Option	Description
Debug (continued)	Show Next Statement	Moves the cursor to the line of code marked by a yellow arrow in the left margin. When you have a large script, using this command is an excellent way to find out where you are in the debugging process. The keyboard shortcut for this command is Alt+Num*. (This is the asterisk on the numeric keypad.)
	Toggle Breakpoint	Turns on or off a breakpoint for the line where the cursor is located. The keyboard shortcut for this command is F9.
Debug	Clear All Breakpoints	Toggles off all breakpoints that have been set. This command will not toggle all the breakpoints you have set back on; you will have to do that breakpoint by breakpoint. The keyboard shortcut for this command is Shift+Ctrl+F9.
	Break on Exceptions exception.	Causes the Debugger to break whenever an exception is thrown and to break on the line that generated the
Window	Cascade	Displays all open script windows so that they overlap.
	Tile	Tiles all open script windows so that they are all visible at the same time.
Help	Contents showing.	Brings up the Debugger help file with the contents
	Index	Brings up the Debugger help file with the index showing.
	About IS Debugger...	Brings up a dialog that tells you what version of the Debugger is running.

Eight of the commands described in Table 12-7 can also be executed from the toolbar if it is enabled. These commands are from the File and Debug pulldown menus. From the File menu the Open command has been implemented as a toolbar button. From the Debug pulldown menu the Go, Break, Step Into, Step Over, Step Out, Show Next Statement, and Toggle Breakpoint commands have been implemented as toolbar buttons. After the Open Toolbar button, the commands on the toolbar are in the following order (from left to right): Toggle Breakpoint, Go, Break, Step Into, Step Over, Step Out, and Show Next Statement. When you place the mouse pointer over a toolbar button, a ToolTip will tell you what the button does.

If you click your right mouse button in the script window, you will get a context menu containing three commands: Insert/Remove BreakPoint, Run to Cursor, and Add to Watch. The Insert/Remove BreakPoint command is the same as the Toggle Breakpoint command on the toolbar or on the Debug pulldown menu. The Run to Cursor command is the same as the command of the same name on the Debug menu. The Add to Watch command is not on any of the pulldown menus or on the toolbar. This command adds a variable to the watch window. You select the variable that you want added by placing the cursor somewhere in the variable's name in the Script window. You can add any word to the watch window but unless this word is a variable name the Value field in the watch window will inform you that there was an error because the symbol could not be found.

THE SCRIPT WINDOW The script window displays your script so that you can view it as you run it. The next statement to be executed is positioned in the window and identified by a yellow arrow. Magenta circles appear in the left margin of lines with breakpoints. A line you have identified by the Run to Cursor command is marked by a blue circle in the left margin.

The title bar of the script window shows the full name of the file displayed in the top script window. Also shown in the title bar is the state of the Debugger. This state can be one of the following: [Break], [Run], or [Waiting for a Break]. Note that you can scroll the window to any location in your script, but that unlike the script editor, the Debugger does not offer the Goto command that would allow you to jump to a specific line number in the script.

The script window scrolls automatically if necessary when you use the Step Into or Step Over commands to trace through a set of statements. Likewise, when script execution is halted at a breakpoint, the window scrolls automatically to the location of the breakpoint.

The Debugger uses color syntax highlighting to display your script in the Script window just as the script editor does. The Options... command on the View pulldown menu will bring up the Properties dialog where you can redefine the colors to be used to color syntax the tokens in the Debugger script window. Property changes made in the Debugger script window do not have an impact on the properties set for the script editor.

When the Debugger is in the [Break] state, the next statement to be executed is identified by a yellow arrow in the left margin. Often you will have scrolled the script so that this marker is not in view: you can bring it back into view by using the Show Next Statement command, which brings the cursor back to the line identified by this yellow arrow. In a large script this is the way to easily get back to where the Debugger has stopped.

THE VARIABLE WINDOW The Variable Window displays the values of the local variables that have been declared in the user-defined function where the Debugger is presently running. When the Debugger moves out of one user-defined function into another, the list of variables displayed in the Variable Window will change.

Variables declared as structures and lists cannot be inspected in the Variable and watch windows. The only way to display the values of structure or list members is to assign the value to a local or global variable: the value of this variable will then display the value of the member.

In the Variable Window, you can change the displayed value of the local variable. You get access to the variable's value by first highlighting the row of the variable and then left-clicking in the Local Value field. This puts you into an edit mode wherein you can change the value. When you are in the edit mode, a context menu is available to you, which you can display by clicking the right mouse button. This context menu provides the Undo, Cut, Copy, Paste, Delete, and Select All commands.

THE WATCH WINDOW Where the Variable Window provides a complete list of all the local variables in your user-defined function, the watch window enables you to choose which variables you want to inspect or watch. You can highlight the first blank row in the watch window and then left-click to put yourself into edit mode. You can then type in the name of the variable that you want to watch, which can be either a local or a global variable.

The easiest way to add a variable to the watch window is to right-click the variable name in the script window and select the Add to Watch command. This will place the variable's name into the Name field of the watch window. If the variable is in scope, the watch window will immediately display the present value assigned to the variable. If the variable is out of scope, the value in the Value field of the watch window will display the following error message:

```
Error: symbol "variable_name" not found.
```

An important global variable you can set in the watch window is LAST_RESULT. This variable displays the value returned from the last function call made in the script and executed by the Debugger. Being a global variable, it does not go out of scope.

TRACING THE EXECUTION OF YOUR SCRIPT

You can use any one of several methods to trace through your script in order to see what is happening. Most of your debugging will consist of your stepping through the script one executable line at a time. Your favorite command to use for this purpose will be the Step Over command (the keyboard shortcut is F10). However, there will be times when you want to get into one of your private functions to see how it is operating; to do this you will use the Step Into command (the keyboard shortcut is F11). When you do go into one of your private functions and you want to get out of it before you reach the end, you will use the Step Out command (the keyboard shortcut is Shift+F10). If you do go to the end of your private function, use either the F10 or F11 command to bring you back to the main entry point function.

When you want to run to a certain point before you start to execute the code line by line, you have two choices. You can place the cursor in the script window where you want to start the step-through operation to begin and then select the Run to Cursor command. You can also set a breakpoint on the executable line where you want to begin your step-through operation and then select the Go command and the Debugger will execute the script up to this point. You can only set breakpoints on executable lines of script. If you try to set a breakpoint on a non-executable line, the breakpoint will actually be set on the first subsequent executable line. If you want to jump from point to point, set a number of breakpoints and use the Go command to jump from one to the next.

If you want to jump into a private function, all you have to do is set a breakpoint in the function where you want the Debugger to stop. This will take you to the desired location. If you do not set breakpoints inside the function, the functionality will be the same as if you had selected the Step Over command when reaching the line where the function was called.

If you do not want to set a breakpoint, you can place the cursor in the line where you want to the Debugger to stop and then select the Run to Cursor command from either the Debug pulldown menu or the context menu that appears when you click the right mouse button.

As you are tracing through your script the Variable Window shows the current values of the variables. You can also change the values of these variables in order to give yourself a better idea of what is happening. The watch window shows where you can see how a specific variable or set of variables are behaving during the execution of your script.

Breakpoints are not saved from one debugging session to another. This functionality may be provided in some future release of the ISWI product.

Summary

In this chapter, you took a close look at the scripting environment to be found in InstallShield for Windows Installer. This scripting functionality enables you to create custom actions using a language that was specifically developed for performing installation-related actions. This chapter is a prerequisite to your upcoming study of the InstallScript language and its capabilities, which are the subjects of the next two chapters. Then in the final chapter of this part we discuss how to use this scripting language to create custom actions.

Chapter 13

Introduction to the InstallScript Language

IN THIS CHAPTER

- Setting up the environment for testing InstallScript
- InstallScript data types
- InstallScript expressions
- InstallScript statements
- Built-in InstallScript functions
- Creating user-defined functions
- Calling functions in a dynamic-linked library

THIS CHAPTER COVERS the basic features of InstallScript, a scripting language that provides a rich set of data types, expressions, statements, and built-in functions. In addition, we will cover how to extend the functionality of the language by using user-defined functions creating functions in a dynamic-linked library. This chapter serves as a prerequisite for the next chapter, which is about how to use the InstallScript language to create functional programs.

Setting up an Environment for Testing the InstallScript Language

As you work through this chapter, you will want to be able to experiment with the code examples that are provided. To make this easy and efficient, you need to set up an environment for running scripts and seeing some output. To create this environment, start with the ScriptTest project that you created at the beginning of Chapter 12. The first thing to do with the Setup.rul script is to delete all the "TO DO:" comment statements along with any other instructional comment statements. This will cut down on the clutter in your script and make things easier to see. The next thing you should do is define a string constant CAPTION that will contain the title text that you will use in your dialog that will provide you with feedback when you run your scripts. You define this string constant before defining the ScriptTest entry point function.

In the ScriptTest function you define some string and number local variables that you will use to run your tests and use as arguments to the SprintfBox function. In this function you also enter a call to the SprintfBox built-in function. You will be adding more variables later when you start testing your script examples. For now this gives you a skeleton with which you can complete the other preparations required to get this function to execute your scripts.

```
///////////////////////////////////////////////////////////////////////
//
//  IIIIIII SSSSSS
//    II    SS                          InstallShield (R)
//    II    SSSSSS (c) 1996-2000, InstallShield Software Corporation
//    II        SS                      All rights reserved.
//  IIIIIII SSSSSS
//
//
//  This template script provides the code necessary to build an
//  entry-point function to be called in an InstallScript
//  custom action.
//
//    File Name:  Setup.rul
//
//  Description:  InstallShield script
//
///////////////////////////////////////////////////////////////////////

#include "isrt.h"
#include "iswi.h"

#define     CAPTION         "Script Test Feedback"

export prototype ScriptTest(NUMBER);


///////////////////////////////////////////////////////////////////////
//
// Function:  ScriptTest
//
// Purpose:   This is the entry point function used to run
//            our scripting test examples
//
//
///////////////////////////////////////////////////////////////////////
```

```
function ScriptTest(hMSI)
STRING     szFormat, szValue;
NUMBER     nValue;
begin

     SprintfBox(INFORMATION, CAPTION, szFormat, nValue, szValue);

end;
```

You now need to create a custom action using the Custom Action wizard. As you did in Chapter 11, right-click the Custom Actions icon in the tree view of the Actions/ Scripts view and select the Custom Action Wizard... option. For each of the panels in this wizard, Table 13-1 shows the values that need to be entered or selected.

TABLE 13-1 CUSTOM ACTION WIZARD ENTRIES

Panel	Field	Value
Basic Information	Name	ScriptTest
	Comment	Custom action for experimenting with InstallScript
Action Type	Type	Run InstallScript code
	Location	Disabled for this type
Action Parameters	Source	ScriptTest
	Target	Disabled for this source
Additional Options	Wait for the action to finish executing	This check box is checked and cannot be unchecked
	Ignore custom action return code	This check box can be checked or left unchecked
	In-Script Execution	Immediate execution
	Execution Scheduling	Always execute

The following remarks provide additional information about the Custom Action Wizard selections that are shown in Table 13-1:

- The “Ignore custom action return code” check box can be left unchecked but for this particular usage of a custom action it doesn’t matter whether it’s checked or not, because you are only working with the script and not actually creating custom actions that have return codes.

- Since you are not installing anything you need to have this custom action run in immediate mode.
- In this example the Execution Scheduling is left as “Always execute,” but it would work just as well to have specified that the custom action is to “Execute only once” or “Execute only once per process.”

What you should now have in your Actions/Scripts view is something that looks like Figure 13-1. The tree control under the InstallScript icon shows a blue diamond with the name of the one function that you have in your script. Your ScriptTest custom action appears under the Custom Actions icon.

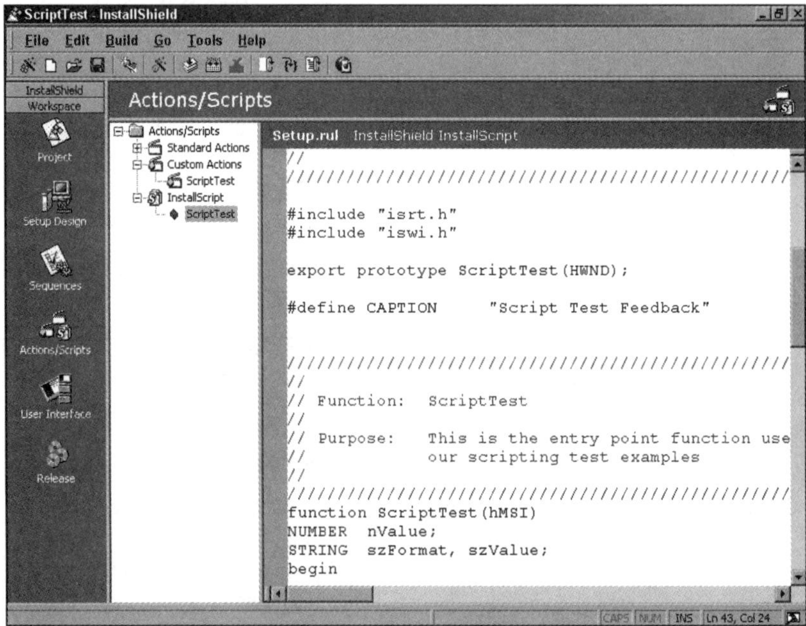

Figure 13-1: Actions/Scripts view with defined function

To finish setting up your test environment you need to insert your ScriptTest custom action into the InstallUISequence. Before you do this, however, you’ll want to strip this sequence of all other actions and dialogs, so that the only user interface you have to deal with is the one that the SprintfBox function will display. When you insert the ScriptTest custom action into the UI sequence, it will be the first and only action in this sequence. Since you are not running the ExecuteAction action the client never passes control to the server process. This means that when you click the OK button on the message box displayed by the SprintfBox function the install process will terminate and you will not have to waste time canceling the installation. When you are finished with this manipulation of the InstallUISequence, your sequences view will look like Figure 13-2.

This project does not need to have any features or components defined. If it doesn't, you will get a warning telling you that there are no files included in the project. You can ignore this warning for your present purposes. This project was named ScriptTest. Since you will not be making any changes to the system when you run our tests you do not have to do anything with respect to the project settings or the setup design.

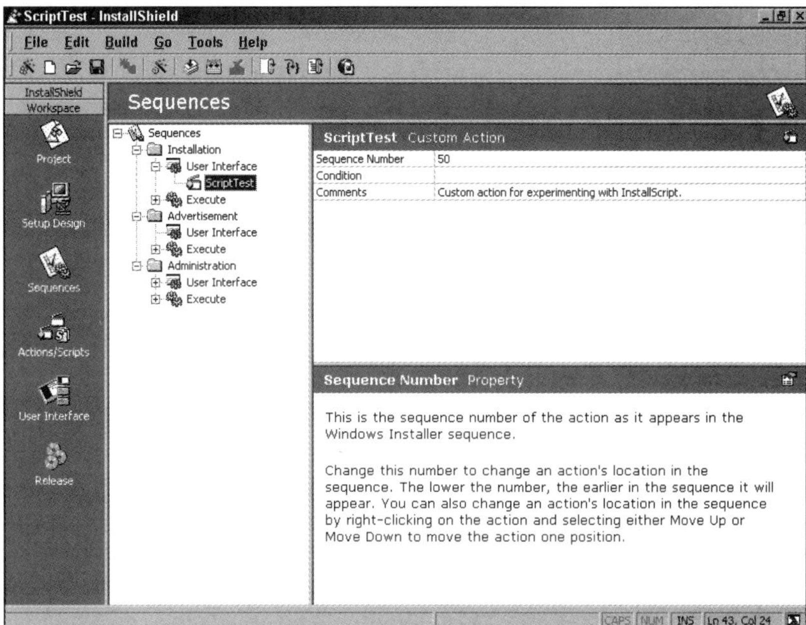

Figure 13-2: The Sequences view of your InstallScript test project

You now need to run the Release Wizard to create the project that you will continue to rebuild as you experiment with the InstallScript language. Run the Release Wizard using a build label of Basic Build and a release name of Version 1.0.0. Take the defaults all the way up to the Advanced Settings panel and then uncheck all the check boxes in the Launcher Settings group before completing the build.

Your script test environment is now constructed, so you are ready to look at the details of the InstallScript language. What you will do to run the test scenarios is to first compile the script to make sure there are no compile-time errors, and then build the project using the Build icon on the toolbar, and finally make a test run using the Test button on the toolbar. Your output will be displayed in a message box created by the SprintfBox script function. You should now look at the SprintfBox function and see what its capabilities are.

The SprintfBox script function

This script function is essentially a wrapper around the Windows MessageBox API and the wsprintf function. The prototype for this function is as follows:

```
SprintfBox(
  NUMBER nType,        // message box style
  STRING szTitle,      // message box title
  STRING szFormat,     // format-control string
  . . .                // optional arguments
);
```

The following describes the parameters to the SprintfBox built-in function:

- *nType* – This specifies the style of the message box to be displayed. A few InstallScript styles are defined that map to the styles in the Windows MessageBox API, but you can use many of the styles defined for this API directly in SprintfBox. In the skeleton code that you created earlier in the chapter, you used the INFORMATION style, which is an InstallScript-defined constant. This provides a message box with an icon that has an *i* in a circle and one OK button.

  You can see the MessageBox API styles that are supported by the InstallScript compiler by looking in the windefs.h header file. You can also add the missing style constants to this file, if you wish. You can find the values for these additional MessageBox styles in the Windows header file winuser.h. This file comes with both Visual C++ and the Platform SDK. You'll find the windefs.h header file in the following location:

  ```
  Program Files\InstallShield\Script\isrt\Include
  ```

- *szTitle* – This is a string that appears as the caption in the title bar of the message box.

- *szFormat* – This string contains the format by which the values to be displayed are formatted. For each argument to be printed you should provide a compatible format specification to print the value. You can also provide text in addition to the format specification. If there were no values to be printed, this format string would contain only text with no format specification. The format specification is as follows:

  ```
  %[-][#][0][width][.precision]type
  ```

  The format specifiers in square brackets (`[]`) are optional, as with the wsprintf function. SprintfBox also supports all the fields supported by this function. Refer to the MSDN Library for a complete description of the wsprintf function.

The InstallScript Data Types

A computer's memory consists of a string of ones and zeros, and for a high-level programming language to make sense out of this it needs to know how to interpret the contents of memory. It does this by declaring that a certain part of memory is to be interpreted as being a particular type of data, which it does in turn by defining something called a data type. All high-level languages have a set of primitive data types and InstallScript is no exception.

Unlike with C language, you cannot assign a value to an InstallScript variable on the same line where you declare the variable. The InstallScript compiler initializes all variables to default values and you cannot change these default values by specifying a value at the point of declaration.

```
int nArg = 1; // OK in C but an error in InstallScript
```

InstallScript has three primitive data types, as described in the following list:

NUMBER — A four-byte signed integer, which means that it can represent numbers from –2,147,483,648 to 2,147,483,647. Any variable declared as a NUMBER type is automatically initialized to zero.

STRING — An array of characters with each character being handled as a two-byte Unicode character on an NT or 2000 machine and as multi-byte characters on a Win 9x machine. Strings in InstallScript are handled without the use of a null terminator, which means that you can have embedded null characters. A null terminator is only added to a string when it is being passed to a DLL function. Any variable declared as a STRING type is automatically initialized as a null string (" ").

VARIANT — A special data type that can contain many different types of information. You can use a VARIANT data type in place of any of the other data types in InstallScript. Variables of this type are initialized as Empty, which means that 0 is used if the variable is being used in a numeric context or a null string (" ") is used if the variable is being used in a string context. The VARIANT data type can be a convenient way to convert between NUMBER and STRING variable types.

The InstallScript language has many aliases for these three primitive data types. These aliases help you remember the purpose for which you are declaring the different variables in your script; they are described in Table 13-2.

Table 13-2 INSTALLSCRIPT DATA TYPE ALIASES

Primitive	Alias	Description
NUMBER	BOOL	Used to represent the conditions of TRUE or FALSE.
	CHAR	Used to represent a single character. A character code fits in the lower byte of the four-byte NUMBER type. Inside a structure this data type is only one byte in size.
	HWND	Used to hold the handle to a window and, more generically, used to hold any handle provided by the Windows operating system.
	INT	Used to represent a four-byte signed integer.
	LIST	Used to identify a LIST that is the InstallScript implementation of a linked list.
	LONG	Used to represent a four-byte signed integer.
	LPSTR	Used as a pointer to a null terminated string.
	POINTER	Used as a generic pointer.
	PSZ	Used as a pointer to null terminated string.
	SHORT	Used to represent a four-byte signed integer. However, in a structure a variable declared as this data type is only two bytes in size.
STRING	STRING	Used to hold a null terminated string of characters.
VARIANT	OBJECT	Used to hold any of the other types of data, or a COM object.

As you can see, there are many aliases for the primitive NUMBER data type. You may be asking yourself how a signed integer, which a NUMBER is, can serve as a pointer to a location in memory or a handle to a window. Everyone knows that there is no such thing as a negative memory address or window handle. The answer is that within InstallScript a pointer can be negative, but when you pass it out to a function, it is used as the required data type. An integer is just four bytes and an address is also just four bytes. When you pass a NUMBER variable to a function that is expecting a pointer argument, the NUMBER variable gets implicitly type cast to a pointer.

You should note that no floating-point data types are defined for InstallScript; in this regard it is just like the Windows Installer. No floating-point data types are used in any of the MSI database tables.

It is very important that you use the correct data type that represents the intended usage of the variable.

It cannot be emphasized enough that you should use the correct data type for the intended use of a variable. For example, even though the CHAR data type is presently implemented as an alias for the NUMBER data type, this may not be the case later on down the line. It is very possible that in future releases of InstallScript the CHAR data type may be changed to be truly just one character and not four bytes like it is now. For your code to continue to compile, you would have to be declaring your data types correctly.

This is so you can be sure that your scripts continue to compile in the future. It is possible that future versions of the InstallScript language will only allow pointer types where a pointer type is required. In other words, future versions of the InstallScript compiler may be made to perform much stricter type checking.

Symbolic constants and variables

In InstallScript we deal with two types of symbols: symbolic constants and variables. You create symbolic constants using the #define preprocessor directive. They are either of type NUMBER or of type STRING. You can define a symbolic constant of type NUMBER by using either decimal or hexadecimal notation. The following lines of code

```
#define    CONSTANT    65
```

and

```
#define    CONSTANT    0x41
```

define the same bit representation for the CONSTANT symbolic constant. The main points to understand about symbolic constants is first that their values cannot be changed and second that even though they are in memory someplace you have no means of accessing that memory. Another important point is that the compiler does not see symbolic constants. The preprocessor makes all the substitutions in the code before the compiler begins to parse the code.

Variables provide you with the means to access memory. A variable essentially gives you a name for a particular location in memory. When you declare a variable, you have to tell the compiler what its data type is so that it will know how the bits that comprise that memory are to be interpreted. The compiler also uses the data type so that it knows how much space in memory the variable is going to occupy. The data type of a variable is also used by the compiler to perform type checking. To create a variable name you can use letters, numbers, and the underscore character (_), but you cannot start the name with a number. There is no practical limit on the length of a variable name, but only the first 63 characters of the name are considered significant in InstallScript. A number of language keywords (as shown in the following list) are reserved by InstallScript and cannot be used as variable names.

`Abort`	`exit`	`program`
`begin`	`EXIT`	`prototype`
`binary`	`external`	`repeat`
`BINARY`	`EXTERNAL`	`return`
`BOOL`	`export`	`set`
`BYREF`	`EXPORT`	`short`
`BYVAL`	`for`	`SHORT`
`case`	`function`	`stdcall`
`catch`	`goto`	`STDCALL`
`cdecl`	`HWND`	`step`
`CDECL`	`if`	`string`
`char`	`int`	`STRING`
`CHAR`	`INT`	`switch`
`default`	`LPSTR`	`then`
`downto`	`LIST`	`to`
`else`	`long`	`try`
`elseif`	`LONG`	`typedef`
`end`	`number`	`until`
`endcatch`	`NUMBER`	`variant`
`endif`	`object`	`VARIANT`
`endfor`	`OBJECT`	`void`
`endprogram`	`pointer`	`VOID`
`endswitch`	`POINTER`	`while`
`endwhile`	`PSZ`	

The following remarks provide specific information about several of the keywords shown above:

- You will use the binary/BINARY keyword when you want to send binary data to a Windows API. Strings in the script are handled as Unicode but the string is translated to ANSI before it is passed to the Windows API. Using this keyword will prevent this translation from occurring when a binary file is being created or read using APIs such as WriteFile() or ReadFile().
- You will use the external/EXTERNAL keyword when you prototype a function that has been defined in a script library that is being linked with the .rul file.
- You will use the void/VOID keyword when you prototype a function that does not return a value.

Before we take a closer look at the various data types, let's discuss some of the conventions used in creating scripts.

Scripting conventions

There are only a few conventions we need to discuss here: these deal with declaring variables, naming variables, and using comments and white space in your script.

DECLARING VARIABLES

Many of the data types such as INT also allow the lowercase version int. Both the uppercase and the lowercase versions mean the same thing and can be used interchangeably. Some of the data types such as LIST and HWND must be rendered in uppercase. By convention, you should declare all variables using the uppercase version of the data-type name.

```
INT   nVal; // Use this form
int   nVal; // Don't use this form
```

As with all coding conventions, the objective here is easier readability of the script.

VARIABLE NAMING

The most important thing that a good variable name does is let the reader of the code know the purpose of the data the variable represents. Since variable names in InstallScript can be up to 63 characters long, you have plenty of opportunity to create meaningful names for your variables. A good variable name is a big step toward self-documenting code. In the InstallScript documentation, the names used for variables employ a limited Hungarian notation.

The term *Hungarian notation* comes from the man who invented this convention. His name is Charles Simonyi, one of the senior programmers at Microsoft, and he happens to be a native of Hungary.

The convention in InstallScript is to use a lowercase prefix that identifies the data type and a qualifier that describes the purpose of the data held in the variable. Qualifiers are normally mixed-case names with each word in the variable name beginning with an uppercase letter. Table 13-3 provides a description of the prefixes commonly used in InstallScript.

TABLE 13-3 COMMON VARIABLE PREFIXES

Prefix	Data Type	Description
b	BOOL	A Boolean variable that indicates a condition of either TRUE or FALSE
c	CHAR	A variable that represents a single character
h	HWND	A variable that represents any type of handle used or returned by a Windows API function
n	INT	A variable that is a four-byte signed number
l	LONG	A variable that is a four-byte signed number
p or lp	POINTER	A value to be used as a pointer; lp stands for *long pointer*, a standard identifier used by Windows APIs
sz or str	STRING	A string that can contain null characters. The sz prefix has been used in the past to signify a null terminated string. The str prefix is now the preferred prefix since strings in InstallScript are no longer null terminated except when they are passed to a DLL function.
v or obj	OBJECT	A variable being used as a VARIANT; most of the time this will be an object created with the CreateObject() InstallScript API

COMMENTS AND WHITE SPACE

InstallScript uses the same comment statement syntax available in C++. You can create block comment statements that cover multiple lines if they are surrounded by the /* and */ identifiers. You can also create in-line or single-line comment statements by using double slashes (//). InstallScript ignores white space outside of a string literal, which allows you to provide more readable code. You are encouraged to make use of white space and comment statements so that other people will be able to understand your code more easily.

The pointer data types

I have already shown that all pointer data types in InstallScript are just aliases for the NUMBER primitive data type. A pointer variable holds the address of another variable. To be able to work with pointers you need to be able to get the address of a variable and, having gotten the address, to get the value that the pointer is pointing at. To do this you have two special operators: you can use the Address operator (&) and the indirection operator (*) to get the address of a variable and to get the value at an address, respectively.

The aliases that declare various types of pointers are POINTER, LPSTR, PSZ, LIST, and HWND. Actually, HWND is not really a pointer; it is an alias for a location in memory. Handles are used in a table where the actual memory address of a window may change because the operating system is moving things about in order to make the most efficient use of the memory resource.

We discuss the LIST data type later in this chapter in the section of the same name, because it plays a special role in the creation of a linked list.

The following code shows the typical use of this data type and the operators previously mentioned:

```
function Foo()
INT         nArg1, nArg2;
POINTER     pArg;
begin

   nArg1 = 3;
   pArg = &nArg1 ; // Set the variable pArg to point at nArg1
   nArg2 = *pArg; // Set nArg2 to be equal to nArg1
end;
```

You cannot use the indirection operator on the left side of the assignment operator. The following code would be valid in C but not in InstallScript.

```
pArg = &nArg1;
*pArg = 3; // This generates an InstallScript compiler error
```

You can, however, use the indirection operator when you pass values to a function, as shown in the following example:

```
nArg1 = 3;
pArg = &nArg1 ; // Set the variable pArg to point at nArg1

// The following message box will display nArg1 = 3
SprintfBox(INFORMATION, "Script Test", "nArg1 = %d", *pArg);
```

You can have pointers to pointers as long as you dereference them one step at a time:

```
function Foo()
INT         nArg1, nArg2;
POINTER     pArg1, ppArg1, pArg2;
begin
   nArg1 = 3;
   pArg1 = &nArg1 ; // Set the variable pArg to point at nArg1
   ppArg1 = &pArg1; // ppArg is now a pointer to a pointer
   nArg2 = **pArg1; // This will cause a compiler error
   pArg2 = *ppArg1; // This will work
   nArg2 = *pArg2;  // nArg2 is now equal to nArg1
end;
```

You can only use the indirection operator (*) with NUMBER data types.

We will examine pointers in more detail in Chapter 14.

The BOOL data type

A BOOL variable holds either a symbolic constant, either TRUE or FALSE. The following is an example of its use. In this example, szArray is an array of strings of nSize size and szSearch is a string being searched for in the array.

```
function Foo()
BOOL bFound;
INT i;
begin
   bFound = FALSE;
   i = 0;
```

```
   while(!bFound && i<nSize)
     if(StrCompare(szArray(i), szSearch) = 0) then
        bFound = TRUE;
        SprintfBox(INFORMATION, "Search Results", "The string: %s\n
                                  was found at index: %d",
                                  szSearch, i);
     endif;
     i = i + 1;
   endwhile;

   if(!bFound) then
      SprintfBox(INFORMATION, "Search Results",
                 "The string %s was not found", szSearch);
   endif;
end;
```

The TRUE symbolic constant is defined to be 1 and the FALSE symbolic constant is defined to be 0.

The CHAR data type

The CHAR data type declares variables that will hold single characters; the exception is when a CHAR data type is declared a member of a structure. Then the size of the CHAR variable is actually only one byte. You can test the fact that a CHAR is only one byte within a structure by implementing the following code in a script:

```
// global declaration
typedef    Test
begin
    CHAR  cArg;
end;

function Foo()
// local declarations in a function
CHAR  cArg;
Test    test;
INT   nArg;
begin
   nArg = SizeOf(cArg); // this returns the value of 4

   nArg = SizeOf(test); // this returns the value of 1
end;
```

What this means is that in a structure you can only hold numbers between 0 and 255 in a structure member if it has been declared as being CHAR. As a character, this structure member will be able to display the complete ASCII character set. Outside of a structure, a variable declared as CHAR can hold values from –2,147,483,648 to 2,147,483,647. If you assign a CHAR structure member a value larger than 255 or smaller than 0, the script will still compile but at run time an exception will be thrown and your script will die.

You can create an array of type CHAR but this would not be the same thing as a type STRING, which is also an array of characters. The array of type CHAR would be treated in InstallScript as if it were an array of integers.

The following are all valid ways to assign the letter A to a variable of type CHAR:

```
function Foo()
// local variable declarations
STRING  szStr;
CHAR     cArg;
begin
   // string assignment
   szStr = "This is A test";

   //  a type CHAR variable assignment
   cArg = "A";
   cArg = 'A';
   cArg = szStr[8];
end;
```

The integer data types

The integer data types are LONG, INT, and SHORT. With one exception, in InstallScript these each represent a four-byte signed integer. The exception is that a type SHORT that is a member of a structure will have a size of two bytes, as shown in the following code:

```
// global declaration
typedef     Test
begin
    SHORT  sArg;
end;

function Foo()
// local declarations in a function
SHORT  sArg;
Test    test;
INT   nArg;
begin
```

```
   nArg = SizeOf(sArg); // this returns the value of 4

   nArg = SizeOf(strucTest); // this returns the value of 2
end;
```

This means that in a structure you can only hold numbers between -32768 and 32767 in a structure member if it has been declared as being SHORT. Outside of a structure, a variable declared as SHORT can hold values from -2,147,483,648 to 2,147,483,647. If you assign a SHORT structure member a value larger than 32767 or smaller than -32768, the script will still compile but at run time an exception will be thrown and your script will die.

The STRING data type

The STRING data type is an array of Unicode or multi-byte characters (that is, not null terminated). The internal implementation of the STRING data type in InstallScript allows for embedded null characters. As I mentioned before, you cannot assign a value to a STRING variable on the same line where you have declared the variable. You can assign a value to a STRING variable as follows:

```
function Foo()
STRING szStr;
begin
   szStr = "This is a string"; // OK in InstallScript
   szStr =  'This is a string'; // Also OK in InstallScript
end;
```

Of course, in C, you cannot initialize a pointer to an array of characters using double quotes unless you are doing it at the same time that you are declaring the variable, and at no time can you initialize a pointer to an array of characters using single quotes.

When you declare a STRING variable, you can specify a minimum size or you can leave the variable unsized and let InstallScript automatically size it for you when you assign it a value. When you specify a minimum size for a string variable, this variable can still grow as needed. It just cannot get smaller than the minimum size defined. InstallScript has an auto-size feature that will always resize the length of a STRING variable to the size required to hold the value assigned. However, a STRING variable will never be sized smaller than the minimum size specified when the variable was declared. You are only required to set the size of a string when a STRING variable is a member of a structure. There are also issues relative to string sizing, when they are being passed to an API exported from a DLL.

Specifying the minimum size of a string variable is done as follows:

```
function Foo()
STRING   szArg[10]; // square brackets are used for string sizing
```

```
INT      nSize;
begin
   szArg = "string";
   nSize = SizeOf(szArg); // nSize will still equal 10

   szArg = "This is a string";
   nSize = SizeOf(szArg);  // nSize will now equal 16
end;
```

We will address the specific string-sizing issues with regard to structures and passing strings to a DLL function in the section "Working with Strings" in Chapter 14.

The following code describes the string-sizing functionality in InstallScript where one STRING variable type is given an initial size of 10 and the other variable is not given an initial size.

```
// szArg1 has a minimum size of 0
// szArg2 has a minimum size of 10
STRING szArg1, szArg2[10];
INT     nArg;
```

The minimum size of szArg1 is 0 since it was not given an initial size when it was declared, and the minimum size of szArg2 is 10 since it was initialized with that size.

```
nArg = SizeOf(szArg1); // nArg is 0
nArg = SizeOf(szArg2); // nArg is 10
```

When a STRING variable is assigned a value, it will automatically be sized to fit the length of the string unless the minimum size of the variable is greater than the length of the string being used for the initial assignment.

```
szArg1 = "Test";
nArg = SizeOf(szArg1); // nArg is 4

szArg2 = "Test";
nArg = SizeOf(szArg2); // nArg is still 10

szArg1 = "This is a test";
nArg = SizeOf(szArg1); // nArg is 14
```

```
szArg2 = "This is a test";
nArg = SizeOf(szArg2); // nArg is now 14
```

Resetting the values of szArg1 and szArg2 to a null string resets their sizes to those used when they were first declared.

```
szArg1 = "";
nArg = SizeOf(szArg1); // nArg is 0

szArg2 = "";
nArg = SizeOf(szArg2); // nArg is 10
```

Using the Resize operator temporarily redefines the size of the string but a new assignment operation again redefines their size.

```
szArg1 = "This is a test";
Resize(szArg1, 20);
nArg = SizeOf(szArg1); // nArg is 20

szArg2 = "This is a Test";
Resize(szArg2, 20);
nArg = SizeOf(szArg2); // nArg is 20

szArg1 = "";
nArg = SizeOf(szArg1); //nArg is 0

szArg2 = "";
nArg = SizeOf(szArg2); // nArg is 10
```

These code examples show that when a STRING type variable is declared without an initial size then its minimum size will be 0 and it will continue to be resized so that it will be able to hold whatever string is assigned to it. Automatic resizing works in both directions as the size of the text string being used to set the value of the variable increases or decreases. When a STRING type variable is given a size when it is declared, this size becomes the minimum size for that variable. All automatic resizing occurs with respect to that minimum size. A STRING variable given an initial size when it is declared cannot be resized to a length less than this initial value. Nothing but practical considerations limit the length of a string that can be assigned to a STRING type variable.

A more detailed description of the use of the SizeOf and Resize operators will be provided later in this chapter in the section "Expressions."

The VARIANT data type

The VARIANT data type in InstallScript can hold either NUMBER or STRING type information. This is the same VARIANT data type used in Visual Basic. You can use it to hold a pointer to an OLE automation object.

We can assign the same VARIANT type variable a string value or an integer value.

```
function Foo()
STRING  szArg;
INT     nArg;
VARIANT vArg;
begin
   vArg = 12345;

   // szArg will be equal to the string "1234567890"
   szArg = vArg + "67890";

   vArg = "12345";

   // nArg will be equal to the value 80235
   nArg = vArg + 67890;
end;
```

These code examples show that you can use the VARIANT data type in place of the NumToStr() and StrToNum() InstallScript functions.

In most cases, when you have two VARIANT data types and you want to use them in an expression, they have to hold the same data type if you are using the + operator. This operator is overloaded to mean addition in an arithmetic expression and to mean concatenation in an expression that contains strings. With the following variables declared, I'll demonstrate various combinations of the VARIANT types vArg1 and vArg2 that work and other combinations that will not work. When both of the VARIANT data types are assigned string values, using the concatenation operator can have the result assigned only to a STRING type variable. When both of the VARIANT data types are assigned integer values, then using the concatenation operator can have the result assigned only to a STRING type variable.

```
function Foo()
STRING     szArg;
INT        nArg;
VARIANT    vArg1, vArg2;
begin
```

```
   vArg1 = "12345";
   vArg2 = "67890";

// This will work and give the value of "1234567890" for szArg
   szArg = vArg1 + vArg2;

   // This will not work and an exception will be thrown
   nArg = vArg1 + vArg2;

   vArg1 = 12345;
   vArg2 = 67890;

   // This will work and give the value of 80235 for nArg
   nArg = vArg1 + vArg2;

   // This will not work and an exception will be thrown
   szArg = vArg1 + vArg2;
end;
```

When the VARIANT data types are assigned an initial value, one with an integer and the other with a string, then using the + operator can have the result assigned only to a NUMBER type variable.

```
vArg1 = 12345;
vArg2 = "67890";

// This will work and give the value of 80235 for nArg
nArg = vArg1 + vArg2;

// This will not work and an exception will be thrown
szArg = vArg1 + vArg2;
```

Adding a symbolic constant to the previous expression will provide enough information to the compiler for it to work.

```
// This will work and give the value of "8023510"
szArg = vArg1 + vArg2 + "10";
```

In the previous statement, vArg1 and vArg2 are first treated as integers and added together. Then the result of the summation is treated as a string and concatenated with the string `"10"`.

I have mentioned that certain code will throw an exception. We'll cover exception handling in Chapter 14.

The LIST data type

InstallScript has a special data type called a LIST. In actuality, this data type is just a pointer to the header of a doubly linked list that is implemented by the runtime engine and not by the InstallScript engine. A list can hold either a string or an integer and as such is something like an array, which also can hold only one type of data. There are a number of built-in functions in InstallScript that you can use in a script to create and manipulate lists. Some of these functions work only with lists that hold strings and others work only with lists that hold numbers. In the next section you are introduced to arrays in InstallScript and this new data type should be used in place of the LIST data type.

The following code shows how to create a string list and add a first member to it.

```
function Foo()
STRING  szArg;
LIST    lList;
begin
   // You would use the constant NUMBERLIST to create a number list
   lList = ListCreate(STRINGLIST);

   // Adding the first element you can use either the
   //BEFORE constant or the AFTER constant
   ListAddString(lList, "This is a string", BEFORE);

   // The following will display this string in a message box
   ListCurrentString(lList, szArg);
   SprintfBox(INFORMATION, "String List", "Current Element: %s,
                                                      szArg);
end;
```

There are three types of built-in functions in InstallScript that you can use to manipulate lists: Those that create and destroy lists, those that search lists, and those that modify lists. The following tables provide brief descriptions of these functions. For the detailed descriptions, refer to the online or the printed Function Reference that comes with InstallShield for Windows Installer.

Table 13-4 lists the functions you can use to create and/or destroy a LIST object. Where the function name contains an asterisk, you can replace the asterisk by either the token "String" or the token "Item." Function names that end with the term "String" work only with lists that contain strings and function names that end with the term "Item" work only with lists that contain numbers.

Table 13-4 FUNCTIONS FOR CREATING AND DESTROYING LISTS

Function Name	Description
ListCreate	Creates an empty list. Pass it the NUMBERLIST constant if you want a number list or the STRINGLIST constant if you want a list that holds strings. This function returns a handle to an initialized list header. You use this pointer as a parameter to all of the other list functions.
ListAdd*	Adds either a number node or a string node to the list, depending on which variation of the function you use. You cannot add a number node to a string list or a string node to a number list. With this function, you can add the new node either before or after the node defined in the header as the current node in the list.
ListReadFromFile	Adds strings to a string list by reading in the values from a text file. Each line in the text file delimited with a new line and carriage return creates one node for the target string list. There is no similar function for number lists, but you could create one in InstallScript.
ListDestroy	Frees up the memory used by the list header and all the nodes that have been created.

Table 13-5 lists those built-in functions you can use to search and access a list once it is created.

Table 13-5 FUNCTIONS FOR SEARCHING AND ACCESSING LISTS

Function Name	Description
ListCount	Returns the number of elements in the list.
ListCurrent*	Depending on the variation used, returns as a parameter either the number value or the string value stored in the element identified in the list header as the current node.

Continued

TABLE 13-5 FUNCTIONS FOR SEARCHING AND ACCESSING LISTS *(Continued)*

Function Name	Description
ListGetFirst*	Depending on the variation used, returns as a parameter either the number value or the string value stored in the element identified in the list header as the first node in the list.
ListGetNext*	Depending on the variation used, returns as a parameter either the number value or the string value stored in the element that comes directly after the node identified in the header as the current node. This node is then set as the new current node.
ListGetType	An undocumented function that returns the list type of the list identifier (pointer) that is passed to it as a parameter. The return value will be equal to either NUMBERLIST or STRINGLIST.
ListFind*	Depending on the variation used, searches for either a specified number or a string in the list. If found, this element is then set as the new current node. The search for a string in a string list is case-sensitive. It starts from the node identified in the list header as the current element. The search will stop when the first matching element is found.
ListSetIndex	Makes a certain element the current element, based on the index that is passed. This function enables you to traversal the list using special constants. Since a list is implemented as a doubly linked list you can traverse the list both forward and backward one element at a time using the appropriate constants in place of the index value. The list index is zero-based.
ListWriteToFile	Writes the contents of a string list to a text file. Each element in the list is created in the text file as a separate line.

Finally, Table 13-6 lists the functions you can use to modify a list after it has been created.

TABLE 13-6 FUNCTIONS FOR MODIFYING LISTS

Function Name	Description
ListSetCurrent*	Depending on the variation used, enables you to change either the value of the number or the string contained in the current element.

Function Name	Description
ListDelete*	Depending on the variation used, enables you to delete either the current number or the current string element. It only deletes the current element and not the list. Even if you were to delete all the elements in the list you would still need to delete the list header using the ListDestroy() function.

You will notice that there are no specific functions you can use to directly sort a list. We discuss the implementation of a simple algorithm for sorting a list in the section "Working with Lists and Arrays" in Chapter 14.

The array data type

An array is a collection of values of a specific data type. You can create arrays of any of your primitive data types and you can even create arrays of structures and lists if you have a mind to do so. An array performs much the same function as does a LIST data type but it does not have or need a set of functions to manipulate it. All you need is an index to either set or get values in the array. Lists are better performing than arrays if you do a lot of inserts and deletions into the list while arrays outperform lists when it comes to random access.

You can declare an array with a defined size or without giving it an initial size. You can then use the Resize operator to change the size of the array if you want it to grow or shrink. Just as in the C language the indexing of an array is zero-based. The following code shows how to declare and work with arrays.

```
function Foo()
INT   nArray(); // No initial size given to the integer array
begin
   // Size the array so that it can hold 5 values
   Resize(nArray, 5);

   nArray(0) = 0;
   nArray(1) = 1;
   nArray(2) = 2;
   nArray(3) = 3;
   nArray(4) = 4;

   // The following will display the value of 4 in the message box
   SprintfBox(INFORMATION, "Script Test", "Value: %d", nArray(4));
end;
```

You need to be careful when using the Resize operator since you can make your array smaller and lose some or all of your data, as shown in the following code.

```
function Foo()
INT   nArray(); // No initial size given to the integer array
begin
   // Size the array so that it can hold 5 values
   Resize(nArray, 5);

   nArray(0) = 0;
   nArray(1) = 1;
   nArray(2) = 2;
   nArray(3) = 3;
   nArray(4) = 4;

   Resize(nArray, 4);

   // The following will throw an exception since nArray(4)
   // no longer exists
   SprintfBox(INFORMATION, "Script Test", "Value: %d", nArray(4));
end;
```

If in the preceding code you make the array smaller and then larger again, the data is lost and the lost value is reset to 0, as shown in the following code.

```
Resize(nArray, 4);
Resize(nArray, 5);

// The following will display the value of 0 in the message box
SprintfBox(INFORMATION, "Script Test", "Value: %d", nArray(4));
```

The array data type in InstallScript is limited to a single dimension. This means that you cannot declare an array as follows:

```
INT nArray(2)(5); // This will give you a compiler error
```

An array is most useful when it represents a table and you want to perform a table lookup based on an index number. It also lends itself to the use of hashing algorithms, which provide very efficient access to the desired value in the table or array.

We'll complete our look at the InstallScript data types by looking at the one data type that permits you to store different primitive data types as a unit. This is the structure data type.

The structure data type

A structure creates a user-defined data type that collects related elements together; these elements can consist of variables that are of different primitive types. This goes beyond the abilities of the LIST and array data types, which can only collect together elements of the same primitive data type. To define a structure you need to use the typedef keyword and create a block that is defined by the begin and end keywords. To create a structure that defines a geometrical point you would do the following:

```
typedef  POINT
begin
      INT  x;
      INT   y;
end;
```

To declare a variable of this type and assign it a value you would do this:

```
function Foo()
POINT    point;
begin
   point.x = 2;
   point.y = 3;
end;
```

To access the members of this structure you have used the structure member operator, which is a period (.). You can define a structure where the members of that structure are themselves structures. You could create a RECTANGLE structure that consisted of two POINT structures, as follows:

```
typedef  POINT
begin
    INT   x;
    INT   y;
end;

typedef RECTANGLE
begin
    POINT     top_left;
    POINT     bottom_right;
end;
```

Using the structure member operator, you can define a RECTANGLE variable Rect and assign it values that define it as a 2×2 square, as shown below:

```
function Foo()
RECTANGLE   Rect;
begin
   Rect.top_left.x = 2;
   Rect.top_left.y = 1;
   Rect.bottom_right.x = 4;
   Rect.bottom_right.y = 3;
end;
```

The following is a structure definition that represents a row in the Feature table. This lets you see how you can use different primitive data types to define a structure and what rules some of these primitive data types need to follow. There are eight columns in the Feature table. The data types of five of these columns are text strings of varying lengths and the other three columns are two-byte integers. You will use the STRING data type for the text string attributes and the SHORT data type for the two-byte integer attributes. Remember from the previous discussion on these data types that any variable declared in a structure as a STRING must be given a size, and that the SHORT data type inside of a structure has a size of two bytes.

```
typedef FEATURE_TABLE
begin
      STRING      Feature[32];
      STRING      Feature_Parent[32];
      STRING      Title[64];
      STRING      Description[255];
      SHORT       Display;
      SHORT       Level;
      STRING      Directory_[72];
      SHORT       Attributes;
end;
```

Instead of accessing the members of this structure with the structure member operator, you will declare a pointer to this structure and access the members using the structure pointer operator, which is a dash followed by the greater-than symbol (->). You declare a pointer to a structure by writing first the name of the structure followed by the POINTER data type identifier, and then the declared name of the structure.

```
FEATURE_TABLE            Feature_Row3;
FEATURE_TABLE POINTER    pFeature_Row3;
```

You now have to assign an initial value to the pointer variable so that it points at the Feature_Row1 structure.

```
pFeature_Row1 = &Feature_Row1;
```

Now, using the structure pointer operator, you will assign values to members of the structure appropriate for the ShapeDraw_Feature feature created for the ISWI Artist application.

```
pFeature_Row3->Feature = "ShapeDraw_Feature";
pFeature_Row3->Feature_Parent = "Main_Feature";
pFeature_Row3->Title = "Shape Drawing";
pFeature_Row3->Description = "This feature allows the user of" +
                             " the application to draw" +
                             " the \"Hello ISWI\" string" +
                             " inside various geometric shapes";
pFeature_Row3->Display = 8;
pFeature_Row3->Level = 100;
pFeature_Row3->Directory_ = "INSTALLDIR";
pFeature_Row3->Attributes = 8;
```

A structure can contain a POINTER variable that points at a variable of its own type. This enables you to create a linked list where the nodes can be used to store data of different types. This is more robust than the linked list implemented by the LIST data type but to create a linked list using a structure you would need to create all your own functions for manipulating this linked list. A node in a linked list is implemented as follows:

```
typedef  tagNODE
begin
      STRING          string_data;
      INT             integer_data;
      tagNODE POINTER  pNext; // pointer to next element in the list
      tagNODE POINTER  pPrev; // pointer to the previous element in
  // the list
end;
```

You could use this type of definition for a linked list node to implement a doubly linked list.

It is now time to move on and discuss the creation of valid expressions in InstallScript. Here is where we look at the various operators and how to use them in generating expressions.

Expressions

An InstallScript expression is composed of some number of operands and optional operators, the number of each depending on the type of expression being formed. Variable names, array names, constants, function calls, array references, and structure references are all expressions. Applying a unary operator to one of these expressions is also an expression. Combining two or more expressions with a binary operator generates another expression.

An expression that can be assigned a value is called an *lvalue*. An lvalue is used on the left-hand side of an assignment expression but it can be on the right-hand side as well if the expression is returning the value of an address. An expression that can provide a value is called an *rvalue*. An rvalue has to be on the right-hand side of an assignment expression and since it can be a constant, it does not have to have an address associated with it.

We will now look at the various types of expressions you can form using InstallScript.

Arithmetic operators

There are five arithmetic operators in InstallScript, as shown in Table 13-7.

TABLE 13-7 ARITHMETIC OPERATORS

Operator	Function	Usage Description
*	Multiplication	x * y: Multiplies the expressions x and y
/	Division	x / y: Divides expression x by expression y
%	Remainder or modulus	x % y: Provides the remainder of the division of integer expression x by integer expression y
+	Addition	x + y: Adds the value of expression x to the value of expression y
-	Subtraction	x – y: Subtracts the value of expression y from the value of expression x

Keep in mind that all numerical operations in InstallScript are integer operations. Therefore, division will truncate the result and not round the result to the closest value.

For example:

```
function Foo()
INT   nResult;
begin
   nResult = 5/2; // Here nResult will equal 2
end;
```

As I mentioned before, in InstallScript you are working with signed integers, so when performing operations on large numbers you need to be careful that you are not making the number go negative when you do not want it to. See the following code.

```
function Foo()
INT   nResult;
begin
   nResult = 3000000000;

   // nResult interpreted as -1294967296
   SprintfBox (INFORMATION, CAPTION, "nResult = %d", nResult);

   nResult = nResult/2;

   // nResult interpreted as -647483648
   SprintfBox (INFORMATION, CAPTION, "nResult = %d", nResult);

   nResult = 1500000000;

   // nResult interpreted as 1500000000
   SprintfBox (INFORMATION, CAPTION, "nResult = %d", nResult);
end;
```

An arithmetic expression is most commonly used on the right-hand side of the assignment operator, but it can also be used wherever a logical statement is expected, such as in an if statement or a while statement. Arithmetic statements can also be combined with the logical operators, which are discussed in the following section.

Relational and logical operators

Relational and logical operators create expressions that evaluate to TRUE or FALSE. These operators are outlined in Table 13-8.

TABLE 13-8 RELATIONAL AND LOGICAL OPERATORS

Operator	Function	Usage Description
!	logical NOT	!x: Evaluates to FALSE if expression x is TRUE and evaluates to TRUE if expression x is FALSE
<	less than	x < y: Evaluates to TRUE if expression x is less than expression y: otherwise it evaluates to FALSE
<=	less than or equal	x <= y: Evaluates to TRUE if expression x is less than or equal to expression y; otherwise it evaluates to FALSE
>	greater than	x > y: Evaluates to TRUE if expression x is greater than expression y; otherwise it evaluates to FALSE
>=	greater than or equal	x >= y: Evaluates to TRUE if expression x is greater than or equal to expression y; otherwise it evaluates to FALSE.
=	equality	x = y: Evaluates to TRUE if expression x is equal to expression y; otherwise it evaluates to FALSE.
!=	inequality	x != y: Evaluates to TRUE if expression x is not equal to expression y; otherwise it evaluates to FALSE.
&&	logical AND	x && y: Evaluates to TRUE if both expression x and expression y are TRUE; otherwise it evaluates to FALSE.
||	logical OR	x || y: Evaluates to TRUE if either or both expression x or expression y are TRUE; if both expressions are FALSE it evaluates to FALSE.

When you're creating a logical expression in InstallScript, any expression that evaluates to something other than 0 will be considered TRUE. Because the equality operator is the same as the assignment operator, you cannot use an assignment operation where a logical expression is expected. If you try this, the compiler will treat the assignment as a check on equality and your variable will not be assigned a value.

As I mentioned before, the equals sign (=) can both assign a value to a variable and evaluate the equality of two expressions. Even in an expression that you would not think is assessing equality you will get some unexpected results. Take a look at the following code:

```
function Foo()
INT   x, y, z;
begin
   x = y = z = 1;
end;
```

You might think that you have just assigned the value of 1 to all three variables. What actually happens is that this statement is evaluated like this:

```
x = (y = (z = 1));
```

First `z` is evaluated to determine if it is equal to 1: the result is FALSE so the expression `z = 1` evaluates to FALSE, which is 0. Then the expression y = 0 is evaluated: this evaluates to TRUE or 1 since it is initialized as 0. The variable `x` is then set equal to the result of the `y = 0` relational expression which is 1.

When you are using the AND (`&&`) logical operator, both expressions must be TRUE for the logical expression to evaluate to TRUE. When you are using the OR (`||`) logical operator, then only one of the associated expressions must be TRUE for the logical expression to evaluate to TRUE. The logical NOT (`!`) operator evaluates to TRUE when its operand is FALSE or 0 and to FALSE if the operand is other than 0 or is TRUE.

Evaluation of logical expressions is performed from left to right. In addition, arithmetic operators have a higher precedence than relational and logical operators do. See the following code:

```
function Foo()
INT   a, b, c, d, e;
begin
   a = 14;
   b = 2;
   c = 3;
   d = 4;

   // This if statement will evaluate to TRUE and the
   // assignment statement will be executed since c *d
   // gets evaluated first then its value is added
   // to the value of b then the relationship is evaluated.
   if(a = b + c * d) then
```

```
      e = 5;
   endif;
end;
```

I recommend that you make liberal use of parentheses to make this type of expression more readable. A liberal use of parentheses becomes very important when you are creating compound relational tests. For an example, see the following code:

```
function Foo()
INT   a, b, c, d;
begin
   a = 2;
   b = 2;
   c = 3;

   // Here the if statement evaluates to FALSE
   if(!a = c-b) then
      d = 5;
   endif;

   // Here the if statement evaluates to TRUE
   if(!(a = c-b)) then
      d = 5;
   endif;
end;
```

You can use function calls in a logical statement. Using a remainder (modulus) operator to get the remainder of a division operation you can determine whether a number is odd or even.

```
// Here the return value from taking the modulus would be 1
// so the number is odd
if((5%2)=0)then
SprintfBox (INFORMATION, CAPTION, "Even");
else
SprintfBox (INFORMATION, CAPTION, "Odd");
endif;
```

In this if statement, I have made an explicit comparison between the result of the modulus operation and 0. You can use a shorthand approach by using the NOT logical operator, as shown below:

```
// If the return value from the modulus operation is
// non-zero then the NOT operator
// would make the if statement FALSE so the
```

```
// else block would get executed. If the number being tested
// was even then the NOT operator would make the if statement
// TRUE and the first block would be executed
if(!(5%2))then
   SprintfBox (INFORMATION, "Script Test", "Even");
else
   SprintfBox (INFORMATION, "Script Test", "Odd");
endif;
```

It's very easy to use the relational operators such as the operator less-than or the inequality operator. You just want to remember to use parentheses to make sure you are getting the evaluation of the conditional statement that you are expecting.

The SizeOf and Resize operators

The SizeOf operator finds the size of variables and structures and the Resize operator modifies the size of strings and arrays. The syntax of the SizeOf operator is as follows:

```
NUMBER SizeOf(variable name);
```

You cannot use this operator to return the size of a data type such as INT, CHAR, or the like. You first have to declare a variable of this type and then set its size. If you set the size of an array, the SizeOf operator will return the number of elements in the array and not the number of bytes of memory being used. For example:

```
function Foo()
INT   nArray(20), nSize;
begin
   // nSize is set to 20
   nSize = SizeOf(nArray);
end;
```

When you use the SizeOf operator with a VARIANT data type, the VARIANT variable must contain an array or a structure or it will throw an exception.

```
function Foo()
INT   nArray(20), nSize;
VARIANT    vVariant;
begin
   vVariant = nArray;

   // nSize is set to 20
   nSize = SizeOf(vVariant);
```

```
   vVariant = "This is a string";

   // This throws an exception
   nSize = SizeOf(vVariant);
end;
```

The Resize operator has the following syntax:

```
NUMBER Resize(array or string name, new size)
```

You can use this operator as follows to set the size of an array that was declared without a size:

```
function Foo()
INT   nArray(), nSize;
begin
   // This sets the size of nArray to 20
   // and returns the value of 20 to nSize
   nSize = Resize(nArray, 20);
end;
```

You can also use the SizeOf operator with the Resize operator to set the size of one array to be equal to the size of another array.

```
function Foo()
INT   nArray1(20), nArray2();
begin
   // This sets the size of nArray2 to be equal
   // to the size of nArray1
   Resize(nArray2, SizeOf(nArray1));
end;
```

When trying to resize a string variable for which a minimum size was set when it was declared, be aware that you cannot resize it to a size below the established minimum. If you attempt to resize an array below the size specified when the variable was declared, it is a no-op so no harm is done. However, the size returned by the Resize operator will be the new size that you specify, but if this size is less than the minimum size, this value will be incorrect.

```
function Foo()
INT      nSize;
STRING  szStr[10];
begin
   szStr = "ABCDEFGHIJKLMNOPQRSTUVWXYZ";
```

```
    // Here the string is resized down to 15
    // and the last letter contained is 0
    nSize = Resize(szStr, 15);

    // This gives the size of the string as 15
    // and this is good
    nSize = SizeOf(szStr);

    // Here the string is left at a size of 15
    // but the value of nSize is 9 which is incorrect
    nSize = Resize(szStr, 9);

    // This gives the size of the string as 15
    nSize = SizeOf(szStr);
end;
```

The Bitwise Operators

A bitwise operator views its operand or operands as a collection of bits. Each bit can contain a value of either 0 or 1. Using these bitwise operators, you can test and/or set individual bits to one of the two allowed values. Table 13-9 shows the bitwise operators implemented in InstallScript.

TABLE 13-9 BITWISE OPERATORS

Operator	Function	Usage Description
~	bitwise NOT	*~x*: Does a NOT on each bit in expression *x*. This converts all 1s to 0s and all 0s to 1s.
<<	left shift	*x* << *n*: Shifts all the bits in expression *x n* places to the left and fills in the bits on the right side with 0s.
>>	right shift	*x* >> *n*: Shifts all the bits in expression *x n* places to the right and fills in the bits on the left side with the bit that is in the sign bit location.
&	bitwise AND	*x* & *y*: Compares each bit in expression *x* with the bit in the same position in expression *y*; if both bits are 1 then the resultant bit at that position will be set to 1; otherwise the bit will be set to 0.

Continued

TABLE 13-9 BITWISE OPERATORS *(Continued)*

Operator	Function	Usage Description
^	bitwise XOR (exclusive OR)	*x* ^ *y*: Compares each bit in expression *x* with the bit in the same position in expression *y*; if either bit but not both is 1 then the resultant bit at that position will be set to 1; otherwise the bit will be set to 0.
|	bitwise OR (inclusive OR)	*x* | *y*: Compares each bit in expression *x* with the bit in the same position in expression *y*; if either or both bits are 1 then the resultant bit at that position will be set to 1; otherwise the bit will be set to 0.

One of the primary uses of the bitwise operators is to store large amounts of information in a small space. They do this by creating what are called *bit flags* wherein each bit in an integer can be set or not set, and this state can be used to signify a certain action to be taken. Also, shifting bits left or right is a very fast way to multiply or divide a number by 2^n.

You can use the bitwise AND operator in masking operations to set specific bits of a data item to 0 and preserve other bits of the data.

```
function Foo()
INT   nVal1, nVal2;
begin
   nVal1 = 25;

   // nVal2 will equal 9
   nVal2 = nVal1 & 77;
end;
```

The following code demonstrates the effect of the bitwise inclusive OR operator. The major effect is that it will preserve all the bits of both operands.

```
function Foo()
INT   nVal1, nVal2;
begin
   nVal1 = 25;

   // nVal2 will equal 93
   nVal2 = nVal1 | 77;
end;
```

The bitwise exclusive OR operator has the property that if a value is exclusive OR'd with itself it will always produce 0 as the result. In addition, the exclusive bitwise OR can do a swap without the use of a temporary variable. See the following for an example:

```
function Foo()
INT   nVal1, nVal2;
begin
   nVal1 = 25;
   nVal2 = 50;

   nVal1 = nVal1 ^ nVal2;
   nVal2 = nVal2 ^ nVal1;
   nVal1 = nVal1 ^ nVal2;

   // In the message box nVal1 will show as 50 and
   // nVal2 will show as 25
   SprintfBox(INFORMATION, "Script Test",
                       "nVal1 = %d\nnVal2 =%d", nVal1, nVal2);
end;
```

The bitwise left-shift operator shifts the bits to the left and inserts 0s on the right. The effect of shifting is to multiply the value by 2^n where n is the number of places that the bits are shifted to the left. However, because you are dealing with signed integers in InstallScript, this will only work until the sign bit becomes 1 and then the number turns negative. If you shift enough spaces, the number will become 0.

```
function Foo()
INT   nVal1, nVal2;
begin
   nVal1 = 1;

   // nVal2 is equal to 1073741824
  nVal2 = nVal1 << 30;

   // nVal2 is equal to -2147483648
   nVal2 = nVal1 << 31;

   // nVal2 is equal to 0
   nVal2 = nVal1 << 32;
end;
```

The bitwise right-shift operator shifts bits to the right and inserts 0s on the right if the number is positive and 1s on the right if the number is negative. This is what is known as a *logical right shift.*

```
function Foo()
INT   nVal1;
begin
   nVal1 = 1;

   // nVal1 is now equal to -2147483648
   nVal1 = nVal1 << 31;

   // nVal1 is now equal to -1
   nVal1 = nVal1 >> 31;

   // nVal1 is now back to 1
   nVal1 = nVal1 ^ -2;
end;
```

Operator precedence

Precedence of operators in InstallScript is the same as in the C language. Table 13-10 summarizes each InstallScript operator, its precedence, and its associativity.

TABLE 13-10 SUMMARY OF INSTALLSCRIPT OPERATORS AND THEIR PRECEDENCES

Operator	Description	Associativity
( )	Function call	Left to right
[ ]	Array element reference	
->	Pointer to structure member reference	
.	Structure member reference	
-	Unary minus	Right to left
!	Logical negation	
~	Ones complement	
*	Pointer indirection	
&	Address	
SizeOf	Size of an object	
Resize	Resize an object	
*	Multiplication	Left to right
/	Division	

<table>
<tr><th>Operator</th><th>Description</th><th>Associativity</th></tr>
<tr><td>%</td><td>Modulus</td><td></td></tr>
<tr><td>+</td><td>Addition</td><td>Left to right</td></tr>
<tr><td>-</td><td>Subtraction</td><td></td></tr>
<tr><td><<</td><td>Left shift</td><td>Left to right</td></tr>
<tr><td>>></td><td>Right shift</td><td></td></tr>
<tr><td><</td><td>Less than</td><td>Left to right</td></tr>
<tr><td><=</td><td>Less than or equal to</td><td></td></tr>
<tr><td>></td><td>Greater than</td><td></td></tr>
<tr><td>>=</td><td>Greater than or equal to</td><td></td></tr>
<tr><td>=</td><td>Equality</td><td>Left to right</td></tr>
<tr><td>!=</td><td>Inequality</td><td></td></tr>
<tr><td>&</td><td>Bitwise AND</td><td>Left to right</td></tr>
<tr><td>^</td><td>Bitwise XOR</td><td>Left to right</td></tr>
<tr><td>|</td><td>Bitwise OR</td><td>Left to right</td></tr>
<tr><td>&&</td><td>Logical AND</td><td>Left to right</td></tr>
<tr><td>||</td><td>Logical OR</td><td>Left to right</td></tr>
<tr><td>=</td><td>Assignment</td><td>Right to left</td></tr>
</table>

Statements

A statement is the smallest independent unit in an InstallScript. It is any valid expression followed by a semicolon, or it is one of the special statements such as a label. Most commonly, a simple statement is an assignment or a function call. A compound statement is a sequence of statements enclosed by the begin and end keywords. Statements are executed in the order in which they occur, unless special flow-of-control statements change this sequential order. These special flow-of-control statements allow for the conditional or repeated execution of expressions. The conditional execution of statements is implemented by the if, if-else, and switch compound statements. The repeated execution of statements is implemented by the for, while, and repeat statements. The following sections address those statements supported by InstallScript.

The if and if-else statements

An if statement places conditions on the execution of a statement or group of statements. There are a number of different constructs of the if statement, all of which will be discussed here. The general format of the simplest of these constructs is as follows:

```
if[(]expression [)] then
      program statement(s);
endif;
```

When *expression* evaluates to a numerical value different from 0, the program statements within this block are executed. The parentheses around *expression* are optional but using them will make the program much more readable.

```
function Foo()
INT    nVal;
begin
   // This will produce the absolute value of nVal
   if(nVal < 0)then
      nVal = -nVal;
   endif;
end;
```

In the majority of situations you will want to do something else if *expression* does not evaluate to a non-0 value. For this reason, we have the if-else construct. The general format for this construct is as follows:

```
if(expression) then
      program statement(s); // executed if expression is non-zero
else
      program statement(s); // executed if expression is zero
endif;
```

One situation in which you might use this construct was already mentioned in this chapter: you want to determine whether a number is even or odd.

```
if(!5%2)then
      SprintfBox (INFORMATION, CAPTION, "Even");
else
      SprintfBox (INFORMATION, CAPTION, "Odd");
endif;
```

In these constructs you can see that any valid statement within the confines of an if or if-else statement is permitted. This means that you can have an if or an if-else statement, thus nesting the if or if-else constructs. The general format for this type of construct is as follows:

```
if[(]expression [)] then
      if(expression) then
           program statement(s);
      else
           program statement(s);
endif;
else // This else belongs to the outside if statement
      if(expression) then
           program statement(s);
      else
           program statement(s);
      endif;
endif;
```

There is no practical limit in InstallScript as to the level to which you can nest these statements. I have tested a nested if statement that was 30 levels deep and found no problems when I compiled or ran it. However, because it is very common to create a decision based on more than just executing one set of code when a condition is true and another set of code when the condition is false a special construct is available to you. This is the elseif construct and its general format is as follows:

```
if(expression1) then
      program statement(s); // executed if expression1 is non-zero
elseif(expression2)then
     program statement(s);  // executed if expression2 is non-zero
else
     program statement(s);  // executed if expression1 and
                            // expression2 are both zero
endif;
```

You could use the elseif construct to count the vowels, consonants, and spaces in a string variable, as shown in the following example.

```
function Foo()
INT         nSize, nIndex;
INT         aCnt, eCnt, iCnt, oCnt, uCnt, conCnt, spCnt;
STRING      szStr;
begin

   szStr = "This is a string";
   nSize = SizeOf(szStr);
```

```
    for nIndex = 0 to nSize-1
       if(szStr[nIndex] = 'a' || szStr[nIndex] = 'A')then
          aCnt = aCnt + 1;
       elseif(szStr[nIndex] = 'e' || szStr[nIndex] = 'E')then
          eCnt = eCnt + 1;
       elseif(szStr[nIndex] = 'i' || szStr[nIndex] = 'I')then
          iCnt = iCnt + 1;
       elseif(szStr[nIndex] = 'o' || szStr[nIndex] = 'O')then
          oCnt = oCnt + 1;
       elseif(szStr[nIndex] = 'u' || szStr[nIndex] = 'U')then
          uCnt = uCnt + 1;
       elseif(szStr[nIndex] = ' ')then
          spCnt = spCnt + 1;
       else
          conCnt = conCnt + 1;
       endif;
    endfor;
end;
```

When you create a long chain of elseif statements like this, they can be hard to read and might cause errors when they have to be modified. A better way to accomplish the same thing is to use the switch statement. You can use a switch statement if the values being tested are any of the InstallScript data types. Before we move on to the switch statement, however, which is the subject of the next section, there is a special version of the if statement in InstallScript you should know about: the if with the goto statement. The general format for this construct is as follows:

```
if [(]expression [)] goto labelname
```

In this construct, if *expression* evaluates to non-zero then program execution will jump to the line containing *labelname*. A label is an identifier followed by a colon. The section on the goto statement addresses this subject in more detail.

The switch statement

The switch statement is another way to choose between two mutually exclusive options. The switch statement is considered by many to be superior to the elseif statement for implementing this type of functionality. It is more readable and easier to maintain than a long chain of elseif statements. The general format of the switch statement is as follows:

```
switch(expression)
    case value1[, valuen]:
       program statement(s);
    case value2[, valuen]:
```

```
      program statement(s);
   case value3[, valuen]:
      program statement(s);
   case value4[, valuen]:
      program statement(s);
   default:
      program statement(s);
endswitch;
```

The switch statement shown here consists of the switch keyword followed by an expression in parentheses. It is the result of this expression that will be evaluated by the switch statement. Following the switch keyword is a set of case labels followed by a constant expression or expressions delimited by commas. The constant expression(s) are compared against the result of the switch `expression` and the success of the comparison determines which program statements are executed. Just before the endswitch statement there is an optional default label. When none of the case label comparisons is successful, then the code under the default label is executed. Finally, the switch statement is terminated by the endswitch statement, which needs to have a semicolon at the end.

The constant expressions that follow the case label can be of any of the InstallScript data types, including a string constant. Unlike in C there is no break statement required because the implementation includes an automatic break. In other words, you can't implement a fall-through where a series of case statements are all implemented. The closest thing to implementing this fall-through is the ability to include more than one constant for a particular case label.

In the following example you will calculate the number of each vowel, space, and consonant in a string using the switch statement. This is the same thing you did in the example for the elseif statement, except that here you will use a while statement instead of a for loop to cycle through the letters of your string.

```
function Foo()
INT         nIndex;
INT         aCnt, eCnt, iCnt, oCnt, uCnt, sCnt, conCnt;
STRING      szStr;
begin
   szStr = "This is a string";

   while(szStr[nIndex] != '\0') // Continue until the
                                //terminating null
     switch (szStr[nIndex])
        case 'a','A': // Check for both lowercase and uppercase
           aCnt = aCnt + 1;
        case 'e','E':
           eCnt = eCnt + 1;
        case 'i','I':
```

```
               iCnt = iCnt + 1;
            case 'o','O':
               oCnt = oCnt + 1;
            case 'u','U':
               uCnt = uCnt + 1;
            case ' ': // Check for the space character
               sCnt = sCnt + 1;
            default:
               conCnt = conCnt + 1; / Count the consonants
         endswitch;

         nIndex = nIndex + 1; // Increment the string index
      endwhile;
   end;
```

In InstallScript the compiler will let you have the same value for multiple case labels, which can definitely cause problems if you are not careful. Using the same value for multiple case labels can easily happen if you are using a cut-and-paste approach to create your initial switch statement. You will not get a run-time error either.

The for loop statement

You have already seen the use of the for loop in some of the previous examples. The important thing to remember about the for loop is that it is designed to loop through a block of statements a fixed number of times. Depending on the condition of the for loop, it may terminate before it executes any statements. The general format of the for loop statement is as follows:

```
for init-expression to | downto expression1 [step expression2]
    program statement(s);
endfor;
```

The *init-expression* sets the initial value of the for loop's index. The index can be assigned a value using any expression that provides a numerical value. The second element of the for loop is either the to keyword or the downto keyword. The to keyword sets the for loop mode of operation so that the loop's index is incremented and the downto keyword sets the mode of operation so that the index is decremented. The purpose of *expression1* is to determine when the looping operation should be terminated. When the for loop's index is incremented or decremented so that is greater or less, depending on the for loop's mode, than the numerical value specified in *expression1* then the program execution exits the loop and continues with the first statement following the endfor keyword.

The default operation of the for loop is to increment or decrement the index by one. You can change this default operation by using the step keyword followed by an expression (*expression2*) that evaluates to a numerical value. This value will then be to the number by which the index is incremented or decremented.

If you use a value of zero for *expression2* you will create an infinite loop. This may be what you want to do but you will need to use a goto combined with an if statement to break out of this infinite loop.

In the example showing the use of the for loop statement you first use a for loop to assign values to an integer array and then use a nested for loop to perform a bubble sort on this array. You sort the array into ascending order as follows:

```
function Foo()
INT         nSize, nIndex;
INT         nArray(20), nVal, i, j;
begin

   nVal = -1;
   nSize = SizeOf(nArray);

   // Use this to initialize the array elements
   // This will create alternating negative and positive values
   for nIndex=0 to nSize-1
      nArray(nIndex) = nIndex * nIndex * nVal + nVal;
      nVal = nVal * -1;
   endfor;

   // Display the values of the array before it is sorted
   for i=0 to nSize-1
      SprintfBox (INFORMATION, "Before Sort",
                      "Array value: %d at index = %d", nArray(i),i);
   endfor;

   // Perform a bubble sort on nArray
   for i=0 to nSize-2
      for j=i+1 to nSize-1

          // We use our bitwise approach for swapping values
          if(nArray(i) > nArray(j)) then
               nArray(i) = nArray(i) ^ nArray(j);
               nArray(j) = nArray(j) ^ nArray(i);
               nArray(i) = nArray(i) ^ nArray(j);
```

```
            endif;
        endfor;
    endfor;

    // Display the values of the array after it is sorted
    // This is to make sure that it worked as expected
    for i=0 to nSize-1
        SprintfBox (INFORMATION, "After Sort",
                       "Array value: %d at index = %d", nArray(i), i);
    endfor;
end;
```

If you want to break out of a for loop statement prior to its completion, you can do this with the special if statement with the goto syntax. You cannot, however, define a label inside a for loop. If you do define a label inside a for loop, you will get a compiler error.

The while statement

The while statement repeatedly executes a block of statements as long as a certain condition remains TRUE. Based on the evaluation of the condition it is possible that the program statements contained within the while statement will not be executed. The general syntax for this statement is as follows:

```
while [(] condition [)]
        program statement(s);
endwhile;
```

The parentheses around `condition` are optional, but using them will make the program much more readable. The while statement is particularly valuable because you do not have to know in advance how many times the program statement is to be executed; you let the `condition` expression determine that. Even the for statement does not require you to know in advance how many iterations you're going to have. The distinguishing characteristic of the for statement is just that index variable is incremented/decremented automatically while the while statement does not have the concept of index variables and can base iterations on a variety of conditions.

The following are two examples of using the while statement in situations where you do not know in advance how many loops will be required. The first example is simple: calculating the greatest common divisor (GCD) of two positive integers. To implement this algorithm you need to use the modulus operator that we discussed earlier in the chapter.

```
function Foo()
INT         nTemp, nNum1, nNum2;
INT         nOrigNum1, nOrigNum2;
```

```
begin
   // Set the values for which the GCD is to be calculated
   nNum1 = 1026;
   nNum2 = 405;

   // Save these values for use in the SprintfBox
   nOrigNum1 = nNum1;
   nOrigNum2 = nNum2;

   // Implement Euclid's procedure for finding the GCD
   while(nNum2 !=0)
      nTemp = nNum1%nNum2;
      nNum1 = nNum2;
      nNum2 = nTemp;
   endwhile;

   SprintfBox(MB_OK, "Script Test", "The GCD of %d and %d = %d",
                             nOrigNum1, nOrigNum2, nNum1);
end;
```

The second example is a little more complicated because you need to use nested while statements. Again, you are using the while statement because you do not know in advance how many loops will be required to obtain the desired result. This example shows how to calculate a certain quantity of prime numbers. The first prime integer is defined as being 2. Again you need to make use of the modulus operator.

```
function Foo()
INT   nTest, nPrimes, nDiv;
INT   nPrimeArray(), i;
BOOL  bIsPrime;
begin
   nTest = 2;
   nPrimes = 1;

   Resize(nPrimeArray, 1);
   nPrimeArray(0) = 2;

   while(nPrimes <= 20)

      // Assume at the start that the nTest is a prime number
      bIsPrime = TRUE;
      nDiv = 2;

      // Test the target number up to one-half its value
```

```
      while(nDiv <= nTest/2 && bIsPrime)
           bIsPrime = nTest%nDiv;
           nDiv = nDiv + 1;
      endwhile;

      if(bIsPrime) then
           nPrimes = nPrimes + 1;
           Resize(nPrimeArray, nPrimes);

           nPrimeArray(nPrimes-2) = nTest;
      endif;

      nTest = nTest + 1;
   endwhile;

   // Print out the values calculated to verify it worked
   for i=0 to 19
      SprintfBox (INFORMATION, "Script Test", "Prime # = %d",
                                                   nPrimeArray(i));
   endfor;
end;
```

As with the for loop statement you cannot define a label inside of a while statement. You can, however, use the special goto with an if statement in order break out of a while loop before it finishes.

The repeat statement

As you have seen with both the for loop statement and the while statement there are situations where these statements might not be executed at all. Also the condition for the execution of these looping constructs must be set outside of the statement structure. With the repeat statement, you are guaranteed that the statement body will be executed at least once because the condition is not evaluated until the end of the loop. The general syntax of this statement is as follows:

```
repeat
    program statement(s);
until [(] condition [)];
```

Note that the parentheses are optional but it is best to use them for the sake of readability. With this construct, the looping will continue until *condition* evaluates to TRUE; then program execution will exit the loop and continue with the first program statement after the repeat statement.

In the following example, I use the repeat statement to reverse the digits of a number and display this operation as it occurs.

```
function Foo()
STRING      szNumber;
INT         nValue;
VARIANT     vRightDigit;
begin
   nValue = 12345;

   repeat
      vRightDigit = nValue%10;

      // Convert the right digit to a string using the
      // properties of the VARIANT data type
      szNumber = szNumber + vRightDigit;

      // Knock off the right-most digit
      //and repeat the operation
      nValue = nValue/10;
      SprintfBox (INFORMATION, "Script Test",
                     "Reversed Number = %s", szNumber);
   until (nValue = 0);
end;
```

If you were to use a while statement to perform this manipulation, you would have to set the condition as nValue != 0. This would, however, prevent you from getting a display if the value of nValue were set to 0.

The goto statement

InstallScript supports the much maligned goto statement. This statement provides unconditional branching from the point where the goto statement is encountered in the code to the location in the code where a label statement is defined. The general syntax for this statement is as follows:

```
goto Label;
```

`Label` is an identifier provided in the code. The `Label` identifier can only be used as the target of the goto statement and this label must be terminated with a colon. You cannot jump from one function to another using this statement, which means that inside a function the target of the goto statement must be defined inside that same function. You are also not allowed to immediately precede the end statement of a function with a label. You can get around this restriction using the null statement like this:

```
Label:;
end;
```

The semicolon by itself is termed a null statement. If you use it as shown above, you can place the label immediately before the end statement.

If you want to read more about the controversy surrounding the goto statement in programming and how that controversy got started, refer to the book *Code Complete* by Steve McConnell (Microsoft Press, 1993). The first section of Chapter 16 of this book provides an excellent discussion on this topic.

The return, exit, and abort statements

The return, exit, and abort statements allow termination of function execution when conditions merit. The return statement ends a function's execution and returns control and a return value to the parent routine at the statement that follows the point where the function was originally called. The general syntax of the return statement is as follows:

```
return [[(]value [)]];
```

You can return the value of any data type supported by InstallScript. Returning an integer value from a function is optional and placing parentheses around the value being returned is also optional.

The syntax of the exit and abort statements is as follows:

```
exit;
abort;
```

The difference between exit & abort is that the former is used to perform normal termination while the latter is used for abnormal termination. You need to be very careful when using these statements because they will shut down the InstallScript engine and you will not be able to execute any further custom actions in the current sequence.

Functions

In a normal programming environment you have a main program and you create the functionality you require in separate code units called functions. These functions are then called from the main program to implement the specific purpose of the application. A function is identified by its name and a list of parameters enclosed in parentheses. A function generates a result that can be returned to the calling program either through the return type of the function, through a parameter passed to the calling function, or both.

In the InstallShield for Windows Installer environment, the units of code that you deal with are functions and only functions. There is no main program from which you call the functions you create. Every function that you create in ISWI is either a private function or an entry-point function that you call to implement a custom action.

There are four types of functions that you can use in creating custom actions in ISWI: built-in functions, user-defined functions, functions implemented in a dynamic-linked library, and event handler functions. These four types of functions are the subjects of the following four subsections.

The built-in functions

The InstallScript engine provides a set of functions that have already been created and made available for use. These functions are described in the online help as well as in the Function Wizard available from the Edit→Insert pulldown menu option. The operation of the Function Wizard has already been described Chapter 12. For the built-in InstallScript functions the isrt.h header file provides the function prototypes for all the built-in functions. The online help provides sample scripts that use each of the built-in functions.

User-defined functions

User-defined functions are the functions that you create to implement a custom action. In general, to create a user-defined function you need to create a prototype for the function and implement the function body. You will create either a private function or an entry-point function. The entry-point function is what you will call to implement a custom action; a private function is what the entry-point function will use in its implementation of the custom action. Each of these two types of functions has a specific syntax that you must use when you create a prototype.

PROTOTYPING USER-DEFINED FUNCTIONS

The syntax for the entry-point function prototype is as follows:

```
export prototype func-name(NUMBER);
```

In this prototype the export keyword identifies the function as an entry-point function. An entry-point function can only have one parameter and the data type of that parameter must be NUMBER. By convention, the name you should use when implementing your entry-point function for this parameter is hMSI. The compiler will not object if you add more parameters to this function, but it will not work as a custom action. The Windows Installer expect a function that only needs the handle to the install session. A function that needs additional parameters will not be called properly: thus the call will fail.

A private function prototype can have as many parameters as it needs to carry out its intended purpose. In fact, a private function can be prototyped to have a variable number of arguments, as shown in the following example. This is the general syntax for prototyping a private function:

```
[external] prototype [return-type]
                        func-name([parameter-data-type-list], [...]);
```

At the beginning of this prototype is the external keyword. This keyword is only required if the function definition is contained in a script library. It lets the compiler know that it does not need to find the implementation of the function in the current script when a call is made to it. It is the job of the linker to locate where this function is defined.

It is also optional to specify the return type for the function. If no return type is specified the default NUMBER return type is assumed. However, you can specify a STRING or a VARIANT return type for a function. If you do specify one of these return types, you also have to specify it in the function definition.

A private function can take as many 16 defined parameters and it can also take a variable number of parameters. When a function is going to take a variable number of parameters, you denote this with an ellipsis (...). When you want to pass a set number of parameters along with a variable set of parameters, the set number of parameters must be first in the parameter list. The variable number of parameters will then follow the predefined number of parameters. The variable number of parameters is handled as an array inside the function being called. There is an example of this in the next section.

When you pass arguments to a private function, you have the option of passing them by value or by reference. When you pass an argument by value, the private function makes its own local copy of the argument and any changes made to this argument within the private function are not seen by the calling function. This is the default operation for any argument that is passed to a private function. However, if you want to send an argument by reference, then you need to use the BYREF keyword when you prototype your function. When you send an argument by reference, the private function does not create a local copy of the argument and any changes that it makes to the value of the argument will be seen by the calling function. Even though the default is to pass an argument to a private function by value there is a BYVAL keyword that can be used in order to make your code more readable.

As an example, you could have a private function that is passed a string literal and the string with the characters reversed is passed back to the calling function through a second argument. You would prototype such a function as follows:

```
prototype ReverseString(BYVAL STRING, BYREF STRING);
```

CREATING AND USING USER-DEFINED FUNCTIONS

The best way to explain the creation and use of a user-defined function is to give an example. In the following example, you have a small private function that sums an undefined quantity of numbers and then returns the result as part of a string.

This gives you a chance to look at the use of a return type other than the default, and also to look at the use of a variable set of parameters.

```
#include "isrt.h"
#include "iswi.h"

#define     CAPTION     "Script Test Feedback"

export prototype ScriptTest(NUMBER);

// Prototype a STRING return type and a variable number of
// parameters to be passed.
prototype STRING SumArray(NUMBER, ...);


///////////////////////////////////////////////////////////////////////
//
// Function:  ScriptTest
//
// Purpose:   This is the entry point function used to run
//            our scripting test examples
//
//
///////////////////////////////////////////////////////////////////////
function ScriptTest(hMSI)
STRING     szFormat, szValue;
begin

     szFormat = "%s";

     szValue = SumArray(10 ,0,1,1,2,3,5,8,13,21,34);
     SprintfBox(INFORMATION, CAPTION, szFormat, szValue);

end;

// The variable number of parameters is handled by
// the nArray parameter
function STRING SumArray(nNum, nArray)
INT   i, sum;
STRING     szResult;
begin

     // Sum the array of numbers passed to the function
     for i=0 to nNum-1
        sum = sum + nArray(i);
```

```
    endfor;

    // Generate the buffer for returning to the calling function
    Sprintf(szResult, "The sum of the array is %d", sum);

    return szResult;

end;
```

In this small example, you have summed the first 10 values of the Fibonacci sequence and returned this calculation as a STRING data type. You didn't really need to pass the number of values to be summed as a parameter; you could have used the SizeOf operator inside the function instead. I used this example solely to show that you can have a mix of defined and variable number of parameters.

When using private functions, you need to be constantly aware of the fact that all variables declared inside your function cease to exist once the function has returned to the calling routine. If you have defined a global and a local variable of the same name, the local variable will take precedence over the global variable. You may ask, How can the value of a local variable be returned to the calling routine and still be valid? The answer is that behind the scenes the compiler assigns your local variable to a global variable and this is how you can return a STRING or VARIANT data type. The name of this global variable is LAST_RESULT and we discussed it in the last chapter when we discussed using the Watch Window in the Debugger.

A common method for returning values from a private function is to pass an [out] variable to the function and have the function fill in the value for this variable. This approach is required when more than one value is to be returned from a function. This variable or variables are then available for use in the calling routine. For a function parameter to be an [out] variable it must be defined as being passed BYREF, meaning that the parameter is being passed by reference and not by value. You could change your previous example so that you get the result back through a parameter instead of as the return value from the function. The following code demonstrates this; since you are not returning anything from the function you can use the VOID keyword to indicate that this is the case.

```
#include "isrt.h"
#include "iswi.h"

#define     CAPTION     "Script Test Feedback"

export prototype ScriptTest(HWND);

// Declare that function as returning VOID since the value
// you desire is being passed through a parameter
prototype VOID SumArray(NUMBER, BYREF STRING, ...);
```

```
///////////////////////////////////////////////////////////////////////
//
// Function:  ScriptTest
//
// Purpose:       This is the entry point function used to run
//            your scripting test examples
//
//
///////////////////////////////////////////////////////////////////////
function ScriptTest(hMSI)
STRING     szFormat, szValue;
begin

      szFormat = "%s";

      SumArray(10 ,szValue, 0,1,1,2,3,5,8,13,21,34);
      SprintfBox(INFORMATION, CAPTION, szFormat, szValue);

end;


function VOID SumArray(nNum, szResult, nArray)
INT   i, sum;
begin

      for i=0 to nNum-1
           sum = sum + nArray(i);
      endfor;

      Sprintf(szResult, "The sum of the array is %d", sum);

end;
```

You now have defined your private function to return the requested information through a passed parameter defined as being passed by reference. If you do not use the BYREF keyword, the compiler defaults to treating the parameter as being passed by value and in this case the function will make its own copy of the parameter and use that in its operation. When the function ends, however, this variable will go out of scope and the calling function will see no change in the parameter that it passed.

The name of every user-defined function you create, whether an exported function or a private function, will appear in the tree control to the left of the Script Editor panel beside a blue icon. This is shown in Figure 13-3.

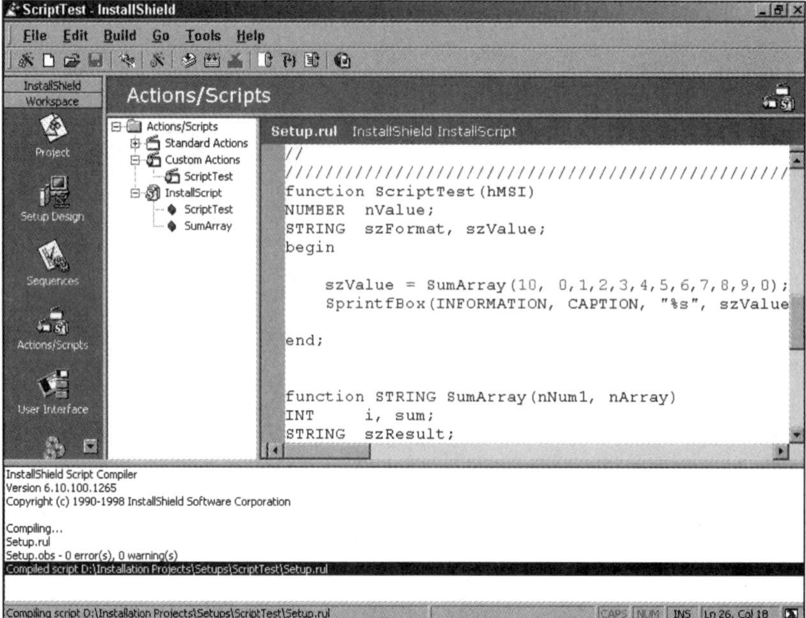

Figure 13-3: Script Function view in ISWI showing tree list of all define functions

Even though all the functions that you define show up in the tree control, only the exported functions are available to you in the Custom Action Wizard. This is useful because it means you can click any function name in the tree control and be taken directly to that function's definition in the script. This is a big help in navigating a large script.

Functions in a dynamic-linked library

With InstallScript, you can create functionality in a dynamic-linked library that you can call from within your script. You can also call Windows APIs from your script. To take advantage of this functionality you need to prototype these functions in a special way.

PROTOTYPING THE FUNCTION

To prototype functions in a dynamic-linked library that you have created yourself, you need to use the following syntax:

```
prototype [calling-convention] DLL-name.exported-func-name
                               ([parameter-data-type-list]);
```

InstallScript has two keywords that you can use to specify the calling convention used by the DLL function. These keywords are stdcall and cdecl. If you do not specify a calling convention then the stdcall convention is used by InstallScript.

Most Windows APIs use the stdcall calling convention where as DLLs created using Visual C++ have a default calling convention of cdecl.

In Chapter 10 there is a sidebar that discusses in detail the various calling conventions as well as the name decoration of exported functions. The title of this sidebar is Calling Conventions, Exporting Symbols, and Name Decoration in Dynamic Link Libraries Create with Microsoft Visual C++.

When you want to prototype one of the Windows APIs, you first need to know from which Windows DLL the API is exported. You can find this out in the MSDN Library description of the particular API you are interested in. For most of your needs the Windows API you want to use will be in Kernel32.dll, User32.dll, or GDI32.dll. For each of these DLLs there is a symbolic constant you can use when you prototype the API. The general syntax to use for prototyping these APIs is as follows:

```
prototype KERNEL32|USER32|GDI32.API-name(parameter-data-type-list);
```

Refer to Chapter 10 for a discussion of name decoration for functions exported from a dynamic-linked library. To properly call an exported function from your script you need to know the exact exported name of that function.

USING THE FUNCTION

To use a function in a dynamic-linked library that you create you need to load that DLL into memory before you can call your functions. To do this you need to use the built-in function UseDLL. UseDLL is essentially a wrapper around a call to the LoadLibrary() Windows API. The UseDLL function has the following declaration:

```
NUMBER UseDLL(
    STRING szDLLName  // Full path to the DLL location
);
```

The return value from this function lets you know the success or failure of the attempt to load this DLL into memory. A failure to load the DLL is most commonly caused by an incorrect path being specified for the DLL's location.

After you have invoked this function, you can make the calls to any of the functions you have exported from this DLL. After you have finished using the functions in the DLL, you need to free the DLL from memory. To do this you will need to use the UnUseDLL built-in function. This function is a wrapper around the FreeLibrary() Windows API. The UnUseDLL function has the following declaration:

```
NUMBER UnUseDLL(
    STRING szDLLName  // Full path to the DLL location
);
```

When you want to call a Windows API function, you do not need to load it into memory or free it from memory since Windows takes care of that for you when it starts up. In Appendix E you will find a list of the Windows APIs that are already prototyped for you.

Event-handler functions

An event handler function is a special function that is automatically executed at the beginning and end of each sequence. There are two of these functions, OnBegin() and OnEnd(), and they are already prototyped in the header file iswi.h. The default implementation of these two event handlers is a no-op, which means that they are empty functions. Use them when you want to perform some special operations at the start and end of each sequence. To do this you would implement these functions in your script and essentially override the built-in implementation.

We discuss the actual use of these two functions in more detail in the Preliminaries section of Chapter 16 when we talk about creating custom actions using InstallScript.

Summary

In this chapter, you have taken an extensive tour through the components of the InstallScript language, including the available data types, the use of operators to create expressions, and the statements that provide you with the ability to control the flow of execution of your programs. At the end you took a look at how you can extend the functionality of the language by creating your own functions either in InstallScript or in a DLL. You have seen that you can also access the many functions provided by the Windows operating system.

This chapter has prepared you for the next chapter, where you get into actually seeing the things you can do with the language. In the next chapter you will use the various capabilities of InstallScript to see the different methods you can develop for extending the base capability of the language. Then, in Chapter 15, you will actually create some practical custom actions using the scripting language.

Part IV

Advanced Concepts

Chapter 14

Advanced InstallScript

IN THIS CHAPTER

- Working with stings in InstallScript
- Passing strings to functions
- Working with the LIST data type
- Working with arrays in InstallScript
- Working with structures
- Using exception handling in InstallScript

NOW THAT YOU KNOW what InstallScript is all about you can take a look at how to use it for typical programming tasks. In this chapter you will work through a number of examples showing how to create meaningful scripts. We start with how to work with strings and then move on to arrays, lists, and structures. We then cover how to perform exception handling in InstallScript and finally how to interface with COM.

Working with Strings

In InstallScript, you can work with strings both as strings and as path names. You can use several special operators and a number of built-in functions when working with strings.

Strings as strings

One of the built-in functions is the StrCompare(szString1, szString2) function, which compares two strings and returns a value that is –1 if string1 is less than string2, 0 if the strings are equal, and 1 if string1 is greater than string2. The only problem with this function is that it does the comparison on a case-insensitive basis.

As a general example of working with strings, try creating a string comparison function that allows you to perform either a case-insensitive or a case-sensitive comparison of two strings. Call this function StrCompareEx(), and in addition to passing in as parameters, the two strings to be compared, pass in a parameter that will tell the function how you want this comparison to be performed. The code for this function is shown below; you will be using it in other examples in this chapter.

```
//////////////////////////////////////////////////////////////////////
//
// Function:  StrCompareEx
//
// Purpose:   This function
// compares two strings for equality. The comparison can be
// performed on case sensitive or non-case sensitive basis.
//
//////////////////////////////////////////////////////////////////////
function StrCompareEx(szStr1, szStr2, bCase)
INT       nReturn, nLen1, nLen2, i;
begin

    // The following assignment is not really necessary
    // since all NUMBER data types are initialized to zero
    // when they are declared. An explicit assignment has been
    // done to make it clear what the starting values are.
    i = 0;
    nReturn = 0;

    // Get the length of each string to be compared
    // All else being equal the longer string is the greater
    nLen1 = StrLength(szStr1);
    nLen2 = StrLength(szStr2);


    // If it is to be a case insensitive comparison
    // change  both strings to be upper case.
    if(!bCase) then
       StrToUpper(szStr1, szStr1);
       StrToUpper(szStr2, szStr2);
    endif;

    // Compare each string character by character
    // and the first character that is different
    // determines the result of the comparison.
    // The comparison with '\0' for strings greater than
    // 260 characters fails in ISWI 1.52 but is fixed in
    // version 2.0
    while(szStr1[i] != '\0' && szStr2[i] != '\0')
       if(szStr1[i] < szStr2[i]) then
```

```
            return -1;
        elseif(szStr1[i] > szStr2[i]) then
            return 1;
        endif;
            i = i + 1;
    endwhile;

    // If all characters are the same up to the end of the
    // shortest string then the string length determines
    // the result of the string comparison.
    if(nLen1 = nLen2) then
        return 0;
    elseif(nLen1 > nLen2) then
        return 1;
    elseif(nLen1 < nLen2) then
        return -1;
    endif;

    return 0;

end;
```

In the above function, you used two of the built-in string manipulation functions. These are StrLength() and StrToUpper(). The condition expression for the while loop provides an example of a complex logical expression and shows that the null terminator for a string is the `'\0'` character. Ten functions are available for manipulating strings as strings. Table 14-1 gives a brief description of each of these functions.

TABLE 14-1 BUILT-IN FUNCTIONS FOR MANIPULATING STRINGS AS STRINGS

Function Name	Description
CopyBytes	Copies a specified number of bytes from one string to another string. You can specify offset indexes into the source and destination strings if you do not want to start copying from the beginning of the string.
NumToStr	Converts a number to a string and returns this value as an [out] parameter of the function.
StrCompare	Performs a comparison of two strings. This comparison is case-sensitive manner.

Continued

Table 14-1 BUILT-IN FUNCTIONS FOR MANIPULATING STRINGS AS STRINGS *(Continued)*

Function Name	Description
StrFind	Determines if one string contains another string. If the string is found, this function will return the index of the first character of the first occurrence of the string. The search is case-insensitive.
StrGetTokens	Extracts sub-strings from a string and places them into a string list. The sub-strings are identified by being separated by a list of one or more characters that make up a set of delimiters.
StrLength	Returns the length of a string in bytes passed to it as a parameter. When working with multi-byte character strings, this will provide an incorrect value as to the true length of a string. You should get into the habit of using the function that is described next. Also, if a string passed to this function has embedded null characters, it will return the length up to the first null character only. To get the length of any string that has embedded null characters, you need to use the SizeOf operator.
StrLengthChars	Returns the number of characters in a string. You can get the correct number of characters even if you pass this function a multi-byte character string. If the string passed to this function has embedded null characters it, it will return the length of the string in characters up to the first null character. To get the length of any string that has embedded null characters you need to use the SizeOf operator.
StrSub	Copies part of a string to another string. The sub-string to copy is defined by a starting point in the source string and the number of bytes to copy.
StrToLower	Converts all the alphabetic characters in a string to lower case.
StrToNum	Converts a string to a number, much like the C function atol(). The first character can be a plus (+) or a minus (-) sign, but the remaining characters in the string must be numeric. After the optional plus or minus sign this function will convert all numeric characters to numbers up to the first alphabetic character it finds. At that point it will return the value already converted. If it finds no numeric characters, the function will fail.
StrToUpper	Converts all the alphabetic characters in a string to upper case.

For a complete description of these string-related functions you need to refer to the on-line language reference. The on-line reference provides examples of the use of these functions.

Two or more strings are often concatenated into one longer string. You can do this easily in InstallScript by overloading the plus (+) sign so that it can operate on strings as well as numbers. The following code snippet shows the use of this operator.

```
function Foo()
STRING  szStr1, szStr2, szStr3;
begin
   szStr1 = "This is string number 1";
   szStr2 = "This is string number 2";

   szStr3 = szStr1 + " and " + szStr2 + " and they " +
                "have been concatenated together";
end;
```

The above code shows that you can concatenate string variables with string literals and that you can continue on multiple lines as long as you terminate the string with either double or single quotes before continuing on the next line.

Sometimes when searching for a sub-string in another string you only need to know if it is there and not what its location is. To accommodate this need InstallScript has the string find operator, which is the percent sign (%). Since this operator only tells you if the sub-string exists in the parent string it returns a Boolean: TRUE or FALSE. You can only use a construct using this operator where a logical expression is allowed. The following code snipped gives an example of the basic function of this operator.

```
parent_string % sub_string
```

You can use this in if, while, and repeat statements, as shown in the following code.

```
function Foo()
STRING   szFormat, szStr1, szStr2;
NUMBER   nNum;
begin

   szFormat = "szStr1 = %s\nszStr2 = %s";

   szStr1 = "1";
```

```
    szStr2 = "8532110";

    // Continue to truncate the number until the number 1
    // is no longer part of the string, and then exit the loop
    while(szStr2 % szStr1)
       StrToNum(nNum, szStr2);
       nvNum = nNum/10;
       NumToStr(szStr2, nNum);
    endwhile;

    SprintfBox(INFORMATION, CAPTION, "Final Result\n" +
                                      szFormat, szStr1, szStr2);

end;
```

In the above code I keep changing the parent string until the character 1 can no longer be found, and then I exit the while loop and print the resulting number. I use several string manipulation functions in doing this, and also show an example of using the string concatenation operator in the construction of the output format string in the SprintfBox function.

Another handy capability available to you when you're working with strings is to be able to use strings that have been entered into a string table. In a string table, a string ID identifies each string value in the table. Using the @ symbol you can use a string identifier wherever you would normally use a string constant. For example, the following line of code would display the string `{&Tahoma8}The disk space required for the installation of the selected features.` in a message box.

```
SprintfBox(INFORMATION, CAPTION, "%s", @IDS__IsFeatureDetailsDlg_6);
```

The InstallScript compiler does not interpret the formatting part of the string as the Windows Installer does but takes the whole string identified by the IDS__IsFeatureDetailsDlg_6 string ID.

When you're working with strings, there are a select group of nonprintable characters and some printable characters that have special meaning and these special characters require special treatment to be used in a string. You can insert these characters into a string if you use them as escape sequences. An escape sequence is a backslash combined with a character, which either performs a special function or permits the display of a character that, if used by itself, would not be displayable. Table 14-2 shows the escape sequences supported by InstallScript.

In the next section you will be using the `\\` escape character, because path strings must contain the backslash character. Now let's move on to looking at how to handle strings that define paths to folders and files.

TABLE 14-2 SUPPORTED ESCAPE SEQUENCES

Escape Character	Description
`\n`	Inserts a carriage return and a line feed into the string.
`\r`	Inserts a carriage return only into a string. This will only work for the display device that supports this type of operation. Otherwise this does the same thing as the `\n` escape character.
`\t`	Inserts a horizontal tab into the string.
`\'`	Inserts a single quote into the string.
`\"`	Inserts a double quote into the string.
`\\`	Inserts a backslash into the string.
`\ooo`	Inserts the character whose octal code is equal to ooo.

Strings as paths

When we speak of paths in a 32-bit environment, we are concerned with both filename length and path length. However, even though you are in a 32-bit environment you still need to worry about short filenames, because some targets for an installation might not support more than the 8.3 file naming convention. InstallScript provides a special concatenation operator and a number of functions to help you manipulate paths.

When we talk about paths we mean absolute paths, relative paths, and universal naming convention (UNC) paths. The term path is generic enough to mean filename as well as hierarchy of folder names. In the 32-bit world we often talk about long filenames. What this means is that filenames are limited to 256 characters and paths are limited to 260 characters. The path limit includes the name of the file. The difference between the path length and the filename length is the space required for the drive letter, colon (`:`), and backslash (\) at the beginning of the path, and the NULL terminator (`'\0'`) at the end of the path.

A UNC path denotes a location on a network server that might not necessarily be mapped to a drive letter on the local machine. In any case the same network drive could easily be mapped to different drive letters on different workstations. The format for a UNC path is as follows:

```
\\server_name\share_name\folder name(s)\filename
```

The component \\server_name\share_name\ of this path is equivalent to the drive letter, colon, and backslash of a standard absolute path.

A path string is no different from any other string. The only thing that sets it apart is that a path string is comprised of components that happen to use the double backslash (\\) as a delimiter. Unlike with most other strings, working with a path string consists of extracting these various components from the string and using them in special ways. You could create your own user-defined functions to access the components that make up a path string. However, since InstallScript provides built-in functions for most – if not all – of your needs in this regard, you are relieved of this extra effort.

The special concatenation operator you use when dealing with paths is called the append-to-path operator and it is the caret (^) symbol. This operator ensures that you have backslashes between a path and the subdirectory or filename you are appending. If you have the correct number of backslashes at the end of your path, this operator will only concatenate the second string. If you do not have the proper number of backslashes, they will be added before the second string is concatenated. The following code snippet demonstrates this functionality.

```
szInstallLocation = "C:\\Program Files\\" ^ "InstallShield";
szInstallLocation = "C:\\Program Files" ^ "InstallShield";
```

Both of these lines of code result in the same legal path to the installation location of InstallShield for Windows Installer. The first line just concatenates the two strings and the second line adds the double backslashes and then concatenates the two strings.

A number of built-in functions also enable you to manipulate path strings. With them you can easily convert from long paths to short paths and back again. You can also parse a path and retrieve significant information, such as the drive letter, filename, or file extension. Table 14-3 provides a list of these functions along with a short description of each.

TABLE 14-3 BUILT-IN FUNCTIONS FOR MANIPULATING STRINGS AS PATHS

Function Name	Description
GetDir	Removes the drive letter and colon from a fully qualified path and returns the remainder of the path in a function parameter. If the supplied path name is formulated according to the universal naming convention, then the server and share names are removed from the string and the remainder of the path is returned. If you pass a string that does not have either a drive letter or a UNC format string, then the return will be a null string.

Function Name	Description
GetDisk	Removes the drive letter and colon from a fully qualified path and returns the drive letter with the colon in a function parameter. If the supplied path name is formulated according to the universal naming convention, then the server and share names are returned. If you pass a string that does not have either a drive letter or a UNC format string, then the return will be a null string.
LongPathFromShortPath	Converts a short path name to its equivalent long path name. The short path name must exist on the system or the function will return the same path that was passed. Your short path name cannot have a trailing backslash or the path will not be converted.
LongPathToQuote	Either places double quotation marks around a long path name or removes the double quotation marks from a long path name. Double quotation marks around a long path name are only necessary if the name contains spaces. You will use this function to remove the quotes around a long path name before you pass it to any other function such as LongPathToShortPath.
LongPathToShortPath	Converts a long path name to its equivalent short path name. The long path being converted must exist on the system or the function will return the same path that was passed to it. For a relative path to be converted the current directory needs to be the root of the relative path or the function will not be able to find the path. You can use the ChangeDirectory function to make the current directory the root of the relative path.
ParsePath	Retrieves the specified part of an existing path string without using direct string manipulation. Works with any valid path, including short paths, long paths, and UNC paths that may or may not include a specific filename.
PathAdd	Adds an additional path specification to a search path in the path buffer. The path buffer must be created with the PathSet function before this operation can take place.
PathDelete	Removes a path specification from a search path in the path buffer. The path buffer must be created with the PathSet function before this operation can take place.

Continued

TABLE 14-3 BUILT-IN FUNCTIONS FOR MANIPULATING STRINGS AS PATHS *(Continued)*

Function Name	Description
PathFind	Searches the path buffer for a specific directory. You can specify the directory with either a fully qualified path or the directory name only. The path buffer must be created using the PathSet function before this operation can take place.
PathGet	Retrieves the search path currently stored in the path buffer. The path buffer must be created with the PathSet function before this operation can take place.
PathMove	Repositions a directory in the path buffer to another location. You can also use this function to position the directory relative to another directory or as the first or last item in the path string. The path buffer must be created with the PathSet function before this operation can take place.
PathSet	Creates the path buffer and stores a search path string in this buffer. You can then manipulate this buffer using the other path functions.
StrRemoveLastSlash	Removes the trailing backslash from a path specification.

For a complete description of the above functions you need to access the InstallScript on-line help, which becomes available when you open the Script Editor.

Passing strings to functions

When you consider the passing of strings to functions, you need to understand the difference between passing a string to a user-defined function and passing a string to a DLL function. By default a string is passed BYVAL to a user-defined function. When the string is passed, you do not need to define a size for the string because auto sizing will be performed on the string inside the function. If you do define the size of a string and then pass it to a user-defined function, the defined size will carry over to the function.

When you pass a string to a DLL function and this string is being passed by reference (BYREF), the string is sized to a length of at least 1024 automatically. You can specifically size it to something higher but the minimum size passed to the DLL function will be 1024. Automatically sizing strings to a minimum of 1024 characters is done so as to provide backward compatibility with older scripts that have assumed this type of functionality. If you pass a string to the DLL function by value (BYVAL), it is not sized to a length greater than that to which the calling function has set it. To demonstrate the passing of a string to both a user-defined function and a DLL function, try creating the capability to reverse the characters in a string. You will do this first with a user-defined function and then using a DLL function.

In the following code you are implementing a small private function that reverses the characters of a string and sends this reversed string back to the calling function through one of the arguments. This shows the actual use of the BYVAL and BYREF keywords. As explained in Chapter 13 you could just as easily have returned the reversed string as the return value of the function instead of putting it into one of the function's arguments.

```
///////////////////////////////////////////////////////////////////////
//
//  IIIIIII SSSSSS
//    II    SS                          InstallShield (R)
//    II    SSSSSS                       (c) 1996-2000,
//    II        SS        InstallShield Software Corporation
//    II        SS                 All rights reserved.
//  IIIIIII SSSSSS
//
//    File Name:  Setup.rul
//
//  Description:  InstallShield script
//
///////////////////////////////////////////////////////////////////////
// include files
#include <isrt.h>
#include <iswi.h>

// function prototypes
// entry point functions
export prototype ScriptTest(NUMBER);

// private functions
prototype ReverseString(BYVAL STRING, BYREF STRING);

// global constants
#define    CAPTION         "Script Test Feedback"


///////////////////////////////////////////////////////////////////////
//
//  Function:  ScriptTest
```

```
//
//  Purpose:   This function is
//             the entry point for a custom action that
//             demonstrates the passing of a string to a private
//             function.
//
///////////////////////////////////////////////////////////////////
function ScriptTest(hMSI)
STRING     szStr, szRevStr;
begin

    // Initialize the string variable
    szStr = "This is a test string";

    // Call the private function
    ReverseString(szStr, szRevStr);

    // Display the results of the function call
    SprintfBox(INFORMATION, "Calling User Function",
        "Input String = %s\nOutput String = %s", szStr, szRevStr);

end;


////////////////////////////////////////////////////////////////////
//
//  Function:  ReverseString
//
//  Purpose:   This function is used to reverse the characters in a
//             string
//
////////////////////////////////////////////////////////////////////
function ReverseString(szStr, szRevStr)
NUMBER     i, j, nLen;
begin

    // Get the length of the input string
    nLen = StrLength(szStr);

    // Explicitly assign the indices
    i = 0;
    j = nLen-1;

    // Loop through one half the string swapping the characters
    while(i < j)
```

```
        szStr[i] = szStr[i] ^ szStr[j];
        szStr[j] = szStr[j] ^ szStr[i];
        szStr[i] = szStr[i] ^ szStr[j];

        // Increment the forward index
        i = i + 1;

        // Decrement the backward index
        j = j - 1;
    endwhile;

    // Set the output string to the reversed string
    // Since the input string was passed BYVAL the original
    // input string does not get changed.
    szRevStr = szStr;

end;
```

The next code example shows you how to implement the previous functionality with a function exported from a DLL. This will demonstrate how to pass a string to a DLL function. Following the InstallScript code is the C++ code that implemented the DLL.

```
////////////////////////////////////////////////////////////////////
//
//  IIIIIII SSSSSS
//    II    SS                     InstallShield (R)
//    II    SSSSSS                 (c) 1996-2000,
//    II        SS        InstallShield Software Corporation
//    II        SS               All rights reserved.
//  IIIIIII SSSSSS
//
//    File Name:  Setup.rul
//
//  Description:  InstallShield script
//
////////////////////////////////////////////////////////////////////
// include files
#include <isrt.h>
#include <iswi.h>

// function prototypes
// entry point functions
export prototype ScriptTest(NUMBER);
```

```
// private functions
// This is the prototype for the DLL function
prototype RevStr.ReverseString(BYVAL STRING, BYREF STRING);

// global constants
#define    CAPTION        "Script Test Feedback"


///////////////////////////////////////////////////////////////////
//
//  Function:  ScriptTest
//
//  Purpose:   This function is
//             the entry point for a custom action that demonstrates
//             the passing of a string to a DLL function.
//
///////////////////////////////////////////////////////////////////
function ScriptTest(hMSI)
STRING     szStr, szRevStr, szDLLName;
NUMBER     nReturn, nSize;
begin

    // Set the path to the DLL and then load the DLL into memory
    szDLLName = "D:\\Installation Projects\\Scratch\\revstr.dll";
    nReturn = UseDLL(szDLLName);

    if(nReturn) then
        MessageBox("Failed to load DLL", SEVERE);
        return ERROR_INSTALL_FAILURE;
    endif;

    // Initialize the input string
    szStr = "This is a test string";

    // Get the size of the input string
    nSize = SizeOf(szStr);

    // Size the string variable being passed BYREF to the DLL
    Resize(szRevStr, nSize+1);

    // Call the DLL function
    ReverseString(szStr, szRevStr);

    // Display the results
    SprintfBox(INFORMATION, CAPTION,
           "Input String = %s\nOutput String = %s", szStr,
```

```
szRevStr);

    // Unload the DLL from memory
    UnUseDLL(szDLLName);

end;
```

The following is the source code for the DLL that exports the ReverseString() function.

```
// stdafx.h : include file for standard system include files,
// or project specific include files that are used frequently, but
// are changed infrequently
//


// Insert your headers here
#define WIN32_LEAN_AND_MEAN      // Exclude rarely-used stuff from
                                 // Windows headers

#include <windows.h>
#include <stdio.h>
#include <string.h>


// stdafx.cpp : source file that includes just the standard includes
// ReverseString.pch will be the pre-compiled header
// stdafx.obj will contain the pre-compiled type information

#include "stdafx.h"

;
; Module definition file for the RevStr.dll
;

LIBRARY    "REVSTR"

DESCRIPTION "DLL for reversing the text in a string"

EXPORTS
      ReverseString   PRIVATE

// ReverseString.cpp : Defines the entry point for the
// DLL application.
//
```

```
#include "stdafx.h"

BOOL APIENTRY DllMain( HANDLE hModule,
                       DWORD  ul_reason_for_call,
                       LPVOID lpReserved
                            )
{
    return TRUE;
}


//
// This function will reverse the characters in a string
//
STDAPI ReverseString(LPCSTR szStr, LPSTR szRevStr)
{
    int i, j, nLen;


    // Get the length of the input string
    nLen = strlen(szStr);

    // Copy the input string into the output string
    // All operations will be done directly on the output string
    strcpy(szRevStr, szStr);

    // Initialize the forward and backward indices
    i = 0;
    j = nLen -1;

    // Loop through half the string and switch values
    while(i < j)
    {
        szRevStr[i] ^= szRevStr[j];
        szRevStr[j] ^= szRevStr[i];
        szRevStr[i] ^= szRevStr[j];

        // Increment the forward index
        ++i;

        // Decrement the backward index
        --j;
    };

    return 0;
}
```

The present default action in InstallScript is to size any string variable being passed BYREF to a DLL function to a size of 1024. In the previous code you specifically went through the procedure of sizing the szRevStr variable to the size of the input string. This was important because this default sizing may not continue to be implemented in the ISWI version of InstallScript and of course the actual size of the stirng may be larger than 1024 characters. Because of the way you explicitly specified the size of szStr, your code will be able to handle any change in this default handling of string lengths.

Working with Lists and Arrays

There are many similarities between lists and arrays in that they have a homogeneous data type and they can be expanded or contracted in size rather easily. An array has an advantage over a list because it can hold the VARIANT data type as well as a STRING or a NUMBER data type. A list can only hold a STRING or a NUMBER data type and it cannot hold a VARIANT data type. It is also easier to sort an array than it is to sort a list. With a list, however, it is easier to insert items at arbitrary locations and to delete items in the middle of the list. The main thing that you do with either a list or an array is hold data and then search the list or array to retrieve that data.

An example of sorting and searching a list

The following example presents a complete Setup.rul file that demonstrates the use of a bubble sort on a list and then a binary search of that list. There are built-in functions that enable you to do a sequential search of a list. When the list is short a sequential search is just as fast as any other mechanism, but when you have a long list then you may want to use other means to speed up the search process. Shown in this example is an implementation that enables you to use the same functions on either a numerical list or a string list. Also demonstrated is the use of a function that can take a variable number of arguments and the ability of the VARIANT data type to switch between numbers and strings. You'll use the StrCompareEx function that you developed earlier to do these string comparisons.

```
///////////////////////////////////////////////////////////////////////////////
//
//  IIIIIII SSSSSS
//    II    SS                         InstallShield (R)
//    II    SSSSSS                      (c) 1996-2000,
//    II        SS     InstallShield Software Corporation
//    II       SS                     All rights reserved.
//  IIIIIII SSSSSS
//
//    File Name:  Setup.rul
//
```

```
//  Description:  InstallShield script
//
////////////////////////////////////////////////////////////////////
// include files
#include <isrt.h>
#include <iswi.h>

// function prototypes
// entry point functions
export prototype ScriptTest(NUMBER);

// private functions
prototype Compare(LIST,...);
prototype GetValues(LIST, NUMBER, NUMBER, BYREF VARIANT,
                                                    BYREF VARIANT);
prototype Sort(LIST);
prototype Swap(LIST, NUMBER, NUMBER);
prototype BinSearch(LIST, VARIANT);
prototype StrCompareEx(STRING, STRING, BOOL);

// global constants
#define CAPTION "Script Test Feedback"


////////////////////////////////////////////////////////////////////
//
// Function:  ScriptTest
//
//  Purpose:  This function is
//            the entry point for a custom action that demonstrates
//            the sorting and searching of an InstallScript LIST.
//
////////////////////////////////////////////////////////////////////
function ScriptTest(hMSI)
INT     nCount, k, i, j, nItem, nStart, nReturn;
STRING  szString[10], szItem, szStr1, szStr2;
LIST    nList, szList;
begin

    // Create a number list
    nList = ListCreate(NUMBERLIST);

    k = -1;

    // Initialize the number list
```

```
// What you create here is an arbitrary set of 21 numbers
for i=0 to 20
    ListAddItem(nList, i*i*k, AFTER);
    k = k * -1;
endfor;

// Create a string list
szList = ListCreate(STRINGLIST);

nStart = 65;

// Initialize the string list
// What you create here is an arbitrary set of 21 strings
for i=0 to 20
    for j=0 to 8
        k = nStart + j;
        szString[j] = k;
        if(k=90) then
            nStart = 97;
        endif;
    endfor;

    // Null terminate each string
    szString[9] = '\0';

    // Add the string to the list
    ListAddString(szList, szString, AFTER);
    nStart = nStart + 1;
endfor;

// Perform a bubble sort on the number list
Sort(nList);

nCount = ListCount(nList);

// Loop through the list and display each number value
for i=0 to nCount-1
    ListSetIndex(nList, i);
    ListCurrentItem(nList, nItem);
    SprintfBox (INFORMATION, "Script Test",
                                "Current Item = %d", nItem);
endfor;

// Search the number list for -100
nReturn = BinSearch(nList, -100);
```

```
    // Display the results of the search
    if(nReturn >= 0) then
        SprintfBox (INFORMATION, "Script Test",
                                "Value found at index = %d", nReturn);
    else
        SprintfBox (INFORMATION, "Script Test", "Value not found");
    endif;

    Sort(szList);

    nCount = ListCount(szList);

    // Loop through the list and display each string value
    for i=0 to nCount-1
        ListSetIndex(szList, i);
        ListCurrentString(szList, szItem);
        SprintfBox (INFORMATION, "Script Test",
                                  "Current String = %s", szItem);
    endfor;

    // Search the string list for the string "bcdefghij"
    nReturn = BinSearch(szList, "bcdefghij");

    // Display the results of the search
    if(nReturn >= 0) then
        SprintfBox (INFORMATION, "Script Test",
                               "Value found at index = %d", nReturn);
    else
        SprintfBox (INFORMATION, "Script Test", "Value not found");
    endif;

end;

///////////////////////////////////////////////////////////////////////////
//
//  Function:  Compare
//
//  Purpose:   This function is used to compare values in a list
//             that are passed as an array of two VARIANTs.
//             If the first value is less than the second value
//             then return -1.
//             If the first value is equal to the second
//             then return 0. If the first value is greater than the
//             second value then return 1.
```

```
//
///////////////////////////////////////////////////////////////////////
function Compare(ListID, Values)
INT     nType, nItem;
STRING  szItem;
begin

    // Get the list type
    nType = ListGetType(ListID);

    // If the list is a number list then
    // do a simple numeric comparison
    // If the list is a string list then perform a
    // case-sensitive string comparison
    if(nType = NUMBERLIST) then
        if(Values(0) < Values(1)) then
            return -1;
        elseif(Values(0) = Values(1)) then
            return 0;
        else
            return 1;
        endif;
    else
        if(StrCompareEx(Values(0), Values(1), TRUE) < 0) then
            return -1;
        elseif(StrCompareEx(Values(0), Values(1), TRUE) = 0) then
            return 0;
        else
            return 1;
        endif;
    endif;

end;


///////////////////////////////////////////////////////////////////////
//
//  Function:  Sort
//
//  Purpose:   This function performs a bubble sort on a list
//
///////////////////////////////////////////////////////////////////////
function Sort(ListID)
INT     nCount, i, j;
VARIANT Value1, Value2;
```

```
begin

    // Get the number of elements in the list
    nCount = ListCount(ListID);

    for i=0 to nCount-2
        for j=i+1 to nCount-1
            // Get the values in the list at indices i and j
            GetValues(ListID, i, j, Value1, Value2);

            // Compare the two list values and
            // if the first value
            // is greater than the second value
            // swap the values
            // because you are sorting in ascending order
            if(Compare(ListID, Value1, Value2) = 1) then
                Swap(ListID, i, j);
            endif;
        endfor;
    endfor;

end;


///////////////////////////////////////////////////////////////////
//
//  Function:  GetValues
//
//  Purpose:   This function returns the values of two list nodes
//             without regard for whether they are strings or
numbers
//
///////////////////////////////////////////////////////////////////
function GetValues(ListID, nIndex1, nIndex2, Value1, Value2)
INT     nType, nItem1, nItem2;
STRING  szItem1, szItem2;
begin

    // Get the list type
    nType = ListGetType(ListID);

    // Using the capabilities of the VARIANT type
    // you can work with either a number list or a
    // string list. You just have to use the correct
    // APIs to access the list. Since the return
    // data type is a VARIANT it can hold either
```

```
    // a number value or a string value.
    if(nType = NUMBERLIST) then
        ListSetIndex(ListID, nIndex1);
        ListCurrentItem(ListID, nItem1);
        ListSetIndex(ListID, nIndex2);
        ListCurrentItem(ListID, nItem2);
        Value1 = nItem1;
        Value2 = nItem2;
    else
        ListSetIndex(ListID, nIndex1);
        ListCurrentString(ListID, szItem1);
        ListSetIndex(ListID, nIndex2);
        ListCurrentString(ListID, szItem2);
        Value1 = szItem1;
        Value2 = szItem2;
    endif;
end;


///////////////////////////////////////////////////////////////////////
//
//  Function:  Swap
//
//  Purpose:   This function does an in-place swap of
//             two elements in a list
//
///////////////////////////////////////////////////////////////////////
function Swap(ListID, nIndex1, nIndex2)
INT     nType, nTemp, nItem1, nItem2;
STRING  sTemp, szItem1, szItem2;
begin

    // Get the list type
    nType = ListGetType(ListID);

    // You just need to know the list type
    // so that you can use the correct APIs for swapping the
    // values and the correct data type for the temporary
    // variable used to hold one of values being swapped
    if(nType = NUMBERLIST) then
        ListSetIndex(ListID, nIndex1);
        ListCurrentItem(ListID, nItem1);
        ListSetIndex(ListID, nIndex2);
        ListCurrentItem(ListID, nItem2);

        nTemp = nItem1;
```

```
        nvItem1 = nItem2;
        nItem2 = nTemp;

        ListSetIndex(ListID, nIndex1);
        ListSetCurrentItem(ListID, nItem1);
        ListSetIndex(ListID, nIndex2);
        ListSetCurrentItem(ListID, nItem2);
    else
        ListSetIndex(ListID, nIndex1);
        ListCurrentString(ListID, szItem1);
        ListSetIndex(ListID, nIndex2);
        ListCurrentString(ListID, szItem2);

        sTemp = svItem1;
        svItem1 = svItem2;
        svItem2 = sTemp;

        ListSetIndex(ListID, nIndex1);
        ListSetCurrentString(ListID, szItem1);
        ListSetIndex(ListID, nIndex2);
        ListSetCurrentString(ListID, szItem2);
    endif;
end;


///////////////////////////////////////////////////////////////////////
//
//  Function:  BinSearch
//
//  Purpose:   This function performs a binary search
//             on a sorted list
//
///////////////////////////////////////////////////////////////////////
function BinSearch(ListID, Search)
INT     nCount, nMid, nLow, nHigh, nType;
INT     nReturn, nItem;
STRING  szItem;
VARIANT vItem;
begin

    // Get the list type
    nType = ListGetType(ListID);

    // Get the number of elements in the list
    nCount = ListCount(ListID);
```

```
    nLow = 0;
    nHigh = nCount - 1;

    // Loop through the list until the element is found
    // or nLow is greater than nHigh meaning that the element
    // is not in the list
    while(nLow <= nHigh)
        nMid = (nLow + nHigh)/2;
        ListSetIndex(ListID, nMid);

        // Use a VARIANT to hold either the
        // number or the string value
        if(nType = NUMBERLIST) then
            ListCurrentItem(ListID, nItem);
            vItem = nItem;
        else
            ListCurrentString(ListID, szItem);
            vItem = szItem;
        endif;

        // Based on the comparison results either continue
        // the search in the upper half of the list
        // or in the lower half of the list
        nReturn = Compare(ListID, vItem, Search);

        if(nReturn = -1) then
            nLow = nMid + 1;
        elseif(nReturn = 1) then
            nHigh = nMid - 1;
        else
            return nMid;
        endif;

    endwhile;

    return -1;
end;


//////////////////////////////////////////////////////////////////////
//
//  Function:  StrCompareEx
//
//  Purpose:   This function performs a comparison
//             of two strings
//             and this will be done on a case-sensitive or case
```

```
//              -insensitive basis depending on the value of bCase.
//
///////////////////////////////////////////////////////////////////////
function StrCompareEx(szStr1, szStr2, bCase)
INT     nReturn, nLen1, nLen2, i;
begin

    i = 0;
    nReturn = 0;

    // Get the length of the two strings
    // that are being compared.
    nLen1 = StrLength(szStr1);
    nLen2 = StrLength(szStr2);

    // If it is to be a case-insensitive comparison
    // change all characters to upper case
    if(!bCase) then
        StrToUpper(szStr1, szStr1);
        StrToUpper(szStr2, szStr2);
    endif;

    // Compare each string character by character
    while(szStr1[i] != '\0' && szStr2[i] != '\0')
        if(szStr1[i] < szStr2[i]) then
            return -1;
        elseif(szStr1[i] > szStr2[i]) then
            return 1;
        endif;

        i = i + 1;
    endwhile;

    // If the characters in both strings are the same
    // then the length will determine the comparison results
    if(nLen1 = nLen2) then
        return 0;
    elseif(nLen1 > nLen2) then
        return 1;
    elseif(nLen1 < nLen2) then
        return -1;
    endif;

    return 0;

end;
```

In the previous code example you implemented sorting and searching that is probably easier to do with an array. The same approach you used above to sort and search a list can be easily converted to sort and search an array. You do not need to repeat the above example for arrays but you should examine another aspect of arrays: how to make an array of structures.

The implementation of arrays in InstallScript

You implement arrays in InstallScript the same way you implement arrays in Visual Basic, using the SAFEARRAY. The SAFEARRAY approach was developed in order to get around the problems inherent in the raw C++ array. These problems include a lack of index protection, no size limit, and no initialization. In C++ a SAFEARRAY is a protected data structure accompanied by a set of system functions that allow you to work on this structure. The C++ SAFEARRAY structure for Win32 machines looks like what is shown in the following code.

```
// The C/C++ SAFEARRAY data structure
struct SAFEARRAY {
   WORD     cDims;
   WORD     fFeatures;
   DWORD    cbElements;
   DWORD    cLocks;
   void     *pvData;
   SAFEARRAYBOUND    rgsabound[1];
};
```

With the SAFEARRAY method you need to use a special approach to pass an array to a DLL function. You learn how to do this in the next section.

Implementing the QuickSort algorithm

The following code demonstrates how to implement the QuickSort algorithm to sort an array. To actually use this example you will need to insert it into your code for implementing a custom action. This would be a private function that is called by the function that you export.

```
///////////////////////////////////////////////////////////////////////////////
//
//  IIIIIII SSSSSS
//    II    SS                    InstallShield (R)
//    II    SSSSSS                 (c) 1996-2000,
//    II        SS        InstallShield Software Corporation
//    II        SS               All rights reserved.
//  IIIIIII SSSSSS
//
//    File Name:  Setup.rul
```

```
//
//  Description:  InstallShield script
//
///////////////////////////////////////////////////////////////////////

// include files
#include <isrt.h>
#include <iswi.h>

prototype void Swap(BYREF VARIANT, NUMBER, NUMBER);
prototype void QuickSort(BYREF VARIANT, NUMBER, NUMBER);


///////////////////////////////////////////////////////////////////////
//
//  Function:  Swap
//
//  Purpose:   This function will swap two values in an array
//
///////////////////////////////////////////////////////////////////////
function void Swap(array, i, j)
VARIANT vTemp;
begin
    vTemp = array(i);
    array(i) = array(j);
    array(j) = vTemp;
end;


///////////////////////////////////////////////////////////////////////
//
//  Function:  QuickSort
//
//  Purpose:   This function implements the QuickSort algorithm
//
///////////////////////////////////////////////////////////////////////
function void QuickSort(array, nLBound, nUBound)
NUMBER nLo, nHi;
VARIANT vMid;
begin
    if(nLBound >= nUBound) then
        return;
    endif;

    vMid = array((nLBound + nUBound) / 2);
```

```
    nLo = nLBound;
    nHi = nUBound;

    while(nLo <= nHi)
        while(nLo < nUBound && array(nLo) < vMid)
            nLo = nLo + 1;
        endwhile;

        while(nHi > nLBound && array(nHi) > vMid)
            nHi = nHi - 1;
        endwhile;

        if(nLo <= nHi) then
            Swap(array, nLo, nHi);
            nLo = nLo + 1;
            nHi = nHi - 1;
        endif;
    endwhile;

    if(nLBound < nHi) then
        QuickSort(array, nLBound, nHi);
    endif;

    if(nLo < nUBound) then
        QuickSort(array, nLo, nUBound);
    endif;
end;
```

The QuickSort algorithm is probably the most widely used sorting algorithm. However, you will notice that the implementation of the QuickSort algorithm uses recursion. As I mentioned earlier, recursion can consume stack space on the machine where it is running.

Passing an array to a DLL function

The following example shows how to create an array of DWORDs so that it can be passed to a Win32 API.

```
///////////////////////////////////////////////////////////////////
//
//  IIIIIII SSSSSS
//    II    SS                     InstallShield (R)
//    II    SSSSSS                  (c) 1996-2000,
//    II        SS          InstallShield Software Corporation
```

```
//    II        SS                All rights reserved.
//  IIIIIII SSSSSS
//
//    File Name:  Setup.rul
//
//  Description:  InstallShield script
//
///////////////////////////////////////////////////////////////////////

// include files
#include <isrt.h>
#include <iswi.h>

// Private functions
prototype STRING StreamArray(VARIANT);
prototype BOOL PSAPI.EnumProcesses(POINTER, LONG, BYREF LONG);
prototype POINTER Array2Pointer(BYREF VARIANT);

// entry point functions
export prototype ScriptTest(NUMBER);

// global variables
// Mirroring the C/C++ SAFEARRAY data structure
typedef _SAFEARRAY
begin
SHORT   cDims;
SHORT   fFeatures;
LONG    cbElements;
LONG    cLocks;
POINTER pvData;
/*rgsabound omitted*/
end;

// Mirroring the C/C++ VARIANT data structure
typedef _VARIANT
begin
    SHORT       vt;
    SHORT       wReserved1;
    SHORT       wReserved2;
    SHORT       wReserved3;
    NUMBER      theRealData;
end;


///////////////////////////////////////////////////////////////////////
```

```
//
// Function: ScriptTest
//
// Purpose: This function is
//          the entry point for a custom action that demonstrates
//          the passing of an array to a DLL function.
//
///////////////////////////////////////////////////////////////////////
function ScriptTest(hMSI)
LONG processIDs(512);
LONG cb, cbNeeded;
begin
    cb = SizeOf(processIDs) * 4; // 4 = SizeOf DWORD

    EnumProcesses(Array2Pointer(processIDs), cb, cbNeeded);

    // Shrink the Array to the no. of
    // items returned by EnumProcesses
    // This is needed to prevent StreamArray
    // from outputting junk
    Resize(processIDs, cbNeeded / 4);

    MessageBox(StreamArray(processIDs), INFORMATION);

    abort;
end;


///////////////////////////////////////////////////////////////////////
//
// Function: Array2Pointer
//
// Purpose: This function will typecast an array pointer to a
//          _VARIANT pointer
//
///////////////////////////////////////////////////////////////////////
function POINTER Array2Pointer(array)
_VARIANT POINTER pVariant;
_SAFEARRAY POINTER pArray;
begin
    pVariant = &array;
    pArray = pVariant->theRealData;
    return pArray->pvData;
end;
```

```
///////////////////////////////////////////////////////////////////////
//
//  Function:  StreamArray
//
//  Purpose:   This function dumps an array into a string. Elements
//             are separated by a space.
//
///////////////////////////////////////////////////////////////////////
function STRING StreamArray(array)
NUMBER i;
STRING s;
begin
    for i = 0 to SizeOf(array) - 1
        s = s + array(i) + " ";
    endfor;

    return s;
end;
```

The important function in the preceding code is the Array2Pointer function. When you declare an array variable, a VARIANT variable is created internally. This VARIANT variable holds the SAFEARRAY implementation of the array. In this sense the Array2Pointer function typecasts the pointer to the array to a _VARIANT pointer. This extracts the SAFEARRAY pointer from the VARIANT variable. The pointer to the actual data is extracted from the _SAFEARRAY pointer. The _VARIANT and _SAFEARRAY typedefs are InstallScript versions of the VARIANT and SAFEARRAY structures defined in C++.

Working with Structures

At the time of this writing it is not possible in InstallScript to generate a linked list where new nodes for the list have to be created at run-time. This makes it somewhat useless to try to create a linked list of structures unless you know at compile time how many nodes you are going to have in the list. Accordingly, I will not provide an example of this type of construct.

However, it is possible to create an array of structures. The following example is a complete working Setup.rul file that demonstrates how to create this type of array.

```
///////////////////////////////////////////////////////////////////////
//
//  IIIIIII SSSSSS
//    II    SS                     InstallShield (R)
//    II    SSSSSS                   (c) 1996-2000,
```

```
//    II         SS     InstallShield Software Corporation
//    II        SS               All rights reserved.
//  IIIIIII SSSSSS
//
//    File Name:  Setup.rul
//
//  Description:  InstallShield script
//
////////////////////////////////////////////////////////////////////
//  include files
#include <isrt.h>
#include <iswi.h>

// function prototypes
// entry point functions
export prototype ScriptTest(NUMBER);

// private functions
prototype OBJECT NewNode();
prototype FillNodeArray(BYREF VARIANT, NUMBER);

// global constants
#define CAPTION "Script Test Feedback"

// global variables
typedef NODE
begin
STRING  szStr[50];
INT nCount;
end;


///////////////////////////////////////////////////////////////////
//
//  Function:  ScriptTest
//
//  Purpose:   This function is
//             the entry point for a custom action that demonstrates
//             the creation of an array of structures.
//
///////////////////////////////////////////////////////////////////
function ScriptTest(hInstall)
INT     nNodes, i;
OBJECT  structArray();
begin
```

```
    nNodes = 15;

   try

     // Create and populate the array of structures
        FillNodeArray(structArray, nNodes);

        // Display the values in the array
        for i=0 to nNodes-1
            SprintfBox(INFORMATION,
                    "Script Test", "String = %s\nLength = %d",
                        structArray(i).szStr,
                                  structArray(i).nCount);
        endfor;

    catch
        SprintfBox(SEVERE, "Script Test", "Exception was thrown");
    endcatch;

end;


///////////////////////////////////////////////////////////////////
//
//  Function:  NewNode
//
//  Purpose:   This function returns a new object of type NODE
//
///////////////////////////////////////////////////////////////////
function OBJECT NewNode()
NODE    node;
begin
    // Creates new local version and then
    // sends it to the global variable
    return node;
end;


///////////////////////////////////////////////////////////////////
//
//  Function:  FillNodeArray
//
//  Purpose:   This function creates and populates an array of
//             structures of type NODE
//
///////////////////////////////////////////////////////////////////
```

```
function FillNodeArray(array, n)
INT     i;
STRING  szi;
OBJECT  obj;
begin

    // Size the array for the number of nodes
    // to be stored in the array
    Resize(array, n);

    // Fill the array with arbitrary strings and numbers
    for i=0 to n-1
        // Create a new node for each element in the array
        set obj = NewNode();
        array(i) = obj;
        NumToStr(szi, i);
        array(i).szStr = "This is string #" + szi;
        array(i).nCount = StrLength(array(i).szStr);
    endfor;

end;
```

The secret here is the function NewNode, which returns into a global variable an object of the type defined for the array. The reason that this is possible is that structures are actually COM objects and there is an external reference counting that keeps them alive in memory.

Exception Handling

When your script does something wrong at run time, it is called an *exception*. Exception handling is the mechanism you implement to do something in your code about the exceptions that occur when your script is executing. There are many ways to do exception handling: you can check return values from functions or create special blocks of code to handle exceptions that are "thrown" by the function or block of code to where they are handled appropriately.

The traditional approach

The traditional approach to checking for and handling exceptions at run time is to evaluate the return values from function calls. An example of this is as follows:

```
function Foo()
INT     nReturn, nFileHandle;
STRING  szPath, szFileName;
```

```
begin
   // Assign the file parameters
   SzPath = "C:\\Scratch";
   SzFileName = "TestText.txt";

   nReturn = CreateFile(nFileHandle, szPath, szFileName);

   if(nReturn < 0) then
      // code to handle situation where
      // where the file was not created.
   endif;
end;
```

In this traditional approach, you handle errors where you are doing your normal processing. Many functions have a whole range of return values that represent different types of errors; if this is the case you might use a switch statement after each call to these functions to try to handle each of the error types in the best way possible. A good example of this type of function is the CopyFile InstallScript built-in function that has seven types of error-return codes. With the InstallScript built-in functions, you are stuck with this traditional approach to handling errors, but in user-defined functions you have a much more elegant approach available to you. This modern approach is the subject of the remainder of this section.

The modern approach

With the modern approach to exception handling, you can take care of exceptions in a different part of the code from where you are performing your normal processing. All modern programming languages, such as C++, Java, Visual Basic, VBScript, and JScript, can perform exception handling. InstallScript also has this same functionality, which is designed along the lines of the exception handling found in VBScript and JScript. This mechanism consists of having functions "raise" or "throw" an exception when a run-time error occurs; this exception is then caught and handled by a special block of code. You place the statements and function calls that you know can throw an exception in another special block of code called the try block. In this way, you can if you wish select only a subset of code that needs to be subject to exception handling.

The general syntax for creating this modern approach to exception handling is as follows:

```
try
      // Statements and function calls that may raise an exception
catch
      // Code that is used to handle the exception when one is
raised
      // by the statements and function calls in the try block
endcatch;
```

The try...catch block can be nested inside another try...catch block to an arbitrary depth. Nesting of these blocks would look like the following:

```
try
     // Statements and function calls that may raise an exception
try
     // Statements and function calls that may raise an exception
catch
     // Code that is used to handle the exception when one is
raised

    endcatch;

catch
    // Code that is used to handle the exception when one is raised
    // by the statements and function calls in the outer try block
   try
    // Statements and function calls that may raise an exception
   catch
    // Code that is used to handle the exception when one is raised
    // by the statements and function calls in the inner try block
   endcatch;

    // Code that is used to handle the exception when one is raised
    // by the statements and function calls in the outer try block
endcatch;
```

This raises the question, How does one go about throwing or raising an exception so that all this new exception handling can go to work? An exception can be thrown in several ways. The InstallScript engine will throw an exception under certain circumstances, and the scripting engine will turn a failure HRESULT return values from COM calls into an exception. Finally, you can raise an exception within the script code you write using the same functionality inherent in the VBScript Err object.

To understand how to handle exceptions that are raised when you're accessing the methods of an automation interface, you need to get into detail about the Err object. You will also want to use the functionality of the Err object when you develop your own user-defined functions to implement exception handling.

THE ERR OBJECT

The Err object in InstallScript is very similar to the same object in VBScript. With this object you can design your user-defined functions to respond well to run-time errors. The Err object is intrinsic to InstallScript and it has global scope. You do not need to create an instance of this object since it is already done for you. When used correctly the Err object will tell you what went wrong and where it went wrong.

The Err object has five properties and two methods that are used to implement exception handling. The syntax of the Err object is as follows:

```
Err.<Property_Name> [= value];
```

or

```
Err.<Method_Name>[(argument_list)];
```

You can read a property value by specifying the name of the property to be read and you set the value of the property using the assignment operator. You invoke a method by providing its name and when necessary a list of arguments. The available properties for the Err object are described in Table 14-4.

TABLE 14-4 ERR OBJECT PROPERTIES

Property Name	Description
Err.Number	The default property of the Err object. This numeric value is set at the point where the error occurs and is normally used in a switch statement for handling the error or exception. The range of the permitted values for an error is 0 to 65535. The final value of the error number is the value chosen bitwise AND'd with 0x80040000.
Err.Source	A string that identifies the procedure or object where the error was generated.
Err.Description	A string that provides a short description of the error that has occurred. This string is displayed to the user if the script is not going to handle the error internally and then continue with the installation.
Err.HelpFile	The fully qualified path to the help file where help for this error has been documented.
Err.HelpContext	The context ID of the topic within the help file where help for this error has been documented. The help file will open up to this topic.
Err.LastDllError	This property holds the return value of the WINAPI function GetLastError(). This is useful since calling GetLastError() directly from a script will not yield the intended result since the scripting engine as part of its normal operations, is itself calling a lot of WINAPI functions that set the last error.

The two methods available with the Err object are documented in Table 14-5.

TABLE 14-5 ERR OBJECT METHODS

Method Name	Description
Err.Clear	Clears all property settings of the Err object. This method does not take any arguments. If you do not use it, any properties not reset will carry over for the next Err object defined. The InstallScript engine automatically calls this method on the Err object whenever an Err object is handled in the catch block and a new Err object has not been initialized.
Err.Raise[(number, source, description, helpfile, helpcontext)]	Used to generate the run-time error. When this method is used, there must be a try... catch block somewhere in the calling chain in order for the exception to be intercepted and handled. This method takes as optional arguments any or all of the five properties associated with this object. None of these arguments is required since all of the properties can be set outside prior to the invocation of the method.

Before we get into the actual use of the Err object you need to examine the exception handling hierarchy, which deals with handling exceptions when there is a chain of calls from one function to another.

THE EXCEPTION HANDLING HIERARCHY

Figure 14-1 shows a typical scenario where the entry-point function calls a private function that in turn calls another private function. In this figure the entry point function ScriptTest calls private function fooA and fooA calls fooB. As shown in the figure all these calls occur in a try...catch block.

When fooB is executed an exception is raised. Since this happens inside a try block the exception handling mechanism takes over and tries to handle the exception within its own catch block. If it cannot handle the exception, it raises another error, which then jumps the execution handling to the catch block of the fooA function. If fooA cannot handle the exception, it raises another exception and the attempt to handle the exception starts again in the catch block of the ScriptTest function.

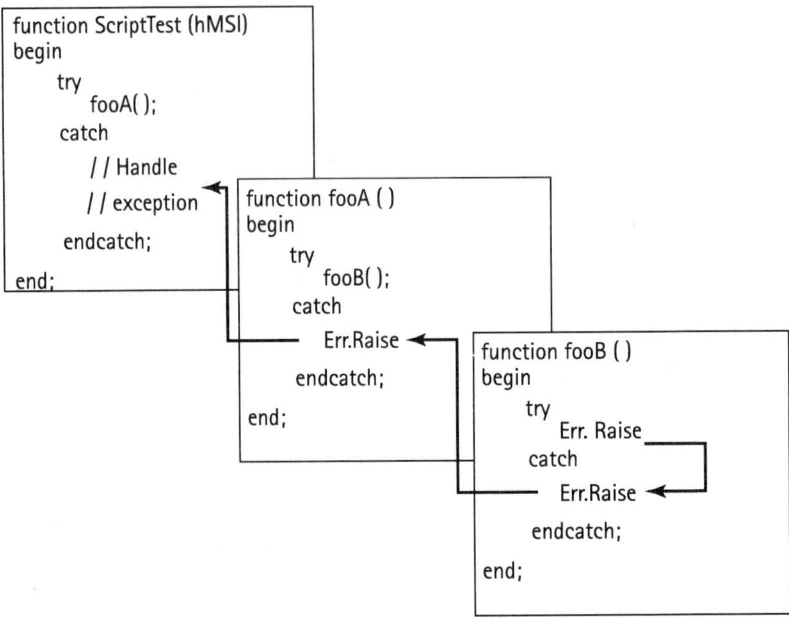
function ScriptTest (hMSI)
begin
try
fooA( );
catch
// Handle
// exception
endcatch;
end;
function fooA ( )
begin
try
fooB( );
catch
Err.Raise
endcatch;
end;
function fooB ( )
begin
try
Err. Raise
catch
Err.Raise
endcatch;
end;

Figure 14-1: A sequence of function calls

Now take the situation where the functions fooA and fooB have not had try...catch blocks implemented. If fooB raises an exception the InstallScript engine will continue up the hierarchy until it can find a function that has an error handler enabled. In this case the function ScriptTest attempts to handle the exception within its catch block.

Now it is time to take a look at how you would actually use the Err object to trap exceptions thrown by the scripting engine or implement exception handling for user-defined functions. First take a look at how you would use the Err object to handle engine-thrown exceptions.

XREF

Chapter 15 covers handling exceptions that are thrown while you're accessing COM.

HANDLING EXCEPTIONS THROWN BY THE INSTALLSCRIPT ENGINE

Table 14-6 lists the seven exceptions that the InstallScript engine will throw based on the circumstances. Most of these exceptions are thrown when something goes wrong when you're trying to access a function in a dynamic-link library.

TABLE 14-6 EXCEPTIONS THROWN BY THE INSTALLSCRIPT ENGINE

Error Number	Description
0x80040701	Occurs when there is an attempt in the script to divide by 0.
0x80040702	Occurs when a dynamic-link library failed to load when the UseDLL() built-in function is called. This can happen if the DLL could not be found, if DLLs on which the DLL that is being loaded is dependent could not be found.
0x80040703	Raised when the DLL function being called cannot be found. This can happen if you are not using the function name as exported from the DLL. If you did not use a module definition file when creating the DLL, the names of the exported functions will be decorated.
0x80040704	Raised when a DLL function call results in a bad stack. This can happen when the prototyping of the function being called in the DLL is incorrect.
0x80040705	Raised when you try to access a string location that is outside the upper bound of the string. For purposes of backward compatibility this exception is not raised until you try to access position 300 in a string that is sized to be less than 300 characters in length.
0x80040706	Raised when you try to use an object variable that is not referring to a valid object.
0x80040707	Raised when you make a call to a DLL function and the DLL function crashes.

The following code shows a generic layout for catching the exceptions thrown by the InstallScript engine. It is a switch statement that provides an error description and then displays this error in a message box. When the user clicks the OK button on the message box, the Windows Installer will get an installation failure message and will abort the installation.

```
function ScriptTest(hMSI)
begin
```

```
try
   // do something that will cause
   // the engine to throw an exception
catch

   switch(Err.Number ^ 0x80040000)
       case 0x701:
          Err.Clear;
          Err.Description = "There was a division by zero";
       case 0x702:
          Err.Clear;
          Err.Description =
             "The installation failed to load a required DLL";
       case 0x703:
           Err.Clear;
           Err.Description =
             "The installation could not find a required DLL
function";
       case 0x704:
           Err.Clear;
           Err.Description =
             " Dll function call resulted in a bad stack because"
+ "of a Possible incorrect function prototype";";
       case 0x705:
           Err.Clear;
          Err.Description = "An attmept was made to access " +
                   "an array location that was out of bounds.";
       case 0x706:
           Err.Clear;
           Err.Description = "An attempt was made to access " +
                                "an object that does not exist";
       case 0x707:
           Err.Clear;
           Err.Description = "A call to a DLL function crashed";
       default:
           Err.Clear;
           Err.Description = "There was an unknown exception" +
                              " thrown by the scripting engine";
     endswitch;

     SprintfBox(SEVERE, "Exception", "Error: %X\n\n%s",
                                   Err.Number, Err.Description);

     // Tell the Windows Installer to abort the installation
```

```
        return ERROR_INSTALL_FAILURE;

    endcatch;

end;
```

In the above switch statement you will notice that I am performing the switch on the value of Err.Number XOR'd with 0x80040000, which will generate the raw error number given in hex used by the case statement. At the time of this writing using just the value of Err.Number for the switch expression generated a compiler error. Another option would have been to use a number variable to store the value of the Err.Number property and then use this in the switch expression.

IMPLEMENTING EXCEPTION HANDLING IN USER-DEFINED FUNCTIONS

In the example shown here you are going to create a wrapper around the CopyFile built-in function. This is a good example of how to make use of the exception-handling capabilities of InstallScript in the functions you write. The following code demonstrates this wrapper function.

```
export prototype ScriptTest(HWND);

prototype VOID MyCopyFile(STRING, STRING);

///////////////////////////////////////////////////////////////////////
//
// Function:  ScriptTest
//
// Purpose:   This is the entry point function used to run
//            your scripting test examples
//
///////////////////////////////////////////////////////////////////////
function ScriptTest(hMSI)
STRING  szSrc, szDest;
begin

    szSrc = "D:\\Installation Projects\\Scratch\\revstr.dll";
    szDest = "E:\\Scratch\\revstr.dll";

    try
        MyCopyFile(szSrc, szDest);
    catch
        switch(Err.Number ^ 0x80040000)
            case 2:
                SprintfBox(SEVERE, "Exception",
```

```
                "Error #: %X\n\nError occurred in function %s\n\n%s",
                            Err.Number, Err.Source, Err.Description);
            case 3:
                SprintfBox(SEVERE, "Exception",
                "Error #: %X\n\nError occurred in function %s\n\n%s",
                            Err.Number, Err.Source, Err.Description);
            case 5:
                SprintfBox(SEVERE, "Exception",
                "Error #: %X\n\nError occurred in function %s\n\n%s",
                            Err.Number, Err.Source, Err.Description);
            case 6:
                SprintfBox(SEVERE, "Exception",
                "Error #: %X\n\nError occurred in function %s\n\n%s",
                            Err.Number, Err.Source, Err.Description);
            case 27:
                SprintfBox(SEVERE, "Exception",
                "Error #: %X\n\nError occurred in function %s\n\n%s",
                            Err.Number, Err.Source, Err.Description);
            case 38:
                SprintfBox(SEVERE, "Exception",
                "Error #: %X\n\nError occurred in function %s\n\n%s",
                            Err.Number, Err.Source, Err.Description);
            case 46:
                SprintfBox(SEVERE, "Exception",
                "Error #: %X\n\nError occurred in function %s\n\n%s",
                            Err.Number, Err.Source, Err.Description);
            default:
                SprintfBox(SEVERE, "Exception",
                "Error #: %X\n\nError occurred in function %s\n\n%s",
                            Err.Number, Err.Source, Err.Description);
        endswitch;

    endcatch;

end;


///////////////////////////////////////////////////////////////////////////////
//
// Function:  MyCopyFile
//
// Purpose:   This is the entry point function used to run
//            your scripting test examples
//
///////////////////////////////////////////////////////////////////////////////
```

```
function VOID MyCopyFile(szSrcFile, szDestFile)
NUMBER  nReturn;
begin

    nReturn = CopyFile(szSrcFile, szDestFile);

    if(nReturn < 0) then
        switch(nReturn ^ 0x80070000)
            case 0x02:
                Err.Number = 2;
                Err.Source = "MyCopyFile";
                Err.Description = "Unable to open the source" +
                                            " file for copying";
                Err.Raise;
            case 0x03:
                Err.Number = 3;
                Err.Source = "MyCopyFile";
                Err.Description =
                        "Unable to copy the source file to" +
                                        " the destination file";
                Err.Raise;
            case 0x05:
                Err.Number = 5;
                Err.Source = "MyCopyFile";
                Err.Description =
                    "The destination drive is read only";
                Err.Raise;
            case 0x06:
                Err.Number = 6;
                Err.Source = "MyCopyFile";
                Err.Description =
                    "Unable to allocate enough memory to" +
                                        " complete the file copy";
                Err.Raise;
            case 0x27:
                Err.Number = 27;
                Err.Source = "MyCopyFile";
                Err.Description = "Unable to create the" +
                                        " destination directory";
                Err.Raise;
            case 0x38:
                Err.Number = 38;
                Err.Source = "MyCopyFile";
                Err.Description =
                    "Not enough space on the target location to" +
```

```
                                        " perform the file copy";
                Err.Raise;
            case 0x46:
                Err.Number = 46;
                Err.Source = "MyCopyFile";
                Err.Description = "The destination file is" +
                                                " read only";
                Err.Raise;
            default:
                Err.Number = 100;
                Err.Source = "MyCopyFile";
                Err.Description = "An unknown error occurred" +
                                        " during the file copy";
                Err.Raise;
        endswitch;
    endif;

end;
```

Summary

In this chapter you took a close look at the InstallScript language and implemented a number of functions that perform generic actions. We saw that InstallScript is a very powerful scripting language and that there is very little you cannot do with it. In the next chapter you will see that it is even more powerful and that with COM you can extend the language to suit your needs.

Chapter 15

InstallScript and COM

IN THIS CHAPTER

- Accessing COM objects form InstallScript
- Using the Windows Installer automation interface
- Using the FileSystemObject
- The capabilities of the Windows Scripting Host object model

FROM INSTALLSCRIPT YOU can access COM objects via the automation interface exposed by any application or DLL. This dramatically increases the capability of this scripting language over and above what is available to it from its own built-in API function set. The purpose of this chapter is to provide a sense of what you can do with this functionality. It is not an in-depth discussion of COM or what an automation interface is. In particular we look at three commonly available automation interfaces and how you might want to take advantage of their exposed methods and properties. These three automation interfaces are the ones exposed by the Windows Installer, the SCRRUN.DLL run-time scripting engine, and the Windows Scripting Host.

Accessing COM

From within a script, you can access the methods and properties of any automation interface that has been registered on the target machine. To do this you need to know the ProgID of the registered interface and you will need to use the set keyword and the CreateObject() function. The general syntax for this is as follows:

```
set object-name = CreateObject("progID");
```

The `object-name` is a variable that you have declared in your script as an OBJECT data type. The `progID` is the programmatic identifier for the automation interface you are accessing, as given in the Registry. The CreateObject() function uses the ProgID to access the CLSID that defines the requested interface. InstallScript supports the standard *object.property* and *object.method* syntax for accessing the properties and methods exposed by an automation interface.

Accessing the Windows Installer Automation Interface

Below is an example script that accesses the Windows Installer automation interface. You can use the same process for any other automation interface you want to access.

```
Function foo()
STRING     szVersion;
OBJECT     Installer;
begin
    try

    // Create an Installer object
    set Installer = CreateObject("WindowsInstaller.Installer");

    // Access the Version property of the Installer object
    szVersion = Installer.Version;

    // Display the results in a message box
    SprintfBox (INFORMATION, CAPTION,
                    "Windows Installer Version: %s",szVersion);
    catch
        SprintfBox (INFORMATION, "Script Test",
                                        "Exception was thrown");
        exit;
    endcatch;
end;
```

In the preceding script sample, you should notice that the Version property is returned as a string. Also note that the script is using a try-catch block to trap any exceptions that are thrown. If you were to capture the Version property as an integer data type, you would see that an exception is thrown. The return value depends on the method or property being accessed and type mismatches can occur when there is no legal conversion from the returned type to the type of the variable that holds the return value. The SprintfBox in the above example displayed on my machine the following string:

```
Windows Installer Version: 1.10.1029.0
```

From within InstallScript you are not able to access the Windows Installer Session object for the current installation process. This is because the Session object is not an object that you can create. A VBScript or JScript custom action has access to the Session object because the Windows Installer provides this object to them as the host in which these types of custom actions are running.

However, there are many other objects and their methods and properties that you can use from InstallScript. Unfortunately, most of these can only operate on an MSI package that has not been opened for installation. Figure 15-1 shows the object model for the Windows Installer automation interface.

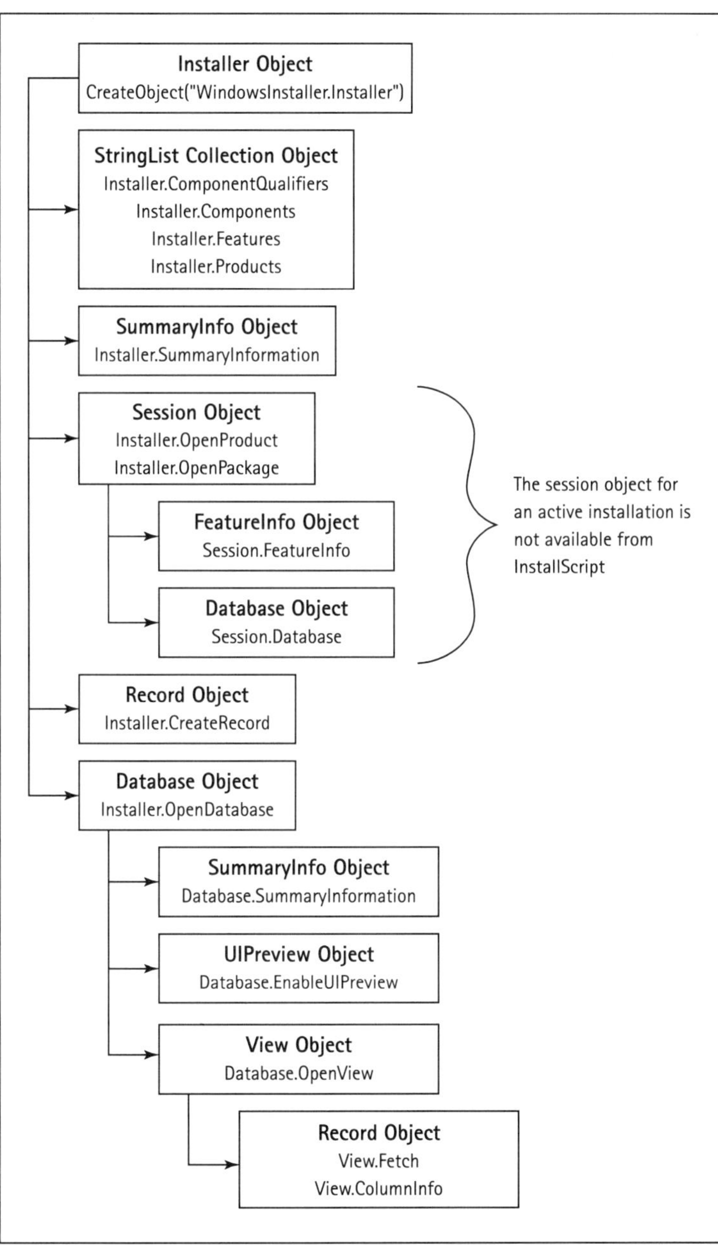

Figure 15-1: The Windows Installer object model

There is a good use of the Windows Installer automation interface that you can implement from InstallScript. That is the use of the OpenProduct or the OpenPackage method of the Installer object. These will allow you to perform the equivalent of a nested installation of another MSI package. You would have to do this from the UI sequence because another MSI installation would be locked out once control had passed to the execute sequence. In the execute sequence you are restricted to running one of the three types of nested installation custom actions that become child installs of the main install.

A potentially useful object exposed by the Windows Installer automation interface is the StringList collection object. Using the ComponentQualifiers, Components, Features, and Products properties of the Installer object you can create a StringList collection object that contains a list of the associated GUIDs or names that have been installed on the system. For the Products and Components properties the StringList contains the associated GUIDs. For the ComponentQualifiers and Features properties the StringList object contains the text string identifier. Using these properties you can find out what is already installed on the target system. The following code provides an example of how to iterate through the products and features installed on the system and display this information in a message box.

```
////////////////////////////////////////////////////////////////////
//
//  IIIIIII SSSSSS
//    II    SS          InstallShield (R), (c) 1996-2000
//    II    SSSSSS     InstallShield Software Corporation
//    II        SS            All rights reserved.
//  IIIIIII SSSSSS
//
//
//      This template script provides the code necessary
//      to build an entry-point function to be called in
//      an InstallScript custom action.
//
//
//    File Name:  Setup.rul
//
//  Description:  InstallShield script
//
////////////////////////////////////////////////////////////////////

#include "isrt.h"
#include "iswi.h"

export prototype ScriptTest(HWND);
```

```
/////////////////////////////////////////////////////////////////////
//
// Function:  ScriptTest
//
// Purpose:   This is the entry point function used to run
//            our scripting test examples
//
/////////////////////////////////////////////////////////////////////
function ScriptTest(hMSI)
NUMBER  nProductCount, nFeatureCount, i, j;
STRING  szFeature, szProduct;
OBJECT  Installer, Features, Products;
begin

    // Since you are dealing with COM you want to do everything
    // inside a try block so you can catch any exceptions
    // that might be thrown.
    try
        // Create the object using the Windows Installer ProgID
        set Installer = CreateObject("WindowsInstaller.Installer");

        // Create a Products collection object using the Products
        // property of the Installer object
        set Products = Installer.Products;

        // Obtain the number of products in the collection
        // so that you can iterate through the collection.
        nProductCount = Products.Count;

        for i=0 to nProductCount-1

            // Create a Features collection object for each
            // product in the Products collection object.
            set Features = Installer.Features(Products.Item(i));

            // Get the number of features in the Features collection
            // object so you can iterate through this collection.
            nFeatureCount = Features.Count;

            // Display the names of each feature for each product
            // registered on the machine.
            for j=0 to nFeatureCount-1
                SprintfBox(INFORMATION, "Products & Features",
                    "Product: %s\n\nFeature: %s",
```

```
                                        Products.Item(i), Features.Item(j));
            endfor;
        endfor;

    catch

        // Announce that an exception was thrown
        SprintfBox(INFORMATION, "Exception",
                                        "An exception was thrown.");

    endcatch;

end;
```

Refer to the Windows Installer help file, found in the SDK, for a complete description of all the objects, methods, and properties exposed by the Windows Installer automation interface.

Using the Capabilities of the Scripting Objects

The Microsoft Script Runtime objects are located in SCRRUN.DLL. These objects can be used from within InstallScript to create custom actions. The only requirement to be able to use these objects is for SCRRUN.DLL to be installed on the target system. The two objects that are available from SCRRUN.DLL are the FileSystemObject object and the Dictionary object.

As an example of using the methods and properties of the FileSystemObject, create a folder and then create a text file in this folder. Then write a line to this text file and get the date and time of its creation by accessing its attributes.

```
function foo()
OBJECT   fso, f, file, MyFile;
begin
    try

        // Create a file system object
        set fso = CreateObject("Scripting.FileSystemObject");

        // Create a new folder named New Folder under Scratch
        // The Scratch folder must already exist; otherwise
```

```
        // an exception is thrown
        set f = fso.CreateFolder("c:\\Scratch\\New Folder");

        // Use the folder object created to display the full path
        SprintfBox (INFORMATION, "Script Test", "Path: %s", f.Path);

        // Create a text file in the folder just created
        set MyFile = fso.CreateTextFile("C:\\Scratch\\New
                                        Folder\\TestFile.txt", TRUE);

        // Write a line of text to the new text file created
        MyFile.WriteLine("This is a test.");

        // Close the text file
        MyFile.Close;

        // Create a file object for the file just created
        set file = fso.GetFile
                   ("C:\\Scratch\\NewFolder\\TestFile.txt");

        // Using the file object DateCreated property display the
        // date and time the file was created
        SprintfBox (INFORMATION, CAPTION, "Date Created: %s",
                                                 file.DateCreated);
    catch
        SprintfBox(INFORMATION,
                      "Script Test","Exception was thrown");
        exit;
    endcatch;
end;
```

The Dictionary object implements an associative array. Each item in the array is associated with a unique key. The key is used to access the items in the array. This key can be an integer or a string. Dictionary objects give you associative arrays whereas InstallScript gives you regular arrays with numeric indices. The Dictionary object can be very valuable if you need a map like functionality. Therefore we will focus our attention on the capabilities of the FileSystemObject object.

Overview of the FileSystemObject Objects

There are eight objects and collections contained in the FileSystemObject model. Figure 15-2 provides an overview of the scripting run-time object model.

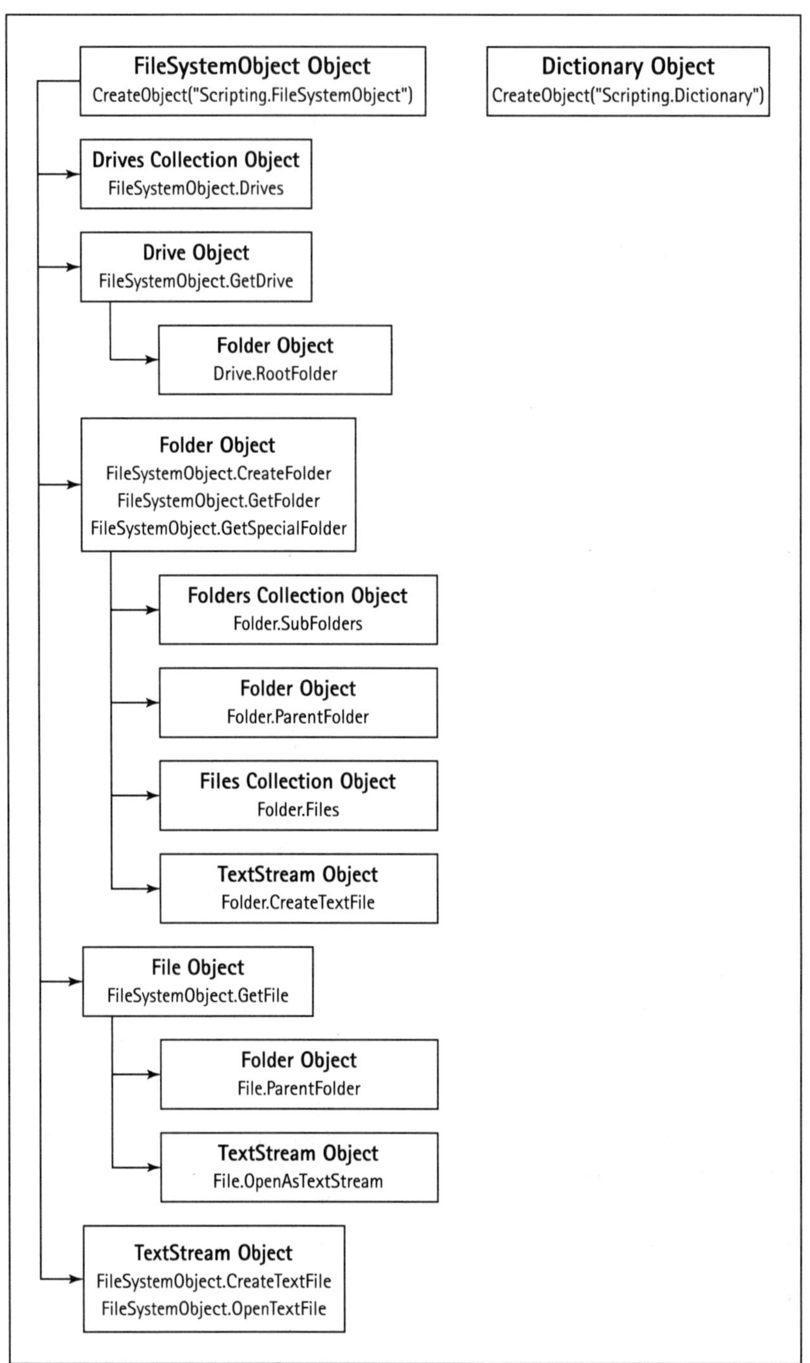

Figure 15-2: The scripting run-time object model

Considering the nature of an installation the FileSystemObject provides a very potent set of methods and properties. With this object you can create, modify, move, and delete folders. You can determine if a folder exists and, if it does, where it is located. You can also create, read, write, and delete files. You can also obtain information about the drives attached to the local machine. These drives can be either local drives or remote drives on a network.

Figure 15-2 has incorporated the methods or property names used to create the identified object. Table 15-1 describes these various objects and collections.

TABLE 15-1 THE FILESYSTEMOBJECT COLLECTIONS AND OBJECTS

Object Name	Description
FileSystemObject	The main object from which all other objects are created. To create this object you need to use the following line of code: `CreateObject("Scripting.FileSystemObject");` Directly from this object you can create a Drives collection object, a Drive object, a Folder object, a File object, and a TextStream object. There are 24 methods exposed by this object and one property.
Drives	Provides a list of all the drives attached to the local system, regardless of type. Of particular importance is that fact that a removable drive does not have to have media in it in order to be in the list. You can only create a Drives collection object from a FileSystemObject through the Drives property.
Drive	Provides a number of methods and properties that enable you to access information about a particular drive attached to the local system. The drive can be of any type including one that is mapped to a network share. You can only create a Drive object by the FileSystemObject's GetDrive method.
Folders	Provides a list of all folders within a folder. You can only create a Folders collection object with a Folder object's SubFolders property.

Continued

TABLE 15-1 THE FILESYSTEMOBJECT COLLECTIONS AND OBJECTS *(Continued)*

Object Name	Description
Folder	Contains the methods and properties that enable you to manipulate folders. You can create, delete, and move folders and query the system for other information about the folders that are present. You can create a folder in a number of ways: with the FileSystemObject methods (CreateFolder, GetFolder, and GetSpecialFolder); with the ParentFolder property of a Folder object; with the RootFolder property of a Drive object (which creates a Folder object that represents the root folder of a specified drive); or with the ParentFolder property of a File object.
Files	Contains a list of all files contained in a particular folder. You can only create a Files collection object with the Files property of a Folder object.
File	Provides you with the methods and properties to manipulate files. You can create, delete, and move files. You can also query the system for pertinent information about the file such as its attributes. You can only create a File object with the GetFile method of the FileSystemObject.
TextStream	Provides you with the methods and properties that enable you to read and write text files. You can create a TextStream object with the CreateTextFile method of the Folder object; with the OpenAsTextStream method of the File object; and with either the CreateTextFile or OpenTextFile methods of the FileSystemObject.

The present capability of the FileSystemObject only enables you to manipulate text files. It is planned in the future to extend this capability to binary files.

At the present time in InstallScript there is no functionality equivalent to the For Each...Next capability in VBScript. This functionality is critical to iterating a collection that you cannot access through a numeric index. This is the case with the Drives collection, which only implements access through a string index. Since you will want to use this capability for one of the examples in the next chapter, in the next section you are going to create a very specialized function for iterating through a Drives collection.

Creating a Drives collection iterator

The following code implements the capability for iterating through a Drives collection object. This is somewhat ugly so we can only hope that this functionality will be added to the InstallScript language in the future. In this example you will take advantage of the intrinsic functionality of exception handling. Trying to access a drive that does not exist will throw an exception. When you catch the exception, you increment the index and proceed with the loop until you have either exhausted all the letters of the alphabet or found all the drives in the collection. You know you have found all the drives in the collection when the number of drives found is equal to the value of the Count property of the Drives collection.

```
////////////////////////////////////////////////////////////////////////
//
//  IIIIIII SSSSSS
//    II    SS          InstallShield (R), (c) 1996-2000
//    II    SSSSSS     InstallShield Software Corporation
//    II        SS            All rights reserved.
//  IIIIIII SSSSSS
//
//
//      This template script provides the code necessary
//      to build an entry-point function to be called in
//      an InstallScript custom action.
//
//
//    File Name:  Setup.rul
//
//  Description:  InstallShield script
//
////////////////////////////////////////////////////////////////////////

#include "isrt.h"
#include "iswi.h"

#define CAPTION     "Script Test Feedback"

export prototype ScriptTest(HWND);

prototype GetDriveTypeText(STRING, BYREF STRING, NUMBER);
prototype GetDrivesAndTypes(BYREF VARIANT, BYREF VARIANT);

////////////////////////////////////////////////////////////////////////
//
// Function:  ScriptTest
```

```
//
// Purpose:   This is the entry point function used to run
//            your scripting test examples
//
///////////////////////////////////////////////////////////////////////
function ScriptTest(hMSI)
STRING  valArray(), txtArray();
NUMBER  i;
begin

    GetDrivesAndTypes(valArray, txtArray);

    for i=0 to 4
        SprintfBox(INFORMATION, "Drives Collection",
            "Drive: %s\n\nDescription: %s", valArray(i),
txtArray(i));
    endfor;

end;


///////////////////////////////////////////////////////////////////////
//
//  Function:  GetDrivesAndTypes
//
//  Purpose:   This function returns as arrays the available drive
//             letters and drive types.
//
///////////////////////////////////////////////////////////////////////
function GetDrivesAndTypes(valArray, txtArray)
NUMBER  nCount, nFound, i;
STRING  szDrive, szIterator, Text;
OBJECT  dc, d, fso;
begin

    // Create a FileSystemObject
    set fso = CreateObject("Scripting.FileSystemObject");

    // From the FileSystemObject create a
    // Drives collection object
    set dc = fso.Drives;

    // Get the number of items in the Drives collection object
    nCount = dc.Count;
```

```
// Size the arrays to hold the number of items in
// Drives collection object.
Resize(valArray, nCount);
Resize(txtArray, nCount);

nFound = 0;
i = 0;

// Loop through all possible drive letters and check if
// they are available on the local machine.
// If a drive letter is available then you add it to the
// valArray. If the drive does not exist an exception gets
// thrown and you increment the index i.
// This will be the code that is replaced once InstallScript
// implements the For Each...Next functionality for iterating
// collections that do not support a numeric indexing.
// Since the switch statement is inside a try block
// you will be able to catch the exception thrown when an item
// you are trying to access does not exist. You handle this
// exception by incrementing the index and continuing with
// loop through the possible list of drives.
while(nFound < nCount)
    try
        switch(i)
            case 0:
                szDrive = dc.Item("A");
            case 1:
                szDrive = dc.Item("B");
            case 2:
                szDrive = dc.Item("C");
            case 3:
                szDrive = dc.Item("D");
            case 4:
                szDrive = dc.Item("E");
            case 5:
                szDrive = dc.Item("F");
            case 6:
                szDrive = dc.Item("G");
            case 7:
                szDrive = dc.Item("H");
            case 8:
                szDrive = dc.Item("I");
            case 9:
                szDrive = dc.Item("J");
            case 10:
```

```
                szDrive = dc.Item("K");
            case 11:
                szDrive = dc.Item("L");
            case 12:
                szDrive = dc.Item("M");
            case 13:
                szDrive = dc.Item("N");
            case 14:
                szDrive = dc.Item("O");
            case 15:
                szDrive = dc.Item("P");
            case 16:
                szDrive = dc.Item("Q");
            case 17:
                szDrive = dc.Item("R");
            case 18:
                szDrive = dc.Item("S");
            case 19:
                szDrive = dc.Item("T");
            case 20:
                szDrive = dc.Item("U");
            case 21:
                szDrive = dc.Item("V");
            case 22:
                szDrive = dc.Item("W");
            case 23:
                szDrive = dc.Item("X");
            case 24:
                szDrive = dc.Item("Y");
            case 25:
                szDrive = dc.Item("Z");
        endswitch;
        szDrive = szDrive + "\\";

        // For the found drive get the drive type
        GetDriveTypeText(szDrive, svText, i);

        // Populate the arrays for the drives that are found
        valArray(nFound) = szDrive;
        txtArray(nFound) = svText;
        nFound = nFound + 1;
        i = i + 1;
    catch
        i = i + 1;
    endcatch;
```

```
    endwhile;

end;


///////////////////////////////////////////////////////////////////////
//
//  Function:  GetDriveTypeText
//
//  Purpose:   This function will be called by the script engine
//
///////////////////////////////////////////////////////////////////////
function GetDriveTypeText(szDrive, svText, index)
INT nType;
begin

    // Call the Windows API to get the drive type identifier
    nType = GetDriveType(szDrive);

    // For the drive type returned create a text description
    switch(nType)
        case DRIVE_UNKNOWN:
            svText = "Unknown drive type";
        case DRIVE_NO_ROOT_DIR:
            svText = "Invalid drive";
        case DRIVE_REMOVABLE:
            svText = "Removable drive";
        case DRIVE_FIXED:
            svText = "Fixed drive";
        case DRIVE_REMOTE:
            svText = "Remote drive";
        case DRIVE_CDROM:
            svText = "CD-ROM drive";
        case DRIVE_RAMDISK:
            svText = "RAM disk drive";
    endswitch;

end;
```

You will use this iterator in the creation of a real-world custom action in Chapter 16.

Refer to the VBScript or JScript documentation for a complete discussion of the methods and properties of the FileSystemObject and Dictionary objects.

Now let's move on and examine another automation interface that can provide some robust functionality. This is the set of objects exposed by the Windows Scripting Host.

Capabilities of the WSH Objects

The Windows Scripting Host comes natively with Windows 98 and Windows 2000 but you have to install it on Windows 95 and Windows NT 4.0. This means that if you are distributing your application to Windows 95 and/or Windows NT 4.0, and you want to use the WSH automation interface methods and properties, you will have to check for the existence of the scripting host and if it is not there install it before trying to access it.

To check for the existence of the Windows Scripting Host you need to see if the file wscript.exe is in the System32 folder. If you need to install the WSH, first obtain the redistributable file WSH.exe and run the installation silently with the following command line:

```
WSH.exe /q
```

You would run this as an executable custom action with the WSH.exe file stored in the Binary table.

Figure 15-3 shows the objects you can access from InstallScript. There are two creatable objects: one that enables access to the Windows shell through a set of methods and properties and one that provides methods and properties that work with networks.

You can download the WSH setup program from the following URL:

```
www.microsoft.com/msdownload/vbscript/scripting.asp
```

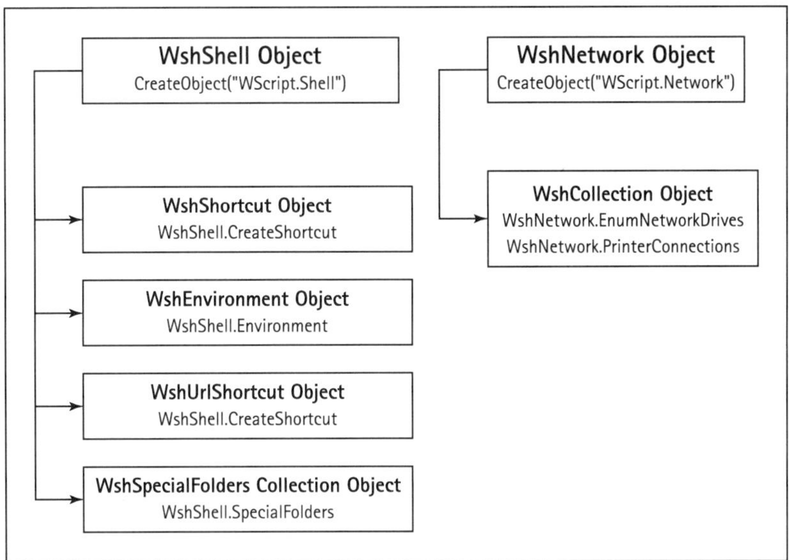

Figure 15-3: The Windows Scripting Host object model

Refer to the MSDN Library for a complete description of the methods and properties available to you from the Windows Scripting Host.

Summary

In this chapter you have received (I hope) a sense of the immense power available to you through this capability in InstallScript to access COM. You have seen three major areas where you can derive major benefit from various automation interfaces. These are the Windows Installer automation interface, the FileSystemObject available from the scripting run-time library, and the Windows Scripting Host, which provides some unique ways to access the Registry and remote drives and printers.

Chapter 16

Using InstallScript to Create Custom Actions

IN THIS CHAPTER

- Getting setup to use InstallScript for custom actions
- Initialization and clean up during an installation
- Working with the Property table
- Setting properties at runtime
- Using custom actions in the user interface
- Working with dynamic link libraries from InstallScript

THE PURPOSE OF THIS chapter is to take what you have learned in the last three chapters about InstallScript and use this knowledge to create some actual custom actions. We will start of with creating a method for determining what sequence you are running in. This will give you a chance to examine the use of the OnBegin() and OnEnd() event handlers.

After this we will examine the Property table in great detail. The Property table is very important since you need to interface with this table to create most custom actions. After looking at the Property table you'll create a custom action that dynamically populates a ListBox control in a dialog box. Finally we'll look at how to create helper functions in a dynamic-linked library.

Preliminaries

In order to run the custom actions you'll create in this chapter you need to build a complete project. You cannot use the project that you were using to investigate the InstallScript language since you took all the actions out of the InstallUISequence table in that project. So the first thing you need to do is to create a small project. This time, create a project with one feature and one component. This way, you'll avoid problems with the Windows Installer when you run this package.

You can create an InstallScript custom action as either an immediate or a deferred category custom action. The one thing you cannot do with an InstallScript custom action is run it asynchronously. The custom actions you are going to create in this chapter will all be of the immediate category and they will all be inserted into the InstallUISequence table. When you create an InstallScript custom action and then highlight this custom action in the Actions/Scripts tree control, you will see that there is a very large number for the custom action type. This is a special number used in the project file to differentiate an InstallScript custom action from the normal custom actions created as described in Chapter 11. This number is the Windows Installer type value summed with 65535. When you create your immediate custom action, you will see the type number for this action as 65536; when you subtract 65535 you get a type of 1. This type, as I described in Chapter 10, is a DLL custom action stored in the Binary table.

Before you start creating some custom actions you need to understand the use of the two event handlers that are part of the scripting environment. These event handlers are the subjects of the next section.

Initialization and Clean-Up

Implemented in InstallScript are two script functions called event handlers. The names of these functions are OnBegin() and OnEnd(). As implemented in InstallScript they are empty functions. However, you can override the internal implementation by adding these functions to your script. When your script is linked, the implementation of these functions in your script will be linked to create the .inx file. The OnBegin() function is called right after the scripting engine is installed and/or started. This function gives you a chance to implement whatever initialization actions are required so that your InstallScript custom actions will run correctly. On Windows NT and Windows 2000 these event handlers are executed twice, once in each process – that is, once in the UI sequence running in the client process and once in the execute sequence running in the service process. On Windows 95/98 these event handlers are executed twice but this time they are executed once in the UI sequence and once in the execute sequence. There is only one process running, however, on Windows 95/98.

The OnBegin() and the OnEnd() event handlers are prototyped in the header file iswi.h, which can be found in the Script\iswi\Include folder under the InstallShield for Windows Installer installation location. In this header file is also defined the __hMsiInstall global variable. This global variable holds the handle to the current installation session and its purpose is to allow the OnBegin() and the OnEnd() event handlers to have access to this handle.

It might be important to know the process or sequence you are in when the OnBegin() or OnEnd() function is executing. You might want to do different things depending on whether you are in the UI sequence or the execute sequence. In the following code you'll create the capability to determine what sequence or process is currently being executed. The core of this code is in the SetSequence() function.

You need to call this function in the OnBegin() event handler prior to any code that depends on the sequence being executed. You must then call the GetSequence() function, which returns a value of 1 if execution is in the UI sequence and a value of 2 if execution is in the execute sequence. You can find this code on the CD-ROM contained in the file WhatSequence.rul under the Chapter 16 folder. In this example the entry point function is named CATest() and is the custom action inserted into the various sequences to test this functionality.

```
////////////////////////////////////////////////////////////////////
//
//  IIIIIII SSSSSS
//    II    SS                      InstallShield (R)
//    II    SSSSSS                    (c) 1996-2000,
//    II        SS     InstallShield Software Corporation
//    II       SS                 All rights reserved.
//  IIIIIII SSSSSS
//
//    File Name:  Setup.rul
//
//  Description:  InstallShield script
//
////////////////////////////////////////////////////////////////////

//  include files
#include <isrt.h>
#include <iswi.h>

// function prototypes
// entry point functions
export prototype CATest(NUMBER);


// private functions
prototype SetSequence();
prototype NUMBER GetSequence();

// global variables
HWND    nSequence; // Only required if the CleanUp custom action
                   // is not passing the session handle


////////////////////////////////////////////////////////////////////
//
//  Function:  CATest
//
```

```
//  Purpose:   This function will be called by the script engine
//             as a custom action
//
///////////////////////////////////////////////////////////////////////////////
function CATest(hInstall)
NUMBER  nReturn;
begin

    nReturn = GetSequence();

    switch(nReturn)
        case 1:
            SprintfBox (INFORMATION, "Script Test",
                                      "We are in the UI Sequence");
        case 2:
            SprintfBox (INFORMATION, "Script Test",
                                 "We are in the Execute Sequence");
        default:
            SprintfBox (INFORMATION, "Script Test",
                                    "We do not know where we are");
    endswitch;

end;


///////////////////////////////////////////////////////////////////////////////
//
//  Function:  OnBegin
//
//  Purpose:   This function will override the predefined OnBegin
//             event handler
//
///////////////////////////////////////////////////////////////////////////////
function OnBegin()
NUMBER  nReturn;
begin

    // Call this function as the first line in
    // the OnBegin event handler
    SetSequence();

    nReturn = GetSequence();

    // In a switch statement like this you would perform any
    // appropriate initialization
```

```
    switch(nReturn)
        case 1:
            SprintfBox (INFORMATION, "OnBegin()",
                                    "We are in the UI Sequence");
        case 2:
            SprintfBox (INFORMATION, "OnBegin()",
                              "We are in the Execute Sequence");
        default:
            SprintfBox (INFORMATION, "OnBegin()",
                                    "We do not know where we are");
    endswitch;

end;


///////////////////////////////////////////////////////////////////
//
//  Function:  OnEnd
//
//  Purpose:   This function will override the predefined OnEnd
//             event handler
//
///////////////////////////////////////////////////////////////////
function OnEnd()
NUMBER  nReturn;
begin

    nReturn = GetSequence();

    // In a switch statement like this you would perform any
    // appropriate clean-up activities
    switch(nReturn)
        case 1:
            SprintfBox (INFORMATION, "OnEnd()",
                                    "We are in the UI Sequence");
        case 2:
            SprintfBox (INFORMATION, "OnEnd()",
                              "We are in the Execute Sequence");
        default:
            SprintfBox (INFORMATION, "OnEnd()",
                                    "We do not know where we are");
    endswitch;

end;
```

```
//////////////////////////////////////////////////////////////////////
//
//  Function:  SetSequence
//
//  Purpose:   This function will set the current sequence in the
//             property table so that it can be retrieved by the
//             GetSequence function.
//
//////////////////////////////////////////////////////////////////////
function SetSequence()
STRING  szWHATSEQName, szWHATSEQValue, strWHATSEQValue;
STRING  szUILevelName, strUILevelValue;
NUMBER  nCharCount, nUILevelValue, nWHATSEQValue;
begin

    // The public property that will be set with the
    // currently executing sequence
    szWHATSEQName = "WHATSEQ";

    // The Windows Installer property that identifies the
    // user interface level being used for the current installation
    szUILevelName = "UILevel";

    // Get the value of the UILevel property
    // from the Property table
    nCharCount = 1024;
    MsiGetProperty(__hMsiInstall, szUILevelName, strUILevelValue,
                                                        nCharCount);
    StrToNum(nUILevelValue, strUILevelValue);

    // Get the value of the WHATSEQ property
    // from the Property table. The first time
    // this property will not exist.
    nCharCount = 1024;
    MsiGetProperty(__hMsiInstall, szWHATSEQName, strWHATSEQValue,
nCharCount);
    // If the property does not exist then
    // nWHATSEQValue will be zero
    StrToNum(nWHATSEQValue, strWHATSEQValue);

    // If the UI level is less than 4 then the installation
    // is being run in either basic or silent mode
    if(nUILevelValue < 4 && nWHATSEQValue = 0) then
        szWHATSEQValue = "2";
```

```
        // Set the global variable to the current sequence for
        // use by the OnEnd event handler. This is only necessary
        // as long as the CleanUp custom action does not define
        // the value of the session handle. This is a situation
        // that should be fixed by the time this book is published.
        nSequence = 2;
        MsiSetProperty(__hMsiInstall, szWHATSEQName,
                                                szWHATSEQValue);

    // If the UI level of the installation is full
    // or reduced and the WHATSEQ property is null
    // then we must be running in the UI sequence
    elseif(nUILevelValue >= 4 && nWHATSEQValue = 0) then
        szWHATSEQValue = "1";
        nSequence = 1;
        MsiSetProperty(__hMsiInstall, szWHATSEQName,
                                                szWHATSEQValue);


    // If the UI level of the installation is full
    // or reduced and the WHATSEQ property is 1
    // then we must be running in the execute sequence
    elseif(nUILevelValue >= 4 && nWHATSEQValue = 1) then
        szWHATSEQValue = "2";
        nSequence = 2;
        MsiSetProperty(__hMsiInstall, szWHATSEQName,
                                                szWHATSEQValue);
    endif;

end;


///////////////////////////////////////////////////////////////////////
//
//  Function:  GetSequence
//
//  Purpose:   This function returns the value of the WHATSEQ
//             property, which determines the current sequence
//             in which the installation is running.
//
///////////////////////////////////////////////////////////////////////
function NUMBER GetSequence()
STRING  szWHATSEQName, strWHATSEQValue;
NUMBER  nCharCount, nWHATSEQValue, nResult;
```

```
begin

    szWHATSEQName = "WHATSEQ";

    nCharCount = 1024;
    nResult = MsiGetProperty(__hMsiInstall, szWHATSEQName,
                                        strWHATSEQValue, nCharCount);

    // If the call to MsiGetProperty was successful then
    // the value of the WHATSEQ property tells you what sequence
    // you are currently running in.
    if(nResult = ERROR_SUCCESS) then
        StrToNum(nWHATSEQValue, strWHATSEQValue);

    // The following is necessary only as long as the CleanUp
    // function does not properly set the session handle. This
    // situation occurs only in the OnEnd() event handler. If you
    // get an invalid handle error when calling the MsiGetProperty
    // API then you assume that you are in the OnEnd()event handler.
    // You base your decision on the value of the nSequence global
    // variable to return the current sequence in which you are
    // running. You need to reset the global variable to 1 so
    // that when the next call to the OnEnd()event handler is made
    // you can return the current value for the current sequence.
    elseif(nResult = ERROR_INVALID_HANDLE && nSequence = 2) then
        nWHATSEQValue = 2;
        nSequence = 1;
    elseif(nResult = ERROR_INVALID_HANDLE && nSequence = 1) then
        nWHATSEQValue = 1;
    endif;

    return nWHATSEQValue;

end;
```

It is important to realize that the first call to the OnBegin() event handler can be made either from the UI sequence or from the execute sequence. However, the first call to the OnEnd() event handler will always be made from the execute sequence.

The above example has also illustrated one of the important features of the InstallScript implementation: when you define a global variable it is available to all custom actions running in a particular sequence. This is similar to the type of communication you can get with the Property table and public properties across the process boundary that separates the client and server processes.

If the implementation of the CleanUp custom action has been corrected by the time this book has gone to press, you do not need to use the nSequence global variable approach to determining the current sequence inside the OnEnd() event handler.

Retrieving and Adding Data to the Property Table

When you create custom actions, you will most likely have to interface with the Property table. You have already gotten a taste of working with the Property table from the code example in the previous section. Because the Property table is so important, there are two special functions provided by the Windows Installer to work with this table. In the next section you'll take a close look at these two functions. Keep in mind that the function of properties in the Windows Installer environment is to act as global variables to the installation.

Working with the Property table

There are two database functions provided by the Windows Installer for working with the Property table at runtime. These functions are MsiGetProperty() and MsiSetProperty().These two functions have been prototyped in the InstallScript fashion in the header file ISMsiQuery.h. This file is in the Script\Include subfolder of the ISWI installation location. You will notice in this header file that even though many of these API functions have both ANSI and Unicode versions that you do not need to specify the ANSI version of the function name when using it. This is because in this header file you will see the following macro defined for all functions that have both versions:

```
#define MsiGetProperty  msi.MsiSetPropertyA
```

The MsiGetProperty() function retrieves that value of an installer property. The MsiGetProperty function has the following format:

```
NUMBER MsiGetProperty(
   NUMBER hInstall,          // handle to installer session
   BYVAL STRING szName,      // case sensitive property name
   BYREF STRING szValueBuf, // buffer for returned property value
   BYREF NUMBER pchValueBuf // in/out buffer character count
);
```

By default, InstallScript sets the size of a string variable passed BYREF to a DLL function to 1024. However, the best approach to setting the size of the buffer that is passed to this function is to first pass an empty string in order to get back the actual size of the number of characters that make up the property value. Then use the Resize operator to set the size of the buffer, making sure to add 1 to the value returned from the function. Then you call the function again with the buffer sized to just accommodate the property value. If a property is not defined, an empty string will be returned as the value of the buffer.

The MsiSetProperty() function is used to set the value of an installer property. The MsiSetProperty function has the following format:

```
NUMBER MsiSetProperty(
    NUMBER hInstall,           // handle to installer session
    BYVAL STRING szName,       // case-sensitive property name
    BYVAL STRING szValue       // property value to set
);
```

You can use this function to remove a property as well as set the value of a property. To remove a property all you need to do is set the value of the existing property to an empty string. This will remove the property from the Property table.

An example custom action for setting the CCP_DRIVE property

The CCP_DRIVE property is a public property used during a competitive upgrade scenario. Essentially, the value of the CCP_DRIVE property contains the root path to a removable volume that contains the signature file or files, which identify the competitive product. This property is used by the RMCCPSearch action along with the file signatures provided in the CCPSearch table to qualify the user for compliance with the installation requirements of the upgrade product. This property provides the root location for any searching to be done by the RMCCPSearch action. The acronym CCP stands for compliance Checking Program and RMCCP stands for Removable Media Compliance Checking Program.

In this example, assume that the removable media that you want to find is the drive letter for the CD-ROM, and that there is only one CD-ROM on the target machine. In a later example you will create a more robust solution wherein, under certain circumstances, the user will be asked to select the root location from which the RMCCPSearch action will start its search. The code for this example is as follows:

```
///////////////////////////////////////////////////////////////////////
//
//  IIIIIII SSSSSS
//    II    SS                      InstallShield (R)
//    II    SSSSSS                    (c) 1996-2000,
//    II        SS        InstallShield Software Corporation
//    II        SS                   All rights reserved.
```

```
//  IIIIIII SSSSSS
//
//    File Name:  Setup.rul
//
//  Description:  InstallShield script
//
///////////////////////////////////////////////////////////////////////////////

//  include files
#include <isrt.h>
#include <iswi.h>

// function prototypes
// entry point functions
export prototype CCP_DRIVE(NUMBER);

///////////////////////////////////////////////////////////////////////////////
//
//  Function:  CCP_DRIVE
//  Purpose:   This function is
//             the entry point for a custom action that will set the
//             CCP_DRIVE property to the drive letter of the CD_ROM
//             on the target system
//
///////////////////////////////////////////////////////////////////////////////
function CCP_DRIVE(hInstall)
NUMBER  nCount;
STRING  szCCPDrive;
LIST    lstCCPDrive;
begin

   // Create the list to hold the list of valid drives
   lstCCPDrive = ListCreate(STRINGLIST);

   // Get just a list of CD-ROM drives and make sure that
   // checking of the minimum drive space does not occur
   GetValidDrivesList(lstCCPDrive, CDROM_DRIVE, -1);

   // Get a count of the number of entries made in the list
   nCount = ListCount(lstCCPDrive);

   // Make sure that there is a CD-ROM drive found
   // before setting the CCP_DRIVE property
   if(nCount > 0) then
       // Assume that the first item in the list is the one you want
```

```
        ListGetFirstString(lstCCPDrive, szCCPDrive);

        // You need to add the colon and backslash to complete the
        // specification of the root search location
        szCCPDrive = szCCPDrive + ":\\";

        // Set the property using the MSI API
        MsiSetProperty(hInstall, "CCP_DRIVE", szCCPDrive);
    else
        // If no CD-ROM drive is found abort the installation
        // after telling the user about the problem
        MessageBox("Cannot find a CD-ROM drive to search", SEVERE);

        // Returning this value will cause the Windows Installer
        // to abort the installation
        return ERROR_INSTALL_FAILURE;
    endif;

end;
```

The simplifying assumption made here is that it is the CD-ROM drive that contains the media from which the qualifying product will be validated. Later in this chapter, when you get to the section on working with the user interface, you will implement a more robust solution to this problem.

Chapter 21 provides more detail about searching for other applications.

An example custom action for setting the ARPINSTALLLOCATION property

The ARPINSTALLLOCATION property is the full path to an application's root folder. This information will appear in the Add/Remove Programs applet information that is part of the new functionality on Windows 2000. In the following example you will take the value of the INSTALLDIR property and use its final value to set the ARPINSTALLLOCATION property. You need to place this custom action in the InstallExecuteSequence to make sure that this property will still be set even if the installation is run in basic or silent mode.

```
///////////////////////////////////////////////////////////////////////////////
//
//  IIIIIII SSSSSS
```

```
//    II    SS                    InstallShield (R)
//    II    SSSSSS                  (c) 1996-2000,
//    II         SS     InstallShield Software Corporation
//    II        SS                All rights reserved.
//  IIIIIII SSSSSS
//
//    File Name:  Setup.rul
//
//  Description:  InstallShield script
//
////////////////////////////////////////////////////////////////////

//  include files
#include <isrt.h>
#include <iswi.h>

// function prototypes
// entry point functions
export prototype SetARPINSTALLLOCATION(HWND);

////////////////////////////////////////////////////////////////////
//
//  Function:  SetARPINSTALLLOCATION
//
//  Purpose:   This function will be called by the script engine
//
////////////////////////////////////////////////////////////////////

function SetARPINSTALLLOCATION(hInstall)
STRING  szPropertyName, szPropertyValue;
NUMBER  nResult, nBufSize;
begin

    // Explicitly initialize the value buffer and buffer size
    // to null values so as to get the size of the buffer needed
    szPropertyValue = "";
    nBufSize = 0;

    MsiGetProperty(hInstall, "INSTALLDIR", szPropertyValue,
                                                        nBufSize);

    // Get the buffer size required and resize the value buffer
    nBufSize = nBufSize + 1;
    Resize(szPropertyValue, nBufSize);
    MsiGetProperty(hInstall, "INSTALLDIR", szPropertyValue,
```

```
                                                    nBufSize);

    // Set the value of the ARPINSTALLLOCATION property to the
    // value of the INSTALLDIR property
    MsiSetProperty(hInstall, "ARPINSTALLLOCATION", szPropertyValue);

end;
```

Even though you may think of INSTALLDIR as an entry in the Directory table it also becomes a property when the Directory table is resolved.

You must set the ARPINSTALLLOCATION property to qualify for the "Certified for Microsoft Windows" logo.

Creating a custom action to view the contents of the Property table

Up to this point you have been working with the Property table one property at a time. Taking a look at all the properties in the Property table is educational, and will also introduce the use of the Windows Installer SQL query language.

An explanation of the Windows Installer SQL query language is provided in Chapter 11.

In the following code you execute a view on the complete Property table and then fetch each record one at a time and write it to a text file.

```
///////////////////////////////////////////////////////////////////////////////
//
//  IIIIIII SSSSSS
//    II    SS                      InstallShield (R)
//    II    SSSSSS                    (c) 1996-2000,
//    II        SS     InstallShield Software Corporation
//    II       SS                   All rights reserved.
//  IIIIIII SSSSSS
//
//    File Name:  Setup.rul
//
```

```
//  Description:  InstallShield script
//
///////////////////////////////////////////////////////////////////////

//  include files
#include <isrt.h>
#include <iswi.h>

// function prototypes
// entry point functions
export prototype GetProperties(HWND);

// private functions
prototype HWND GetPropertyTableView(HWND, STRING);
prototype WritePropertyTableToFile(HWND, STRING, STRING);
prototype OBJECT CreateTextFile(STRING, STRING);


// global constants
#define NAME_FIELD          1
#define VALUE_FIELD         2
#define NAME_FIELD_BUFSIZE  73
#define TAB_DELIMITER       "\t"


///////////////////////////////////////////////////////////////////////
//
//  Function:  GetProperties
//
//  Purpose:   This function will be called by the script engine
//
///////////////////////////////////////////////////////////////////////
function GetProperties(hMSI)
HWND    hView;
begin

    // Get the persistent property values
    hView = GetPropertyTableView(hMSI, "Property");

    // Write the persistent property values to a text file
    WritePropertyTableToFile(hView, "C:\\Scratch", "Property.txt");

end;
```

```
///////////////////////////////////////////////////////////////////
//
// Function: GetPropertyTableView
//
// Purpose:  This function returns a view of all the records in
//           the named Property table
//
///////////////////////////////////////////////////////////////////
function HWND GetPropertyTableView(hInstall, szTableName)
STRING  szQuery;
NUMBER  nResult;
HWND    hView, hDataBase;
begin

    // Select all columns and all rows in the named table
    szQuery = "SELECT * FROM " + szTableName;

    // Obtain a handle to the active database
    hDataBase = MsiGetActiveDatabase(hInstall);

    if(hDataBase = 0) then
        MessageBox("Unable to open active database", SEVERE);
        exit;
    endif;

    // Create a view object as specified by szQuery
    nResult = MsiDatabaseOpenView(hDataBase, szQuery, hView);

    if(nResult != ERROR_SUCCESS) then
        MessageBox("Error opening view.", SEVERE);
        exit;
    endif;

    // Execute the view object and make it
    // ready for retrieving records
    nResult = MsiViewExecute(hView, NULL);

    if(nResult != ERROR_SUCCESS) then
        MessageBox("Error executing view.", SEVERE);
        exit;
    endif;

    return hView;

end;
```

```
////////////////////////////////////////////////////////////////////////
//
//  Function:  WritePropertyTableToFile
//
//  Purpose:   This function will write the records of the Property
//             table to the specified text file
//
////////////////////////////////////////////////////////////////////////
function WritePropertyTableToFile(hView, szFolder, szFileName)
NUMBER  nResult, nBufSize;
STRING  szPropertyName, szPropertyValue, szStr;
HWND    hRecord;
OBJECT  file;
begin

    // Get the text file to which the records will be written
    set file = CreateTextFile(szFolder, szFileName);

    // Fetch the first record of the Property table
    nResult = MsiViewFetch(hView, hRecord);

    // Loop through all the records of the Property table
    // and write them one at a time to the text file.
    while(nResult = ERROR_SUCCESS)

        // You know the name field of the Property table is 72
        // characters in size so set the buffer size to that
        nBufSize = NAME_FIELD_BUFSIZE;
        MsiRecordGetString(hRecord, NAME_FIELD, szPropertyName,
                                                    nBufSize);

        // Explicitly set the value buffer to an empty string
        // so you can obtain the required buffer size
        szPropertyValue = "";
        nBufSize = 0;
        MsiRecordGetString(hRecord, VALUE_FIELD, szPropertyValue,
                                                    nBufSize);


        // Now that you know the required buffer size set the
        // buffer size and get the property value
        nBufSize = nBufSize + 1;
        Resize(szPropertyValue, nBufSize);
        MsiRecordGetString(hRecord, VALUE_FIELD, szPropertyValue,
                                                    nBufSize);
```

```
        // Create a tab delimited string to write to the text file
        szStr = szPropertyName + TAB_DELIMITER + szPropertyValue;

        // Write the line to the text file
        file.WriteLine(szStr);

        // Fetch the next record in the view
        nResult = MsiViewFetch(hView, hRecord);

    endwhile;

    // Close the text file after you have fetched and
    // written all the records.
    if(nResult = ERROR_NO_MORE_ITEMS) then
        file.Close;
        return 0;
    else
        MessageBox("Error fetching view.", SEVERE);
        return -1;
    endif;

end;


//////////////////////////////////////////////////////////////////////
//
//  Function:  CreateTextFile
//
//  Purpose:   This function will use the FileSystemObject to
//             create a text file
//
//////////////////////////////////////////////////////////////////////
function OBJECT CreateTextFile(szFolder, szFileName)
OBJECT  fso, folder, file;
begin

    // Create a file system object
    set fso = CreateObject("Scripting.FileSystemObject");

    // Create a folder object if it does not already exist
    if(!fso.FolderExists(szFolder)) then
        set folder = fso.CreateFolder(szFolder);
    endif;

    // Create the absolute path to the text file
```

```
    szFileName = szFolder ^ szFileName;

    // Create a text stream object
    set file = fso.CreateTextFile(szFileName, TRUE);

    return file;

end;
```

In the preceding code you have made use of a number of new Windows Installer API functions. These functions helped you to access the Property table as a whole by creating a view and then fetching the records of that view one at a time. Table 16-1 describes each of these functions.

TABLE 16-1 DATABASE MANIPULATION FUNCTIONS

Function Name	Description
MsiGetActiveDatabase	Returns a handle to the database that was opened during the present installation session. This function must be called first in order to provide the database handle required as input by other MSI functions.
MsiDatabaseOpenView	Opens a view object using a SQL query. This query must be created using the special syntax accepted by the Windows Installer. From this function you get a handle to the view object used by the other functions that work with the view object.
MsiViewExecute	Executes the SQL query on the specified table and prepares the view for fetching the records. This function must be called only once per view, before any attempt is made to fetch a record. Refer to Chapter 11 for a discussion of how to use the parameter record argument to this function.
MsiViewFetch	Retrieves the next sequential record in the view. Once you have obtained the record handle you can use a number of different functions to read and write the columns in the record.
MsiRecordGetString	Gets the string value of a record column. You can use a number of Get and Set functions to retrieve or set string and integer types of column data. For binary column data you can use a pair of Set and Read functions to manipulate binary data as a stream.

Refer to the MSI help file for a complete description of the record manipulation API functions available from the Windows Installer.

Table 16-2 describes the properties that are persisted in the Property table. You will notice that some of these properties are not documented in the MSI help file because they have been authored by ISWI.

TABLE 16-2 LIST OF PROPERTIES WRITTEN TO THE PROPERTY TABLE AT RUN TIME

Property Name	Property Value
ARPHELPLINK	`http://www.iswiartco.com`
ARPHELPTELEPHONE	555-555-1234
ARPNOREPAIR	0
ARPURLINFOABOUT	`http://www.iswiartco.com`
ARPURLUPDATEINFO	`http://www.iswiartco.com`
DefaultUIFont	Tahoma8
DialogCaption	InstallShield for Windows Installer
DiskPrompt	[1]
DiskSerial	1234-5678
Display_IsBitmapDlg	1
ErrorDialog	SetupError
InstallChoice	AR
INSTALLLEVEL	100
Manufacturer	ISWI Art Company
NewFolder	NewFolder-NOTUSED
PIDTemplate	12345<###-%%%%%%>@@@@@
ProductCode	{F1E244D0-C12A-4B8A-BFD4-3EDC00710E6D}
ProductID	None
ProductLanguage	1033

Property Name	Property Value
ProductName	CATest
ProductVersion	1.0.0.0000
ProgressType0	install
ProgressType1	Installing
ProgressType2	installed
ProgressType3	installs
RebootYesNo	Yes
Registration	No
ReinstallFileVersion	o
ReinstallModeText	omus
ReinstallRepair	r
SetupType	Typical
UpgradeCode	{A82A9247-D63F-46EA-BD2B-913D26276B32}

We have pretty much exhausted the Property table so now it is time to see how to work with the user interface using custom actions.

Custom Actions and the User Interface

Custom actions are about the only method you can use when you want to do something dynamic with the user interface. In particular you need to use a custom action if you want to dynamically populate a ListBox, ComboBox, or a ListView control in a dialog box. There is also a DoAction control event that executes a custom action based on the action of the control with which it is associated. In the following section you will work with a ListBox control and learn how to dynamically populate it using a custom action.

Dynamically populating a list box during an installation

In this example you are going to create the capability that will enable the user to choose the drive on which the RMCCPSearch action will search for the qualifying product. This will give you experience with a list box control and the DoAction control event. In this example you need to create three entry-point functions: one to populate the ListBox control and two to be associated with the DoAction control event assigned to the two buttons in the dialog box you will have to create.

Before you start generating the custom actions, generate the dialog box you are going to populate with your custom action. In Chapter 9, you learned how to work with the user interface using the Dialog Editor. Therefore, I will only show the dialog you need to create. Figure 16-1 shows this dialog.

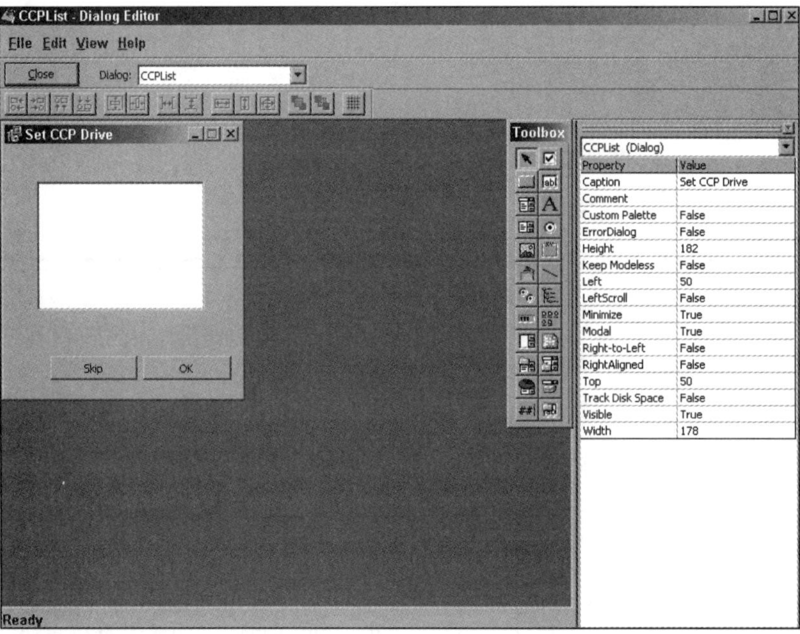

Figure 16-1: Dialog box with ListBox control showing the list of available drives on the local machine

When you create this dialog box, you will want to assign the property DRIVELIST to the ListBox control. It is through this property that all of the local drives will be associated so that they will all show up as a group in the ListBox control. Now let's move on to looking at the code to manage this dialog box. In the following code you are creating three entry point functions, three helper or private functions, and you are accessing one DLL function. The three entry point functions are the targets of the three custom actions that you will need to create. The three private functions are used to provide functionality that is needed by the three entry point functions. We also need to prototype one of the Windows Installer functions that has not been prototyped for us in the iswi.h file. You should enter this code yourself and make sure that it compiles correctly. Following this code I discuss the steps you need to take to make use of the functionality that you have created.

```
///////////////////////////////////////////////////////////////////////////
//
//  IIIIIII SSSSSS
//    II    SS                     InstallShield (R)
//    II    SSSSSS                   (c) 1996-2000,
//    II        SS     InstallShield Software Corporation
//    II        SS                All rights reserved.
//  IIIIIII SSSSSS
//
//    File Name:  Setup.rul
//
//  Description:  InstallShield script
//
///////////////////////////////////////////////////////////////////////////

// include files
#include "isrt.h"
#include "ISWI.h"
#include "winapi.h"


// function Prototypes
// entry point functions
export prototype SetDriveList(HWND);
export prototype SetCCP_DRIVE(HWND);
export prototype ClearCCP_DRIVE(HWND);

// private functions
prototype AddListBoxRecord(STRING, INT, STRING, STRING, HWND);
prototype GetDriveTypeText(STRING, BYREF STRING, NUMBER);
prototype GetDrivesAndTypes(BYREF VARIANT, BYREF VARIANT);

// DLL functions
prototype MSI.MsiCloseHandle(HWND);

// global constants
#define PROPERTY     "DRIVELIST"
```

```
///////////////////////////////////////////////////////////////////////
//
//  Function:  SetDriveList
//
//  Purpose:   This function will be called by the script engine
//             to populate the ListBox control
//
///////////////////////////////////////////////////////////////////////
function SetDriveList(hMSI)
NUMBER  nReturn, nSize, i, nBufSize;
STRING  valArray(), txtArray(), szDisplay;
STRING     szQuery, szDrive, szValue;
HWND   hDataBase, hView;
begin

      i = 1;

    // Define the SQL query for accessing the ListBox table
    szQuery = "SELECT * FROM ListBox";

    // Get the active database handle
    hDataBase = MsiGetActiveDatabase(hMSI);

    if(!hDataBase) then
        return ERROR_INSTALL_FAILURE;
    endif;

    // Create the view object based on the SQL query
    nReturn = MsiDatabaseOpenView(hDataBase, szQuery, hView);

    if(nReturn != ERROR_SUCCESS) then
        MsiCloseHandle(hDataBase);
        return ERROR_INSTALL_FAILURE;
    endif;

    // Obtain an array of drive letters and another
    // array of drive types. The values in these arrays
    // will be used to populate the ListBox control
    GetDrivesAndTypes(valArray, txtArray);

    // Get the array size so you know how many drives
    // are on the local machine. This will be the number
    // of rows that you need to add to the ListBox table
    nSize = SizeOf(valArray);
```

```
    // Loop thorugh all the values in the arrays and add
    // them to the ListBox table
    for i=0 to nSize-1

        // Create the string that will be displayed in the
        // ListBox control
        szDisplay = valArray(i) + " - " + txtArray(i);

        // Add the record to the ListBox table
        nReturn = AddListBoxRecord(PROPERTY, i+1, valArray(i),
                                                  szDisplay,hView);

        if(nReturn < 0) then
            MsiCloseHandle(hDataBase);
            MsiCloseHandle(hView);
            return ERROR_INSTALL_FAILURE;
        endif;

    endfor;

    // After everything is completed close all the handles
    MsiCloseHandle(hDataBase);
    MsiCloseHandle(hView);

    return ERROR_SUCCESS;

end;


//////////////////////////////////////////////////////////////////////
//
//  Function:  SetCCP_DRIVE
//
//  Purpose:   This function will be called by the DoAction
//             control event assigned to the OK button
//
//////////////////////////////////////////////////////////////////////
function SetCCP_DRIVE(hMSI)
NUMBER  nReturn, nBufSize;
STRING     szValue;
begin

    // Get the value of the DRIVELIST property
    // This will be equal to the choice made by the user
```

```
    // in the ListBox control on the dialog
    szValue = "";
    nReturn = MsiGetProperty(hMSI, PROPERTY, szValue, nBufSize);

    nBufSize = nBufSize + 1;
    Resize(szValue, nBufSize);

    nReturn = MsiGetProperty(hMSI, PROPERTY, szValue, nBufSize);

    // Set the value of the CCP_DRIVE property to be equal
    // to the selection made by the user in the ListBox control
    nReturn = MsiSetProperty(hMSI, "CCP_DRIVE", szValue);

    if(nReturn != ERROR_SUCCESS) then
        return ERROR_INSTALL_FAILURE;
    endif;

end;


//////////////////////////////////////////////////////////////////////
//
//  Function:  ClearCCP_DRIVE
//
//  Purpose:   This function will be called by the DoAction
//             control event assigned to the Skip button
//
//////////////////////////////////////////////////////////////////////
function ClearCCP_DRIVE(hMSI)
NUMBER  nReturn;
begin

    // Set the value of the DRIVELIST property to an empty
    // string so that it will be removed from the Property table
    nReturn = MsiSetProperty(hMSI, PROPERTY, "");

    if(nReturn != ERROR_SUCCESS) then
        return ERROR_INSTALL_FAILURE;
    endif;

end;


//////////////////////////////////////////////////////////////////////
//
```

```
//  Function:  AddListBoxRecord
//
//  Purpose:   This function adds records to the
//             ListBox table
//
///////////////////////////////////////////////////////////////////////
function AddListBoxRecord(szProperty, nOrder, szValue, szText,
hView)
NUMBER  nReturn;
HWND    hRecord;
begin

    // Create a record object so you can add your values to it
    hRecord = MsiCreateRecord(4);

    if(!hRecord) then
        return ERROR_INSTALL_FAILURE;
    endif;

    // Populate the four fields of the record object
    MsiRecordSetString(hRecord, 1, szProperty);
    MsiRecordSetInteger(hRecord, 2, nOrder);
    MsiRecordSetString(hRecord, 3, szValue);
    MsiRecordSetString(hRecord, 4, szText);

    // Add this record to the ListBox table
    // These changes will not be persistent since the
    // in-memory database is read only
    nReturn = MsiViewModify(hView, MSIMODIFY_INSERT_TEMPORARY,
                                                        hRecord);

    if(nReturn != ERROR_SUCCESS) then
        MsiCloseHandle(hRecord);
        return ERROR_INSTALL_FAILURE;
    endif;

    // Close the record handle
    MsiCloseHandle(hRecord);

    return ERROR_SUCCESS;

end;


///////////////////////////////////////////////////////////////////////
```

```
//
// Function:   GetDrivesAndTypes
//
// Purpose:    This function returns as arrays the available drive
//             letters and drive types
//
///////////////////////////////////////////////////////////////////////
function GetDrivesAndTypes(valArray, txtArray)
NUMBER  nCount, nFound, i;
STRING  szDrive, szIterator, svText;
OBJECT  dc, d, fso;
begin

    // Create a FileSystemObject
    set fso = CreateObject("Scripting.FileSystemObject");

    // From the FileSystemObject create a
    // Drives collection object
    set dc = fso.Drives;

    // Get the number of items in the Drives collection object
    nCount = dc.Count;

    // Size the arrays to hold the number of items in the
    // Drives collection object
    Resize(valArray, nCount);
    Resize(txtArray, nCount);

    nFound = 0;
    i = 0;

    // Loop through each possible drive letter and check if
    // that drive letter is available on the local machine.
    // If the drive letter is available then add it to the
    // valArray. If the drive does not exist and an exception is
    // thrown increment the index i.
    // This will be the code that is replaced once InstallScript
    // implements the For Each...Next functionality for iterating
    // collections that do not support numeric indexing
    while(nFound < nCount)
        try
            switch(i)
                case 0:
                    szDrive = dc.Item("A");
                case 1:
```

```
        szDrive = dc.Item("B");
    case 2:
        szDrive = dc.Item("C");
    case 3:
        szDrive = dc.Item("D");
    case 4:
        szDrive = dc.Item("E");
    case 5:
        szDrive = dc.Item("F");
    case 6:
        szDrive = dc.Item("G");
    case 7:
        szDrive = dc.Item("H");
    case 8:
        szDrive = dc.Item("I");
    case 9:
        szDrive = dc.Item("J");
    case 10:
        szDrive = dc.Item("K");
    case 11:
        szDrive = dc.Item("L");
    case 12:
        szDrive = dc.Item("M");
    case 13:
        szDrive = dc.Item("N");
    case 14:
        szDrive = dc.Item("O");
    case 15:
        szDrive = dc.Item("P");
    case 16:
        szDrive = dc.Item("Q");
    case 17:
        szDrive = dc.Item("R");
    case 18:
        szDrive = dc.Item("S");
    case 19:
        szDrive = dc.Item("T");
    case 20:
        szDrive = dc.Item("U");
    case 21:
        szDrive = dc.Item("V");
    case 22:
        szDrive = dc.Item("W");
    case 23:
        szDrive = dc.Item("X");
```

```
                case 24:
                    szDrive = dc.Item("Y");
                case 25:
                    szDrive = dc.Item("Z");
            endswitch;
            szDrive = szDrive + "\\";

            // For the found drive get the drive type
            GetDriveTypeText(szDrive, svText, i);

            // Populate the arrays for the drives that are found
            valArray(nFound) = szDrive;
            txtArray(nFound) = svText;
            nFound = nFound + 1;
            i = i + 1;
        catch
            i = i + 1;
        endcatch;

    endwhile;

end;


//////////////////////////////////////////////////////////////////////
//
//  Function:  GetDriveTypeText
//
//  Purpose:   This function will be called by the script engine
//
//////////////////////////////////////////////////////////////////////
function GetDriveTypeText(szDrive, svText, index)
INT nType;
begin

    // Call the Windows API to get the drive type identifier
    nType = GetDriveType(szDrive);

    // For the drive type returned create a text description
    switch(nType)
        case DRIVE_UNKNOWN:
            svText = "Unknown drive type";
        case DRIVE_NO_ROOT_DIR:
            svText = "Invalid drive";
        case DRIVE_REMOVABLE:
```

```
            svText = "Removable drive";
        case DRIVE_FIXED:
            svText = "Fixed drive";
        case DRIVE_REMOTE:
            svText = "Remote drive";
        case DRIVE_CDROM:
            svText = "CD-ROM drive";
        case DRIVE_RAMDISK:
            svText = "RAM disk drive";
    endswitch;

end;
```

The SetDriveList function is the entry point of a custom action that will collect the information found on the target system of the installation and add rows to the ListBox control in the dialog that you created earlier. In this function you have created an SQL query that is used to get a view of the ListBox table. Using the GetDrivesAndTypes private function you obtain an array of drives and their descriptions that will be used to populate the ListBox table. You then call the AddListBoxRecord function that will add the rows to the ListBox table.

The AddListBoxRecord private function first creates an empty record of four columns and then, using the Windows Installer functions MsiRecordSetString and MsiRecordSetInteger, adds values to this record. After setting the values for the columns in the record, the record is used by the Windows Installer function MsiViewModify to add rows to the ListBox table. It is important to realize that all tables in the running database are read only. When you create records at run time for a specific table, these records are not persisted in the database after the installation is complete. This is why you need to use the MSIMODIFY_INSERT_TEMPORARY constant when you call the MsiViewModify function.

In the above code there are two other exported functions, which are the entry points for two additional custom actions. The SetCCP_DRIVE function is used to set the CCP_DRIVE property to the location selected by the end user. The ClearCCP_DRIVE function is used to set the CCP_DRIVE property to null. The custom actions defined using these two entry point functions are attached to the two buttons in the dialog shown in Figure 16-1.

The steps that you need to take to get this example to work are given in the following list. It is assumed that you have already created the dialog box shown in Figure 16-1 and that you have entered and compiled the code shown above.

1. Using the custom action wizard create an immediate custom action that uses the SetDriveList entry point function.
2. Insert this custom action into the InstallUISequence table right after the SetupInitialization dialog.

3. Right after this custom action insert the dialog that contains the ListBox control and which is shown in Figure 16-1.
4. Create another immediate custom action that uses the SetCPP_DRIVE entry point function.
5. Using the dialog editor go to the Behavior icon for the new dialog and define a DoAction control event for the button that is to be used to set the CCP_DRIVE property. The argument for this control event is the name of the custom action that you created in the previous step. The condition on this control event needs to be 1 so that it will always execute.
6. Create the final immediate custom action that will use the ClearCCP_ DRIVE entry point function.
7. Using the dialog editor go again to the Behavior icon for the new dialog and define a DoAction control event for the button that is to be used for clearing the CCP_DRIVE property. The argument for this control event is the name of the custom action that you created in the previous step. The condition on this control event needs to be 1 so that it will always execute.

Once you have completed the above steps you need to build your project and test it. When you run your installation user interface, you should see a dialog box in which all the drives on your test machine are displayed.

We now need to move on and look at how to create custom actions where dynamic link libraries need to be accessed from InstallScript.

Working with Dynamic Link Libraries

There will often be times when you want to implement functions in a DLL that you can call from your script. The problem that arises is how does one get this DLL onto the system then find it. After the installation is complete the question is how to remove this DLL from the system. The solution to this is to stream your DLL into the *Binary* table and then stream it out into the location defined by the SUPPORTDIR system variable. This system variable is a temporary location that gets cleaned up at the end of the installation by the CleanUp custom action that is launched at the end of each sequence.

The following code shows how to incorporate a DLL into the *Binary* table and to stream it out and then call a function in this DLL. The DLL that we are using for this example is the one we created to reverse a string passed to it. This DLL was created in Chapter 14.

To be able test this code example you will need to stream the DLL into the *Binary* table. You do this by using the Power Editor in ISWI. For this new row you will create in the *Binary* table you want to use the name of REVSTR for the entry. You then need to identify in the second column the build location of the revstr.dll. When you build your project, this file will be streamed into the *Binary* table without any further effort on your part.

```
////////////////////////////////////////////////////////////////////
//
//  IIIIIII SSSSSS
//    II    SS                     InstallShield (R)
//    II    SSSSSS                   (c) 1996-2000,
//    II         SS     InstallShield Software Corporation
//    II        SS                 All rights reserved.
//  IIIIIII SSSSSS
//
//    File Name:  Setup.rul
//
//  Description:  InstallShield script
//
////////////////////////////////////////////////////////////////////

// include files
#include "isrt.h"
#include "ISWI.h"
#include "winapi.h"


// function Prototypes
// entry point functions
export prototype CATest(HWND);

// private functions
prototype StreamFileFromBinary(HWND, STRING, STRING);

// DLL functions
// This function is not already prototyped in winapi.h
prototype KERNEL32.WriteFile(NUMBER, BINARY, NUMBER,
                                            BYREF NUMBER, NUMBER);
// This function is not already prototyped in ISMsiQuery.h
prototype MSI.MsiCloseHandle(HWND);

// This is the prototype for our own DLL function
prototype revstr.ReverseString(STRING, BYREF STRING);
```

```
// global variables
// This is a constant associated with the
// WriteFile Windows API function
#define CREATE_ALWAYS   2


///////////////////////////////////////////////////////////////////////
//
//  Function:  CATest
//
//  Purpose:   This function will be called by the script engine
//
///////////////////////////////////////////////////////////////////////
function CATest(hMSI)
STRING  szBinaryKey, szFileName;
STRING  szStr, svStr;
NUMBER  nReturn;
begin

    // Intialize the string that we are going to reverse
    szStr = "This is a string.";

    // Identify the row in the Binary table
    // where our DLL is stored
    szBinaryKey = "REVSTR";

    // Create the path to where we are going
    // stream out our DLL
    szFileName = SUPPORTDIR ^ "revstr.dll";

    // Stream out the DLL
    nReturn = StreamFileFromBinary(hMSI, szBinaryKey, szFileName);

    if(nReturn != ERROR_SUCCESS) then
        return ERROR_INSTALL_FAILURE;
    endif;

    // Load our DLL into memory
    nReturn = UseDLL(szFileName);

    if(nReturn < 0) then
        return ERROR_INSTALL_FAILURE;
    endif;

    // Call our exported function in our DLL
```

```
    revstr.ReverseString(szStr, svStr);

    // Display the results of reversing the string
    SprintfBox(INFORMATION, "DLL Streaming",
            "Input string: %s\n\n Output string: %s", szStr, svStr);

    // Unload our DLL from memory
    nReturn = UnUseDLL(szFileName);

end;


//////////////////////////////////////////////////////////////////////
//
//  Function:  StreamFileFromBinary
//
//  Purpose:   This function will stream out a file from the
//             the Binary table.
//
//////////////////////////////////////////////////////////////////////
function StreamFileFromBinary(hInstall, szBinaryKey, szFileName)
NUMBER  nReturn, nvBufSize, nWritten;
STRING  szQuery, szStream;
HWND    hDataBase, hBinaryView, hBinaryRecord, hFile;
begin

    //Get the handle to the active database.
    hDataBase = MsiGetActiveDatabase(hInstall);

    if(hDataBase = 0) then
        return ERROR_INSTALL_FAILURE;
    endif;

    // Get a view of the binary table based on an SQL Query
    szQuery = "SELECT * FROM Binary WHERE Name='"
                                              + szBinaryKey + "'";

    // Create the view object for that contains the one
    // row that we are interested in
    nReturn = MsiDatabaseOpenView(hDataBase, szQuery, hBinaryView);

    if(nReturn != ERROR_SUCCESS) then
        MsiCloseHandle(hDataBase);
        return ERROR_INSTALL_FAILURE;
    endif;
```

```
// Execute the view before getting the record
nReturn = MsiViewExecute(hBinaryView, NULL);

if(nReturn != ERROR_SUCCESS) then
    MsiCloseHandle(hDataBase);
    MsiCloseHandle(hBinaryView);
    return ERROR_INSTALL_FAILURE;
endif;

// Fetch the first and only record in the view
nReturn = MsiViewFetch(hBinaryView, hBinaryRecord);

if(nReturn != ERROR_SUCCESS) then
    MsiCloseHandle(hDataBase);
    MsiCloseHandle(hBinaryView);
    return ERROR_INSTALL_FAILURE;
endif;

// Create the file in that location using the
// CreateFile Windows API.
hFile = CreateFileA(szFileName, GENERIC_WRITE, 0, 0,
                    CREATE_ALWAYS, FILE_ATTRIBUTE_NORMAL, 0);

if(hFile = INVALID_HANDLE_VALUE) then
    MsiCloseHandle(hDataBase);
    MsiCloseHandle(hBinaryView);
    MsiCloseHandle(hBinaryRecord);
    return ERROR_INSTALL_FAILURE;
endif;

nBufSize = 1023;
// Repeat our extraction of the file until there are
// no more bytes to stream out of the Binary table
repeat

    //Read the stream into a buffer, 1023 bytes at a time
    nReturn = MsiRecordReadStream(hBinaryRecord, 2, szStream,
                                                     nBufSize);

    // If the operation to stream out the file fails
    // then close all handles and return failure. The Windows
    // Installer will then terminate the installation.
    if(nReturn != ERROR_SUCCESS) then
```

```
            MsiCloseHandle(hDataBase);
            MsiCloseHandle(hBinaryView);
            MsiCloseHandle(hBinaryRecord);
            CloseHandle(hFile);
            return ERROR_INSTALL_FAILURE;
        endif;

        if(nBufSize > 0)then
            //Write the buffer to a file.
            nReturn = WriteFile(hFile, szStream, nBufSize,
                                                    nWritten, 0);

            // If the operation to write the file fails
            // then close all handles and return failure.
            // The Windows Installer will then
            // terminate the installation.
            if(nReturn == 0) then
                MsiCloseHandle(hDataBase);
                MsiCloseHandle(hBinaryView);
                MsiCloseHandle(hBinaryRecord);
                CloseHandle(hFile);
                return ERROR_INSTALL_FAILURE;
            endif;
        endif;
    until(nBufSize = 0);

    //Close all handles
    CloseHandle(hFile);
    MsiCloseHandle(hBinaryRecord);
    MsiCloseHandle(hDataBase);
    MsiCloseHandle(hBinaryView);

    return ERROR_SUCCESS;

end;
```

A good location for handling your DLLs that you want to use from your script is the OnBegin() event handler. You could create one DLL that exports all the functions needed by your script and load this DLL in this handler. You could then unload this DLL in the OnEnd() event handler. Based on the sequence in which you are running, you could load a different DLL. You would use the code shown earlier in this chapter for determining what sequence you are in.

Summary

In this chapter we have taken a look a number of ways you can use InstallScript to implement custom actions. We have discussed the OnBegin() and OnEnd() event handlers and the important use we can make of these special functions. We have also investigated the very important *Property* table and taken a look at what we can use it for. We have been reminded that this table is the equivalent of the definition of global variables in a structured programming environment. Finally we looked at how to handle a DLL that we need to call from our script. We saw how to stream this file into the *Binary* table and how to stream it out again into a temporary location that will automatically get cleaned up at the end of the installation.

Chapter 17

Creating and Sharing Components

IN THIS CHAPTER

- ◆ How the operating system handles dynamic-link libraries
- ◆ The rules to follow when creating components
- ◆ How to properly modify components
- ◆ How to use InstallShield for Windows Installer to create components
- ◆ Using merge modules to deliver components to an installation package
- ◆ How the Windows Installer keeps track of the components already installed
- ◆ The installation of special types of components

THIS CHAPTER ADDRESSES one of the core concepts of creating Windows Installer packages. This core concept is the proper creation of components and how the Windows Installer handles these components.

Component Sharing and the Operating System

From its very inception, the Windows operating system was based on the concept of different applications sharing code. Initially, much of the code that comprised a Windows application was found in a dynamic-link library (DLL), which exported various functions that the main application executable used to perform various operations. If these operations are of generic value, other applications can use these same DLLs for implementing their functionality without having to develop the same code over again. All installing these DLLs into a central location where all applications that need them can find them is all that is necessary. Typically, if a DLL were only shared among the applications of a specific company, then it would be installed to a folder that has a format similar to the following:

```
<Drive>:\Program Files\Common Files\<company-name>\Shared
```

If a DLL is installed in this location, all the clients that use this file need to know the path to locate the file, so that it can be found and loaded into memory.

If the DLL is shared across applications of different companies, the standard location for installing this type of file is the following:

```
<WindowsFolder>\System32
```

A globally shared DLL that is installed in the System32 folder can always be found because this location is part of the standard search path used by the operating system for finding DLLs.

Dynamic-link libraries that are not shared are installed into the install location of the using application executable or in a subdirectory of this location. In this situation, the client executable always knows the relative path to this DLL and can always find it.

If you look at a COM server instead of a Win32 DLL, the Registry now provides the location of the server. You find this location by querying the registry for the class ID and not through a search path as you use with a Win32 DLL.

How the OS handles a dynamic-link library

Regardless of how an application finds its DLLs, only one copy of this DLL is in memory. This section of memory is called the global heap and this DLL gets mapped into the separate address space of each application that is using the DLL. On Windows 95, Windows 98, and Windows NT 4, each application runs in its own process space, which is one of the major advances that these 32-bit operating systems make over the older 16-bit Windows OS. This functionality is shown in Figure 17-1.

The problem comes when two different applications need different versions of the same DLL. After the first application launches, it loads the DLL that it needs into memory and it works the way it was designed. However, after the second application launches, the operating system finds that a DLL already exists by the requested name in memory, so that the OS maps this DLL into the address space of the second application. Unfortunately, this is not the version of the DLL that this second application needs, and thus it fails to function properly or possibly will not run at all. This is the conflict between versions of DLLs we've referred to as DLL Hell.

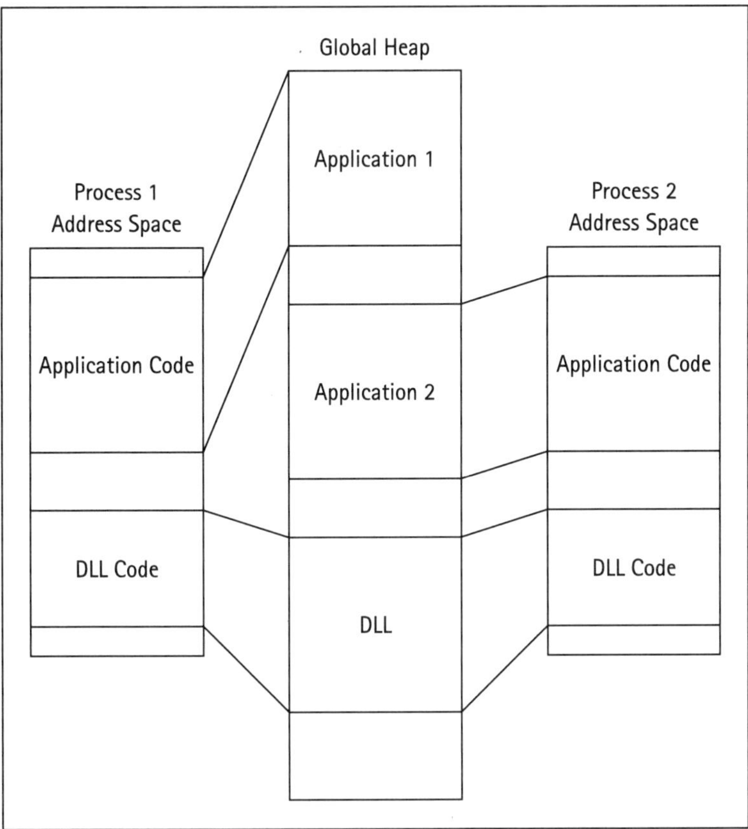

Figure 17-1: The mapping of a DLL into the address space of two different applications

What causes DLL Hell?

Version conflicts between DLLs are caused primarily because newer versions of DLLs that get installed onto a machine are not completely backward compatible. After the newer DLL is installed into a shared location, it will overwrite the older version that is already on the machine. You find other causes of DLL Hell, such as introducing new DLLs that have bugs, which break functionality that used to work or the overwriting of newer DLLs with older versions, because the installation program did not check for the version before it copied the file. However, the lack of complete backward compatibility between new and old DLLs is the primary cause.

How new versions of are changing things

The new versions of the Windows operating systems – Windows 2000, Windows 98 SE, and Windows Me – implement new functionality to help reduce the problems that have arisen in the past due to the conflict between different versions of DLLs. One area addressed is the destabilization caused to the operating system itself by the indiscriminate replacement of system components with the wrong versions of these components. This functionality is termed System File Protection and is discussed in the next section. System File Protection has only been implemented in Windows 2000 and Windows ME.

Another functionality implemented in these new operating systems is the capability to have more than one version of the same DLL in memory at the same time. This capability allows for what is called side-by-side sharing, where each application can use the version of a DLL that it needs and with no version conflict. Side-by-side sharing has been implemented in Windows 2000, Windows 98 SE, and Windows ME. This creation of private components is discussed in the sections that follow the discussion of System File Protection.

SYSTEM FILE PROTECTION

System File Protection (SFP) is a new functionality that protects the system files from being updated or deleted by applications that try to modify the files that are in the System32 folder and other protected folders. If an application tries to copy over or delete one of the files that is on the File Protection List, the copy or delete operation will appear to succeed, but the correct file will be replaced, so that the system is brought back to the same state as when it was first installed.

The files that are protected by this new functionality are the .sys, .exe, .dll, .ocx, .ttf, and .fon files that are installed from the Windows 2000 CD-ROM. If a file is copied to a protected folder, the System File Protection will receive a directory change notification. After this notification is received, the System File Protection determines which file was changed. If the file is on the system file protection list, the SFP checks the file signature in a catalog file to determine whether the new file is the correct version. If the version is not correct, the file is replaced with the correct version from the dllcache folder under the System32 directory or the file is replaced from the original distribution media for the operating system.

You find approximately 2700 to 2800 files on the file protection list, depending on the flavor of the operating system that you are talking about. The question that arises is how to update these files if the operating system has them protected. Only four mechanisms support changing the files that are on the file protection list. These are listed as follows:

- Windows 2000 Service Packs (Update.exe)
- Hot-fix distributions (Hotfix.exe)
- Operating system upgrades (Winnt32.exe)
- Windows Web Update

The Windows Me operating system implements System File Protection in a different manner. Windows Me uses catalogs that describe protected files. The protection of files on Windows Me requires that the file be on the file protection list with a catalog with the version information. This functionality permits the update of protected files with the installation of an application if the information for the file is updated with a system file protection catalog.

SIDE-BY-SIDE SHARING

In Windows 2000, Windows 98 SE, and Windows Me, you find a new functionality that permits applications to privatize the DLLs that they need to make sure are not changed out by the installation of another application with a version of the DLL with which they cannot work. This functionality is called side-by-side sharing, which allows multiple versions of a DLL to be loaded into memory at the same time.

Two approaches to side-by-side sharing exist and the type you use determines how an installation is structured. These approaches are shown in the following list:

- Creating new components: Creation of a new component, designed from scratch and used by only one application.
- DLL redirection: Reconfiguration of an existing application so that the DLLs that provide its functionality are isolated, and another application that installs a newer version will not prevent the already installed application from using the version of the DLL that it needs.

The primary focus of creating new components that make use of the side-by-side sharing capabilities of the new operating systems is to prevent future versions of the component from being the one that is used by the original application. The primary focus of DLL redirection is to insulate existing applications from being disabled by the installation of other applications that install incompatible versions of the same DLL.

The Componentization Rules

You need to follow a number of strict rules when creating components. These rules need to be followed because components are sharable between features in a single application, as well as across applications and across companies. These rules are critical to the proper reference counting of components and if this is not done correctly, then applications can get disabled when uninstalling a component that is required. A situation is also possible where you can leave orphaned resources behind on a machine after uninstalling components that were not created in the proper manner. Proper reference counting is also critical to the proper performance of major upgrades using the *Upgrade* table.

When creating components, the basic guideline to follow is to build small components that include all the resources required by the file or files in the component. The reason for small components is to make modification of the component less necessary. Adding or removing files from a component is not possible while still keeping the same component ID. If you want to be able to add or remove files from an application, you want to be able to do this by adding or removing components and not adding or removing files from a component.

As you deal with the installations for medium to large applications, creating larger components is necessary. This becomes necessary to both simplify the creation of the installation package as well as to minimize the bloat caused to the registry by the large amount of component information that needs to be added. However, making larger components does generate component management problems when it comes time to version the component. Thinking of a component in the same light as COM interface that has been shipped is appropriate. Once shipped, a COM interface is immutable. The only way to add functionality to a COM server is to add a new interface. The same goes for components. After you create a component and actually ship it as part of an application, you do not want to change it in any fashion. If you need to add additional resources to a component, then you need to think about creating a new component with a new component ID.

You now look at the rules to follow when creating a component. You also look at how a component can legally be modified, as well as at the impact that breaking the rules for component creation can have.

Creating new components

With components being the atomic unit of an application, defining the components correctly is important. One of the important reasons for defining the components correctly is so that the mechanism used for reference counting the components works as designed. The refcounting of components plays an important role in many areas, such as the performance of major upgrades. Below is a list of rules that to follow when creating components:

- **Never create two components that install a resource under the same name and target location.** If a resource must be duplicated in multiple components, change its name or target location in each component. Apply this rule across applications, products, product versions, and companies.
- **Note that the previous rule means that no two components can ever have the same keypath file.** The keypath value points to a particular file or folder belonging to the component, which the installer uses to detect the component. If two components have the same keypath file, the installer is unable to distinguish which component is installed. Two components, however may share a keypath folder.
- **Never create a version of a component that is not compatible with all previous versions of the component.** Apply this rule across applications, products, product versions, and companies.

- **Don't create components that contain resources, which need to be installed into more than one directory on the user's system.** The installer installs all the resources in a component into the same directory. Installing some resources into subdirectories is not possible.
- **Define a new component for every .exe, .dll, and .ocx file.** Designate these files as the keypath files of their components. Assign each component a component code GUID.
- **Define a new component for every .hlp or .chm help file.** Designate these files as the keypath files of their components. Add the .cnt or .chi files to the components holding their associated .hlp and .chm files. Assign each component a component code GUID.
- **Define a new component for every file that serves as a target of a shortcut.** Designate these files as the keypath files of their components. Assign each component a component code GUID.
- **Identify any files, registry keys, shortcuts, or other resources that are shared across applications and which can be provided by existing components available as merge modules.** You must not include any of these resources in the components you author. Instead obtain these components by merging the merge modules into your installation package.
- **Group all the remaining resources into folders.** All resources in each folder must ship together. If a pair of resources may ship separately in the future, put these in separate folders. Define a new component for every folder. Try to keep the total number of components low to improve performance. Divide the application into many components when it is necessary to have the installer check the validity of the installation thoroughly. Designate any file in the component as the keypath file. Assign each component a component code GUID.
- **Add registry keys to the components.** Any registry key that points to a file should be included in that file's component. Other registry keys should be logically grouped with the files that require them.

These above rules are not necessarily hard and fast but used with an understanding of why they are there. The rules basically aim to insure that no two applications will ever require different versions of the same file, removal of one application does not break another application, and no resources are orphaned on a machine regardless of the order in which products are uninstalled.

Modifying a component

Authors may need to introduce new components or modify existing components. If the addition, removal, or modification of resources effectively creates a new component, then the component code must also be changed.

CREATING A NEW COMPONENT

Introduce a new component and assign it a unique component code when making any of the following changes:

- Any change not shown by testing to be compatible with previous versions of the component. In this case, you must also change the name or target location of every resource in the component.
- A change in the name or target location of any file, registry key, shortcut, or other resource in the component. In this case, you must also change the name or target location of every resource in the component.
- Addition or removal of any file, registry key, shortcut, or other resource from the component. In this case, you must also change the name or target location every resource in the component.

When introducing a new component, authors need to do one of the following to ensure that the component does not conflict with any existing components:

- Change the name or target location of any resource that may be installed under the same name and target location by another component.
- Guarantee that the new component is never installed into the same folder as another component, which has a resource under a common name and location. This includes localized versions of files with the same filename.
- When changing the component code of an existing component, also change the name or target location of every file, registry key, shortcut, and other resource in the component.

CREATING A NEW VERSION OF A COMPONENT

A new version of a component is assigned the same component code as another existing component. Modifying a component without changing the component code is only optional in the following cases:

- Testing the changes to the component prove it to be backward compatible with all previous versions of the component.
- The author can guarantee that the new version of the component will never be installed on a system where it conflicts with previous versions of the component or applications requiring a previous version.
- The component code results in two components sharing resources, such as registry values, files, or shortcuts.

What happens if the rules are broken

The following describes ways that authors sometimes break the recommended component rules and the possible consequences.

An author adds resources to a component without changing the component code.

- Products installed with the old component have no information about the added resources in their installation database.
- If both a new product, which has the added resources, and an old product are installed on the same computer, the resources can be left behind if the new product is uninstalled first.
- An old product without the added resources cannot repair the newer version of the component. Reinstalling the old product does not restore the added resources.

An author removes resources from a component without changing the component code.

- Products installed with the new component have no information about the removed resources in their installation database.
- If both an old product, having the resource information, and a new product are installed on the same computer, the resources can be left behind if the old product is uninstalled first.
- A new product with the removed resources cannot repair the older version of the product. Reinstalling the new product does not restore the removed resources.

An author includes a file that is incompatible with previous versions without changing the component code.

If an author includes an incompatible file in a component without changing the component code, default file versioning causes the installer to overwrite the original file with the more recent incompatible file. This overwrite can damage old products needing the original file. It may also prevent the installer from repairing the old product because the version of a component's keypath file determines the version of the component. If a newer version of the keypath file is already installed, the installer does not install the older version of the component. For more information, see File Versioning Rules in the Windows Installer help. In this case, the new product must be removed before the old product can be reinstalled.

- Default file versioning causes the installer to overwrite the original file with the more recent incompatible file.
- Old products that need the original file are damaged.

- An overwrite may also prevent the installer from repairing the old product because the version of a component's keypath file determines the version of the component. If a newer version of the keypath file is already installed, the installer does not install the older version of the component. For more information, see File Versioning Rules in the Windows Installer help. In this case, the new product must be removed before the old product can be reinstalled.

An author includes the same resource in two different components.

If two components have a resource under the same name and location, and both components are installed into the same folder, then the removal of either component removes the common resource, which damages the remaining component.

- Uninstalling either component removes the resource and breaks the other component.
- The component reference-counting mechanism is damaged.

Special issues relating to component creation

Several special issues need to be addressed when creating components. These issues are the use of self-registration for COM components, the sharing of COM components between features, the use of the SharedDLLs key in the registry, and the various ways that a KeyPath can be defined for a component. These topics are discussed in the following four subsections.

SELF-REGISTRATION OF COM COMPONENTS

The self-registration of COM components has long been the solution to correctly making the entries in the registry so that the COM component can be properly initialized and loaded into memory when the client application needs it. In the new world of the Windows Installer, self-registration is should not be done because self-registration is a black box that cannot be managed by the Windows Installer service. If the Windows Installer does not know what has been done to the system by the running of the DllRegisterServer function in a COM DLL, it cannot know how to properly handle the registry keys this function has created during other operations.

Not using self-registration is strongly recommended for installation package authors. Instead, they should register modules by authoring one or more of the other tables provided by the installer for this purpose. These tables are the *Class*, *TypeLib*, and *ProgId* tables. Many of the benefits of having a central installer service are lost with self-registration, because self-registration routines tend to hide critical configuration information.

- A rollback of an installation with self-registered modules cannot be safely done using DllUnregisterServer because you have no way of telling if the self-registered keys are used by another feature or application.

- The ability to use advertisement is reduced if Class or extension server registration is performed within self-registration routines.
- The installer automatically handles HKCR keys in the registry tables for both per-user and per-machine installations. DllRegisterServer routines currently do not support the notion of a per-user HKCR key.
- If multiple users are using a self-registered application on the same computer, each user must install the application the first time they run it. Otherwise the installer cannot easily determine that the proper HKCU registry keys exist.
- The DLLRegisterServer can be denied access to network resources, such as type libraries, if a component is both specified as run-from-source and is listed in the SelfReg table. This can cause the installation of the component to fail to during an administrative installation.
- Self-registering DLLs are more susceptible to coding errors because the new code required for DllRegisterServer is commonly different for each DLL. Instead, use the registry tables in the database to take advantage of existing code provided by the installer.
- Self-registering DLLs can sometimes link to auxiliary DLLs that are not present or are the wrong version. In contrast, the installer can register the DLLs using the registry tables with no dependency on the current state of the system.

The order in which the installer registers or unregisters self-registering DLLs cannot be specified by the order in which the entries are made in the SelfReg table. Also the SelfReg table cannot be used to implement the registration of a self-registering executable. For this type of executable, authoring the correct database tables is necessary if this registration is to take place during the installation.

SHARING A COM COMPONENT BETWEEN FEATURES

You cannot share a COM component between features under certain circumstances. If you do not self-register your COM component and you want to share this component between two features where one of these features is not a child of the other, then it is not possible to create the Class table where your COM component is entered twice, once for each feature. This is because the name of the feature with which a COM component is associated is not part of the primary key of the Class table and you cannot have duplicate primary keys in any table. When you build your Windows Installer package, ISWI will make only one entry in the Class table and will not make the second entry. You would then have the possibility of not installing the feature that actually registers the COM component thus causing the other feature to fail because the COM registration has not been created.

You have a few solutions to this dilemma. One possible approach is to make one of the features that are going to use this COM component a child of the other feature that will also use this COM component. You would then associate the COM component with the parent feature and you would never be able to install the child without installing the parent, but you could install the parent without installing the child. You could also define this COM component as self-registering, but then you would start to cripple some of the functionality that was described in the previous section.

MIXING LEGACY AND MSI APPLICATIONS ON THE SAME MACHINE

Before the advent of the Windows Installer, applications kept track of shared DLLs in the following registry key:

```
HKEY_LOCAL_MACHINE\SOFTWARE\Microsoft\Windows\CurrentVersion\
SharedDLLs
```

Under this key, every DLL installed to a shareable location is entered here and given a reference count. Every application that comes along increments the reference count after installing the same DLL to the same location. Any uninstalled application that was decrements the reference count. When the reference count on the shared DLL becomes zero, the DLL gets removed from the system under the assumption that no other application needs it. This was a way to keep the system as clean as possible, so that it would not clutter up with a lot of unused files.

The Windows Installer keeps track of shared DLLs independently of the shared DLL reference count in the registry. For the purpose of backward compatibility with the older form of reference counting shared components, a Windows Installer component can be marked as being shared. This marking tells the Windows Installer to reference count the file in the component using the older format as well as with the newer format. If a reference count for a shared DLL exists in the registry, the installer always increments the count when it is installing the file and decrements the count when it is uninstalling, regardless if the component is marked as being shared. If a component is not marked as being shared and the reference count does not already exist, the installer will not create a reference count under the SharedDLLs key. Also, on Windows NT and Windows 2000, if a file is installed to the System32 folder, the file automatically receives an entry under the SharedDLLs key, even if the component is not marked as being shared.

If a component is not identified as being shared, another application can remove the component under certain circumstances even if the component is still needed. The following scenario demonstrates how this can occur:

- An application that uses the Windows Installer installs a shared component.
- A component is not marked as being shared with no reference count already under the SharedDLLs registry key, so that the installer does not begin a reference count.

- A legacy application, which also installs the DLL in the above component, is installed, and this legacy application creates and increments a reference count for the shared DLL.
- The legacy application is uninstalled.
- The reference count for the shared component is decremented to zero and the component is removed.
- The application that used the Windows Installer is now broken because it no longer has access to the DLL that was removed by the legacy application.

To avoid these scenarios, always mark a component as being shared so that it makes the proper entries under the SharedDLLs registry key.

DEFINING THE KEYPATH FOR A COMPONENT

The keypath for a component is normally the name of a file in the component, but it can also be a folder or a registry entry. If the keypath is a folder, then the component installs in this folder. It is not possible to have two keypath values for any component and this value cannot be shared between two components. This goes along with the rule that the same file cannot be installed by two different components. The use of a folder as the keypath value for a component is appropriate for a component that contains a number of files and where no particular files stands out as being a good candidate. This situation may occur for a component that installs a bunch of clip art, for example.

The keypath value is how the Windows Installer is able to locate the component on the system after it is installed. The health of a component is evaluated through the keypath. If the keypath for a component to be installed is missing, then this enables the self-repair functionality of the Windows Installer. If a component has a missing keypath and that component is associated with a feature that contains the target of a shortcut, then the Windows Installer attempts to reinstall the component that has the missing keypath after the user activates the shortcut. If the component is not associated with such a feature, then the self-repair is implemented from within the application itself.

Creating Components in ISWI

You can use two approaches to create components directly in an ISWI installation project. You can do this by using the various context menus to create components, add files, create shortcuts, and so forth. You can also make use of the Component Wizard to create components that require special handling. These types of specialized components can be COM components, NT Services, ODBC components, and Font components. The next two sections discuss each of these two approaches for adding components to a project.

Another method can be used to deliver components to a project, which is the creation of components outside of the project and then merging these components into the Windows Installer database at build time. This approach deals with the subject of Merge Modules, which are covered in a separate section later in this chapter.

Creating components directly in the ISWI IDE

No matter what approach you use to create components, you need to associate them with a feature. After you define your features, you can right-click a feature name to get a context menu that provides you with a number of options that relate to components. The component related options on this context menu are described in the following list:

New Component	Creates an empty component with a default name. All the input required to define this component is entered through the IDE.
Insert Components...	Launches a dialog that enables you to associate components that have already been created with other features in the project. Because you cannot add the same component twice under the same feature, this functionality only permits the sharing of components between features.
Component Wizard...	Launches the Component Wizard that helps you create specialized components. Using this wizard is the subject of the next section.
Merge Module Wizard...	Enables the selection of Merge Modules to associate with a feature or set of features. Using this wizard is discussed later in this chapter.

In this section, you will be covering the first two options in the previous list. After you select the New Component option, ISWI creates a component with the default name of NewComponentX, where X represents a sequence number used to distinguish components from one another. The name that you use for the component identifies the component in the *Component* table and because this component is the primary key in this table, this name has to be unique within the project. If you try to create two components with the same name, ISWI gives you an error message stating that a component with that name defined in the project already exists.

After you create a component by using the New Component option, you add all the files and associated information that is necessary to completely define the component. First, you want to look briefly at the context menu options after you right-click a component name in the IDE. After you right-click a component name, you get the following listed options:

Remove	Disassociates the component with the present feature. It does not remove the component from the project and it can still be seen in the Setup Design – Components view as well as under any other features with which it is still associated. This particular command is only available in the global view where both features and components are displayed together. Using the Insert Components... command, described in the previous section, you can re-associate a removed component with the feature or to move it to another feature. You cannot create another component with the same name as a removed component because it is still resident in the project.
Delete	Permanently removes a component from the project and if you want the component back, you have to recreate it. After a component is deleted, you can then create another component with the same name.
Rename	Allows you to change the name of a component.

Associated with each component in the ISWI IDE is a property page in which you enter data. When you define components in this property page, you are specifying the entries that are made in the *Component* table. Under each component is a tree of icons where you enter data that is associated with the component. If you enter data here, you are defining values that get entered into other tables. Each of these other tables has a foreign key into the *Component* table or has a foreign key into a table that has a foreign key into the *Component* table. To be able to create components in a knowledgeable fashion, you need to take a look at the fields of the *Component* table. Table 17-1 provides a description of the fields in the *Component* table.

TABLE 17-1 THE FIELDS IN THE COMPONENT TABLE

Column	Description
Component	The primary key for the table and an identifier that is unique for the product.

Continued

Table 17-1 THE FIELDS IN THE COMPONENT TABLE *(Continued)*

Column	Description
ComponentId	A GUID, which by definition, must be unique. The Windows Installer uses this value to register the component in the registry. If this value is null, then the component will not get registered and the Windows Installer will not be able to either remove or repair it. Notice that all the letters in the above values are uppercase letters, which is necessary for this to be a valid component ID. The GUIDGEN utility generates GUIDs that can have some lowercase letters, which have to be changed to uppercase before they can be used in this table.
Directory_	A foreign key into the *Directory* table. The value in the *Directory* table is a property that contains the path to where the component is to be installed.
Attributes	The value in this column is used to define how components are to be handled by the Windows Installer. This field is used to define whether a component can or cannot be run from source or whether this functionality is optional. Other options can be set as well, such as whether a component is permanent, or transitive, and so on.
Condition	A condition is an expression that evaluates to TRUE or FALSE. If the result of a condition is TRUE, the component will install, otherwise it will not install. If this column is null, then is the result is the same as if the condition is evaluated to TRUE.
Keypath	The Windows Installer uses the value to detect the existence of the component. Normally, this value is called the key file of the component, but it can also be a registry entry or a folder. If this column is null, then the value in the Directory_ column is used as the keypath.

Now that you see what is entered into the *Component* table, you look at the component properties page in ISWI to see how each of the entries that you make are used to populate the *Component* table. Figure 17-2 shows the component property page in ISWI.

Table 17-2 describes all the properties shown in Figure 17-2.

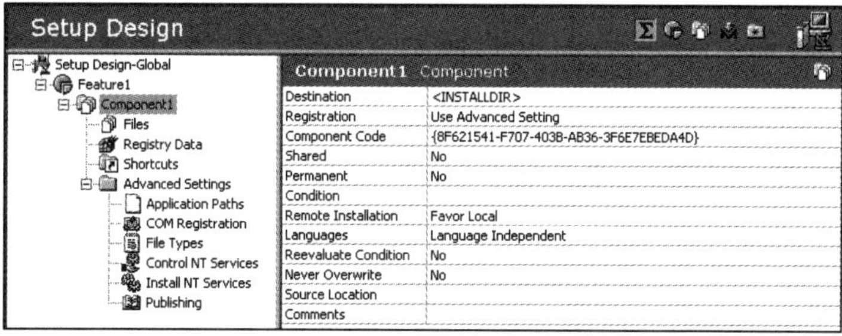

Figure 17-2: The component properties page in ISWI

Table 17-2 DESCRIPTION OF THE COMPONENT PROPERTIES IN THE ISWI IDE

Property	Description
Destination	This property sets the value of the Directory_ field in the *Component* table. You can add hard coded folders under this location that is configurable by the end user through the custom setup dialog, or you can have the component installed to a predefined location, such as the System32 folder.
Registration	This property relates to COM servers and how the registration information is extracted. For components that are not COM servers, this setting is meaningless. In your installation project, you can choose to have the COM information extracted after the MSI database is created. You can also use the Component Wizard to extract this information and if you do, the information does not change from build to build. If you extract the COM registration, every time you build the database, the COM information is written to the Log file, which is created for each build.
Component Code	This property is the GUID that makes each component unique. These GUIDs are not the same GUIDS used to define COM class IDs. This property sets the value of the ComponentId field of the *Component* table.

Continued

TABLE 17-2 DESCRIPTION OF THE COMPONENT PROPERTIES IN THE ISWI IDE *(Continued)*

Property	Description
Shared	This property is used to set a bit flag in the Attributes field of the *Component Table*. The purpose of this bit flag is to maintain compatibility with legacy applications that may be installing the same files that make up this component. The SharedDLLs key in the registry maintains this compatibility where a reference count is kept of all applications that use the same shared file.
Permanent	This property sets another bit flag in the Attributes field of the *Component* table that determines whether this component will be uninstalled or left on the machine.
Condition	This property is a condition that controls whether a component is installed or not. This property is used to set the value of the Condition field in the *Component* table.
Remote Installation	This property sets another bit flag in the Attributes field of the *Component* table that determines whether this component can be run from source only, run locally only, or run in either mode.
Languages	This property relates to the build environment of ISWI where it is possible to filter components based on the language that is set here. A build can be made to bring in only components identified with a set of languages. Components that are designated as Language Independent are included in all builds.
Reevaluate Condition	This property sets another bit flag in the Attributes field of the *Component* table that determines whether the condition in the Condition field of the *Component* table is reevaluated on a reinstall of the application. This property is primarily used under the circumstances where the OS has been upgraded and the component originally installed needs to be switched out with another component. Setting this property to Yes identifies the component as a transitive component. Without this bit flag being set, the condition statement is not reevaluated during the reinstallation.
Never Overwrite	This property sets another bit flag in the Attributes field of the Component table that determines whether this component will be overwritten during an installation or a reinstallation.

Property	Description
Source Location	This is an ISWI specific property that allows you to configure the media layout to be different from the layout of folders of the installed product. By default, the media layout of files is the same as what is seen after installing the product.
Comments	This property is an internal comment that only is inserted into the project file and is never built into the MSI database.

After you have entered the data that defines the component, you need to start making entries for the tree of icons that are below the component name. This tree of icons, shown in Figure 17-2, shows that you have some basic input that can be made and then you have number of areas in the IDE where you can create the Advanced Settings. The basic settings that you can make are the addition of files to the component by clicking on the Files icon, definition of registry entries that are to be made when the component gets installed, and the definition of a shortcut that is associated with the component. The Advanced Settings area provides the capability to define an entry under the App Paths key in the registry, define COM registration information, create a file association, define the installation and control parameters of an NT service, and define the component as being a member of an array of components. Refer to the entries for several of the basic and advanced settings described in detail in Chapter 7. Next, you look at the background of each of these settings and only discuss those details not already covered.

ADDING FILES TO A COMPONENT

After you create a component and click the Files icon, you have two methods to use to add files to the component. By default, the File List panel appears after you click the Files icon. This is shown in Figure 17-3.

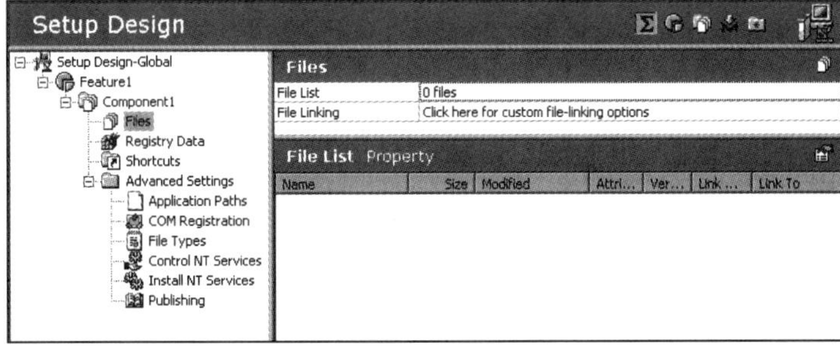

Figure 17-3: The File List property page in the ISWI IDE

If you right-click in this page, you get a context menu that has an Add... option. Selecting this option launches a browse dialog where you can navigate to the location of the files that you want to add to the component. After you select the files that you want to add to the component, ISWI asks you to supply the name of a path variable for this location if one isn't defined already. After the files are added the context menu, by right-clicking you find a number of additional options that are enabled. You can set a file to be the keypath for the component. After installation, you can also remove a file or set the properties of the file to be different than what they are on the build machine by selecting the appropriate option.

The most important of these options is the Set Key File option, which allows you to designate the file that is highlighted as the keypath of the component. If you do not define any file as the keypath and you do not designate an associated registry entry as being the keypath for the component, you find the keypath in the folder in which the component is installed.

Using the previous method creates what is termed a static link to the files. You can also create a dynamic link, which is a link to a folder and not any specific file or files. Dynamic links are good if the added files to the component are likely to change on a regular basis during development. This functionality makes performing nightly builds much more efficient, without having to continuously add and remove files from the project before the build is made.

To get to the property page where you can create a dynamic file link to a folder, you need to click the mouse on the File Linking text at the top of the Files page. A property page, which looks like Figure 17-4, appears.

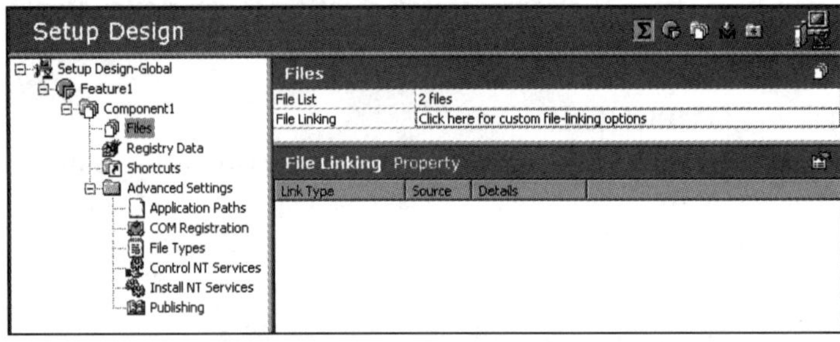

Figure 17-4: The File Linking Property page in the ISWI IDE

If you right-click the mouse in this property page, you get a different set of options in the resulting context menu. Before any dynamic link is created, the only enabled option is the New Dynamic Link option. If you select this option, you obtain the Dynamic File Link Settings dialog, which is shown in Figure 17-5.

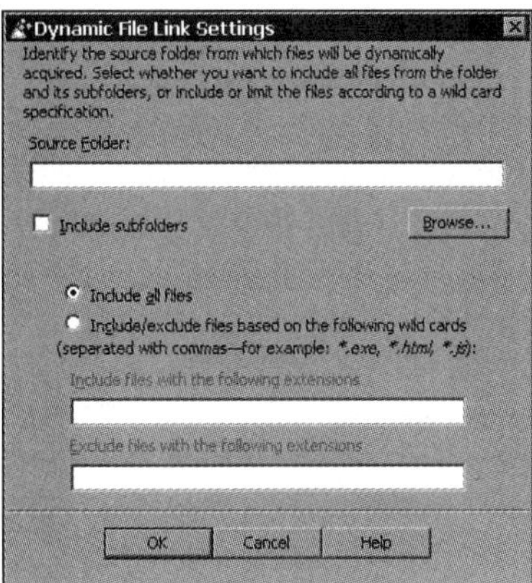

Figure 17-5: The Dynamic File Link Settings dialog

In this dialog, you can browse the folder that contains the files to be added to the component. You have the option to include subfolders. If you do, the linking automatically creates a new component for the files in the subfolder. You can add and delete files from these folders and the dynamic link gets updated so that the new files are added to the component, and the missing files are dropped from the component at the next build. You cannot add new folders after the dynamic link is created and have the new folder used to create another new component. You have to remove the dynamic link and create a new one that encompasses the additional subfolder.

At the bottom of the Dynamic File Link Settings dialog you are provided with the option to include all files in the designated folders or to include and exclude files based on a file specification. The specification for including and\or excluding files can use wild cards. By necessity, you need at least one file in a dynamically linked folder that is excluded if a file is to be used as the keypath for the component. It is only possible to identify a statically linked file as the keypath, which only makes sense if you understand that a dynamic link is only relative to a particular folder and has no knowledge with regard to the files in the folder.

Regardless of how you add files to a component, the outcome of the operation is to eventually make the entries in the *File* table. One of the fields in this table is a foreign key into the *Component* table. These files do not get copied to the target system unless the associated component gets installed to run locally. The files do not get copied for any other state of the component, such as if the component were to run from source.

ADDING REGISTRY DATA

Clicking the Registry Data icon in the component tree, the visual registry editor presents itself. Using this editor, you can define the entries made in the registry after the component gets installed. You can also right-click the top node in the visual registry editor and choose to import the contents of a .REG file. You can also export the information that you enter in this editor to a .REG file. This visual registry editor is shown in Figure 17-6.

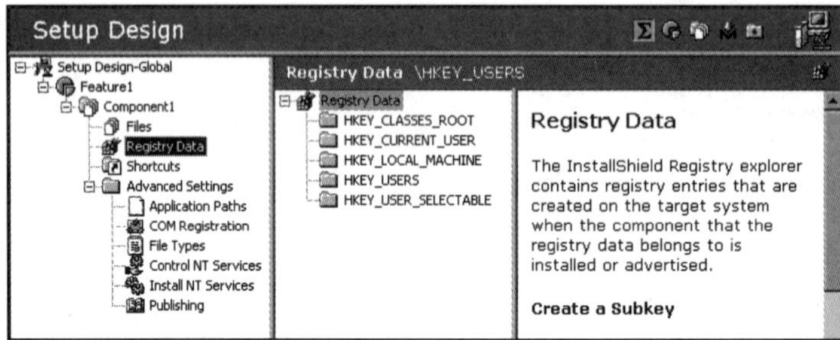

Figure 17-6: The Visual Registry Editor in the ISWI IDE

The values that you enter here are used to populate the *Registry* table when the Windows Installer package is built. To create a key, you left-click the name of the root key and right-click to bring up the context menu. The options offered are to create a new key or to perform a search of the keys, value names, and/or value data. After you select the New Key option, you get a key with a default name, which you can rename as necessary. If you right-click on this new key, you are offered the options to create another new key, rename the key, delete the key, or to perform a search of the entries made in the registry editor.

A special key in the registry editor may look unfamiliar. This registry key has the name of HKEY_USER_SELECTABLE. This key allows you to define registry values that get written to HKEY_CURRENT_USER if the install is for the current user or to HKEY_LOCAL_MACHINE if the install is for the machine. To make this work properly, it is first necessary to create a key named SOFTWARE under this key before any other keys and values are created. Creating a key is necessary because the SOFTWARE key is the only key that can be written under both HKEY_CURRENT_USER and HKEY_LOCAL_MACHINE.

After you create a key, you can then create value names and value data by right-clicking in the farthest right panel. You get the (Default) value name provided for you and you can set the value by typing in the value data field, which is shown in Figure 17-7.

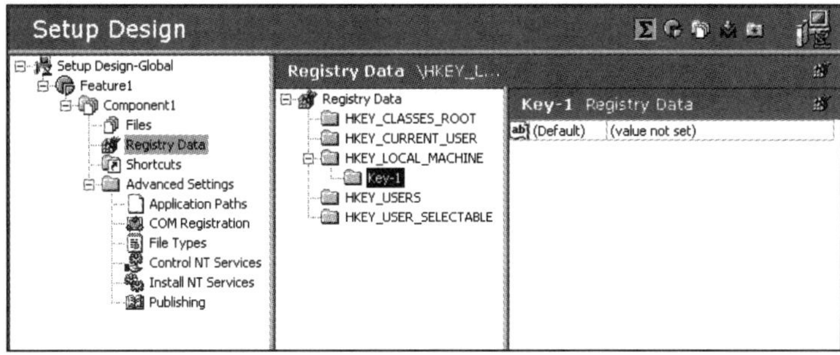

Figure 17-7: Creating value names and value data for registry keys

If you right-click in the Registry Data panel, you get a context menu that offers the capability to create a string value, a binary value, or a DWORD value. You are also able to delete or rename a value name and you can define a particular value name and value data pair as the keypath for the component. A number of formatting issues need to be understood when creating keys or value name and value data pairs. These issues are discussed in the following sections. In general the creation of a key, a value name, and value data use formatted strings, which means that the replacement mechanism of using the square brackets in a formatted string can be used to insert the value of properties, environment variables, *File* table keys, and *Component* table keys into the registry keys and values that are created at install time.

CREATING KEYS As you have already seen, you can enter key names by hard coding them in the visual registry editor. However, you can use the replacement functionality of a formatted string to create the actual key names themselves at run time. You can use four possibilities to create key names at install time. These are using the value of a property, the value of a user environmental variable, the path to the installation folder of a component, and the complete path to a file. The format for each of these is shown in the following list:

[*property-name*]	If you put the name of a property inside square brackets, the value of the property is inserted at run time and the property name and the square brackets is removed.
[%*environmental-variable*]	If you precede a name with the % sign, you tell the Windows Installer to replace the square brackets with the value of the user defined environmental variable. Note that this will only capture the user environmental variable value and not the system environmental variable.

[$*component-name*]	If you precede a name with the $ sign, you tell the Windows Installer to replace the square brackets with the install directory of the component. The *component-name* is a key into the *Component* table.
[#*file-key*]	If you precede a name with the # sign, you tell the Windows Installer to replace the square brackets with the full installation path of the file. The *file-key* is a key into the *File* table.

When you use these replacement mechanisms, you get a tree of sub-keys with a new sub-key being created for every backslash in the replacement string. For example, if you use the [#*file-key*] format for creating a key comprising the full path to a file, you make an entry similar to Figure 17-8.

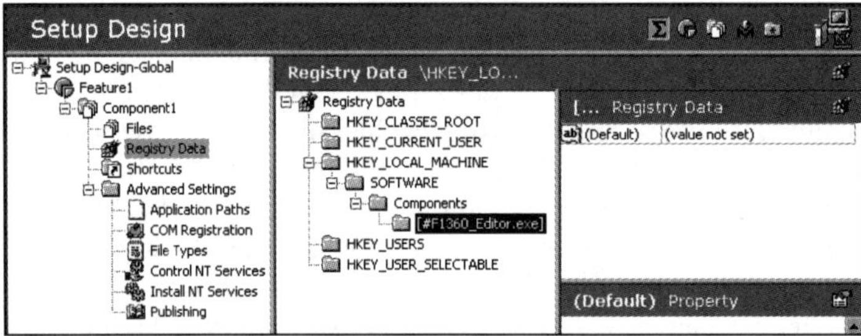

Figure 17-8: Using a key into the file table to create a registry key at install time

In Figure 17-8, note that the key into the *File* table is not file name but a decorated version of the file name. This decorated name is used as the primary key in the *File* table, and for any file this decorated name can be read from the File List property page after you click the Files icon under the component name in the IDE. For any particular file, this key into the *File* table is found from the farthest right-hand column in the File List property page.

When you run the installation and install, this component for the previous example you gets the registry entry, as shown in Figure 17-9. From this figure, you can see that you get a key structure where every backslash in the file path creates another sub-key.

When you create keys, you have some options about how they are to be handled during the installation or uninstallation. By default, any key that you define in the visual registry editor is created at install time and removed during uninstallation. You can, however, define a key that is created at install time but will not be removed at uninstallation. Conversely, you can define a key that is not created at install time but if it exists is removed at uninstallation.

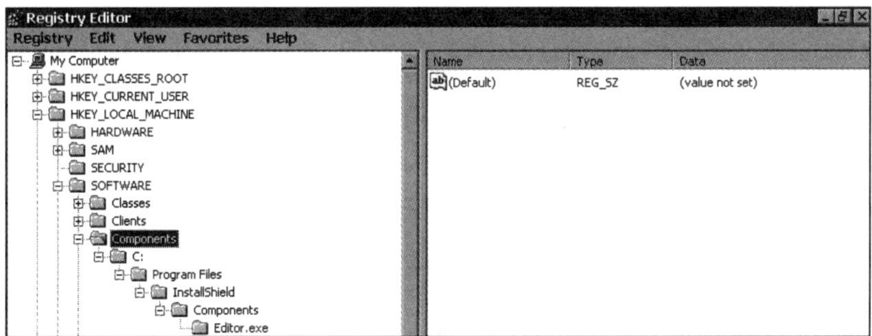

Figure 17-9: The Registry entry for a key created by using a key into the file table

In Figure 17-10 is shown the format where you can have a key created during the installation but the key is not removed during uninstallation.

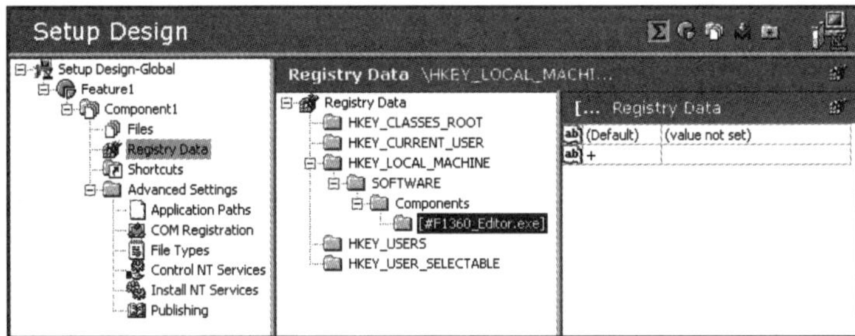

Figure 17-10: Defining a registry key that will get created but not removed

To create this key, you create a dummy value name that has no value data. In place of a value name you enter the plus + sign. This sign tells the Windows Installer to create a key but that during uninstallation, this key should not be removed. If you want to create a key that would not be created during the installation but would be removed, if it existed, during uninstallation, you would replace the + sign with the minus - sign. The default for registry keys defined in ISWI uses the asterisk * and this defines that the registry key is to be created during installation and removed during uninstallation.

CREATING VALUES When you create values, you first create a value name and then you give it a value that can be interpreted as a REG_SZ, REG_MULTI_SZ, REG_EXPAND_SZ, REG_DWORD, or REG_BINARY depending on the formatting that is used. When you create string type data, you can use the same replacement mechanism that was described when creating keys. When creating binary data or DWORD data, the only replacement option that can be used is the [*property-name*] mechanism. The value for the particular property name to be replaced has to be of the correct data type.

When you create string data and you do not use any specific formatting, the data is interpreted as being of type REG_SZ. With a little formatting, you can create either a REG_MULTI_SZ or a REG_EXPAND_SZ data type. Figure 17-11 shows the entries that need to be made for all of the various data types.

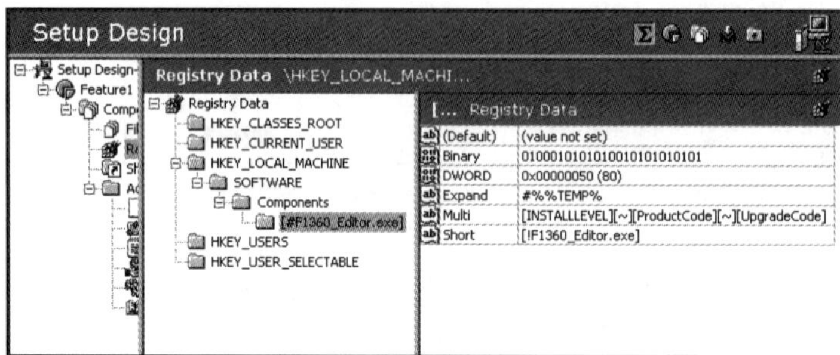

Figure 17-11: Creating the various registry data types

If you want to create a string data type that is interpreted as type REG_EXPAND_SZ, you need to prefix the string to expand with #%. If you want to create an expandable string value in the registry for the TEMP environmental variable, you enter the #%%TEMP% string in the ISWI visual registry editor, as shown in Figure 17-11. To create a data type that to be interpreted as type REG_MULTI-SZ, you need to use the [~] sequence of characters to represent the null delimiter between the various components that make up this registry data type. Figure 17-11 shows the entry that needs to be made if you want to create null-delimited list of property values. Here you use the [~] sequence of characters between three property names enclosed in square brackets. The use of the [~] sequence of characters can be used to either append or prefix a null-delimited list of strings to an existing registry entry. The complete use of this sequence of characters is shown in the following list:

- The use of the character sequence [~] within a string value separates the individual strings and is interpreted and stored as a null character.
- If a [~] character sequence precedes the string list to be written into the registry, the strings are appended to any existing registry value strings. If a string being appended already exists in the registry value, the original occurrence of the string is removed.
- If a [~] follows the end of the string list, the strings are prefixed to any existing registry value strings. If the string to be prefixed already exists in the registry value, the original occurrence of the string is removed.
- If a [~] character sequence is at both the beginning and the end or at neither the beginning nor the end of the string list to be written to the registry, the strings are to replace any existing registry value strings.

If creating string data that will be interpreted as type REG_SZ, you use a special form of the *File* table key replacement. If you use the [!*file-key*] format for this replacement, you get as data a short file name path to the referenced file. This is the only location where this replacement form can be used. If the replacement form is used in any other location, it is treated as if you used the # sign instead.

Figure 17-12 shows the actual registry entries that are made for the input in the visual registry editor that is depicted in Figure 17-11.

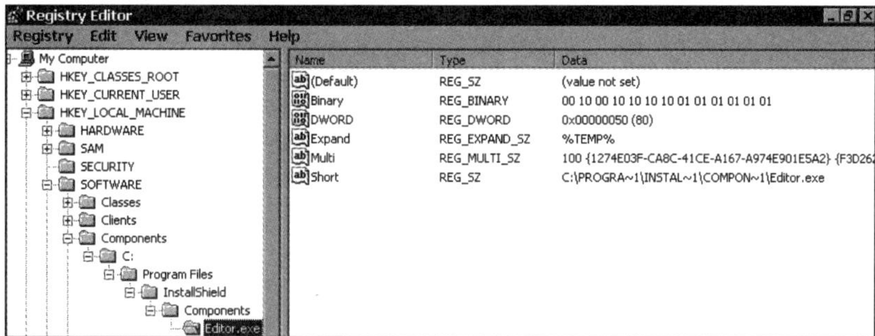

Figure 17-12: The registry entries created from the input shown in Figure 17-11

When you create DWORD, type REG_DWORD, data values in the visual registry editor, you need to select whether you are entering the values as decimal numbers or hexadecimal numbers. You should set the type of input being made before the number is actually entered. The value is always shown in hexadecimal format with the decimal equivalent shown in parentheses. You can use a property name within square brackets here as long as the value of the property is a number.

When you create a data of type REG_BINARY, you would normally cut and paste the binary data from another source into the data field in the registry editor. You can also define a property name within square brackets and the value of the property name is used at install time. Because you can programmatically create a string of binary data in the *Property* table, this is the best method of creating this data. It is recommended that if the binary data exceeds 2048 bytes, then this data should be stored as a file and only the name of the file stored in the registry. Do this to reduce registry bloat and to increase the efficiency of the registry.

Within the ISWI IDE, angle brackets (<>) are used to enclose the names of properties or *Directory* table entries. When you build your project, these angle brackets are converted to the square brackets that are understood by the Windows Installer. This angle bracket mechanism only works if the properties are authored in the Property Manager or authored in the *Directory* table using the Power Editor. If you try to use angle brackets for a property or *Directory* table that does not exist at build time, the angle brackets will be entered into the MSI database as is and when the Windows Installer tries to run the installation, it generates an installer error.

CREATING SHORTCUTS

In Chapter 7, you go through the details of creating a shortcut and discuss each of the properties defined for a shortcut. Creating a shortcut in the ISWI IDE provides the information that is required in order to populate the Shortcut table when the Windows Installer is built. When you create a shortcut, you do not have to create it only on the Start | Programs menu. You can create a folder and create shortcuts to various features of the application inside this folder. You can also create shortcuts and folders in the Start | Programs | Startup menu, directly on the Start menu, and in the Desktop and SendTo folders in a user's profile. The options to create either a shortcut or a folder are provided via the context menu if you right-click the appropriate icon in the Shortcuts tree under a component name.

When you want to create a folder in which to place several shortcuts, you need to make sure that for every shortcut to go into this folder, you use the exact folder name and description. So that you do not have perform a copy and paste operation, you can do this simply through the use of string identifiers. Both the displayable name and description of the folder get assigned a default string ID after it is first created. You can then go into the String Table editor that is accessed at the bottom of the shortcut property page and redefine the string ID to a name that is more meaningful. After you create the folder and subsequent shortcuts that are to go into this folder, all you need to do is select the string ID in the Display Name property that was created the first time the folder was entered. The same process goes for the folder description.

When creating shortcuts or folders for shortcuts, the name that you first create is not important and it is not used. The display name is the important name, which is placed in the Name column of the *Shortcut* table.

If you want to create a shortcut directly on the Start menu itself or on the Desktop, you do this same way that you create a shortcut on Start | Programs menu. However, if you want to create a shortcut in the SendTo folder, you need to make sure that you create a standard shortcut and not an MSI shortcut. This means that you need to identify the target of the shortcut and not depend on the keypath file to be the target. If you create an MSI shortcut, then the Send To command on the context menu in Windows Explorer won't work.

If you are creating an installation package for an application to obtain the "Certified for Windows" logo, you need to be aware of the requirements and recommendations that are listed in the "Application Specification for Microsoft Windows 2000 for desktop applications." These requirements and recommendations are given in the following list:

- You cannot place shortcuts to documents, such as read me files, in the Start Menu. If you have important information that the user should see, you need to consider displaying that information during the install process.

- You cannot put shortcuts to help files in the Start Menu. Users need to access help as soon as they launch the application.
- You cannot place shortcuts to perform an uninstallation in the Start Menu. The Add/Remove Program control panel applet is available to provide this functionality.
- Do not place an icon to launch an application directly under Start | Programs, and if possible, you need to avoid placing it in a folder under programs. In particular, you should not create a folder in the Start Menu in which you only put one item.
- Do not put anything at the top of the Start Menu because users consider this their own personal space.
- If the product supports applications, such as tools or utilities that are associated with the application, put all the icons under a single folder in the Start Menu.

It is possible for any particular installation to disable the creation of MSI shortcuts, which is accomplished through the setting of the DISABLEADVTSHORTCUTS property. Because this line is a public property, it can be set at the command line. A common use of this property is when an administrator wants to disable the capability to advertise an application for roaming users that move between environments that support and do not support advertisement. Advertisement is not supported on Windows 95 and Windows NT 4.0 where the version of SHELL32.DLL is less than 4.72.3110.0.

THE APPLICATION PATH

The first icon under the Advanced Settings tree under the component name is where you create the application path for an application. Chapter 7 covers the actual creation of an application path. Here I discuss what an application path is and where this information is placed in the MSI database.

Essentially the concept of a per-application path was introduced with Windows 95. When you define an application path in ISWI, you are defining two entries that will be made in the *Registry* table when the installation package is built. The registry key that is created is the name of the executable that runs the application. This key is created in the following location:

```
HKLM\SOFTWARE\Microsoft\Windows\CurrentVersion\App Paths\<exe-name>
```

The default value data is the complete path to the executable and this allows you to type in the name of the executable in the Run dialog accessed from the Start menu and run the application. Also, you create a Path value name if the application uses dynamic-link libraries. The value data for this value name is a semicolon-delimited list of folder paths that contain the DLLs that the application needs to load. This list of paths is appended to the system PATH environment variable, and thus they get included in the standard search path that the operating system uses to find DLLs.

COM REGISTRATION

The next advanced settings icon is used to define COM Registration information for the component. Here you have a visual editor that is similar in function to the registry editor discussed in the previous section. You create the values that get entered into the *Class* table, *ProgId* table, and the *TypeLib* table when the database is built. The alternative to making these entries manually is to have the Component wizard extract this information for us. The Component Wizard is discussed later in this chapter.

Reading the discussion earlier in this chapter about not using self-registration for COM servers is important.

FILE TYPES

You have already gone through the process in Chapter 7 of creating a file association. What I want to discuss here are the rules imposed by the "Certified for Windows" logo about creating file associations.

Having an associated registered file-type for every file that does not have the hidden bit set that is created by the application in a location that is not in the install location of the application is necessary. This includes files that are created during the installation, implementation and data files, and user created files that are native to the application.

If the file-type is already registered, you do not have to create a file association unless you want to take over the association that is already resident on the target machine. If the file-type is not already registered, creating an association for each new file type is necessary. When you create a file association, you need to include the following items:

- Provide an icon so that none of the files that the application creates is identified by the default Windows icon.
- Provide a friendly type description for the file type that makes for easy identification of the file in Windows Explorer.
- Ensure that each file-type has an associated action when double-clicked, such as launching the application and loading the file.

The NoOpen designation may be used for files that you do not want users to open. If the user double-clicks a file marked as NoOpen, the operating system automatically provides a message informing the user that the file cannot be opened. If an action is associated with a NoOpen file type, the NoOpen designation is ignored.

To create a NoOpen designation for a particular file type, you create a ProgId and extension as you have done in the past. After you do this, you right-click the ProgId and select the Rename option. You right-click again and select to copy this ProgId to the clipboard. You now move to the Registry Data icon under the same component and create a new key under HKEY_CLASSES_ROOT. You replace the default name of the new key with the name of the ProgId that you copied to the clipboard. Now against this key, you create a new string value and give it a value name of NoOpen. For the value data for this NoOpen value name, you enter a message that gets displayed by the operating system.

An exception is made if the application allows the user to save or export file types that are not native to the application. In this case, the user may choose to save a file as a type that has no association on the user's computer. The application may save the file as requested by the user, even though the file will have a default Windows icon.

For every file extension that you define, you can create a MIME type so that the file can be opened with a helper application if the file is sent across the Internet. To register a MIME type for a particular file extension, you right-click the file extension that you have created under the File Types icon in ISWI and select the New MIME Type option. After you do this, you get a default MIME type that you needs to change to the correct value for your file extension. A MIME type consists of a major type and a subtype. For example, the MIME type for a text file is `text/plain`, which indicates a normal ASCII file. Also, when you create this MIME type, you have the option to identify the CLSID of an ActiveX server that can handle your file. The CLSID information is optional.

CONTROL NT SERVICES

Under this icon in the Advanced Settings tree, you define the entries that get built into the *ServiceControl* table. The Windows Installer uses the entries in this table to control NT services that are on the target machine or are being installed as part of the application installation.

INSTALL NT SERVICES

Under this icon in the Advanced Settings tree, you define the entries that get built into the *ServiceInstall* table. The Windows Installer uses the entries in this table to install an NT service.

PUBLISHING

The final icon in the Advanced Settings tree is where you create what may be thought of as an array of components. The entries you make here are entered into the *PublishComponent* table when the MSI database is built. The information from this table is entered into the registry during the installation of the application and this information can then be used from within the application to allow the user to choose which component to use for a particular operation. The entries made here have nothing to do with enabling advertisement of an application. A complete description of how to use the entries made here to create qualified components is provided later in this chapter.

Using the component wizard

In the previous sections, you looked at the many entries that you can make to define a component. For large applications, creating components in this fashion can be time consuming and subject to error. To help ease the burden of creating components, ISWI has a Component Wizard that you can use to create components from a group of files and it can also be used to guide you through the creation of specialized components.

The Component Wizard is accessed from the context menu displayed after you right-click a feature name in the Setup Design view. The option to launch the Component Wizard is the next to the last command on this context menu. After you launch the wizard, you get the welcome dialog that gives two options. You can choose to create components using "Best Practices" (componentization rules) or you can choose to create specialized components. This welcome dialog is shown in Figure 17-13.

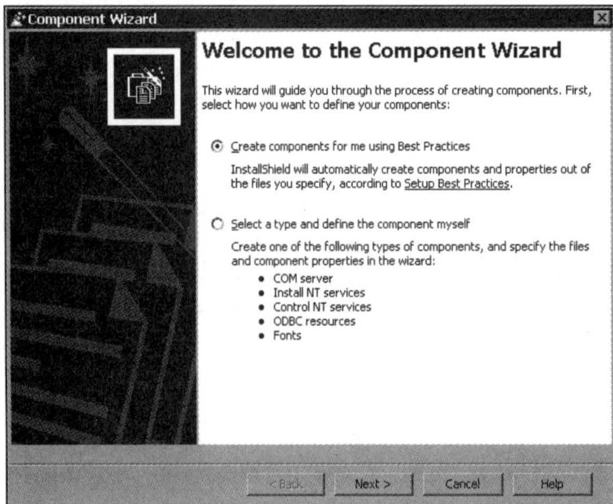

Figure 17-13: The welcome dialog for the Component Wizard

In the following two sections, you look at both of the options that are offered by the Component Wizard.

GLOBAL COMPONENT CREATION

After you select to create components using the componentization rules, you get a number of created components based on a subset of all the rules that were described earlier in this chapter. A list of rules used to create components are below:

- Every .exe, .dll, and .ocx file needs to be placed in its own component and this file has to be the keypath of the component.

- Every .hlp and .chm file needs to be placed in its own component. For a component that has an .hlp file, the .cnt file needs to be included in the component. For a component that has a .chm file, the .chi file needs to be included as part of the component. The .hlp file and the .chm file need to be the keypath for the component.
- The same file cannot be included in more than one component.
- No file that is available in a merge module can be included in an authored component.

When the Component Wizard runs, it creates components based on the above rules. Any file that does not fall into one of the above categories is grouped into a single component using the AllOther<*feature-name*>Files naming convention. The other components are given a name that is the same as the keypath file name.

When you use the Component Wizard to create components based on the above rules, only standard components are created with the exception that if the .exe, or .dll are COM servers, then the COM registration information is extracted after the component is created. By definition, an .ocx is a COM server, so that the COM information is always extracted when the component is created. Special components for NT Services, ODBC, and Fonts cannot be created using this particular option of the Component Wizard.

After you launch the Component Wizard and you move to the dialog following the welcome dialog, you are prompted to specify the installation location to be used for all the components to be created. This dialog provides a dropdown list of the standard locations that are set by the Windows Installer at run time, as well as the INSTALLDIR variable, which is the default location. This dialog is shown in Figure 17-14.

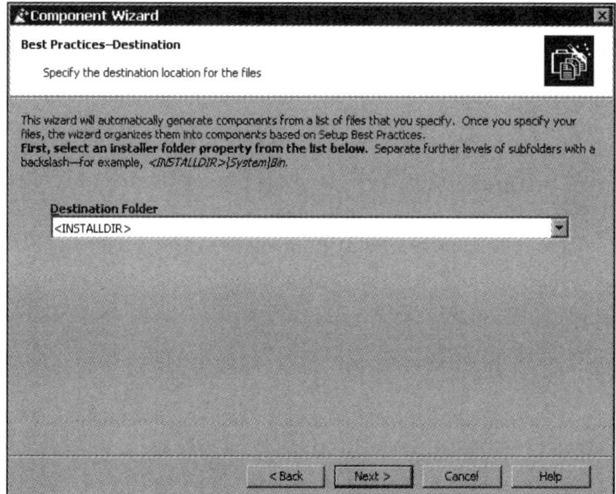

Figure 17-14: The Best Practices-Destination dialog of the Component Wizard

After the destination dialog, you get a dialog that enables you to select the files to use to create the components. This dialog is shown in Figure 17-15.

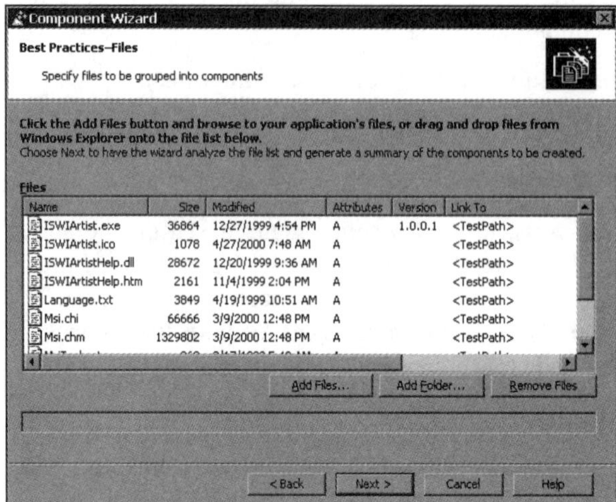

Figure 17-15: The Best Practices-Files dialog of the Component Wizard

You can browse to a particular location using the Add Files... button on this dialog and select a group of files, or you can click the Add Folder... button and browse to a folder and after the folder is selected, all the files in the folder are used to create the components. You can also do a combination of both by selecting individual files as well as pulling in all the files out of a particular folder or folders. Files can be removed from the group of files by selecting one or more files and clicking the Remove Files push button.

When you click the Next button on this dialog, the Component Wizard starts the process of creating the components. For each .exe, .dll, and .ocx it will attempt to self-register the file and then compare the applicable areas of the registry for any COM information that may have been written. Once this snap shot has been taken then the file is unregistered. At the completion of this process the Component Wizard displays a Summary dialog as shown in Figure 17-16.

In this dialog it can be seen what components were created and the files that are included in each of these components. Now that the components have been created you can start to modify them by performing such actions as defining shortcuts, registry entries, renaming the components, etc. When the wizard runs it looks for the OLESelfRegister string in the version resource of the file. If it finds it this string and the file is either a .dll or an .ocx then the wizard runs REGSVR32.EXE *<file-name>*. After collecting the COM registration information it runs REGSVR32.EXE /u *<file-name>* to unregister the file. If the file is an .exe the command *<file-name*.exe> /regserver is run to register the COM server and then the command *<file-name*.exe> /unregserver is run to remove the registration.

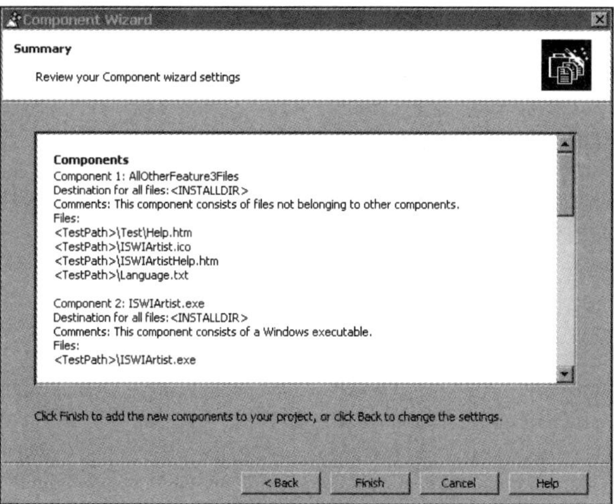

Figure 17-16: The Summary dialog of the Component Wizard

Now that you have seen how to use the Component Wizard to create components in a global fashion, you can look at the second option where you can create specialized components one at a time.

CREATING SPECIALIZED COMPONENTS

By selecting the second option on the welcome dialog of the Component Wizard, you are able to create five different types of specialized components. After you click the Next button on the welcome dialog, you get the Component Type dialog that shows these five component types. You can choose to create a COM Server, Install NT Services, Control NT Services, ODBC Resources, or Fonts component. The Component Type dialog is shown in Figure 17-17.

In this dialog, you first select the component type that you want to create, and then you give the component a name by entering it into the Component Name edit field. The only type of component that does not allow the specification of a component name is the ODBC Resources component type, because the Component Wizard creates a number of different components for ODBC. In the following sections, you examine each of the five types of specialized components that you can create.

COM SERVER COMPONENTS After you select to create a COM server component, the Component Wizard gives you two dialogs where you specify the required parameters to define this type of component. Table 17-3 describes each of the dialogs in the wizard that come after the Component Type dialog.

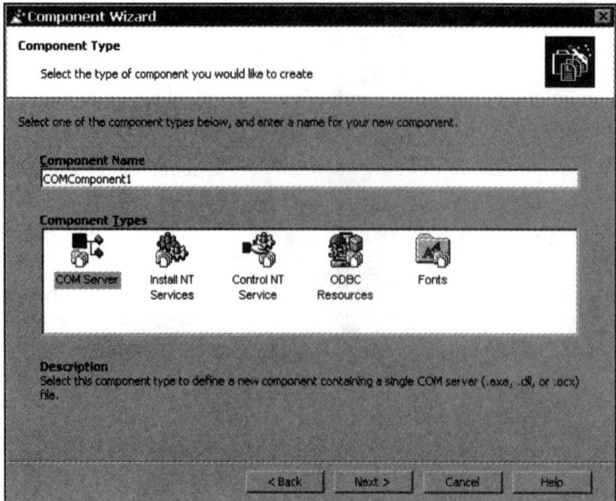

Figure 17-17: The Component Type dialog of the Component Wizard

TABLE 17-3 THE CREATION OF A COM SERVER COMPONENT USING THE COMPONENT WIZARD

Dialog Name	Description
COM Server-Destination	In this dialog, you define the folder where the component gets installed. A dropdown list offers a choice of the operating system defined locations that you can select or the INSTALLDIR location. The INSTALLDIR location is the configurable location that can be set by the end user during the installation. If you want your component to go to a subdirectory of the INSTALLDIR location, then you can add the name of that subfolder in this edit field of the dropdown list.
COM Server Executable	You identify the file that is the COM server to be the key file for the component you are creating. You have the option of specifying that the Component Wizard extract the COM registration information from the file. If you do, then this information gets entered into the project file and every time you build the installation package, the proper tables in the database get populated. If you want to extract the COM information during the build, you would not check this option for extraction during the component creation process. If the identified file is executable, you can also identify it as being a COM NT service.

Dialog Name	Description
Summary	This dialog provides a list of all the COM information that is extracted from the COM server. If you click the Back button, you can go back to the previous dialog and either change any of the settings or just have the information re-extracted.

After you have created the COM component, you can view and modify the results of the COM registration extraction by clicking the COM Registration icon under the components Advanced Settings tree. If no extraction was performed because it is to be done at build time, the COM information is only shown in the build log file and not in the IDE.

Unlike the approach used by the Component Wizard, when components are being created using the componentization rules, the file is not checked for the OLESelfRegister string in the version resource when creating a single COM component. If the file is not self-registering and is an .exe, then the file gets launched. You need to be careful that the file is an actual COM server.

COM extraction only captures the information that is actually related to COM. If the DllRegisterServer function in a COM DLL makes entries in the registry that are not related to COM, these entries are not captured by the Component Wizard. This is because only the COM related keys in the registry are monitored during the extraction process. Non-COM registry entries have to be entered into the Registry table.

INSTALL NT SERVICE COMPONENTS After you select that you want to create an Install NT Service component, the Component Wizard gives you five dialogs where you specify the parameters that are required to define this type of component. Table 17-4 describes each of the dialogs in the wizard that follow the Component Type dialog. The entries that you make when creating an Install NT Service type of component are used to populate the *ServiceInstall* table in the database.

TABLE 17-4 THE CREATION OF AN INSTALL NT SERVICE COMPONENT USING THE COMPONENT WIZARD

Dialog Name	Description
NT Service Executable	In this dialog, you identify the executable file being used to house the NT service or services that are going to be installed by this component. For each service that you are installing, you need to identify the name of the service by which this service is to be known by the Service Control Manager. You do this by clicking the Add button and providing this name. You can also remove a service name by using the Remove button. The context menu you get after you click the right mouse button offers the same functionality. In addition, you can use the context menu to rename a service.
Service Information	In this dialog, you get a dropdown list of all the services that you defined in the previous dialog. For each of these services you can define a display name that is used by the Service Control Manager. By default, this display name is the same as the service name that you specified. At the bottom of this dialog, you specify whether the service shown in the dropdown list is to run in its own process or whether it is to be a thread in the same process as other services. You also need to define when to start the service. This dialog provides five options for starting a service.
Service Load Order	In this dialog, you identify how the services that you have defined get loaded. This incorporates the definition of a load-ordering group to which a service may belong, as well as the names of other services to start before this service can be started. If the service does not belong to a load-ordering group, then this edit field is left blank. In the dependencies edit field, you can identify both load ordering groups and other services to start before the service you are installing can be started. To identify a load ordering group, you need to precede its name with the plus (+) sign, so that the windows Installer knows that it is not a service. If you want to identify more than one service as dependencies, you need to separate the name of each service with a comma.

Dialog Name	Description
Error Control	In this dialog, you specify how to handle an error. The selection you make here affects how the entries are made in the *ServiceControl* table for this service.
Service Logon	This dialog allows you to identify whether the NT service is to be installed to the local system account or whether it is to be installed for a particular user and password. For a service that is being installed to the local system account, you can identify whether it will interact with the desktop or not.
Summary	This final dialog displays a list of the selections that you made in the wizard and gives you the opportunity to go back and change your selections before the component is created.

After you create the Install NT Service component, you can view and modify the results created by the wizard by clicking the Install NT Services icon under the components Advanced Settings tree.

CONTROL NT SERVICE COMPONENTS After you select that you want to create a Control NT Service component, the Component Wizard gives you four dialogs where you specify the parameters that are required to define this type of component. Table 17-5 describes each of the dialogs in the wizard that follow the Component Type dialog.

TABLE 17-5 THE CREATION OF A CONTROL NT SERVICE COMPONENT USING THE COMPONENT WIZARD

Dialog Name	Description
Specify Service	In this dialog, you specify the service that you are controlling with this component. You can specify a service already installed or one being installed with the present installation package.
Installation Events	In this dialog, you specify what events you want to occur when the NT service is installed. You can start, stop, and/or delete a service during the installation. You also can specify that no event is to occur during the installation.

Continued

TABLE 17-5 THE CREATION OF A CONTROL NT SERVICE COMPONENT USING THE COMPONENT WIZARD *(Continued)*

Dialog Name	Description
Uninstallation Events	In this dialog, you specify what events you want to occur when the NT service is uninstalled. You can start, stop, and/or delete a service during the uninstallation. You also can specify that no event is to occur during the installation.
Wait Type	In this dialog, you specify the wait type for the NT service being controlled before the installation or the uninstallation is to proceed.
Summary	This final dialog displays a list of the selections that you made in the wizard and gives you the opportunity to go back and change your selections before the component is created.

After you create the Control NT Service component, you can view and modify the results created by the wizard by clicking on the Control NT Services icon under the component's Advanced Settings tree.

FONTS COMPONENTS After you select that you want to create a Fonts component, the Component Wizard gives you a maximum of two dialogs where you specify the parameters that are required to define this type of component. Table 17-6 describes each of the dialogs in the wizard that follow the Component Type dialog.

TABLE 17-6 THE CREATION OF A FONTS COMPONENT USING THE COMPONENT WIZARD

Dialog Name	Description
Add Installed Fonts	In this dialog, you select from the fonts installed on the build system those that you want to install as part of the installation. In this dialog, you can also choose to include font files that are not already installed on the build system.
Add New Fonts	When you select to include fonts that are not installed on the system, you get this dialog, where you need to enter the title of the font and the name of the font file name.
Summary	This final dialog displays a list of the selections that you have made in the wizard and gives you the opportunity to go back and change the selections before the component is created.

After you create the Fonts component, you can view and modify the results created by the wizard by clicking the Files icon under the component's basic settings tree. Unlike with other types of components that are created with the Component Wizard, no special icon is in the component's settings tree where the definition of the component can be viewed because all you have actually done is select and/or specify a number font files to be included in the component. The one thing that you want to do is go to the property sheet for the Fonts component and mark the component as being permanent. You need to do this because there is no mechanism for reference counting font files in the operating system.

If you do not mark a font component as being permanent then when you uninstall your application the fonts will be deleted and they will no longer be available on your system.

ODBC RESOURCE COMPONENTS After you select that you want to create ODBC Resource components, the Component Wizard gives you three dialogs where you specify the required parameters to define this type of component. Table 17-7 describes each of the dialogs in the wizard that follow the Component Type dialog.

TABLE 17-7 THE CREATION OF ODBC RESOURCE COMPONENTS USING THE COMPONENT WIZARD

Dialog Name	Description
Specify ODBC Drivers	In this dialog, you get a list of all the ODBC drivers that are installed on the build system. You select those for which you want to create components. You are not able to add any drivers that are not already on the system. However, when you highlight a driver in the left-hand panel, you can add, modify, or delete attributes for this driver in the right hand panel of this dialog. To add or delete an attribute, you right-click the mouse and choose the desired option from the context menu. To modify an existing attribute, you left-click the mouse on the attribute to be changed and type in the changes.

Continued

TABLE 17-7 THE CREATION OF ODBC RESOURCE COMPONENTS USING THE COMPONENT WIZARD *(Continued)*

Dialog Name	Description
Specify ODBC Data Sources	In this dialog, you are given a list of the ODBC data source names that have been installed on the build system. Here you can add new data source names by right-clicking in the left hand panel and you can add, modify, and delete attributes for any highlighted data source name. To add or delete an attribute, you right-click the mouse and choose the desired option from the context menu. To modify an existing attribute, you left-click the mouse on the attribute to be changed and type in the changes. To set any data source name to be installed to the local system account, you highlight the data source name in the left-hand panel and check the System DSN check box at the bottom of the dialog.
Specify ODBC Translators	In this dialog, you get a list of the code page translators installed on the build system. You cannot add new translators and you cannot add or delete attributes. You can modify an attribute by left-clicking in the attribute value cell and making the desired changes.
Summary	This final dialog displays a list of the selections that you have made in the wizard and gives you the opportunity to go back to change any selections before the component is created.

For the other components, except for fonts, you find an icon in a component's Advanced Settings tree where you can create the component without having to use the Component Wizard. For ODBC Resource components, you find no icon until after you have run the Component Wizard. After the wizard is run, then you can go to view and modify the settings that were entered after the wizard was run.

Delivering Components to the Application

Merge modules are a mechanism used at design time whereby diverse development groups can work independently and create components that can be shipped to a central location where the installation for the complete application is developed.

Merge modules depend on the capability of the Windows Installer to be able to take two MSI databases and combine them into one.

Merge modules are the choice if you want to create shared components shared between applications. If the components you are create are used by only one application with no possibility that the component will be shared across applications, then creating the component directly in the application without the use of a merge module is better. Creating merge modules are important so that two different setup developers do not try to create a component for the same file using two different component codes. If this happens, the component reference count is done incorrectly, particularly concerning the interface with legacy installations that use the SharedDLLs key in the registry.

The use of merge modules becomes particularly important when an application is designed to use the Windows Installer API in order to perform feature level install-on-demand and to perform self-repair operations. In this situation, creating the component IDs during the development process instead of during the creation of the installation becomes necessary. For the correct component IDs to be used for the installation, the developer of the application needs to create the components making sure that the component IDs used are the ones that were used inside the application for implementing the desired functionality.

Merge modules also have a function if a development team is located in different parts of the country or even the world. This scenario can happen for large applications. Here the various development organizations need to package their part of the application in merge modules to ship these to the central location where the installation for the application is being created. In this case, it only is necessary for the setup developer to know to which features in the application each merge module is to be associated.

Merging MSI databases

To be able to merge two MSI databases, the databases must have the same code page. If the code pages are different for the databases to be merged, then any attempt to merge them will fail. Chapter 19 covers database code pages and localization. In addition, for two databases to merge, all corresponding tables in each database must have the same schema, meaning each table that appears in both databases must have the following:

- Equal number of primary keys
- Equal number of columns
- Each corresponding column must have the same column type
- Each corresponding column must have the same name

If the schema of any two corresponding tables is different, then the merge will fail.

Another scenario can occur where the merge will not fail outright but you still have a problem. If a row or rows in corresponding tables of the databases to be merged have the same primary key(s) but the data is different, a problem occurs. The problem is called a row merge conflict and when this occurs, the merge process creates a new persistent table that is used to keep track of the row merge conflicts. This table identifies the table name and for each table it gives the number of row merge conflicts in that table.

Occasionally, temporary columns are added to a table to perform some particular operation. Columns that are not persistent do not affect the schema definition and therefore do not affect a merge operation.

The structure of a merge module

A merge module is a simplified msi database that is constructed in a fashion so that you have no possibility of having a row merge conflict. A merge module cannot be installed but instead has to be merged with a full MSI package. A merge module has an .msm extension and delivers components to an MSI package. After a merge module is merged, it has no further use relative to that particular installation.

Six database tables must be present in all merge modules, which are the *Component*, *Directory*, *FeatureComponents*, *File*, *ModuleSignature*, and *ModuleComponents* tables. After a merge module is merged with an MSI database, the *ModuleSignature* and the *ModuleComponents* tables become part of this database. The *ModuleDependency* and the *ModuleExclusion* tables are optional and only used if identifying modules that are required to also be present or those that cannot be used with a particular merge module is necessary. After the merge, these tables become part of the MSI database.

Six sequence tables can occur in a merge module, but these tables are never merged into the MSI database. The tables are only used to identify where actions and/or dialogs are to be inserted into the standard sequence tables found in an MSI database. These module sequence tables have the naming format Module* where the asterisk stands for the name of the equivalent table in the MSI database. If any of these tables is authored into a merge module, an empty copy of the equivalent table in the MSI database also has to be included in the merge module. A copy is included to allow the merge utility to know the schema of the table into which the actions and/or dialogs in the merge module will be inserted. A *ModuleIgnoreTable* table is optional in a merge module. This table identifies those tables in the merge module that are not to be merged with the MSI database. This table is never added to the MSI database during the merge operation.

Nine database tables cannot occur in merge module. These are the *BBControl*, *Billboard*, *CCPSearch*, *Error*, *Feature*, *LaunchCondition*, *Media*, *Patch*, and *Upgrade* tables. All the other database tables can occur in a merge module. Whether you include the tables or not depends on the functionality that is authored in to the merge module.

A merge module is described in the Summary Information stream that it contains. The module GUID is given in the Revision Number property of the Summary Information stream. This same property in a Windows Installer package defines the Package Code. Using this GUID and modifying it in a special way and then appending the GUID to a readable string, you get the Module ID. You can think of the readable string as the name of the merge module. The modifications that you need to make to the module GUID are as follows:

- Remove the curly braces ({}) from the ends of the GUID.
- Change all the dashes (-) in the GUID to underscores (_).
- Delimit the module name from the modified module GUID with a period (.).

For example, if you have merge module name of "Object" and you have a module GUID of {94366786-F5EF-11D3-8213-204C4F4F5020} in the Revision Number property of the Summary Information stream, then you get a Module ID as follows:

```
Object.94366786_F5EF_11D3_8213_204C4F4F5020
```

This Module ID is the entry in the first column of the *ModuleSignature* table. In addition, this modified Module GUID is used to make the primary key in every table unique in the merge module. This is to prevent the possibility of a conflict between the rows in the merge module and the database with which the merge module is to be merged. A conflict occurs when the database and the merge module have the same primary key and different data. If this occurs, the row in the database is not overwritten with the row in the merge module. The place where this naming convention in a merge module is not used is where the primary key in the merge module is not by definition already unique. Such a situation occurs in the Class and TypeLib tables where part of the primary key is made up of a GUID already. The modified Module GUID is not used in this case to make the primary key unique because it already is unique. In fact, to modify a GUID with another GUID makes the registration of a class be incorrect after the COM component is installed.

Every file that is delivered to an installation project by a merge module is stored in a cabinet (CAB) file that is streamed into the merge module. The name of this embedded cabinet file is always MergeModule.CABinet. The names of the files in this CAB file need to match the names of the files given in the first column of the *File* table in the merge module database. Any files that are in the CAB file but not listed in the *File* table are not installed when the main installation package is run. It is this mechanism that allows the creation of multiple language merge modules.

Chapter 19 briefly discusses the creation of multiple language merge modules.

As can be seen from the previous discussion, the creation of a merge module is a complex process. This complex process is greatly eased by using ISWI. This product handles all the complexities of creating the correct primary keys, and so forth, for you. All you concern yourself with is the proper creation of the components that comprise the merge module, which is the subject of the next section.

Creating a merge module

If you want to create a merge module, you open a merge module project that is created by selecting the Blank Merge Module Project icon in the Create a new project... view, as shown in Figure 17-18.

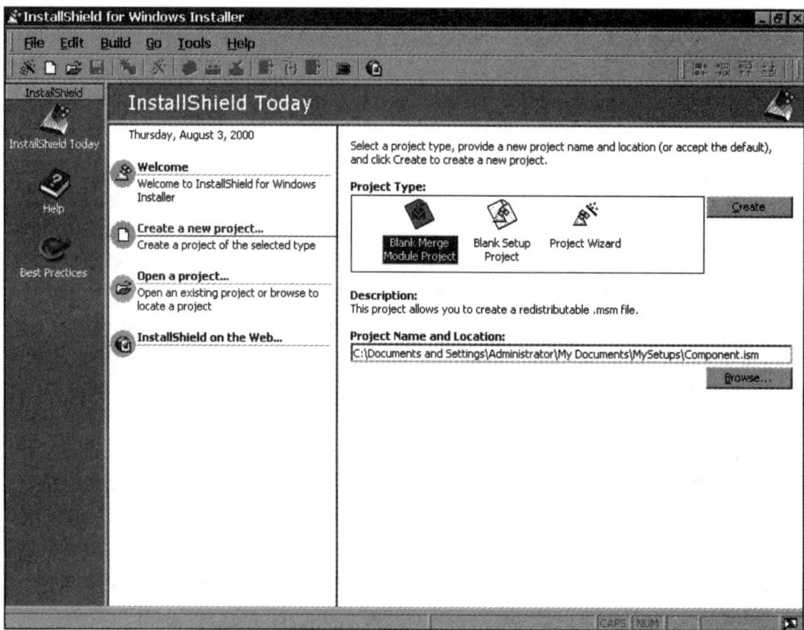

Figure 17-18: Creating a Merge Module Project

The project file that is created has the same .ism extension as for a standard installation project except that when this file is built, the file creates an .msm file and not an .msi database. After the merge module is created, it is inserted into any project you're using. A number of merge modules are shipped with ISWI where many of these come from Microsoft and a few are provided to enable the migration from projects created by the InstallShield Express product. The Microsoft merge modules that ship with ISWI are found in the Modules\i386 folder under the root ISWI install location. The merge modules that enable the migration from Express are found in the Objects folder under the root ISWI install location.

When you create merge modules and want to copy them to a central location for use by multiple projects, the merge modules are copied by default to the Merge-Modules folder under the MySetups folder. On Windows NT 4.0, the MySetups folder is under the Personal folder in a user's profile. On Windows 2000, this folder is under the MyDocuments folder in the Documents and Settings\\<*user-name*> folder. You can modify the location of all merge modules by going to the Tools | Options dialog and clicking the File Locations tab. At the bottom of this particular property sheet is an edit field where you can add new locations and modify the default locations.

Now you need to take a look at the basic merge module project to see how it differs from the creation of a standard installation project.

CREATING AND BUILDING THE MERGE MODULE PROJECT

When you first open a new merge module project, nothing dramatic tells you that this is a merge module project, but several items are different from a normal install project. First, in the View Bar on the right side of the screen, you see only five icons instead of six that can be used to show the major views in a project. The one view that is missing is the Sequences view. Also, you can note that in the Project view, you do not see the Windows 2000 Properties icon, and you have a Merge Module Properties icon instead of a Product Properties icon. The path variables are the same as in the standard install project, but both the Property Manager and the String Tables editor are empty. These tables are empty because a merge module cannot run without first being merged with a standard MSI package, so that no properties need to be authored unless the component(s) included in the merge module require them. Also, having a user interface is not common for a merge module, so that no displayable strings are needed to be part of the default merge module project. The Merge Module Properties page is shown Figure 17-19.

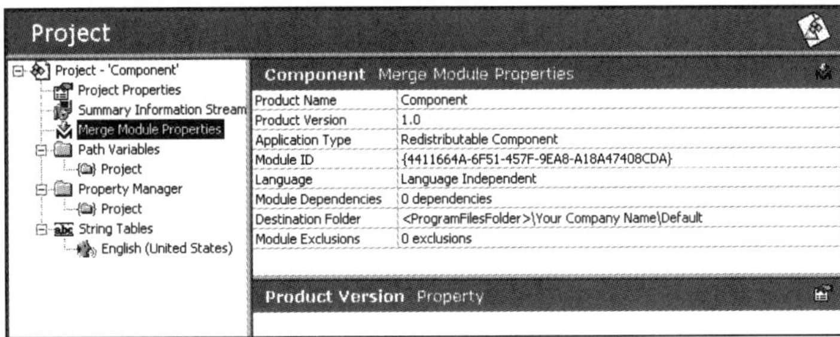

Figure 17-19: The Merge Module Properties page

Because the Merge Module Properties in the Project view is the only item that is different from what you have seen in a standard install project, you need to look at the properties to be entered here. Table 17-8 discusses the values to be entered in this property page.

Table 17-8 THE MERGE MODULE PROPERTIES

Property Name	Description
Product Name	The text you enter in this field is used as the Module Name, which along with the modified module GUID, forms the Module ID that is used to identify the merge module in the *ModuleSignature* table.
Product Version	The value that you enter here is used to version the merge module. This value is placed in the Version column of the *ModuleSignature* table when the merge module is built.
Application Type	An internal type identification is used only in the project file, which used to create the merge module. This is not placed in the merge module itself.
Module ID	The Module GUID is used in a modified form, along with the Product Name value described in this table, to create the Module ID that is used in the *ModuleSignature* table as the identifier that uniquely describes the merge module.
Language	The language identifier of the default language for the merge module whose value is entered into the Language column of the *ModuleSignature* table. If this value is shown as language independent, then 0 is entered into the Language column.
Module Dependencies	This property defines those other merge modules that are necessary for the present merge module to function correctly. After you click this cell, you get a property sheet at the bottom of the screen where you enter the necessary information to define the merge modules on which this merge module is dependent. If you right-click a row in this property sheet, you have the option of creating a dependency entry from scratch by selecting the New option or a merge module that is already in the Merge Module Gallery. In the Name column, you enter the value of the Subject property in the Summary Information Stream. In the Version column, you enter the version string that is in the Version column of the *ModuleSignature* table. For the Language and Module ID columns, you enter the values in the equivalent columns of the *ModuleSignature* table. After you select a merge module in the gallery, all these columns are filled in for us.

Property Name	Description
Destination Folder	In this property, the initial value of the INSTALLDIR property of the merge module is defined. In a following section, I discuss the merge module's destination.
Module Exclusions	The entries made for this property are similar to those made for defining the module dependencies. This property defines those merge modules where the present merge module cannot work. The additional information here is that you define both the minimum and maximum versions of the merge modules to be excluded. You also define the languages of those modules to exclude based on the various formats. If you define the Language to be language independent, then you exclude no merge module based on its language. Otherwise, you can exclude merge modules based on the language you enter into the Language column or you can exclude all languages except the one identified in the Language column. You do this by double-clicking the Language column and launching special Exclusion Languages dialog. Based on one of the two options in this dialog, you exclude the identified language or you exclude all languages except the selected language.

When you move to the Setup Design view, you see that you can only create components. Components are created in a merge module in the same fashion as discussed earlier in this chapter for a standard installation project. These components can be created manually or you can create them by using the Component Wizard.

In the Actions/Scripts view, you cannot create custom actions using InstallScript. You have the Custom Action Wizard available, but you are not allowed to create nested install custom actions, yet you can create all the other types of custom actions. You can create custom actions in the same manner as described in Chapter 11. If all you do is create these actions, you can then insert them into the proper location in the sequence tables in the standard installation project after the merge module has been incorporated. You can also define within the merge module where the custom action is supposed to go relative to the actions in the target packages sequence tables. The next section discusses how you accomplish this creation.

The User Interface view does not have any predefined dialogs but you can create dialogs if a particular merge module requires them. As stated in the previous paragraph, a merge module only needs a user interface in unusual circumstances. If all you do is create these dialogs, you can then insert them into the proper location in the sequence tables in the standard installation project after the merge module is incorporated. You can also define within the merge module where the dialog is supposed to go relative to the actions in the target packages sequence tables. How you accomplish this is also discussed in the next section.

Finally, the Release view provides the same functionality that is available in the Release view of a standard installation project. The only item that is different is the property page for a particular release label. Here only those properties that can change for a merge module can be set, while the other properties are read-only. When building a release from the Release view, the merge module is not copied to the MergeModules folder in the default build location.

Maximum control over a build is gained by running the Release Wizard to create the merge module. In this version of the Release Wizard, you find one additional dialog than in a standard installation project and some fields are disabled because a merge module only contains components and no features, while a merge module cannot perform an installation on its own. In the Filtering Settings dialog, the Release Flags edit field is disabled because this option only applies to features.

The new dialog in the merge module Release Wizard is the Merge Module Options dialog, which allows you to copy or not copy the merge module to the MergeModules folder. This dialog is shown in Figure 17-20.

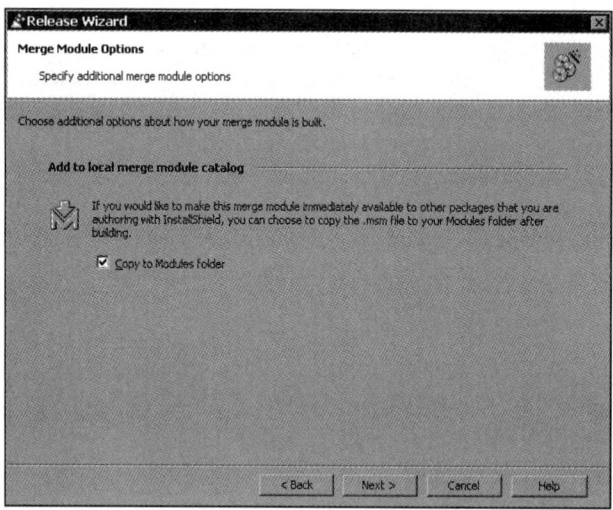

Figure 17-20: The Merge Modules Options dialog in the Merge Module Release Wizard

In the Advanced Settings dialog, the Launcher Settings are disabled because these all pertain to the creation of a boot strapping capability. This capability is not needed here because a merge module cannot run independently.

Chapter 7 covers in detail the Release Wizard for a standard installation project.

CONTROLLING WHERE A MERGE MODULE GETS INSTALLED

As discussed in the previous section, every merge module requires a *Directory* table in order to add directories to the main installation database. Directories defined in the merge module cannot replace any directories already defined in the *Directory* table of the main installation database. ISWI provides a default destination location for a merge module in the Modules Properties panel and it also allows you to specify specific locations for the installation of each component in the Setup Design view. If you merge a merge module in the main installation project, you use the Merge Module Wizard. After you run this wizard, the Merge Module Destination dialog asks where in the directory structure of the main installation you want to add the merge module. You need to look at the various options that you have for setting the destination where the files in a merge module are copied after the installation is run.

In a merge module, you have two main choices for defining the merge module destination in the Modules Properties panel. These choices are a full path or just a folder name, which can be considered a relative path to where the merge module files get installed. For the destination property for the component in the Setup Design view, you also have two main choices. You can specify the component destination to be the INSTALLDIR variable that gets set at run time, or you can define the destination to be a predefined location, such as CommonFilesFolder\Folder-Name. After you run the Merge Module Wizard to insert the merge module into the main installation project, you have three main choices after you get to the Merge Module Destination dialog. You can specify "(Use merge module's default destination)," or "INSTALLDIR," or some predefined location that is set by the operating system. The file destinations described in Table 17-9 are the various combinations that you can set for the destination in the merge module, along with the choices you can select after the Merge Module wizard runs.

Table 17-9 MERGE MODULE FILE DESTINATION MATRIX

Merge Module Destination Settings	Main Project Destination Setting	File Installation Location
The Destination Folder property in the Merge Module Properties property sheet defines an absolute path value and the Destination property for the as INSTALLDIR.	Any of the three possible types of selections, that is (Use merge module's " default destination)," "INSTALLDIR," or a predefined location.	The files are copied to the absolute path defined in the Destination Folder property in the Merge Modules Properties sheet.
The Destination Folder property in the Merge Module Properties property sheet defines a relative path value and the Destination property for the component is defined as INSTALLDIR.	The selection made when inserting the merge module by using the Merge Module Wizard is "(Use merge module's default destination)."	The component files are copied to the following location: ROOTDRIVE\Relative-Path If the ROOTDRIVE property is not authored into the *Property* table, the Windows Installer sets the files to the local drive that can be written to and which has the most component is defined free space.
The Destination Folder property in the Merge Module Properties property sheet defines a relative path value and the Destination property for the component is defined as INSTALLDIR.	The selection made after inserting the merge module by using the Merge Module Wizard is "INSTALLDIR."	The component files are copied to he following location: tINSTALLDIR\Relative-Path
The Destination Folder property in the Merge Module Properties property sheet defines a relative path value and the Destination property for the component is defined as INSTALLDIR.	The selection made after inserting the merge module by using the Merge Module Wizard is a predefined location.	The component files are copied to the following location: Predefined-Location\ Relative-Path

Merge Module Destination Settings	Main Project Destination Setting	File Installation Location
The Destination Folder property in the Merge Module Properties property sheet defines either a relative path value or an absolute path value and the Destination property for the component is defined as a predefined location.	Any of the three possible types of selections, that is "(Use merge module's default destination)," "INSTALLDIR," or a predefined location.	The component files are copied to the predefined location that is defined for the component Destination property.

Provided later in this chapter is a full discussion of the Merge Module Wizard.

One of the aspects that you notice from the previous table is that none of the possibilities described include having the component files go to the root directory of an installation. To make this happen, you must make a special entry in the *Directory* table of the main installation database. For example, assume that the merge module has a Module GUID of {9376C8F3-784D-11d4-9837-0010A4ECA 65E}. You find this same value as the Module ID property in the ISWI Merge Module Properties property sheet. The entry you then need to make in the *Directory* table of the main installation database is shown in Table 17-10.

Table 17-10 DIRECTORY TABLE ENTRY TO FORCE MERGE MODULE FILES TO GO TO THE ROOT INSTALLATION LOCATION

Column Name	Value
Directory	INSTALLDIR.9376C8F3_784D_11D4_9837_0010A4ECA65E
Directory_Parent	INSTALLDIR
DefaultDir	.

The entry in the Directory column is what appears in the Directory table of the merge module. The Module GUID is modified to conform to the rules for naming primary keys in a merge module. The Directory_Parent column essentially equates the merge module location to be equal to the value of the INSTALLDIR location. The period (.) in the DefaultDir column is placed there because you are not interested in any sub-folders under INSTALLDIR, yet this column cannot be NULL.

CONTROLLING THE SEQUENCE OF ACTIONS AND DIALOGS WITHIN THE MERGE MODULE

For many merge modules that you create, all you do is deliver files and other component resources to a standard Windows Installer installation package. However, if your merge module needs to include actions and/or dialogs, and you want to control where and how they are used in the main installation package, you then need to author special sequence tables in the merge module. You do this so that these actions and dialogs get inserted correctly when the merge module is merged into the main Windows Installer package.

Controlling the sequence of actions from within a merge module depends on the proper authoring of the special sequence tables that can only be included in a merge module. The names of these sequence tables follow the format Module<*name of equivalent .msi sequence table*>. For example, the name of the sequence table in a merge module that controls the user interface during installation has the name *ModuleInstallUISequence*. The schema of these special tables is different than the tables in an MSI database. This schema is described in Table 17-11.

TABLE 17-11 THE SCHEMA OF THE MERGE MODULE SEQUENCE TABLES

Column Name	Description
Action	The name of an action to insert into sequence of the main installation database, this action can be one of the standard actions known to the Windows Installer, or it can be an entry in the merge module's *CustomAction* table or *Dialog* table. If it is the name of a standard action, then the BaseAction and After columns of the record must be Null.
Sequence	If a standard action is defined in the Action column, then this column contains the recommended sequence number for this standard action. If the sequence number in the merge module differs from that for the same action in the main installation database sequence table, the merge operation uses the sequence number from the main installation database and not the sequence number that is entered here. If a custom action or dialog is entered into the Action column, this field must be set to Null.

Column Name	Description
BaseAction	The BaseAction column can contain a standard action, a custom action specified in the merge module's custom action table, or a dialog specified in the module's dialog table. The BaseAction column is a key into the Action column of this table. This means that every standard action, custom action, or dialog listed in the BaseAction column must also be listed in the Action column of another record in this table.
After	The number placed in this column is a Boolean value that determines whether the entry in the Action column comes before or after the entry in the BaseAction column. If it is to come before the value in the BaseAction column, you need to use 0 and if you want it to come after then you need to 1.
Condition	This condition is an expression that evaluates to either True or False. If it evaluates to True, the action is executed, and if it is False, the action is not executed. If this column is left Null, the condition is considered to be True. This entry becomes the condition in the Condition column of the sequence table in the main installation database.

The concept of these tables is to provide information to the tool that is performing the merge about where to insert the action or dialog into the sequence table of the main installation database. A good example of the use of these tables is the Access97 merge module that is distributed with ISWI version 1.52. You can find this merge module in the Objects folder under the location where ISWI is installed. Except for a situation where you are inserting a standard action that does not already occur in the sequence table of the main installation database, a minimum of two rows needs to be authored into the module sequence table.

INSERTING A MERGE MODULE INTO THE MAIN INSTALLATION PROJECT

After you create your merge modules or receive them from the developer, you need to consume them in the main installation project. First, you need to make sure that these merge modules are copied to the MergeModules folder in the location where your builds are being made. Next, you need to make sure that you know which features to associate with each merge module. Then you start the process of inserting each merge module that you want to use by launching the Merge Module Wizard. Right-clicking a feature and selecting the last option on the resulting context menu accesses this wizard.

The first dialog in this wizard is the welcome screen that is shown in Figure 17-21.

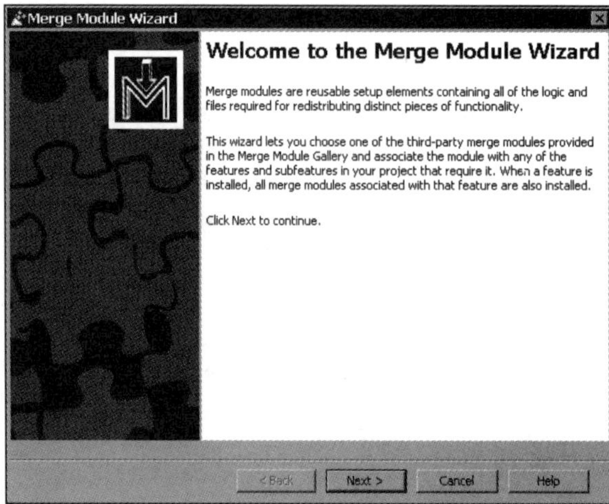

Figure 17-21: The Welcome dialog of the Merge Module Wizard

As shown in this dialog, the wizard provides access to all the merge modules that you find in the merge module locations specified in the options dialog. After you click the next button, you get the Merge Module Gallery dialog that provides access to the merge modules in the specified locations. The string provided in the Subject property of the merge module information stream identifies the merge modules in the gallery. The Merge Module Gallery dialog is shown in Figure 17-22.

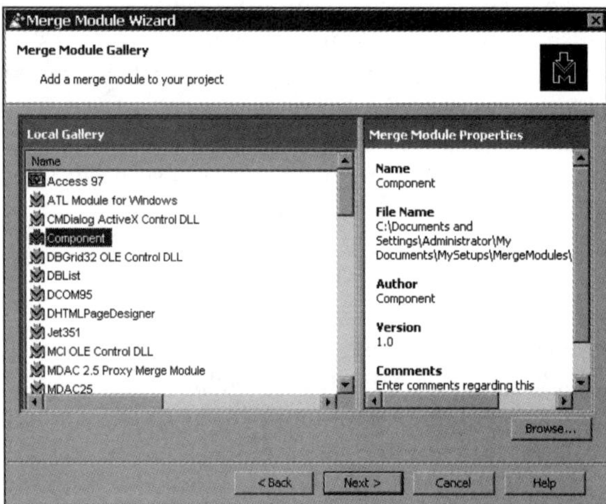

Figure 17-22: The Merge Module Gallery dialog of the Merge Module Wizard

In this dialog, you find two panels, the Local Gallery on the left and the Merge Module Properties on the right. In the left panel, you can display the available merge modules in list form, as shown in Figure 17-22, or you can right-click to have the merge modules displayed using large icons. After you click a merge module in the Local Gallery, you get a display of its properties in the right panel. The Name property is the same as shown in the left hand panel and this is the value of the Subject property in the Summary Information Stream. The File Name property shows where the merge module is located on the build machine, The Author property is the value of the Author property in the Summary Information Stream, The Version property is obtained from the Version field of the *ModuleSignature* table, and the Comments property is the value of the Comments property in the Summary Information Stream.

You can also browse for a merge module by clicking on the Browse button. When you select a merge module in this manner, its location will be added to the standard search path used for merge modules. Thereafter merge modules in this new location will appear in the Merge Module Gallery.

You select the merge module that you want to associate with your feature and click the Next button. Selecting more than one merge module at a time is not possible. After you click the Next button, you get the Merge Module Destination dialog. This dialog is shown in Figure 17-23.

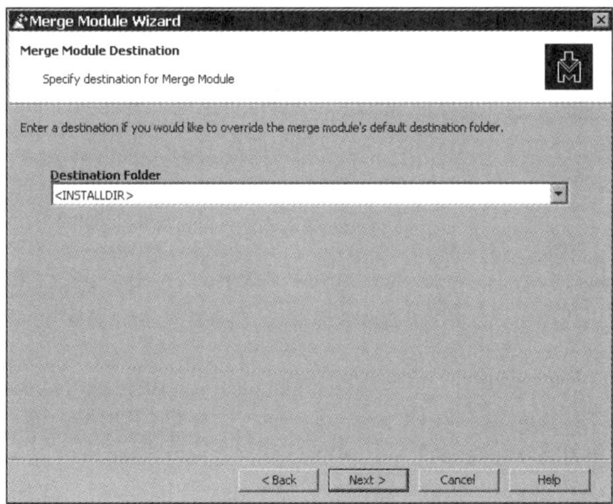

Figure 17-23: The Merge Module Destination dialog of the Merge Module Wizard

In this dialog, you can make some choices where to install the merge module. In this dialog, a dropdown list provides a list of operating system defined locations as well as the standard INSTALLDIR location. You also can choose to have the merge module installed to the default location specified in the merge module *Directory* table. A full discussion of defining the destination for a merge module is provided earlier in this chapter.

After you have select how to handle the destination of the merge module, you move on to the next dialog in the wizard. This dialog is the Associate Merge Module with Features dialog that is shown in Figure 17-24.

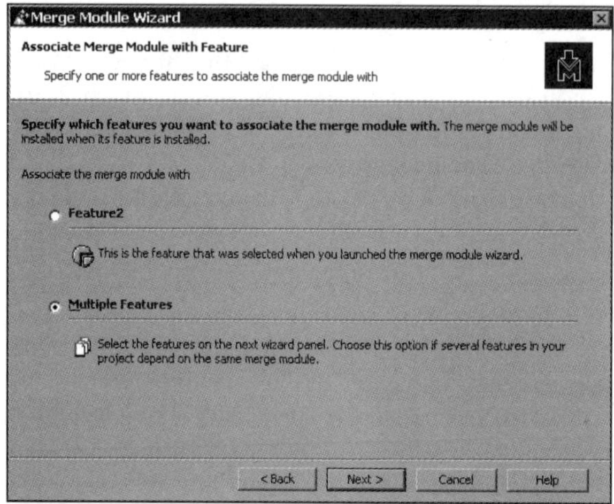

Figure 17-24: The Associate Merge Module with Feature dialog of the Merge Module Wizard

In this dialog, you have the opportunity to associate the merge module with more than just the feature from which you launched the wizard. If you select to associate the merge module with multiple features, you then get the dialog shown in Figure 17-25.

In this dialog, you are given a list of all the other features in the project, and you can choose to associate the merge module with some or all of the other features. After you finish with this selection, you go to the final dialog in the wizard, which is the Summary dialog. This dialog is shown in Figure 17-26.

This dialog, as with all summary dialogs, shows all the selections that were made in the wizard and gives you the chance to go back and change them. After you click the Finish button on the Summary dialog, a pointer to the merge module is created and associated with the designated features. If you highlight a merge module that has been inserted, you get a property sheet that provides a view of the properties for the merge module. This is shown in Figure 17-27.

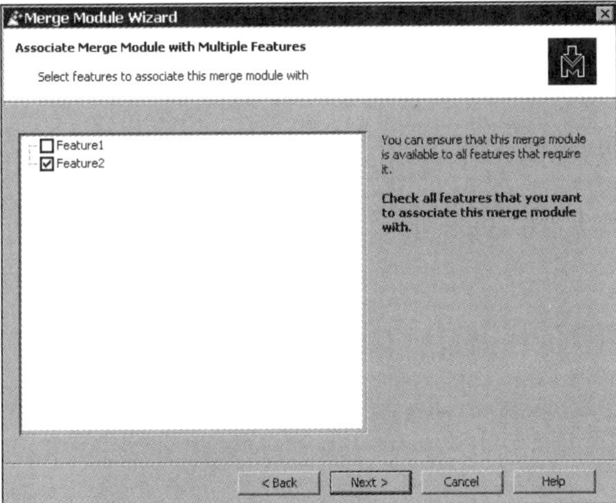

Figure 17-25: The Associate Merge Module with Multiple Features dialog of the Merge Module Wizard

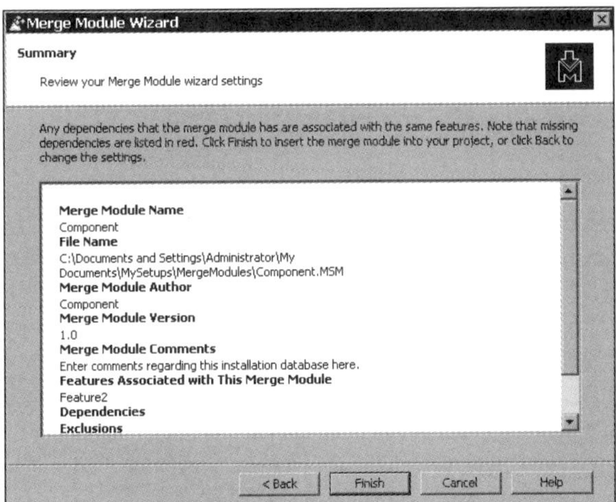

Figure 17-26: The Summary dialog of the Merge Module Wizard

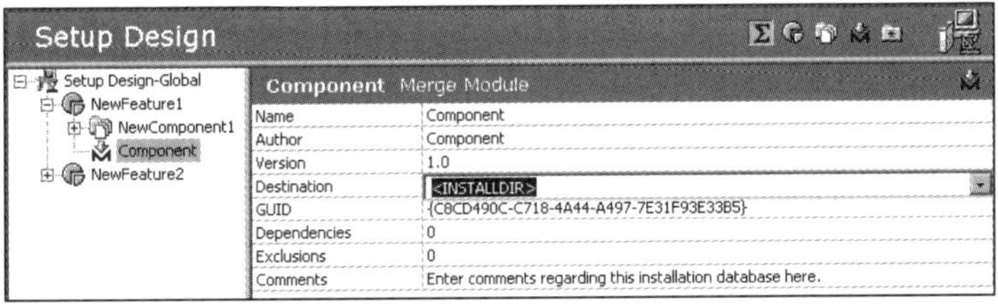

Figure 17-27: The viewable properties in the Setup view for a Merge Module

All of these properties are read-only with the exception of the Destination property. You can change this value without having to reinsert the merge module. After you have the merge module inserted into the main installation project, all you have to do is build the project. The merge modules will merge during this process. Not incorporating the merge modules into the project .ism file is important. After you change a merge module, all you have to do is rebuild the installation project and this merges the new merge module with the MSI database that is created.

Installing Shared Components

With the Windows Installer, components are refcounted in the registry but using a different approach than is used for non-Windows Installer based installations. For the non-Windows Installer installation, a shared component (file) is given a refcount in the SharedDlls key in the registry. This approach normally is used for DLLs and most of these DLLs are installed to the Windows System32 folder, which only reference counted the file itself and does nothing with regard to the registry entries and other information that are associated with this DLL.

Windows Installer components, however, are refcounted as a whole. This means that all resources that comprise a component are refcounted.

How the system keeps track of installed components

One of the primary mechanisms in the Windows Installer is the new approach to the reference counting of components. Instead of just counting the number of applications that are using a shared component, the Windows Installer counts all aspects of the component, which means that all the resources that comprise a component are counted. Because the present SharedDLLs key in the registry is not designed to handle this counting, a more robust type of reference counting with a different approach has to be used. The location where this reference counting is performed for both per-machine and per-user installed applications is under the following registry key:

```
HKEY_LOCAL_MACHINE\SOFTWARE\Microsoft\Windows\CurrentVersion\
Installer\Components\
```

Under the Components key are sub-keys that are packed component GUIDs of all the components that have been installed to either run locally or to run from source. The value names under each of these sub-keys are the packed product GUIDs of all the products that have installed the component. The value data for each of these packed product GUIDs is the keypath for the component as defined for the product that installed it. If a product is uninstalled, its value name and data are removed from the registry. If no more products are associated with a particular component, then the Windows Installer removes the component and all its resources from the system.

As has been stated in other chapters that discuss the use of the registry by the Windows Installer, you need to be aware that what I have said here only relates to version 1.2 and earlier of the Windows Installer. The next versions of the Windows Installer will be changing the way information about an application is stored.

One of the properties discussed earlier in this chapter is the property that defines the component as being permanent. This means that the component never get uninstalled even if no products are registered as using the component. The creation of a packed product GUID that consists of all zeros accomplishes this. Because this will never represent an actual product that has been installed on the system, the component will never be uninstalled because one value name and data will always be associated with the component.

Installing Win32 and COM DLLs

Shared files come in two categories, globally shared components and side-by-side shared components. In this section, you discuss where to put globally shared components.

If a shared component is only shared between the applications created by a single software vendor, then these shared components are installed into a folder under the following location:

```
%ProgramFiles%\Common Files\Company-Name
```

It is also acceptable to install shared components for a single software vendor to the following directory:

```
%ProgramFiles%\Company-Name\Shared Files
```

When more than one software vendor uses a shared component, this type of component needs to be installed into the following location:

```
%WindowsFolder%\System32
```

When installing to this global location and you want to obtain the “Certified for Windows” logo, documenting all cases where files are copied to this location is necessary.

If you try to copy files that are on the Windows File Protection list into the System32 folder on Windows 2000, Windows 98 SE, or Windows Me, this action will fail. On these operating systems, having the application use the system files provided by the operating system is necessary.

The ideal situation on the new operating systems is to privatize the components of an application so that there is no opportunity for one application to place a globally shared component on the system with which another application cannot work. How this is accomplished is the topic of the next section.

Isolating a component

If you want to privatize a component on Windows 2000, Windows 98 SE, or Windows Me so that only the application that needs the component uses it, you need to isolate this component. When you isolate a component using the Windows Installer, you are implementing DLL redirection. To implement DLL redirection using the Windows Installer, you need to define the components that are going to run in a side-by-side manner in the *IsolatedComponent* table. The Isolate-Components action reads this table and enables the proper handling of the affected components so that they get installed properly. Table 17-12 describes the entries that need to be made in the *IsolatedComponent* table.

TABLE 17-12 THE ISOLATEDCOMPONENT TABLE SCHEMA

Column Name	Description
Component_Shared	The entry in this column is a foreign key into the Component table and identifies the component that contains the shared file. This shared file should be the key file for this component and it must be a different component than the one that installs the client of the shared file. For this component, setting the Shared property to Yes in the Component property sheet is necessary. This is necessary to protect the shared copy of the component being isolated so that other applications that are using the shared copy are not be broken by an uninstallation.
Component_Application	The entry in this column is a foreign key into the *Component* table and identifies the component that contains the client executable of the shared file. The .exe should be the key file for this component and it must be a different component than listed in the Component_Shared column.

DLL redirection is implemented by making a copy of the shared file in the install location of the client executable. In this same location, a zero byte file is created with the same name as the executable but with a .LOCAL extension added. For example, if the name of the executable is MyApp.exe, the zero byte file has the name of MyApp.exe.LOCAL. When the system loader on Windows 2000, Windows 98 SE, or Windows Me detects that a .LOCAL file is in the same directory, it alters the search path for loading DLLs or OCXs. It does not matter whether the executable is performing a LoadLibrary call using an absolute path to the shared location, the local version of the DLL gets loaded into memory. The same applies to COM servers where the registration contains the absolute path to the shared location of the DLL or OCX. The isolated version is loaded instead.

The IsolateComponents action needs to be placed between the CostInitialize and the CostFinalize actions and can only be used when performing an INSTALL top-level action. In other words, component isolation cannot be implemented during an administrative installation or when an application is being advertised. This action makes sense when the IsolateComponents action runs it queries the *Isolated-Component* table and makes entries in the DuplicateFile table, which is queried by the DuplicateFiles action. The reason that the IsolateComponents action has to be placed as I describe previously is because of the need to have an accurate file cost calculation, which can only be done after the DuplicateFile table has been populated. When the Windows Installer detects that it is running on a system that supports DLL redirection, it sets the RedirectedDLLSupport property. Using this property, conditioning the IsolateComponents action is possible so that it only runs when the installation is being performed on Windows 2000, Windows 98 SE, and Windows Me.

When the InstallFiles action runs, it copies the shared files to the shared location and then the DuplicateFiles action makes a copy of these files to the location where the client executables is installed.The InstallFiles action also creates the .LOCAL file at this time. The duplication of the shared files to a private location only occurs if the client executable gets installed.

Earlier in this chapter, you mention a true side-by-side functionality that does not rely on creating a .LOCAL file for COM components. A new application is designed at the beginning to take advantage of the capability to have two or versions of the same DLL in memory at the same time. Part of this functionality relies on registering a COM server with a relative path instead of an absolute path. To have the Windows Installer register a COM server with a relative path instead of an absolute path, you need to set a special attribute. In ISWI when you have a COM component and you have extracted the COM registration information by using the Component Wizard, you have the class information displayed under the Advanced Settings. If you click the COM Registration icon and then expand the Class icon in the right hand panel, you see the class description. If you click this description, a property sheet is displayed and you can then set the relative attribute, as shown in Figure 17-28.

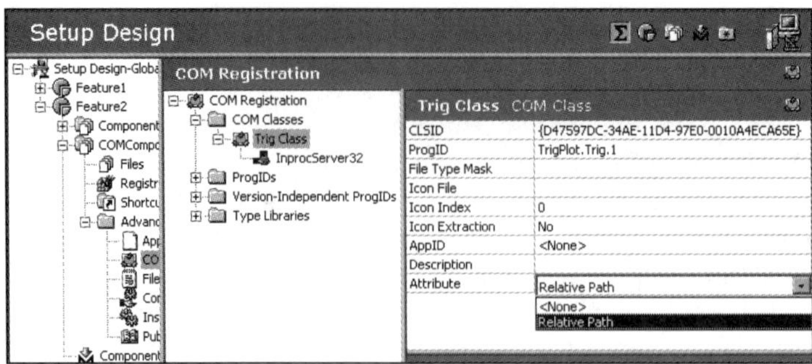

Figure 17-28: Setting the relative attribute for a COM Class

Setting the relative attribute for a class when extracting the COM information at build time is not presently possible.

Creating an array of components

A special capability of the Windows Installer allows for the creation of a category of components. Components that belong to a defined category are called Qualified Components and can be thought of as an array of components. The Windows Installer makes special registry entries for qualified components, which allows applications to access these components to provide particular capabilities to the user. Qualified components are defined in the *PublishComponent* table and this table is read by the PublishComponents action, which makes the needed registry entries. Just because the term "Publish" is used here does not mean that this functionality has to do with advertising. This is a completely different use of the word publish.

Because you are concerned here with the authoring of the *PublishComponent* table, you need to look at the fields that need to be filled in for this table. Table 17-13 describes the entries that are required in this table.

TABLE 17-13 THE PUBLISHCOMPONENT TABLE SCHEMA

Column Name	Description
ComponentId	This value is a GUID that defines the category of components being grouped together. This is the GUID for the category of qualified components and is not the same GUID appearing in the ComponentId column of the *Component* table.

Column Name	Description
Qualifier	This qualifier is a text string that qualifies the value in the ComponentId column. This qualifier is used to distinguish multiple forms of the same component, such as a component that is implemented in multiple languages. These are the qualifier text-strings returned by MsiEnumComponentQualifiers.
Component_	A foreign key in the first column of the *Component* table, this identifier refers to the qualified component's record in the Component table.
AppData	An optional and localizable text string, which describes the qualified component, is commonly parsed by the application and is displayed to the user. This string is retrieved from the registry by using the MsiEnumComponentQualifiers function.
Feature_	This is a foreign key into the first column of the *Feature* table and is the feature that is installing the qualified component.

In ISWI the entries made in this table are created for each component using the Publishing icon under the Advanced Settings. After you click the Publishing icon, you see a panel to the right where you can right-click to generate a GUID that serves as the ComponentId in the PublishComponent table. Under the GUID is a default qualifier string, which you can rename to whatever you want. After you highlight the qualifier, you can add an optional string to be placed in the AppData column. In order to include other components in the same group, copying the ComponentId GUID from the first component to the other components is necessary. To copy the GUID to the clipboard, you right-click the first GUID generated, select the Rename option, and then right-click again and select the Copy command. This copies the GUID to the clipboard where it can be used to generate the same ComponentId for the other components that are to be grouped together. Orca is an example of the use of published components. Orca creates an array of components for the three validation suites defined in three different .cub files. You can see this if you open up the Orca .msi file using Orca and go into the PublishComponent table.

The ISWI IDE where the qualified components are defined is shown in Figure 17-29.

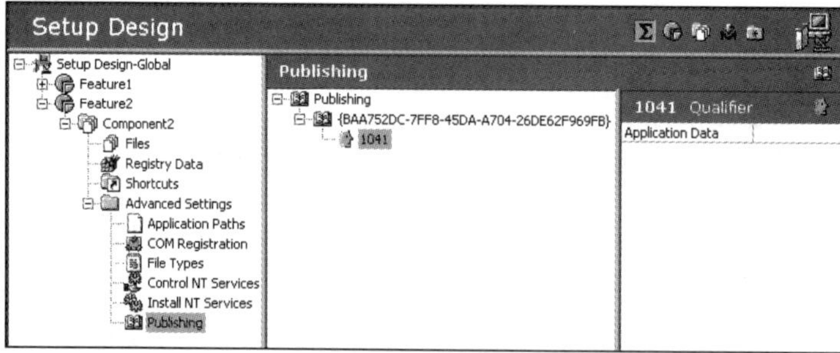

Figure 17-29: Creating qualified components by using the Publishing advanced settings

When the PublishComponents action queries the *PublishComponent* table, it makes entries into the registry that a number of Windows Installer API functions can use to retrieve information about these components. The names of the API functions that use this information are MsiProvideQualifiedComponent, MsiProvideQualifiedComponentEx, and MsiEnumComponentQualifiers. These functions read the information in the registry that defines the qualified components. The registry entries for qualified components are made in one of two locations depending on whether the installation was performed for the current user or for the machine. These locations are as follows:

```
HKEY_CURRENT_USER\SOFTWARE\Microsoft\Installer\Components
```

for a per-user installation and

```
HKEY_LOCAL_MACHINE\SOFTWARE\Classes\Installer\Components
```

for a per-machine installation. The sub-keys under these locations are the packed ComponentId GUIDs from the *PublishComponent* table. Under these sub-keys, the value names are the component qualifiers and the value data for each of these qualifiers is a Darwin Descriptor concatenated with the AppData string from the *PublishComponent* table. A Darwin Descriptor is a combination of the ProductCode property, feature name, and component code.

You need to be aware that after version 1.2 of the Windows Installer the usage of the registry will be changing. What I have shown here could very well be changing in the future. This information is provided so that you can get a feeling about how the Windows Installer works underneath.

Summary

You start this chapter by looking at how operating systems handle the loading of dynamic link libraries into memory. You examine how the older operating systems handle this function, and then you look at the changes introduced by Windows 2000, Windows 98 SE, and Windows Me. This new functionality is where more than one version of the same DLL can be loaded into memory at the same time. You then look at the rules set down to guide you in the creation of components and look at what happens if you do not follow these rules. You also look at the guidelines that should be followed to change a component and when the component code needs to be changed, thus creating a new component.

Next, you took a close look at the many ways that components can be created using the features in ISWI. You see how a component can be created by using the Component Wizard. The Component Wizard had two modes of operation, one where a number of files can be used to create components following the componentization rules, and the second where you can create special types of components. These special types of components are those that install NT Services, ODBC, Fonts, and COM Servers.

After looking at the creation of components, you then look at the means that have been provided by the Windows Installer for delivering components to an application. For any component that is to be shared between applications, the recommended method is to create the component in a merge module. You look at the structure of a merge module and then investigate the features in ISWI where you can create merge modules and then insert them into an installation project.

Finally, you look at how the Windows Installer registers components and how to install special types of components. These special types of components are those that support side-by-side sharing as well as the creation of an array of components. An array of components allows applications to access various components that belong to a family of components all of which have a parallel functionality.

Chapter 18

The Creation and Use of Transforms

IN THIS CHAPTER

- ◆ Understanding what transforms are, and what they are not
- ◆ Learning the structure of a transform file
- ◆ Learning the various types of transforms
- ◆ Creating of transforms
- ◆ Applying transforms at both design time and at run time
- ◆ Using and manipulating transforms in special ways

TRANSFORMS ARE A major component of the Windows Installer functionality. They can play important roles at design time and at run time.

What Are Transforms?

Simply put, a transform is the difference between two MSI packages. Unlike a merge module, which we discussed in Chapter 17, a transform can be used not only to add resources to a MSI package but also to modify entries in a MSI database. You learned in Chapter 17 that a merge module was only used for delivering components at design time to a MSI package. Like a merge module a transform can be used for delivering a component to a MSI package, but unlike a merge module it can also be used to add features to a package.

You might ask, What is the good of a merge module when I can do everything with a transform? The answer is that a merge module can be authored and a transform is only generated as the difference between two MSI packages. When I say that a transform cannot be authored I mean that there are no APIs available from the Windows Installer that provide direct access to the components of a transform. It is possible to create a tool, such as InstallShield Tuner, that gives the impression that you are directly manipulating the internals of a transform. With a transform there is no structure to ensure that applying a transform to a MSI package will avoid conflicts. With a merge module, the structure of this type of file is specifically designed to avoid conflicts that are possible when merging two databases. A merge module can contain a CAB file but a transform cannot.

When authoring a merge module, you can control whether it can be applied to an MSI package by using the ModuleDependency, ModuleExclusion, and ModuleIgnore tables in the merge module. (In Chapter 17 we discuss these tables.) When creating a transform, you can use the Error and Validation flags to control the database to which it can be applied. These flags are stored in the Character Count property of the Summary Information Stream inside the transform file.

You can apply a transform either at design time or at run time. When applied at design time, it will permanently alter the target MSI package much as a merge module does. A transform can also be applied at run time. When you do this, the MSI package is modified only in memory and the target package is not permanently modified. A merge module has no such functionality.

Transforms are a very important feature of the Windows Installer technology. You can use them by themselves or to help implement other features in the Windows Installer. You can use transforms in multilanguage merge modules or to implement patch packages. They also play a major role in the deployment functionality of Windows 2000. Transforms are the de facto standard for customization of an MSI package. Tools available in the market for authoring transforms are InstallShield Tuner for any MSI package and Office Customization wizard only for Microsoft Office.

The Structure of a Transform File

A transform (an .mst file) is a COM-structured storage file but it is not an MSI database and so you can't open it with Orca. You can use a transform to add, update, or delete a row in the reference database; you can also use it to add or delete a table or add a column to the reference database. As of this writing, you cannot delete a column with a transform. If you open a transform using the DocFile viewer that comes with Visual Studio, you will see something that looks very much like an MSI database. The difference is that the streams in the transform are different from those in an MSI package.

A transform is made up of a Tables catalog, a Columns catalog, and individual streams for tables in which rows will be added, updated, or deleted. A transform makes use of masks to determine whether a particular operation is to add, update, or delete a particular entity in the reference database. The Tables catalog contains the information for the tables that are to be added or deleted. The Columns catalog contains information about the columns to be added. The table streams make use of the masks to define whether the entry in the stream is to be used to add a new row, update a row, or delete a row from the associated table.

The transform Summary Information Stream

Because a transform is a COM-structured storage file, it has a Summary Information Stream. Appendix B contains a complete description of the properties found in a transform Summary Information Stream and the use that each of these properties is put to. One property that we should discuss in more detail is the Character Count property.

The Character Count property in the Summary Information Stream of a transform holds information that determines whether a transform can be applied to the reference database or not. It also holds information that determines whether the application of a transform will fail or not. The Character Count property is a four-byte integer where the upper word contains the transform's validation flags and the lower word contains the error condition flags. The validation flags determine whether a transform can be applied to a particular database and the error flags determine the conditions under which the application of the transform will succeed or fail. In either case the term *reference database* refers to the database to which the transform is being applied.

The error flags in actual fact define the error conditions to be suppressed when a transform is applied to a database. If none of the error flags is set then any of the possible error conditions will cause the application of the transform to fail. Table 18-1 describes the various error flags .

TABLE 18-1 TRANSFORM ERROR CONDITION FLAGS

Error Flag	Description
0x00000000	When the error flag is 0, any of the possible errors described in the remaining rows of this table will cause the application of the transform to the reference database to fail.
0x00000001	Suppresses the error that would be generated when a transform tries to add a pre-existing row to the reference database.
0x00000002	Suppresses the error that would be generated when a transform tries to delete a nonexistent row from the reference database.
0x00000004	Suppresses the error that would be generated when a transform tries to add a pre-existing table to the reference database.
0x00000008	Suppresses the error that would be generated when a transform tries to delete a nonexistent table from the reference database.
0x00000010	Suppresses the error that would be generated when a transform tries to update a nonexistent row in the reference database.
0x00000020	Suppresses the error that would be generated if the code page for the transform and the code page for the reference database do not match and neither is neutral.

As I mentioned earlier, the validation flags you can set in the transform determine whether a transform can be applied to a particular database. Also, as with the error flags I just described, you need to add the validation flags for the various types of validation to occur when a transform is applied. Table 18-2 describes the possible validation flags. The validation flags fall into one of four groups as shown in the table. In the general group any combination of flags is allowed, but in the other groups only one of the flags can be selected.

TABLE 18-2 TRANSFORM VALIDATION FLAGS

Flag Group	Validation Flag	Description
General	0x00000000	If the upper word in the Character Count summary property is 0, there will be no validation to determine if the transform can be applied to the reference database. The transform will just be applied.
	0x00000001	When this flag is set, the default language of the transform must match the default language of the reference database or the transform will not be applied.
	0x00000002	When this flag is set, the product code of the transform must match the product code contained in the Property table of the reference database or the transform will not be applied.
Product Version	0x00000008	When this flag is set the transform and the reference database will be compared using only the major version.
	0x00000010	When this flag is set the transform and the reference database will be compared using the major and minor versions.
	0x00000020	When this flag is set the transform and the reference database will be compared using the major, minor, and update versions.

Flag Group	Validation Flag	Description
Product Version Relationship	0x00000040	When this flag is set the comparison of product versions in the transform and the reference database will be validated if the product version in the transform is less than the product version in the reference database or the transform will not be applied.
	0x00000080	When this flag is set the comparison of product versions in the transform and the reference database will be validated if the product version in the transform is less than or equal to the product version in the reference database or the transform will not be applied.
	0x00000100	When this flag is set the comparison of product versions in the transform and the reference database will be validated if the product version in the transform is equal to the product version in the reference database or the transform will not be applied.
	0x00000200	When this flag is set the comparison of product versions in the transform and the reference database will be validated if the product version in the transform is greater than or equal to the product version in the reference database or the transform will not be applied.
	0x00000400	When this flag is set the comparison of product versions in the transform and the reference database will be validated if the product version in the transform is greater than the product version of the reference database.

Continued

TABLE 18-2 TRANSFORM VALIDATION FLAGS *(Continued)*

Flag Group	Validation Flag	Description
Upgrade Code	0x00000800	When this flag is set the Upgrade Code property of the transform must match the UpgradeCode property of the reference database or the transform will not be applied.

We have gone into detail here about the error condition and validation flags you can set to determine whether a transform is applied or not. These flags are important and you will come into contact with them again when you create a transform in this chapter using the ISWI Transform Wizard. You will also meet up with them again in Chapter 20 when we look at the creation of patch packages. Now let's take a look at the various types of transforms that have been defined.

The Types of Transforms

Transforms can be embedded in the MSI package to which they are to be applied. This type of transform only has relevance in a run-time environment. A transform can also be stand-alone: this type of transform is relevant to both the design-time environment and the run-time environment. In the design-time environment you can perform only a static application of the transform to the target MSI package that permanently changes the package. In the run-time environment, stand-alone transforms get much more interesting. For this type of transform you need to be concerned about the proper caching of transforms as well as how many transforms are to be applied and in which order. In the run-time environment stand-alone transforms are either *secured* or *unsecured*. Depending on the security designation of a stand-alone transform the place where a transform is cached will change after the installation has been completed. Table 18-3 describes each type of transform.

Transforms associated with a product are entered into the registry. The type of transform is indicated in the registry by the entry's formatting. If you are installing on a per-user basis, the transform entries in the registry are the value data for the Transform value name associated with the following key:

```
HKCU\SOFTWARE\Microsoft\Installer\Products\{ProductCode}
```

If you are installing on a per-machine basis, the transform entries in the registry are the value data for the Transform value name associated with the following key:

```
HKLM\SOFTWARE\Classes\Installer\Products\{ProductCode}
```

TABLE 18-3 DESCRIPTION OF THE TRANSFORM TYPES

Transform Type	Description
Embedded Transform	Stored inside the MSI package; as such these types of transforms are always available to the user. Because of this, this type of transform is never cached on the end user's system.
Stand-alone Secure-At-Source Transform	Has a source at the root of the MSI package. When the product is either installed or advertised, the transform is cached on the system in a location where the user does not have write privileges.
Stand-alone Secure-Full-Path Transform	Has a source located at the fully qualified path specified in the TRANSFORMS property. When the product is either installed or advertised, the transform is cached on the system in a location where the user does not have write privileges.
Stand-alone Unsecured Transform	Cached on the local system when the package is either installed or advertised. The cache location is the Application Data folder in the user's profile; here the user has write privileges. If you are installing on a per-machine basis, the transform is cached in %Windows%\Installer\{*ProductCode*} folder.

In either of these registry locations the value data for the Transform value name are a semicolon-delimited list of the associated transforms for the product. If a transform is a Secure-At-Source transform type, the name of the transform in the list is preceded by an at symbol (@). If the transform is a Secure-Full-Path transform type, the entry for the transform in the list is a fully qualified path to the transform preceded by the pipe symbol (|).

If the transform is stand-alone and unsecured and the install was performed on a per-user basis, the cached location of the transform is shown in the list using what is called a *shell-folder path*. If the installation was performed on a per-machine basis, the transform is shown in the list with a fully qualified path to its cached location. Embedded transforms are stored in the list with the storage token, a colon (:) preceding the name of the transform.

Creating and Applying Transforms

The main thing to keep in mind about transforms is that you can author them as you author an MSI database. The only way to create a transform is to use the appropriate Windows Installer APIs to create the transform as the difference between two MSI databases. Another thing to keep in mind is that transforms only describe the difference between the tables in two MSI databases; they do not do anything with source files or the Summary Information Stream in an MSI file.

You can apply a transform at design time or at run time. When you apply a transform at design time, the target database to which you apply the transform is permanently changed. When you apply a transform at run time the MSI database is changed only in memory; the changes are not persisted in the database.

Creating a transform using ISWI

You can access the ISWI Transform Wizard from the Tools pulldown menu. You can use this wizard to create a transform as the difference between two MSI databases. For creating a transform the wizard is wrapper around the MsiDatabaseGenerate-Transform and MsiCreateTransformSummaryInfo Windows Installer APIs. You will use the Transform Wizard to create a transform between the Schema.msi database found with the Windows Installer SDK and the MSI package you created earlier for the ISWI Artist application. Schema.msi is an empty database that you used in chapters 4 and 5 to create your first installation package the hard way. In order for Schema.msi to work correctly in this example you have to make two entries into the Property table using Orca. You need to enter one row containing the ProductVersion property and set this property to be the same as that for the ISWI Artist application. You also need to add a row for the ProductCode property and again make the value the same as for the ISWI Artist application. Once you have done these two things you can proceed with creating the transform. Finally, you need to add a PackageCode value to the Summary Information Stream of Schema.msi. You can get a package code value by using the GUIDGEN.EXE utility that comes with Visual C++. Once you are done modifying the Schema.msi database you can move on to creating the transform.

When you access the Transform Wizard from the Tools pulldown menu, you will see the Welcome dialog shown in Figure 18-1.

In this Welcome dialog the default selection is to create a transform so all you need to do is click on the Next button. This brings you to the Specify Files dialog where you identify the two MSI databases to be used to create the transform. This dialog is shown in Figure 18-2.

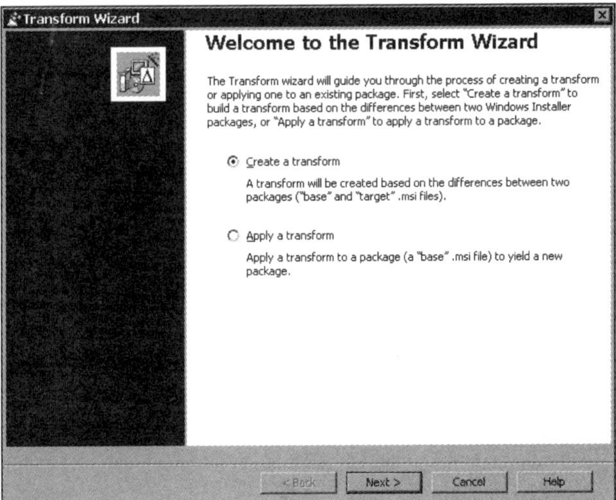

Figure 18-1: The Welcome dialog of the Transform Wizard

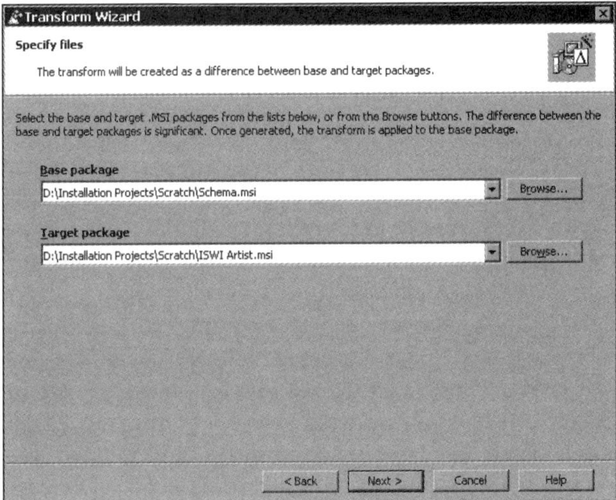

Figure 18-2: The Specify Files dialog of the Transform Wizard (transform creation mode)

In this dialog you can see that you need to identify a base package and a target package. The base package is the database without any changes. The base package is sometimes called the reference database and it is the one to which you apply the transform in order to obtain the target package. Figure 18-2 shows that Schema.msi is the base package and ISWI Artist.msi is the target package.

The dialog in the Transform Wizard is the Validation Settings dialog, shown in Figure 18-3.

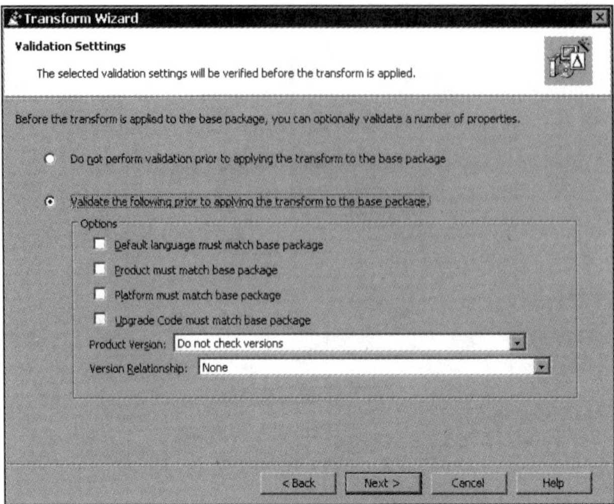

Figure 18-3: The Validation Settings dialog of the Transform Wizard (transform creation mode)

In this dialog you set the validation flags that determine whether a transform can be applied to a particular package or not. (These flags were described in Table 18-2.) In the example you are running you won't want to perform any validation because you will be applying this transform to an empty database. The next dialog in the Transform Wizard is the Suppress Error Conditions dialog, where you can decide which errors to suppress at application time. Any errors that occur and are not suppressed will cause the application to fail. The Suppress Error Conditions dialog is shown in Figure 18-4.

In this dialog you check all possible error conditions to be suppressed. By doing this you ensure that the transform will be applied regardless of whether any of the possible error conditions actually exist.. The next dialog in this wizard is where you determine the name of the transform and where it is to be created. The Specify output file name dialog is shown in Figure 18-5.

As you can see in this figure the transform is named ISWI Artist.mst and it will be created in the same location where the two databases are located. (You could of course browse to another location.) The next dialog in the Transform Wizard is the Summary dialog, shown in Figure 18-6. Here you can review all the settings you have made and if necessary go back and change them.

Clicking on the Create button in this dialog creates the transform and presents the Completing the Transform Wizard dialog. This dialog is shown in Figure 18-7: it tells you that the transform was created successfully and provides you with a sample command line for applying this transform at run time.

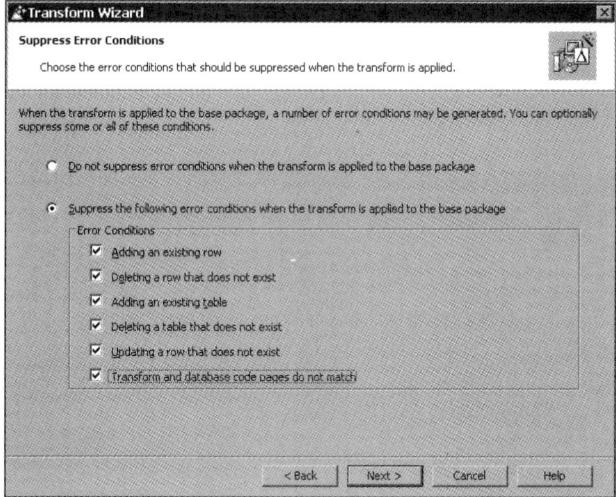

Figure 18-4: The Suppress Error Conditions dialog of the Transform Wizard (transform creation mode)

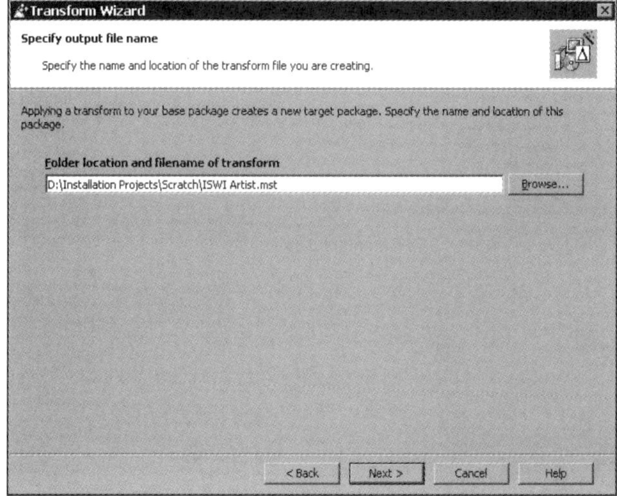

Figure 18-5: The Specify output file name dialog of the Transform Wizard (transform creation mode)

Now that the transform has been created, you can get rid of the original ISWI Artist.msi file and rename Schema.msi as ISWI Artist.msi. Now you also have to copy the source file tree to the location of the ISWI Artist.msi and ISWI Artist.mst files. You are now ready to install the ISWIArtist application using the essentially empty database and a transform.

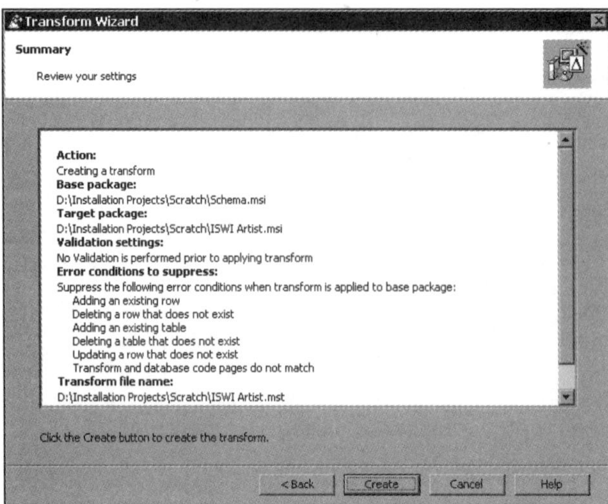

Figure 18-6: The Summary dialog of the Transform Wizard (transform creation mode)

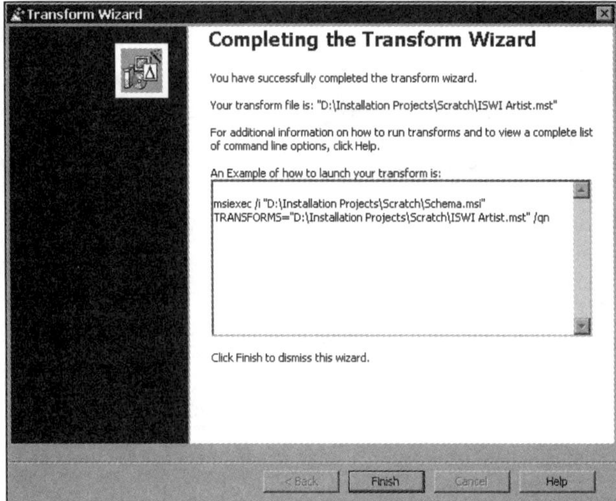

Figure 18-7: The Completing the Transform Wizard dialog of the Transform Wizard (transform creation mode)

Before you use the transform you have just created, you need to understand the business of applying transforms, both at run time and at design time.

Applying transforms at run time

To apply a transform at run time you need to run the installation from the command line or programmatically where the command line is passed to the CreateProcess Windows API. When using a transform at run time to modify an installation package, you need to be aware of the fact that this transform must always be available to perform maintenance operations on the original install.

Transforms have many run-time uses. Network administrators use transforms to modify the feature set of a product depending on the workgroup to which the product is assigned. In Chapter 19 you will see how the run-time application of transforms is used to permit multilingual installations. The key to applying transforms at run time is using the TRANSFORMS public property. This property takes a value that is a semicolon-delimited list of transforms that the Windows Installer is to apply to the base MSI package when the installation is run. Before you take a look at some of the various example command lines for applying transforms, you need to understand how transforms affect the resource resiliency and how setting system policy comes into play.

RESOURCE RESILIENCY AND SYSTEM POLICY

The main concern with transforms is that unless they are embedded in the MSI package they can be deleted or lost. Once this happens you can't perform any further operations on the installed product. This can have a negative impact on resource resiliency. Resource resiliency is one of the key features of the Windows Installer functionality. How the Windows Installer will handle deleted or lost transforms can be controlled by using either a specific public property or by setting a per-machine policy in the registry. The appropriate formatting of the command-line value for the TRANSFORMS property can also control the caching of transforms. Essentially what we are talking about here is generating one of the two types of secure transforms described in Table 18-3. A secure transform is just a transform that is cached on the target system in a location where the user does not have write privileges.

A secure transform only has meaning if the user installing the application that uses a transform does not have administrative privileges. If the user has administrative privileges the transform cannot be located in any place that cannot be written to by the user because an administrator has access to all locations on the machine.

To define a secure transform to the Windows Installer you can set the TRANSFORMSSECURE property to 1, you can set the TransformsSecure policy to 1, or you can use either the @ or | symbol in front of the name of the transform on the command line. This may look like redundant functionality, but in fact each of these methods of securing a transform has a different scope. If you set the TRANSFORMSSECURE property in the MSI database to have a value of 1, you have determined that regardless of the machine on which this package is installed the associated transforms will be secure. When you set the TransformsSecure system policy, you have limited the scope to the machine but it will apply to all packages using transforms installed on the machine. When you use the special symbols, you have limited the scope to just the current installation package on the current machine.

USING THE TRANSFORMSSECURE PROPERTY Authoring the TRANSFORMSSECURE property into the MSI database is the only sure method that a setup developer has of forcing all applied transforms to be secure transforms. When you use this property, the Windows Installer distinguishes between a Secure-At-Source and a Secure-Full-Path transform from the command line. If the transform list only includes the names of the transform files to be applied without any path qualification, the transforms are considered Secure-At-Source transforms. If the transform list includes the full path for each transform in the transform list, then the transforms are considered Secure-Full-Path transforms.

A property called TRANSFORMSATSOURCE was available with the version 1.0 of the Windows Installer. This property is no longer used and if version 1.1 of the Windows Installer comes across this property in any MSI database it will treat it just as it treats the TRANSFORMSSECURE property.

SETTING THE TRANSFORMSSECURE MACHINE POLICY Setup developers have no control over the machine policies to be set; this is the domain of the network administrator. The key where the machine policies are set is as follows:

```
HKLM\SOFTWARE\Policies\Microsoft\Windows\Installer
```

The value name created for this key is TransformsSecure and the value data given to it is 1. When this policy is set, the Windows Installer distinguishes between a Secure-At-Source and a Secure-Full-Path transform from the command line. If the transform list only includes the names of the transform files to be applied without any path qualification, the transforms are considered to be Secure-At-Source transforms. If the transform list includes the full path for each transform in the transform list, then the transforms are considered to be Secure-Full-Path transforms.

A per-user system policy called TranformsAtSource was available with version 1.0 of the Windows Installer. This system policy is no longer used and, if version 1.1 of the Windows Installer comes across this policy, it will treat it as if the TransformsSecure per-machine system policy had been set.

CACHING AND SEARCHING FOR TRANSFORMS When you install an application using Secure-At-Source transforms or unsecured transforms, these transforms are cached on the system (see Table 18-3). If these transforms become unavailable, the Windows Installer will try to restore them as it would an unavailable MSI package. This search pattern is prescribed by the SourceList entries in the registry for each product.

When you install an application using Secure-Full-Path transforms, these transforms are also cached on the system as described in Table 18-3. If these transforms become unavailable, they can only be restored using the location specified by the full path associated with them. The Windows Installer in this instance will not search as it would if an MSI package needed to be restored.

EXAMPLE COMMAND LINES

You are not allowed to mix types of transforms at the command line except to identify embedded transforms along with any other type. For example, if you have Secure-At-Source transforms, you cannot include any Secured-Full-Path or Unsecured transforms in the transforms list. You could include any embedded transforms that needed to be applied. Table 18-4 shows a number of example transform lists that are valid values for the TRANSFORMS property.

TABLE 18-4 VALID TRANSFORM LISTS

Transform List	Description
@transform1.mst;transform2.mst	Secure-At-Source transforms. Setting TRANS FORMSSECURE or the TransformsSecure system policy would be redundant and have no effect.
|transform1.mst;transform2.mst	Secure-Full-Path transforms. Setting TRANS FORMSSECURE or the TransformsSecure system policy would be redundant and have no effect.
@transform1.mst;:transform2.mst	transform1.mst is a Secure-At-Source transform and transform2.mst is an embedded transform. Setting TRANSFORMSSECURE or the Transforms Secure system policy would be redundant and have no effect, because transform1.mst has already been identified as a secure transform and transform2.mst's being embedded is not cached on the system.

Continued

TABLE 18-4 VALID TRANSFORM LISTS *(Continued)*

Transform List	Description
\\server\share1\transform1.mst; \\server\share2\transform2.mst	Unsecured transforms if the TransformsSecure system policy and the TRANSFORMSSECURE property are not set. If either of these is set both of the transforms are Secure-Full-Path transforms.
transform1.mst;transforms2.mst; :transform3.mst	Unsecured transforms if the TransformsSecure property and the TransformsSecure system policy are not set. If either of these is set these transforms are Secured-At-Source transforms. In all cases transform3.mst is an embedded transform.

The help that comes with the Windows Installer SDK provides many more examples of valid command lines.

You can now run the ISWI Artist.msi installation package using the following command line:

```
msiexec /i <path to ISWI Artist.msi> TRANSFORMS="ISWI Artist.mst"
```

When you run this command line, you get the normal installation user interface and the application installs just as it did earlier in the book. The only difference is that the transform is cached in the %Windows%\Installer\{*ProductCode*} folder. When you uninstall the application, you will still see the transform cached on the machine until you reboot the system. After the reboot the transform will have been removed. If you change this command line as follows, you will see that the transform is cached in a different location.

```
msiexec /i <path to ISWI Artist.msi> TRANSFORMS="@ISWI Artist.mst"
```

Now the transform is cached in the %Windows%\Installer\{*ProductCode*}\SecureTransforms folder. You can experiment with the different command lines if you want to see what happens in other situations.

Applying a transform at design time using ISWI

Now let's look at the design-time use of transforms. Essentially, the design-time purpose of transforms is to efficiently propagate the differences between two databases to a third database. Being able to do this automatically is much more efficient than having to author the changes into the third database using ISWI or Orca.

Now let's go through the ISWI Transform Wizard using the Apply a Transform option from the Welcome dialog shown in Figure 18-1. The Apply Transform operation of this wizard is a wrapper around the MsiDatabaseApplyTrnasform Windows Installer API. When you select this option and click the Next button, you get the dialog shown in Figure 18-8.

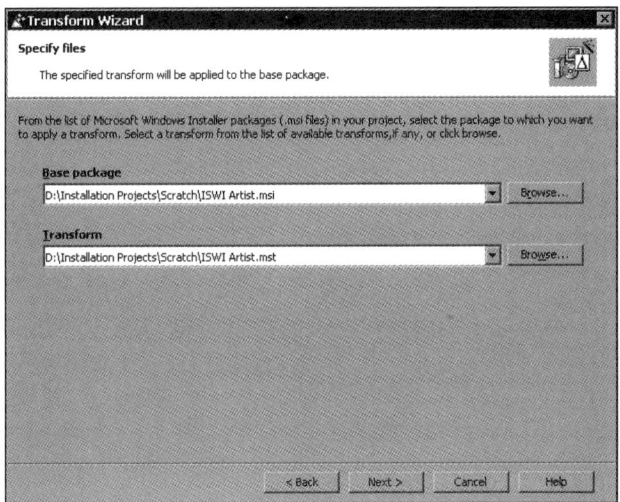

Figure 18-8: The Specify Files dialog of the Transform Wizard (apply transform mode)

In this dialog you are asked to select the MSI database to which the transform is going to be applied, and to select the transform to apply. Once you have browsed to these two files you proceed to the next dialog, shown in Figure 18-9.

This dialog looks exactly like the dialog shown in Figure 18-4, which appears when you are creating a transform. This dialog appears again when you are applying a transform in order to give you the opportunity to override the error-suppression flags you added to the Summary Information Stream of the transform. For the purpose of this example you should keep the same settings, which suppress all error conditions that might occur when you apply the transform. After making sure that you have selected to suppress all error conditions, move onto the next dialog in the wizard. This dialog is the Specify output file name dialog and it is shown in Figure 18-10.

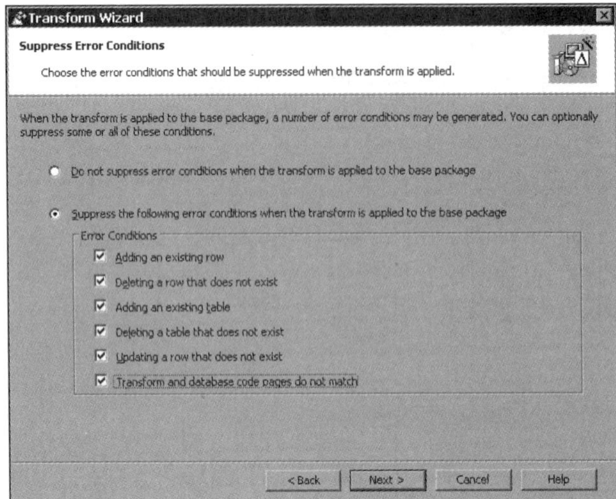

Figure 18-9: The Suppress Error Conditions Dialog of the Transform Wizard (apply transform mode)

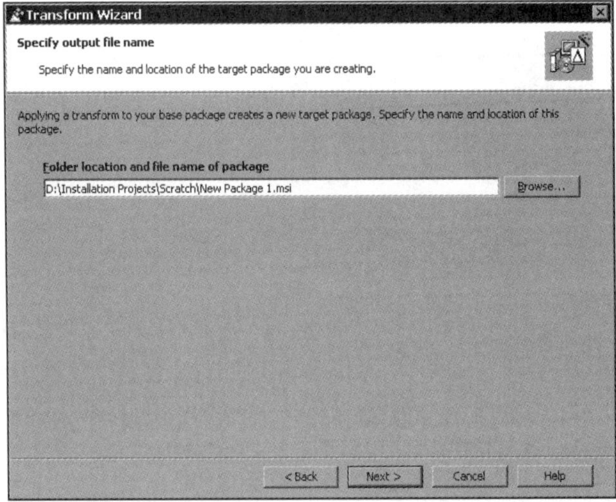

Figure 18-10: The Specify output file name dialog of the Transform Wizard (apply transform mode)

In this dialog you specify the name of the resulting MSI file that will be created when the transform is applied. In this case you can just leave the default name for now. You can rename it after we finish with the wizard. The next dialog in the wizard is the Summary dialog where you can review all the selections you have made in the various wizard dialogs. This dialog is shown in Figure 18-11. When you click the

Apply button, the transform is applied and you see the final dialog, that tells you that the application of the transform was successful, and also shows you the name and location of the MSI file that was created.

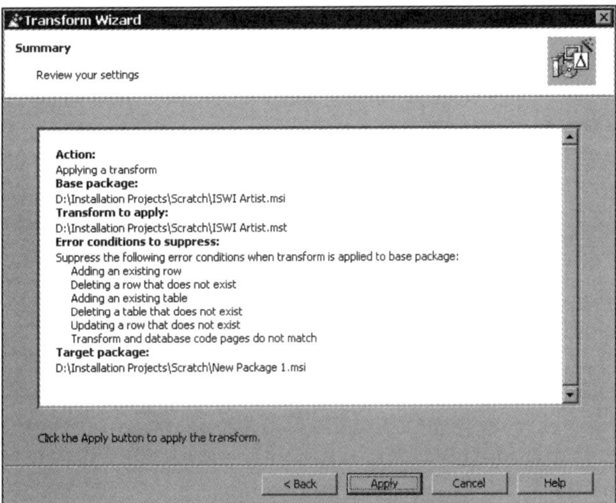

Figure 18-11: The Completing the Transform Wizard dialog of the Transform Wizard (apply transform mode)

Before you test this new MSI package you need to rename it as ISWI Artist.msi. You need to do this because every product identified by a specific ProductCode property value must have the same package name. You can give the same package name to different products, but if you change the package name used to install a product you need to change the ProductCode. Once you have changed the name, double-click this file and make sure that it runs correctly. If ISWI Artist was already on the system the install will launch into the maintenance mode and you can uninstall it.

Now that we have covered the basics of transforms we should look at a few special issues.

Using a Transform to Add Resources

As you have seen you can only use transforms to modify the MSI database. You cannot modify the Summary Information Stream or the files that comprise the application. When you are adding new files to an installation, you'll normally want to associate these new files with components and features. The transform should add one or more new components to the installation database to contain the additional files. The transform should not add resources to a component that already exists in the installation.

The transform should also add one or more new features to the installation database to contain the new components. These new features should not be the parents of any existing features, but new parent and child features may be introduced together. New features should be given names that are unique across all other transforms for this product. No two transforms should ever add a feature to this product that has the same name listed in the Feature column of the Feature table and contains different components or resources.

Viewing the Contents of a Transform

You cannot look at a transform with Orca or any tool like it. One of the ways you can look at the contents of a transform is like what you did in the above exercise: you can merge it with a blank MSI database such as Schema.msi and then open up the database with Orca. Using Orca, you can then export all the tables and import those with data in them into an Excel spreadsheet. This approach, however, is fairly cumbersome and lacks a certain amount of elegance.

The more elegant solution to viewing the contents of a transform is to use the _TransformView table. This is a read-only temporary table specifically created to enable you to view the contents of a transform. Using this table, however, requires you to do some programming. In this chapter we will only look at the steps you would need to take if you were going to create a utility to view a transform using this special table.

To invoke this table you need to use the MsiDatabaseApplyTransform API and the MSITRANSFORM_ERROR_VIEWTRANSFORM error condition bit flag. Using this flag stops the transform from being applied to the database and dumps the contents of the transform into the _TransformView table. The first thing to do is to take a look at the attributes of this database table. Table 18-5 describes each column in the _TransformView table.

TABLE 18-5 THE ATTRIBUTES OF THE _TRANSFORMVIEW TABLE

Column	Data Type	Key	Description
Table	Identifier	Y	Contains the name of an altered table in the database.
Column	Text	Y	The name of the altered column, if a row has been modified. If the table was added or deleted, then the keyword CREATE or DROP is entered in this column. If a row has been added or deleted from the table, the keyword INSERT or DELETE is entered in this column.

Column	Data Type	Key	Description
Row	Text	Y	Contains a tab-delimited list of the values of the columns that comprise the primary key for the table. If one of these columns is null, a single space is entered. If the table is being added or removed, this column is null.
Data	Text		Holds the data in the field, which can be a string, integer, or a binary stream. If the data is a binary stream, this column holds the column definition. If the table is being added or removed, this column holds the column definition. A column definition string consists of a single letter that defines the data type followed by a number that defines the width of the column. If the letter is uppercase, then the column can be null.
Current	Text		If the reference database has a value that is going to be modified, this column holds the current value of the column data. Otherwise it holds a column number.

Once you populate this table with the contents of a transform, you can look at the table to get the details. Since this table is not persisted when the database is closed you cannot open it up and look at it using Orca after the transform has been applied. What you need to do is access the rows in this table using SQL queries and save the information to a text file or display it in a window of the utility you created to perform this operation.

Chapter 11 covers the syntax of the SQL used in Windows Installer.

A VBScript file that uses the _TransformView table to view the contents of a transform comes with the Windows Installer SDK. The name of this script file is WiLstXfm.vbs and you can run it using the console executable of the Windows Scripting Host. If you want to view the transform you created for the ISWI Artist application and capture it to a text file, run the following command line:

```
cscript wilstxfm.vbs "ISWI Artist.msi" "ISWI Artist.mst" >
                                                    Transform.txt
```

This will give a very large text file that is somewhat cryptic so it is not necessarily very valuable.

Editing a Transform

There will be times when you will want to be able to edit the contents of a transform. The problem with trying to edit a transform is that there are no Windows Installer APIs that enable you to directly access the structure of a transform file. To edit a transform you need to apply it to a database, edit the database, and then recreate the transform. You can do this programmatically or use ISWI. The ideal situation would be to create a utility to perform this operation and read the required changes from an initialization file. Table 18-6 describes the process of editing a transform both programmatically and using ISWI.

TABLE 18-6 PROCESS STEPS FOR EDITING A TRANSFORM

Step	Programmatic Approach	ISWI Approach
1	Make a temporary copy of the reference database. The name of this temporary copy does not matter.	Make a temporary copy of the reference database. The name of this temporary copy does not matter.
2	Using the MsiOpenDatabase API, open the temporary copy of the database using the MSIDBOPEN_TRANSACT persist mode.	Using the Transform Wizard, apply the transform to be edited to the temporary copy of the reference database.

Step	Programmatic Approach	ISWI Approach
3	Apply the transform to be edited to the temporary copy of the database using the MsiDatabaseApply Transform API.	Open this MSI database using Orca and make the changes in the tables that are affected. You could also use this database to create an ISWI project and make the changes in the IDE. However, to rebuild the database you would have to make sure all the source files for the application were available so that you could make the build without creating any build errors.
4	Edit the database by applying the transform to the temporary copy of the reference database. This entails creating and executing a view and then fetching and modifying a record. When you have done this, commit the database using the MsiDatabase Commit API. (Chapter 11 provides more detail on this type of operation.)	Using the Transform Wizard, create a new transform between the modified temporary database and the original reference database.
5	Open the reference database in read-only mode.	Replace the original transform with the new transform just created.
6	Generate a new transform as the difference between the reference database and the modified temporary database. This will require the use of the MsiDatabase GenerateTransform and MsiCreateTransform SummaryInfo APIs.	
7	Close the two open databases and replace the original transform with the new transform.	

Creating a command-line utility to automatically edit a transform is a good exercise that gives you experience with the Windows Installer database functions. Of course you could use the InstallShield Tuner product and save yourself a lot of effort.

Embedding a Transform in an MSI Package

You learned from the discussion on the types of transforms that a transform can be embedded in the MSI package. Version 1.5 of ISWI does not provide any post processing that enables you to embed a transform in an MSI package. To do this you have to work with the _Storages table. When you embed a transform in an MSI package, you create a sub-storage that will hold the stream containing the transform.

Since the _Storages table is the mechanism that the Windows Installer uses to create a sub-storage in an MSI package, you should take a look at this table. Table 18-7 describes the attributes that comprise this table.

Table 18-7 ATTRIBUTES OF THE _STORAGES TABLE

Column	Data Type	Key	Description
Name	Text	Y	A unique identifier that is the name to be used as the name of the sub-storage in MSI database. The length of this identifier cannot exceed 31 characters.
Data	Binary		Comprises the file to be streamed into the MSI database.

You work with this table as you would work with any of the tables in the database. You need to create and execute a view to this table, fetch a record, and then set the values in this record using the MsiRecordSetString and MsiRecordSetStream APIs. After you have done this you need to use the MsiViewModify API to insert the record into the _Storages table. When you call the MsiDatabaseCommit API, the Windows Installer will use the information in this table to actually create the substorage in the database. The _Storages table is only a temporary table and is not persisted with the database.

Windows Installer SDK comes with a VBScript file that provides command-line functionality for creating sub-storages in an MSI database. The name of this script file is WiSubStg.vbs and you can use it on the command line as long as the Windows Scripting Host is installed. The command line you would use to embed the ISWI Artist.mst transform into the ISWI Artist.msi MSI database is as follows:

```
cscript wisubstg.vbs "ISWI Artist.msi" "ISWI Artist.mst"
```

This will create a sub-storage in the ISWI Artist.msi database. The name of this sub-storage will be ISWI Artist.mst. After you have embedded the transform in the MSI package, you can run the installation using the following command line:

```
msiexec /i <path to the ISWI Artist.msi file>
                                    TRANSFORMS=":ISWI Artist.mst"
```

The source code for the WiSubStg.vbs file is the place to go to find out more about how to remove sub-storages from an MSI database or how to get a list of the sub-storages that might be in a database.

Summary

In this chapter you learned how to use transforms both at design time and at run time. We discussed the various types of transforms and how they are cached on the system at run time. This caching is necessary in order for the Windows Installer to be able to support maintenance operations on an installed product. Transforms are cached in different locations depending on whether they are secured or unsecured. Embedded transforms are not cached since they remain with the MSI database when it is cached on the system.

You learned how to add resources to an MSI package using a transform. Since transforms only make modifications to a database you cannot use them to directly change the files in an installation or to change the Summary Information Stream in the MSI package. You learned what steps to take to edit a transform, which essentially requires that the transform be applied to the reference database, the changes made to this database, and the transform recreated. You also looked at some of the VBScript files that come with the Windows Installer SDK and saw how you could use them to view the contents of a transform or to embed a transform in an MSI package.

Part V

Solving Real-World Problems

Chapter 19

Localizing an Installation

IN THIS CHAPTER

- The issues related to localizing an installation
- The support provided by Windows 2000 for running localized applications
- Common installation scenarios that come up during localized installation
- How a Windows Installer database gets localized
- The features in ISWI that enable you to create localized installations
- How to use the ISWI features to create various localized installations
- How to add a new language to ISWI

THE PC HAS BECOME the standard global computing and communications tool and this globalization has created the need to distribute products around the world. It is incumbent on us to provide our customers with product installations in many different languages. Creating numerous international editions of a product has therefore become a major effort that entails creating and managing localized versions of products and their installations.

Using the features of InstallShield for Windows Installer you can take a big step toward managing all the aspects of distributing software internationally. In this chapter we'll look at a number of issues related to localizing Windows Installer packages.

The Issues of Globalization and Localization

The globalization and localization of an installation is not really much different than the globalization and localization of an application. *Globalization* refers to the process by which software is made locale-independent; *localization* refers to the practice of modifying software so that it displays its user interface in the language of the user. When it comes to the globalization activity in the creation of an installation package, all you are doing is creating a database with a neutral code page. A *code page–neutral installation database* is one that only contains characters that can be handled by any code page. Once you have this type of installation database you can localize it by first setting the code page of the database and then adding the appropriate localized strings to the various fields in the affected database tables.

Once you have the neutral code page installation database you need to be able to localize it according to the needs of the end user. Doing this at run time is the subject of this chapter. However, before we can get to the point of running an installation in the language of the end user you need to take a quick look at the issues involved in creating an installation for a particular locale. A *locale* is a set of user preferences that relate to language, cultural conventions, and environment. These user preferences are represented as a list of values used to identify such things as input language, keyboard layout, sorting order, and the formats to be used for numbers, dates, currencies, and time.

If you're creating a localized installation, translating all the displayable strings is the task that will undoubtedly take the most time and effort. Creating the appropriate bitmaps and icons to be displayed on the dialogs making up the installation user interface will also take a lot of time. The creation of the correct graphics can often be overlooked, resulting in the display of graphics that have either no meaning to the end user or might even be considered by the end user to be offensive.

Generally English strings to be translated are totally developed and then sent to a translation firm where they are translated into the various languages required by the installation. It's important to provide the translator with the context in which the English string is being used. This is because an English string can be translated in different ways depending on the context in which it is being used.

Something else you should keep track of is the length of the translated string relative to the length of the English string. Sometimes the translated string will not fit into the same space as the English string. This will cause the resizing of text and button controls and could even affect the size of the dialog box itself. Since all dialogs in a wizard sequence should be of the same size, this is an important consideration.

Windows 2000 Language Support

Windows 2000 has the best international language support of any Windows operating system that has been released so far, largely because all international versions of Windows 2000 use the same set of binary files. Because of this it is now possible to develop multilingual installations on the same machine without having to switch between various localized versions of the operating system. Of course you should still test your installations on the various localized version of the OS before releasing the product.

Windows 2000 is available in either localized versions or in a multilingual version. There are 24 localized versions of Windows 2000. These localized versions are English, German, Japanese, Traditional Chinese, Simplified Chinese, Korean, Arabic, Hebrew, Spanish, French, Italian, Swedish, Dutch, Brazilian, Norwegian, Danish, Finnish, Czech, Polish, Hungarian, Russian, Portuguese, Greek, and Turkish. Each of these localized versions has the same ability to handle input, processing, and display of text in any of the languages supported in Windows 2000. For example, with the proper selection of a user locale, input locale, and system locale a user could create and display a Japanese document on an English version of the operating system.

There are differences among the localized versions of Windows 2000 when it comes to some language-specific items. The following is a list of cases in which a particular language version of Windows 2000 would provide additional functionality over another.

- Greater migration and upgrade support for the language of the OS
- More extensive compatibility for applications written in the language of the OS
- More language-specific fonts available for the specific language of the OS
- Greater selection of Input Method Editors available for the specific language of the OS
- Special tools available for the specific language of the OS
- More local drivers are available for such peripherals as modems and printers
- Legacy support for DOS and earlier BIOS versions
- The user interface is localized in the language of the OS
- All documents – such as readme files, release notes, and help – are in the localized language of the OS

The multi-language version of Windows 2000 essentially wraps all the localized versions into one version. This product enables the switching of the user interface between the various supported languages. On the same machine one user could run the user interface in Japanese and another user could run the user interface in German. Not only as menus and dialogs would be shown in the selected language but the help files, readme files, and so forth would also be in the selected language. The main benefit to corporations purchasing this version of Windows 2000 is a reduction in the total cost of ownership because they don't have to support separate language versions of the OS in a multilingual environment.

There is very little difference between the Multi-Language version of Windows 2000 set to a particular user interface language and the localized version of Windows 2000 in that same language. The main difference is that for the Multi-Language version of Windows 2000 the install language is English. Also not localized with this version of Windows 2000 are all 16-bit code, bitmaps, registry keys, registry values, folder and file names, and .inf files.

For those who want to delve into the international aspects of Windows 2000 in more depth the following Web site is a good place to start: `http://www.microsoft.com/globaldev/`. This Web site is a repository of information about developing applications that take advantage of the new multilingual features of Windows 2000.

Language-Specific Installation Scenarios

Along with the new international capabilities offered by Windows 2000 comes a more complex set of installation options. It is now possible to enable the user to choose the language of the installation and in so doing select the language version of the product to be installed. No longer do you have to check the language version of the operating system and make that the default language for both the installation and the product.

We can group the various language installation scenarios into one of three categories. The first category is the simplest: the product is language-specific and the language of the installation is the same as the language of the product. In the second category there are a number of different language versions of the product on the distribution media and the user can choose the language in which to run the installation. The choice of installation language determines the language version of the product that is installed. Finally, in the third category there is one application that ships with multiple language resources. In this scenario the end user chooses which language to use for the installation as well as the language resources to be installed. The following sections address these categories in more detail. Then, after a discussion of how a Windows Installer database is localized, we'll look at three example installations that demonstrate each of these three categories.

Installing a single-language product

This is the simplest scenario, wherein the product is defined to be of one language only. Typically you would set the language of the installation to be the same as the language of the product. With this type of setup the end user does not choose the language of the product or the language to be used during the installation. However, it is possible to offer the user a selection of languages in which to run the installation. This can be valuable in a multilingual environment where the person doing the installation is not the person who will be using the application. With Windows 2000 this becomes totally feasible, but with the Windows Installer there is a small problem related to the proper registration of the product language. We discuss this particular problem at the end of this chapter.

Installing a product whose language is set during installation

In this scenario the end user is offered a list of languages in which to run the installation and the selection that is made also determines the language version of the product being installed. Implementing a scenario like this requires that an installation package be constructed of components that support all the languages to be offered during the installation. These components are then conditioned on the ProductLanguage property and only those components that support the selected language are installed. Alternatively, the user may be given a selection of languages in which to run the installation, while the components are still conditioned on the language of the operating system. You could develop other variations, but they would all be very similar to these.

Installing a product whose language is set when the product is run

It is possible to create a multi-language application wherein the user can change the language of the user interface. Applications such as these are normally created using satellite resource DLLs. In this method, each supported language has its resources in a separate DLL, which means that there is a separate component for each of these DLLs. Each DLL uses the same resource identifiers, but also contains strings and other language- or locale-dependent resources in the appropriate language. Each DLL is named according to the language of its resource.

When generating the installation package for this type of application, you need to focus on the structure of the feature tree because you need to enable the end user to select the languages to be supported by the application. As in the previous two scenarios, you can also provide a selection of languages in which the end user can run the installation.

The Localization of a Windows Installer Database

Before we get into a discussion of how to use ISWI to create a localized install, we should discuss the inner workings of the Windows Installer and how it handles language issues. In this discussion you will learn about the MSI database, the Summary Information Stream, and multi-language merge modules. These three subjects are covered in the following three subsections.

Basics of Windows 2000 national language support

In this section we'll take a brief look at what national language support is and a few definitions that relate to creating installations in different languages. National language support is a broad subject so we will only scratch the surface here.

National language support provides an API set that enables you to set the user locale, user language identification, and retrieve strings formatted correctly for a specific language and location. It also includes support for keyboard layouts and language-specific fonts.

Languages are installed on Windows 2000 in the form of language groups. For any particular language group the system locale determines which code pages are used on the system by default. The user locale determines which settings are used for formatting dates, times, currency, and numbers by default for each user. It also determines the sort order for text. When it comes to creating localized installations, you do not need to know any more about the intricacies of national language support.

For a complete discussion of national language support in Windows 2000 a good source is the MSDN Library.

Now let's take a closer look at what these particular terms mean. To do this, look at the Regional Options applet accessed from the Control Panel. This dialog is shown in Figure 19-1.

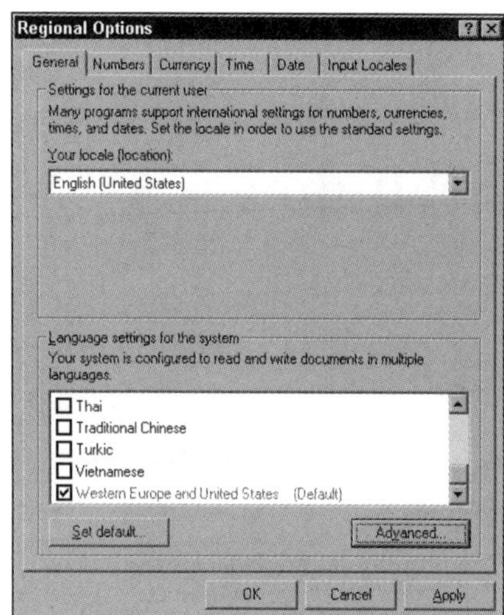

Figure 19-1: The Regional Settings dialog from the Windows 2000 Control Panel

LANGUAGE GROUP

When you install a language group, you are controlling which system locale and user locale can be selected. When you're installing the English version of Windows 2000, the Western Europe and United States language group is installed by default. This particular language group cannot be uninstalled. In Figure 19-1 you can see that a number of other languages can be installed. If you decided to check the Japanese language group in the Regional Settings dialog and then click the Apply button, you would be asked for the CD-ROM from which the original installation of Windows 2000 was performed so that this additional language group could be installed.

When an additional language group is installed, Windows 2000 copies the necessary keyboard files, Input Method Editors (IMEs), TrueType Font files, bitmap font files, and national language support files (.nls). This operation also adds registry entries for font linking and installs scripting engines for complex script languages such as Arabic and Hebrew. The fact that a language group has been copied to the system does not mean that this new language group has been activated. Any number and combination of language groups can be installed on any Windows 2000 version.

There are 16 language groups in addition to the Western Europe and United States language group. These language groups are Arabic, Armenian, Baltic, Central Europe, Cyrillic, Georgian, Greek, Hebrew, Indic, Japanese, Korean, Simplified Chinese, Thai, Traditional Chinese, Turkish, and Vietnamese. When any of these language groups is copied to the system, Windows 2000 will require that the system be rebooted.

SYSTEM LOCALE

The system locale determines which code page is used on the system by default. The system locale setting only affects those applications that are not fully Unicode-compliant. When you set the system locale to a certain language, Windows 2000 is instructed to emulate a non-Unicode-based operating system that is localized to the language you have selected. This does not mean that the dialogs and menus of the operating system are changed to the selected language. Setting the system locale only affects the dialogs and menus of the applications of the system that are not fully Unicode-compliant.

For example, once you have installed the Japanese language group and want the code page for this language to become the default UI code page, click the Set default... button in the Regional Options dialog and you will get the Select system locale dialog shown in Figure 19-2.

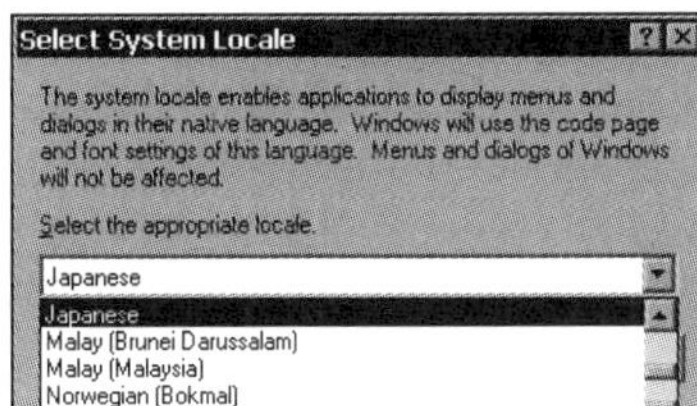

Figure 19-2: The Windows 2000 Select system locale dialog

In this dialog you select Japanese from the combo box and click the OK button. Back in the Regional Options dialog, click the Apply button and you are offered the choice of recopying the language group from the original CD-ROM or using the files you have already copied. Click the Yes button in this message box to use the files you have already copied; you are immediately notified that the system needs to restart for the new settings to take effect. After the restart you'll notice that Japanese is now shown as the default in the Regional Options dialog, shown in Figure 19-3.

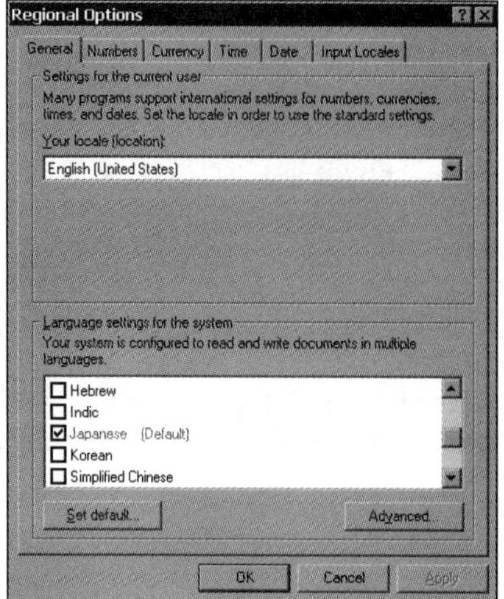

Figure 19-3: The Regional Options dialog with Japanese as the default language

The Japanese code page is now the default UI code page in the MSI documentation. Note that Japanese cannot now be deselected; if you scroll down to the Western Europe and United States language group you'll see that it is still checked that you cannot deselect this language group either, even though it is no longer shown as the default. If you want to deselect Japanese, you would first have to change the default back to the Western Europe and United States language group and then uncheck the Japanese language group. Then clicking on the Apply button would remove this language group from the system.

USER LOCALE

The user locale determines the default sort order and the default settings for formatting dates, times, currency, and numbers. The user locale is set by using the Your locale (location): combo box at the top of the Regional Settings dialog. The user locale is not considered a language setting. It just handles formatting issues for displayable text. Even though Japanese is currently selected as the default language you can still continue to use the formatting criteria for United States English. When you apply a particular user locale, you don't need to restart your computer.

CODE PAGE

A code page defines a collection of characters, numbers, punctuation, symbols, and special characters for a particular language. Each character in a code page is assigned a numeric value called a *code point*. Computer hardware, software, and operating systems exchange information for a particular language or group of languages using these code points.

For historical reasons the Windows code page currently in effect is referred to as the ANSI code page. The original Windows ANSI code page was developed for use with Windows 3.1 and was targeted for use in the United States and Western Europe. This code page was called code page 1252, Latin 1, or Windows ANSI. The explosion of computer usage around the globe necessitated the creation of many new single-byte and double-byte code pages. All of these code pages are still referred to as the ANSI code page.

Localizing a Windows Installer package

Now that you understand a little about how Windows 2000 handles the complex issues of language support, take a close look at what you need to do to localize an MSI package to a particular language. You need to examine three areas in particular: the database, the Summary Information Stream, and the handling of multiple language merge modules. Each is the subject of one of the following three subsections. Before you go on, however, look at how strings are stored in the MSI package. This discussion applies to both the MSI database and merge modules, but it does not apply to the Summary Information Stream.

THE STRING POOL

In order to minimize the size of the database all strings are stored in a single array, called the *string pool*. In other words, all strings are actually in the database only once even if they are used in more than one location in the database. Each table that uses a string has only an index into the string array; it does not actually contain the string itself. Case-sensitive string comparisons are accomplished very quickly since all they require is the comparison of the indices of two strings. Fast string comparisons are required, for one example, during database queries. When you open an MSI database using Orca and see a string in a particular column, what you are seeing is the string being indexed by that column. The string is not actually stored in the column.

The string pool actually consists of two sets of data stored in a stream called _StringPool. One set of data consists of an array of refcounts, attributes, and string lengths. Attributes deal mainly with the type of string – whether it is a double-byte character set string (DBCS), the display style, or other. The other set of data contains the strings that are all concatenated together without the NULL terminator. The code page of the database is stored in the header of the _StringPool stream.

It is important to validate the string pool when creating a localized installation database because it is possible to have a corrupt string pool. The only means of validating the string pool is to use the MSIINFO.EXE tool in the Windows Installer SDK. String pool verification consists of two main checks: a check for unsupported extended characters and a string reference count verification.

The check for unsupported extended characters can happen in one of two ways depending on whether the database has a neutral code page or not. For packages with a neutral code page a check is made to see if any characters are extended character. If such a string is found, it is flagged and a message is displayed saying that the code page of the database is invalid because these characters require a specific code page to be rendered consistently on all systems.

If the database has a code page, each string is scanned for an invalid extended character. This check requires that the code page of the database be installed on the system. If there is a code page problem, a message is displayed saying that the code page of the database is invalid because these characters require a specific code page to be rendered consistently on all systems. You can fix the problem by using the pseudo _ForceCodepage table to force the code page of the database to the appropriate value. The next section describes the use of this pseudo table.

To verify the reference counts of all strings, every table is scanned for string values, a count of each distinct string is kept, and the result is compared to the stored reference count in the database string pool. If there is a string reference count problem, the database is considered to be corrupt. You can fix this problem by exporting each table of the database using the MsiDatabaseExport API. This function creates a text archive file for each table exported. These text archive files are then used to create a new database using the MsiDatabaseImport API. The new database will have the same content as the old database, but the string reference counts will be correct. Adding data to or deleting data from a database with a corrupt string pool can increase corruption of the database and loss of data.

LOCALIZING THE MSI DATABASE

When you want to localize an MSI database, you need to concern yourself with not only the localized strings that make up the authored installation user interface and those that are added to the system during installation, but also with the code page of the database, the ProductLanguage, ProductCode, and PackageCode properties, and the localization of the Error and ActionText tables. First we need to discuss how to set the code page of an MSI database.

THE DATABASE CODE PAGE Before we get into a deeper discussion of setting the code page for an MSI database we need to discuss the concept of a code page neutral database. A code page neutral database contains only those characters that can be translated using any code page. This means that all characters must be contained in the ASCII character set. This is because all code pages share this character set, which is the lowest 128 characters (0x00 to 0x7F). The code-page entry in the string pool header for a code page neutral database is 0.

You define the code page of an MSI database by importing a text archive file for a pseudo table with the name of _ForceCodePage. The first two lines in the file are to be blank; on the third line there is to be a numeric code page number followed by a tab delimiter and the string _ForceCodePage. You can import this text archive file using the MSIDB.EXE utility found with the Windows Installer SDK on the CD-ROM at the back of the book, or you can add it programmatically with the MsiDatabaseImport database function or the Import method of the Database object available as part of the Windows Installer automation interface. Once you have set the code page of an MSI database you need to stamp all further text archive table imports with the same code page; otherwise the import action will fail.

You can also set the code page of a neutral database by importing a text archive file that includes non-ASCII characters. A text archive file that contains non-ASCII characters is stamped with the appropriate code page. When you import this file with the MsiDatabaseImport API function, the code page of the database is set to the code-page stamp of the text archive file. After this, only text archive files that are code page neutral or have the code page of the original text archive file can be imported. All other text archive files will cause failure of the import action.

All strings are stored in an MSI database as ANSI strings regardless of the operating system on which the database was built. This is because an MSI package must run on Windows 9x just as easily as it runs on Windows NT/2000. The main thing to remember about the code page for an MSI database is that its primary function is to correctly translate the strings being added to the database and the strings being extracted from the database for use during an installation. Except in one minor way, which we discuss in the next section, the database code page does not have any function in the actual display of the strings when the installation is run.

On Windows 9*x* the strings in the database are displayed at run time based on the active code page as defined by the system locale. If the system locale code page does not support some of the characters authored into the database, these characters will not appear correctly during the installation. On Windows NT/2000 the strings in the database are translated from ANSI to Unicode and are thus displayed properly. The only requirement is for the database code page to be on the system so that the translation can occur. ANSI strings are translated to Unicode by the MultiByteToWideChar Windows API with the database code page being used as input to this function.

ADDING LOCALIZED STRINGS TO THE DATABASE In the last section we touched on the issue of adding localized strings to the database by importing text archive files. You add localized strings to an MSI database in two ways: by importing text archive files or by programmatically adding strings using the Windows Installer API. Since we have already covered the importing of localized text archive files in the last section, in this section we'll look at the programmatic approach.

When you add localized strings to a database, there are four things that you have to be concerned about: the operating system of the authoring environment, the code page of the database, the system locale code page, and the code page required to support the characters in the strings being added to the database. Programmatically modifying a database means that you are going to open the database, create a view, modify all records that contain localizable strings using the MsiRecordSetString API, and then commit the changes to the database.

When you author a database on a Windows 95/98 system, the code page of the database must match the current code page of the system. The strings being passed to the database then require the code page of the database for proper display. The code page of the database can be neutral (0) and in this case you would only be able to pass strings that use the original ASCII characters – that is, there could be no extended characters.

The situation changes when you author a localized database on a Windows NT/2000 system. On these operating systems the only requirement is that the code page of the database be on the system when the strings are being passed to the database. The code page of the database does not have to be the code page currently in effect on the build system. You start the process of localizing a Windows Installer database by setting the code page of the database before you add any strings. You do this by importing the _ForceCodePage pseudo table. The next step is to convert the ANSI strings from your authoring environment to Unicode using the MultiByteToWideChar API function with the database code page as input. Then use the resulting string as input to the Unicode version of the MsiRecordSetString function. When the database is committed, the Unicode string passed to it is translated back to ANSI using the code page of the database. This process results in a properly localized database.

However, if you pass an ANSI to the ANSI version of the MsiRecordSetString API function, Windows NT or Windows 2000 converts this ANSI string to Unicode using the current code page of the system. When the database is committed, the Unicode string is then converted back to ANSI using the code page of the database. If the current system code page is different from the code page of the database, this could result in corruption of the strings in the database. Also, in the event that you change the code page of the database when it already contains non-ASCII characters, the non-ASCII strings will be translated to the new code page. This will also corrupt the database if the existing strings have characters not supported by the new database code page.

Finally, consider the display of text in controls that populate a dialog box. Essentially it is important that the DefaultUIFont property be set to one of the predefined styles listed in the TextStyle table. If this property is not set, the Windows Installer will use the system font and if the code page of the database is different from the system locale code page it is possible that the Windows Installer will incorrectly display text strings in the User Interface Wizard of the installation. Also, there is an attribute you can set for the Text, ListBox, and ComboBox controls that enables you to specify whether the database code page or the system locale code page is to be used to create the fonts shown in these controls. The name of this attribute is UsersLanguage. When this bit flag is set, the system locale code page is used; when it isn't, the database code page is used. If you have a database that is not code page neutral, you will want to use the code page of the database to display strings. If your database is code page neutral, then you can set the bit flag so that the code page of the system locale is used to display the strings.

LOCALIZING THE ACTIONTEXT AND ERROR TABLES The ActionText and Error tables provide an important part of the text displayed in the installation user interface. The ActionText table contains localizable text that is displayed in a progress dialog box describing the action currently being executed. The text in this table is also written to a log file when logging is enabled. The format of this table is shown in Table 19-1.

TABLE 19-1 THE FORMAT OF THE ACTIONTEXT TABLE

Column	Data Type	Key	Description
Action	Identifier	Y	Contains the name of the action with which the action text is associated. This is the primary key for this table.
Description	Text		Contains the localized text that will be displayed when this action is being executed.
Template	Template		Contains the localized template string that displays the action data associated with the action listed in the first column.

The Error table is used by the Windows Installer to look up error message-formatting templates when processing an error that has a defined error number. Error messages are also localizable strings and you need to handle the translation of these error messages when localizing an MSI database. Table 19-2 shows the format of the Error table.

Table 19-2 THE FORMAT OF THE ERROR TABLE

Column	Data Type	Key	Description
Error	Integer	Y	Contains the error code. This code is a positive integer used to find the message to be displayed when an error occurs. The Windows Installer uses a set of reserved error codes ranging from 0 to 33. There is another set of error codes that start at 1000 and go through 1999. These are what are called *ship error codes* and they are authored into this table along with the other reserved error codes. Error codes greater than 1999 are considered internal errors and not authored into the database. The range of error codes from 25000 to 30000 is reserved for use by custom actions.
Message	Template		Contains the localized template that is displayed when an authored error occurs.

The Windows Installer SDK includes localized versions of the ActionText and Error tables for all languages supported by the Windows Installer. You can import these tables into an MSI database by using the MSIDB.EXE utility found in the SDK or by using the MsiDatabaseImport API.

ISWI automatically includes localized versions of these tables when you add a supported language to your installation project. With these tables already available, the only thing you need to do when you author an MSI package is make sure that you localize any custom strings you have authored.

SETTING THE PROPERTIES When localizing an MSI database, you need to make sure that the ProductCode, ProductLanguage, and PackageCode properties are set correctly. One of the simple rules you need to follow is that every language version of a product must be considered a separate product. An English and a French version of the same product must each have different ProductCode properties because they are considered different products. The PackageCode is set in the Revision property of the Summary Information Stream and must be different for each package.

There is, however, an instance where two different products can be installed from the same package. This can happen when a base package is modified at run time by a transform. The transform modifies the package so that it installs a particular language version of the product. It changes the ProductCode property as part of the transform operation but the package code remains unchanged since it is not affected by the transform. All that is required is for the bootstrap executable that launches the installation to query the user for the language version of the product to be installed.

THE SUMMARY INFORMATION STREAM

Two properties in the Summary Information Stream are important when you are localizing an MSI database. In the Template property you identify a list of languages supported by the database. Entering a comma-delimited list of numeric language IDs in this property specifies the supported languages. If the language ID entered is 0, the database is identified as being language-neutral. The whole purpose of identifying the supported languages in the Summary Information Stream is so that when transforms are being applied to the database validation can be performed against the language of the database. If the supported languages identified in the Summary Information Stream do not match the language of the database, you can define that the transform not be applied.

The other property to set is the Codepage property. The Codepage property is the numeric value of the ANSI code page used for any strings stored in the Summary Information Stream. This property translates the strings in the Summary Information Stream into Unicode when the contents are being displayed in windows Explorer. You must set the Codepage property before setting any property strings in the Summary Information Stream. This is not the same code page that is in the header of the _StringPool stream in the database.

Chapter 18 addresses in detail the creation and application of transforms.

MULTIPLE-LANGUAGE MERGE MODULES

In Chapter 17 you learned about merge modules and using them to deliver components to an installation database. In this section we'll briefly touch on a special type of merge module that contains components that support more than one language. Version 1.52 of ISWI does not support the creation and merging of multiple-language merge modules.

The basic concept of a multiple-language merge module is that it is comprised of components that ship files in different languages. The merge module is identified as having a default language both in the Template property of the Summary Information Stream and in the Language column of the ModuleSignature table. The Template property contains a comma-delimited list of all the languages supported by the merge module with the first language in the list being the default language. The cabinet file embedded in the merge module contains all the files that comprise the components in the merge module.

For every language supported by the merge module there is an embedded transform inside the merge module that is applied when the module is opened during a merge operation. Which transform is applied to the merge module prior to its being merged depends on the requested language at merge time. The merge tool is responsible for requesting the language and then applying the transform to the merge module before actually merging it with the installation database.

The Localization Features of ISWI

You enable the localization features of ISWI when you install one of the language packs. There is an East language pack and a West language pack that provide translated text for all the dialogs that come with ISWI as well as the localizable text in the ActionText and Error tables. When you look at the localization features of ISWI, you will see that both build-time and run-time functionality have been made available. The core of the build-time functionality is the string table.

The string table

In Chapter 7 you learned about the basic functionality and concept of a string table, and you do not need to go back over that material again. What we'll discuss here is the string table with respect to the localization of an installation. In order to add languages to an installation you need to go to the Project Properties icon in the Project view and select the Setup Languages property. When you do this, you will see at the bottom right of the screen a list of languages that you can add to your setup project. If you were to select French, German, and Spanish in addition to English, you would see something like what is shown in Figure 19-4.

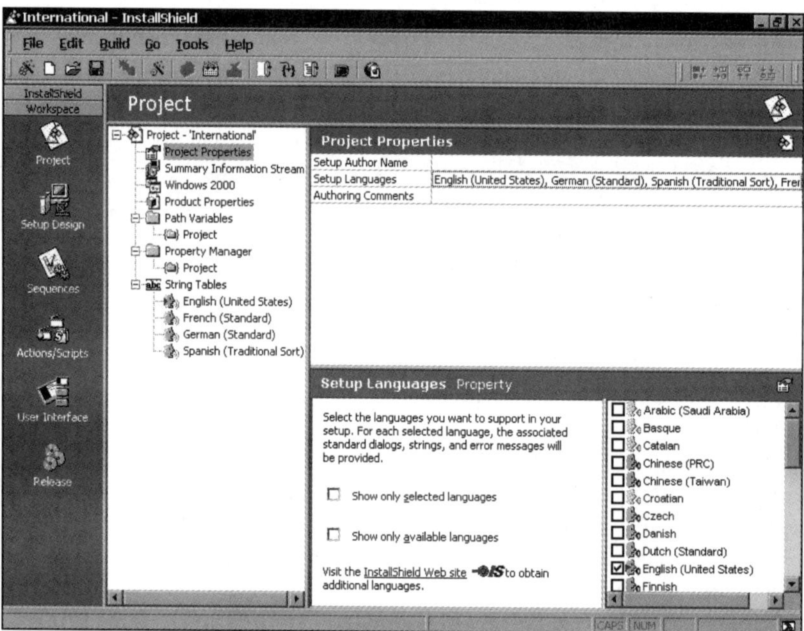

Figure 19-4: A selection of four setup languages

If you click any of the four string tables under the String Tables icon in the Project view, you will see the standard text in the particular language you chose. Also, you can see that a red arrowhead identifies the English string table in Figure 19-4. This tells you that this is the default language that will be used throughout the ISWI IDE. You can set any of the other languages as the default IDE language by right-clicking one of the non-default languages and selecting the Make default option from the context menu. If you were to do this for French, you could then go to the Power Editor, open up the ActionText table, and see all the localizable strings in French.

You need to set the default language to the one you will be using to author the setup package. When you create custom strings, such as feature display names, these strings will be placed into the default string table. When the setup project is complete, you can export these strings to a tab-delimited text file for translation into the other languages. You would, of course, make sure that you had set all the string identifiers to your format before exporting these custom strings. If the formats that you use for all the new string identifiers do not all sort together, you can get them to sort contiguously by sorting on the Modified column instead of the Identifier column. The Modified column provides the date and time that the strings were placed into the string table.

The Dialog Editor

In the Dialog Editor, accessible through the User Interface view, the default language you set in the Project view plays an important role. In the User Interface view you can access and edit dialogs in each language for which you have defined a setup language. Each dialog in every language will always have the same controls. The default language you set in the Project view under the String Tables icon has no meaning in the Dialog Editor. Whatever you do to any dialog, regardless of the language, will affect that dialog for all the languages. The only control attributes that are not propagated to other dialogs are the size, position, and right-to-left (RTL) attributes. When you change the position or size of a control in one dialog, the change does not apply to the other language versions of that dialog.

Filtering components on language association

One of the things you can do in ISWI is identify a component with a language or set of languages. When you click a component in the Setup Design view, you see that there is a property called Languages. This is not a Windows Installer property but a property defined by ISWI. By default all components are indicated as being Language Independent. However, if you click the Languages property for a component you can see that a list of languages appears in the bottom right corner of the screen. This list looks like the list you get when setting the setup languages but here you get not only the languages but also all the sub-languages defined for the Windows operating system. Also, you do not need to install the language packs for this list to be functional.

After you have set the Languages property for the component you make use of this property when you build the installation package. In the Release Wizard there is a dialog called Filtering Settings. This dialog is shown in Figure 19-5.

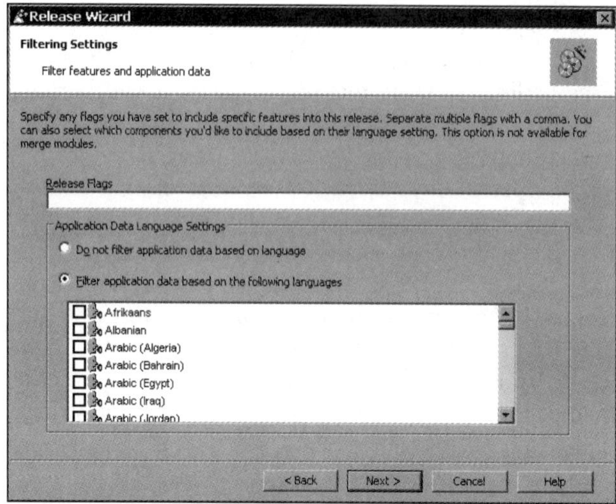

Figure 19-5: The Filtering Settings dialog of the Release Wizard

In the Application Data Language Settings group box you can filter the components for the current build based on language. As soon as you select the option to filter the components the list of languages in the list box is enabled. You then select the component languages that you want included in the build. The Release Wizard will include only those components that have a Languages property value that matches the languages selected in the Filtering Settings dialog. The Release Wizard will also include all components identified as being Language Independent.

Just because you can filter components based on language doesn't mean that you can create different language versions of a product from one project file simply by filtering the components. You need to keep in mind that every language version of a product requires a different value for the ProductCode property. Also, if there are to be separate packages for each language version of a product then there will need to be different PackageCode values. There is also the consideration of whether the UpgradeCode property should be changed or not between the different language versions of a product.

Multilingual installations

With ISWI you can create multilingual installations. The first aspect of multilingual installations you need to understand is another of the dialogs in the Release Wizard and the functionality it controls.

THE SETUP LANGUAGES DIALOG IN THE RELEASE WIZARD

The Setup Languages dialog is shown in Figure 19-6.

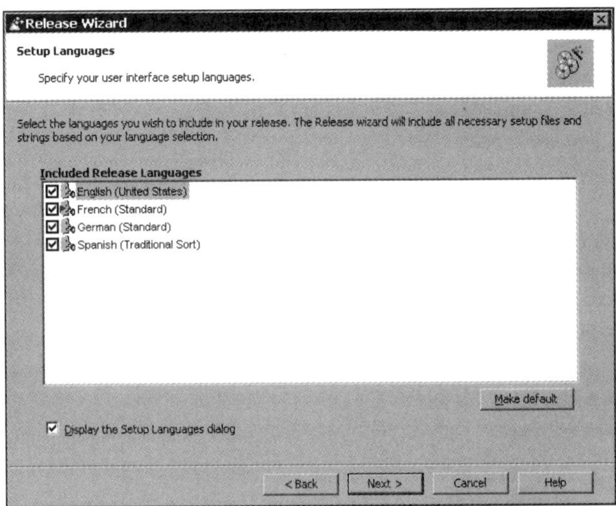

Figure 19-6: The Setup Languages dialog in the Release Wizard

In this dialog you are presented with a list of the setup languages that you have added to the project. It is in this dialog that you control how the specific build in progress will be constructed with regard to language support. You can see that in this dialog a default language is identified. Identifying a default language in this dialog does not have the same meaning as identifying a default language in the Project view. Here you are specifying the language or possible languages in which the installation will run. The default language specified here is the language in which the installation will be run. Any of the languages in this dialog can be deselected except the language designated as the default language. To change to a different default language all you need to do is select another language and click the Make default button.

At the bottom left in the Setup Languages dialog is a check box with the title Display the Setup Languages dialog, which when checked forces SETUP.EXE to display an initial dialog from which the user can select the language in which the installation is to run. Once the user has chosen a language SETUP.EXE launches the installation using that language.

BUILDING THE MEDIA

Regardless of whether the Display the Setup Languages dialog check box is checked or not, the SETUP.EXE and SETUP.INI files must be part of your installation package. SETUP.EXE implements the functionality of the multilingual installation and it gets the information it needs from the SETUP.INI file. There are two locations in the SETUP.INI file where information is found. This information is used to control the installation of an application when you select more than one language in the Setup Languages dialog of the Release Wizard. The first section is the startup section as follows:

```
[Startup]
CmdLine=<Command line to be passed to Setup.exe>
Product=<Product name>
PackageName=<Package file name>
MsiVersion=<Windows Installer Version>
EnableLangDlg=[Y | N]
```

The EnableLangDlg key has a value string of Y if the Setup Languages dialog is to be launched by SETUP.EXE; otherwise the value string is N. The other section in SETUP.INI that is important to running a multilingual installation is as follows:

```
[Languages]
count=4
default=407
key0=409
key1=40C
key2=407
key3=40A
```

Under this section you get a total count of all the languages; then a language ID in hexadecimal notation identifies the default language. The default language is followed by the language ID for all the languages selected in the Setup Languages dialog of the Release Wizard.

When more than one language has been selected in the Setup Languages dialog, the build creates a media image that consists of a code page neutral MSI database and a separate transform for each language selected. The code page neutral database is one that contains no tables that have columns that have localizable columns. Creating a temporary MSI database for each language and then generating the transform as the difference between this language specific database and the code page neutral database creates the language transform for each of the selected languages.

You run into a problem on Windows 9x if you want to create a multilingual installation package for languages that require different code pages such as English, German, or Greek. Either the German or Greek strings in the MSI database will be corrupt depending on whether the system locale on the build machine is set to code page 1252 (Western Europe and United States) or code page 1253 (Greek). Both German and Greek have different extended character sets, and only the characters supported by the system locale code page will be translated correctly.

It is possible that a multilingual installation package could be created successfully with only English and Greek as the selected setup languages because generally English characters can be translated by the ASCII character set, which all code pages support. You would need to set the system locale of the build machine to the Greek (1253) code page so that the Greek characters would be properly translated.

RUNNING THE INSTALLATION

If the Setup Languages dialog has been enabled, the user is presented with a dialog that contains a combo box that lists all of the languages included in the installation as setup languages. Choosing one of these languages launches the setup in this language. To launch the setup, SETUP.EXE launches the code page neutral MSI database and applies the appropriate language-specific transform to it. Since this operation only transforms the in-memory version of the database, the language transform along with the code page neutral database is cached on the machine for use during maintenance operations.

On Windows 9x machines, if the current system locale code page does not support the selected install language, then SETUP.EXE will check to see if any of the other languages identified as setup languages during the build are supported. If one of these languages is supported, then the install will run in that language. If none of the languages is supported, then SETUP.EXE will display an error and the installation will not continue.

On Windows NT/2000 it is only necessary that the code page of the selected language be installed on the system; the code page does not necessarily have to be the current system locale code page. If the code page is not installed, SETUP.EXE will look at the other possible setup languages and if an installed code page supports one of these then it will be used to run the installation. Otherwise SETUP.EXE will display an error message and terminate the installation.

If the Setup Languages dialog is not enabled and more than one language is selected during the build, the installation will be run in the language designated as the default language. If the default language is not supported by the target system, SETUP.EXE will look in SETUP.INI for another language supported by the system.

THE PRODUCT LANGUAGE AND PRODUCT CODE PROBLEM

One of the things that you'll notice immediately when you create multilingual installations is the fact that the ProductCode property will stay the same regardless of the language of the installation. Also, the ProductLanguage property will be set to the language of the install, which may not be the language of the product that is getting installed.

To follow the rules you need a different ProductCode value for each language of a product. Using the default functionality of ISWI you cannot do this. It is necessary to post process the transforms created for a multilingual installation so that each of the transforms has a different ProductCode. By doing this you ensure that you can install different language versions of a product on the same machine.

The ProductLanguage property is set to the language of the install so that if the Windows Installer displays an internal message during the installation it will be in the language in which the install is being performed. However, this property also identifies in the registry the language of the product that is installed. This language can be used to identify products in the Upgrade table that are to be removed after the completion of a major upgrade. Here there is no neat solution since once the ProductLanguage property is set so that it will show the correct language for the built-in messages it will also be used to identify the language of the product that has been installed.

You can decide to accept Windows Installer messages in an incorrect language or you can accept the incorrect product language entry in the registry. If you want to ignore the possibility of the Windows Installer displaying messages in the wrong language, you can post process the language transforms so that they include the language of the product and not the language of the installation. A better approach is to create installations in the same language as the language of the product and not provide the end user a choice of install language.

Now that you know all about the localization features in ISWI let's look at a few scenarios to see how to create various types of installations.

Using the Localization Features of ISWI

Let's look at three scenarios and list the actions you would need to take to create the appropriate installation packages. There are no example packages for these scenarios – just a set of steps you need to follow and issues you need to consider.

Creating an installation for a single localized product

In its simplest form this type of installation is no different from the installation packages that we have been talking about throughout this book. This is where there is one product in a particular language and the installation is created in the same language. If you want to create an installation in German for a German product, all you have to do is select German as a setup language, change the default language to German, and deselect the English language. (You would do all this in the Project view.) You would select or deselect the setup languages in the Project Properties panel and change the default language under the String Tables icon.

A more complex scenario is one in which you build a project that contains components of various languages and from this one project build a package for a particular language version of the product with the same language being used for the installation. In this case you need to identify each component by its language association. You can do this in the Setup Design view where one of the properties you can assign to a component is a language. During the build you can filter out all components that do not possess the correct language affiliation. You set the filtering criterion to be used in the build in the Filtering Settings dialog of the Release Wizard (see Figure 19-5). The next setting you have to make is in the Setup Languages dialog of the Release Wizard (see Figure 19-6). Here you have to identify the language of the product to be the default language and to make sure that all other languages are deselected. You need to make sure that the ProductLanguage property is set properly. This will only happen if you make the language you use in the installation the same as the language of the components in the product.

When you have a project that includes components for multiple language versions of a product, you need to be careful about changing the ProductCode property when you build each language version. The Windows Installer considers two different versions of the same product to be different products.

Finally you need to understand what it takes to create an installation for a single-language product but we want to offer the end user a selection of languages in which the installation can be run. In this scenario you will still want to filter the components so that you get only those components applicable to the language version of the product you want to install. However, you will need to check all the languages you want to include in the selection offered to the user in the Setup Languages dialog of the Release Wizard (see Figure 19-6), and you will also want to check the Display the Setup Languages dialog check box at the bottom of this dialog.

When you build, you get a code page neutral MSI database and a transform file for each of the installation languages you want offered to the end user. Now you have to post process the transform files so that they all contain the same value for the ProductLanguage property. You need to give this product language property the language ID that corresponds to the language of the product. If you do not do this, then the product language entered into the registry will be the language in which the installation is run and not necessarily the language of the product itself.

You can post process the language transforms as described in Chapter 18 where it discusses how to edit a transform.

If you post process the language transforms for a single-language product in order to offer a selection of languages in which the installation can be run, you run the risk of Windows Installer internal messages being displayed in a language different from the language of the installation. For example, if you have a French product and the end user selects to run the installation in Arabic, the Windows Installer will display any internal messages in French because you have set the ProductLanguage property in all the language transforms the French language ID.

Creating an Installation for a Set of Localized Products

Here there is only one main scenario, the installation of a particular localized product based on the language selected for use in the installation user. When creating the install package, you need to condition each component that is not language-independent on the value of the ProductLanguage property. This scenario requires that you do not filter the components based on language association when building the installation package. You should also select all languages in the Setup Languages dialog of the Release Wizard and make sure to check the Display the Setup Languages dialog check box so that the language selection dialog is enabled at run time. This will give you a build comprised of a code page neutral MSI database and a language transform for each language in which the product has been created.

Using the technique described in Chapter 18 you need to edit each of the language transforms you created when you built the install package. For each of these transforms you need to modify the ProductCode so that each transform has the product code that corresponds to the language of the product. Now when the user selects a language for the installation the transform that implements that language will be applied to the code page neutral database and only those components that are language-independent and of which the condition on the component is true will get installed.

Creating an installation for a product that ships multiple-language resources

The main scenario for this category of localized installation is very much like the installation of a single-language product with the language of the installation being selected by the user at run time. The languages that the product to be installed will support after installation are selected in the custom setup-type dialog where the feature tree is comprised of not only the main functionality features but also the features from which you can select the languages to be supported.

When building the install package, you should not filter any of the components based on language association. You can have either a single language for the installation user interface or you can enable the user select the language in which the install will run. If you want present the user with a selection of install languages, you will need to edit the language transforms in order to set the ProductLanguage property to be the language of the product being installed. It would be acceptable to set the product language for this type of product to be the default language that the product will use in its user interface. You could also set it to the primary language ID if all the languages supported by the product are in the same family.

Depending on the language selected for the installation user interface, the Windows Installer may display internal messages in a language different from the one being used during the installation.

Adding a New Language

ISWI provides a method for adding new languages that are not available using the language packs that are offered by InstallShield Software Corporation. You can access the New Language wizard from the Tools pulldown menu by selecting the Add New Language... option. This option is only enabled if there are no open projects. When you select this option and click the Next button on the Welcome dialog, you get a dialog that looks like what is shown in Figure 19-7.

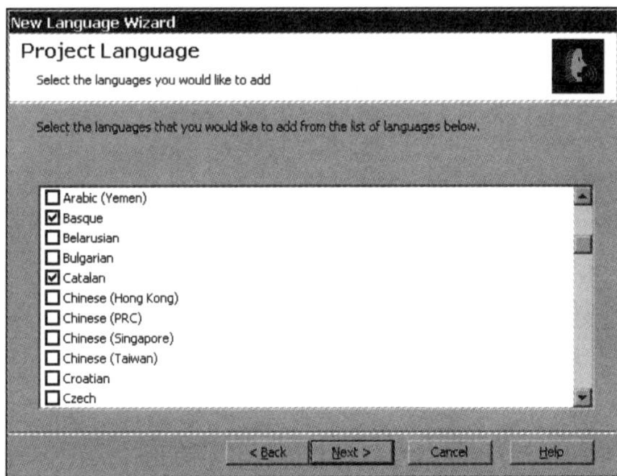

Figure 19-7: The Project Language dialog in the New Language Wizard

In this dialog you are presented with a list of languages that you can add to past projects as well as to future projects. When you select one or more languages from this list, the Next button is enabled and you can proceed to the next dialog in the wizard. That dialog is the Project Files dialog, shown in Figure 19-8.

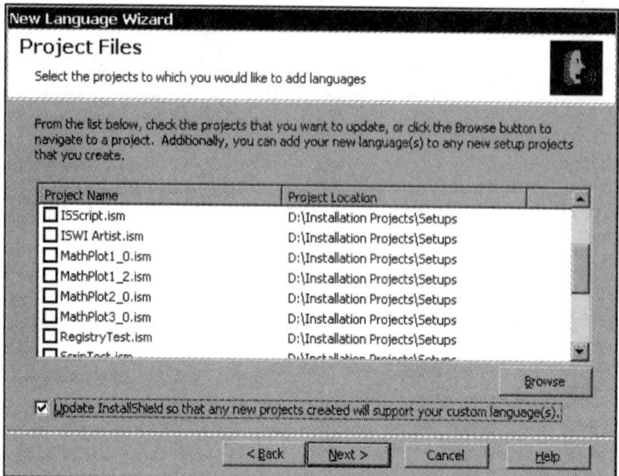

Figure 19-8: The Project Files dialog in the New Language Wizard

In this dialog you are given a list of all the projects you have created and you can select some or all of these to which to add a new language. You can also choose to include the new language or languages in all future projects: just check the check box at the bottom of the Project Files dialog. When you click the Next button, you get to the Summary dialog. When you click the Finish button, the selected projects and templates are updated. The Summary dialog is shown in Figure 19-9.

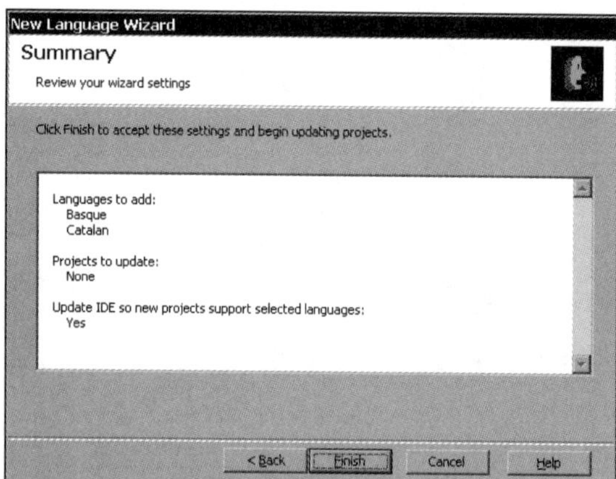

Figure 19-9: The Summary dialog in the New Language Wizard

When you add a new language to an existing project you are able to then select that new language as one of the setup languages. What you get is a copy of the default language string table, which you then have to translate into the new language. The standard approach to performing this translation is to export the string table as a tab-delimited text file and send it to a translator. Once the translation is complete you import the translated text file and it will overwrite the default language strings in the string table.

When you add a new language so that it will be included in all new projects, you are modifying the templates used to create new installations or merge module projects. However, every time you create a new project you will have to translate the strings for the new language unless you have preserved the previous text file that was translated and then import this file each time you create a new project that needs to use this language. A better way would be to modify the template files used to create new projects so that you do not have to worry about losing the translated text file or having to always import it. The project template files are found in the Support\0409 directory where ISWI is installed. The three template files you want to modify are as follows:

IsProjTpl.ism	The template used by the Project Wizard to create new projects
IsProjBlankTpl.ism	The template you use to create a new project directly in the IDE without going through the Project Wizard
IsProjBlankMMTpl.ism	The template used to create a new merge module project

Since these files have the regular project file format you can open them up directly in ISWI. In these files you can temporarily add the new language as a setup language and then translate this new language. After the text file is translated you can import the new language, save the project file, and then deselect this language as one of the setup languages. After you do that you can create new projects where this new language will be immediately available because it is now included in the project template.

Summary

In this chapter you learned what it takes to localize a Windows Installer package. You saw that this is not a simple activity, but you also saw how ISWI simplifies many of the tasks involved. In particular you looked in detail at how the code page of the database and the current code page of the build system affect the creation of a localized database, both in a Windows 9x build system and in a Windows NT/2000 build system environment. Learning how a Windows Installer package gets localized you were able to easily create a localized package using ISWI.

You saw a number of scenarios where creating a multilingual installation for a single-language product necessitated the post processing of the language transforms. You needed to post process these transforms in order to set the ProductLanguage and the ProductCode properties correctly. In the Windows Installer world, you discovered that two different language versions of a product are considered two different products and thus need to have different ProductCode property values.

Finally, you saw how we could extend the language offerings that are available for ISWI by adding your own languages. You can add these new languages to existing projects and also to the templates, so that these new languages will automatically be available to all new projects.

Chapter 20

Handling Updates and Upgrades of a Product

IN THIS CHAPTER

- Performing updates and upgrades
- Updating a product by reinstallation
- Performing major upgrades by using the Upgrade table
- Patch package structure
- Creating patch packages
- Handling updates of the operating system

THIS CHAPTER COVERS one of the most important subjects relating to the installation of software, which is how to upgrade an application that has already been installed.

Description of the Example Products

In this chapter, you work with an application called MathPlot. On the CD-ROM at the back of the book, you can find four versions of this product. Both the source code for this application and the setup projects are available there. Figure 20-1 provides a diagram of this simple application. This application draws some trigonometric functions with more capability being added with each higher version.

The difference between versions 1.0 and 1.2 is that version 1.2 draws two additional curves. A COM DLL implements the plotting functionality and is available in both an ANSI and a UNICODE version. This application follows the rules as to when the component code of a component is to be changed. All the components in this application are backward compatible with the component codes remaining from version to version. After you add the Symbol_Font component to the Main_Feature feature, you force a change in the ProductCode property and thus the major version of the product changes. You find the rules of when you need to change the Product Code property a little later in this chapter.

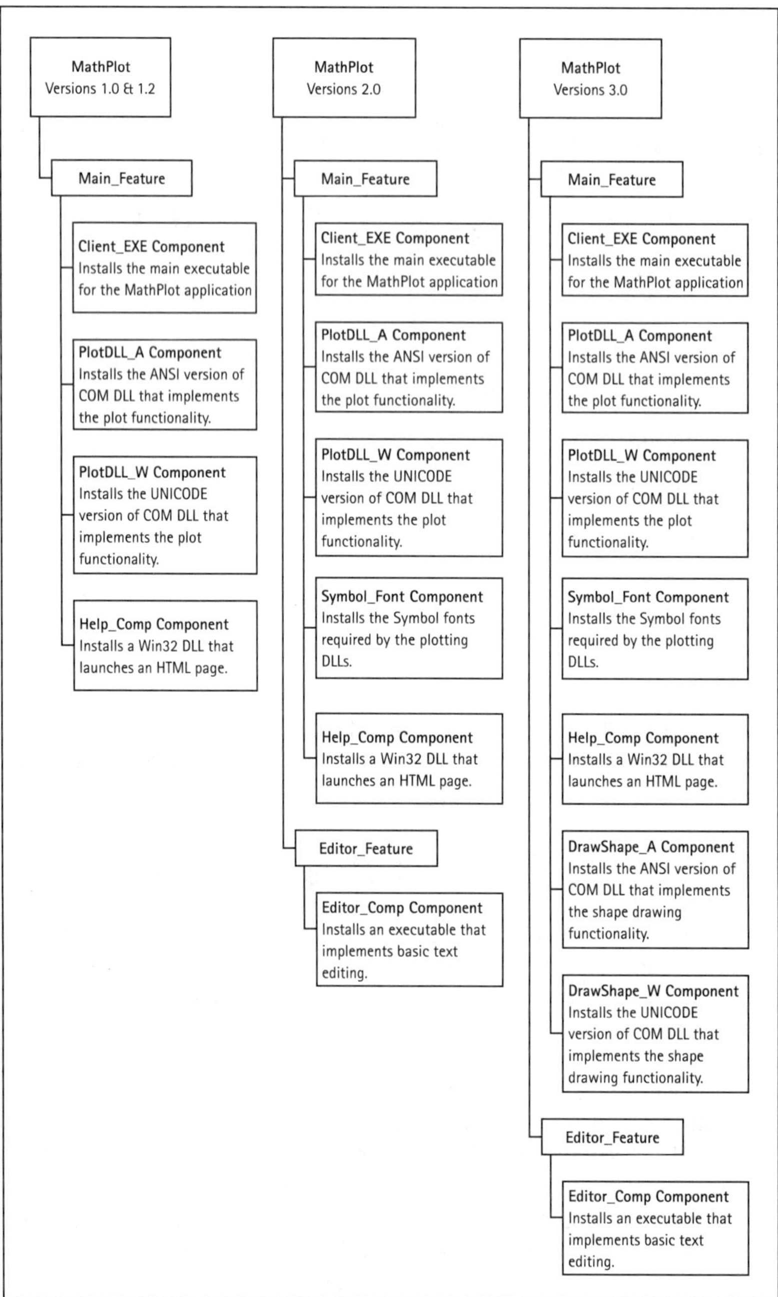

Figure 20-1: The MathPlot application

Types of Updates and Upgrades

The Windows Installer provides a robust functionality for updating or upgrading an application. This functionality applies to an application that is installed on the local machine or is installed as an administrative image on a network drive. The Windows Installer defines three types of updates or upgrades, which are a small update, a minor upgrade, and a major upgrade. Each of these types of update or upgrades can be distributed as either a full installation package or as a patch package.

As you may expect, the difference between the three types of upgrades to a product is how major the changes are to the product. The three types of upgrades are discussed in detail in the following three sections. Based on the significance of the changes being applied to the application, the ProductCode may require no changes. Also, the ProductVersion properties or only the ProductVersion may need to change or both properties need to change. In all cases, however, the PackageCode of the cached installation package will need to change.

The use of patch packages to perform an upgrade to an application has advantages over the approach of using a full installation package. A patch package can contain an entire file as part of the upgrade process, but the patch package also can contain just those bits required to modify part of a file. This approach has the advantage of allowing for a much smaller download by the end user than is necessary if the whole product had to be downloaded.

Only two types of images can receive an update or an upgrade, which are a local installation or an administrative installation. You cannot update or upgrade features that have not been installed. You find more information about the three types of updates and or upgrades in the following sections.

The small update

For a small update, you have a situation where a small number of files that make up the application require some minor changes. If you have this situation and do not want to change the product version, you can perform a small update. But you find a problem with this situation because no efficient means is available to detect whether a user is using the original product or the one with the updated files. This situation poses a problem for the technical support organization if the changes made in the affected files fixed any bugs.

You can use three methods to deliver a small update to a product that has already been installed either locally or as an administrative image on a network drive. These three methods are as follows:

- Perform a reinstallation of the product.
- Apply a patch to a local installation of the product.
- Apply a patch to an administrative image of the product, followed by reinstalling the clients of that administrative install.

Upgrading a product

When you get away from making only minor changes to a few files, you get into the business of upgrading a product. Here you start to make changes in some of the important properties in the MSI database. The two types of upgrades are the minor upgrade and the major upgrade. Both of these upgrades are discussed in the following sections.

THE MINOR UPGRADE

A minor upgrade is different from a small update in that a minor upgrade does change the product version. The product code does not change with a minor upgrade. The propagation of a minor upgrade to the end user is implemented in the same fashion as described in the previous section for small updates. One new issue arises after you propagate a minor upgrade that doesn't occur with a small update. You need to make sure that you do not inadvertently downgrade an existing version to a lower version. Changing the product version also mandates that you maintain an order to the application of minor upgrades. For example, if you have a version 1.0 for which you create a patch to upgrade it to version 1.1, and then you create another patch to upgrade version 1.0 to version 1.2, you need to be cognizant of the fact that you need to apply the patches in the appropriate order to go from version 1.0 to version 1.2.

In general, you can control the order of patch application by setting the product version validation bits in the transforms that comprise part of a patch package. However, if you propagate a minor upgrade through the reinstallation of the product, you need to take special care to author into your installation packages the logic required to prevent the downgrading of a higher version to a lower version. For example, you do not want a version 1.0 product to be able to reinstall over a version 1.2 product.

THE MAJOR UPGRADE

As you may assume, a major upgrade of a product requires a change to both the ProductVersion and the ProductCode properties. Major upgrades change the major version number of a product whereas a minor upgrade changes only the minor version number of a product.

PREPARING AN APPLICATION FOR AN EVENTUAL MAJOR UPGRADE To be able to perform a major upgrade, be sure to include an UpgradeCode in the *Property* table in the database. The UpgradeCode is a GUID and it is an indicator of a family of related products. For example, version 1.0 and version 1.2 of a particular product should all use the same UpgradeCode. You also need to have the ProductCode, ProductVersion, and ProductLanguage properties, which are required properties and always need to be in the *Property* table. The UpgradeCode property identifies an installed application as being a member of the family to which a major upgrade applies. You can see how this property operates later in the chapter. First look at the rules that you need to follow before deciding to change the ProductCode property.

WHEN TO CHANGE THE PRODUCTCODE Before you change the ProductCode, follow these specific rules to decide whether the changes are necessary. These rules are:

- If having both the original product and the upgraded product on the machine at the same time is necessary, then the ProductCode properties need to be different between the two versions. If the ProductCode properties are not different, trying to install the upgraded version of the product puts you into a maintenance mode where you can change the existing product that is already on the machine.
- If the name of the MSI package file is to change, then you need to change the ProductCode property. The reason this change is necessary is because of the information the Windows Installer writes to the registry for each product. One of the values that is written to the registry is the PackageName against the SourceList key that is associated with each product that is installed. In the case of a per-user installation this information is written to the following key:

  ```
  HKCU\SOFTWARE\Classes\Installer\Products\{ProductCode}
  \SourceList
  ```

  In the case of a per-machine installation this information is written to the following key:

  HKLM\SOFTWARE\Classes\Installer\Products\{ProductCode} \SourceList All sources identified for a particular product are paths to folders only and do not include the name of the package. A source can be the location of some media, a network location, or a URL. The PackageName value is then appended to these folder paths to get the fully qualified path to the MSI package. Regardless of the actual source for a product, the name of the package is identical
- The ProductCode needs to change if the component code for an existing component changes. Once again this is because of how components are refcounted in the registry. This refcounting of components is done under the following registry key:

  ```
  HKLM\SOFTWARE\Microsoft\Windows\CurrentVersion\Installer
  \Components\{Component Code}
  ```

  Under each of the component codes is a list of value names comprised of the ProductCodes of the products that have installed the component. The installed state of the component can be either local or run-from-source. The data associated with each of these value names is the key path for the component. From this it can be seen that if we change the component code of an existing component without changing the ProductCode, we will still have the original component still refcounted in addition to the component with the new component code. This is, of course, not desirable and would break the component refcount functionality of the Windows Installer.

- If you add a new component to an existing feature or remove a component from an existing feature, you need to change the ProductCode. The association between features and components is written to the registry under the flooring key:

  ```
  HKLM\SOFTWARE\Microsoft\Windows\CurrentVersion\Installer
  \Features\{ProductCode}
  ```

  The value names under each of the ProductCode keys are the names of features that have been installed locally or run-from-source. The value data for each feature is the compressed component codes of all components contained within that feature. At the end of this string of compressed component codes is the name of the parent feature if one exists. If you do not change the ProductCode after adding or removing a component from a feature, this information in the registry will be incorrect. If this information is incorrect, then the installer functions that use this information will not function correctly.

- If you make an existing feature into the child of another existing feature, you need to change the ProductCode property. The Windows Installer keeps track of the feature tree of a product in one of two locations depending on whether the installation was performed per-user or per-machine. For a per-user install the registry key is as follows:

  ```
  HKCU\SOFTWARE\Microsoft\Installer\Features\{ProductCode}
  ```

  For a per-machine installation the registry key where this information is recorded is as follows:

  ```
  HKLM\SOFTWARE\Classes\Installer\Features\{ProductCode}
  ```

  The value names for each of the ProductCode keys are the names of the features in the product and the value data is the name of the parent feature for the feature. If the feature has no parent, the value data is null. If the structure of the feature tree changes without changing the ProductCode, then you will create incorrect information in the registry for the product that is already registered.

  If you remove an existing child feature from its parent feature, you also need to change the ProductCode. The reason for this is the same as stated for when we make an existing feature into the child of another existing feature.

This book is showing the registry entries that are made with versions 1.2 or lower of the Windows Installer. In future versions of the Windows Installer the use of the registry will be different. The purpose of showing you these registry entries is to give you an idea of the basis for the rules that have been setup by Microsoft. You should not depend on these registry entries being there in the future.

In the section above, I mention ProductCodes and ComponentCodes and their use in the registry. In all these cases, these codes will not look the same as you see them in the installation projects because they have been entered into the registry in packed or compressed form. This manipulation of these codes by the Windows Installer is done in order to enhance searching functionality and to save space in the registry.

Summary of valid upgrade methods

Three types of updates or upgrades are discussed in the previous sections and various methods shown to implement these changes. Table 20-1 summarizes all this information and shows where you can use each of the methods that are available.

TABLE 20-1 SUMMARY OF THE METHODS USED TO UPDATE OR UPGRADE A PRODUCT

Upgrade Method	Upgrade Type	Discussion
Reinstallation	Small Update	Small update works because the Windows Installer recognizes the product is already installed on the machine through the ProductCode being the same.
	Minor Upgrade	Minor upgrade works because the Windows Installer recognizes that the product is already installed on the machine through the ProductCode being the same.
	Major Upgrade	The reinstallation cannot be used to perform a major upgrade because a change in product code exists and the new MSI package does not recognize that the old product is on the system.
Patching	Small Update	Small update works because the patch package created uses the original package and the new package as the sources for creating the difference that needs to be added to the installed version of the product.

Continued

TABLE 20-1 SUMMARY OF THE METHODS USED TO UPDATE OR UPGRADE A PRODUCT *(Continued)*

Upgrade Method	Upgrade Type	Discussion
Patching	Minor Upgrade	Minor upgrade works because the patch package created uses the original package and the new package as the sources for creating the difference that needs to be added to the installed version of the product.
	Major Upgrade	Major upgrade works because the patch package was created by using the original package and the new package as the sources for creating the difference that needs to be added to the installed version of the product. In the case of a major upgrade, the old product has to be removed by using the functionality contained in the Upgrade table approach.
Fresh Install	Small Update	The Fresh Install cannot be used to perform a small update because no product version difference exists between the product on the system and the package that is making the changes.
	Minor Upgrade	Even though the Fresh Install can be used to identify older versions on the system, the ProductCode property has not changed so that the Windows Installer will attempt to perform a maintenance operation on the current installation.
	Major Upgrade	Major upgrade works because the Fresh Install contains the definition of those older products that have to be removed after the installation of the new product.

In the following sections, you can investigate a number of the scenarios shown in the above table. You can use the sample applications found on the CD-ROM at the back of the book and discussed in the first section of this chapter.

Updating or Upgrading a Product by Reinstallation

If you update an installation by performing a reinstallation of the product, you can perform a complete reinstallation or a partial reinstallation. Generally, a reinstallation is performed from the command line setting the REINSTALL and REINSTALLMODE properties appropriately. However, you can also perform a complete reinstallation of a product in a programmatic fashion.

The basic command line syntax for performing a reinstallation of a product is as follows:

```
msiexec /i [path to new .msi file] REINSTALL=[feature list]
                                      REINSTALLMODE=vomus
```

In this command line, you need to identify that path to the new MSI package because it contains the modified files that comprise the small update. You cannot use the product code in place of this new .msi file because that only uses the cached package already on the machine, and the package does not reference the correct files. For a complete reinstallation, the REINSTALL property is set to a value of ALL. This value signifies that all features already installed on the local machine will be reinstalled. To perform a reinstall of just the features that are impacted by the changed files comprising the small update, the REINSTALL property is set equal to a comma delimited list of the names of the affected features.

The value string used to set the REINSTALLMODE property defines the type of reinstallation to perform. Each letter in this string specifies how the reinstallation treats files, registry entries, and shortcuts. Table 20-2 describes the meaning of each of these five reinstallation modes.

TABLE 20-2 REINSTALLATION CODES

Option	Description
v	Using the specified MSI package runs the reinstallation, which is used to re-cache the local package on the target machine.
o	A file is reinstalled if the file is missing or if an older version of the file on the system exists. The files that change need to have a more recent version. Or if they are not versioned, then they need to show a later file creation date.

Continued

TABLE 20-2 REINSTALLATION CODES *(Continued)*

Option	Description
m	Rewrite all required registry entries from the Registry table that go to the HKEY_LOCAL_MACHINE or HKEY_CLASSES_ROOT registry hive. Rewrite all information from the Class table, Verb table, PublishComponent table, ProgID table, MIME table, Icon table, Extension table, and AppID table regardless of machine or user assignment. Reinstall all qualified components.
u	Rewrite all required registry entries from the Registry table that go to the HKEY_CURRENT_USER or HKEY_USERS registry hive.
s	Reinstall all shortcuts and re-cache all icons overwriting any existing shortcuts and icons.

An optional command line approach for performing a complete reinstallation of a product is to use the repair mode switch and not the installation switch. The command line for the repair mode switch is as follows:

```
msiexec /fvomus [path to new .msi file]
```

If you want to programmatically initiate a complete reinstall, you use the MsiReinstallProduct() Windows Installer API function. Use the Windows Installer SDK documentation for the correct parameters to pass to this function.

A minor upgrade example by using the reinstallation approach

On the CD-ROM at the back of the book are setups that are created for version 1.0 and version 1.2 of the MathPlot application. For each of these versions, you find a Release-1. Work with the Release-1 by first installing version 1.0 and then upgrade it to version 1.2 by using the following command line:

```
msiexec /i [path to version 1.2 .msi file] REINSTALL=ALL
                                            REINSTALLMODE=vomus
```

This command performs a minor upgrade of the MathPlot application by using a complete reinstall of the product. After you run the command line, you see the SetupResume dialog display, which is modified to show both the value of the Preselected property and the RESUME property. This dialog was modified in the version 1.2 setup package. After you click the Next button, the reinstall takes place and the new product is immediately available for use.

The above process shown for performing a minor upgrade is the same that you would use to perform a small update.

Performing a Major Upgrade by Using the Upgrade Table

The approach to performing a major upgrade is to first find all related products that are already installed on the system and then to remove these products after the new product is installed. A related product is one that has the same UpgradeCode as the product to be installed while the product version and product language match the product version range and list of valid languages that are identified in the *Upgrade* table against the UpgradeCode. The FindRelatedProducts action implements the process of finding the related products on the system. For every product found on the system, the FindRelatedProducts action appends the associated product code to a property identified in the ActionProperty column of the *Upgrade* table.

The RemoveExistingProducts action uses this list of product codes to initiate the uninstallation of these found products. To make sure that this public property gets sent across the process boundary to the InstallExecuteSequence table, make the ActionProperty a part of the SecureCustomProperties property. This property adds the ActionProperty property to the list of restricted public properties. Then the ActionProperty property will still be sent across the process boundary, even if the application is being managed and the public properties that can be sent across to the execute sequence are restricted.

During an upgrade, you can have the same feature states of the installed application maintained after the upgrade process. Using the MigrateFeatureStates action maintains the features, but this is only useful if the feature tree has not changed significantly between the original product and the new product.

The following is a summary of the process of performing a major upgrade using the *Upgrade* table:

- In the setup of the new product, identify all the products that you are replacing with this image by authoring rows in the *Upgrade* table.
- By using the FindRelatedProducts action in the new setup of the product, find all the products on the system that match the criteria provided in the *Upgrade* table.
- The Installer adds the ProductCode property for each product that is found to the value of the property name identified in the ActionProperty column in the *Upgrade* table. The value of this property ends up being a semicolon-delimited list of all the product codes found on the target system.

- Add the name of the ActionProperty as a value for the SecureCustom Properties property. Do this by authoring the value into the *Property* table using the ISWI Property Manager. You do this so that the execute sequence still passes from the ActionProperty in the case where the product is being installed as a managed application in a Windows NT/2000 environment.
- Using the RemoveExistingProducts action, the installer uninstalls all the older products that it finds on the system by the FindRelatedProducts action.
- If you want to maintain the same feature states in the product that existed in the old product, use the MigrateFeatureStates action in both the user interface sequence and the execute sequence and add the appropriate attribute in the *Upgrade* table.

The next section takes a closer look at the FindRelatedProducts, MigrateFeature States, and RemoveExistingProducts actions. The *Upgrade* table is covered in detail in the major upgrade example.

The FindRelatedProducts action

As stated in the previous section, the FindRelatedProducts action queries the *Upgrade* table to get the UpgradeCode that is used to search the registry for any installed products that have this UpgradeCode. The UpgradeCode for each product is written in the registry in one of two locations depending on whether the installation of the product was done per user or per machine. You find another location where this action is also written, but that location is only for future use. If an installation is performed for the current user, the UpgradeCode is written to the following registry key:

```
HKCU\SOFTWARE\Microsoft\Installer\UpgradeCodes\{UpgradeCode}
```

If an installation is performed for the machine, the UpgradeCode is written to the following registry key:

```
HKLM\SOFTWARE\Classes\Installer\UpgradeCodes\{UpgradeCode}
```

The other location where the UpgradeCode is written for all installations but is reserved for future use is under the following registry key:

```
HKLM\SOFTWARE\Microsoft\Windows\CurrentVersion\Installer
\UpgradeCodes\{UpgradeCode}
```

The UpgradeCode properties are written in a packed format and under each of these keys is a list of value names that consist of the ProductCode property of the products that are associated through the UpgradeCode. The ProductCode is also written in a packed format. There is no value data written to the registry for any of these value names.

Once again you need to be aware that this book is showing the registry entries that are made with versions 1.2 or lower of the Windows Installer. In future versions of the Windows Installer the use of the registry will be different. The purpose of showing you these registry entries is to give you an idea of the basis for the rules that have been setup by Microsoft. You should not depend on these registry entries being there in the future.

Using the ProductCode associated with the UpgradeCode, the FindRelatedProducts action finds the ProductVersion and ProductLanguage and decides whether the criterion in the Upgrade table is met. If the action is met, it unpacks the ProductCode and appends it to the value of the ActionProperty property specified in the *Upgrade* table. The action unpacks this ProductCode because it needs to be in the original format for use in eventually performing an uninstallation using a nested-install custom action.

Because this action finds the product codes to uninstall, the action needs to be placed prior to either the MigrateFeatureStates or the RemoveExistingProducts action. Because of the possibility of a silent upgrade being performed, the action needs to be placed in both the user interface sequence and the execute sequence. The FindRelatedProducts action is designed to run only once. If the action runs in the user interface sequence, then it will not run in the execute sequence. Place this action in the sequence right after the LaunchCondition action, which is the default location.

The MigrateFeatureStates action

The MigrateFeatureStates action uses the results of the FindRelatedProducts action to determine what relevant products are already on the target system. Then if the msidbUpgradeAttributesMigrateFeatures bit flag has been set in the Attributes column of the *Upgrade* table, this action will query the registry for the feature states of the installed product and then will set the feature states for the new application to be the same as for the installed product. Of course, this action is only possible for those features that have the same names in both old and new products.

Feature states are written to the registry by the PublishFeatures action. The MigrateFeatureStates action is placed immediately after the CostFinalize action because the feature states are not finally set for the new product installation until the CostFinalize action queries the *Condition* table. You do not want the feature states modified by the MigrateFeatureStates action until the internal process of setting the feature states is complete. If the Preselected property is set, the MigrateFeatureStates action will not run. The Windows Installer sets this property whenever there is a resumed installation, such as after the reboot of the system or if the selection of features is made from the command line.

The RemoveExistingProducts action

The main concern with the use of the RemoveExistingProducts action is where it should be placed in the execute sequence. To place this action in the correct location, you need to understand that you are combining two events into one. Instead of first uninstalling the old product before we install the new product, or installing the new product and then later uninstalling the old product, you are combining these two events into one installation package. The whole functionality of the combining of theses two events depends on the proper refcounting of components. By using this action, older files that are still needed by the new product are not removed after the RemoveExistingProducts action is executed.

You essentially have two choices where to place the action in the execute sequence, before any changes are made to the system by the install of the new product or after all changes are made to the system by the install of the new product. You definitely do not want to remove the old product during the making of changes to the system because that removes files, registry entries, and so on before the components of the new product are refcounted. The most efficient placement of this action is after the InstallFinalize action, because this action keeps the install of the new product from having to reinstall files that were not changed between the old and the new products. The RemoveExistingProducts action only runs during an initial install and not during a maintenance installation.

An example using the Upgrade table approach to perform a major upgrade

To upgrade either version 1.0 or version 1.2 of the MathPlot application to version 2.0, you only have to make one entry into the *Upgrade* table in the version 2.0 installation package. Use the Power Editor under the Tools pulldown menu in ISWI. Table 20-3 shows the entries that need to be made in the *Upgrade* table.

Table 20-3 ENTRIES IN THE UPGRADE TABLE OF THE VERSION 2.0 PACKAGE

Row #	Column Name	Attribute Value
Row 1	UpgradeCode	{E04C6575-37E0-11D4-97E4-0010A4ECA65E}
	VersionMin	
	VersionMax	1.20.0000
	Language	
	Attributes	513
	Remove	
	ActionProperty	OLDPRODUCTS

The following remarks provide more detail for the entries that are described in Table 20-3:

- ◆ The value used in this table for the UpgradeCode comes from the value used for that property in both the version 1.0 and version 1.2 installation packages.
- ◆ Leave the VersionMin column null, which means that no lower bound is on the minimum version to which this upgrade can be applied.
- ◆ Leaving the VersionMin field null means that you have to enter a value for the VersionMax field. Enter the value of the highest product version to which this upgrade can be applied. In this case that value is 1.20.0000.
- ◆ Leave the Language column null, so that this upgrade applies to all languages.
- ◆ In the attributes column, tell the Windows Installer to include in the search for installed products those attributes that include the version specified in the VersionMax column. You also want to migrate feature states, so that the final result is 512 + 1 as the bit flag to be entered into the Attributes column.
- ◆ Leave the Remove column null to indicate that you want to remove all features of the old product. Otherwise, you can provide a comma-delimited list of feature names you want removed, and only those names would be uninstalled after the RemoveExistingProducts action is executed.
- ◆ In the last column of the *Upgrade* table, specify the name of the public property that is to hold the product codes of the installed older products.

In addition to entering the above row into the *Upgrade* table, enter into the *Property* table the SecureCustomProperties property name with a value of OLDPRODUCTS. This installation package is available on the CD-ROM at the back of the book. One feature added to this installation package is the value of the OLDPRODUCTS property, which is displayed in the InstallWelcome dialog box. To perform the upgrade, run the installation for version 2.0 of the MathPlot product.

Preventing the Downgrading of a Higher Version with a Lower Version

Authoring your installations so that some time in the future they cannot be used to downgrade a higher version to a lower version is another application of the *Upgrade* table. This action presupposes that you know the UpgradeCode to be used in future versions, which may not be possible. But I can go through an explanation of how to implement this functionality, by assuming that a version 3.0 of the MathPlot product exists and that it has the same UpgradeCode as in version 2.0.

To implement this type of logic requires the use of the UpgradeCode and SecureCustomProperties properties, the Upgrade, Property, and CustomAction tables, and the FindRelatedProducts action. The key here is to use the same UpgradeCode property for all major versions in the same family of products. Then by using the FindRelatedProducts action, a designated property is set if a product is found that is a member of this family. This property is then used as a condition on an Error custom action that displays an error message and then terminates the reinstallation if the user is trying to downgrade the present version on the computer.

The following is a summary of the process to prevent a lower version from installing over a higher version:

1. In the setup of a particular product, identify all the higher versions of the product by authoring rows in the *Upgrade* table that will detect these higher version products if they have already been installed.
2. Using the FindRelatedProducts action in the older setup of the product, find all the products on the system that match the criteria provided in the *Upgrade* table.
3. Add the ProductCode property for each product that is found to the value of the property name identified in the ActionProperty column in the *Upgrade* table. The value of this property ends up being a semicolon-delimited list of all the product codes found on the target system.
4. Add the name of the ActionProperty as a value for the SecureCustom Properties property. Do this by authoring into the *Property* table using the ISWI Property Manager. Add this value so that in the case where the product is being installed as a managed application in a Windows NT/2000 environment, the ActionProperty still passes to the execute sequence.
5. Using an Error (Type 19) custom action prevents the installation of a lower version over a higher version. This custom action is conditioned using the name of the property entered in the ActionProperty column of the *Upgrade* table. If a newer product is found, this property gets set, and the condition on the custom action evaluates to TRUE, which lets the custom action execute. The custom action displays a message and then terminates the installation after the user clicks the OK button.

To demonstrate how this all works, the assumption is made that four versions of the product is already produced. These are version 1.0, version 1.2, version 2.0, and version 3.0. The following tables show the entries that need to be made to implement the logic in the MSI package for version 2.0, so that it does not install if version 3.0 is already installed, but will upgrade versions 1.0 and 1.2. You can author the version 1.0 and version 1.2 MathPlot packages to not install over versions 2.0 and 3.0, as long as you know in advance the UpgradeCode properties that you use in these later versions. You can use the same UpgradeCode property for all versions of the MathPlot application to make the changes easier, but in this example I used a different upgrade code for the version 1.x products than I did for versions 2.0 and 3.0.

The first change is to add an additional row to the *Upgrade* table. This additional row is shown in Table 20-4 as Row 2. Shown as Row 1 in Table 20-4 is what you have already entered when you did the major upgrade example in the previous section.

TABLE 20-4 ENTRIES IN THE UPGRADE TABLE OF THE VERSION 2.0 PACKAGE

Row #	Column Name	Attribute Value
Row 1	UpgradeCode	{E04C6575-37E0-11D4-97E4-0010A4ECA65E}
	VersionMin	
	VersionMax	1.20.0000
	Language	
	Attributes	513
	Remove	
	ActionProperty	OLDPRODUCTS
Row 2	UpgradeCode	{E04C65B6-37E0-11D4-97E4-0010A4ECA65E}
	VersionMin	2.00.0000
	VersionMax	
	Language	
	Attributes	2
	Remove	
	ActionProperty	NEWPRODUCTS

In the following remarks, I have provided more detail about the entries shown in Table 20-4:

- Row 1 is the same as what you already entered to perform the major upgrades of either version 1.0 or version 1.2 of the MathPlot application.
- The UpgradeCode used in Row 2 is the value that is assigned to both version 2.0 and version 3.0 of the MathPlot install packages.
- Set the VersionMin column to 2.00.0000, but do not set the inclusive attribute in the Attributes column, which means that all versions greater than 2.00.0000 will be detected but not version 2.0 itself.

- In the Attributes column, set the msidbUpgradeAttributesOnlyDetect bit flag so that there will only be detection but not installation of the products found.
- In the ActionProperty column, identify the public property to contain the product codes of all products found on the target system that match the criteria specified in this row of the *Upgrade* table.

The next step is to enter this new ActionProperty property as part of the value for the SecureCustomProperties property. You do this by using the Property Manager in ISWI found in the Project view. We use a semicolon delimiter to separate the two action properties. Table 20-5 shows what this row in the *Property* table looks like.

TABLE 20-5 ENTRIES IN THE PROPERTY TABLE OF THE VERSION 2.0 PACKAGE

Row #	Column Name	Attribute Value
Row x	Property	SecureCustomProperties
	Value	OLDPRODUCTS;NEWPRODUCTS

The final step is to create the Error custom action that halts the installation of the earlier version over the later version. You cannot use the Custom Action Wizard in ISWI to do this, but you can do this directly in the IDE. After you right-click on the Custom Actions icon in the Actions/Scripts view, select the New option form the context menu instead of the Custom Action Wizard option. Then make the entries directly in the property screen, as shown in Figure 20-2.

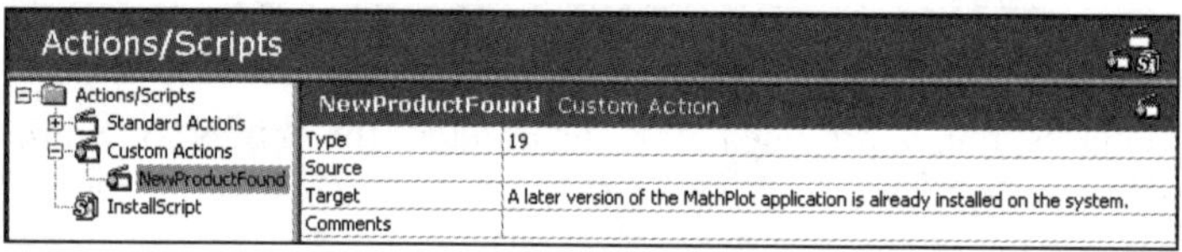

Figure 20-2: Creating the error custom action

As you can see from the figure, you enter **19** for the Type of the custom action, leave the Source field null, and enter the message to be displayed in the message box in the Target field.

Running the example

You find the projects for both version 2.0 and version 3.0 of the MathPlot application on the CD-ROM at the back of the book. To see how this works, just install version 3.0

and then try to install version 2.0. The installation of version 2.0 will be stopped immediately by the custom action.

Patching

Patching is a technique that is used to update a file with only those bits that are different. Using this technique is the best means of delivering upgrades of products in the smallest possible form. Patching can have great value when delivering product upgrades via the Internet. With the Windows Installer, a patch package contains an update or upgrade, which combines both the means to upgrade the files in a product as well as the means to upgrade the associated MSI database. You can only use a patch package to perform a small update, minor upgrade, or a major upgrade. The first subject we need to discuss is the structure of a patch package.

The structure of a patch package

A patch package is a COM structured storage file, but it does not contain a database such as a normal installation package. A Summary Information Stream comprises a patch package with at least one transform sub-storage and at least one cabinet file stream. A patch package has an .msp file extension and this extension is registered to the following command:

```
msiexec /p "%1"
```

However, double-clicking on an .msp file can only perform a major upgrade of a local installation. The small update and the minor upgrade need to be run from the command line with certain other parameters being set, which will be discussed in detail later in this chapter.

THE SUMMARY INFORMATION STREAM

The following is the Summary Information Stream for the patch package as a whole. Each transform sub-storage has its own Summary Information Stream, which is described in the following sub-section. Four properties need to be set, as listed below. For a description of the other properties that can be set, see Appendix B.

Revision Number property	A GUID that uniquely identifies the patch package. A list of patch code GUIDs follow this GUID, which designates the patches to be removed after this patch is applied. The patch codes for the patches to be removed are concatenated with no delimiter separating the GUIDs in the list.
Template property	A semicolon-delimited list of product codes that designate the products that are valid targets for the patch package.

Last Saved By property	A semicolon-delimited list of the transform sub-storages contained in the patch package. This list is given in the order in which these transforms are applied.
Keyword property	Contains a semicolon-delimited list of sources used for the patch.
Word Count property	Specifies the patch engine used to create the patch files. Windows Installer version 1.1 requires a value of 1. This value indicates that the Microsoft library of functions was used to create the file patches. The file MSPATCHC.DLL provides this library of functions that need to be used for creating patch packages. The functions found in MSPATCHC.DLL presently constitute the only mechanism for creating patch packages that is currently supported.

THE TRANSFORM SUB-STORAGE

The transforms included in a patch package are used to modify an application's database. As discussed in Chapter 15, a transform can add, delete, or modify information that is contained in an application's MSI package. For each database that is the target of the patch package, you have separate transform sub-storages. Both sub-storage contain two transforms. One transform is used to change the target database to the new version of the product. The second transform is used to add entries to the *Patch, PatchPackage, Media, InstallExecuteSequence,* and *Admin ExecuteSequence* tables. These entries provide instructions to the Windows Installer for performing file patching.

THE CABINET FILE STREAM

The cabinet file stream in a patch package contains the files or the parts of files that are required to update or upgrade an application. The cabinet file stream can contain three types of files, as listed below:

Patch files	Contain only that information required to change an older version of a file into a newer version of the same file. Modifying more than one file with a single patch file is possible.
New files	Not included in the original distribution of the application and as such, are not present on the machine.
Replacement files	Replace an older version of the same file. The most common use for including this type of file in a patch package is if the patch file is larger than the new version of the file.

Patch creation basics

Creating a patch package is a complex process, which you can only accomplish by using the API exported from the Microsoft supplied file PATCHWIZ.DLL. In this section, we discuss how to use this API to create a patch package. To use this API, we first need to create a patch creation properties file (.pcp). Using the API and a .pcp file, we work through an example of how to create a patch package.

THE PATCH CREATION PROPERTIES FILE

A patch creation properties file is a COM structured storage file that has the same format as an MSI database, except that it has a .pcp file extension. This database does not use any of the tables that are used in an MSI database, but instead it has its own database schema. This schema is shown in Figure 20-3.

You can use nine tables in a patch creation properties file, but only four of these tables are required. The tables identified with an asterisk in Figure 20-3 are the required tables. The other five tables are used to specify additional information for more the creation of complex types of patch packages. The File table shown in the schema is not part of the .pcp file. The table is shown because many of the tables reference either the *File* table in the target image or the *File* table in the upgraded image. A patch package is created as the difference between these two images of the product. We take a close look at the four required tables in the Patch Creation Properties file because these four tables are populated by the ISWI Patch Creation Wizard.

The API that uses the patch creation properties file is UiCreatePatchPackage with the only function exported from PATCHWIZ.DLL. The ISWI Patch Creation Wizard invokes this API after it creates the patch creation properties file. We can also create a patch package using the MSIMSP.EXE utility that is available with the MSI SDK. However, we need to first create the patch creation properties file using the Orca database-editing tool. Using the ISWI Patch Creation Wizard is much easier.

The creation of a basic patch package uses just the *Properties, ImageFamilies, TargetImages,* and *UpgradeImages* tables. The steps for creating a basic patch package are as follows:

1. Define the global properties to use in creating the patch package in the *Properties* table.
2. Define the product images to upgrade by the patch package in the *TargetImages* table.
3. Define the product images in the *UpgradedImages* table as they will appear after the application of the patch package.
4. Define a family of upgraded images in the *ImageFamilies* table.

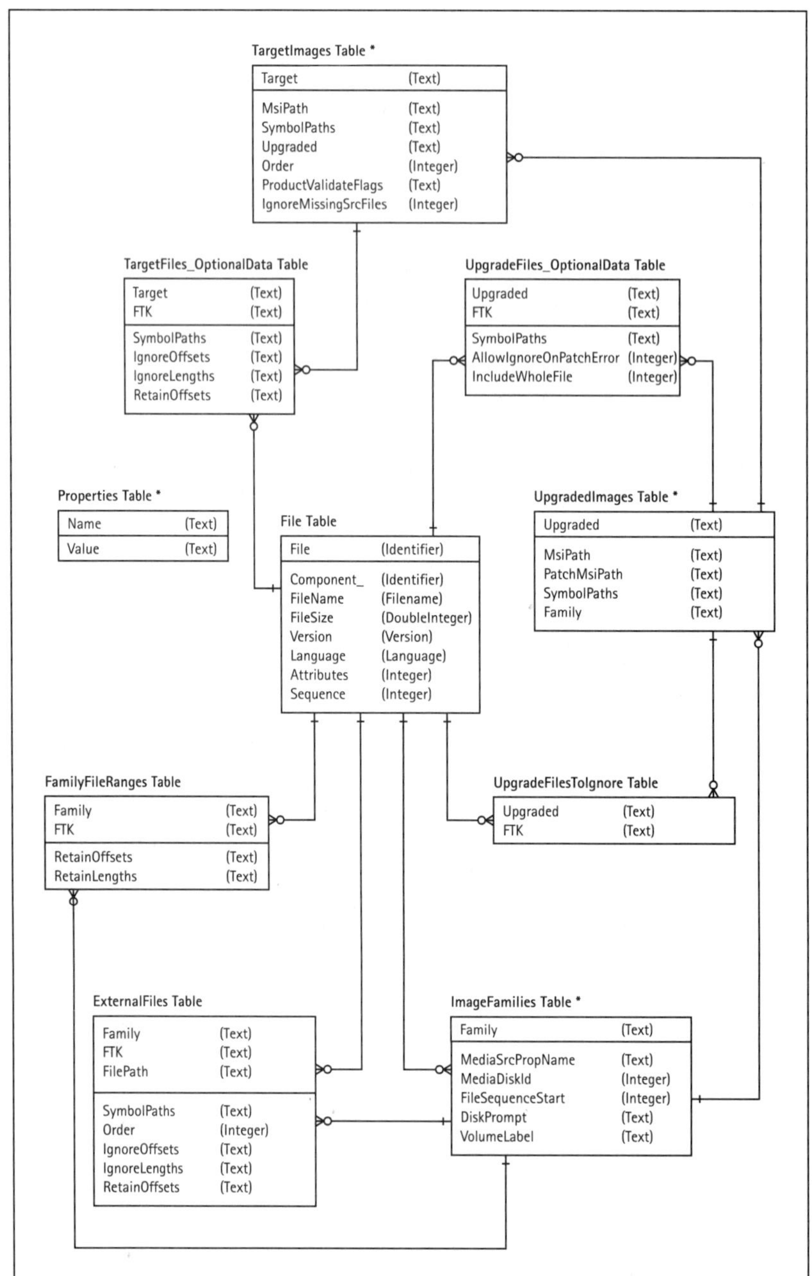

Figure 20-3: Database schema for a patch creation properties file

The remaining tables provide optional enhanced functionality so that they may be empty for simple patches. Frequently you need to treat specific files differently. Sometimes a file may need to be patched, which contains a range of bits that may contain unpredictable contents. (For example, past versions of Microsoft Office would stamp some user registration data into the executable.) This presents a problem when patching is determining if a current file on an end-user's machine matches the Target image as well as how to patch just the needed bits while retaining the user specific bits. In order to accommodate this need, fields were added to specify ranges of bits to ignore when identifying the file as well as ranges for bits that should never be overwritten.

The first table that we want to look at is the *Properties* table. Unlike the other tables, the *Properties* table contains a number of prescribed entries for which values need to be provided. However, these entries do not limit the addition of other rows to this table if rows are required for other purposes. We see how ISWI adds an additional row to this table. The *Properties* table has two columns with the first column the name of the property and the second column holding the value of the property. Table 20-6 shows the twelve required properties and gives a description of the purposes of these properties.

TABLE 20-6 DESCRIPTION OF THE PROPERTIES TABLE IN A PATCH CREATION PROPERTIES FILE

Name of Required Property	Purpose of Required Property
PatchGUID	A unique identifier for the patch package that is to be created from the patch creation properties file. This unique identifier is a GUID in the same form as the ProductCode property. This is a required property for every patch package that is created.
PatchOutputPath	The full path, including filename, of the patch package file that is to be generated. This information can pass directly to the UiCreatePatchPackage function. If the information passes, this property can be NULL. Otherwise this property is required.

Continued

TABLE 20-6 DESCRIPTION OF THE PROPERTIES TABLE IN A PATCH CREATION PROPERTIES FILE *(Continued)*

Name of Required Property	Purpose of Required Property
ListOfPatchGUIDsToReplace	A non-delimited list of PatchGUID identifiers that identifies all the patches that can be unregistered during the application of the new patch package. This identifier allows older patches whose changes are incorporated into this patch to be un-registered and no longer used. A typical use of this is a service pack that replaces several hotfixes. To un-register a patch package means to remove the information in the registry that associates these patches with a product and to remove the patch transforms from the list of transforms that are to be applied to the MSI database associated with the product. This property can be NULL.
ListOfTargetProductCodes	A semicolon-delimited list of ProductCode property values for the products that may receive the patch being created. If this list begins with an asterisk, the list of product codes is generated from the .msi files of the targets listed in the *TargetImages* table. Additional product codes can be entered after a leading asterisk, and they get appended to the list that replaces the asterisk. This property is required.
PatchSourceList	A source used to locate the .msp file for the patch in the event that the locally cached copy becomes unavailable. This value is added to the source list of the patch after it is applied to a product. This property can be NULL.
AllowProductCodeMismatches	Set to 1 if the ProductCode property may differ between the upgraded images listed in the *UpgradedImages* table and the target images listed in the *TargetImages* table. If the value of this property is NULL or 0, a patch package will not include any of the products where there is a difference in the ProductCode properties.

Name of Required Property	Purpose of Required Property
AllowProductCodeMismatches *(continued)*	If we are creating a patch that will perform a major upgrade, this property needs to be set to 1.
AllowProductVersionMajorMismatches	Set to 1 if the major version field of the ProductVersion property may differ between the upgraded images listed in the *Upgraded Images* table and the target images listed in the *TargetImages* table. If the value of this property is NULL or 0, a patch package will not include any of the products where there is a difference in the major version field of the ProductVersion properties. If we are creating a patch that will perform a major upgrade, then this property needs to be set to 1.
ApiPatchingOptionFlags	A 32-bit integer in hex format that represents the combination of patch option flags to use when creating a binary file patch. The default for this property is to automatically select the best patching approach and to fail the creation of the binary patch if the resulting file is larger than compressing the new file itself. This approach is the slowest of all the creation options. You can find a complete list of the patch symbol usage flags in the PATCHAPI.H file in the MSI SDK. All these flags start with the sub-string PATCH_OPTION_.
ApiPatchingSymbolFlags	A 32-bit integer in hex format that represents the combination of patch symbol usage flags to use when creating a binary file patch. The default value for this property is zero. A complete list of the patch symbol usage flags can be found in the PATCHAPI.H file in the MSI SDK. All these flags start with the sub-string PATCH_SYMBOL_.

Continued

TABLE 20-6 DESCRIPTION OF THE PROPERTIES TABLE IN A PATCH CREATION PROPERTIES FILE *(Continued)*

Name of Required Property	Purpose of Required Property
ApiPatchingSymbolFlags *(continued)*	If Microsoft Visual C++ is on the machine creating the patch and if symbol files are provided, the resulting binary patch may be smaller. A working binary patch will still be created if no symbol files are provided or if the symbol files provided to the patch creation dll are unable to be used (only symbol files created with Microsoft Visual C++ will be recognized). Subdirectories of symbol file folders are not traversed when searching for symbol files.
MsiFileToUseToCreatePatchTables	The full path to a template .msi file from which to export the Patch table and PatchPackage table. This property is optional.
DontRemoveTempFolderWhenFinished	Set to 1 if the temporary folder containing the transforms, the byte-level patches, and the entire new files are not being removed after creating the patch package. These files constitute the contents of the .msp file before they are embedded into the patch package. This property can be useful for debugging patches. Setting this property to 0 or NULL forces the temporary folder to be removed after the creation of the patch package.
IncludeWholeFilesOnly	Set to 1 if the files being changed are to be included in their entirety when creating the patch package instead of creating a binary file patch. The patch packages will be larger in size, but the creation of the patch package will be faster. Setting this property to 0 or NULL means that a binary file patch will be created.

The next table that we look at is the *ImageFamilies* table. The *ImageFamilies* table provides information to be added to the Media table during the patching process. The family name is prefixed with PCW_CAB_ to generate the cabinet's stream name when embedded into the patch package file. The installer embeds a cabinet stream in the Windows Installer patch file for each family in the table. The cabinet contains the binary patches and new files required to update a target image into an upgraded image of the product.

A *family* is a group of related Upgraded Images that share one or more common files. Each Upgraded Image must belong to one and only one Family; a Family contains one or more Upgraded Images. Each Family has its own cabinet file in the Windows Installer patch file. This cabinet file contains the binary patches and new files necessary to update the file differences between Target and Upgraded Images.

A family cabinet file, shared among several upgraded images, does not replicate the binary patches and new files for common files. Any foreign key into the File table (FTK) shared between two or more upgraded images within a family must represent the same common file; these common files must be identical between all the upgraded images in a family. A common file must share the same FTK in each upgraded image to contribute to a smaller cabinet file. Two or more unrelated upgraded images can be associated in one family, but the Windows Installer patch will not be any smaller and there are disadvantages. You can create a Windows Installer patch that patches the target images of more than one family. But for download efficiency, avoid this patch and create separate patch packages for each family.

Table 20-7 describes the purpose of the six columns that comprise *ImageFamilies* table.

TABLE 20-7 THE ATTRIBUTES OF THE IMAGEFAMILIES TABLE IN A PATCH CREATION PROPERTIES FILE

Column Name	Data Type	Key	Description
Family	Text	Y	The value entered in this field is an identifier for a group of related product images that have been updated to the most recent version of the product. This identifier is limited to a total of eight alphanumeric characters or underscores.
MediaSrcPropName	Text		This property is entered into the Source column of the *Media* table. This property identifies the location of the cabinet file containing the patch files or any new files added by the patch. A different source needs to be specified for these files, because the source of the patch package can be stored separately from the product's source. The patch package transform adds this property to the *Media* table.

Continued

TABLE 20-7 THE ATTRIBUTES OF THE IMAGEFAMILIES TABLE IN A PATCH CREATION PROPERTIES FILE *(Continued)*

Column Name	Data Type	Key	Description
MediaDiskId	Integer		The Windows Installer enters this value into the DiskId field of the Media table record created after the patch package is applied. This value must be greater than any current DiskID in any of the target MSI databases, including previous patches
FileSequenceStart	Integer		This field is the sequence number for the starting file. This same file sequence number must not exist in two patches for the same product. To ensure this, the value in this field must be greater than all sequence numbers used in previous patches or in the original installation package. The greatest sequence number in a patch can be determined by adding the total number of entries in the patch cabinet file to the FileSequenceStart number for that patch.
DiskPrompt	Text		The Windows Installer enters the value in this column into the DiskPrompt field of the *Media* table record crated after the patch package is applied.
VolumeLabel	Text		The Windows Installer enters the value of this attribute into the VolumeLabel field of the *Media* table record created after the patch package is applied.

The next table that we look at is the *UpgradedImages* table. The *UpgradedImages* table provides information specific to the upgraded image of the product to which the targets will be patched. The upgraded image needs to be an administrative image of the latest version of the product because patching does not replace existing versioned files with lower versions. The upgraded image can also be an uncompressed build of the upgraded image as created by the ISWI Release Wizard. Table 20-8 describes the purpose of the five columns that comprise this table.

TABLE 20-8 THE ATTRIBUTES OF THE UPGRADEDIMAGES TABLE IN A PATCH CREATION PROPERTIES FILE

Column Name	Data Type	Key	Description
Upgraded	Text	Y	An arbitrary identifier to connect the target images with an upgraded image of that product.
MsiPath	Text		Specifies the path to the installation database at the root of the upgraded image. This path includes the name of the MSI database. This field is required.
PatchMsiPath	Text		Points to another copy of the upgraded installation database that contains additional authoring specific to the patch installation process; an example may be additional dialogs or custom actions conditioned on the PATCH property. This filed is optional.
SymbolPaths	Text		A semicolon-delimited list of folders that are searched for Visual C++ symbol files that can be used to optimize the generation of the binary patch. Visual C++ must be installed on the computer generating the patch and used to create the symbol files. This field is optional.
Family	Text		A foreign key into the *ImageFamilies* table. An upgraded image can only belong to one image family.

The next table that we look at is the *TargetImages* table. This table provides information for target images similar to the information provided by the *Upgraded Images* table for the upgrade images of the product. Table 20-9 describes the purpose of the seven columns that comprise this table.

Table 20-9 THE ATTRIBUTES OF THE TARGETIMAGES TABLE IN A PATCH CREATION PROPERTIES FILE

Column Name	Data Type	Key	Description
Target	Text	Y	An identifier for a target image. The patch package updates the target image specified in this column to the upgraded image specified in the Upgraded column. You can have one or more target images for each upgraded image. As with the upgraded image, the target image must be a fully uncompressed administrative image of the product or an uncompressed build created by the ISWI Release Wizard. The value in this field is used with the value in the Upgraded field to generate the names of the transforms that the installer adds to the patch package.
MsiPath	Text		Specifies the path to the installation database at the root of the target image. This path includes the name of the MSI database. This field is required.
SymbolPaths	Text		A semicolon-delimited list of folders that are to be searched for Visual C++ symbol files that can be used to optimize the generation of the binary patch. Visual C++ must be installed on the computer generating the patch and used to create the symbol files. This field is optional.
Upgraded	Text		A foreign key into the *UpgradedImages* table.
Order	Integer		Specifies the relative order of the target image, which is commonly from the oldest to the newest image. Because multiple targets can be patched to an upgraded image, the Order field provides a means to sequence the transforms in the patch transforms list.

Column Name	Data Type	Key	Description
ProductValidateFlags	Text		Used to specify product checking to avoid applying irrelevant transforms to a target image. The flags used here are the same validation flags that are used to create the Summary Information Stream in a transform. These flags force validation of the target database before the transform is applied. Chapter 18 covers this topic in detail.
IgnoreMissingSrcFiles	Integer		If this field is set to 1, then the Windows Installer ignores the files that are missing from the target image and leaves the files unchanged during patching. This field enables patches to be made without requiring the entire administrative image; only the changed files of the product and the .msi file are required. This may reduce the time required to generate the patch.

We have taken a very detailed look at the four tables that make up every patch creation package file because this information is important in the proper use of the ISWI Patch Creation Wizard. Before we leave this section, we want to take a brief look at the other five tables that are used for advanced patching implementations.

In order to create the smallest patch packages as possible, make a build using the Release Wizard to optimize the build using the option provided in the Media Type & Patch Optimization panel. This optimization makes sure that the same files in two MSI packages use the same *File* table keys (FTK). When creating a patch package, two files that have the same FTK are assumed to be the same file and those files that do not have the same FTK are assumed to be different files.

THE UPGRADEDFILES_OPTIONALDATA TABLE The UpgradedFiles_OptionalData table provides information specific to individual files of an Upgraded Image. If the symbol files for a file are not in the image's SymbolPaths, you can use the SymbolPaths field to add the specific path. (See the glossary for more information on symbol files). If you encounter a file that is cannot be patched, you can use the AllowIgnoreOnPatchError field to indicate that the file patch is non-vital (for example, a readme file); this field allows patching to continue without failing and halting. If you want to include the whole file instead of creating a binary patch, the IncludeWholeFile field can be set to a non-zero value.

THE FAMILYFILERANGES TABLE The FamilyFileRanges table provides information specific to individual files of an Upgraded Image that have ranges that should never be overwritten. The offsets and sizes of these ranges to avoid are specified in the RetainOffsets and RetainLengths fields respectively.

THE TARGETFILES_OPTIONALDATA TABLE The TargetFiles_OptionalData table provides information specific to individual files of a Target Image. If the symbol files for a file are not in the image's SymbolPaths, you can use the SymbolPaths field to add the specific path. (See the glossary for more information on symbol files.) If the UpgradedFiles_OptionalData specifies file ranges to retain, the RetainOffsets field specifies the offsets for those ranges in the Target file; the UpgradedFiles_OptionalData table derives lengths. If ranges need be ignored only for determining the signature of a file, use the IgnoreOffsets and IgnoreLengths fields; the file binary patch may still overwrite these ranges. Note: bound files are automatically unbound before determining their signature so that the binding data does not need to be specifically excluded.

THE EXTERNALFILES TABLE The ExternalFiles table provides information just as the TargetFiles_OptionalData but for files that are not part of a Target Image. Files that need this capability are those that are part of the product but may be encountered because they may have been updated by another product or process. The FilePath field locates the file, and in the event that you have multiple external files of the same FTK value, the Order field provide sequencing information. The other fields are similar to those in the TargetFiles_OptionalData table.

THE UPGRADEDFILESTOIGNORE TABLE In some instances, you may not want to update some of the changed files of the product and want to keep them in the Upgraded Image. You can do this by using the UpgradedFilesToIgnore table. Files that are only part of an administrative image can cause an unnecessary increase in size in patch packages targeted for client machines. If you exclude these files with the UpgradedFilesToIgnore table, the administrator should be instructed in how to update these files separately.

Applying a patch package

Use a patch package to perform all three types of upgrades and apply these upgrades to either locally installed images of a product or administrative images of a product. One of the main reasons that an administrative installation unpacks all compressed files is to allow it to be upgraded through the use of a patch package. In the following subsections, we look at how to apply a patch package to both a locally installed product and to an administrative image of the product.

THE SMALL UPDATE OR MINOR UPGRADE OF A LOCALLY INSTALLED IMAGE

The application of a patch package to the local installation of a product is done from the command line or by using one of the programmatic approaches that are available. The command line for applying a patch package looks very similar to the one used to do a reinstallation of the product. The general syntax of this command line is as follows:

```
msiexec /p[path to .msp file] REINSTALL=[comma delimited feature
                                   list] REINSTALLMODE=omus
```

Note that you do not have to identify the product to which this patch is being applied, because this information is contained in the Summary Information stream of the .msp file. The application of the patch package does not permanently change the database in the cached MSI package. The changes to the database required by the patch package are made only in memory and are applied each time the product installation is run in maintenance mode or if the product is uninstalled. These database changes are implemented by the transforms that comprise the patch package.

When a patch is applied a number of registry entries are made. For installations performed for the current user entries are made under the following keys:

```
HKCU\SOFTWARE\Microsoft\Installer\Products\{ProductCode}\Patches
```

and

```
HKCU\SOFTWARE\Microsoft\Installer\Patches\{PatchGUID}\SourceList
```

Under the first key shown above is a value name of patches with the value data being a REG_MULTI_SZ list of patches that are associated with the product. For each patch listed there is a value name of the patch code with the value data being semicolon delimited list of transforms that are applied by the patch. Under the second key shown above is provided the information related to the source locations for the patch packages. This information is provided in the same fashion as is provided for the sources each product. Installations performed on a per-machine basis are written to the following two keys with the same value names and value data as described above for the per-user installs.

```
HKLM\SOFTWARE\Classes\Installer\Products\{ProductCode}\Patches
```

and

```
HKCU\SOFTWARE\Classes\Installer\Patches\{PatchGUID}\SourceList
```

For all installations, regardless of whether they are per-user or per-machine, entries are made under the following registry key:

```
HKLM\SOFTWARE\Microsoft\Windows\CurrentVersion\Installer\Patches
\{PatchGUID}\
```

The value name for each PatchGUID is LocalPackage and the value data associated with this value name is the path to the cached .msp file. All ProductCode and PatchGUID keys are in a packed format.

Once again you need to be aware that this book is showing the registry entries that are made with versions 1.2 or lower of the Windows Installer. In future versions of the Windows Installer the use of the registry will be different. The purpose of showing you these registry entries is to give you an idea of the basis for the rules that have been setup by Microsoft. You should not depend on these registry entries being there in the future.

The patch package patches the application files that are already installed on the target system. When dealing with the application files, the patch package ignores the original source for the application. If any components exist that we identified in the original installation to run-from-source, these components are changed in the database so that they are installed locally during the application of the patch package. After these components are installed locally, the files affected by the small update or minor upgrade are modified by the patch package. A side effect of this patch is that you cannot reinstall any of these components to run-from-source as long as the patch package is on the system.

THE MAJOR UPGRADE OF A LOCALLY INSTALLED IMAGE

Performing a major upgrade using a patch package is easier than doing a small update or a minor upgrade because we do not have to do it from the command line. All we have to do is double-click the patch package, and the installation is upgraded. We can also run the following command line:

```
msiexec /p [path to .msp file]
```

When doing a major upgrade using a patch package, we also need to author the upgraded image to uninstall the old application. Do this in the same fashion as explained in the previous section on performing upgrades using the *Upgrade* table.

PATCHING AN ADMINISTRATIVE IMAGE

You can apply a patch package to an administrative installation by virtue of the fact that this type of installation has unpacked all compressed application source files. The application of a patch package to an administrative image is performed in the same fashion for all three types of upgrades. In fact, one of the purposes of creating administrative installations in this fashion is to specifically enable the application of a patch package to the product. After an administrative installation is updated through a patch package, the propagation to the end user of the revised application is through the installation or reinstallation of the product from the patched administrative image. In other words, getting an updated application on the user's machine through the patching of an administrative image is a two-step process. First, you apply the patch to the administrative image, and then the user comes to where this image is located and installs the updated product.

The syntax for the command line required to apply a patch package to an administrative installation is as follows:

```
msiexec /a [path to the administrative image .msi file] /p [path to
                                                        the .msp file]
```

After an administrative image is created, sometimes the SHORTFILENAMES property will need to be set to the value of 1. Do this if the network operating system does not support long file names. If this is the case, then this property also needs to be set when applying the patch package to the administrative image.

The reinstallation of the patched administrative image, explained in the previous section, is performed through either a complete or partial reinstallation. Of course, for any user that has not already installed the application, a normal installation is all that is required because the patching of an administrative installation permanently changes the msi database and source files. This reinstallation is different from the patching of a local installation where the transforms that comprise the patch package get applied every time that a maintenance operation is performed for the application.

How transforms affect patching

If you're installing a patch and one or more customization transforms to an application, you usually install the patch first, followed by the customization transforms. By design, the patch is not broken by the subsequent installation of the customization transforms. However, installing the transforms first, followed by the patch, may break the customization.

For example, a break in the customization occurs if a patch is used to update a product from version 1 to version 2 and a customization transform that works for version 1 does not work for version 2. In this case, the version update patch cannot be applied to a customized product without first uninstalling and then reinstalling the original product.

Note that version validation used by the Microsoft Office Customization Wizard permits customizations to be used across changes in the product version. The developer is responsible for authoring their customization transforms to be compatible across all versions if this is necessary for the product.

Using the ISWI Patch Creation Wizard

We can create a patch creation properties file using the Orca database-editing tool, and then create the patch package using the MSIMSP.EXE utility. This, however, is a lot of work, so instead, we are going to use the ISWI Patch Creation Wizard to create the patch packages that we need. As an example of how to use this wizard, we will create a patch package that will upgrade either version 1.0 or version 1.2 of the MathPlot application.

We access the wizard from the Tools pulldown menu by selecting the Create Patch... option. You do not need to have an open ISWI project to create a patch package. After we first launch the Patch Creation Wizard, we get the welcome panel shown in Figure 20-4.

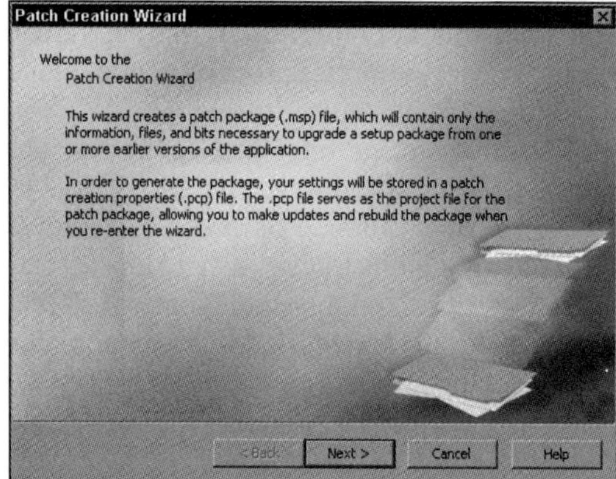

Figure 20-4: The welcome panel of the ISWI Patch Creation Wizard

Click next to get a panel that asks us either to name the patch creation properties file that we want to create or to select an existing file. We will browse to a folder where we want the patch created and provide a name for the patch creation properties file as shown in Figure 20-5.

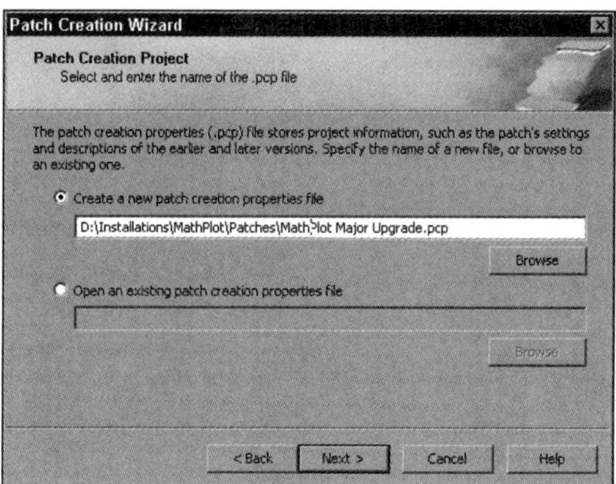

Figure 20-5: Naming the patch creation properties file

After naming the patch creation properties file, click next to get a panel where we are asked to name the target images to which the upgrade patch will be applied. The first action that we need to take is to create identifiers for the target images. We do this by right-clicking on the Previous Version icon and selecting the Add Package option. We need to create two identifiers here because we are targeting two versions of the MathPlot application to be handled by this one upgrade. After creating the two identifiers, click on one of the identifiers, and you get a screen shown in Figure 20-6.

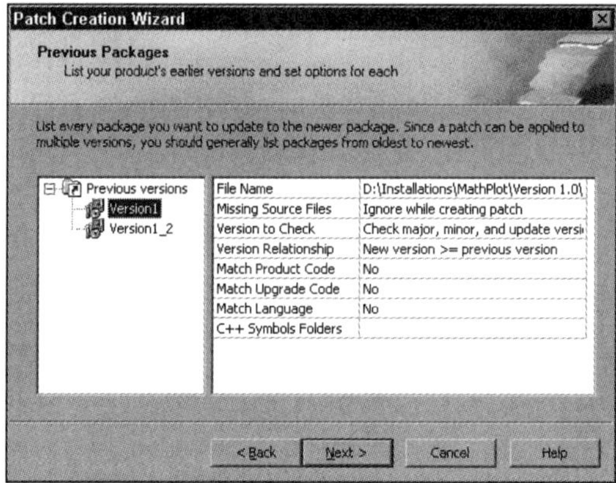

Figure 20-6: Describing the target images to upgrade

Each of the identifiers that we create will be inserted into the Target column of the *TargetImages* table in the patch creation properties file that we are authoring. Because we are creating two identifiers, two rows will be in the *TargetImages* table.

Each of these identifiers has a set of attributes that we need to enter. Except for the naming of the target MSI package, we are given a set of default attributes that we may need to change depending on the circumstances. The attributes that we set in this panel of the wizard are used to populate the columns of the *TargetImages* table. Because we are creating a major upgrade patch package, some changes need to be made. Table 20-10 shows the entries that need to be made in the right hand panel for each of the two identifiers.

TABLE 20-10 ATTRIBUTES FOR TARGET IMAGES OF THE MATHPLOT APPLICATION

Attribute	Value	Discussion
File Name	[path to MSI package]	For the Version1 identifier, we supply the complete path, including the file name, to the MSI package for version 1.0 of the MathPlot application. This MSI package needs to be at the root of the source files that comprise this version of the MathPlot application. For the Verson1_2 identifier, we supply the same information, which is the path to the version 1.2 MSI package. This information populates the MsiPath column of the *TargetImages* table.
Missing Source Files	Ignore while creating patch	The default setting for this attribute is set with the IgnoreMissingSrcFiles column of the TargetImages table to '1'. This tells the Patch Creation Wizard to ignore any missing source files in the target images.
Version to Check	Check major, minor, and update versions	The default value for this attribute is set and it specifies that all three fields of the ProductVersion property will be checked when the patch package transforms are applied to the target database. This information is used along with the next four attributes to set the ProductValidateFlags column in the *TargetImages* table.

Attribute	Value	Discussion
Version Relationship	New version >= previous version	The default value for this attribute is set and it specifies how the version checking is to be done. This information is used along with the previous attribute and the next three attributes to set the ProductValidate Flags column in the *TargetImages* table.
Match Product Code	No	The default value for this attribute is Yes. We need to change this to No because we are performing a major upgrade in this example. Setting this to No means that the patch package transforms will still be applied, even when the ProductCode property of the target image is different than the ProductCode property in the transforms. This information is used along with the previous two attributes and the next two attributes to set the ProductValidateFlags column in the *TargetImages* table.
Match Upgrade Code	No	The default value for this attribute is Yes. We need to change this to No because we are performing a major upgrade in this example. Setting this to No means that the patch package transforms will still be applied even when the UpgradeCode property of the target image is different than the UpgradeCode property in the transforms. This information is used along with the previous three attributes and the next attribute to set the Product ValidateFlags column in the *Target Images* table.

Continued

TABLE 20-10 ATTRIBUTES FOR TARGET IMAGES OF THE MATHPLOT APPLICATION *(Continued)*

Attribute	Value	Discussion
Match Language	No	No is the default value for this attribute. The No value means that the patch package transforms will still be applied even when the ProductLanguage property of the target image is different than the ProductLanguage property in the transforms. This information is used along with the previous four attributes to set the ProductValidateFlags column in the *TargetImages* table.
C++ Symbols Folders		This value is left NULL because we are not trying to use the Visual C++ symbol files to make the binary file patches smaller. If we enter a path here, this information would be used to populate the SymbolPaths column of the *TargetImages* table.

The order column of the *TargetImages* table is populated by the order in which the identifiers are created in the lefthand screen of the Previous Packages wizard panel. We create these identifiers in an older to newer sequence as recommended. The Upgraded column in the *TargetImages* table is automatically filled in by the Patch Creation Wizard to be the same as the one row that will be created in the *UpgradedImages* table.

After we click the Next button in the Previous Packages panel, we get the Newer Package wizard panel. In this panel, we are asked to provide the complete path to the MSI package for the upgraded image. This upgraded image is the MSI package and source files of Version 2.0 of the MathPlot application. The path to the MSI package for the upgraded image is used to populate the MsiPath column of the *UpgradedImages* table. This panel of the Patch Creation Wizard is shown in Figure 20-7.

Also in this panel, we are asked to identify the Visual C++ symbol file folders for the upgraded image of the MathPlot application. Because we are not using symbol files, we leave this edit filed blank. If we had identified a path to a folder holding symbol files, this information would be used to populate the SymbolPaths column of the *UpgradedImages* table in the patch creation properties file.

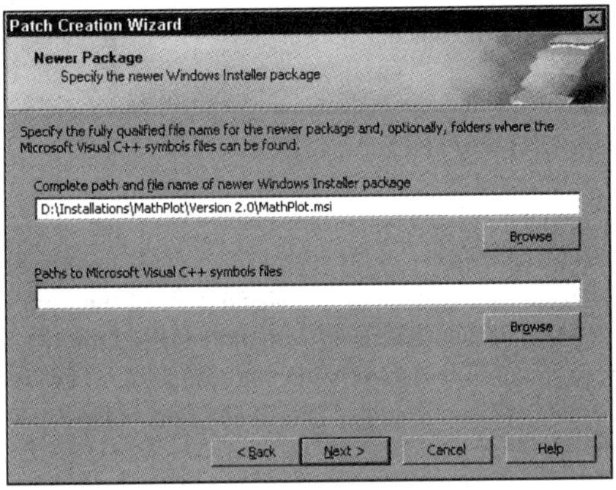

Figure 20-7: Identifying the upgraded image

We click the Next button to get to the next panel of the wizard, which is the Patch Package Identity panel. In this panel, we are asked to identify the name of the patch package (.msp file) being created. We are provided with a default name that is in the same location as the .pcp file and uses the same name as this file except that the extension is .msp instead of .pcp. For our purposes we can use the default name and path that is provided us. We also have the opportunity to specify a GUID to be used to uniquely identify the patch package that will be created by the wizard. We can take the value that is offered to us. This panel is shown in Figure 20-8.

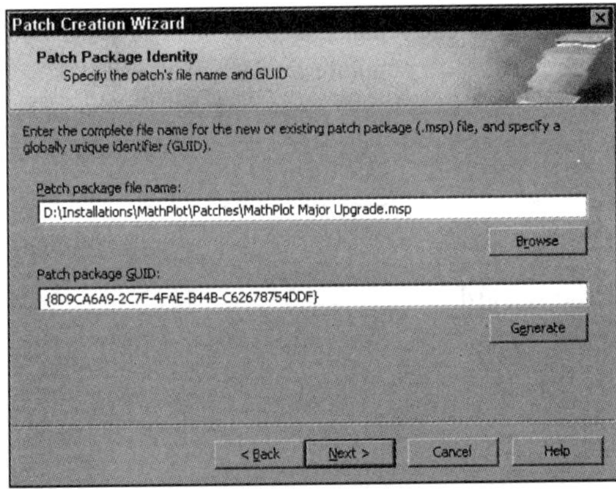

Figure 20-8: Identifying the patch package to create

The information as to the name and location of the patch package file being created by the wizard is used to populate the PatchOutputPath column of the *Properties* table. Populating the PatchGUID column of the *Properties* table is the patch package GUID value.

The next panel in the wizard is the Previous Patches panel. In this panel, you find three edit fields that are described in Table 20-11.

TABLE 20-11 THE ENTRIES IN THE PREVIOUS PATCHES PANEL

Edit Field Name	Value	Description
Disk ID	2	2 is a value that written to the *Media* table of the target images MSI database after it is upgraded using the patch package. The default value here is based on being one greater than the largest DiskID attribute value found in any of the identified target image MSI databases. The DiskID column of the *Media* table needs to be unique because it is the primary key for that table.
File sequence start	9	The default number here is a value that is larger than any file sequence number in either of the target image MSI databases. It is also one larger than the last file sequence number in the upgraded image MSI database, because this value has to be greater than any file sequence number for any previous patches that may have been applied, as well as greater than the original installation database.
List of patch GUIDs to replace		This edit field enables us to specify the PatchGUID properties of any patches that should be unregistered after the current patch package is applied. The data we enter here is used to populate the ListOfPatchGUIDsToReplace property in the *Properties* table. We have nothing to enter in this edit box.

Shown in Figure 20-9 is the panel in the wizard.

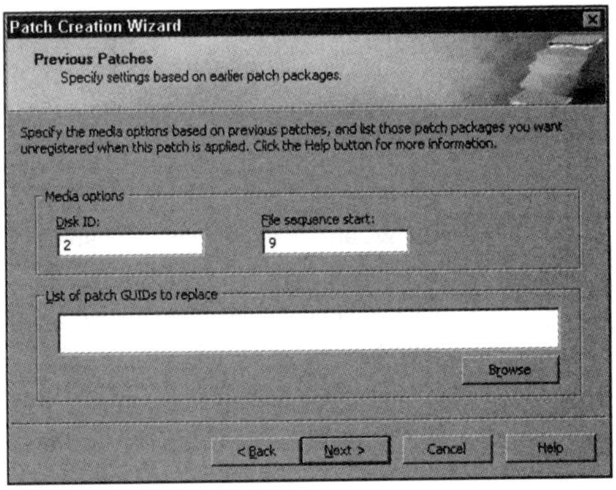

Figure 20-9: The Previous Patches wizard panel

The next panel in the Patch Creation Wizard is the Patch Creation Settings dialog. In this dialog, we select some additional settings that control how we create the patch package. This panel is shown in Figure 20-10.

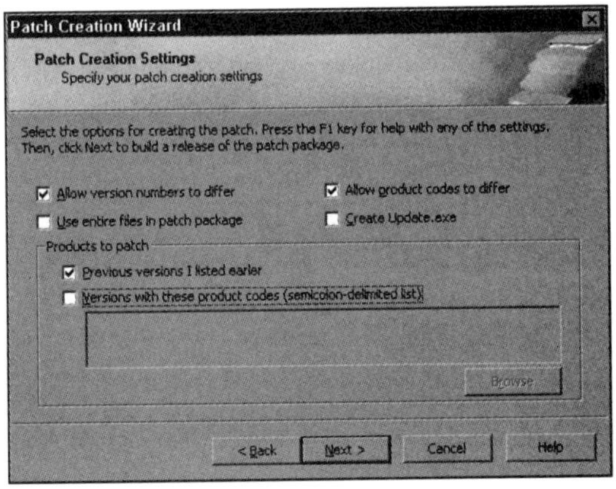

Figure 20-10: The patch creation settings panel

In this panel, you find six check boxes with the purpose of each check boxes described in Table 20-12.

Table 20-12 SELECTING THE PATCH CREATION SETTINGS

Check Box Title	State	Description
Allow version numbers to differ	Checked	Checking this box controls whether the wizard actually creates a patch package or not. If this box were not checked and we tried to create a patch package for the situation where the target and the upgrade images had differences in the major version of the products, then the patch package would not get created. This check box only governs the creation of a patch package and not the application of the patch package. If this control is checked, the AllowProductVersion MajorMismatches property of the *Properties* table will be set to 1.
Use entire files in patch package	Unchecked	This check box governs whether a patch package will include binary file patches or just whole files that have to be replaced. Because we want to have binary file patches to give us a smaller patch package, we leave this box unchecked. If this control is checked, the IncludeWholeFilesOnly property of the *Properties* table is set to 1.
Allow product codes to differ	Checked	Checking this box controls whether the wizard will actually create a patch package or not. If this box were not checked and we tried to create a patch package for the situation where the target and the upgrade images had differences in the values for the ProductCode property, the patch package would not get created. This check box only governs the creation of a patch package and not the application of the patch package. If this control is checked, the Allow ProductCodeMismatches property of the *Properties* table will be set to 1.

Check Box Title	State	Description
Create Update.exe	Unchecked	This check box defines whether the Patch Creation Wizard creates a file called Update.exe where the patch package is embedded inside this file. This file is a means of delivering a patch package and allowing the user just to double-click this file in Windows Explorer. This has nothing to do with how the patch is created. Because we are doing major upgrade, we leave this control unchecked.
Previous versions I listed earlier	Checked	Leaving this box checked means that the patch package will be created using the target images that have already been identified in the *TargetImages* table through the Previous Packages panel. If this control is checked, the ListOfTargetProduct Codes property in the *Properties* table will begin with an asterisk.
Versions with these product codes (semicolon-delimited list)	Unchecked	If this control is checked, we can enter additional product codes that will get appended to the list of product codes identified in the *TargetImages* table. We leave this box unchecked because we do not have any additional products that need to be updated with this patch package.

After we click the Next button, we start the creation of the patch package and see a wizard panel that provides the progress of this creation, which is shown in Figure 20-11.

After the creation of the patch package is complete, we get the final panel in the wizard. This wizard displays the results of the creation process. We can scroll down in this panel and see if any errors were produced during the creation of this patch package. This final panel in the wizard is shown in Figure 20-12.

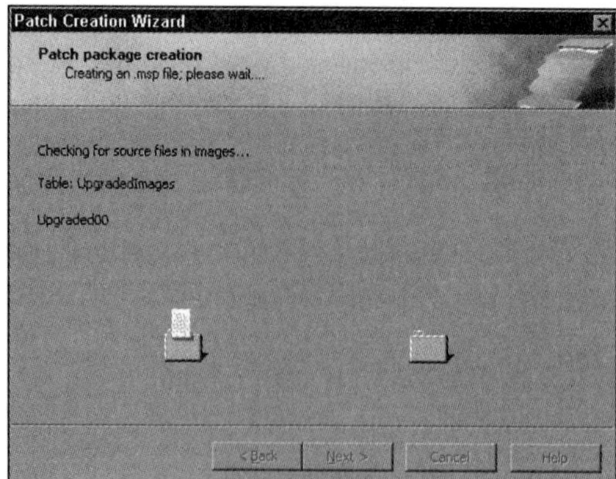

Figure 20-11: The Patch Creation progress panel

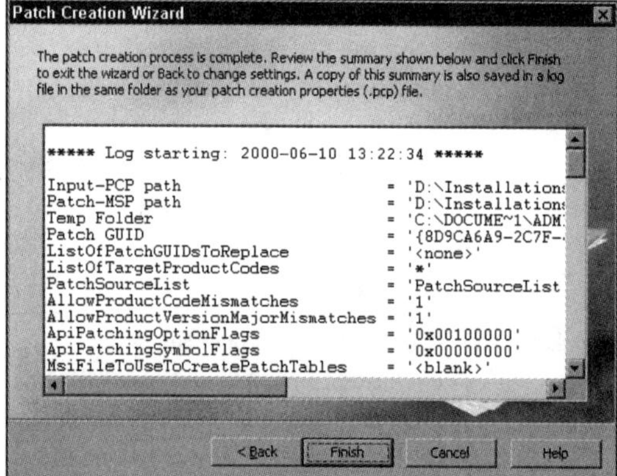

Figure 20-12: The final Patch Creation Wizard panel

Now that we created our patch package that will perform a major upgrade on either version 1.0 or version 1.2 of the MathPlot application, we can run the upgrade just by double-clicking on the .msp file in Windows Explorer. But before we do that, we need to make sure that we authored into version 2.0 a row in the *Upgrade* table that will handle the uninstallation of either of the earlier versions. Unless this is in the version 2.0 package, the old version will be upgraded, but it will not be removed from the system.

On the CD-ROM at the back of the book, you find both a major upgrade patch package and a minor upgrade patch package. The major upgrade is from versions 1.0 and 1.2 to version 2.0 of the MathPlot application, and the minor upgrade is form version 1.0 to version 1.2 of the MathPlot application. If you want to look at the .pcp files that are created for these patch packages, you can open them by using the Orca database editing tool and exporting to tab-delimited text files. These files can be imported into an Excel spreadsheet for formatting and printing.

The Handling of Operating System Upgrades

One feature a product needs is to handle the upgrade of an operating system. The most common scenario is to have a product installed on Windows 98 and then have the operating system upgraded to Windows 2000. If the product needs to have different components installed because of the change in the OS, the product needs to go through an upgrade process by being reinstalled. The purpose of the reinstallation is to switch out those components that only run on Windows 98 with those components that run on Windows 2000.

Under normal circumstances, performing this reinstallation does not cause a reevaluation of the conditions on the components that were already installed on Windows 98. To make this reevaluation take place during the reinstallation, we need to set a certain property on the components that need to be changed out. This property, called the Reevaluate Condition property, is in the property sheet for each component. This property sheet is accessed by going to the Setup Design view in ISWI and clicking a component name. For the properties that are OS dependent, we want to set this property to Yes.

A good example where you want to do this is with the MathPlot application. The PlotDLL_A and the PlotDLL_W components need to be changed out if the OS is ever upgraded. We already have these components conditioned based on the version of the operating system. The PlotDLL_A component only gets installed if the application is installed on a Windows 9.x machine, and the PlotDLL_W component only gets installed if the application gets installed on a Windows NT/2000 machine. For each of these components the Reevaluate Condition property for these two components has been set to yes in the install packages provided on the CD-ROM at the back of the book.

Summary

In this chapter, we see a number of methods that can be used to upgrade the installation of a product. You can accomplish a small update and a minor upgrade by reinstallation or through the use of a patch package. A major upgrade can be performed using the *Upgrade* table or by using a patch package. We also looked at using the *Upgrade* table to prevent a lower version from installing over a later version of a product. The creation on a patch package is investigated in detail by going through all the tables that comprise a patch creation properties file. The ISWI Patch Creation Wizard is examined during the creation of a patch package and all the panels in this wizard were related to the specific tables in the patch creation properties file that were being authored. Finally, we saw how to author an installation package that would handle the upgrading of the operating system from Windows 9x to Windows NT/2000.

Appendix A

MsiExec Command Line Options

THIS APPENDIX PROVIDES A comprehensive explanation of all the command line switches that you can use with MSIEXEC.EXE. Examples are provided for most of the common usages of the command line.

General

The command line options available for running the Windows Installer can be put into one of four different categories. These categories are listed as follows:

- Initiates one of the three top-level actions
- Modifies an already installed product
- Modifies one of the above two categories
- Sets the value of public properties
- Has miscellaneous functionality

All the command line options discussed here relate to the Windows Installer executable MSIEXEC.EXE. This executable runs all the installations while also returning error codes that are discussed at the end of this appendix. The format of the command line is as follows:

```
msiexec  /<switch>[optional modifiers] <parameters> [/<additional
switches>]
```

or

```
msiexec  [/<additional switches>]  /<switch>[optional modifiers]
<parameters>
```

The switches used are position independent, but you cannot separate a switch from its parameters. All switches are also case independent. When specifying the location of an MSI package or other file, you can provide the absolute path, just the file name if the name is in the current directory, or a relative path if the file is in a lower directory from where you are located. Using the parent directory notation (..) to identify a relative path to the file does not work.

Invoking the Top-Level Actions

Three top-level actions correspond to the three major components of functionality of the Windows Installer. These top-level actions are INSTALL, ADMIN, and ADVERTISE. The following three sections cover the command to invoke each of these top-level actions.

The INSTALL top-level action

To invoke the INSTALL top-level action, use the following command line:

```
msiexec /i <MSI package | ProductCode> [properties ...]
```

If the product is not installed or advertised, the only valid parameter that you can use is the name of the MSI package. If the product is advertised, you can use either the MSI package or the ProductCode property to run the installation. If using the ProductCode property, make sure that you include the curly braces on each end of the GUID, otherwise `msiexec.exe` will not recognize the parameter. With an advertised product using either the MSI package or the ProductCode, the installation runs you through the complete user interface. This guidance does not happen if you try to run an advertised product from the Start | Programs menu. In this case, only basic UI is displayed without providing any option for the user to interface with the user interface. If the product is already installed, using either parameter will put you into the maintenance mode where you have the option to Modify, Repair, or Remove the product.

Three modifying switches can be used with the /i switch, which are listed below and described in detail in a later section.

/l	This switch allows for the creation of a Windows Installer log file that can display all the actions that are being taken to install the product.
/q	This switch sets the user interface level to be used for the installation.
/m	This switch generates an SMS status .mif file.

The ADMIN top-level action

To invoke the ADMIN top-level action, use the following command line:

```
msiexec /a <MSI package> [properties...]
```

Using this command line places an administrative image of the product on a network drive. If the source files for the product are compressed, they will be uncompressed in this operation and placed in a tree as defined by the DefaultDir column of the *Directory* table. In the special case where a patch package is applied to an administrative image, this command line is also used in conjunction with the command parameters that identify the patch package. This command line is discussed in the section on invoking maintenance operations.

There are three modifying switches that can be used with the /a switch and they are listed below and described in detail in a later section.

/l This switch allows for the creation of a Windows Installer log file that can display all the actions that are being taken to install the product.

/q This switch sets the user interface level that is to be used for the installation.

/m This switch generates an SMS status .mif file.

The ADVERTISE top-level action

To invoke the ADVERTISE top-level action, use the following command line:

```
msiexec /j[u|m] <MSI package>
```

Running this command line advertises the product so that its icon appears on the Start | Programs menu, but no files are installed. On a pre-Windows 2000 operating system, this command line only works if Active Desktop is installed. Two optional parameters can be used to modify the /j switch, which are described as follows:

u This switch specifies that the advertised product is only available to the current user of the machine.

m This switch specifies that the advertised product is available to all the users of the machine.

If you do not use either of the optional switches, then the default action is make the advertised product available to all users of the machine. After this operation is complete, the product is installed the first time a user tries to access it from the Start | Programs menu. When advertising a product from the command line, you can additionally apply a list of transforms or specify a language ID. The switches to do this are described as follows:

/t Applies a list of transforms to the advertised package in the same fashion as setting the public TRANSFORM property on the command line when running the INSTALL top-level action. If you have to apply more than one transform, then you delimit the list of transform files with semicolons.

/g Using this switch sets the ProductLanguage value in the Property table to the ID specified.

Possible command lines that implement this functionality are as follows:

```
msiexec /j[u|m] <MSI package> /t transform.mst
msiexec /j[u|m] <MSI package> /g 1034
msiexec /j[u|m] <MSI package> /t transform.mst /g 1034
```

Three additional modifying switches can be used with the /j switch, which are listed below and described in detail in a later section.

/l This switch allows for the creation of a Windows Installer log file that displays all the actions being taken to install the product.

/q This switch sets the user interface level to use for the installation. This switch is only valid to choose between basic and no UI. Full and reduced UI are not available for advertise installs.

/m This switch generates an SMS status .mif file.

This option ignores properties that are passed on the command line.

Invoking Maintenance Operations

In this context, maintenance operations consist of repair, removal, or upgrading by using a patch package. If an installation package is authored with a maintenance mode capability, then re-running an installation of a product that is already installed and making the appropriate choice in the maintenance type dialog can also obtain both the repair and removal options. You also have the option to change the installed features, which you cannot do through the use of any special command line option.

Repairing a product

The command line for performing a repair operation on an installed product is as follows:

```
msiexec /f[p|o|e|d|c|a|u|m|s|v] <MSI package | ProductCode>
```

As with the /i switch described in the previous section, either the package name or the product code is specified to indicate which product the repair operation is to be performed. As can be seen from the previous command line, ten optional modifiers can be used with the /f switch. Unlike the optional modifiers for the advertisement case, these modifiers are not mutually exclusive. If none of these are specified, then the default used is pecms. Table A-1 provides a functional description of each of these modifiers.

TABLE A-1 DESCRIPTION OF THE REINSTALL OPTION CODES

Code	Description
p	Reinstall a file only if the file is missing.
o	Reinstall a file if it is missing or if an earlier version of the file is on the machine.
e	Reinstall a file if it is missing or if a file with the same version or an earlier version is on the machine.
d	Reinstall a file if it is missing or a different version of the file is on the system.
c	Reinstall a file if it is missing or if the stored checksum does not match the calculated value. This code only works for executables and dynamic link libraries that are compiled with the correct linker switch so that a checksum is created. In addition, attributes column in the *File* table also have to be set appropriately.
a	This code forces all files to reinstall.
u	This code forces all user specific registry entries to be rewritten.
m	This code forces all machine specific registry entries to be rewritten.
s	This code forces all shortcuts to be overwritten.
v	This code re-caches the local package.

This option list has the same specifications as the REINSTALLMODE property. Be careful when using the default options. If the original installation was done on a per-user basis, the default options won't write any of the per-user registry entries.

Three additional modifying switches are used with the /f switch, which are listed below and described in detail in a later section.

/l This switch allows for the creation of a Windows Installer log file that can display all the actions that are being taken to install the product.

/q This switch sets the user interface level that is to be used for the installation.

/m This switch generates an SMS status .mif file.

Removing a product

The command line to uninstall a product is as follows:

```
msiexec /x <MSI package | ProductCode>
```

This command line enables you to remove an installed or advertised product. The rules for the package and product code parameters follow the same rules as for a normal installation.

Three additional modifying switches are used with the /j switch, which are listed below and described in detail in a later section.

/l This switch allows for the creation of a Windows Installer log file that can display all the actions that are being taken to install the product.

/q This switch sets the user interface level that is to be used for the installation.

/m This switch generates an SMS status .mif file.

Upgrading a product

Upgrading a product is applying a patch package or completely reinstalling over the old version of the product. A patch package can be applied to a local installation or to a local installation. For complete details of patching and upgrades, see Chapter 17. To apply a patch to a local installation, use the following command line:

```
msiexec /p <patch package>
```

To apply a patch package to an administrative image on a network server, use the following command line:

```
msiexec /a <MSI package on network server> /p <patch package>
```

To upgrade a local installation of a product by using the complete reinstall approach, use the following command line:

```
msiexec /fvomus <Updated MSI package>
```

or

```
msiexec /i <Updated MSI package> REINSTALL=ALL REINSTALLMODE=vomus
```

To upgrade a local installation of a product by using a partial reinstallation, use the following command line:

```
msiexec /i <Updated MSI package> REINSTALL=[Feature List]
                                        REINSTALLMODE=vomus
```

To use this command line, however, you need to know the names of the features that have been changed by the update.

Using Generic Modifying Switches

For many of the command line options described in the previous section, a set of optional switches allow you to modify the base operation of the command line action. The following three sections describe these modifying switches in more detail.

Setting the user interface level

The Windows Installer has four user interface levels, which define what dialogs the installation user interface displays. Not specifying the user interface level will display the full user interface, which is normal. To modify this default, use the following switches:

/qf This switch displays the full user interface, which is the same as not using this switch at all. Using the /qf+ switch also works but it performs in the same manner as the /qf switch.

/qr This switch displays the reduced user interface. A reduced user interface is where only the authored modeless dialog boxes that are part of the user interface are displayed. Commonly, this dialog is just the progress dialog showing the status of the installation. If an error occurs during the installation, then the error is displayed in a modal dialog box. After clicking the OK button, the installation rollbacks the system to the state it was before the installation started.

/qb This switch displays the basic user interface. The basic user interface only shows those dialogs built into the Windows Installer engine. Because using this interface level bypasses the UISequence table, no authored dialog boxes are shown. If an error occurs during the installation, a modal error dialog box announces the error. After you click the OK button, the installation rollbacks the system to the state it was prior to the start of the installation.

/qb+ If the previous switch is enhanced by using a plus (+) sign, then a modal dialog box is displayed at the end of the installation that say the installation is completed successfully. Modal error dialog boxes also display if an error occurs, and then the final dialog display states that the installation has failed.

/qb- If the /qb switch is modified with a minus sign (-), then this suppresses any error message dialog boxes. If an error occurs, the Windows Installer automatically rollbacks the system to its prior state at start of the installation.

/qn This switch provides the silent install or silent uninstall functionality where no user interface is displayed. The /q switch can also be used to provide the same functionality. If an error occurs during the installation, the error is not displayed, and the Windows Installer automatically performs a rollback. The only indication of the failure is the fact that no icon is on the Start | Program menu.

/qn+ If you enhance the previous switch by using a plus (+) sign, then a modal dialog box is displayed at the end of the installation that says the installation is completed successfully or that the installation failed depending on the circumstances. If an error occurs during the installation, this error is not displayed and the Windows Installer automatically performs a rollback.

The user interface level switches /qn-, /qr-, /qf-, and /qb+- are not supported and using them causes a Windows Installer command line error message box to display.

Logging Windows Installer actions

Logging the Windows Installer permits the installation, uninstallation, product advertisement, product repair, administrative installation, and patching actions. The command line to perform this logging operation for an installation is as follows:

```
msiexec /i <MSI package | ProductCode>
/l[i|w|e|a|r|u|c|m|o|p|v|+|!|*] <path to log file>
```

The optional modifiers to the /l switch are not mutually exclusive and these modifiers enable you to get the types of messages that you want. Table A-2 provides a list of these codes and their description.

Table A-2 DESCRIPTION OF THE LOGGING OPTION CODES

Code	Description
i	Log only status messages.
w	Log only non-fatal warnings.

Code	Description
e	Log all error messages.
a	Log the start of all actions.
r	Log all action-specific records.
u	Log all user requests.
c	Log the initial UI parameters.
m	Log any out-of-memory or fatal exit information.
o	Log out-of-disk-space messages.
p	Log any terminal properties.
v	Provide verbose output.
+	Append the log file to an already existing log file.
!	Flush line to the log.
*	Log all information without using the verbose mode of output.

A common command line that logs all information is as follows:

```
msiexec /i <MSI package | ProductCode> /l*v <path to log file>
```

Generating an SMS status .mif file

To generate a SMS status .mif file, use the following command line:

```
msiexec /i <MSI package | ProductCode> /m <path to .mif file>
```

This command line option writes a number of attributes of the Windows Installer package into the .mif file, as shown in Table A-3. For this command to work, the file ISMIF32.DLL needs to be on the machine and in the path from which the installation is being executed. Normally you find this file in the Windows folder. The file exports the function *InstallStatusMIF*, which is used to create this status file. The Summary Information Stream in the MSI package extracts most of the information that gets entered into this file.

Table A-3 INSTALLATION STATUS INFORMATION WRITTEN INTO AN SMS STATUS FILE

Status Field	Information Provided
Manufacturer	The Author property in the Summary Information Stream fills in this field. The Author property in turn is normally set from the Manufacturer property that is found in the *Property* table of the installation database.
Product	The Revision Number property in the Summary Information Stream fills in this field. The Revision Number property is a GUID that identifies a particular package. This GUID is referred to as the package code, which is unique for every package that is created.
Version	The Subject property in the Summary Information Stream fills in this field. The Subject property is normally set from the ProductName property found in the *Property* table of the installation database.
Locale	The Template property in the Summary Information Stream fills in this field. The Template property provides the platform and the language versions supported by the installation database.
Serial Number	The Windows Installer does not set this field.
Installation	ISMIF32.DLL to "DATETIME" sets this field.
InstallStatus	The Windows Installer sets this field to either Success or Failed.
Description	This field is used to display error messages. These error messages are provided in the following order: 1. Error messages generated by the Windows Installer. 2. Resource from MSI.DLL if the installation does not begin or if a user initiates exit. 3. System error message. 4. The Windows Installer generating a formatted message.

Setting Properties at the Command Line

Two types of properties are found in the *Property* table, public properties, and private properties. Public properties are denoted by the fact that the names of these properties are in all uppercase letters. Public properties are named as such because the user can set them at the command line. The command line for setting a public property is as follows:

```
msiexec /i <MSI package | ProductCode> INSTALLLEVEL=50
```

Even though only public properties can be set from the command line, the name of the public property as used does not have to be in all-uppercase. The following command line also works:

```
msiexec /i <MSI package | ProductCode> installlevel=50
```

Setting properties from the command line is only valid if using the /i, /a, or /x switches for initiating wither the INSTALL, or ADMIN top-level actions, or the uninstallation of a product.

When we are talking about public properties that can be set on the command line, we are referring to those public properties that are not restricted. A restricted public property is one that cannot be set by the user in a managed environment. The user has a default list of public properties that can be set in a managed environment, and the setup developer can modify this list. See Chapters 7 and 9 for more discussion relative to restricted public properties.

Miscellaneous Switches

Three switches fall into the miscellaneous category. These switches are not particularly useful, but to be thorough, they are documented here. These switches are listed below:

/? or /h — Using either of these switches displays the copyright information for the Windows Installer. The switch displays the error message box that gets displayed after incorrect command line parameters are used, such as trying to set a public property between a switch and its parameter. This command line look like the following:

```
msiexec /?
```

/y — This switch performs the same function as REGSVR32.EXE, which is a manual registration of a self-registering module. The one difference is that using this switch does not provide any feedback as to the success or failure of the operation. This switch is used to add information to the registry that is not possible to place in the registry related tables in the MSI database.

	Use this switch if you need to order the self-registration of a number of files, and then MSIEXEC.EXE is used as a custom action with this switch, and perform the self-registration in the order required. An example of using this switch is shown below: `msiexec /y shapeartist.dll`
/z	This switch performs the same function as REGSVR32.EXE /u, which is to manually unregister a self-registering module. The one difference is that using this switch does not provide any feedback as to the success or failure of the operation. Use this switch to remove information from the registry that is not possible to identify in the registry related tables in the MSI database. Use this switch when you need to order the self-unregistration of a number of files, and then MSIEXEC.EXE is used as a custom action with this switch, and perform the self-unregistration in the order required. An example of using this switch is shown here: `msiexec /z shapeartist.dll`

Windows Installer Error Codes

Refer to the list of Win32 Error Codes that you find in the Microsoft MSDN Library for a complete list of possible error codes that can be returned by the Windows Installer API, MSIEXEC.EXE, and INSTMSI.EXE.

Appendix B

Summary Information Stream Reference

THIS APPENDIX PROVIDES FOUR tables that describe in detail the property descriptions for each of the four types of Windows Installer files that store information in a Summary Information Stream. These four files are listed below with their file extensions:

- A full installation database file with the .msi file extension
- A merge module database file with the .msm file extension
- A transform file with the .mst file extension
- A patch package with the .msp file extension

Microsoft is reviewing what properties of these four file types is actually required. If authoring one of these types of files, considering that they are all required is the safe approach.

Table B-1 provides the description for the properties used when authoring an installation database package. This type of package is the only one of the four file types that can actually perform an installation.

TABLE B-1 MSI DATABASE SUMMARY INFORMATION PROPERTY SET

Property Name	Property Description
Codepage (PID = 1)	This property is set to the numeric value of the ANSI code page to use for any strings that are stored in the Summary Information stream. This property identifies the code page used if displaying the Summary Information in the property sheet in Windows Explorer. Also, use this property to translate the strings in the Summary Information stream into Unicode when calling the Unicode API functions. This property needs to be set prior to setting any of the string properties in the summary Information stream. The value type is a 2-byte signed integer. Note: This code page property has nothing to do with the strings in the installation database.

Continued

TABLE B-1 MSI DATABASE SUMMARY INFORMATION PROPERTY SET *(Continued)*

Property Name	Property Description
Title (PID = 2)	This property is a short description of the type of Windows Installer package in which this Summary Information stream resides. For an installation database, this string is similar to "Installation Database". This string informs users about the purpose of the file. The value type is a counted null terminated string. The representation is an initial DWORD byte count, which includes the terminating null, followed by a string that contains that many bytes. The code page property described previously indicates the character set to use.
Subject (PID = 3)	This property is the name of the application being installed and is normally set from the value of the ProductName property found in the *Property* table. The value type is the same as for the Title property described previously.
Author (PID = 4)	This property is the name of the company that created the product being installed and is normally set from the value of the Manufacturer property found in the *Property* table. The value type is the same as for the Title property described previously.
Keywords (PID = 5)	File browsers, such as Windows Explorer, use these values to perform keyword searches for a file. If you enter more than one keyword, separate them by commas. Typically, one enters the keywords- Installer, MSI, Database. In addition, product specific keywords can be used here, and this location can also be used for performing versioning on the MSI package during development. The value type is the same as for the Title property described previously.
Comments (PID = 6)	This property conveys the general purpose of the installer database. By convention, it is set to: "This installer database contains the logic and data required to install *<product name>*." The value type is the same as for the Title property described previously.

Property Name	Property Description
Template (PID = 7)	This property specifies both the platform and the language versions supported by the installer database. The format for this is: [platform][,platform][,...];[language id][,language id][,...]. The platform values that you use most likely are Intel and Alpha. If a platform is not specified, then the package is considered to be platform independent. Specifying zero for the language ID means that the package is language neutral. Examples of valid strings are: Intel;1033 Alpha,Intel;1033 The value type is the same as for the Title property described previously.
Last Saved By (PID = 8)	The Windows Installer sets this value to the name of the user that is logged on to the system during an administrative installation. The Windows Installer never uses this property, which should always be NULL in a database that is being shipped. You can use this property during construction of the MSI package to keep track of the last person to modify the database. The value type is the same as for the Title property described previously.
Revision Number (PID = 9)	The value of this property is the package code of the installer package. This code is a GUID. The value type is the same as for the Title property described previously.
Total Editing Time (PID = 10)	The Windows Installer service does not support this property, but the property is shown here because it is part of the standard set of Summary Information stream properties.
Last Printed (PID = 11)	This value is a date and time that can be set during an administrative installation to record when the administrative image is created. For a normal installation, this property is the same as the Create Time/Date property defined next. The value type is a 64-bit FILETIME structure, which the Platform SDK documentation defines. Essentially, this structure defines the number of 100-nanosecond intervals that have occurred since January 1, 1601.
Create Time/Date (PID = 12)	This property records the time and date when the MSI database is created. The value type is the same as for the Last Printed property described previously.

Continued

Table B-1 MSI DATABASE SUMMARY INFORMATION PROPERTY SET *(Continued)*

Property Name	Property Description
Last Save Time/Date (PID = 13)	The value of this property specifies the last time the MSI database was modified (saved). This property gets updated every time the database is changed. When the database is initially created, this value is set to NULL to indicate that no modifications have taken place. The value type is the same as for the Last Printed property described previously.
Page Count (PID = 14)	The value of this property contains the minimum version of the Windows Installer that is required for running the installation database. This value is stored as the Major Version * 100 plus the Minor Version. For Windows Installer 1.1, this value is 1 * 100 + 10 = 110. The value type is a 4-byte signed integer.
Word Count (PID = 15)	The value of this property is a bit field that indicates the type of source file image. This value provides information to the Windows Installer about whether long or short file names are being used, whether the source files are compressed or uncompressed, and whether the source files are from the original media or from an administrative image on a network drive. The details of creating the values for this property are given below: At the present time, only the first three bits of this 4-byte integer are used. Bit 0: If this bit is 0, then long file names are being used. If this bit has a value of 1, then short file names are being used. Bit 1: If this bit is 0, then the source files are uncompressed. If this bit is equal to 1 (integer 2), then the source files are compressed. Bit 2: If this bit is 0, then the source is the original media. If the value of this bit is 1 (integer 4), then the source is an administrative image created by an administrative installation. These bits can be combined in the following manner to create the possible values that you can use for this property. 0: This value means that the source is uncompressed and is using long file names. The source tree for these files is defined in the *Directory* table. 1: This value means that the source is uncompressed and is using short file names. The source tree for these files is defined in the *Directory* table. 2: This value means that the source files are compressed into a cabinet using long file names and the source of this cabinet is defined in the *Media* table.

Property Name	Property Description
	3: This value means that the source files are compressed into a cabinet using short file names and the source of this cabinet is defined in the *Media* table. 4: This value means that the source is an administrative image and is using long file names. The source tree for these files is defined in the *Directory* table. 5: This value means that the source is an administrative image and is using short file names. The source tree for these files is defined in the *Directory* table. The value type is a 4-byte signed integer.
Character Count (PID = 16)	This property is not used for installation packages but only for transforms. The value type is a 4-byte signed integer.
Thumbnail (PID = 17)	This property is not supported by the Windows Installer service, but is shown here because it is part of the standard set of Summary Information Stream properties.
Creating Application (PID = 18)	The value of this property is the name of the application used to author the installation database. The value type is the same as for the Title property described previously.
Security (PID = 19)	The value of this property identifies how to open this package. If the value is 0, there is no restriction. If the value is 2, then read-only is recommended. And if the value is 4, then read-only is enforced. For installation packages, the property value is set to 2. The value type is a 4-byte signed integer.

Table B-2 describes all the entries that are valid for a merge module database. A merge module is a simplified MSI database file that is missing those tables that allow the file to be installed on its own. Instead a merge module needs to be merged with a standard MSI database so that its contents can be installed. A merge module is used to deliver components to a standard installation database.

TABLE B-2 MERGE MODULE SUMMARY INFORMATION PROPERTY SET

Property Name	Property Description
Codepage (PID = 1)	This property is set to the numeric value of the ANSI code page that is used for any strings that are stored in the Summary Information Stream. This property identifies the code page to use when displaying the Summary Information in the property sheet in Windows Explorer. It is also used to translate the strings in the Summary Information Stream into Unicode when calling the Unicode API functions. This property is set prior to setting any of the string properties in the Summary Information Stream. The value type is a 2-byte signed integer. Note: This code page property has nothing to do with any of the localizable strings in the merge module database.
Title (PID = 2)	This property is a short description of the type of Windows Installer package in which this Summary Information Stream resides. For a merge module database, this string is similar to a "Merge Module." This property informs users about the purpose of the file. The value type is a counted null terminated string. The representation is an initial DWORD byte count, which includes the terminating null, followed by a string that contains that many bytes. The character set used is as indicated by the code page property described previously.
Subject (PID = 3)	This property is the name of the application being installed and is normally set from the value of the ProductName property found in the *Property* table. The value type is the same as for the Title property described previously.
Author (PID = 4)	This property is the name of the company that created the product being installed and is normally set from the value of the Manufacturer property found in the *Property* table. The value type is the same as for the Title property described previously.

Property Name	Property Description
Keywords (PID = 5)	File browsers, such as Windows Explorer, use these values to perform keyword searches for a file. If more than one keyword is entered, they are separated by commas. Typically one would enter the keywords, MergeModule, MSI, Database. In addition, product specific keywords are used here and this location can also be used for performing versioning on the MSI package during development. Because the end user uses these values, they are candidates for localization when creating merge modules for other languages. The value type is the same as for the Title property described previously.
Comments (PID = 6)	This property conveys the general purpose of the merge module database. The property can be set to: "This merge module database contains the logic and data required to install <component name(s)>." In general this comment string should be complete enough to adequately describe the merge module and its components. The value type is the same as for the Title property described previously.
Template (PID = 7)	This property specifies both the platform and the language versions supported by the merge module database. The format for this is: [platform][,platform][,...];[language id][,language id][,...]. The platform values that you most likely use are Intel and Alpha. If a platform is not specified, then the package is considered to be platform independent. Any number language IDs can be specified, but if there is more than one a multi-language merge module is indicated. Specifying zero for the language ID means that the package is language neutral. Examples of valid strings are: Intel;1033 Alpha,Intel;1033 The value type is the same as for the Title property described previously.
Last Saved By (PID = 8)	The value type is the same as for the Title property described previously.

Continued

Table B-2 MERGE MODULE SUMMARY INFORMATION PROPERTY SET *(Continued)*

Property Name	Property Description
Revision Number (PID = 9)	The value of this property is the merge module ID. This code is a GUID, which needs to be used in its raw form and not in the modified form that is used to make the primary keys in the database unique. The raw form has the curly braces at each end and uses dashes to separate the various fields that comprise the GUID. The value type is the same as for the Title property described previously.
Total Editing Time (PID = 10)	This property is not supported by the Windows Installer service but it is being shown here because it is part of the standard set of Summary Information Stream properties.
Last Printed (PID = 11)	This value is not used by merge modules and is set to NULL.
Create Time/Date (PID = 12)	This property records the time and date when the merge module database is created. The value type is the same as the Last Printed property described previously.
Last Save Time/Date (PID = 13)	The value of this property specifies the last time the MSI database was modified (saved). This property gets updated every time the database is changed. When the database is initially created, this value is set to NULL to indicate that no modifications have taken place. The value type is a 64-bit FILETIME structure, which is defined in the Platform SDK documentation. Essentially, this structure defines the number of 100-nanosecond intervals that have occurred since January 1, 1601.
Page Count (PID = 14)	The value of this property contains the minimum version of the Windows Installer that is required by this merge module database. This is stored as the Major Version * 100 plus the Minor Version. For Windows Installer 1.1, this value is 1 * 100 + 10 = 110. The value type is a 4-byte signed integer.
Word Count (PID = 15)	"0" Note that merge module files are always inside an embedded cabinet file regardless of the value of this property. The value type is a 4-byte signed integer.

Property Name	Property Description
Character Count (PID = 16)	This property, not used for merge modules, is set to NULL. The value type is a 4-byte signed integer.
Thumbnail (PID = 17)	This property is not supported by the Windows Installer service but is shown here because it is part of the standard set of Summary Information Stream properties.
Creating Application (PID = 18)	The value of this property is the name of the application used to author the merge module database. The value type is the same as the Title property described previously.
Security (PID = 19)	The value of this property identifies how this package is opened. If the value is 0, there is no restriction. If the value is 2, then read-only is recommended. And if the value is 4, then read-only is enforced. For merge module packages, the property value is set to 2. The value type is a 4-byte signed integer.

A transform is a COM structured file that defines the difference between two installer databases. A transform is not, however, a database in itself and as such is not viewable using the Orca tool. Being a COM structured storage file, it does have a Summary Information Stream. The values used for the properties of this file type are given in Table B-3.

TABLE B-3 TRANSFORM SUMMARY INFORMATION PROPERTY SET

Property Name	Property Description
Codepage (PID = 1)	This property is set to the numeric value of the ANSI code page that is used for any strings that are stored in the Summary Information Stream. This property identifies the code page used when displaying the Summary Information in the property sheet in Windows Explorer. The property is also used to translate the strings in the Summary Information Stream into Unicode after calling the Unicode API functions. This property is set prior to setting any of the string properties in the Summary Information Stream. The value type is a 2-byte signed integer. Note: This code page property has nothing to do with the strings in the transform.

Continued

Table B-3 TRANSFORM SUMMARY INFORMATION PROPERTY SET *(Continued)*

Property Name	Property Description
Title (PID = 2)	This property is a short description of the type of Windows Installer package in which this Summary Information Stream resides. For a transform, this string, such as "Transform" informs users about the purpose of the file. The value type is a counted null terminated string. The representation is an initial DWORD byte count, which includes the terminating null, followed by a string that contains that many bytes. Use the character set as indicated by the code page property described previously.
Subject (PID = 3)	The value of this property is a short description of the purpose of the transform and this description normally contains the name of the product. The value type is the same as the Title property described previously.
Author (PID = 4)	This property is the name of the company that created the product that is the focus of the transform and the value of the property is normally set from the Manufacturer property found in the *Property* table. The value type is the same as for the Title property described previously.
Keywords (PID = 5)	File browsers, such as Windows Explorer, use these values to perform keyword searches for a file. If more than one keyword is entered, they are separated by commas. Typically one would enter the keywords, Transform, MSI, Installer. In addition, product specific keywords are used here. Because the end user uses these values, they are candidates for localization when creating installations for other languages. The value type is the same as for the Title property described previously.
Comments (PID = 6)	This property conveys the general purpose of the installer database. By convention, the property is set to: "This transform contains the logic and data required to modify <*product name*>." The value type is the same as the Title property described previously.

Property Name	Property Description
Template (PID = 7)	This property specifies both the platform and the language versions of the installer database that are compatible with the transform. This property may be left blank if there are no restrictions and only one language can be specified. The format for this is: [platform][,platform][,...];[language id][,language id][,...]. The platform values that you most likely use are Intel and Alpha. If a platform is not specified, then the package is considered to be platform independent. Specifying zero for the language ID means that the package is language neutral. Examples of valid strings are: Intel;1033 Alpha,Intel;1033 The value type is the same as the Title property described previously.
Last Saved By (PID = 8)	The value of this property specifies the platform and language of the transformed database. The syntax for this property is the same as previously described for the Template property. The value type is the same as the Title property described previously.
Revision Number (PID = 9)	The value of this property is a list of values that start with the original product code and original product version. Using a semicolon delimiter, this string is then followed by the new product code and the new product version. The last item in the list is the upgrade code delimited from the rests of the string with a semicolon. No delimiter is used between product codes and product versions. This string value looks as follows: <original product code><original product version>;<new product code><new product version>;<upgrade code> Of course, the product codes and the upgrade code are GUIDs. The value type is the same as the Title property described previously.
Total Editing Time (PID = 10)	This property is not supported by the Windows Installer service but it is shown here because it is part of the standard set of Summary Information Stream properties.
Last Printed (PID = 11)	This property is not used and therefore is set to NULL.6

Continued

Table B-3 TRANSFORM SUMMARY INFORMATION PROPERTY SET *(Continued)*

Property Name	Property Description
Create Time/Date (PID = 12)	This property records the time and date when the transform is created. The value type is the same as the Last Printed property described previously.
Last Save Time/Date (PID = 13)	The value of this property specifies the last time the transform was modified (saved). This property gets updated every time the database is changed. When the transform is initially created, this value is set to NULL to indicate that no modifications have taken place. The value type is the same as the Last Printed property described previously.
Page Count (PID = 14)	The value of this property contains the minimum version of the Windows Installer required for processing the transform. This property is set to the greater of the Page Count property values belonging to the two installer database used to create the transform. This is stored as the Major Version * 100 plus the Minor Version. For Windows Installer 1.1, this value is 1 * 100 + 10 = 110. The value type is a 4-byte signed integer.
Word Count (PID = 15)	This property is not used and its value needs to be set to NULL. The value type is a 4-byte signed integer.
Character Count (PID = 16)	The value of this property specifies the validation and the error condition flags sued with this transform. The lower 2 bytes of this value are used to specify those error conditions that are suppressed after the transform is applied. The upper 2 bytes of this value specify the properties that are validated to verify that the transform can be applied to the target MSI database. The properties that can be validated are the default language, the product, the product version, the relationship between the product versions, and the upgrade code. A complete description of these error condition and property validation flags is provided in the documentation of the MsiCreateTransformSummaryInfo Windows Installer database function. This document is found in the MSI Help, which is on the MsiSdk found on the CD-ROM at the back of the book. The value type is a 4-byte signed integer.

Property Name	Property Description
Thumbnail (PID = 17)	This property is not supported by the Windows Installer service but it is shown here because it is part of the standard set of Summary Information Stream properties.
Creating Application (PID = 18)	The value of this property is the name of the application used to create the transform. The value type is the same as the Title property described previously.
Security (PID = 19)	The value of this property identifies how this package is opened. If the value is 0, there is no restriction. If the value is 2, then read-only is recommended. And if the value is 4, then read-only is enforced. For transforms, the property value is set to 4. The value type is a 4-byte signed integer.

A patch package is a COM Structured storage file but such as a transform, it does not contain a database and therefore cannot be viewed using the Orca utility. Being a COM structured storage file, a patch package does have a Summary Information Stream. Table B-4 provides the description of the values for the properties that comprise the patch package Summary Information Stream.

TABLE B-4 PATCH PACKAGE SUMMARY INFORMATION PROPERTY SET

Property Name	Property Description
Codepage (PID = 1)	This property is set to the numeric value of the ANSI code page used for any strings stored in the Summary Information Stream. This property identifies the code page used when displaying the Summary Information in the property sheet in Windows Explorer. It is also used to translate the strings in the Summary Information Stream into Unicode after calling the Unicode API functions. This property needs to be set prior to setting any of the string properties in the Summary Information Stream. The value type is a 2-byte signed integer. Note: This code page property has nothing to do with any strings that may be in the patch package.

Continued

Table B-4 PATCH PACKAGE SUMMARY INFORMATION PROPERTY SET *(Continued)*

Property Name	Property Description
Title (PID = 2)	This property is a short description of the type of Windows Installer package where this Summary Information stream resides. For a patch package, this string, such as "Patch" informs users about the purpose of the file. The value type is a counted null terminated string. The representation is an initial DWORD byte count, which includes the terminating null, followed by a string that contains that many bytes. The character set used is as indicated by the code page property described previously.
Subject (PID = 3)	The value of this property is a short description of the purpose of the patch package and this description normally contains the name of the product. The value type is the same as for the Title property described previously.
Author (PID = 4)	This property is the name of the company that created the product that is the focus of the patch package, and the value of the property is normally set from the Manufacturer property found in the *Property* table. The value type is the same as the Title property described previously.
Keywords (PID = 5)	The value of this property is a semicolon-delimited list of the sources for the patch package. The value type is the same as the Title property described previously.
Comments (PID = 6)	This property conveys the general purpose of the installer database. By convention, the property is set to: "This patch package contains the logic and data required to modify <*product name*>." The value type is the same as the Title property described previously.
Template (PID = 7)	The value of this property is a semicolon-delimited list of product codes that can accept the patch contained in this package. The value type is the same as the Title property described previously.

Property Name	Property Description
Last Saved By (PID = 8)	The value of this property is a semicolon-delimited list of product The value of this property is a semicolon-delimited list of transform sub-storage names. The order of this list defines the order in which these transforms are applied to the target administrative or local installation. The value type is the same as the Title property described above.
Revision Number (PID = 9)	The value of this property is a list of GUIDs. The first GUID in the list is the patch package code for the patch. Following this GUID is a list of patch code GUIDs for those patches to be removed after this patch package is applied. These GUIDs are concatenated together without the use of any delimiter separating them. The value type is the same as the Title property described previously.
Total Editing Time (PID = 10)	This property is not supported by the Windows Installer service but is shown here because it is part of the standard set of Summary Information Stream properties.
Last Printed (PID = 11)	This property is not used by patch packages and needs to be set to NULL.
Create Time/Date (PID = 12)	This property records the time and date when the patch package is created. The value type is the same as the Last Printed property described previously.
Last Save Time/Date (PID = 13)	The value of this property specifies the last time the patch package was modified (saved). This property gets updated every time the patch package changes. When the patch package is initially created, this value is set to NULL to indicate that no modifications have taken place. The value type is the same as the Last Printed property described previously.
Page Count (PID = 14)	This property is not used by a patch package and needs to be set to NULL.

Continued

TABLE B-4 PATCH PACKAGE SUMMARY INFORMATION PROPERTY SET *(Continued)*

Property Name	Property Description
Word Count (PID = 15)	The value of this property specifies the patch engine that was used to create the patch package. Currently, the only supported patch engine comes from Microsoft and it is called MSPATCH. The value used for this value is 1, which indicates that the patch package is created using MSPATCH. The value type is a 4-byte signed integer.
Character Count (PID = 16)	This property is not used for patch packages and needs to be set to NULL. The value type is a 4-byte signed integer.
Thumbnail (PID = 17)	This property is not supported by the Windows Installer service but is shown here because it is part of the standard set of Summary Information Stream properties.
Creating Application (PID = 18)	The value of this property is the name of the application used to author the patch package. The value type is the same as the Title property described previously.
Security (PID = 19)	The value of this property identifies how this package is opened. If the value is 0, there is no restriction. If the value is 2, then read-only is recommended. And if the value is 4, then read-only is enforced. For patch packages, the property value is set to 4. The value type is a 4-byte signed integer.

Appendix C

InstallScript Run-Time Architecture

IN THIS APPENDIX we discuss the mechanism that allows InstallScript to be used to create custom actions. First we investigate what happens at build time when a custom action has been created using InstallScript. After the build-time discussion we then look at the mechanism used to run InstallScript custom actions during an installation. The only focus we have in this appendix is what happens when we do have custom actions and we do not address any issues that are not related to this subject. The two scenarios that we have to look at are an installation where there is only one language involved and an installation that has been created where the user is allowed to select the language of the installation.

Single Language Installations

A single language installation is where there is only one possible language that can be used in the user interface of the installation. It does not mean that this type of an installation cannot target operating systems of different languages or install localized versions of a product. What we are discussing here is an installation that can have only one possible language used in the Install wizard.

Building the MSI Package

Just creating exported functions using InstallScript does not force any special action from ISWI when you build an MSI package. You actually need to define a custom action as being of the InstallScript type before any different action is taken during the building of the package. However, you do not have to insert these InstallScript custom actions into any of the sequence tables for these special build actions to take place. It is only necessary for these InstallScript custom actions to be in existence.

Four tables in the MSI package are impacted by using InstallScript to implement custom actions. These tables are the *CustomAction, Binary, InstallUISequence,* and *InstallExecuteSequence* tables. Below we look at each of these tables as they would appear after having created a custom action called MyCustomAction, beginning with Table C-1.

Table C-1 THE CUSTOMACTION TABLE GENERATED FOR AN INSTALLSCRIPT CUSTOM ACTION IN A SINGLE LANGUAGE INSTALLATION PACKAGE

Action	Type	Source	Target
CleanUp	513	ISScriptBridge.DLL	CleanUp
EngineStartup	577	ISScriptBridge.DLL	EngineStartup
Rollback_CleanUp	1281	ISScriptBridge.DLL	CleanUp
MyCustomAction	1	ISScriptBridge.DLL	f0
StartUp	513	ISScriptBridge.DLL	StartUp

Remarks:

- The CleanUp custom action is a function exported from the source DLL and it function is to perform clean up at the end of each sequence in the installation. What these actual clean up duties consist of is discussed in the section on the run-time architecture. The 513 type number for this custom action indicates that this custom action is provided by a DLL that is stored in the *Binary* table and that it will execute only once per process. This custom action is of the immediate category, which means that it will be executed as soon as it is encountered in the sequence table by the Windows Installer.
- The EngineStartup custom action is another function exported from the ISScriptBridge.DLL dynamic-link library. The function of this custom action is to install the engine that is used to execute the InstallScript code. How this engine is installed is covered in the run-time architecture section. The 577 type for this custom action indicates that it is provided by a DLL stored in the *Binary* table, that it will execute only once per process, and that the Windows Installer is to ignore any exit codes from this custom action. This custom action is of the immediate category, which means that it will be executed as soon as it is encountered in the sequence table by the Windows Installer.
- The Rollback_CleanUp custom action is implemented by the same function exported from the ISScriptBridge.DLL dynamic-link library as for the CleanUp custom action discussed above. The function of this custom action is to perform all required clean up activities in the event of the installation being prematurely terminated. The 1281 type for this custom action indicates that it is provided by a DLL stored in the *Binary* table and that it will be executed in a deferred mode and only during a rollback if one becomes necessary.

Since this custom action is one sub-categories of deferred custom actions it gets written into the execution script for processing during that phase of the installation.

- The MyCustomAction is the name of the custom action that has been implemented using InstallScript. You will notice that the target for this custom action is shown as f0. This target is one of 1001 predefined exported function names from ISScriptBridge.DLL. How this is used is discussed in the section on the run-time architecture. The 1 type for this custom action defines that it is implemented in a DLL that is stored in the *Binary* table. This is an immediate custom action and that will always be executed. Through the Custom Action Wizard you have the facility to define your InstallScript custom action to run in deferred mode and to have the Windows Installer ignore return values. However, InstallScript custom actions at the time of this writing can only be run synchronously so the Wizard will not let you choose the option to run asynchronously.
- The final custom action that we need to discuss is the StartUp custom action. The function of this custom action is to get everything up and running after the InstallScript engine has been installed. As with the other custom actions it is a function exported from the ISScriptBridge.DLL and its type is that same as for the CleanUp custom action.

The next table that we want to look at is the *Binary* table. This is shown in Table C-2 and it is provided in the form that it would appear when there has only been the one custom action created with no other modifications made to the default project. This means that no new dialogs have been added with the uses of any new graphics. The complete table is being shown because it will be much different when a multi-language installation is created and it is important to explain the reason for the differences.

Table C-2 THE BASIC BINARY TABLE CREATED FOR A SINGLE LANGUAGE MSI PACKAGE WHEN USING AN INSTALLSCRIPT CUSTOM ACTION

Name	Data
_ISRES.DLL	_ISRES.DLL.ibd
Binary10	Binary10.ibd
Binary11	Binary11.ibd
Binary12	Binary12.ibd
Binary13	Binary13.ibd

Continued

TABLE C-2 THE BASIC BINARY TABLE CREATED FOR A SINGLE LANGUAGE MSI PACKAGE WHEN USING AN INSTALLSCRIPT CUSTOM ACTION *(Continued)*

Name	Data
Binary14	Binary14.ibd
Binary15	Binary15.ibd
Binary16	Binary16.ibd
Binary17	Binary17.ibd
Binary18	Binary18.ibd
Binary19	Binary19.ibd
Binary20	Binary20.ibd
Binary21	Binary21.ibd
Binary22	Binary22.ibd
Binary6	Binary6.ibd
Binary7	Binary7.ibd
Binary8	Binary8.ibd
Binary9	Binary9.ibd
InstallScript	InstallScript.ibd
IsConfig.INI	IsConfig.INI.ibd
ISRT.DLL	ISRT.DLL.ibd
ISScript.Msi	ISScript.Msi.ibd
ISScriptBridge.DLL	ISScriptBridge.DLL.ibd
String1033.txt	String1033.txt.ibd

Remarks:

- What is shown in the Data column is what you would see if you exported this table using Orca. In Orca you would only see the string [Binary Data] in this column. What is shown in the above table is the name of the file into which the binary data has been streamed.
- The rows that have an entry in the Name column of the format Binaryxx, where xx is a number, are the icons and bitmaps used in populating the dialogs that make up the installation user interface. What we really want to discuss here is all the other entries in this table.

- In the first row of the table is the English resource DLL for all the external dialogs available through InstallScript.
- The InstallScript entry in the table is the compiled script (.inx) file that will be read by the InstallScript engine to implement the custom actions that have been defined.
- The IsConfig.ini entry in the table is a configuration file that maps an exported function in ISScriptBridge.dll to a call to the entry point function defined in your script.
- The ISRT.DLL entry in the table is the implementation of the InstallScript API function set. Most calls to one of the API functions gets sent by the scripting engine to this DLL.
- The ISScript.Msi entry in the table is the MSI package that installs the engine on the target machine if it is not already installed.
- The ISScriptBridge.DLL entry in the table is the custom action DLL that implements the scripting engine initialization and clean up custom actions as well as serves as the transfer point between the installation process and the scripting engine process.
- The String1033.txt entry in the table is the English string table file that can be accessed from within the script using the @ symbol. This file is in Unicode.

The next table that we look at is the *InstallUISequence* table. We need to understand the additional entries made in this table and in the *InstallExecuteSequence* table. The entries in the *InstallExecuteSequence* table are shown in Table C-4. First we look at the entries made in the *InstallUISequence* table and these are given in Table C-3.

TABLE C-3 THE DEFAULT ENTRIES MADE IN THE INSTALLUISEQUENCE TABLE FOR AN INSTALLSCRIPT CUSTOM ACTION

Action	Condition	Sequence
SetupCompleteError		-3
SetupInterrupted		-2
SetupCompleteSuccess		-1
EngineStartup	Not Installed	1
StartUp		2

Continued

Table C-3 THE DEFAULT ENTRIES MADE IN THE INSTALLUISEQUENCE TABLE FOR AN INSTALLSCRIPT CUSTOM ACTION *(Continued)*

Action	Condition	Sequence
LaunchConditions		50
SetupInitialization		100
FindRelatedProducts		150
AppSearch	APPS_TEST	200
CCPSearch	CCP_TEST	250
RMCCPSearch	Not CCP_SUCCESS And CCP_TEST	300
ValidateProductID		350
CostInitialize		400
FileCost		450
IsolateComponents		500
CostFinalize		550
MyCustomAction	Not Installed	575
MigrateFeatureStates		600
InstallWelcome	Not UITEST And Not Installed	650
SetupResume	Not UITEST And Installed And (RESUME Or Preselected)	700
MaintenanceWelcome	Not UITEST And Installed And Not RESUME And Not Preselected	750
SetupProgress	Not UITEST	800
ExecuteAction		850
CleanUp		851

Remarks:

- The first line we want to look at is the one with the EngineStartup action. This is a custom action exported by the ISScriptBridge.DLL that installs the script engine and related files. This custom action has a sequence number of 1 so it will be the first action taken during the installation.

- The next line that has the StartUp action is the custom action that loads the scripting engine and streams out the compiled script from the *Binary* table. During the initialization of the scripting engine the OnBegin event handler of the script is executed.
- The last line in this table is the CleanUp action. This is a custom action that is responsible for closing the script file and shutting down the scripting engine. During this process the OnEnd event handler is executed.

The other sequence table that we need to look at before we go on to the discussion of the run-time architecture is the *InstallExecuteSequence* table. The entries made in this table are shown in Table C-4.

TABLE C-4 THE DEFAULT ENTRIES MADE IN THE INSTALLEXECUTESEQUENCE TABLE FOR AN INSTALLSCRIPT CUSTOM ACTION

Action	Condition	Sequence
EngineStartup	Not Installed	1
StartUp		2
LaunchConditions		50
FindRelatedProducts		100
AppSearch	APPS_TEST	150
CCPSearch	CCP_TEST	200
RMCCPSearch	Not CCP_SUCCESS And CCP_TEST	250
ValidateProductID		300
CostInitialize		350
FileCost		400
IsolateComponents		450
CostFinalize		500
SetARP		525
SetODBCFolders		550
MigrateFeatureStates		600
InstallValidate		650

Continued

Table C-4 THE DEFAULT ENTRIES MADE IN THE INSTALLEXECUTESEQUENCE TABLE FOR AN INSTALLSCRIPT CUSTOM ACTION *(Continued)*

Action	Condition	Sequence
InstallInitialize		700
Rollback_CleanUp		701
AllocateRegistrySpace	NOT Installed	750
ProcessComponents		800
UnpublishComponents		850
UnpublishFeatures		900
StopServices	VersionNT	950
DeleteServices	VersionNT	1000
UnregisterComPlus		1050
SelfUnregModules		1100
UnregisterTypeLibraries		1150
RemoveODBC		1200
UnregisterFonts		1250
RemoveRegistryValues		1300
UnregisterClassInfo		1350
UnregisterExtensionInfo		1400
UnregisterProgIdInfo		1450
UnregisterMIMEInfo		1500
RemoveIniValues		1550
RemoveShortcuts		1600
RemoveEnvironmentStrings		1650
RemoveDuplicateFiles		1700
RemoveFiles		1750
RemoveFolders		1800
CreateFolders		1850
MoveFiles		1900

Action	Condition	Sequence
InstallFiles		1950
DuplicateFiles		2000
PatchFiles		2050
BindImage		2100
CreateShortcuts		2150
RegisterClassInfo		2200
RegisterExtensionInfo		2250
RegisterProgIdInfo		2300
RegisterMIMEInfo		2350
WriteRegistryValues		2400
WriteIniValues		2450
WriteEnvironmentStrings		2500
RegisterFonts		2550
InstallODBC		2600
RegisterTypeLibraries		2650
RegisterComPlus		2700
InstallServices	VersionNT	2750
StartServices	VersionNT	2800
SelfRegModules		2850
RegisterUser		2900
RegisterProduct		2950
PublishComponents		3000
PublishFeatures		3050
PublishProduct		3100
InstallFinalize		3150
RemoveExistingProducts		3200
CleanUp		3201

Remark:

- The custom actions inserted into this table are the same as described for the *InstallUISequence* table.

What Happens at Run-Time for a Single Language Installation

As has already been discussed above, at run time the ISScriptBridge.DLL host for the script related custom actions is streamed out of the *Binary* table by the Windows Installer. The Windows Installer then calls the exported EngineStartup function in this DLL and this gets the scripting engine installed if it is not already installed. The Windows Installer then calls the StartUp custom action and this launches the scripting engine, streams the compiled script and other files out of the *Binary* table, and opens the compiled script. The compiled script is streamed out as InstallScript.tmp into a folder in the TEMP directory with the name of this folder formed from the Product GUID. At this point the scripting engine is up and running with the compiled script open. The OnBegin() event handler is now executed as part of the initialization process. If the compiled script has not implemented any functionality for this event handler then this becomes a no-op.

Now everything is ready to execute calls to the entry point functions that have been defined in your script. For every entry point function defined in your script an entry has been made in the *CustomAction* table. The source of the custom action is always ISScriptBridge.DLL and the target of the custom action is f0 through fn where n represents the last entry point function defined in your script. ISScriptBridge.DLL has exported functions with the names f0 through f1000. When the Windows Installer calls one of these exported functions ISScriptBridge will map this exported function name to the actual name of the entry point function in your script. This mapping is done through the file ISConfig.ini file that was streamed out into the temporary folder under the TEMP directory. The real name of the function is then used to implement your custom action via the scripting engine.

At the end of the installation the Windows Installer calls the CleanUp custom action. The first thing that this custom action does is execute the OnEnd() event handler. Just as with the OnBegin() event handler if there is no code in your script for this event handler then this is a no-op. After this the CleanUp custom action closes the script, shuts down the scripting engine, and deletes all the temporary files.

Multi-Language Installations

In this section we will discuss the differences in both the build and the run-time actions that take place when a multi-language installation is created and run. First we want to discuss the build-time actions that are implemented to create this multilingual installation package.

Building the MSI Package for a Multi-Lingual Installation

When creating a multi-language installation the only table of the four we discussed in the previous section that is changed is the *Binary* table. Many other tables that are not related to custom actions are different in a multi-language MSI package. For the sake of completeness, it is probably worthwhile to mention what is going on here. The general approach taken when creating a multi-language installation package is to strip out all language dependent information from all the applicable tables. This language dependent information is used to create various language transforms. The transforms that are actually created depend on the languages that will be offered up to the end user for choosing the language in which the install is to be done. The choice of language is provided by the SETUP.EXE file, which then applies the appropriate transform once the user makes their decision on what language to use.

As far as InstallScript custom actions go, the only table we need to look at is the *Binary* table. The content of this table when creating a multi-language installation package is shown in Table C-5.

TABLE C-5 THE BINARY TABLE GENERATED FOR AN INSTALLSCRIPT CUSTOM ACTION IN A MULTI-LANGUAGE INSTALLATION PACKAGE

Name	Data
InstallScript	InstallScript.ibd
IsConfig.INI	IsConfig.INI.ibd
ISRT.DLL	ISRT.DLL.ibd
ISScript.Msi	ISScript.Msi.ibd
ISScriptBridge.DLL	ISScriptBridge.DLL.ibd

Remark:

- The one point to notice here is that all the language dependent files are now missing from the *Binary* table. This includes all the Binaryxx files as well as the _ISRES.DLL file and the string table file. These files are now contained in a transform, which will be applied at run time depending on the choice the user makes at the start of the installation.

What Happens at Run-Time for a Multi-Language Installation

At run time the only thing that is different than already described for the single language installation is the fact that all language dependent table entries get added to the database at run time via the application of a particular language specific transform. Once the transform is applied everything proceeds as described for the single language installation.

Appendix D

System Reboots

THE WINDOWS INSTALLER CAN automatically handle system reboots or it can be controlled so that the setup developer can specify when and if a reboot should be initiated. Inserting actions into the sequence can control reboots of the system. These actions include certain standard actions built in to the Windows Installer service, as well as those forced by a custom action. In all cases both standard actions and custom actions need to have an associated condition that executes the action only if the environment is appropriate. Setting a particular property from the command line can also be used to initiate a reboot without having to insert an action into a sequence table. One of the most common scenarios that will cause a reboot during an installation is the trying to copy over a file that is in use by another process.

In the following sections we explore the different methods for initiating and controlling system reboots through the Windows Installer, staring with how the Windows Installer handles files that are in use when an installation is run.

Replacing Files That Are in Use

There is one particular situation where the Windows Installer will generate a reboot of the system even if there are no special actions placed in the sequence table. This situation occurs when an executable file being installed is found by the Windows Installer to be in use at the time of the installation. When this happens the Windows Installer will display the FilesInUse dialog box, which permits the end user to shut down the processes that are holding the files that are shown as being in use. The FilesInUse dialog is displayed when the InstallValidate action detects the situation that the files being installed are already in use by another application.

Determining if a file is open is done during file costing. During the file costing, if a file is detected as being opened by another process, an entry is made to an internal table with the name of FilesInUse. This table has two columns with the first column containing the name of the file that is open and the second column the full path of the open file.

When the InstallValidate action executes the internal FilesInUse table is queried for any entries. If any entries are found in this table then an entry for each unique process that has a file open is made in the *ListBox* table in the MSI database. The entries made in the *ListBox* table columns are shown in Table D-1.

TABLE D-1 ENTRIES IN THE LISTBOX TABLE USED IN THE FILESINUSE DIALOG

Column	Value
Property	FileInUseProcess
Order	The order of the process as found in the internal table FilesInUse.
Value	Name of the process that holds the open file that needs to be placed.
Text	The caption of the main window of the process identified in the Value column.

After the *ListBox* table is populated the InstallValidate action displays the FilesInUse dialog. The FilesInUse dialog box is an authored dialog that has certain requirements but can be modified within these requirements as seen fit by the setup developer. The design of this dialog is covered in the next section.

The FilesInUse Dialog

This dialog needs to be authored into the MSI database and it is required that the name for this dialog be FilesInUse. This dialog box must have a ListBox control and this control needs to be associated with a property named FileInUseProcess. It is normal for this dialog box to have three pushbuttons with the captions of Exit, Retry, and Ignore. These buttons are not all required and can be modified by the setup developer; however, it is necessary to return certain values to the InstallValidate action in order for this dialog box to function properly. Each button in this dialog is tied to the EndDialog control event and the arguments to this control event return these values. The FilesInUse dialog is shown in Figure D-1.

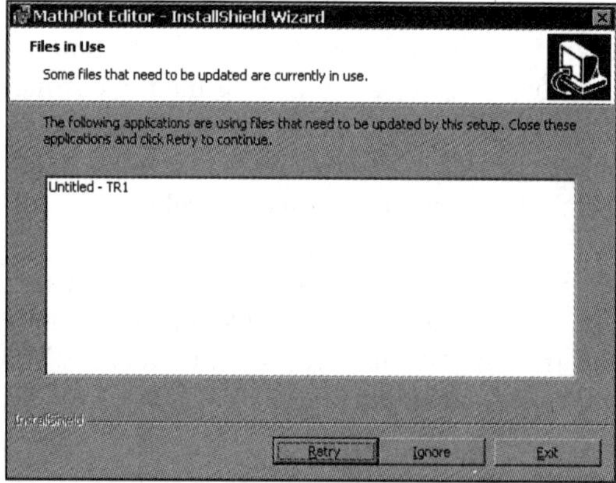

Figure D-1: The FilesInUse Dialog

The Retry button uses the Retry argument on the EndDialog control event. The FilesInUse dialog is closed and control returns to the InstallValidate action. The InstallValidate action causes all values added to the *ListBox* table to be cleared and the file costing process is repeated. If there are still processes identified as holding open a file that is to be replaced, the process just described above is started over. If there are no more processes identified, the InstallValidate action returns success to the Windows Installer and the installation or uninstallation process continues. The Exit button uses the Exit argument on the EndDialog control event and the Ignore button uses the Ignore argument on the EndDialog control event.

This dialog will not be displayed if one of the following listed conditions is true.

- The files in use are not executable files. In other words, if the file in use is a text file or some other file that is not a Portable Executable (PE) file, the FileInUse dialog will not be displayed.
- The Windows Installer is not actually trying to install the files that are in use.
- The process that is holding the files that are in use is the process that launched the installation.
- The process that is holding the files in use does not have a window that has a window title associated with it.

In the situation where the user does not shut down all processes holding files that are to be overwritten, a prompt to the user to perform a reboot is displayed giving the user the opportunity to reboot immediately or to reboot later. This prompt can be suppressed with the use of the REBOOTPROMPT property. If a reboot is determined to be necessary by the Windows Installer when this property is set to Suppress or S, the reboot will happen automatically without the display of a prompt.

If the user decides to not shut down the process that is holding open a file that will be overwritten by an installation, then the Windows Installer will set a property called `ReplacedInUseFiles`. This property can be used to condition custom actions that may be needed to handle this particular type of situation.

Controlling System Reboots

In the previous section we saw that the Windows Installer will automatically prompt the user to reboot the computer if it detects that a file in use has been overwritten by the installation. This occurs if the user chooses to ignore the FilesInUse dialog and does not shut down the process that is holding the file that is in use. However, we do not need to depend on the Windows Installer to identify the need for a reboot. We have several methods that can be used to either create a reboot at the end of an installation or to have one occur during the middle of an installation. These are discussed in the next two sections.

Controlling the Reboot at the End of an Installation

To control the reboot at the end of an installation we have a standard action and a property that we can use. The standard action is called ScheduleReboot and we can insert this action in to the sequence at any location and the Windows Installer will reboot the system at the end of the installation. If the installation is being run in silent mode, there will be no prompt for a reboot; otherwise, there will be a prompt displayed. The installation will not be considered complete until the reboot has occurred.

We also have the REBOOT property, which gives us control on whether a reboot will happen or not. This property can have one of three values as shown in the following list:

- F for Force: When the REBOOT property has this value a reboot will occur at the end of the installation. If the user interface sequence is run then there will be a prompt at the end of the installation for a reboot. If it is a silent installation then the reboot will occur automatically.
- S for Suppress: Using this value for the REBOOT property will suppress all Windows Installer initiated reboots as well as any reboots caused by the insertion of the ScheduleReboot action. It will not suppress any reboots generated by the ForceReboot action. This action is the subject of the next section.
- R for ReallySuppress: Using this value will suppress all reboots of the system including those that are generated by the ForceReboot action.

Controlling the Reboot during an Installation

When we want to reboot during the middle of an installation the system will reboot and then the installation will continue. It is important to realize that the Windows Installer will pick up the installation by starting to execute the install from the beginning. This is because the Windows Installer has no way of knowing where it left off when it rebooted. A different user interface is displayed because the conditions during this resumption of an installation are different. When a ForceReboot action is encountered the Windows Installer will display a prompt for a reboot at that point in the installation as long as the user interface sequence has been run. If it is a silent installation, the reboot will happen automatically without a prompt.

With a ForceReboot action it is necessary to prevent this action from continuing to force a reboot every time the installation is resumed after the last reboot. This means that we have to condition this action so that it only occurs during the first pass through the sequence table. The Windows Installer provides a public property called AFTERREBOOT can be used to create this condition. This property is set to 1 by the Windows Installer on the resumption of an installation after a ForceReboot.

Since this property is not set during the first pass through the sequence table the condition that can be used on the ForceReboot action can be as follows:

```
Not AFTERREBOOT
```

This condition will allow the ForceReboot action to execute the first time and not during the resumed installation.

The behind-the-scenes resumption of the installation after the reboot occurs is accomplished by the writing to the RunOnce registry key with the following command line:

```
msiexec /i <.msi package> AFTERREBOOT=1
```

The ForceReboot action must come between the InstallInitialize and the InstallFinalize actions. Also it is highly recommended that the ForceReboot action come after the RegisterProduct action otherwise the Windows Installer will require the source of the installation package. In fact the ForceReboot action should be sequenced after the following group of actions in the execute sequence.

- Registerproduct
- RegisterUser
- PublishProduct
- PublishFeatures
- CreateShortcuts
- RegisterMIMEInfo
- RegisterExtensionInfo
- RegisterClassInfo
- RegisterProgIdInfo
- ForceReboot

Appendix E

What's on the CD-ROM

THE CD-ROM THAT ACCOMPANIES this book is loaded with a number of valuable resources as listed below.

A complete electronic copy of the book is also included and permits easy text searching.

Source Code, Projects, and Sample Applications

Throughout the book there have been many examples used to illustrate the various features of the Windows Installer and InstallShield for Windows Installer. Copies of all complete examples provided in the book are available on the CD-ROM.

Programs

The following full-featured programs are included.

Microsoft's Windows Installer SDK – Version 1.1

The SDK provides the latest information about the Windows Installer as well as many tools that allow you to directly edit MSI packages, validate packages, etc. The latest vesion of the Windows Installer SDK can be downloaded form the MSDN Web site at the following URL:

```
http://msdn.microsoft.com/com/downloads/sdks/platform/wininst.asp
```

Microsoft Internet Explorer 5.5

This is the latest version of the popular Web browser from Microsoft and it plays an important part in enabling your PC to full advantage of Windows Installer capabilities.

InstallShield® for Windows® Installer 1.52

If you do not already own this product, you can install the version on the CD-ROM and you will be able to do most of the examples provided in the book. You can also install an evaluation copy of the latest version, InstallShield Professional – Windows Installer Edition, as described in the next section. To obtain the password required to install this version, go to `http://www.installshield.com/books/iswidg/`.

Evaluation Copies of the Latest InstallShield Software Products

Using a simple registration process you are provided with a password that allows you to install any of the following InstallShield products.

INSTALLSHIELD® PROFESSIONAL – STANDARD EDITION

The de facto industry standard development tool for creating professional Windows installations, InstallShield Professional allows developers to create setups of any size and complexity that can be distributed by CD, DVD, and the Internet. Used by top software vendors targeting consumer applications worldwide, InstallShield Professional has earned its place as the Windows developers' choice, earning PC Magazines' Editors Choice and many other industry awards.

More information can be found at `http://www.installshield.com/ispro/`.

INSTALLSHIELD® PROFESSIONAL – WINDOWS® INSTALLER EDITION

InstallShield Professional – Windows Installer Edition is the comprehensive setup solution for Microsoft's Windows Installer service. The powerful features of this new service combined with InstallShield's innovative and time saving capabilities to deliver the solution of choice for professional developers. Professional – Windows Installer Edition allows you to meet installation requirements for the Windows 2000 logo and take advantage of the Windows Installer service's TCO-reducing features.

More information can be found at `http://www.installshield.com/iswi/`.

INSTALLSHIELD® EXPRESS

InstallShield Express produces reliable Windows installations entirely in a visual, point-and-click environment. InstallShield Express includes pre-built objects that automatically handle installation of common components. InstallShield Express provides the most built-in support of any visual installation development tool. With its step-by-step installation checklist, InstallShield Express makes setup as quick and easy as possible.

More information can be found at `http://www.installshield.com/express/`.

INSTALLSHIELD® ENTERPRISE – MULTI-PLATFORM EDITION 4.0

InstallShield Enterprise – Multi-Platform Edition 4.0 is the multi-platform installation solution for large scale, distributed applications. Co-developed with IBM, Enterprise – Multi-Platform Edition extends the universally recognized InstallShield Wizard to multiple platforms including OS400, AIX, and OS2 in addition to the existing support for Windows, Solaris, and four Linux distributions. Developers targeting multiple platforms can now write a single installation that will run on multiple platforms while ensuring a consistent, Windows-like, end-user experience every time.

More information can be found at `http://www.installshield.com/iemp/`.

INSTALLSHIELD® PROFESSIONAL – MULTI-PLATFORM EDITION 4.0

InstallShield Professional – Multi-Platform Edition 4.0 is the flexible, multi-platform installation development solution from the leader in installation technology. Co-developed with and used by IBM. Professional - Multi-Platform Edition extends the de facto industry standard InstallShield Wizard to multiple platforms including Linux, Solaris, Windows, AIX and OS/2. Developers targeting multiple platforms can now write a single installation that will do exactly what they want it to do on multiple platforms while ensuring a consistent, Windows-like, end-user experience every time.

More information can be found at `http://www.installshield.com/ipmp`.

INSTALLSHIELD® EXPRESS – MULTI-PLATFORM EDITION 4.0

InstallShield Express – Multi-Platform Edition 4.0 is the quick and easy multi-platform installation development solution. Co-developed with and used by IBM, Express – Multi-Platform Edition extends the de facto industry standard InstallShield Wizard to multiple platforms including Linux, Solaris, Windows, AIX, and OS/2. Developers targeting multiple platforms can now write a single installation that will run seamlessly on multiple platforms while ensuring a consistent, Windows-like, end-user experience every time.

More information can be found at `http://www.installshield.com/ixmp`.

INSTALLSHIELD® TUNER

InstallShield Tuner allows systems administrators to take a Windows Installer setup package from an ISV or internal developer and customize it before you deploy it. You'll create MST transform files that customize your setup during installation. You'll control which features, registry entries, and shortcuts install on your users' systems. And only InstallShield Tuner offers an intuitive user interface that allows administrators to customize ANY Windows Installer package.

More information can be found at `http://www.installshield.com/ist/`.

INSTALLSHIELD® DEMOSHIELD®

InstallShield DemoShield is a multimedia-authoring tool that allows software developers, marketers, trainers, consultants, and multimedia authors to quickly develop demonstrations on CD-ROM or for the Web. Whether you need to create pre-sales demos, CD Browsers, tutorials, or quick tours, DemoShield's easy-to-use interface makes it the ideal solution for anyone looking to create exciting, informative multimedia presentations.

More information can be found at `http://www.installshield.com/demoshield/`.

INSTALLSHIELD® PACKAGEFORTHEWEB

InstallShield PackageForTheWeb provides developers with a single, easy solution for packaging files, applications, and ActiveX controls for Internet or Intranet distribution. You can deploy your application as a self-extracting single-file .exe, localized in 29 different languages and digitally signed with Microsoft's Authenticode technology. PackageForTheWeb is easy for you, and more importantly, easy for your customers.

More information can be found at `http://www.installshield.com/pftw/`.

Index

Symbols and Numbers

A

Continued

E

F

G

H

I

Continued

N

Q

R

S

Continued

U

Continued

Z

Hungry Minds, Inc.
End-User License Agreement

READ THIS. You should carefully read these terms and conditions before opening the software packet(s) included with this book ("Book"). This is a license agreement ("Agreement") between you and Hungry Minds, Inc. ("HMI"). By opening the accompanying software packet(s), you acknowledge that you have read and accept the following terms and conditions. If you do not agree and do not want to be bound by such terms and conditions, promptly return the Book and the unopened software packet(s) to the place you obtained them for a full refund.

1. **License Grant.** HMI grants to you (either an individual or entity) a nonexclusive license to use one copy of the enclosed software program(s) (collectively, the "Software") solely for your own personal or business purposes on a single computer (whether a standard computer or a workstation component of a multi-user network). The Software is in use on a computer when it is loaded into temporary memory (RAM) or installed into permanent memory (hard disk, CD-ROM, or other storage device). HMI reserves all rights not expressly granted herein.

2. **Ownership.** HMI is the owner of all right, title, and interest, including copyright, in and to the compilation of the Software recorded on the disk(s) or CD-ROM ("Software Media"). Copyright to the individual programs recorded on the Software Media is owned by the author or other authorized copyright owner of each program. Ownership of the Software and all proprietary rights relating thereto remain with HMI and its licensers.

3. **Restrictions On Use and Transfer.**

   (a) You may only (i) make one copy of the Software for backup or archival purposes, or (ii) transfer the Software to a single hard disk, provided that you keep the original for backup or archival purposes. You may not (i) rent or lease the Software, (ii) copy or reproduce the Software through a LAN or other network system or through any computer subscriber system or bulletin-board system, or (iii) modify, adapt, or create derivative works based on the Software.

   (b) You may not reverse engineer, decompile, or disassemble the Software. You may transfer the Software and user documentation on a permanent basis, provided that the transferee agrees to accept the terms and conditions of this Agreement and you retain no copies. If the Software is an update or has been updated, any transfer must include the most recent update and all prior versions.

4. **Restrictions on Use of Individual Programs.** You must follow the individual requirements and restrictions detailed for each individual program in Appendix E "What's on the CD-ROM" of this Book. These limitations are also contained in the individual license agreements recorded on the Software Media. These limitations may include a requirement that after using the program for a specified period of time, the user must pay a registration fee or discontinue use. By opening the Software packet(s), you will be agreeing to abide by the licenses and restrictions for these individual programs that are detailed in Appendix E and on the Software Media. None of the material on this Software Media or listed in this Book may ever be redistributed, in original or modified form, for commercial purposes.

5. **Limited Warranty.**

   (a) HMI warrants that the Software and Software Media are free from defects in materials and workmanship under normal use for a period of sixty (60) days from the date of purchase of this Book. If HMI receives notification within the warranty period of defects in materials or workmanship, HMI will replace the defective Software Media.

   (b) HMI AND THE AUTHOR OF THE BOOK DISCLAIM ALL OTHER WARRANTIES, EXPRESS OR IMPLIED, INCLUDING WITHOUT LIMITATION IMPLIED WARRANTIES OF MERCHANTABILITY AND FITNESS FOR A PARTICULAR PURPOSE, WITH RESPECT TO THE SOFTWARE, THE PROGRAMS, THE SOURCE CODE CONTAINED THEREIN, AND/OR THE TECHNIQUES DESCRIBED IN THIS BOOK. HMI DOES NOT WARRANT THAT THE FUNCTIONS CONTAINED IN THE SOFTWARE WILL MEET YOUR REQUIREMENTS OR THAT THE OPERATION OF THE SOFTWARE WILL BE ERROR FREE.

   (c) This limited warranty gives you specific legal rights, and you may have other rights that vary from jurisdiction to jurisdiction.

6. **Remedies.**

   (a) HMI's entire liability and your exclusive remedy for defects in materials and workmanship shall be limited to replacement of the Software Media, which may be returned to HMI with a copy of your receipt at the following address: Software Media Fulfillment Department, Attn.: *The Official InstallShield® for Windows® Installer Developer's Guide,* Hungry Minds, Inc., 10475 Crosspoint Blvd., Indianapolis, IN 46256, or call 1-800-762-2974. Please allow four to six weeks for delivery. This Limited Warranty is void if failure of the Software Media has resulted from accident, abuse, or misapplication. Any replacement Software Media will be warranted for the remainder of the original warranty period or thirty (30) days, whichever is longer.

(b) In no event shall HMI or the author be liable for any damages whatsoever (including without limitation damages for loss of business profits, business interruption, loss of business information, or any other pecuniary loss) arising from the use of or inability to use the Book or the Software, even if HMI has been advised of the possibility of such damages.

(c) Because some jurisdictions do not allow the exclusion or limitation of liability for consequential or incidental damages, the above limitation or exclusion may not apply to you.

7. **U.S. Government Restricted Rights.** Use, duplication, or disclosure of the Software for or on behalf of the United States of America, its agencies and/or instrumentalities (the "U.S. Government") is subject to restrictions as stated in paragraph (c)(1)(ii) of the Rights in Technical Data and Computer Software clause of DFARS 252.227-7013, or subparagraphs (c) (1) and (2) of the Commercial Computer Software - Restricted Rights clause at FAR 52.227-19, and in similar clauses in the NASA FAR supplement, as applicable.

8. **General.** This Agreement constitutes the entire understanding of the parties and revokes and supersedes all prior agreements, oral or written, between them and may not be modified or amended except in a writing signed by both parties hereto that specifically refers to this Agreement. This Agreement shall take precedence over any other documents that may be in conflict herewith. If any one or more provisions contained in this Agreement are held by any court or tribunal to be invalid, illegal, or otherwise unenforceable, each and every other provision shall remain in full force and effect.

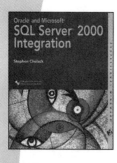

Installation Instructions

The CD-ROM that accompanies this book contains useful applications, demo programs from InstallShield, and source code from the chapters, as well as a complete copy of the book.

To install the items from the CD to your hard drive, follow these steps:

1. Insert the CD into your computer's CD-ROM drive.
2. Start Windows Explorer and select your CD-ROM drive.
3. Open the folder you wish to view and the files in the directory will be shown in your window.

To open the electronic copy of the book (.pdf files), make sure you have Adobe Acrobat Reader installed on your computer. Then open the chapter folder and file you wish to read.

For more information about the components of this CD, turn to Appendix E "What's on the CD-ROM."